THE ORGANIZATION OF SPACE
IN DEVELOPING COUNTRIES

The Organization of Space in Developing Countries

E. A. J. JOHNSON

Harvard University Press
Cambridge, Massachusetts, and London, England

Fourth Printing, 1976

Library of Congress Catalog Card Number: 74–122216
ISBN 0–674–64338–0

Printed in the United States of America

TO VIRGINIA   For years of love and loyalty

PREFACE

The passion for economic growth, an entirely commendable ideal, has led to some rather strange contradictions. Despite the mounting evidence that large cities in both developed and underdeveloped countries are convulsed by endemic poverty, the widely accepted economic cosmogony still asserts with almost theological confidence that true growth can only be expected in the matrix of core region urbanization. That great cities have been, and still are, incubators of change cannot be denied, but this ought not blind us to their limitations; metropolitan centers are both creative and parasitic, elegant and squalid, majestic and pathetic. At what price has their partial and fading splendor been achieved? Yet, even though huge cities, whether named New York or Calcutta, Chicago or Manila, are becoming ungovernable and unmanageable, this unhappy conjecture ought not tempt us to seek escape in Pre-Raphaelite romanticism. With technology now available to every nation, the choice need not be between the saccharine sentimentality of Gandhi's wholly unwarranted panegyric for fusty villages and unquestioning opting for the cruel and unsatisfying dynamism of core-periphery dualism. We have far better choices. It is the object of this essay to show what these alternatives are and to suggest how a more benevolent spatial distribution of enterprise, employment, and creative effort can be achieved.

This study lies somewhere between economic history and economic theory, somewhere between micro and macrogeography, interblending description and analysis, prescription and policy. It is really not very original, but it does, I hope, synthesize elements that have not before been fused. Whether the result is revelation or pedantry is for readers to decide. Because I have lived more than ten years in Korea, Greece, Italy, Yugoslavia, and India with an uncomfortable amount of responsibility for spending more millions of other peoples' money than I like to remember, I address myself to the problem of spatial restructuring with considerable, rather evident reformist zeal; and since this essay is both an analysis and a tract, readers should not be surprised to encounter frequent repetition of certain arguments and themes. The reiteration is quite intentional.

Aside from material that I have transcribed from my *Market Towns and Spatial Development in India* and from some further investigations I made for an International Seminar held at Kanpur in 1967, this essay does not pretend to represent original research. Nor can I even claim that all the bottles into which I have poured old wines, after blending and fortifying them, are of my own making. I owe, of course, a great debt to geographers, who have long wrestled with spatial problems, only to be ignored by most of the economists. I acknowledge particular indebtedness to John P. Lewis, one of the few economists who has sensed the critical role that spatial restructuring must play in any genuinely meliorative development program, and to Laurence Hewes Jr., whose wise counsel and constructive criticism in India helped me to isolate some of the really fundamental spatial problems. Two other acknowledgments are necessary. First versions of three sections in Chapter 6, "The Inseparability of Agrarian and Industrial Development in Progressive Economies," "Incentives for Farmers," and "Spatial Aspects of the Farmer Incentive Problem," were prepared for the International Seminar on the Urban and Industrial Growth of Kanpur held at Kanpur, India, January 2–February 4, 1967, and have been published in *Regional Perspective of Industrial and Urban Growth: The Case of Kanpur,* edited by P. B. Desai, I. M. Grossack, and K. N. Sharma, Bombay, 1969, pp. 171–190. The last two sections of Chapter 11, which together serve as a coda to the whole composition, were prepared for the Second and the Third International Conferences on "The Development of Science and Technology and Their Impact on Society," held at Herceg Novi, Yugoslavia, July 1–8, 1966, and June 27–July 4, 1969, respectively. The first of these two essays was published by the Polish Academy of Science in *Zagadnienia Naukoznawstwa: Studia i Materiały,* 2, No. 4 (8) (1966), 164–173.

To the East-West Center I am very much beholden not merely for the opportunity to spend an academic year in its stimulating milieu (where one breaks lances with charming yet formidable colleagues) but for the faultless amanuenses it provided. Because I literally wear out thesauri seeking words that will precisely convey my veriest meaning, my handwritten manuscripts are dreadful blurs of inserted phrases, crossed-out words, and erasures. Only the patience derived from Oriental heritage can explain the mystery of how my jumbled, illegible, and transposed words could have been converted into typed discourse. For these acts of mercy, courtesy, and amazing competence I am indebted to Lorraine Tani, Norma Wong, Ember Chung, Judy Levens, Satoko Koga, Kathleen Matsumoto, and Diane Koga. For invaluable assistance I want to thank Leroy Tsutsumi, who not only prepared maps and collected data but helped in many, many other tasks; Robert Miura, whose skill and imagination made artistic creations out of my crude sketches; and Hazel Tatsuno and Arline Uyeunten, whose gracious assistance in numberless ways made my ten months at the Center so pleasant and fruitful.

E. A. J. Johnson
Honolulu, Hawaii

CONTENTS

FIGURES

FIGURES

TABLES

THE ORGANIZATION OF SPACE IN DEVELOPING COUNTRIES

CHAPTER 1 THE NATURE OF LANDSCAPES IN HUMAN GEOGRAPHY: PURPOSES UNDERLYING THE ORGANIZATION OF TERRESTRIAL SPACE

The Argument

Differences between "developed" and "less-developed" countries (or between "progressive" and "backward" areas within countries) can to a useful degree be assessed in terms of the ways whereby terrestrial space is organized. For, whatever the dominant organizing principles may be, they will necessarily shape and influence the affected landscapes. Thus, if military control of an area is a chief object of policy, the landscape will be studded with forts, castles, cantonments, and other military or paramilitary institutions strategically located; and the building, maintenance, staffing, and provisioning of these installations may require such a large share of resources and manpower as to arrest or limit seriously the development of nonmilitary institutions and activities.

Somewhat different effects on a landscape may result when a priestly group controls the people who occupy a given compass of land. The chief concern of the controlling elite will be to propagate some ethical doctrine, and to this end the landscape will be divided into appropriate units consistent with certain sacerdotal objectives. Thus, in Christianized Europe a network of dioceses and parishes was established, each with its complement of clergy. Churches and chantries were built, progressively enlarged and beautified. This elaborate infrastructure was designed for catechizing the laity; for the religiously dedicated, another, more or less parallel, set of institutions came into being comprising, inter alia, monasteries, nunneries, and cathedral chapters. But this western version of sacerdotal organization of landscapes was not at all unique; the temples of ancient Egypt, the Buddhist and Hindu shrines of South and Southeast Asia, the Shinto fanes of Japan, and the mosques of Islamic regions called for some corresponding organization of people, and each type profoundly influenced the character of landscapes.

More skeletal, but nonetheless of great importance, is that type of spatial organization which centers around juridical institutions. If justice is to be administered in a territory, a network of courts, assizes, and other adjudicative agencies must be created and sustained to insure an operative set of procedures. This juridical structure will perforce require provisional or permanent political jurisdictions within which courts can function and wherein, if appeals are permitted, a hierarchy of appellate jurisdictions will link the whole complex into a juridical system. Historically, the effect of this development on landscapes has been very important; courts have established guidelines for social and economic conduct, permitting the evolution of certain institutions whose utility various cultures have come to acknowledge. Thus, the pattern of landholding, one of the most important economic aspects of a landscape, has depended for its stability and continuance on legal rules enforced by courts. So have contracts, trusts, wills, deeds, and the rights of inheritance. Very clearly, then, the juridical organization of a territory will profoundly influence the nature of a landscape.

A fourth variety might be administrative control over both land and people in a dependent area, although such control must obviously be based on power, a desideratum which can be achieved either by force, as in military contexts, or by persuasion, as in sacerdotal contexts. But given some tolerable degree of acquiescence, the control can become essentially administrative. Thus, a conquered territory will pay tribute to collectors of revenue, or a God-intoxicated culture will contribute offerings or tithes. The landscape in either case will be under the influence of "collectors," tithe gatherers or tax farmers, and its structure, its capacity for improvement by means of investment will be singularly conditioned by the character of the administrative procedures and by the incidence of the taxes and contributions.[1]

1. This was pointed out with clarity in the latter years of the seventeenth century by Sir William Petty, that remarkable physician-economist who was asked to make a political and economic survey of portions of conquered Ireland. See especially his *Treatise of Taxes and Contributions*, London, 1662, and his *Political Anatomy of Ireland*, London, 1691.

A fifth, and by all odds the most important, means for organizing a landscape is a hierarchy of markets that interlinks the economic activities of the people of an area into some meaningful arrangement. By making exchange of goods and services possible this scheme of things not only permits specialization of tasks and division of labor but creates beneficial interconnections between regions and persons that hold society together, not by force or preachment but by choice. It should be noted, however, that a military organization of a landscape will require some of this economic mechanism for its operation. So will a sacerdotal, a judicial or an administrative system. What really determines the nature of a landscape, therefore, is the extent to which military, sacerdotal, juridical, administrative, or economic influences predominate. It will be the argument of this essay that in less-developed countries (or areas) landscapes have been inadequately influenced by market forces and considerably more affected by military, sacerdotal, juridical, or administrative forces. Some historical examples will make this argument clearer.

Types of Military Landscapes

In vast areas of the world, military force has been employed to organize terrestrial space. The organizing impact has taken several contrasting forms of which three kinds are readily distinguishable. In the United States, particularly in the area west of the Mississippi, cavalry posts were established to control Indian tribes and to protect trappers, herdsmen, traders, and settlers. By reason of the limited military personnel, the posts were located at considerable distance from one another, and consequently the degree of protection was a function of the mobility and availability of mounted troops. Figure 1–1 shows the dispersion of forty-seven military posts in the western United States, 1870–1892. The circles (of which the posts are centers) give a very rough indication of the territory over which each military post tried to provide a measure of protection. Within the shelter of the military establishments a few nonmilitary institutions could grow up: the "store" of a licensed trader, the headquarters of a land company, the office of a lawyer or doctor. Outlying mines, stores and other businesses would, of course, be more vulnerable to attack by Indians or bandits. Yet however insecure the total landscape, there were some places of refuge in

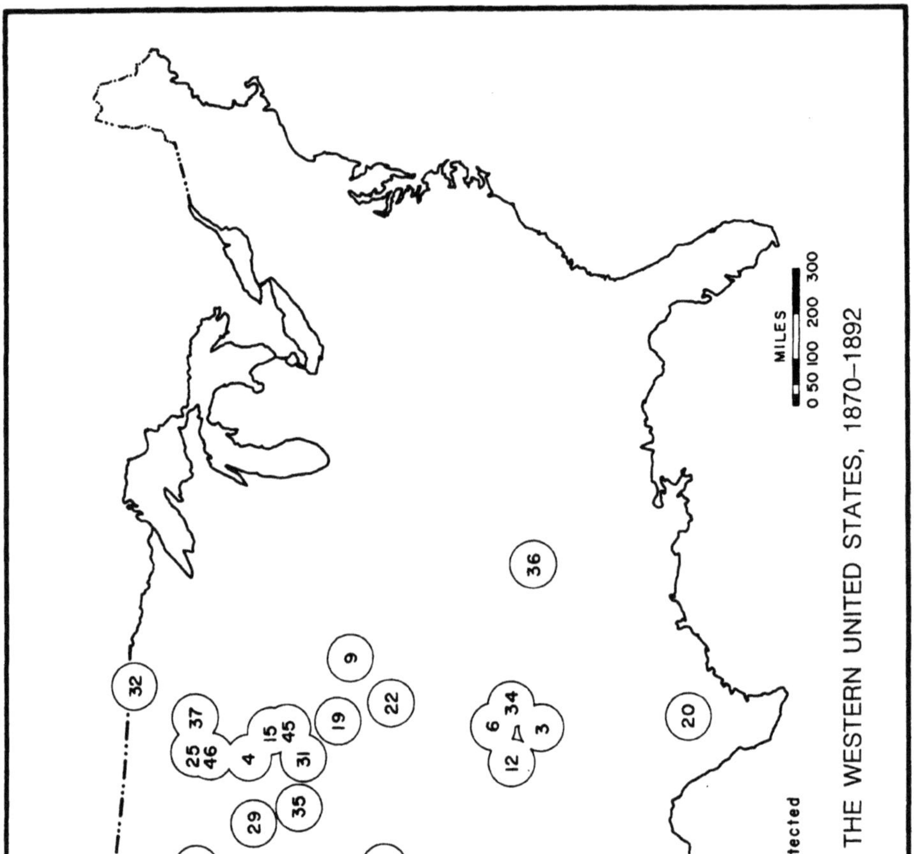

MILITARY POSTS IN THE WESTERN UNITED STATES, 1870–1892

Figure 1–1 Military Posts in the Western United States, 1870–1892

1. Fort Apache, Arizona
2. Fort Assiniboine, Montana
3. Fort Beach, Oklahoma
4. Fort Bennett, South Dakota
5. Fort Cameron, Utah
6. Fort Cantonment, Oklahoma
7. Fort Carlin, Nevada
8. Fort Crawford, Colorado
9. Fort Crook, Nebraska
10. Fort Custer, Montana
11. Fort DuChesne, Utah
12. Fort Elliott, Texas
13. Fort Fizzle, Montana
14. Fort Grant II, Arizona
15. Fort Hale, South Dakota
16. Fort Hall II, Idaho
17. Fort Hancock, Texas
18. Fort William Henry Harrison, Montana
19. Fort Hartsuff, Nebraska
20. Fort Sam Houston, Texas
21. Fort Huachuca, Arizona
22. Fort Jewell, Kansas
23. Fort Keogh, Montana
24. Fort Lewis, Colorado
25. Fort Abraham Lincoln, North Dakota
26. Fort Logan, Colorado
27. Fort McKinney, Wyoming
28. Fort Maginnis, Montana
29. Fort Mead, South Dakota
30. Fort Missoula, Montana
31. Fort Niobrara, Nebraska
32. Fort Pembina, North Dakota
33. Fort Rawlins, Utah
34. Fort Reno, Oklahoma
35. Fort Robinson, Nebraska
36. Fort Logan H. Roots, Arkansas
37. Fort Seward, North Dakota
38. Fort Sherman, Idaho
39. Fort Spokane, Washington
40. Fort Stambaugh, Wyoming
41. Fort Thomas, Arizona
42. Fort Thornburgh, Utah
43. Fort Tularosa, New Mexico
44. Fort Washakie, Wyoming
45. Fort Whetstone, South Dakota
46. Fort Yates, North Dakota
47. Fort Yellowstone, Wyoming

moments of danger. Hence the military organization of the landscape certainly helped to set in motion a process of economic development. In essence, then, the role of the military in this context was to create perimeters wherein investments could be made with reasonable safety.

Not all militarily organized landscapes have been quite so benevolently conceived. Where military forces have been used to conquer lightly populated areas, the object more frequently has been to exploit the territory and the people for the benefit of the invaders. The deployment of military forces in such instances would have to be spatially planned to achieve the required degree of control over the subject population. If the object were simply to appropriate a share of the product of the "going concern," the program might be wholly indifferent toward any change in economic structure or any modification of the customary economic activity of the people of the occupied area. The Ottoman control over Macedonia, Serbia, Bosnia, and Hertzegovina was essentially of this type. Large military fiefs were created, and by means of these semifeudal institutions the countryside and the conquered people were effectively controlled. The outcome, with few exceptions, was a stagnant type of agriculture but a fairly benign local government controlled by the overlord Turks and, to some extent, by favored sycophant minorities.[2] By and large, however, the landscape which emerged was not one that was structurally or ideationally dynamic, and there is no mystery why that portion of the Balkans controlled by the Turks continued to be an underdeveloped area for centuries, despite the elemental vigor of the conquered people and the mineral and agronomic potential of the region.

When a more densely populated area is organized by military means, the consequences are partly similar and partly quite different. The military conquest of Northern India might serve as an example. After the Sepoy Mutiny large military establishments were created with regional headquarters in urban cantonments and with smaller military compounds in outlying towns. (See Figure 1–2.) In the cantonments

Figure 1–2 Location of Major British Military Cantonments in India

1. Agra	20. Dehra Dun	39. Mathura
2. Ahmedabad	21. Deolati	40. Meerut
3. Ahmednagar	22. Dinapore	41. Mhow
4. Allahabad	23. Faizabad	42. Nainital
5. Almora	24. Fatehgarh	43. Nasirabad
6. Ambala	25. Ferozepore	44. Pachmarhi
7. Amritsar	26. Jalapahar	45. Poona
8. Aurangabad	27. Jhansi	46. Ramgarh
9. Bakloh	28. Jabalpur	47. Ranikhet
10. Banaras	29. Jullundur	48. Roorkee
11. Barrackpore	30. Jutogh	49. St. Thomas Mount
12. Bareilly	31. Kamptee	50. Saugor
13. Belgaum	32. Kanpur	51. Secunderabad
14. Cannanore	33. Kasauli	52. Shahjahanpur
15. Chakrata	34. Kirkee	53. Shillong
16. Clement Town	35. Landour	54. Subathu
17. Dagshai	36. Lansdowne	55. Wellington
18. Dalhousie	37. Lebong	
19. Delhi	38. Lucknow	

2. Among these were the Bogomils against whom a pogrom had rather tactlessly been commenced by the Pope on the very eve of the Turkish invasion. For details see Jozo Tomasovich, *Peasants, Politics, and Economic Change in Yugoslavia*, Stanford, Calif., 1955, pp. 93ff.

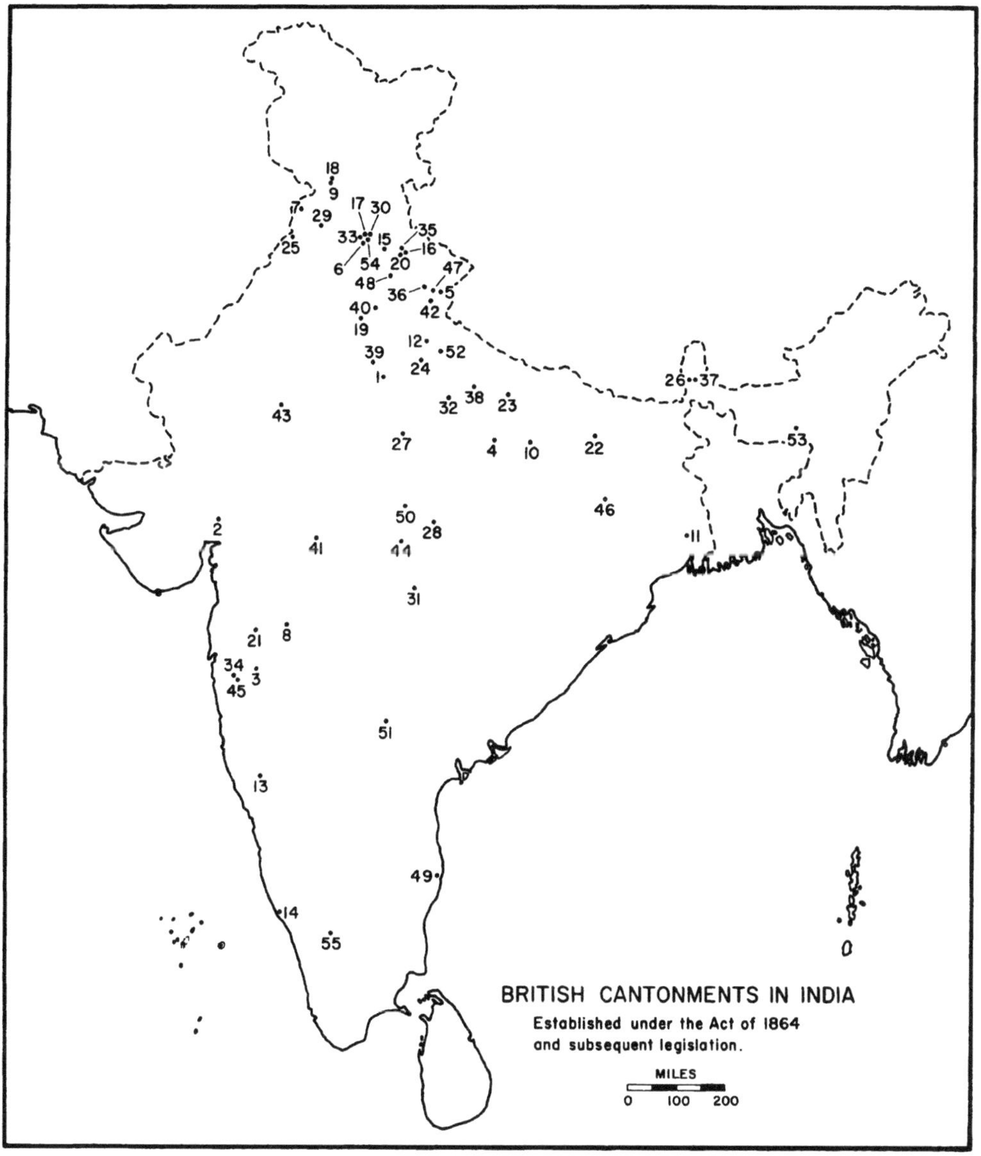

BRITISH CANTONMENTS IN INDIA
Established under the Act of 1864
and subsequent legislation.

were to be found not only military personnel with their servants and retainers but foreign businessmen, Anglo-Indians, other Eurasians, and "native" people to whom the military decision makers chose to accord privileges and rights,[3] which were more or less extraterritorial. This elaborate military control widened steadily into a bureaucratic system which has had a profound and seemingly permanent effect on the Indian economy, projecting its stultifying influences far beyond the moment of Indian liberation. For this elaborate system of military surveillance required the extended use of "native" soldiers and "native" bureaucrats, thereby establishing norms of procedure, conduct, even of thought, which, after generations of inculcation and acceptance, came to be regarded by many Indians as proper and right. But not by all! The arrogance of the privileged Europeans, the favoritism enjoyed by their native servants, soldiers, and concessionaires bred increasing resentment, jealousy, and anger. Indian businessmen saw the best ventures dominated by foreigners or by their hireling "managing agents." Moreover, the economic development of a landscape, such as it was, had an imperialist orientation, one whose epicenter was London, Liverpool, or Manchester rather than Kanpur, Lucknow, Benares, or Allahabad.

Sacerdotal Landscapes

The influence that churches, temples, fanes, mosques, or other places of worship will have on landscapes depends on doctrinal concepts and on liturgical practices. If the sacerdotal institution is a place where congregational worship occurs at fixed times, it will need to be within convenient access of its adherents. Parish churches came, therefore, to be located in villages and small towns, as well as in portions of cities;

3. The cantonments "started as temporary encampments of the military and their camp followers" but in due course "became permanent camps with residential accommodations of the bungalow type for officers." Gradually the population of the cantonments increased as quarters were built for dependents, servants, and camp followers and especially when certain persons were allowed to erect accommodations at their own expense. In most cantonments, "bazaar areas" were designated in which civilians were allowed to build houses or shops, although some of these concessions extended beyond the bazaar sections. All sites, however, remained the property of the (British) government and were "resumable on a month's notice and on payment of compensation for the authorized superstructures." India. Central Committee on Cantonments, *Report,* New Delhi, 1952, pp. 2–3, 16.

similarly, mosques were built at places where all the residents of a transport-determined compass of land could regularly attend the services. These forms of congregational worship consequently tended to convert a landscape into a polka-dot pattern of churches or mosques; and a great number of these religious meeting places became nuclei for markets, for shops of small craftsmen, and for other types of business enterprise.

In some instances, and seventeenth-century New England is a good example, the laying out of new towns on the frontier was under the surveillance, indeed under the direction, of the church. By a process of segmentation a church in an established community would permit some of its members[4] to "gather" a new congregation; this group of persons would then move out on the frontier and establish a new church which would become the spiritual, social, and economic center of a new community. In much the same way settlements in French Canada grew up in the neighborhood of churches, and all over Latin America churches have been the points of social and economic confluence.

Sacerdotal institutions, however, are by no means all congregational. Chantries, shrines, and other revered places may have no regular services, no resident priests or clergy, no congregations. Like Hindu temples they may be places for individual contemplation or individual ablution,[5] or, like the chantries built in honor of St. Elias in the Greek or Anatolian mountains, they may be places of occasional individual pilgrimage. More famous shrines—the medieval church of St. Olaf in Trondheim, the church of the Holy Sepulcher in Jerusalem, or Canterbury Cathedral—might attract hundreds of pilgrims from far distant places. The influence of sacerdotal institutions on landscapes will therefore vary rather widely. In Europe and in uninhabited countries settled by Europeans, churches tended to subdivide a landscape into dioceses (if they were episcopate) and into parishes (whether they were episcopate or not). Every church location could become a potential village or

4. Church membership in early New England was a much-prized privilege reserved for a limited number of properly qualified persons and had none of the voluntaristic characteristics of modern church membership.

5. Some of the elaborate South Indian temples, richly endowed with lands and money, attracted merchants and artisans, and thereby furthered some central-place functions. See Burton Stein, "The Economic Function of a Medieval South Indian Temple," *Journal of Asian Studies*, 19, No. 2 (February 1960), 163–176; and also his "The State, the Temple, and Agricultural Development: A Study in Medieval South India," in *Economic Weekly Annual*, February 4, 1961, pp. 178–187.

town site, and a wide proliferation of villages and towns was thereby encouraged.

A hierarchy of churches will tend to parallel a hierarchy of central places, with parish churches in villages, larger churches in towns, and cathedrals in cities.[6] Which is cause and which effect is hard to know, but the more important the sacerdotal function, usually the greater would be the social and economic confluence. To the cathedral city the farmers would bring their calves, grain, fruits, or wool, and in a great number of cathedral towns markets were held within the cathedral close.[7] In the Islamic world the great mosques in the large cities similarly attracted a wide range of mercantile and light manufacturing enterprises, since to the great mosques would come a steady flow of worshipers; and even today it is to the rug buyers near the great mosques that the weavers from scores, even hundreds, of Middle Eastern villages still bring their rugs and *juvals* (tent-bag faces) to sell.

The widely dispersed Indian temples do not seem to have had this coagulative effect, nor do the Buddhist temples in China, Korea, and Japan. Even great clusters of temples such as the eighty-four fabulous, statue-decorated fanes of Khajuraho[8] did not result in any encircling urbanization; nor did the charming painted rock caves of Ajanta or the elegant sculptured temples of Ellora hewn out of a Maharashta cliff. The neutral effect of these sacerdotal institutions is not, however, something that derives from a peculiar Indian culture; the influence on urbanization of most Western monastic foundations was equally negative. Great British abbeys such as Woburn, Iona, Tintern, and Melrose, for example, did not become market or industrial centers. The explanation is not very obscure. The monasteries were devotional centers for their own members, not assembly places for peasants, tradesmen, and craftsmen; by choice the monks or nuns had withdrawn from the world to a cloistered life of contemplation and worship.

6. There are exceptions. Among famous English cathedrals, Ely and Wells are located in small towns. For the most part, however, throughout Christendom the cathedral was to be found in a sizable city, as in Milan, Cremona, Bologna, Reims, Amiens, Gloucester, Durham, Exeter, Salisbury, Cologne, Antwerp, and Lisbon.

7. This is still done at Dinan in Brittany.

8. Only about a dozen of these exquisite structures still remain in a good state of preservation, but enough still exist to dazzle the observer. One temple alone has 900 life-sized sculptured "heavenly nymphs," carved so lovingly that the total effect is indescribably beautiful. For an account of these exquisite temples see Mulk Raj Anand, Charles Fabri, and Stella Kramrisch, *Khajuraho,* Bombay, 1962.

Even so, the monasteries played a role in shaping landscapes, since most of them derived income from lands which they owned or controlled. "There can have been few parishes in England in 1500," writes a very careful student, "the products of whose fields and pastures were not contributing in some way toward the maintenance of one or more of the over eight hundred religious communities."[9] As landlords, the monasteries syphoned off resources that might have been used for purposes quite different from stocking the wine cellars of the monks, provisioning their tables, or beautifying or extending their refectories, hostels, and churches. The same resources might have built grist mills, stables, and granaries or made possible a wide range of amenities for the peasantry—better houses, furnishings, clothes, medicines, and foods. In short, the social cost of building and maintaining the monasteries should be set over against the putative utility of these co-opted revenues had they been invested in inanimate or in human capital. This aspect of the church, namely its capacity to absorb a large share of agrarian income, is still a powerful deterrent to agricultural investments in virtually the whole of Latin America, and there is no modern Henry VIII in sight who will dare to end this heavy drain of resources—resources that are so urgently needed in the agrarian landscape to increase the productivity of poor peons.

Juridical Landscapes

One type of influence that courts have had on the shaping of landscapes can be illustrated by the development of courthouse towns in the American midwest. For whereas the westward movement of population into a raw frontier (that was ultimately to become a checkerboard of farms) led to the emergence of a polka-dot pattern of villages spaced quite evenly one from another, the political division of the territory into counties led often to fierce competition between villages for the right to become the county seat.[10] The assumption was that the county seat would very likely become a larger than average village because it

9. See Joyce Youings' essay "The Church" in Ch. 5, "Landlords in England," in *The Agrarian History of England and Wales,* Vol. IV, 1500–1640, ed. Joan Thirsk, Cambridge, 1967, p. 306.

10. So that Cambridge, Illinois, could become the county seat, the files were moved secretly at night from Morristown to prevent Geneseo from laying claim to the honor. Some of this data is now recorded on a historical marker on the road between Geneseo and Cambridge.

would have the county courthouse and for that very reason would attract more lawyers, surveyors, banks, and a larger number and greater variety of business enterprises. In short, the expectation was that a county seat would become a regional market center and gradually grow into a city where real estate values could rise. The hope that juridical and political centrality would have such a salubrious effect on the growth of the favored communities was quite consistently realized, particularly because county seats normally also became station towns when railway routes were planned,[11] thus adding another locational factor conducive to the development of the courthouse communities.

Berry's account of the village- and town-making process in southwestern Iowa shows very clearly that among the original trade centers which had sprung up in the late 1840's and the early 1850's only those that could consistently attract enough trade would survive. Consequently intervillage competition became very intense, and "success was often based on the acquisition of some additional attribute of centrality." Thus "all the centers that survived were the sites of grist mills," but "perhaps the most important additional factor determining survival of a center was designation as the county seat," since this "provided added reason for farmers to visit one center rather than another."[12]

Because a system of rectangular survey had been employed in dividing up the American public domain into square miles, midwestern counties tended to be more or less rectangular and fairly uniform in size. As a consequence, the courthouse towns were approximately equidistant, and this historical circumstance provided the wide stretches of the American subcontinent with a grand total of 3,077 county seats, most of which had good prospects of becoming regional market towns. Dividing the total land area of the United States by the total number of counties gives an average size of all these potential market areas of 962 square miles, an average which is, of course, very greatly distorted by the large counties in the arid and mountainous parts of the Southwest and the Rocky Mountain regions. For the area east of the Mississippi and for most of the western watershed of the Mississippi, the courthouse

11. Unless topography made this very difficult. Thus Sandisfield, which was the original county seat of Berkshire County, Massachusetts, had to yield this honor to Pittsfield which became a station town whereas Sandisfield did not.

12. Brian J. L. Berry, *Geography of Market Centers and Retail Distribution*, Englewood Cliffs, 1967, pp. 6–7. This study was partly based on the work of John A. Laska, Jr., "The Development of the Pattern of Retail Trade Centers in a Selected Area of Southwestern Iowa," Master's thesis, University of Chicago, 1958.

towns were the centers of market areas small enough to be reached by the farmers without difficulty even before the age of the automobile. It was therefore a rather lucky accident that the proliferation of the juridical system could have had such a wholesome and stimulating effect on the American landscape.

How fortunate America was can be seen by considering a contrasting system for the administration of justice, one based not on a permanent pattern of sturdy, stone or brick courthouses scattered regularly over a landscape but on a mobile juridical apparatus that left no central places whatever. An example of this can be found in northern and central India in the age of the Moguls. Having come from central Asia, the Mogul emperors brought with them nomadic traditions, and even though they built elaborate forts with palatial quarters, mosques, audience halls, and stables, their empire, as Irvine has pointed out, "never had a fixed capital."[13] Wherever the emperor happened to be *was* the capital and was also the court of justice. Hence "the whole apparatus of government was carried wherever the emperor went. All the great offices of state followed him, and all the imperial records moved with them." According to a contemporary chronicler, when Aurangzeb traveled, the official records were carried on eighty camels, thirty elephants, and twenty carts.[14] A huge army of officials, soldiers, servants, sutlers, and traders moved with the emperor, who was accompanied by his harem and his astrologers. Such elaborate travel was not an unusual or occasional event, "for the five years of his reign, Bahōdur Shah never slept in any building."[15] Like him, most of the emperors spent the greater part of their life under canvas, whether they were expanding their territories by force of arms or administering the areas they had conquered.[16]

The administration of justice was a peripatetic activity carried on in an ambulatory, canvas "audience hall," closely protected by guards and officials. It was to such a "traveling city" that subjects had to re-

13. William Irvine, *The Army of the Indian Moghuls: Its Organization and Administration,* New Delhi, 1962, p. 190. For an excellent analysis of the exploitation of the Indian villagers by the Mogul ruling classes, see Irfan Habib, "Potentialities of Capitalistic Development in the Economy of Mughul India," *Journal of Economics History,* 29, No. 1 (March 1969) 32–78.

14. François Catrou, *Histoire général de l'empire du Mogul,* Paris, 1715, IV, 49.

15. Ibid.

16. For further information on the relation of the Mogul rulers and the rural population, see N. A. Siddiqui, "A Classification of Villages under the Mughals," *Indian Economic and Social History Review,* 1, No. 3 (January–March 1964), 73–82.

pair for the adjudication of their legal problems. Once the administrative and juridical matters at a given resting place were finished, the vast entourage would move on. For a time the encampment had been not merely a royal palace but a court of justice and a bazaar; but after the tent pins had been pulled, and the elephants, camels, and horses, stirring up dense clouds of dust, had moved the treasure, archives, food, water, weapons, and tents on toward the next stopping place, the mobile city became nothing but an empty, well-trodden field. The juridical process had left the landscape unchanged and undeveloped.

Contrasting Effects on Landscapes of Administrative Control over Land and People

Once a landscape has been organized, whatever the means may have been, it is administered. In many modern societies this administration is largely accomplished by owner-occupiers of land and by owners or managers of business enterprises, with limited interference or assistance from governmental authorities. Even in a country such as Sweden, which is considered a rather advanced type of welfare state, about 95 percent of all enterprises are privately owned and operated, and consequently, despite the extent of government surveillance, the main task of administration is assumed by the persons, groups, or companies that own or control the Swedish enterprises. There is, in fact, as there is in all modern countries, a clear division of authority between the public and the private sectors. What has occurred in Sweden is largely this: the traditional, late medieval type of administrative control over landscapes by landlords, military groups, or the church has been almost wholly superseded by a popularly approved type of surveillance whose purpose is to benefit the largest number of citizens, but which leaves the major tasks of administration to the private owners of farms, forests, factories, and all other types of enterprise.[17]

The difference between avowedly "socialist" countries such as Sweden, Denmark, Finland, and Austria and countries such as the United States which profess to be nonsocialistic is largely semantic. The public sector is expanding in all modern countries, and in coun-

17. The clear mandate given the Social Democrats in the September 1968 election indicates that the majority of Swedish voters are apparently satisfied with the type of administrative supervision developed by the Socialists during the past thirty-five years.

tries engaged in nuclear competition or in the competitive conquest of outer space, the ratio between the private and the public sector has radically changed since the end of World War II.[18] In all "advanced" or "developed" countries—France, Britain, Japan, Italy, the United States, Canada, for example—the administration of landscapes has become the fairly clearly distinguished responsibility of government on the one hand and of persons, groups of persons (e.g., cooperative societies or trade unions), and legal organizations (corporations, unincorporated companies, or partnerships) on the other.

In less-developed areas there are trends pointing in the same direction. Thus in India, Ghana, and Mexico new experiments are being made not only to widen the administrative control of the state over economic enterprise but to limit the traditional administrative power of landlords (such as the Indian *zamindars*), military leaders, and churches, temples, and other sacerdotal institutions. But this task of "modernization" is extremely difficult because certain institutions are so deeply entrenched. Over centuries powerful, self-perpetuating systems of administration have rooted themselves into the legal, social, economic, and intellectual fabric of cultures, and it remains to be seen whether this control can be changed without recourse to violence and revolution.

The history of the Turkish conquest and continued occupation of the Balkans provides a vivid example of how permanent a systematic type of administration can become, "affecting for centuries the political, cultural, and economic developments."[19] From the tragic battle of Kosovo in 1389 until the Serbian Revolts in 1804—a period of over four hundred years[20]—the Osmanli Turks and their agents dominated the Balkan landscape, and as Lybyer has so clearly explained, "the military and the adminstrative organization" of the Empire "was one and the same thing."[21] By controlling communication lines, towns, and strategic points, the conquered areas could be easily reduced to a tribute-paying status. Oddly enough there was little effort to proselyte;

18. In the United States in 1968 about one-third of all capital formation was in the public sector.

19. Tomasovich, *Peasants, Politics, and Economic Change,* p. 22.

20. Full control over the area comprising the present "republics" of Serbia, Bosnia, and Herzegovina was not complete until Smederevo was captured (1459), Bosnia was crushed (1463), and Herzegovina humbled (1482).

21. Albert H. Lybyer, *The Government of the Ottoman Empire in the Time of Suleiman the Magnificent,* Cambridge, Mass., 1913, pp. 45–61, 90–113.

the Christian population was "left in peace . . . free to preserve its religious beliefs and church organization" and at liberty to engage in customary economic activities provided only that there was unfailing payment of taxes and tithes and rendering of the corvée. Here, then, was a rather benign form of government, but one in which "the state paid little or no attention to the promotion of economic activity"[22] and in which "the idea of labor for the public welfare or of effort toward progress was not present."[23] The system classified all land in the occupied area into tithe lands, tribute lands, and state lands,[24] but the actual administration envisaged only two types: a limited amount of land on which the government collected taxes and tithes directly[25] and the bulk of the land administered as military fiefs by feudal *spahis* (calvary leaders).

The idea underlying Turkish feudalism was derived from the *Sheri* law based on the Koran, which considered that all land taken from infidels was God's land to be held in trust by the Sultan, as head of the state. Hence, although it was assigned in varying-size parcels to the *spahis,* the ownership continued regalian, and whereas the *spahis* could live on their fiefs, which were generally passed on from father to son, they could not alienate the land, farm out the collection of rents or tithes, or act as judges over the farmers who tilled the fiefs. In short, the task of the *spahis* was exclusively administrative: to collect, on a share basis, the rents, tithes, and dues on a portion of God's land.

The position of the servile agrarian population was strangely different. Whereas the *spahis* could be summarily removed from their fiefs and lose all rights to income and residence, the serfs (mostly Christian but some Moslems) "held their land in heritable fashion"[26] and could not be evicted as long as they worked the land.[27] There were, of course, the obligations that went with this security of tenure: the payment of tithes to the *spahis,* the payment of taxes (via the *spahis*) to the Sultan and to the local government, and the rendering of a

22. Tomasovich, *Peasants, Politics, and Economic Change,* p. 23.

23. Lybyer, *Government of Ottoman Empire,* pp. 193–194.

24. Ibid., pp. 31–32.

25. These *mulk* lands were granted to Turkish settlers and to Mohammedanized peasants in Bosnia and Herzegovina; chief among the latter were the Bogomils whose Gnostic and Neo-Manichaean tenets had been condemned as heretical by both the Roman Catholic Church and the Eastern Orthodox Churches.

26. Tomasovich, *Peasants, Politics, and Economic Change,* p. 29.

27. Only if land remained unworked for three years could tenants (*reaya*) be evicted.

fixed amount of corvée. The tithes (originally tenths) could be paid only in produce, which was delivered to the farmsteads of the *spahis*. Unlike the situation in other feudal societies,[28] commutation of produce tithes into money payments was forbidden, a prohibition that kept the whole system rigid and almost changeless. The Sultan's taxes, however, were payable in money. They were assigned as a lump sum by the Belgrade Pashalik, apportioned among the *knežine* (units of local government), and then by each of these units to the individual taxpayers.

Skillfully designed to force the *spahis* to "tend to the business of the state rather than their personal interest",[29] the system emphasized stability and discouraged change. Gradually the peasants came to consider the lands they cultivated as "their full heritable property," subject, of course, to feudal obligations. This is why, after centuries of quiet submission, an angry revolt exploded when the eighteenth-century descendents of the fifteenth-century *spahis* began claiming the military fiefs as their own, fully heritable property and dared to assert they had the right to evict peasants who would not accept new conditions of tenancy.

It would be a mistake, however, to assume that the South Slavs completely accepted a condition of tithe-paying servitude. One effect of the Turkish conquest on the Balkan landscape was a gradual migration of the more energetic and ambitious young men, thus leeching the countryside of talent and energy. Two types of migration occurred, a movement of people into the mountainous areas[30] and an out-migration, particularly of young men, into the territory of the Hapsburgs, where they manned the "military frontier," a belt of settled soldiers that ultimately stretched from the Adriatic to the Carpathian Mountains. Both movements of population had retarding effects on the South Slav landscapes.[31] The flight to the mountains meant a decrease in field-crop agriculture and an increase in hilltop animal husbandry.[32]

28. See for example R. H. Tawney, *The Agrarian Problem in the Sixteenth Century*, London, 1912.

29. Tomasovich, *Peasants, Politics, and Economic Change*, p. 32.

30. Thousands moved into the rugged fastness of Montenegro, from which the Turks could not dislodge them and from which they launched guerilla sorties against the Turks.

31. During the "Great Migration" into Hungary in 1691, some 30,000 people were said to have migrated.

32. It was not an accident that the leader of the second Serbian revolt, Miloš Obrenović, was a herdsman.

The out-migration from the area of Turkish control often meant that whole areas were deserted, thus hastening the tendency toward decay and stagnation.

The Role of a Hierarchy of Markets in the Organization of Economic Landscapes

Contrasting with the organization of a landscape by military clique, religious leaders, tax gatherers, or other bureaucrats is the organization by producers of goods and services together with merchants and traders —in brief, by buyers and sellers. In complex, highly differentiated economies we are so accustomed to this form of spatial organization that we take it for granted, but there are vast areas of the world community which are hardly commercialized at all and even greater areas which are very imperfectly provided with exchange facilities. Admittedly, virtually all economies, even very backward ones, have some minuscule market arrangements. A random scattering of small market points where exchange of goods or services occurs occasionally is a far cry, however, from a systematic organization of a landscape by means of an interpenetrating market system. A truly effective exchange arrangement, which will permit producers to specialize, depends upon local collection points and larger regional assembly centers that are interlinked by a sales and payments system which provides incentives for producers and at the same time facilitates the distribution of goods in accordance with consumer preferences. A mechanism of this type, capable of integrating production, distribution, and payment, is normally a product of historical forces, not something that can be fashioned or created quickly. But, although it cannot be devised at will, its emergence can be hastened by planning and wise policies.

When a landscape is organized by such market forces a hierarchy of exchange centers ("central places") will normally evolve. Small local assembly and distribution activities will be found in villages and hamlets, and these markets will cater to the needs of people living in a relatively small encircling area. The perimeters of such local market areas will depend on the nature of the topography and on the road, rail, and water transport facilities. But these small markets, which for convenience may be called village markets, are interrelated with larger markets located in towns and cities. Surplus products from the village markets move to the town markets, while goods too specialized for villages to produce move from the towns to the villages. As an economy becomes more urbanized, still larger markets will develop in certain cities, particularly in urban centers strategically located for trade (at ports, river junctions, and railway centers) or for specialized production (near deposits of natural resources, near water power, or favored by other important locational factors). To these city markets both town markets and village markets will be delicately attuned, so that the entire hierarchy of exchange facilities will operate as an economic organism influencing the growth and development of an entire region. Moreover, some parts of the market system, usually (but certainly not always) the city components will be inter-related to varying degrees with foreign markets. Through these complex interconnections consumers in far distant cities will transmit their demands for meat, wool, cotton, eggs, or grain to remote village markets while producers in foreign countries will supply the tea, jade, coffee, or style goods for shops in domestic city, town, or village markets.

If such a system were developed in a region where there were no topographical variations that would interfere with the most direct travel and where there were no legal constraints that would prevent the construction of adequate roads, the pattern of market organization could be visualized as shown in Figure 1–3. In the center of the plain would be a city representing the largest single component of the regional market system. By the dictates of geometry the city would be surrounded by a band of six towns, each controlling a trade area roughly one-seventh of the total regional area dominated by the central city.[33] The trade area of each town market in turn would be divided into village trade areas (one of which is shown in the upper hexagon in Figure 1–3). In this ideal market allocation the entire region would be fully commercialized since all persons would be within convenient reach of some part of the market system.

One of the best examples of how a poor, relatively backward country, long organized by military leaders and feudal administrators, was able to make a fairly swift transition to an economy organized by market forces is provided by the nineteenth- and early twentieth-century history of Denmark. Ever since the separation of Denmark from Sweden in 1520, Denmark had all the characteristics of "a rapidly declining power." War with Sweden (1563–1570), involvement in the Thirty

33. This assumes that the central city itself would cater to the equivalent of a town market and would therefore perform two functions.

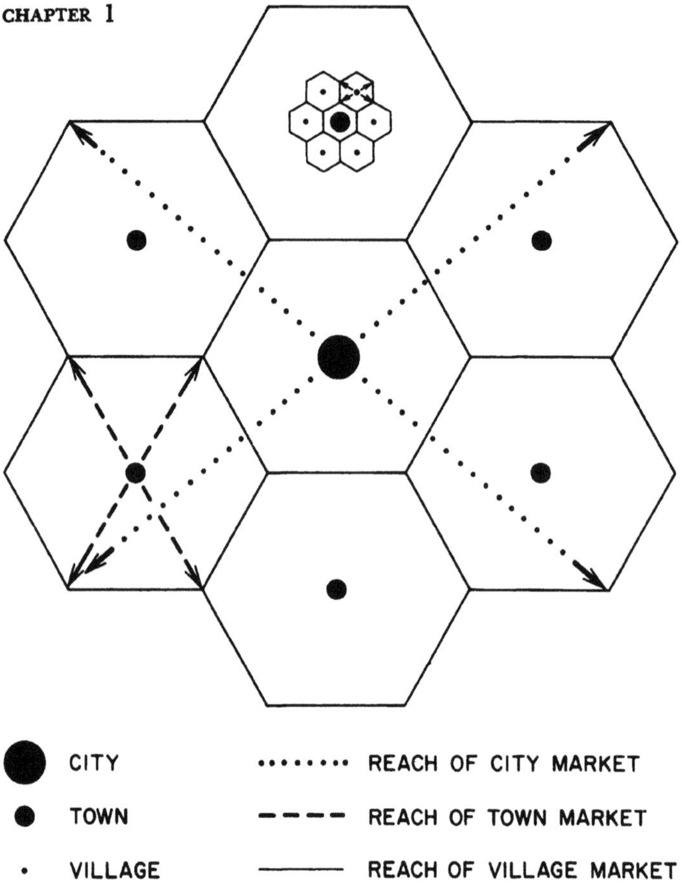

Figure 1–3 A Hierarchy of Market Centers and Market Areas

Years War, and another war with Sweden (1659) had led not only to the invasion of Jutland but to the surrender of two Norwegian provinces and loss of the rich south Swedish provinces.[34] These humbling events, however, did not lead to any loosening of military or feudal control over the Danish landscape. A military law of 1701 forbade peasants to leave the estates on which they were born, a restriction on mobility not relaxed until 1790.[35]

34. For a compact account of these unhappy events see William J. Harvey and Christian Reppian, *Denmark and the Danes,* London, 1915, Chapter 5.

35. The restriction first applied to the age bracket fourteen to thirty-five, but this was extended later to age fifty.

The eighteenth and nineteenth centuries brought yet more troubles. Through blunders in diplomacy, Denmark was plunged into war with both Sweden and Great Britain. Defeated in naval battles, her capital city bombarded, deserted by her presumed allies, Denmark had to sue for peace. The price was very high: after four hundred years Denmark lost Norway to Sweden (and Heligoland to England). The end was still not in sight! In 1848 the German-speaking population of Holstein and Schleswig rose in revolt against Danish rule, and their cause was championed by Prussia. After a momentary military success in 1849, the Danish army was vanquished, and in 1863 Holstein, Lauenberg, and Schleswig were lost. After the surrender of southern Sweden, Norway, and the southern provinces of Jutland, there was not much left of Denmark; it was an impoverished, wretched, exhausted country with poor, sandy soil, no minerals and few forests.[36] The consensus was that "the days of Denmark as a nation were numbered."[37]

In view of all these unfortunate vicissitudes, how was it possible for Denmark to make a transition to a dynamic, efficient, and democratic market economy? First there was cautious political preparation. A new constitution, promulgated in 1849, began the gradual erosion of the king's absolute power, and the right of the people to elect members of the *Folketing* (Lower House) soon led to the development of political parties. (Of these the Socialists were to become the ultimate policy makers, but that came much later.)[38] It was a radical branch of the democratic parties that led the assault on privilege, militarism, and the autocratic practices of the Prime Minister and prepared the way for governments in which the radical and Socialist parties progressively increased their popular support. But it was education rather than politics that set this remarkable transformation in motion.

Two quite different educational institutions were seminally influential in modernizing the Danish landscape. The first were the

36. "Whipped by fierce gales from the North Sea, which from time to time swept in over its western coast, 2800 square miles of [Jutland's] surface were waste—sand, which engulfed cultivated farms and even buildings; bogs, where the 'marsh king' reigned and wild swans and ducks found refuge; *Heden,* whose purple heather stretched unbroken mile on mile, solemn, silent, deserted. The independent peasantry of Jutland, longest to resist the enslaving power of the nobility, were . . . living in greatest poverty" Olive Dame Campbell, *The Danish Folk School, Its Influence on the Life of Denmark and the North,* New York, 1928, p. 26.

37. Harvey and Reppian, *Denmark and the Danes,* p. 85.

38. The early history of the Socialist party was extremely precarious. Meetings were prohibited, and leaders were imprisoned or deported to America.

Folkehöjskoler, the Danish Folk Schools, sometimes called the Peoples' High Schools. These wonderfully successful ventures in systematic adult education owed their inspiration to unorthodox clergymen and dedicated teachers who were dissatisfied with the formalism of traditional education. Chief among these movers and shakers were Christian Flor, who founded Rödding Folk School in 1814; Kristian Kold, a shoemaker's son who developed an evangelical zeal for the education of peasants; and, above all, N. F. S. Gruntvig, who propounded the educational philosophy that lay behind these inspiring institutions. The Folk Schools were not vocational schools; quite the reverse. Their object was to open up for young persons between the ages of eighteen and thirty-five a whole educational vista comprising such subjects as history, literature, mathematics, sociology, science, and music. The reformers felt that this intellectual richness should not be the privileged possession of the few, particularly of the city dwellers, but should be the heritage of all the people whatever their occupation or economic status. The schools succeeded because of the zeal of their organizers, even though they were privately organized and only gradually obtained state assistance. In 1900, fifty-three Folk Schools were in existence, by which time it had already become the custom for the sons and daughters of peasants to attend lectures and discussion at the schools in their vicinity.[39]

The agricultural schools, in contrast, were from the beginning rigorously vocational. Even so, a very close relation existed between them and the Folk Schools.[40] The agricultural schools were also privately owned, by individuals or associations, and received but very modest state subsidies in their formative years. An entering student was expected to have had three or four years' practical work on a farm and, preferably, a winter term at a Folk School. Once enrolled in an

39. For a vivid picture of these schools as seen through the eyes of a visiting Scottish-American, see Campbell, *The Danish Folk School,* particularly Chapters 7, 8, 9, and 10.

40. Campbell puts it this way: "The folk school is firmly attached to the soil. It seeks to relate the culture of books and art to the culture of the soil. . . . It does not forget the economic, and it never aims to divorce the farmer from his profession, the worker from his trade. It has in mind the well-being, the entire well-being of the Danish countryside." *Danish Folk School,* p. 184. The impact of the Folk School on the rural population can be appreciated when one learns that almost one-third of the rural population of Denmark have been students at these schools. On their cultural importance and their relation to the Danish economy, see Peter Manniche, *Living Democracy in Denmark,* Copenhagen, 1952.

agricultural school, however, he concentrated on subjects such as chemistry, farm crops, animal husbandry, dairying, agronomy, seeds and seed testing, meadow management, and other subjects designed to make him a better farmer. Eventually as cooperative creameries were established, more technical subjects had to be included in the curriculum so that graduates would be prepared to operate pasteurizing and other increasingly complex equipment and to cope with problems of cost accounting, warehousing, and marketing. The agricultural schools, of which twenty-two had been established by 1928,[41] represented a growing appreciation that, in order to overcome the handicaps visited upon her by military defeat, land alienation, and loss of manpower by emigration, Denmark would need to make the very best possible use of her natural and human resources. It was gradually recognized by intellectuals, by liberal-minded political leaders, and by reflective peasants that the key to the entire development problem was the creation of incentives that would induce farmers to convert heathland into pastures and to modernize every branch of agriculture. For without deposits of coal or iron, without waterpower or basic industrial raw materials, any important industrial transformation such as had occurred in western Germany, Belgium, and Great Britain seemed most unlikely. Denmark would have to find its economic salvation in the agrarian realm. The problem was how to do it.

The whole agrarian pattern had to be changed. Great estates had to be divided into peasant holdings. In the face of growing competition from cheap American and Canadian wheat, farms had to convert their grain fields into permanent pastures and concentrate on the production of butter, and cheese. But not wholly: feed crops for pigs and poultry needed to be produced, although as export markets for eggs, butter, and bacon widened, it became profitable to import a larger share of feed grains, fertilizers, and oil cakes. By the aid of an enlightened public policy, far-reaching land reforms were authorized. The scattered strips of peasant holdings were consolidated,[42] and eccleciastical tithes were

41. Three of these were horticultural schools and three were specially designed for the benefit of smallholders.

42. Only Sweden can match the thoroughness with which land fragmentation was ended. The very precise studies of Folke Dovring show that in 1950 only 5 percent of Swedish and Danish agricultural land was in need of consolidation. This contrasts with 50 percent in Germany, 30 percent in France, 28 percent in Belgium, and 40 percent in Austria. See Folke Dovring, *Land and Labor in Europe in the Twentieth Century,* The Hague, 1965, p. 40.

capitalized (at twenty-five years' purchase), so that with government aid peasants could buy land that was tithe-free. Great estates were purchased by the government and divided into freeholds which peasants could buy on credit. By 1919 this revolution in land ownership was essentially completed. Landlordism had been liquidated. Over 94 percent of the land was owned by farmers, and in a landscape which was predominantly feudal in 1850, only 306 estates of 600 acres or more were left in 1929.[43]

Yet for all that is said about the wisdom of land reform and the virtues of cooperation (which was developed into an elaborate system in Denmark), the cause of the transformation of the Danish landscape is to be found chiefly in the development of a network of markets. Rather parodoxically, Denmark, which had been handicapped by surviving medieval agrarian institutions,[44] stood to gain from her medieval urban heritage. It should be recalled that medieval Denmark was a great power controlling such large territories in what now is Sweden, Norway, Germany, and Russia (Estonia) that "the Baltic had become a Danish Mediterranean."[45] The collection of maritime tolls and the transhipment of goods had fostered the growth of a number of port cities, while the building of churches and other religious institutions had provided nuclei for other central places, giving the area of contemporary Denmark a total of seventy provincial towns.[46] These urban centers played a most important role in the commercialization of the Danish landscape after 1870. For although Copenhagen grew somewhat faster,[47] the population of the provincial towns doubled in a thirty-year period. In the process of growth the character of the towns changed. The guild system, which had been entrenched in the eighteenth century, was progressively challenged by a new group of entrepreneurs who catered to the needs of the owner-occupiers of the adjacent farms. The emergence of this new group of small businessmen had been made possible by the Trade Act of 1857, which forbade any restrictions on "free and equal access to trade," thereby undermining

43. For a brief account of the "Passing of Landlordism" see Frederic C. Howe, *Denmark the Co-operative Way,* New York, 1936, Chapter 20.

44. Landlordism, ecclesiastical tithes, land fragmentation, and taxes in kind.

45. Harvey and Reppian, *Denmark and the Danes,* p. 71.

46. Harold L. Westergaard, *Economic Development in Denmark before and during the World War,* Oxford, 1922, p. 20.

47. Its population grew from 198,000 in 1871 to 477,000 in 1901, an increase of 141 percent in thirty years, or 4.7 percent a year.

the monopoly power that town-located guilds had so long exercised.[48] The dynamism imparted to the economy by freedom of entry into trade and industry is reflected in the rapid growth of Denmark's industrial and commercial work force, which increased 2½ times between 1857 and 1911.[49] At the same time a series of group activities and legislative measures had stabilized and increased the buying power of the growing urban population. The organization of trade unions in the 1880's led to a rise in the level of urban wages despite the opposition of employers' associations, while the rapid growth of Friendly Societies provided continued spending power for many of the sick, unemployed, and aged. Then came swift progress in social insurance patterned after German models, covering compensation for industrial accidents, old-age pensions, invalid insurance, unemployment benefits, and pension grants for widows and orphans.[50] Although it is difficult to quantify the contribution these measures made to the improvement of urban incomes, it is surely no coincidence that between 1882 and 1909 the earning of artisans rose 50 percent, the pay of unskilled laborers 67 percent, and the compensation of women 58 percent.

It was by this domestic urban progress and by an even swifter growth of industrial cities in Britain, Belgium, and Germany that Danish agriculture was reciprocally stimulated. This rush to the city as Clapham called it,[51] increased the total demand for food in city markets at a time when a vast expansion of cereal growing in the United States and Canada together with a reduction in both rail and ocean transport markedly lowered the delivered price of all the bread grains. Whereas this was a momentary hardship to Danish farmers, in the long run it worked to their advantage. For cheap grain meant cheap flour and bread for urban dwellers in all European industrial countries, leaving relatively more of family budgets available for dairy products and meat. To this situation the Danish farmers progressively adapted themselves by shifting away from cereals to the production of butter, cheese, bacon, beef, eggs, and dressed poultry. The first step was to

48. For the relation of the Trade Act to the general principles underlying the Free Constitution of 1849 see Westergaard, *Economic Development in Denmark,* p. 17.

49. Ibid., p. 21.

50. For a concise account of these early experiments with social security, see Westergaard, *Economic Development in Denmark,* pp. 30–66.

51. J. H. Clapham, *The Economic Development of France and Germany, 1815–1914,* Cambridge, 1928, p. 279.

raise cattle and export marketable animals on the hoof,[52] but in the nineties the Danes began slaughtering both cattle and hogs and exporting meat.[53] Meantime the export of butter had increased almost fifteenfold.[54] Indeed it soon became evident that the largest export demand was for butter, bacon, and eggs.

In this widening market system, large central places—industrial cities in Britain or in the Ruhr—relayed their demand to smaller central places in Denmark, which, in turn, transmitted attractive price offers to villages and farms. The much-heralded Danish cooperative system, was, for the most part, a response to this latent market pull rather than a cause of it. For as Dovring has so wisely explained, cooperation is essentially a technique whereby producers whose scale of operation is too small to afford the needed "internal economies" can achieve the advantages of scale for the procurement of inputs, the marketing of outputs, and the obtaining of credit.[55] Yet at the same time the cooperative creameries, slaughterhouses, or egg-assembling centers could actually widen demand by insuring uniform, consistent, and dependable quality of all their branded products. For that reason Danish ("Lur" brand) butter, Danish packaged bacon, and Danish dated eggs became famous throughout Europe.

The economic history of Denmark from 1860 to 1914 (when development was briefly distorted by World War I) affords one of the most instructive examples of the transformation of a medieval type of economic landscape, stagnant and patently inefficient, into a closely interlocked market mechanism whereby the entire economy was changed, rationalized, and technologically modernized. The effects reveal themselves in many vivid ways. The Danish farmer has now the highest land-man ratio in continental Europe,[56] and although much of his work calls for careful attention to detail,[57] the labor applied per hectare is well below the German, Finnish, Dutch, Belgian, and Italian requirements.[58] Output per man in Danish agriculture had risen in 1960 to the equivalent of what had been achieved in the United States in the early 1940's. This

52. The export of live cattle increased from about 50,000 a year in 1870 to about 100,000 in 1885.

53. Westergaard, *Economic Development in Denmark,* p. 68.

54. From about 5 million kilos in 1870 to 70 million in 1900.

55. Dovring, *Land and Labor in Europe,* pp. 202–205.

56. Dovring, *Land and Labor in Europe,* p. 63.

57. For example, milking, feeding animals, grading of eggs.

58. Dovring, *Land and Labor in Europe,* p. 92, table 12.

contrasts with a British output in 1960 which was close to what the United States had achieved in the middle 1930's. With about 97 percent of farm area in the hands of owner-occupiers (96 percent of the number of farms)[59] the Danish land distribution is unique and unrivalled. By means of popular education and judicious public policy, and with the help of a rather fortuitous growth of foreign demand on which Denmark, because of her strategic location, could capitalize, a fairly swift restructuring of the Danish landscape could occur, making fuller and more effective use of human and natural resources. "The Danish rural reforms," as Dovring has said, "were intelligent and timely,"[60] but this is only one key to this agreeable episode. The transformation of Denmark into a modern, market-organized economy, with adequate safeguards against the abuses so frequently associated with unregulated enterprise-oriented systems, demonstrates quite clearly that "a socio-economic structure is not just a mechanism manned by people who operate it and live within it"; it gives expression to a mentality, to value systems, beliefs, culture, and a way of life.[61] What the Danes achieved, therefore, was not merely an economic rationalization of their landscape but a harmonious adaptation of this structure to an ideology —an ideology that was acceptable to the great majority of the Danish people!

59. Ibid., p. 168, table 30; p. 169, table 31.
60. Ibid., p. 388.
61. Ibid., p. 384.

CHAPTER 2 THE EARLY ORGANIZATION OF SPACE IN COUNTRIES NOW CONSIDERED "DEVELOPED"

The Thesis

In the long, long history of "economic development"—despite the modernity of the term the process is a very old one—a great deal of experimentation has been made in spatial organization. The complex metamorphosis of the manor is really a chapter in the search for tolerably satisfactory patterns of agrarian resource allocation, and so is the history of truncated Norwegian farms with their *saeters* (mountain pastures) often many miles from the home farms to which they belonged. In recent times the Russian attempt to operate townless agrarian landscapes is yet another chapter in this ceaseless search for workable patterns of spatial organization. But except for the Soviet ventures, which are based on the assumption that traditional municipal economic functions can be performed by *kolkhozes* and machine tractor stations, a successful configuration has consistently had a market town as its economic center. Consequently the key to the economic development of countries or regions is normally to be found in the historical relations between town and country. The more contexts in which this phenomenon is studied, the clearer it becomes that development is a function of agrarian commercialization and that the rationalization of agrarian conduct under a pecuniary stimulus calls for a network of conveniently located central places where efficient exchange of goods and services can occur. The overall relation of such a hierarchy of central places to development is examined in Chapters 3 and 4. It is the purpose of this chapter merely to lay some groundwork for this general theory by examining a few historical examples of relatively early development.

In choosing these examples it becomes necessary to advance some definition of a "developed country," and since this is a relative term, the parameters will necessarily be somewhat imprecise. In general, however, a developed country has characteristics such as the following. It has diversified its economic activities, thereby permitting people to engage in tasks and occupations for which they are best suited by aptitude and training. It has availed itself, whether by invention or adoption, of enough modern technology so that the productivity of its work force is of a high order, and it is this degree of productivity that permits the earnings of producers of goods or services to be sufficiently large so that average consumption insures a satisfactory standard of living. The whole economy is effectively integrated by means of an interdependent market structure, an infrastructure of transport, and a sensitive banking and financial system. Personal and institutional savings are regularly accumulated, thus making capital formation a normal and regular occurrence. Some of the currently generated capital is used for improving or maintaining the efficiency of the productive mechanism directly; some is allocated as social capital for such institutions as schools, hospitals, and research laboratories, which help to increase the supply of high-grade manpower and to stimulate discoveries, inventions, and innovations. Lastly, even though there may be very great differences in wealth and income, a developed country will normally be more egalitarian than one less-developed because both the incentives and the opportunity for increasing status are present in societies that put a premium on achievement.

Since it is possible to quantify only some of the performance characteristics of a developed country, such as gross national product, rates of savings, input-output ratios, man-hour productivity, and not possible to measure many other aspects, such as the will to work or the penchant for the maintenance of equipment, any attempt to designate the truly developed countries in the world community is fraught with considerable risk. But there is little disagreement about some countries that have quite clearly reached enviable levels of economic performance. The early history of four such countries, Britain, Belgium, Japan, and the United States, are therefore briefly examined here. All have experienced notable economic development, although they differ markedly in ethnic characteristics, geography, and resource equipment. Some of them "developed" earlier than others, and for some the development was partial rather than nationwide. Even so, they all have certain common characteristics, and it is these general factors that are the main concern of this discussion.

England in the Sixteenth Century

By 1500 England was no longer, if she ever had been, a collectivity of self-supporting rural communities.[1] She was well supplied with market towns where farmers and graziers could sell their produce or their animals and buy their farm supplies or consumer goods. Scattered through the landscape were at least 760 market towns, some of them newly created in the Tudor era, but many of venerable age.[2] The region of greatest market-town density was the eastern portion of England (see Figure 2–1), because, of course, that part of the country was better located for trade with the Continent than the north or the Midland counties. Even so, it is remarkable to observe (Fig. 2–2) how well organized in a market sense most of the central counties actually were. Only in the north (Fig. 2–3) was there a noticeably thin pattern of market towns. But since this area was primarily a cattle-raising economy, and since live animals can move quite long distances without any serious impairment of their value, the market towns in the northern counties could, quite properly, be spaced farther apart.

What seem to have been the locational factors that had created this polka-dot landscape of market towns? Some markets had come into existence because of peculiar circumstance; for example, a new Elizabethan wool market was established at Marshfield (Gloucestershire) because Bath was "infected and greatly visited by the plague." But the establishment of most markets had a more general explanation: the need to provide exchange facilities for an adjacent agricultural region of a certain scope. Depending on their functions, market towns were of several major types. The smaller centers, with populations of from six

1. In the preparation of this section I have drawn extensively on an excellent chapter by Alan Everitt, "The Marketing of Agricultural Produce," in *The Agrarian History of England and Wales*, Vol. IV, *1500–1640*, ed. Joan Thirsk, Cambridge, 1967.

2. Of thirty-four market towns in Gloucestershire "all but five had been founded before the Black Death [1348]" (Everitt, "The Marketing of Agricultural Produce," p. 466).

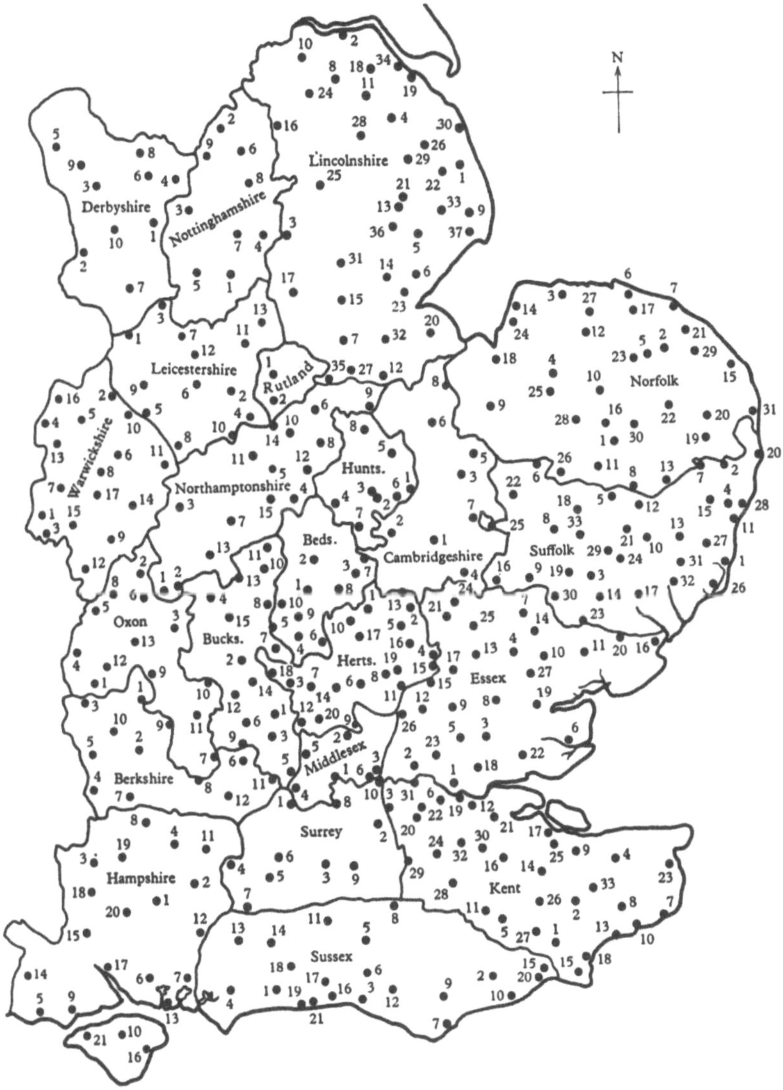

Figure 2–1 Markets in Eastern England, circa 1500–1640
SOURCE: *The Agrarian History of England and Wales*, Vol. IV, ed. J. Thirsk, Cambridge: Cambridge University Press, 1967, p. 473.

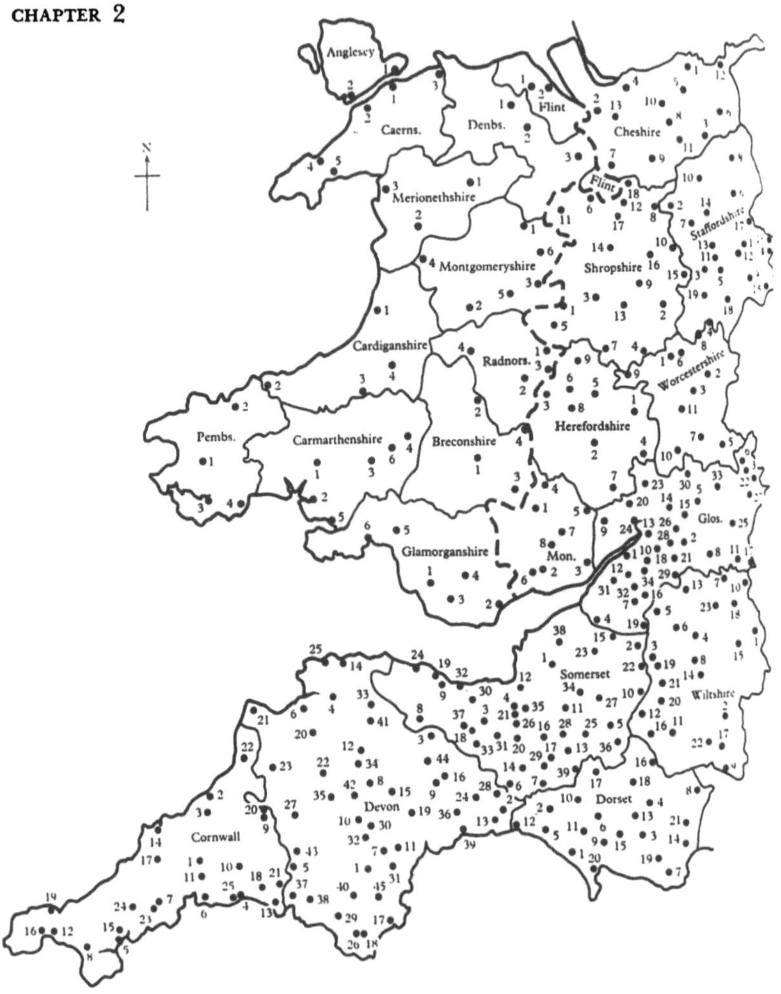

Figure 2–2 Markets in Western England and Wales, circa 1500–1640
SOURCE: *The Agrarian History of England and Wales,* Vol. IV, ed. J. Thirsk, Cambridge: Cambridge University Press, 1967, p. 470.

hundred to a thousand people, served a hinterland of perhaps 7 or 8 square miles,[3] and these were probably the most typical components of England's market network. These smaller markets, however, usually had a satellitic relation to "shire" towns, which had populations of

3. If the maximum reach of a small market were $2\frac{1}{2}$ miles, the area served would be about 7.85 square miles.

several thousand, more varied crafts and specialized occupations, and which exerted an economic influence in one way or another over a wide countryside of fields, pastures, villages, and hamlets. Even larger were provincial cities which were not merely centers for the sale and assemblage of farm produce but consumption centers. Thus Ipswich with its

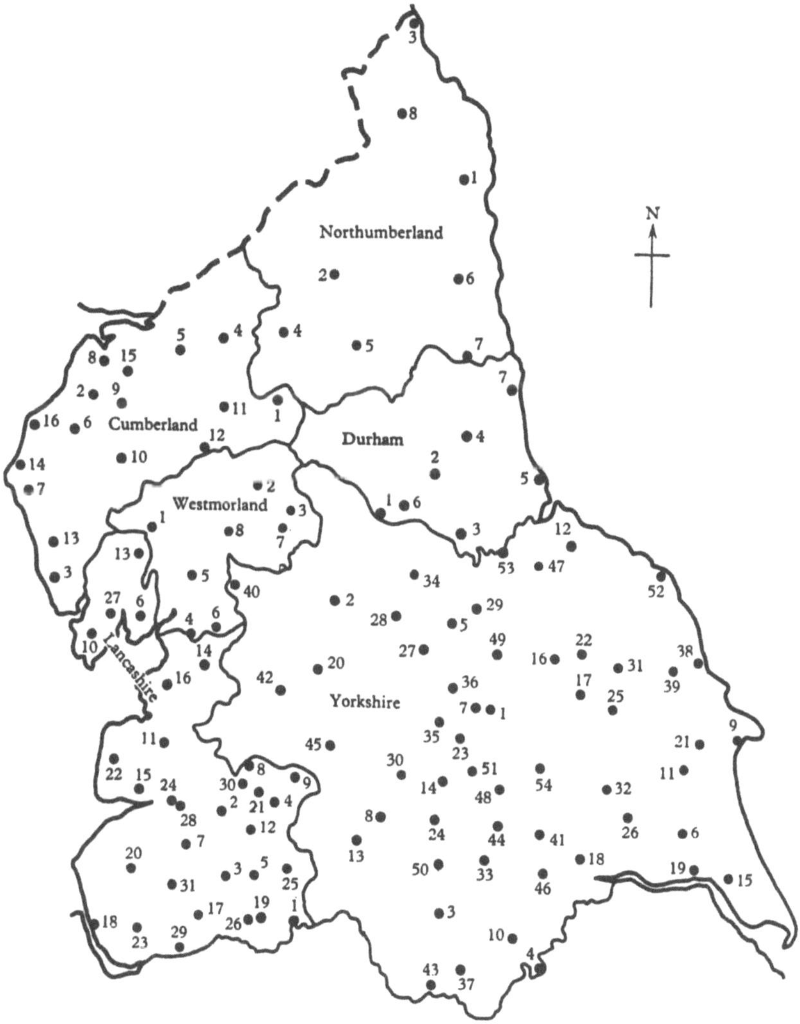

Figure 2–3 Markets in Northern England, circa 1500–1640
SOURCE: *The Agrarian History of England and Wales,* Vol. IV, ed. J. Thirsk, Cambridge: Cambridge University Press, 1967, p. 468.

fourteen churches, Norwich with its skillful wool workers, York and Salisbury with their famous cathedrals, and Coventry with its metal industries were central places with populations ranging up to twelve thousand people.

One cannot particularize the factors that had led to the location of all these market towns. Some were at road crossings, others at ferry sites on navigable rivers. But all that survived were suitably located in relation to a hinterland which supplied the marketable produce and were accessible to itinerant buyers of staple produce—grain, wool, cattle, butter, cheese—and to the even more mobile sellers of shoes, clothing, household supplies, and other consumer goods. In addition to the itinerant merchants, most market towns, except the smallest, had a coterie of resident artisans whose shops stood near enough to the market cross to lure country people and tempt them to buy their wares. But a market town was not merely a trade center. It was, as Everitt has so aptly said, "the focus of the rural life around it. Its square and taverns provided the meeting place for yeomen and husbandmen, not only to buy and sell, but to hear the news, listen to sermons, criticize the government or organize insurrection. Its carpenters, wheelwrights, ploughwrights and other craftsmen existed to minister to the needs of the dependent villages. Its society was closely intertwined with that of the countryside."[4] It was, in short, an organizing mechanism which had transformed the countryside into an enchainment of agro-urban communities.

The degree to which the English network of agro-urban market centers commercialized the countryside can be seen from the relatively small size of the market areas they served. Figure 2–4 shows quite clearly a crescent of counties arching around London from Dorset to Suffolk that had market hinterlands of less than 30,000 acres (47 square miles); in such areas, theoretically, no one would be more than four miles from a market. Farther west in Cornwall and Devon, in the "home counties,"[5] and in Kent the market areas were a little larger, 30,000 to 37,500 acres (between 47 and 58 square miles), and here the maximum distance from the market, theoretically, would not exceed 4½ miles. In the Midlands, in Norfolk, Sussex, Hampshire, and Lancashire the market areas ranged in size from 37,500 acres to 45,000 (from 58 to 70 square miles), making the theoretical maximum distance well under 5 miles. In Lincoln, Chester, Shropshire, Hampshire, and Surrey the market areas

4. Everitt, "The Marketing of Agricultural Produce," p. 488.
5. Buckinghamshire, Bedfordshire, Hertfordshire, and Essex.

covered from 45,000 to 55,000 acres (70 to 80 square miles), and here the greatest average distance from a market would, theoretically, be slightly over 5 miles. It was only in the wolds of Yorkshire and the hills and mountains of the northwest counties that market areas were really large, ranging from 55,000 acres up to 100,000 acres (80 to 156 square

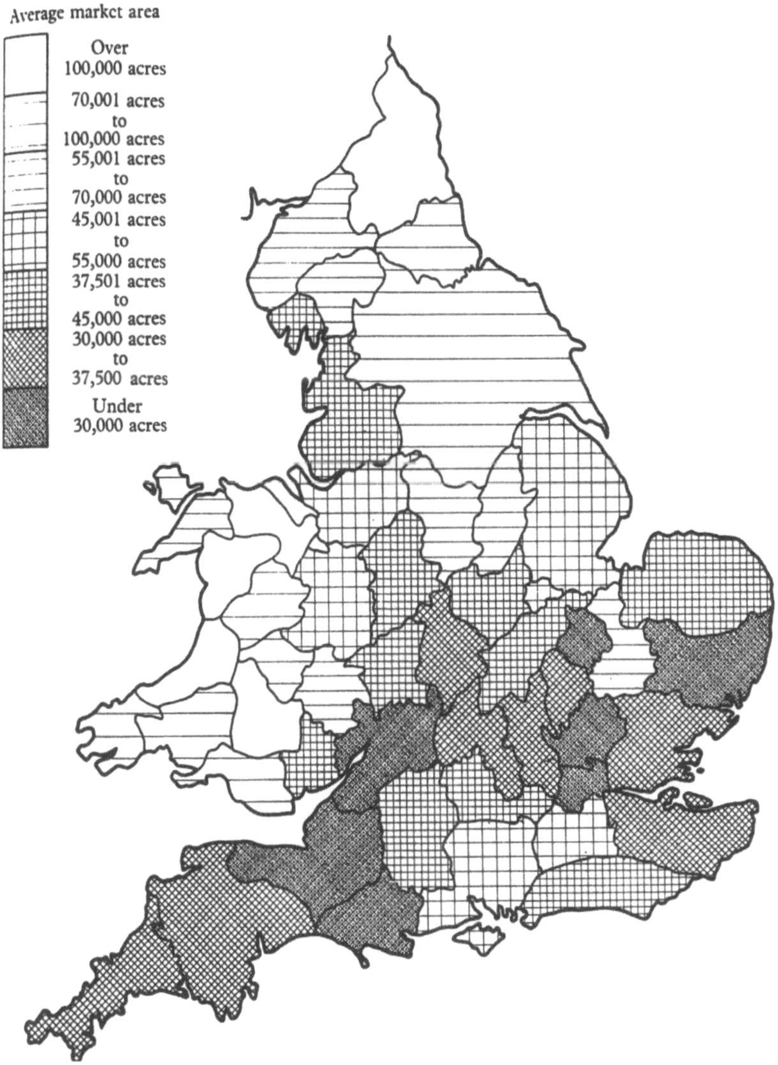

Figure 2–4 Size of Market Areas in England and Wales, circa 1500–1640
SOURCE: *The Agrarian History of England and Wales,* Vol. IV, ed. J. Thirsk, Cambridge: Cambridge University Press, 1967, p. 497.

miles), and here the perimeter of a market area might be an average of 7 miles from a market-area center. But all these estimates are based on a very unrealistic assumption, namely, that England was a perfectly level plain and that topography and complete freedom to cross anyone's property would permit people to travel on the radii of circles. This, of course, was not the case. The actual distance to market was considerably greater because travelers had to follow roads that would wind around hills, over mountains, through defiles or detour along the boundaries of fields or woodlands. Yet even when all these contour and property factors are considered, the majority of country people, as Table 2–1 indicates, were within 10 miles of a market, and, except in the north, only a small minority had to travel 20 miles or more to reach a market town.

Table 2–1 Distances Traveled to Tudor Markets (percentage of people traveling)

Region	1–5½ miles	6–9½ miles	10–19½ miles	20 miles or more	Total under 10 miles	Total under 20 miles
South	31	38	31	0	69	100
East	60	25	13	2	85	98
West	25	35	25	15	60	85
Midlands	36	14	29	21	50	79
North	17	13	20	50	30	50
All England	39	26	20	15	65	35

SOURCE: *The Agrarian History of England and Wales,* Vol. IV, ed. J. Thirsk, Cambridge: Cambridge University Press, 1967, p. 498.

It ought not be assumed, however, that all agricultural produce would be sold in the most accessible market. Sellers, then as now, would seek whichever market offered prospects of the highest prices. Consequently some products would tend to be sold in more specialized markets, and for that reason high-value goods of low weight would travel farther than low-value goods of high weight. Perimeters are therefore traceable which roughly measure the travel range of various goods, and these isovectures (equal-transport cost points forming a market perimeter) will more accurately reflect the market pull of particular markets. The data available for Tudor England indicates that farmers selling grain seldom traveled more than ten miles to their markets and usually less than five.[6] Livestock was brought from a much larger hinterland, and whereas eleven or twelve miles was the typical distance in south-central England, in the north of England drovers moved their herds forty or even fifty miles. Wool, which is bulky but light, was brought by pack animals from distances ranging from twenty to forty miles. Thus, as Figure 2–5 shows, the "reach" of markets was not uniform for all commodities, and it was this variable reach that made the marketing system more sensitive and more efficient.

Another aspect of the English market system should be noted. Because of the large number of central places, particularly, in the east,

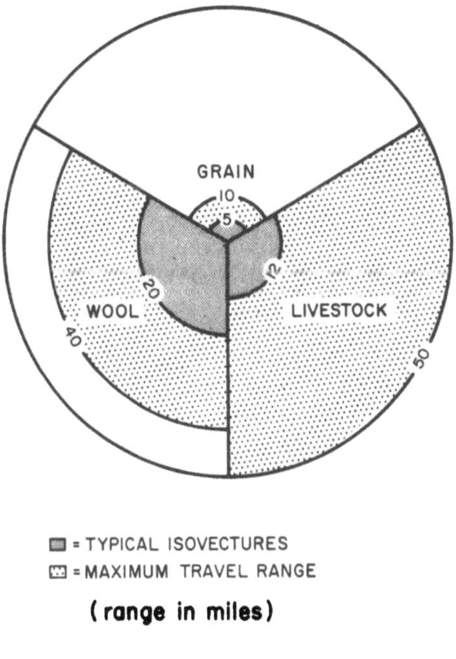

Figure 2–5 Travel Range of Sample Products in Tudor England
SOURCE: Data from *The Agrarian History of England and Wales,* Vol. IV, ed. J. Thirsk, Cambridge: Cambridge University Press, 1967, p. 499.

6. Data I compiled in India (Kanpur region in Uttar Pradesh) in 1966 indicate that food grains, on the average, were hauled in bullock carts more than twice this distance (up to 23 miles). This, of course, indicates the relatively inadequate commercialization of the Indian countryside, not half as well supplied today with markets as Britain was in 1600. For more details on Indian market isovectures, see p. 111.

many farmers were not bound to a single local market but could choose the best among several nearby selling places. To put it another way, markets trespassed on the trade areas of other markets, luring sellers or buyers by better prices. Not all farmers could avail themselves of the price differentials that emerged, but many large farmers could, as the Shuttleworths of Lancashire did when they "sold their beans and wheat at Preston and Ormskirk, their meal at Padihan, their horses at Wigan, their heifers at Blackburn, their sheep at Haslingden and their geldings in London."[7] The great majority of small farmers had a smaller range of choice; for the most part they sold locally to grain buyers, horse traders, or other dealers, who, in turn, disposed of their purchases in larger city markets or sold to merchants with cross-Channel business connections. Through them the English market system became progressively linked with the trade centers of Flanders, France, Holland, and Spain. Wool had long been England's chief export, but grain was also very important.[8] As British farming became more specialized, many other products proved to be profitable exports: malt, butter, cheese, and hops were added to traditional exports such as leather, sheepskins, cattle, and horses. All these commodities served as payment goods for a great variety of imports from relatively more-advanced industrial areas in the Low Countries, South Germany, Northern France, and Italy, thereby linking the rapidly developing British economy with progressive and dynamic areas of continental Europe.

It ought not be assumed, however, that all was well in England's green and pleasant land. Ecclesiastical landlordism had been abruptly ended by the seizure of the vast properties of monasteries, but the Crown rather hastily alienated these lands, thereby enlarging many existing great estates or creating new ones. Estate farming, however, was declining. More and more land was being leased to energetic yeomen whose cash incomes were rising steadily as their productivity improved and as prices for farm produce increased. But rising prices worsened the economic condition of agricultural laborers and of many landlords who had rented their land on long leases and who now were not able to save or invest. As a consequence more and more of the costs of maintaining fences, buildings, and other agricultural capital were

7. John Harland, ed., *The House and Farm Accounts of the Shuttleworths of Gawthorpe Hall,* 1856. See Everitt, "The Marketing of Agricultural Produce," p. 501.

8. For details see N. S. B. Gras, *The Evolution of the English Corn Market,* Cambridge, Mass., 1926.

being transferred to tenants.[9] The articulation of the market system was therefore steadily transforming the character of English landscapes.[10] Despite tensions and strains, which were to intensify until they were contorted and further inflamed during the Civil War, very real progress and development was occurring. Farm productivity was steadily increasing as higher yields proved the wisdom of more effective crop rotations, heavier manuring of fields and pastures, reclamation of wasteland, and the use of better farm tools.[11] A veritable passion for increased production became the fashion; "men were imbued with the conviction that everything could and should be employed and improved. With economy and ingenuity every living thing, where possible, was pressed into the service of man—wild fruits, wild animals, weeds, wildflowers, insects—all found a use in agriculture or as medicines to promote the health of men and stock."[12] Notable progress was made in developing better varieties of wheat, rye, barley, oats, and beans. Industrial crops were planted: dyestuffs such as woad, madder, and saffron, and a variety of other plants, among which tobacco and hops became very popular. All these changes were stimulated by the network of markets where buyers stood ready to reward innovating farmers with prices that left good margins over costs.

Perhaps the most important effect of the network of market towns was their capacity to stimulate agrarian savings and investment; and, more and more, it was the farmers who had leased land from landlords and the small owner-occupiers who were chiefly engaged in capital formation. They could buy better breeding stock or better tools, drain or marl their land, build new stables and granaries because their cash incomes were increasing. It took capital to engage in livestock fattening, which had become a specialized branch of English farming by 1550,[13] as it did to build up large dairy herds. But to an ever greater extent specialization became the order of the day as farmers responded to new

9. For a very careful analysis of these trends, see a chapter by Peter Bowden, "Agricultural Prices, Farm Profits, and Rents," in *The Agrarian History of England and Wales,* IV, particularly, pp. 674–695.

10. R. H. Tawney's *The Agrarian Problem in the Sixteenth Century,* London, 1912, very vividly describes this transformation by detailed sample regional studies.

11. For details see Joan Thirsk's chapter, "Farming Techniques," in *The Agrarian History of England and Wales,* IV, pp. 161–199.

12. Ibid., p. 161. This passion for productivity found perhaps its most complete expression in the writings of Nehemiah Grew. See my *Predecessors of Adam Smith,* New York, 1937, Ch. 7.

13. Bowden, "Agricultural Prices," p. 644.

opportunities, and as more critical consumers, whose tastes and desires were transmitted through the market system, insisted on better-quality vegetables and fruits, on beef from yard-fed steers, on fresh eggs and well-made butter. When one asks why Britain took such a lead in economic development in the eighteenth century, it is well to recall the remarkable progress in economic development she had already made years before the death of Queen Elizabeth or the publication of William Shakespeare's plays.

The Rise of the Belgian Towns

The history of the Low Countries[14] provides an instructive example of how a rather bleak agrarian landscape that had been organized before the eleventh century by counts or bishops, who were, respectively, the leaders of military or ecclesiastical authority, was gradually but progressively transformed as traders, merchants, and artisans established themselves at strategic growth points. So thorough was the change that by the sixteenth century the entire region was studded with renowned market towns and cities, and Flanders, Brabant, Hainault, and Holland were considered to be among the most developed areas of Europe.[15] But, as Pirenne the distinguished historian of Belgium has pointed out, this process of urbanization came much later than corresponding town and city development in Italy, in the Rhineland, or in the upper Danube region.[16] What was it that set this powerful, albeit belated, town-making process in motion?

Geographic factors were no doubt very important since the Low Countries lay athwart important caravan- or water-borne trade routes between southern Europe and the Hansa-controlled trade areas of northwest Europe. The initial town nucleation, however, antedated the great trade organization centered in the Baltic and had therefore a

14. The term is here used to comprehend the territory now comprising modern Belgium, Holland, and the French Departments of Nord and Pas-de-Calais.

15. English economic literature of the seventeenth century is replete with praise and admiration for "Dutch" economic policies and practices. As an example, see Andrew Yarranton, *England's Improvement by Sea and Land, or How to Beat the Dutch Without Fighting*, London, 1677. The oft-repeated argument was that if England really wanted economic development, she should follow the wise expedients that had been so successful in the Low Countries.

16. Henri Pirenne, *Belgian Democracy: Its Early History*, Manchester, 1915, p. 1.

more local origin. Pirenne has explained the process in this sequence.[17] In order to defend their territories the counts built castles, not as permanent residences but as places of refuge for their followers and their serfs, and by the seventh century the landscape was dotted with these *castra*. At the same time bishops had established episcopal churches and palaces which became nuclei for communities of monks, clerics, and their servants. But neither the military strongholds nor the episcopal sees were really towns. Nor had the small states as yet developed any capital cities, for like the Moghul Emperors in India of a later period,[18] the Low Country counts traveled through their rural dominions, dispensing justice and collecting taxes. A few of the strategically located castles did become places where tolls were collected, whether from wagoners or boatmen, and here small markets grew up for victualing the local inhabitants and the travelers. But most of the castle communities and many of the ecclesiastical centers failed to grow into towns or cities since they were "essentially military and administrative posts" rather than market towns capable of organizing the economy of their hinterlands. It was therefore neither the military nor the ecclesiastical organization of the Belgian landscape that was responsible for the development of the remarkable network of genuinely functional urban centers that grew up in the Low Countries.

What did happen was that at nodal trading points—the head of a gulf (Bruges), a bridge site (Maestricht), the confluence of two rivers (Liege), or a portage place (Louvain)—merchants, teamsters, boatmen, or stevadors would congregate, and these places gradually became genuine economic centers. They increased in size as traffic grew and required a dependable food supply from the adjacent rural area. Such a community (*portus*) became a permanent commercial center, and its growth, indeed its very survival, depended on continuous commercial activity. It attracted people of all manner of skills and aptitudes: strong laborers as porters and warehousemen, bright young men who could become bookkeepers and money changers, quick-witted people who could learn how to buy cheap and sell dear, or fearless serfs who dared to run away from the lands to which they were legally bound (*ascriptiti terrae*). For this motley group a body of law was needed rather different from the stereotyped manorial or canon law, a code that would compre-

17. Ibid., Chapter 1.
18. See pp. 13–14.

hend not merely criminal law but would be flexible enough to cover the needs of a pulsing business community. What emerged was "merchants' law" (*jus mercatorum*), which facilitated business transactions by reason of its simplicity and its democratic application.

These trading centers grew up *de facto* not *de jure*. Shrewd counts saw no reason to restrain a type of development that promised to increase their revenues and their reputation, and whereas they may at times have harassed the new communities, they did not suppress them. As for the bishops, they largely ignored the new trade communities until they discovered that the merchant centers were beginning to challenge their authority, when they tried "to subject them to their own unlimited paternal rule."[19] This proved much more difficult than the tradition-bound prelates had expected. A passion for self-government flamed up in the new market towns, and the burghers soon developed considerable skill in arousing the town dwellers against the bishops.[20] The freedom which the town dwellers sought was by no means wholly political; they wanted exemption from feudal obligations and ecclesiastical tithes; and an end to the church prohibitions on usury, regrating, and forestalling. They wanted the right to carry on business as they thought proper, and by skillfully pitting the counts against the bishops they steadily increased their rights to control municipal markets and obtained other privileges such as exemption from military duties and from other servile obligations.

As the Belgian landscape became dotted with "active and flourishing towns," the agrarian hinterlands became progressively commercialized. New opportunities for nimble-fingered young people opened up in the town-centered textile industries, and by reason of their economic and social attraction, the market towns grew while the castle communities and many of the old ecclesiastical centers moldered or disappeared. The towns had actually replaced the *castra,* rendering not only the services—mainly protection—that the castles had provided but also supplying the country people with outlets for their farm produce and with an increasing variety of consumer goods.

Since from the beginning the population of the towns was heterogeneous, the rights of all kinds of people had to be respected. "Town

19. Pirenne, *Belgian Democracy*, p. 29.

20. As early as 1077 the artisans and traders of Cambrai rose in revolt and declared their town a commune. It is, as Pirenne says, "highly significant that it was an episcopal city which first saw the birth of economic enfranchisement." Ibid., p. 32.

air makes men free" was the familiar proverb, and even though there were great social and economic contrasts among the burghers, in the eyes of the emergent municipal law the richest merchant and the poorest porter were presumably equal. For a time this egalitarian aspect of development[21] revealed itself more vividly in the Belgian cities than in any other part of Europe. By about the year 1000, the Belgian landscape was therefore quite well provided with market towns. A few, like Brussels, had grown up around castles;[22] others, such as Tournai or Liege, were originally ecclesiastical centers. The more typical towns and cities, however, had begun as trading sites, which soon attracted craftsmen catering to local urban and rural needs, and, in some instances, produced a new breed of skillful entrepreneurs who built up large export-oriented industries which provided employment for large numbers of workers recruited from a sizable rural area.

It was the rise of the large textile and metalworking industries that gradually led to a decline of the early town democracy. The first group of trading-town settlers were, as de Meeüs has said,[23] men very much like nineteenth-century American pioneers, strong-willed persons with "explosive energy" who made no political distinctions between any of their fellow immigrants. But this equality, which is characteristic of practically all communities whose existence is precarious,[24] was gradually eroded as differentials in wealth and income emerged, as the artisans' groups separated from the traders because their interests were different, and as a body of wage earners came to be dependent on the wealthy operators of an impersonal "putting-out" system of manufacture. This very interesting chapter in political history is much too complicated to be explained here.[25] The chief concern of this discussion is the role played by the towns in organizing the Belgian agrarian land-

21. See p. 29.

22. The city, built on ground once marshy, was first called the "Castle in the Marsh." See Adrien de Meeüs, *History of the Belgians,* translated by G. Gordon, New York, 1962, p. 53.

23. Ibid., p. 51–52.

24. The seventeenth-century Puritan settlers in the Massachusetts Bay Colony called such a beleaguered society a "community of peril" and argued that in such a community there must be perfect equality. For details, see my *American Economic Thought in the 17th Century,* London, 1935, p. 236; reprint ed., New York, 1961, p. 236.

25. The rise of the "patrician" class and their gradual usurpation of governmental control led to a series of violent revolts. For the history of these social and economic movements and their contribution to democratic thought and institutions, see Pirenne, *Belgian Democracy,* Chapters 5–10.

scape, and political interests must be laid aside to chronicle as accurately as possible the effects of the emergence of a powerful business oligarchy on Belgian regional development. It is important to note that the rise of a plutocracy in the larger Belgian towns had much to do with the emergence of a "dual economy."[26]

"The most striking feature" of a town, Pirenne has correctly pointed out, "is its sterility."[27] Since it cannot, by reason of its emphasis on commerce and industry and its neglect of agriculture,[28] feed or otherwise provision its inhabitants, it must perforce work out reciprocal trade relations with producers in the immediate proximity, or, failing that it must import food, fuel, or raw materials from more distant agricultural regions. In either case the town must produce or acquire payment goods acceptable to some rural population. These payment goods —the shoes, clothing, and utensils made by local craftsmen or the imported spices, salt, and pepper—proved to be something more than mere requital for the meat, grain, firewood, fruits, and vegetables that the peasants brought to town markets; they acted as incentive goods that tempted the agricultural groups to sow more wheat, raise more apples, increase their flocks of sheep or their herds of swine. More than that, the cash income that peasants received made it possible for them to commute their manorial labor services into money payments, to rent or buy more land, and thereby to increase the scale of their farming operations. But the stimulating effect of the growth of towns was not confined to immediate agrarian hinterlands. As the towns grew in size, wholesale lots of wine, fish, or grain were brought in—supplies that had been assembled in more distant rural areas where prices were lower or where the quality of goods was superior. In these transactions the payment goods would probably be wholesale lots of textiles or other products of the large-town industries.

Thus the Belgian towns exerted two rather different transforming effects. On an immediate hinterland the products of local tailors, carpenters, blacksmiths, potters, glovers, and tinsmiths were exchanged for farm produce, and this reciprocal dependence came to have a very pervasive, stimulating effect on farm practices. Agricultural yields, low to be sure by modern standards, rose to levels unknown before in

26. See Chapter 5 of this book.

27. Pirenne, *Belgian Democracy*, p. 77.

28. This neglect of agriculture was not complete. Most medieval towns had some fields, pastures, and animal herds. But as the towns grew, their agricultural holdings became increasingly inadequate to provision their inhabitants.

history; hence it was no accident that new farm tools, new crops, and better rotations were borrowed by British farmers from the Low Countries.[29]

Whereas the history of the Belgian towns affords a clear example of how agro-urban communities developed and how burghers and peasants were brought into mutually beneficial economic relations, there is, unfortunately, another side to the story. As large-scale industrial operations in the manufacture of woolen cloth and in the metal industries developed, at Dinant, Ghent, Ypres, Bruges, Donai, and Louvain, a sharp economic distinction arose between the wealthy merchant-entrepreneurs, on the one hand, and their faceless mass of wage earners. Unlike the local craftsmen, these workers owned neither the materials on which they worked nor the tools they employed in their manufacturing operations. They were triply dependent on their employers: for jobs, for materials, and for wages. Separated from the buyers of the goods they produced, their employment, their income, their very existence for themselves and their families depended on the wisdom, honesty, and innate decency of their employers. They had become increasingly an industrial proletariat, and in some of the large Belgian industrial towns they and their dependents constituted a majority of the population.[30] As these large industries developed, in spite of uprisings and rebellions, the wageworkers' lot had deteriorated. They lived "in miserable hovels hired by the week. They hardly ever owned anything but the clothes they stood up in. They wandered from town to town, offering the labor of their hands for hire."[31] Most of these workers (or their parents) had been lured from their rural birthplaces by what they thought would be the freedom and the greater opportunity of an urban center. Here then we find an early example of a "dual economy," one in which large cities had leeched the countryside of energetic and talented young people and instead of rewarding their daring and ambition had exploited their productive power with shameless avarice. In this Belgian example is a prototype of what is occurring today in all

29. One of the great Belgian inventions was a new type of horse collar which made it easy for horses to pull heavy loads. See de Meeüs, *History of the Belgians*, p. 56. The "Dutch plow" made it possible for British farmers to convert marshlands heavily matted with weeds and sedge into usable fields. See *Agrarian History of England and Wales*, IV, p. 164.

30. At the beginning of the fourteenth century, Ghent had over 4,000 weavers in a population of less than 50,000. At Ypres a century later more than half the city's work force was employed in clothmaking.

31. Pirenne, *Belgian Democracy*, p. 95.

too many developing countries.[32] This type of interaction between town and country, which is so patently undesirable, will be analyzed later in some detail. The Belgian episode is particularly apposite and instructive because it shows that whereas freedom to buy and sell goods or services in one type of agro-urban community may be beneficial to all concerned, in another context the same degree of freedom (to buy and sell labor services) may have consequences that are extremely inequitable to one of the contracting parties.

Yet, however heartless it may seem, one must admit that the ruling oligarchy in the great Belgian towns utilized their ill-gotten gains in ways that contributed greatly to the further growth and development of the Low Countries. They built and improved roads, dredged and deepened waterways, designed and dug miles of canals, and this "infrastructure," as it is now fashionable to call it, made the whole market system much more efficient. It was the "patrician" civic authorities who built the magnificent cloth halls that made Belgian cities famous for their architecture, as it was the corporations of great merchant-employers who made certain that their cities would have water systems, adequate wharfs and warehouses, suitable canal locks and portage facilities, handsome and well-built bridges as well as a whole network of water mills and windmills.[33] Nor was the infrastructure wholly physical; it also involved a well-planned set of financial institutions, a system of posts that linked together major cities and fairs, and arrangements for municipal borrowing and taxation that made possible the necessary types of capital formation in the public sector. Belgian municipal authorities eventually challenged the right of the Church to have a monopoly of schools and in this act of defiance not merely laid the foundations for secular public elementary education but perhaps unwittingly established a tradition which was to provide the Low Countries with some of the most famous universities of Europe.[34] Not least

32. For a rather shocking analysis of this trend toward a dual economy in India, see J. F. Bulsara, *Problems of Rapid Industrialization in India,* Bombay, 1964.

33. The windmill, an Arab invention, proved to be of great economic importance in a flat, marshy region that could not develop very much power from waterwheels.

34. William Harvey, who discovered the circulation of the blood, studied at Leyden, as did William Petty, that extraordinary physician-economist, and Nehemiah Grew, Britain's leading botanist in the early eighteenth century. Whereas the most ancient European universities emphasized philosophy, theology, and law, the Belgian and Dutch universities made notable progress in medicine, physics, and optics, reflecting the more practical interests of communities concerned with commerce and industry.

of the patricians' contributions were the town hospitals, which represent a type of infrastructure concerned with conserving a community's human resources—a rather paradoxical development when one considers the concurrent ruthless wastage of manpower in the slum-cursed industrial cities.

How large were the Belgian towns that were exerting such an influence on the Low Country landscapes? Ghent and Bruges may have reached populations of 40,000 and 50,000[35] respectively. Other large cities, such as Louvain, Brussels, Liege, and perhaps Ypres, had from 20,000 to 30,000 inhabitants. The majority of the Belgian cities were apparently in the 10,000 range, a size comparable with that of Frankfurt, Basel, and Freiburg circa 1450. These figures seem to confirm a view that a profound transforming influence can be exerted on rural hinterlands by cities that are not very large.[36] If one draws circles with 15-mile radii using only the more familiar Belgian towns as centers, practically all of the Low Country landscape will be included. If smaller towns are added to the hierarchy of central places, virtually every farmstead would lie within convenient travel distance to some type of market town.

The Japanese Rural Transformation

The modernization of Japan in the latter part of the nineteenth century and the first part of the twentieth century, a process that steadily gathered momentum, provides yet another example of the importance of a functional interaction between agriculture and industry, between town and country. The economic transformation that occurred following the Meiji Restoration (1868) proceeded with such speed that it literally catapulted Japan into the ranks of developed countries. Yet here presumably was a backward economy of about 30 million people of whom "the overwhelming majority were unfree, poverty-stricken peasants";[37] it achieved a phenomenal increase in agri-

35. De Meeüs avers that because Ghent could field an army of 15,000 in the middle of the fourteenth century, it must have had a population of 60,000 (*History of the Belgians*, p. 86), but Pirenne concludes that Ghent never surpassed, if it even reached, 50,000 people.

36. I developed this view in my *Market Towns and Spatial Development in India*, New Delhi, 1965.

37. William W. Lockwood, *The Economic Development of Japan: Growth and Structural Change, 1868–1938*, Princeton, 1954, p. 3.

cultural output[38] which facilitated the utilization of the productive power of more and more people, men and women, in an increasing variety of industrial pursuits. But, as contrasted with what had occurred in other developing countries, Japan increased her industrial output without reducing the rural-dwelling fractions of her work force.[39] It was therefore not gigantic city-located industries that were mainly responsible for pre-1914 growth; it was "the expansion of Japan's basic economy—agriculture and small-scale industry built on traditional foundations—which accounted for most of the growth of national productivity and income during this period."[40] There was an increase in the tempo of change, and this gave a dramatic character to a transition that had been long developing. What occurred in the Meiji period was the spread of more and more labor-intensive, small-scale industries into country towns, which increased rural cash earnings and thereby increased the volume of consumption in scores and presently in hundreds of communities. To meet the demand for more food, fibers, fuel, and other farm products, local farmers raised their output by using larger inputs of fertilizer, by double-cropping more land, by the use of superior seeds and more modern tools, and, above all, by better farm practices. Their cash incomes augmented as workers in the export-oriented rural industries—sericulture, pottery, embroidery, paper, and laquer—earned more and spent more for farm produce. The spending was not entirely for food or other farm products, however; town and country people bought clothing, furniture, household utensils, and a widening variety of domestic goods made in both cities and country towns. A process of organic growth was occurring, stimulated partly by export demand but mostly by a release of latent domestic demand, which the old order of things had frowned on or suppressed.

It would be a mistake, however, to assume that these changes had not been long in preparation, and the most egregious error would be to assume that "rural" industries in the Meiji period were only farm handicrafts. Although there were exceptions, these "rural" manufactur-

38. A 35 to 40 percent increase in the two decades 1894–1914.

39. In the United States, for example, the "rural" population (persons dwelling on farms and in communities of less than 2,500 persons) decreased from 80 percent in 1860 to 50 percent in 1910. Similar trends occurred in Britain, Germany, and other industrializing countries. In Japan the urban population ultimately overtook and surpassed the agricultural population, but this shift came very much later than in other maturing countries.

40. Lockwood, *Economic Development of Japan*, p. 25.

ing operations were mainly carried on in market towns. What brought these market towns into existence? As late as 1590 Japan had only four real cities—Kyoto, Fushimi, Osaka, and Sakai—with a total population of perhaps 400,000 people and all so near to one another that a circle with a radius of 25 miles would have contained them all. The rest of the country was "a rural fastness broken, when at all, merely by small local markets and widely scattered ports and castle towns."[41] Beyond clusters of partly commercialized villages near the few towns and cities there lay what was seemingly "a limitless hinterland of villages where subsistence farming still held sway and men had yet to feel the first sharp tremors of change emanating from the towns."[42] But change was imminent, for ten years later, at the battle of Sekigahara in 1600, Tokugawa Ieyasu "won undisputed leadership over Japan."[43]

Almost immediately a town-building program, already begun, was quickened, one in which the castle town (*jōkamachi*) "assumed an importance out of all proportion to other types of urban communities."[44] As contrasted with the traditional administrative cities that provided residence for a court bureaucracy,[45] the castle towns were both administrative and economic, and progressively economic functions became pre-eminent. Yet their origins were chiefly administrative; the "re-feudalization" of Japan in the sixteenth century had led to a decentralization of authority among some two hundred daimyo, (feudal lords) and the task of building regional administrative centers had begun before the Tokugawa victory made vassals out of the regional daimyo. The result was "a curious blend of centralization and local feudal autonomy"[46] in which each feudal lord was put on his mettle to develop his territorial domain. Completely new cities were built with castles as their nuclei, and "the achievement was made all the more remarkable by the dramatic suddenness with which these operations were carried

41. Thomas C. Smith, *The Agrarian Origins of Modern Japan*, Stanford, Calif., 1959, p. 4.

42. Ibid.

43. For a compact account of this important episode, see Richard K. Beardsley, John W. Hall, and Robert E. Ward, *Village Japan*, Chicago, 1959, pp. 28–57.

44. John W. Hall, "The Castle Town and Japan's Modern Urbanization," *Far Eastern Quarterly*, 15, No. 1 (November 1955), 38.

45. As was the case in China, these administrative cities were larger than their European counterparts, but they were less stable, since trade and industry was of secondary importance. Consequently, when Kyoto and Nara lost their political importance, they were able to survive by becoming famous for their temples.

46. Hall, "The Castle Town," p. 43.

out."[47] Most of the castle towns were built in a thirty-year period 1580–1610,[48] and it "would be hard to find a parallel period of urban construction in world history."[49] There followed a period in which the power of the daimyo was consolidated, when lesser castles were destroyed, so that military strength could be concentrated in the sites best located for defense and, at the same time, well situated for trade. By this process citadels became the gathering place for merchants and artisans and became rudimentary market towns. Once the daimyo and their vassals had taken up residence in the new towns, they became dependent on merchants to link their community with other towns and cities, to provide them with military supplies and consumer goods, and to "bridge the gap between town and countryside."[50] Out of this feudal-economic competition came a progressive rearrangement of commercial activity. Daimyo offered special privileges to merchants and artisans who would settle in their castle towns; as a consequence the old guild system was undermined (as it was in Belgium) by the freer markets in the new towns. Hated by the old guildsmen, courted by the daimyo, the merging group of merchants (*chōnin*) flourished under the patronage and protection of a new feudal order.

The two basic functions of the merchants were to accumulate produce from the agrarian hinterland and to link the castle-town communities with the national market system. The first function often degenerated into a monopoloid operation in which the peasants were outbargained;[51] the second function was more competitive, although the large rice merchants and the financiers often held the whip hand over small-town dealers. Yet even though merchants had been importuned to enter the service of the daimyo, they did not long have the freedom to operate as they thought best, for in the Confucian social theory that prevailed in the Tokugawa era merchants were relegated to a low social status, and as a consequence all forms of commercial

47. Ibid., p. 44.

48. Among the cities founded during this period were Himeji, Osaka, Kanazawa, Wakayama, Tokushima, Kōchi. Takamatsu, Hiroshima, Edo, Wakamatsu, Okayama, Kōfu, Fushimi, Takasaki, Sendai. Fukuoka, Kumamoto. Tottori, Matsuyama, Hikone, Fukushima, Yonezawa, Shizuoka, and Nagoya.

49. Hall, "The Castle Town," p. 44.

50. Ibid., p. 47.

51. "Since the peasant sold either in a free market, or in one rigged against him in favor of monopoly merchants to whom he was required by law to sell, he was periodically caught in a cost-price squeeze." Smith, *Agrarian Origins of Modern Japan*, p. 160.

activity came under the scrutiny and presently under the regulation of the administrative class.[52] The latent dynamism of the new network of urban centers was therefore only partially released, and the merchant group saw their erstwhile days of freedom fade as they faced ever-increasing regimentation.

Despite these disabilities, the activities of the *chōnin* enlarged as the population grew and as old and new cities expanded. Feeding the urban consumers had become really big business by the middle of the eighteenth century, when Edo (Tokyo) had over a half-million inhabitants; Osaka and Kyoto each in the neighborhood of 400,000; Nagoya and Kanazawa 50,000 to 60,000; and when over forty castle towns each had populations of 10,000 or more. Probably as much as 22 percent of the Japanese people now lived in cities of 10,000 persons or over, and few villages were "more than 20 miles from a town of fair size."[53] The enormous quantities of grain, fish, fibers, and timber needed to feed, clothe, and shelter the urban population required the systematic gathering up of supplies from farming and fishing villages, and this task was performed by the town merchants.[54] The growing demand not only hastened the commercialization of the castle-town hinterlands but led steadily toward regional agricultural specialization.

More and more industrial crops were needed: mulberry leaves for silkworms, cotton for the expanding textile industry, sugar cane, indigo; and all these plants required different ecological environments. The mixed subsistence type of farming was progressively superseded by concentration on cash crops suited to soil, rainfall, and temperature. By the time of the Meiji Restoration there were provinces where over 50 percent of the farm incomes were derived from cotton, vegetables, and indigo. As a peasant now received cash payments for most of his

52. In the social fabric of the Tokugawa period the merchants stood beneath the samurai, the farmer, and the artisan. Their ancestors had not, like those of the samurai, performed meritorious services for the state, nor did they, like the farmer and the artisan, produce any visible product. They were profiteers who urged people to buy expensive goods, thereby encouraging luxury. They were considered "a good-for-nothing and unproductive class" by the samurai. For a vivid account of contemporary opinion see Eijiro Honjo, *The Social and Economic History of Japan,* New York, 1965, Chapter 9.

53. Estimates of Furishima Toshi quoted in Smith, *Agrarian Origins of Modern Japan,* p. 68.

54. The complicated nature of the necessary commercial apparatus has been described by Yasukazu Takenaka. See his "Endogenous Formation and Development of Capitalism in Japan", *Journal of Economic History,* 39, No. 1 (March 1969), 141–162.

produce,[55] he could buy cloth, paper, harness, fertilizers, tools, tobacco, and other household and farm supplies. Markets which before the Tokugawa period had mainly provided luxury goods for the samurai were now cluttered with plain and ordinary goods for plain and ordinary people.

Linked with the castle-town markets were smaller village markets, serving areas with a radius of 4 to 5 miles,[56] which helped to commercialize the entire landscape. Above the castle-town markets in the hierarchy of central places, were city markets that specialized in particular commodities. The reach of large market places, such as the great silk market at Fukushima, must have been many times that of the general produce markets in typical market towns. These specialized markets increased in number; there were, for example, twenty-four silk markets in a single prefecture (Gumma) actually functioning in the very year that the Meiji Restoration occurred. This indicates that the organization of economic space was well advanced when the shogunate fell.[57] The countryside was engaging in more and more industrial tasks, so that by 1860 over 90 percent of the silk cloth coming into Edo (Tokyo) was "country stuff." For all the protest of the Kyoto silk makers' guild, the outward movement of industry was to continue.

Much like the famous wool clothiers of the west of England in the fifteenth and sixteenth centuries,[58] the Japanese merchants of the Tokugawa era perfected an efficient "putting out" system in cotton textiles. Local merchants gathered up cotton and shipped it to Osaka, where it was ginned. It was then distributed to provincial merchants who supplied it to peasants for conversion first into yarn and then into cloth. In one province (Echigo) hemp cloth was produced under somewhat different arrangements: after an inexpensive method of bleaching had been discovered, the peasant weavers, believing they were being victimized by a monopoly of local merchants, formed small companies (*nakama*) and began to ship their cloth direct to Edo. Thus by one

55. The peasants paid their land tax in rice, usually 40 to 50 percent of the yield of their paddy fields, and it was for the judicious sale of their surplus rice that the daimyo had to have the services of the reviled *chōnin*.

56. Estimated by Smith, *Agrarian Origins of Modern Japan*, p. 73.

57. G. C. Allen observes, "The popular conception of a people living for centuries under a system of picturesque feudalism and suddenly awakened to practical ambitions by the guns of foreign warships is far from the truth." *A Short Economic History of Modern Japan, 1867–1937*, New York, 1963, p. 13.

58. Whose amazing business activities have been graphically described by E. Lipson in his *History of the English Woolen and Worsted Industries*, London, 1921.

means or another various industries steadily penetrated into the countryside, so that by the late Tokugawa period most villages and all market towns were manufacturing something for *chōnin* to distribute and sell.[59]

Both regional and functional specialization resulted from the increasingly sensitive market network. Sericulture became a major activity around Fukushima, sugar refining in Sanuki Province, hemp weaving on the coast of the Sea of Japan at Echigo. Meantime, within the several expanding rural industries production was being broken down into separate operations performed by different families or groups of producers. Thus, in the textile industry, spinning, weaving, napping, and dyeing became separable tasks in a chain of productive operations. In the silk industry there is an illustration of a type of specialization which was both regional and technical; one region suitable for mulberry gardens bought silkworm eggs and sold cocoons; another region bought cocoons, reeled the silk, and sold silkworm eggs and raw silk; a third group of places bought raw silk, wove it into cloth, and sold silk cloth.[60]

Whereas part-time industrial employment of peasants working in a putting-out" system was probably the most typical trend, a considerable number of large industrial operations had developed in the castle towns and even in villages by the closing years of the Tokugawa period. A cotton mill in Izumi Province had eighty looms in operation in 1837, an enterprise producing silkworms employed thirty workers, oil-pressing mills used waterpower in their enlarging scale of operations, sugar makers had invested in expensive vats and presses, and there were "innumerable brewers employing between 50 and 100 workers."[61] A new class of wealthy peasants (*gōnō*) emerged, about whose alleged luxurious habits of life there was bitter complaint by the defenders of the traditional Confucian stratification.[62] The parvenus were able to lend money to other peasants, even to daimyo. How have they become so wealthy? asked a contemporary writer: "not by farming alone; most make *sake*

59. As early as 1773 there were 208 licensed oil makers in Yamato Province, many of them using waterpower. See Smith, *Agrarian Origins of Modern Japan*, p. 79.

60. Research by Shōji Kichinosuke quoted by Smith, *Agrarian Origins of Modern Japan*, p. 80.

61. Smith, *Agrarian Origins of Modern Japan*, p. 169.

62. The rise of these rural "capitalists" has been vividly described by Thomas C. Smith in an excellent article, "Landlords and Rural Capitalists in the Modernization of Japan," *Journal of Economic History*, 16, No. 2 (June 1956), 165–181.

or vegetable oil, or operate pawn shops."[63] But they were engaged in many other activities: dyeing textiles, silk production, or sugar making. They were undermining the old manufacturing monopolies of the city-dwelling guildsmen.

These wealthy peasants were probably often the leading operators of the widening putting-out system, mainly in the silk industry. Here their investment was in raw materials and in stocks of finished goods. When they shifted their attention to sake or sugar production, fixed investments were required. But even though their industrial activities expanded, the *gōnō* still continued their farming operations. Here they had an advantage over their village neighbors; they could buy more fertilizers (oil cakes, dried fish, night soil) and thereby get higher yields; they could afford more outlays for irrigation or for building new rice paddies; they could take the risks of experimenting with new strains of rice[64] or barley. These Japanese counterparts of Elizabethan yeomen had a great deal to do with consolidating resentment against the daimyo and more coyly against the shogun, and they certainly "helped to give the [Meiji] revolution direction as well as power."[65]

How commercialized had the castle-town and village -market network made an average farm in the late Tokugawa period? Careful reconstruction of probable farm-family budgets, based on diaries and official data and made by competent Japanese scholars,[66] suggest that a farm family at the end of the eighteenth century might produce enough rice and wheat to feed its members and to pay the land tax in kind. Its cash income would be derived from the sale of straw, cotton, or vegetables and from income received for weaving cotton or making straw matting. The cash outlays would be for fertilizers, for farm tools, for the wages of hired laborers, and for a family-wide range of consumer goods. Where data over a spread of time are available, the progressive commercialization of the countryside can be traced. One family kept diaries for 222 years, and from these Professor Toya Toshiyuki was able to show how self-sufficiency in a village in Musashi province was superseded by com-

63. Ibid., p. 168.

64. The number of varieties of rice increased, according to Professor Tōbata Seiichi, from 177 in the seventeenth century to 2,363 by the middle of the nineteenth century. All this experimentation occurred in the so-called stagnant Tokugawa period. Ibid., p. 174.

65. Ibid., p. 165.

66. Notably Toya Toshiyuki in a 1946 study. For further details see Smith, *Agrarian Origins of Modern Japan*, p. 220, note 27 to Chapter 6.

mercial farming.[67] In the process, the crops, the farm techniques, the types of investment, the administration of the work force, and the attitude toward "wealth, work, and neighbors changed." It was the rich peasants, with cash incomes from industrial operations, who constructed ponds, dug irrigation ditches, and utilized water-lifting machines.

The commercialization of the Japanese landscape also had a powerful influence in transforming the composition of the agrarian work force. Traditionally hereditary servants (*fudai*) had made possible the enlargement of blood families, since by their adoption as children the *fudai* actually became members of extended rural families. As trade began to integrate the village into a larger town-centered economy, and as the resultant industrial demand for labor increased, fewer poor persons were compelled to bind their children into servitude. For why should a family sell their children when they could merely sell their children's daily labor power?[68] The *fudai* were progressively replaced by persons hired for a fixed period and for agreed wages (*hōkōnin*), and a shortage of agricultural labor soon developed as rural industries further expanded. Gradually the rural work force became more mobile, migrating from village to village, from one lord's jurisdiction to another, from village to town, or from town to city. Thus the Tokugawa commercialization of the countryside prepared the way for the accelerated industrialization of the Meiji period, which was to require the recruitment of a large urban work force to man large textile mills and the heavy industries in metals, mining, and engineering.[69]

It can be recognized, therefore, that the modernization of Japan had only proximate origins in the early Meiji period; its deep origins are to be found in the Tokugawa period. More influential than anything else in triggering change was the division of Japan into 250 fiefs and the consequent rise of the castle towns which the daimyo built or enlarged in almost all of these local jurisdictions. Outlying villages came to be linked with these castle towns by trade, and in these emergent agro-urban communities more and more rural industries developed. Out of the Tokugawa experience came then a spatial dispersion of industries,

67. For further details, see Smith, "Landlords and Rural Capitalists," p. 175.

68. The population registers of a Shinshū village reveal that the average size of a family declined from 12.3 persons in 1755 (when the extended family was characteristic) to 3.8 in 1830. For further details see Smith, *Agrarian Origins of Modern Japan,* p. 147.

69. For a succinct account of the rise of these industries see Allen, *Short Economic History of Modern Japan,* Chapter 5.

a process that intensified rapidly when Japan began expanding her exports after 1893.[70] This explains why 84 percent of the population lived in places with less than 10,000 persons in 1893, why out of a total population increase from 1893 to 1898 of 3.3 million over 2 million were rural-born, and why, even as late as 1930, two of every three Japanese lived in places with less than 10,000 people.[71] By expanding old and developing new industries, mostly export-oriented, in rural areas, a much fuller use of the active population could be made by bringing more females into the industrial work force.[72] Because most production units in light manufacturing remained small,[73] close supervision of the workers could insure a type of quality control that steadily widened the market for exports; "Hence the labor-intensive rural industries very greatly aided the whole Japanese industrialization programme by making available foreign exchange with which the nation could purchase machinery and equipment for the new heavy industries, for armament works, and for public utilities."[74] Since rural workers already had places to live, the spread of rural industries for a time "kept pressure off the large urban areas for housing and municipal facilities." But only for a time; rapid urbanization began in the 1920's and by 1940 more than 40 percent of the Japanese people lived in cities of over 100,000 people,[75] and the evils of a dual economy had already become evident.[76]

The vitality of the merchant-organizers of rural industries and the drive and resourcefulness of enterprising peasants had made the political structure of the late Tokugawa period baneful and incongruous. The maintenance of "hordes of idle retainers" absorbed a large fraction of the daimyo's revenues, and whereas the samurai might despise and

70. Japan's exports increased from an annual value of 22 million yen in 1873–1877 to 139 million yen in 1894–1898 and 496 million yen in 1909–1913. See Allen, *Short Economic History of Modern Japan,* p. 213, Table 22.

71. Ibid., p. 62.

72. Nine out of every ten workers in silk filatures and in textile weaving were women at the turn of the century.

73. As late as 1930, 53 percent of Japanese workers were employed in enterprises with less than five employees, 59 percent in ventures with less than nine employees. Allen, *Short Economic History of Modern Japan,* p. 198, Table 7.

74. E. A. J. Johnson, *Market Towns and Spatial Development in India,* pp. 33–34.

75. Lockwood, *Economic Development of Japan,* pp. 482–484.

76. This hasty, poorly planned surge of urbanization was characterized by harsh treatment of factory workers, slum housing, high accident rates, and a wanton disregard for suffering. See John E. Orchard, *Japan's Economic Position,* New York, 1930, pp. 342–345.

ridicule the *chōnin*, the merchants, manufacturers, and rich peasants were in the saddle. By reason of a long, long period of peace "the bulk of the *samurai* became functionless."[77] Only those daimyos who were able to adapt themselves to a commercialized countryside, to a money economy, and to the use of an economically enfranchised rural work force were able to make the transition from the dying old order to the emergent new order.[78] The Meiji government, for all its interest in modern, large-scale, automated heavy industries, was wise enough to encourage the further expansion of rural industries. To the time-honored silk industry was added ceramics, lacquerware, and fish canning, while by a system of subcontracting many labor-intensive components for the metal trades came to be manufactured in rural market towns.

How extensive this dispersed rural industrialization actually became may be indicated by Lockwood's estimate that half of Japan's 5½ million farm families had some nonagricultural employment in the 1930's and that for about one-fourth of these farm families the income from industry exceeded that derived from farming.[79] The additional cash income (which in sampled households varied from 31 percent to 67 percent of total family cash income) markedly increased the spending power and the saving capacity of Japanese farm families, increasing the demand function in the entire economy. Rural industries had also another very important industrial consequence: they schooled millions of young country people, boys and girls, in the rudiments of technology. In small rural industries young people learned skills and became familiar with an industrial discipline. Those who migrated to cities came already "half-trained." Rural industry, as Thomas Smith has said, had given Japanese workers "a certain quickness of hand and eye, a respect for tools and materials, an adaptability to the cadences and confusion of moving parts; and city industry . . . was not technically so far advanced as to make his skills irrelevant. Few countries have em-

77. Allen, *Short Economic History of Modern Japan*, p. 26.

78. An excellent example was the Lord of Satsuma who advocated the study of western ideas and practices and founded a cotton-spinning mill (using British equipment) as well as several other new industries. Ibid., pp. 22–23, 33, and 71.

79. Lockwood, *Economic Development of Japan*, p. 491. Not all regions of Japan shared in this income-increasing opportunity. The Meiji expansion of rural manufacturing occurred mostly in areas near ports or major population centers. Mountainous regions supplied relatively more migrants who sought employment in city factories.

barked on [large-scale, automated] industry with a superior labor force at hand."[80] It was not only industrial workers who had been trained in rural industries. The restructuring of Japanese agrarian landscapes in the Tokugawa period had made possible the training of thousands of businessmen. The refusal of the *chōnin* to desist from their money-making ventures in castle-town communities had gradually undermined caste patterns and allowed people with organizing ability to move into positions of larger responsibility, first in private enterprise and after the Meiji Restoration even into governmental positions. But whereas the *chōnin* triumph came in 1869, when feudalism was formally abolished and when entry into all professions and trades was thrown open to all, the new era was to require a cadre of key persons familiar with foreign techniques, management methods, and financial procedures. The sons of the captains of rural industries stood ready to become the trainees for the new era, both at home in the newly established engineering, mining, and agricultural colleges, or abroad in British, German, and American colleges and universities. Once again the developmental role of the castle-town agro-urban community was revealed!

The Rationalization of American Midwestern Landscapes

The three foregoing examples of early organization of space, in Britain, Belgium, and Japan respectively, reveal that great progress had been made over time in the building up of a network of regional markets that made possible not only a better distribution of goods but, by reason of these spatial arrangements, an increasing specialization in productive activities, which rather consistently resulted in cost-reducing techniques and practices. But whereas these early "developing" countries benefited richly from a spatial reordering of their landscapes, a persistent obstacle to a fuller achievement of economies of scale was the primitive character of transportation. Pack animals and carts were the means of land transport in sixteenth-century Britain as they had been in fourteenth-century Belgium, and as they were to be in eighteenth-century Japan. The only advance over the movement of goods by porters, pack animals, carts, or wagons was the use of boats and barges on inland and coastal waterways, but here topography and stream flows

80. *Agrarian Origins of Modern Japan*, p. 212.

limited the use that could be made of this cheaper form of transport.[81] In all three countries, however, a large share of the goods that moved in interregional trade was actually waterborne. England was blessed with numerous gently flowing rivers navigable by small boats or barges. Belgium was equally fortunate and could easily interlink her slow-moving streams with connecting canals. Japan was not so lucky; a mountain spine in Honshu and even more rugged landforms in Kyushu compelled the Japanese to rely on coastal waters for the low-cost movement of grain, timber, and other bulky goods by junks or other sailing crafts.

One reason for the acceleration of economic progress in Japan after the Meiji Restoration was that railroads overcame many of the topographic limitations on the Tokugawa landscapes. It should be remembered that when the Meiji government took control in 1868 not 1 mile of railroad had yet been built, and it took another three years before Japan had the 18 miles of railroad that connected Yokohama with Tokyo. Thirty-five years later, by contrast, Japan had 6,000 miles of railways, and between 1880 and 1910 the traffic moved by rail increased from 848,000 tons to over 40.6 million tons,[82] a forty-seven-fold increase. The great surge of Japanese economic growth is therefore very neatly correlated with the adoption of a railway system of transport, although in the period from 1868 to 1914 domestic waterborne traffic also increased remarkably.[83]

The great stretches of the American Midwest were mostly settled after the railway had passed beyond its experimental stage; hence the influence of an essentially linear form of transport on a landscape can be discovered from the resulting pattern of villages and towns in states such as Illinois, Iowa, and the Dakotas.[84] The railroad in fact tended to

81. In seventeenth-century Britain, Nehemiah Grew, a sharp-eyed scientific observer, concluded that the draft power needed to move 1 ton by road could move 12 tons in canal boats. See E. A. J. Johnson, *Predecessors of Adam Smith,* New York, 1937, p. 121.

82. William W. Lockwood, "The Scale of Economic Growth in Japan, 1868–1938," in *Economic Growth: Brazil, India, Japan,* ed. Simon Kuznets, Wilbert E. Moore, and Joseph J. Spengler, Durham, N.C., 1955, p. 146.

83. Since no figures measuring domestic waterborne freight were kept, the exact growth is not known. But the fiftyfold increase in the tonnage of steamships (1873–1913) and the fivefold increase in the tonnage of small vessels (1888–1910) suggests that the expansion was very rapid.

84. A locomotive can pull a train of cars only on a prepared track; hence its goods-moving capacity is "linear." Pack animals, in contrast, can go anywhere that

reinforce certain rigidities that were already present and had their origin in the system of rectangular land survey that had been adopted in 1785 for the entire unalienated public domain. This system of survey, which had so much to recommend it from the security it gave to every landowner from "overlapping claims," from "lost or forgotten bounds," and from the ease with which titles could be recorded, nonetheless had many shortcomings.[85] Regardless of the topography, the agronomy, or the climate of a region, the public domain was divided up into townships each 6 miles square; hence each was divisible into 36 square-mile units ("sections"). Where general farming was technically possible each square mile (640 acres) tended to be divided into four "quarter section" (160-acre) farms. A township with its fixed number of "sections" therefore tended to divide into 144 farms, so that, if a blood family of, say, 5 persons lived on each farm, an average midwestern township might have a rural population of about 720 persons. It would seem that such a number of producers and consumers living in a compass of land 6 miles square might constitute a satisfactory market-centered community. The trouble was that the symmetry of the survey system required all roads to be boundary roads of the "sections." Consequently, even if a village market center were to grow up in the exact center of a township, persons living in the outer limits of a township would be 3, 4, 5, or 6 miles from the village. Had there been provision for diagonal roads that would bisect sections, the most remote corner of each township would not have been 6 miles but only 4½ miles distant from a centrally located village (see Figure 2–6).

The rectangular survey, which required that a strip of land 44 feet wide bordering all "sections" should be reserved for public roads, had given a certain linear accent to spatial development before the advent of the railroad. Contrast this with what happened in frontier settlement before the adoption of a uniform rectangular survey, and very clear permanent differences in the organization of space become apparent. Figure 2–7 shows the present road pattern in an area around Keene,

---

topography permits, wagons can travel on any reasonably firm surface, and ships can go wherever there is deep enough water. It is the linear characteristic of rail transport that explains why this form of transport has made a distinctive, if not always a beneficial, imprint on economic landscapes.

85. For a detailed account of the origin, adoption, and actual implementation of the rectangular survey system, see Payson Jackson Treat, *The National Land System, 1785–1920*, New York, 1910, especially Chapter 8.

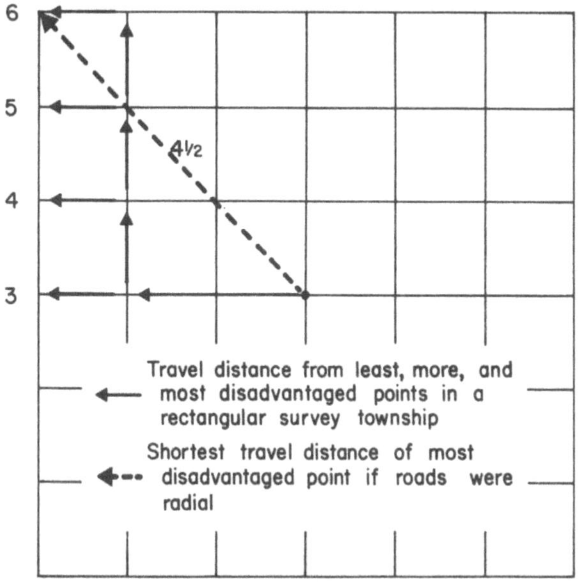

Figure 2–6 Travel Distances in a Township Six Miles Square

New Hampshire, and Figure 2–8 pictures an equally large area around Redfield, South Dakota. It will be evident that, whereas Keene is the hub of a wheel whose spokes are roads radiating in all directions, Redfield is simply a junction of two major roads and consequently exhibits a much weaker centrality. The difference stems of course from the contrast between the principles underlying the system of settlement in New England, on the one hand, and those governing the settlement of midwestern states, on the other.

The New England settlement was a planned advance into frontier areas. Each new town was "laid out" by its "proprietors" who by patent, grant, purchase, or other means had acquired a legal claim to a compass of land. Each new town established a central settlement with its gristmill, sawmill, town hall, church, and common. Here the shareholders in the joint venture would have their "home lots," and here too would be the lots reserved for a marketplace, for a "pound" (stock yard), for school purposes, and for a burying ground.[86] But no less important than the

86. Joseph Schafer has called this procedure of settlement "controlled expansion." Prominent men would form a provisional organization and ask the "general court" (colonial legislature) for a grant of land. The court would appoint "viewers" to

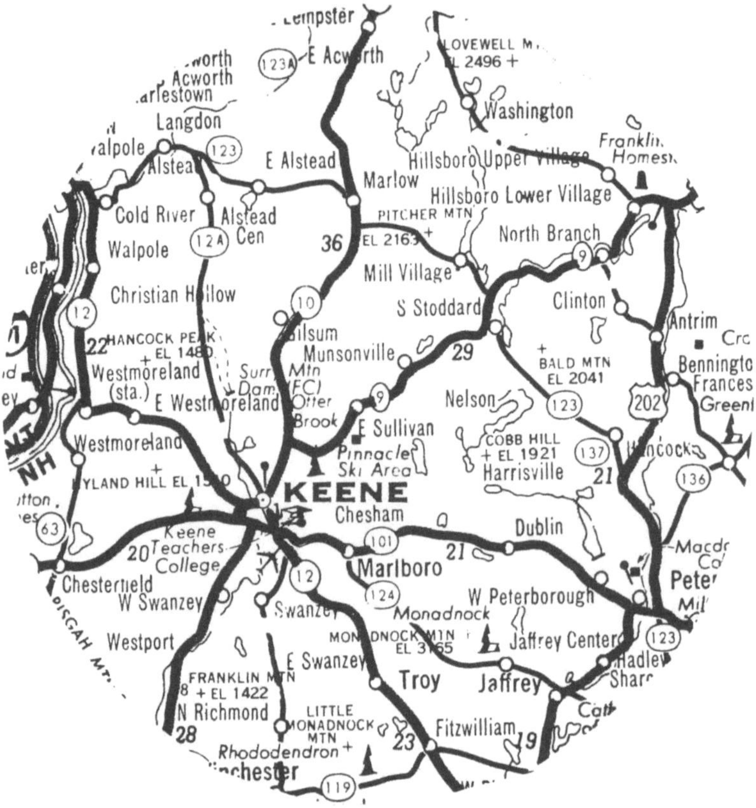

Figure 2–7 A Radial Road System Sample

SOURCE: *Rand McNally Road Atlas: Canada, United States, Mexico.* Chicago: Rand McNally & Co. Map of New Hampshire, p. 44. Copyright by Rand McNally & Company, R. L. 69–Y–44.

designing of the community center and the allocation of the township land was the planning of the roads that would connect the new town with other communities and link outlying areas with the town's central place. New England town records faithfully listed all these road-building activities, giving any number of examples of how new communities

---

visit the chosen tract and help to have the land surveyed. Once the grant was made, the "proprietors" would divide the township into shares and receive applications for full or fractional shares. When actual settlement occurred, the settlers would organize themselves into a "town." *Social History of American Agriculture,* New York, 1936, pp. 8–9.

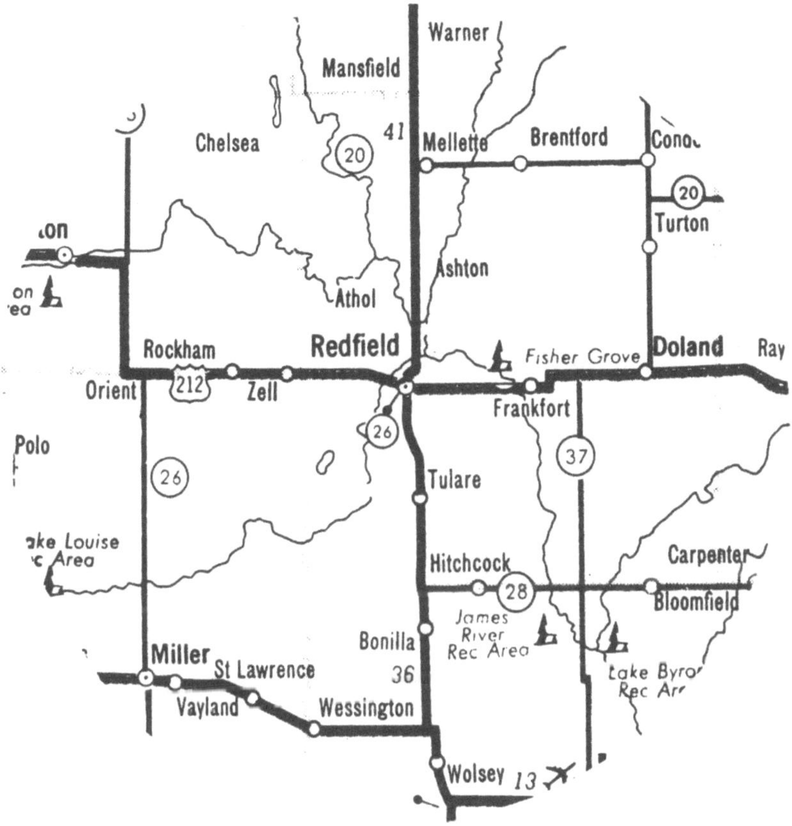

Figure 2–8 A Rectangular Road System Sample

SOURCE: *Rand McNally Road Atlas: Canada, United States, Mexico.* Chicago: Rand McNally & Co. Map of South Dakota, p. 69. Copyright by Rand McNally & Company, R. L. 69–Y–44.

built the infrastructure that would unify their communities and join them with both older and emergent settlements.[87]

The theory underlying the settlement of the Midwest was quite different. Since all unalienated government land was for sale,[88] as was also

87. Thus the proprietors of Housatonic (Mass.) built several roads, and the proprietors of Keene (N.H.) connected their town with Townshend (Mass.). These are only examples of scores of entries in New England town records. On this subject see Roy Hidemichi Akagi, *The Town Proprietors of the New England Colonies,* Gloucester, Mass., 1963, especially Chapter 4.

88. Sizable portions of the public domain had been given to military and naval veterans, some was claimed by foreigners, and many special grants had been made

some land that had previously been disposed of,[89] any person could purchase from the government, or from other owners, as much land as he wanted or could pay for. The community centers that developed, whether towns, villages, or crossroad stores, were not organically planned. They grew up in response to the consumer needs of an encircling area, and their capacity for survival depended on the demonstrated utility of their economic functions. Instead of planning a community and then settling the area where it was to be, which was the New England principle, in the Midwest, with few exceptions, settlement came first, and the central places gradually emerged in response to the urgent needs of the settlers. The consequence was that originally all midwestern central places were tentative.

Whatever nucleation occurred was almost wholly experiential. When a gristmill brought settlers to it, a retail store might presently be located nearby, and a saddler might find it a suitable place to set up shop, as a blacksmith might also do. Where could such a miniscule cluster of enterprises grow up? At a road crossing no doubt, but usually where there was water enough to turn a wheel or where the water table was near enough to the earth's surface so that shallow wells could provide water for men and beasts. Very likely the settlement would be near stands of trees, although as the prairie country was reached this could no longer be a locational factor. This early type of midwestern central-place emergence is illustrated by Figure 2–9, which shows the actual location of some eleven rudimentary market centers in a part of southwestern Iowa in 1868. Almost all of these minute market centers were located in or near woodland areas, and all that survived were gristmill sites. Circles around each center could be drawn with an arbitrary radius of ten miles on the assumption that settlers would travel that maximum distance to a gristmill, a blacksmith's shop, or a "general store." What seemed to be developing in the fifties and sixties was a spatial dispersion of emergent central spaces over this portion of the Iowa landscape.

Figure 2–10 shows what happened when two east-west railroads were built through the area in 1868 and 1869: the Mississippi and Missouri

---

for a variety of purposes. On this tangled topic see Treat, *National Land System,* Chapters 4 ("Foreign Titles"), 10 ("Land Grants for Military and Naval Services"), and 11 ("Special Grants").

89. Especially the land which had been granted to railway companies. On this subject there is a huge literature, but as a very good sample see Paul W. Gates, *The Illinois Central Railroad and Its Colonization Work,* Cambridge, Mass., 1934.

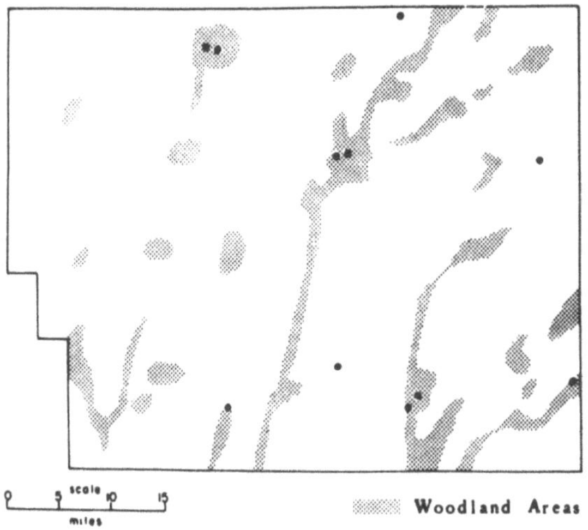

Figure 2–9 Emergence of Central Places in Western Iowa
SOURCE: Brian J. L. Berry, *Geography of Market Centers and Retail Distribution,* © 1967, p. 6. Reprinted by permission of Prentice-Hall, Inc., Englewood Cliffs, New Jersey.

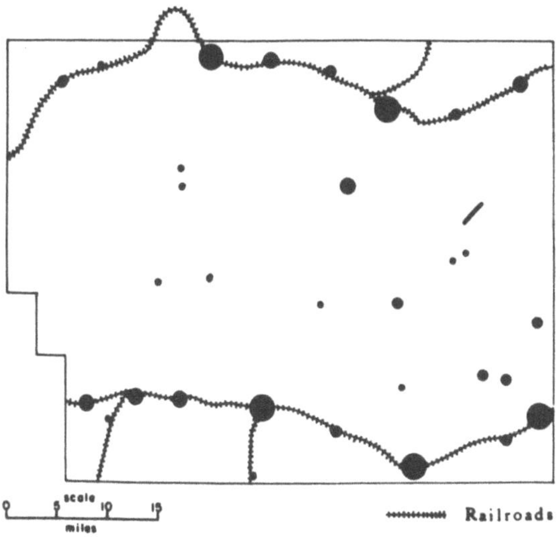

Figure 2–10 Emergence of Central Places in Western Iowa
SOURCE: See Figure 2–9

(from Davenport to Omaha) and the Burlington and Missouri River (from Burlington to Pacific Junction).[90] The dispersion which had begun has now been arrested, and new central places have grown up on the railroad lines at points 5 or 10 miles from one another. The pattern is not the kind of cobweb shown in Figure 2–7 but resembles strings of separated beads of varied sizes, although there are actually only two chief varieties along the railroads: the larger towns and the smaller villages. The settlements through which the first railroads did not pass show little or no growth, and unless they are to be rescued by branch railroads, or main roads, they will either remain hamlets or disappear. Figure 2–11 shows how branch railroads and a system of farm-to-market roads had modified the extreme linearity characteristic about 1879 (Fig. 2–10). By 1904 the construction of north-south railroads and roads had resuscitated some of the moribund hamlets. Yet the beadlike pattern of spatial organization persists; the only difference is that there are now four strings rather than two. Little change in design occurs in the next fifty-two years, except that by 1956 (Fig. 2–12) there has been a sharp reduction in the total number of central places.

The mortality had been almost entirely among the villages and hamlets that were not on major transport axes. The number of central places had reached a peak about 1900, after which time better roads had somewhat lengthened the reach of the larger markets even before the advent of the automobile. When the Model T Ford superseded the horse-drawn buggy or wagon, the reach of better markets rapidly lengthened, particularly when more and more roads were hard surfaced. The full measure of what had occurred in this progressive rationalization of a midwestern landscape can be seen in Figure 2–13, which pinpoints all the central places that had disappeared in the 105-year period 1851–1956. No less than seventy-four central places had failed to survive, whereas forty-three had demonstrated their more permanent economic utility. Thus out of a total of 117 market ventures, only a little more than 1 in 3 (36.8 percent) was needed when hard roads, automobiles, and trucks had lengthened the isovectures of the superior market centers.

It is not only the 63.2 percent shrinkage in the total number of market centers that deserves notice in this historical example. A hierarchy of interrelated central places had emerged rather promptly after the construction of the first railroads. The factors making for relatively

90. For a map showing these railroads see Richard C. Overton, *Burlington Route: A History of the Burlington Lines*, New York, 1965, p. 88.

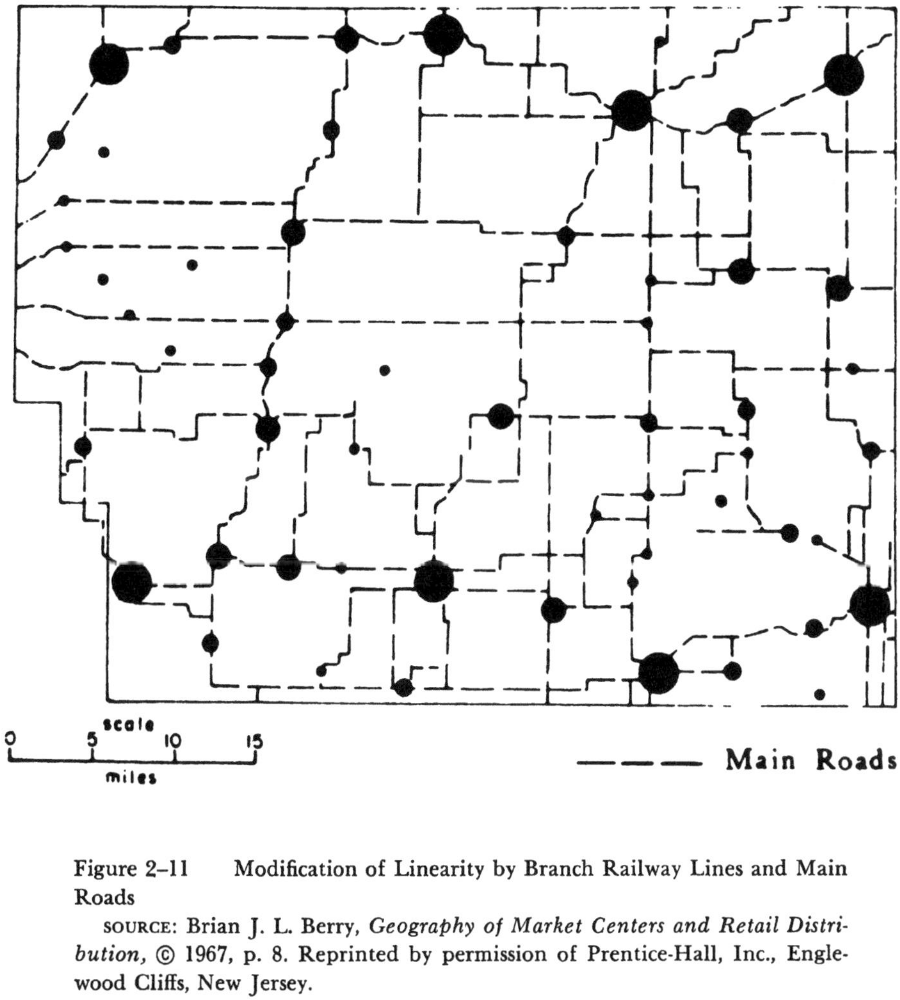

Figure 2–11 Modification of Linearity by Branch Railway Lines and Main Roads

SOURCE: Brian J. L. Berry, *Geography of Market Centers and Retail Distribution,* © 1967, p. 8. Reprinted by permission of Prentice-Hall, Inc., Englewood Cliffs, New Jersey.

greater centrality were mainly, but not wholly, economic; political and administration factors were also influential. Towns that were chosen as county seats survived even if they did not have genuine locational advantages.[91] For the most part, however, the centers best placed for

91. Professor Berry has pointed out that when Lewis was chosen as the county seat of Cass County, two nearby villages dwindled and died. In the same way Frankfort, which had flourished when it was the county seat of Montgomery County, was soon

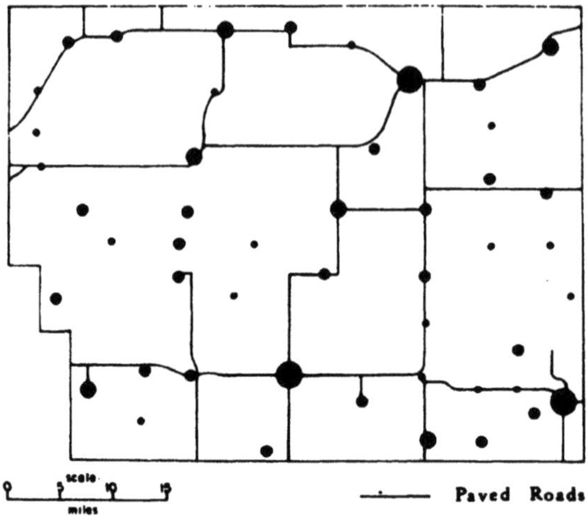

Figure 2–12 Reduction of Number of Central Places
SOURCE: Brian J. L. Berry, *Geography of Market Centers and Retail Distribution,* © 1967, p. 9. Reprinted by permission of Prentice-Hall, Inc., Englewood Cliffs, New Jersey.

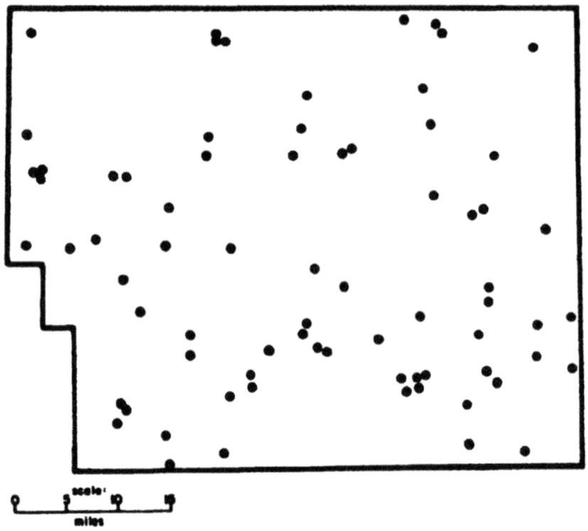

Figure 2–13 Number of Central Places Eliminated in a 105-Year Period
SOURCE: See Figure 2–12

retail, processing, and service activities became the nodal points in the regional market network, and it was the functional interrelation of town and village that gave a structural unity to the whole spatial

deserted after the county seat was moved to Red Oak. *Geography of Market Centers,* p. 7.

apparatus. The element of linearity, however, had produced an unevenness in the availability of markets. Farms near railroads consistently had the shorter distance to towns or villages, and until these disadvantages were partly overcome by the advent of paved roads and automotive transport, the outlying areas were at a distinct competitive disadvantage—a handicap that was reflected in the differentially lower value of their farms.[92]

The villages in the Iowa sample had average populations of a little more than 500 people, and in 1960 they provided about twenty-five kinds of retail or service facilities by about forty establishments. The reach of these small centers was approximately 5 miles, which meant that each had a market area of about 70 square miles.[93] The towns, the next size in the central-place hierarchy, had populations of around 1,500 persons; they performed about fifty kinds of market services by some hundred establishments. The reach of these markets was about 8 miles; hence they served an area of about 200 square miles. By reason of their larger clientele they could provide services not available in villages.[94] The third category of central places, the small cities with populations of about 6,000, carried on some ninety kinds of business by some three to four hundred establishments. Their reach of a little less than 20 miles gave them market areas of about 1,000 square miles populated by about 20,000 additional consumers and producers. These small cities had an even wider range of specialized enterprises than the towns.[95] The only other category of central places besides the three just mentioned were the hamlets with populations of 100 or less. They

92. The initial differential in the value of land near a railway was roughly estimated by the Illinois Central Railroad when it made its first offering of land it had obtained from a Federal grant (all lying within 15 miles of the railroad): prices ranged from $5 to $20 per acre at a time (1854) when public domain land sold for $1.25 an acre. See Gates, *Illinois Central Railroad,* Chapter 8; for other examples of market prices for well-located land in Illinois in the 1850's and 1860's, see Margaret Beattie Bogue, *Patterns from the Sod: Land Use and Tenure in the Grand Prairie 1850–1900,* Springfield, Ill., 1959, pp. 45 ff. In pricing land it offered for sale, the Illinois Central Railroad took into consideration not only the agronomical character and availability of water but the nearness to towns, villages, churches, post offices and the distance from timber groves, coal mines, and stone quarries. Gates, *Illinois Central Railroad,* pp. 167–168.

93. Sixteenth-century English market centers in Lincoln, Chester, Shropshire, Hampshire, and Surrey had market areas of about this size.

94. The towns, for example, had dentists, doctors, dry cleaners, insurance agencies, and funeral parlors. See Berry, *Geography of Market Centers,* p. 15.

95. Such as jewelry, shoe, clothing, and liquor stores; and florists, newspaper printing plants, and auto accessory supply houses.

provided very limited facilities: a general store, a gas station, a roadside restaurant, and perhaps a farm machinery agency.

Although a few hamlets were served by railroads—and these almost always had grain elevators—most of the centers served by railroads were larger and more important than the villages and hamlets without railroads. The railroad villages and towns not only had grain elevators (where farmers could either sell their oats, wheat, or barley outright or store it in anticipation of higher prices) but also banks where money could be deposited or borrowed, hardware stores, lumber yards, and cooperative societies where farm supplies and fertilizer could be purchased. They had yards and loading chutes for cattle or hogs that were to be shipped to market on the railroad, mills for grinding stock feed, repair facilities for motor vehicles and farm machinery. They provided the kinds of organizational skills needed to link the encircling farm community with the regional market, the national market, and, indeed, with international markets. For each type of market area there had come into being the appropriate processing industries, the necessary type of forwarding and shipping facilities, the proper variety of service industries, and an adequate range of retail outlets catering to community needs.

This sample is doubly instructive. The growth and development of the American Midwest was made possible by a pragmatic improvement of spatial organization. Out of this process of "creative destruction"[96] there emerged a regional hierarchy of central places that served to rationalize a rural landscape by a thoroughgoing process of commercialization. A variety of goods locally available provided minimally necessary supplies and equipment for increased output, while the proximity of larger supply centers, with their tempting variety of consumer and producer goods, steadily increased the incentives for greater output and productivity. Progress occurred because spatial patterns were restructured, because improperly located villages were allowed to wither, and because the total number of central places was reduced as market isovectures lengthened.

Comparison of central places in the American Midwest with those in a majority of underdeveloped regions reveals a striking difference. It is not that the underdeveloped regions lack central places, for some have

96. I am, of course, indebted to Joseph Schumpeter for this useful term. See his *Theory of Economic Development*, Cambridge, Mass., 1934.

too many! What is amiss is that they rarely constitute a functional hierarchy, and for this reason they fail to provide an intermeshed system of exchange that will provide the requisite incentives for increased application of labor, capital, and human skills. The American midwestern experience shows that in order to achieve even a tolerably satisfactory degree of regional productive efficiency, the pattern of central places and their functions must be progressively restructured and rationalized.

CHAPTER 3 MARKETING SYSTEMS AND SPATIAL DESIGN

Limitations of Village-Structured Economies

Even though there may be large cities in underdeveloped countries, the typical landscape reveals a predominating village economy. A majority of the people, usually a very large proportion, live in dwellings clustered together in hamlets or villages that consist of only a few hundred people. In India, for example, the 1960 census reported a total of 564,718 villages with an average population of 637 persons; and in these half-million small communities lived 82 percent of the Indian people. Such dispersion of population is to be found not only in Asia but in the Middle East,[1] in Africa, and in Latin America, as well as in Oceania.[2] These thousands upon thousands of villages have various origins deriving from diverse cultures and from complex historical factors. Some villages were built by closely related members of clans,[3]

1. The well-known Hamadan rugs are not made in the city of Hamadan but in some 150 nearby villages. See Arthur T. Gregorian *Oriental Rugs and the Stories They Tell*, Boston, 1957, p. 45.

2. In the 97 inhabited islands of the 2141 islands that constitute the "Trust Territory," settlements range in size from a low of 8 to 13 persons to a high of as many as 4,000, with the median in the neighborhood of 300 persons.

3. In describing the settlement of Šumadija (Northern Serbia) Joel Martin Halpern writes, "Immigrants to Orašac did not arrive as a group but rather as small family units, usually brothers accompanied by their wives and children. Because they were settling in a new homeland these pioneers founded clan groups. . . . Once settled in their new homes the pioneers encouraged relatives who had remained behind . . . to join them. . . . Nuclear family households were rare, and Serbian peasants lived in *zadrugas* comprising as many as four or five married men with their families." *A Serbian Village*, New York, 1958, pp. 11, 13, 26.

others were formed by religious groups[4] or other associated persons. Settlers on frontiers in ancient as in modern times crowded together for mutual defense. Military leaders who needed continuing control over conquered territories rather consistently dispersed their liegemen throughout a landscape, and the settlements of the leaders with their followers, serfs, or slaves, became nuclei for socially differentiated communities.

Whatever the origins—and they are legion—the main economic reason for the village community in field-crop agricultural economies is clear enough: the cultivators need to be near their fields. Except in nomadic economies (where mobility of herds is a requisite for a tolerably satisfactory use of pastureland,[5] and where temporary villages are only places of residence for relatively short periods of time) villages tend to become centers (or near-centers) of spatial areas, and these village-centered units[6] constitute the normal and customary small building blocks of an economic landscape. As these territorial units nest themselves together, a more or less symmetrical honeycomb design will tend to emerge. Some illustrations will make this clearer.

Figure 3–1 is entirely conceptual. It assumes the existence of a group of seven villages, each with encircling land, scattered evenly over an agricultural plain uniformly fertile. Each village would tend to have a market influence over a circular compass of land whose radius would be a maximally convenient transport distance. Since circular areas cannot nest together without leaving blank areas (see Figure 3–2), a full utilization of space would result in overlaps. If these overlaps were bisected, however, all transport distances for all villages would be minimized, and the entire territory would be equitably divided between the several villages. The hinterland of each village would then take the shape of a hexagon rather than a circle.

Skinner's study of rural markets in China shows how actual spatial geography roughly approximates this simplistic model. Figure 3–3 attempts to show the boundaries of a number of historical market areas in

4. The settlement of New England by Puritan dissenters is only one illustration among hundreds of historical instances of the migration of groups of people to new locations for ideological reasons.

5. This use of space often creates difficult territorial disputes. Thus the Laps claim pasture rights for their reindeer herds not only in Sweden but in Finland and Norway; the Kurds claim grazing rights in Iraq, Turkey, and Azerbaijan.

6. On the factors that influence their size see Folke Dovring's penetrating analysis in *Land and Labor in Europe*, The Hague, 1965, chapter 1.

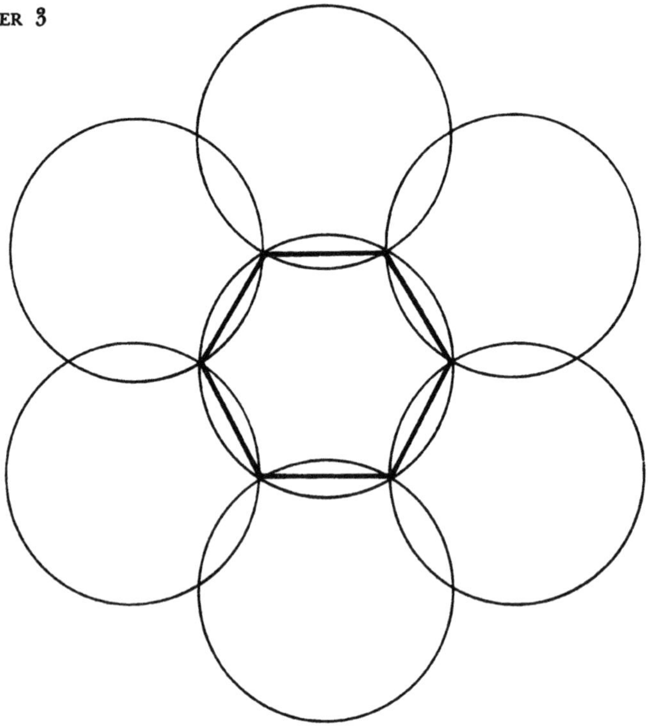

Figure 3–1 Compression of Circular Areas into Hexagons

a portion of Szechwan, near Chengtu.[7] It must be pointed out however, that Skinner's map shows the hinterlands of market towns, not those of agricultural villages; indeed, each of these Chinese market centers constitutes a focal point for the marketing activities of about a score of villages.[8] The point is simply that village hinterland hexagons fit together (with more or less geometric irregularity)[9] into larger configurations, which also tend to be hexagonal. The character of the resulting spatial design is of critical importance in the study of economic development. Just as a happy conjuncture of the right soil, the right rainfall, the right

7. G. William Skinner, "Marketing and Social Structure in Rural China," *Journal of Asian Studies,* 24 (November 1964), 25.

8. "In the 1870's the average number of villages per rural market was 17.9 in Hsiang-shan *hsien* and 19.2 in Ch'ii-chiang *hsien,* both in Kwantung. The classic field study of Chinese rural marketing, that of C. K. Yang in the 1930's in Tsou-p'ing *hsien* Shantung, shows 21.4 villages per standard . . . market." Skinner, "Marketing and Social Structure," p. 18.

9. These irregularities are caused by topographic, agronomic, and other geographical differences. No real landscape is ever an isotropic plain.

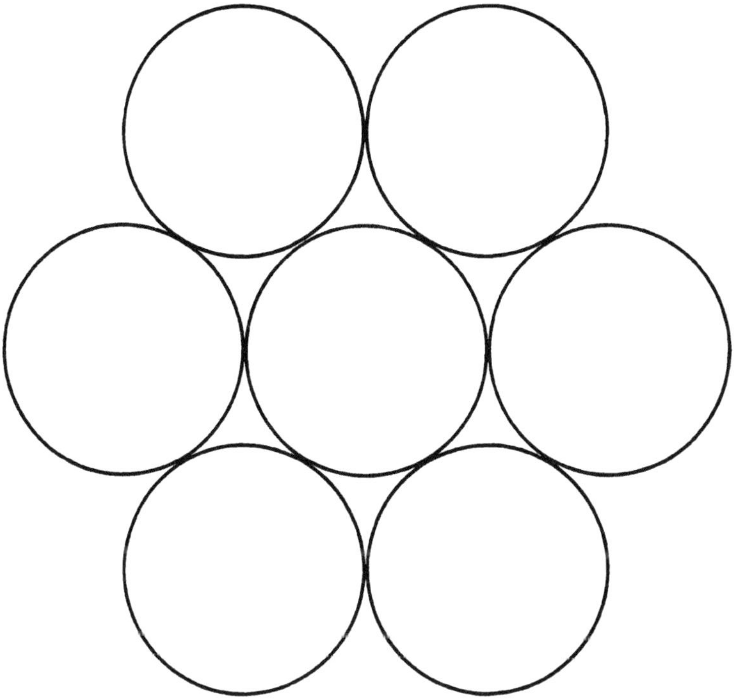

Figure 3–2 Unfilled Space Left by Tangent Circles

temperatures, and the right amount of sunshine can produce grapes that yield a vintage wine, the proper spatial organization of a landscape can provide incentives that will induce people to do their very best to maximize the productive capacity of an economic region.

In this quest for satisfactory spatial design, a community's marketing performance is the critical factor. Nor is it only backward countries recently liberated from some imperial power that have been cursed with an improper organization of space. Before the advent of hard roads and low-priced automobiles, vast stretches of the agrarian landscapes in the United States were badly structured. This variety of faulty spatial design can be illustrated by the limited market reach and the over-extended range of enterprises trying to operate profitably within an inadequate market area in a northern Illinois village, when market perimeters were largely determined by the difficulties of travel over earth roads, incredibly dusty in summer and nothing less than mud bogs for several autumn, winter, and spring months. The people served by this

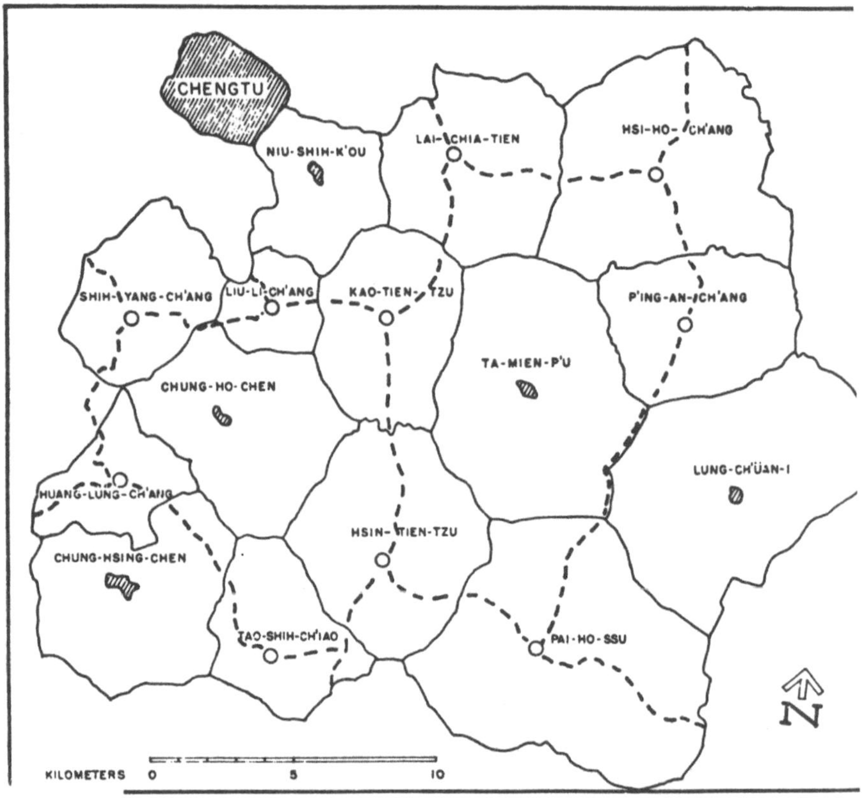

Figure 3–3 A Portion of Szechwan near Chengtu

SOURCE: Brian J. L. Berry, *Geography of Market Centers and Retail Distribution*, © 1967, p. 67. Reprinted by permission of Prentice-Hall, Inc., Englewood Cliffs, New Jersey.

particular market center, located in an area of exceptionally rich farming land, consisted of about 800 residents of the village plus about 850 people who lived on farms located within a 6-mile radius, making a total market of not over 1,650 people.

When the area was initially settled in 1837, only a general store and a saloon represented the future village. After two railways built their tracks so that they crossed only a half mile from the emergent village, the expectation was that this place might become a really flourishing market center. Quite steadily, therefore, the variety and number of enterprises increased: two lumber yards—one on each railway—three "general" stores, two livery stables to provide horses for visiting salesmen, two drugstores. A local newspaper was soon started, and after 1890 a telephone exchange. By 1910 no less than eighty-one enterprises and professional offices had come into being, all trying to make money by catering to variable fractions of the 1,650 consumers.[10] The outcome was mostly a story of low incomes and chronic financial difficulties. Only by planting large kitchen gardens, by scrupulous and penurious economy, and by the generous use of child labor could the families of most of the small-scale entrepreneurs and of the professional men (there were virtually no professional women) eke out a precarious income, living constantly in fear that some of their bills could not be paid and that the mortgages on their modest homes might any day be foreclosed.

The trouble was not that there was any lack of industry or of honest effort. The basic cause of low incomes was the miniscule scale of average operations, which was in turn a function of the inadequacy of the market for each enterprise, or the insufficient number of patients, students, or customers for each doctor, dentist, music teacher, or tailor. The net effect was uniformly low levels of income and a corresponding limited capacity to save and invest. Because average incomes were low,

10. The full list, in 1910, was as follows:

3 general stores
2 drug stores
3 barber shops
2 implement dealers
2 livery stables
3 doctors
3 building contractors
2 lumber yards
2 blacksmith shops
1 baker
1 cobbler
1 furniture dealer and undertaker
1 plumber and tinsmith
1 well driller
1 carpet weaver
2 saloons
2 teamsters
1 cement-block maker
1 house mover
2 realtors
1 concrete contractor
1 creamery
2 garages
2 livestock shippers
2 veterinarians
2 painting and decorating contractors
2 tailors
2 restaurants
2 hotels
2 masons
1 printer and newspaper editor
2 banks
1 dentist
1 harness maker
1 wagon maker
1 jewelry store
1 cigar maker
1 insurance company
1 millinery store
1 poultry-dressing plant
1 kerosene distributor
1 photographer
1 butcher
1 shoe store
1 theatrical company
1 telephone company
1 local light plant
1 market gardener
2 steam engine operators
2 music teachers
1 junk dealer
1 feed mill
1 electrical contractor
1 ice company

a general sentiment for holding down local taxes persisted, leading inevitably to very skimpy and inadequate appropriations for schools and virtually none for public health! A large number of boys and girls did not remain in school beyond the eighth grade, and for a young man to leave the community for college or university study was an exceptional event. Since for the time there seemed little likelihood that the market would widen materially (a rural system of paved roads was as yet only a dream), the prospects were not bright.

Why did not the two railways bring about the requisite market expansion? The answer, as Holmstrom has shown, is that railways elongate and polarize economic development by reason of their linear character.[11] By cheapening the long-distance movement of goods, they permit industrial enterprises at the extremities of railway axes to increase the scale of their operations. At such railway poles (or at major railroad junctions) unit costs of production can be reduced not only because of the economies of scale but because when a sizable range and number of industries locate there, when a disciplined work force is attracted and trained, and when auxiliary and service industries develop, certain economies become available that are "external" to any particular firm and are available for all enterprises. But not every chance railway crossing will become such a "growth point," only those that have clear locational advantages for many types of production.

Before the automobile age, the products made in polarized industrial centers were sold in every country village that could be reached by the railway network. To the extent that economy of scale and competition between sellers lowered prices, consumers in country villages benefited, but their capacity to purchase industrial goods was severely limited by their low incomes. Moreover, since agricultural communities could purchase industrial products only with the money they derived from the sale of grain, cotton, hogs, cattle, potatoes, and other farm products, their buying power depended on the level of farm-product prices in relation to the level of industrial-product prices. But because the demand for all primary commodities is relatively inelastic, and because the prices of industrial goods, then as now, were for the most part "administered," the normal consequence of city-village trade was that the terms of trade tended to move against the village. As a result, the inhabitants of most rural villages not only were handicapped by an in-

11. J. Edwin Holmstrom, *Railways and Roads in Pioneer Development Overseas: A Study of their Comparative Economics*, London, 1934, pp. 265–267.

adequate local market but their economic well-being was adversely affected by forces that were molding a "dual economy."[12]

Still a third factor was jeopardizing economic well-being in American village communities before the automobile age. Almost every small community, such as the one just described, was honeycombed with petty monopolies. If there were scarcely enough customers for one butcher, he could only stay in business by charging high prices although these relatively high prices might not allow him to obtain an adequate income. If there were two drug stores, a rather different situation might exist, a duopolistic balance where neither firm would dare to make prices competitive lest its capacity to survive would be imperiled. The sole funeral director could, of course, charge whatever the traffic would bear, and the sheer inconvenience of going to a larger village by road, or to a city by train, would give monopoloid advantages to implement dealers and local furniture stores. For certain unusual or infrequent purchases, the villagers actually did go farther afield, but a major share of their purchases were regularly made in the local market. Limited outside competition came from mail-order houses, but this had little effect on the local prices of bread, vegetables, meat, and other perishable items of consumption. Effective competition and real consumer's choice had to await the lengthening of market radii.

This process of market widening, which had begun in a feeble way with the use of bicycles, was rather rapidly achieved when automobiles became technically dependable and cheap enough so that many people, not just the fortunate few, could buy them.[13] For whereas a horse-drawn wagon or buggy traveling at 3 miles an hour would take four hours to traverse a 6-mile radius to and from a village market, a 1915 Model T Ford moving at 15 miles an hour could whisk over a 30-mile radius in the same travel time (four hours). If in an agrarian landscape villages were spaced 7 or 8 miles apart, a horse-drawn farmer had but little choice; he could go to the nearest village, or, at the best, he could choose one of two markets. By contrast a farmer with a Ford could take his

12. See Chapter 5.

13. This process was greatly facilitated by the popularization of installment selling, no easy task since it involved a sharp break with the "folklore of capitalism," which postulated that only wastrels bought things "on time," whereas dependable people always paid cash for everything except their houses. Once these prejudices were overcome, a rapidly growing number of car buyers made possible economies of scale so that a Model T. Ford (available in any color provided it was black!) could be sold for $390 f.o.b. Detroit.

choice of any one of some thirty villages contained in a 30-mile radius. (See Figure 3–4) He would most likely go to the largest market center he could reach within such a travel-time radius, since here his range of choice would be greatest.

Yet this very real advantage of choice would be only the static aspect of the situation. With potential customers that could be attracted from a 30-mile radius by lower prices, better quality merchandise, and a more attractive combination of goods and services, business enterprises at superior locational sites could expand the scale of their operations, vary the proportion between their factor inputs (usually in the direction of capital intensivity), distribute their fixed costs over an enlarged output,

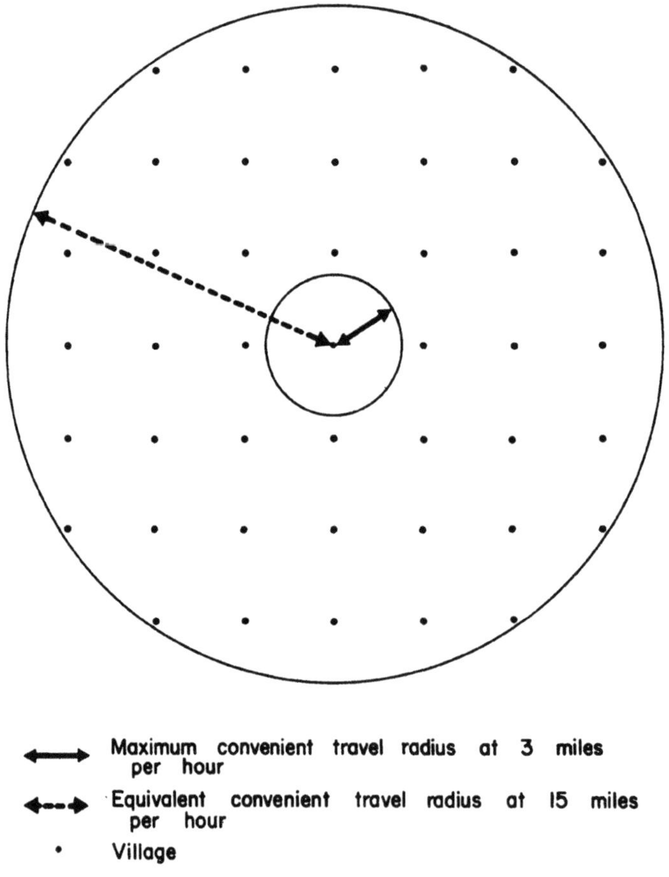

Figure 3–4 Effect of Increase in Speed of Travel on Spatial Market Choices

and by these several means achieve lower unit costs, which in turn would attract still more customers and allow enterprises to "deepen" their capital further. Since a circular market area will increase by the square of a lengthened diameter, it becomes clear that, if the density of population is uniform (as it virtually was in rural areas of northwestern Illinois in 1910), the potential number of buyers in a market area with a 30-mile radius will not be five times that of a market area with a 6-mile radius but twenty-five times as large. In such a market area, comprising, for example, a territory of over 2,800 square miles and a population of over 45,000 people, one or more sizable market towns could ultimately emerge, strategically located not only for trade but for various processing, light manufacturing, and service activities.

In such a market town there would be room for several producers of the same commodity or of the same product-mix, thus generating both price and quality competition from which all consumers would benefit. Moreover, in the same way (although to a lesser extent) that railway poles acquired external economies in the form of power facilities, warehouses, machine shops, repair facilities, insurance companies, and specialized financial institutions, so could regional market centers increase the effectiveness of all the firms engaged in production and marketing. At the same time workers could better adapt their skills and talents to their work by reason of a widening choice of occupations. In addition, workers would now, for the most part, find employment in a more technological scheme of production, and the availability of skilled labor would soon create an additional locational advantage for both old and new enterprises situated in a growing market town.

The integration of dispersed village-centered areas into larger agro-urban communities in developed countries such as Denmark, Sweden, and the United States was partly an autonomous response to market forces and partly the consequence of cautious and experimental planning. The autonomous action consisted of a gradual but progressive shifting of buying and selling activities away from village merchants and artisans toward the larger market centers where greater volume and better factor proportions had given enterprises an advantage over local village trade monopolies. But actually this shifting of more regional business toward larger commercial centers could take place because a certain amount of infrastructure had been planned. It was the civic leaders of the emergent market towns who persuaded voters to approve bond issues for hard roads or for such public utilities as water, gas, and street railway systems. This chapter in embryonic small-region planning was pragmatic and experimental. It was both formal and informal, the formal planning undertaken by county and municipal authorities, the informal by Chambers of Commerce or by groups of citizens who advocated such new departures as consolidated schools and county hospitals.

All these integrative forces were occurring before the principles of overall economic planning were understood.[14] For that reason, as I have pointed out elsewhere,

> the transition from a village-structured economy to a market-town economy was slow, groping and wasteful. No scientific attention was given to locational factors which should have governed the selection of the new (production and marketing) centres. What happened was that several [village] communities concurrently attempted to become regional centres, and this competition, although it did help to invigorate markets, led to a waste of resources invested in both productive equipment and infrastructure. Experience has therefore shown that the creation of necessary market towns cannot wisely be left wholly to atomistic market forces. [The process] needs to be guided, assisted, quickened, and induced by careful overall preplanning even as it should be properly implemented by integrating the whole market-town-making programme with a nation's overall planning of patterns, targets and goals.
>
> A developing nation must therefore make a choice. Its leaders must decide whether they will wait for the slow, hesitant, groping, local market forces painfully and planlessly to bring regional market centres into being or whether they will set in motion a systematic rationalisation of the market and production structure of their rural economy. For one thing is quite certain: adequate regional market and production centres must come into being before there can be any real capacity for organic development and transformation. The longer this decision is postponsed or evaded, the lower the real-income yield on net national investment, and the slower the rate of

14. In the United States the need for regional and national planning was not really recognized before the depression of the mid-1930's, when books such as Barbara Wootton's *Plan or No Plan* and *Planned Society: Yesterday, Today, and Tomorrow*, ed. Findlay MacKenzie, appeared, and when Wesley Mitchell gave a series of lectures on "National Planning" at Cornell University.

improvement in real wages. For in modern societies productivity is not merely the resultant of a ratio between a man and his tools; it is this in relation to the organizational efficiency which the enterprise, the regional market community, and the entire economy provides.[15]

Types of Rural Landscape Design: Dendritic Market Systems

The degree of integration between town and country or, more specifically, between village-centered areas and agro-urban communities, is markedly different in developed and in underdeveloped countries. Not only is the ratio between villages and towns much lower in developed countries but the gradations in the central-place hierarchy are far less abrupt. Berry made the latter point very clear in describing the spatial design of the American Midwest: "As one travels along the highways between county seats, very regular progressions of places are encountered: county seat, village, town, village, all approximately evenly spaced."[16] This, of course, does not mean there is a town for every village, because from this beadlike arrangement there are side roads leading off to outlying villages. Even so, the ratio between villages and market towns is remarkably low, probably about 16 to 1,[17] as contrasted with a ratio ranging from a low of about 50 to 1 to a high of over 300 to 1 in India,[18] and 600 to 1 in Yemen. The contrast can be expressed in a more dramatic way: if India were to have the same village to market-town ratio that the United States now has, she would need more than 47,000 market towns. She now has less than 2,000.

The relative dependence of a village community on a large trading center is a measure of the degree of a community's integration with a larger economic system. But this integration is not the result merely of the village to town ratio. Studies of Indian villages have shown extraor-

15. E. A. J. Johnson, *Market Towns and Spatial Development in India,* New Delhi, 1965, pp. 5–6.

16. Brian J. L. Berry, *Geography of Market Centers and Retail Distribution,* Englewood Cliffs, N.J., 1967, p. 20.

17. As more and more satellite towns come into existence, the ratio is distorted; but since many of these suburban towns serve partly as market centers for adjacent agrarian areas, it is not accurate to disregard them entirely.

18. Johnson, *Market Towns and Spatial Development in India,* p. 140. In an area surrounding Kanpur, India, a city of 1.3 million people, there are some 11,239 villages that can be said to belong to the Kanpur region. Dispersed through the region are twenty-four towns and cities. On the average then, there are 468 villages for every urban center.

dinary variations in the utilization that villages make of nearby towns. Mukherjee and Gupta's survey of eight villages in western Uttar Pradesh revealed that, whereas all these villages were within five miles of a railway and were connected with market towns by serviceable all-weather roads, some villages made almost four-fifths of their purchase outside their local community, and other villages made two-thirds of their purchases inside their own villages and only a third outside.[19] It is therefore not the simple ratio between villages and towns that determines whether agrarian communities are being integrated with a larger regional and national economy but the degree to which village people are willing and able to carry on more transaction in larger trade centers. One factor that has seriously restricted the capacity of villagers to avail themselves of market-town facilities has stemmed from the chronic indebtedness of so many village people to local money lenders, compelling them to trade inside their villages even though they pay more for their purchases and receive less for what they have to sell. But a failure or an incapacity to utilize the superior market facilities of a trading center larger than the village, whether it stems from inertia or debt servitude, does not make the village-town ratio any less consequential for long-run development considerations. Thus in Yugoslavia it was because the 400 years of Turkish administration (under town-dwelling officials) had developed a village-town ratio of about 20 to 1[20] that the integration of rural areas with a dispersed industrial program could proceed so swiftly once an overall development plan was formulated, financed, and implemented. It was the existing village-town ratio that gave Yugoslavia, as it had given Denmark two generations before, an advantage that countries such as Iran, Pakistan, and Egypt do not yet have.

It is a common misjudgment of assume that, because an economy has visible markets where people can buy and sell things, it is, for that reason, adequately monetized and capable of obtaining the long-heralded Smithian benefits of a division of labor. Moreover, even if the markets are in some way interlinked with a system of larger and smaller exchange centers, it does not necessarily follow that the market structure is really capable of promoting development. In Haiti, a notoriously poor and unprogressive country, there are nearly 200 "regular and

19. P. K. Mukherjee and S. C. Gupta, *A Pilot Survey of Fourteen Villages in U. P. and Punjab*, New Delhi, 1959, pp. 67–68.

20. Halpern, *A Serbian Village*, p. 8.

recognized rural market places, and more than 100 urban market places."[21] Since the land area of Haiti is only about 10,700 square miles, the ratio between markets and land area served would seem to be exceptionally low.[22] The trouble is obviously not in the number of markets but in the way they function.

Sidney Mintz's very careful analysis of the Haitian marketing system provides an instructive example of how a basically rural society[23] has become inextricably dependent upon a system of markets whose structure, control, and modus operandi seriously limits the capacity of the peasantry to change perceptibly their debased standard of life. The structure of the market system is essentially dendritic (See Figure 3–5). Goods destined for export (e.g., coffee, sisal) and a wide variety of provisions for the urban population (e.g., pork, beef, poultry, eggs, pulses, grain) are gathered up in or near rural markets, bulked or processed in a few "strategic" markets, and moved to port-cities by migrant traders (*révâdèz*). Conversely, consumer goods which peasant-community artisans cannot produce move from port-cities through strategic (wholesale) markets to local markets. Because of their need for some cash income, the peasants unwittingly play into the hands of the traders, and the whole system tends to keep the peasants' terms of trade persistently adverse. Admittedly, political factors have much to do with Haitian poverty, particularly when main portions of public revenue for both the local governmental units (*arrondissements*) and the state government are derived from taxes on marketing operations—taxes that are "ubiquitous, continuous, and severe."[24]

It is the organization of the market system, however, as well as the control, that frustrates any really progressive and equitable integration of town and country. For the very structure, the essentially dendritic

21. Sidney Mintz, "A Tentative Typology of Eight Haitian Market Places," *Revista de ciencias sociales,* 4, No. 1 (March 1960), 16.

22. Even if Haiti were a level plain, which it most certainly is not, the average market area would be only 35 square miles.

23. It is estimated that more than 85 percent of the Haitian population over fourteen years of age engage in agricultural work of some sort. See Paul Moral, *L'Economie haitïenne,* Port-au-Prince, 1959, p. 84.

24. Licenses are required for the right to purchase designated export commodities; peasants must pay for tethering their horses near a market; merchants are taxed on the stocks of goods they bring to or near a market; processors must pay taxes for the privilege of butchering hogs or cattle. "These endless taxing operations," writes Mintz, "and the numberless petty bureaucrats who collect them (and are supported by them) are the clearest manifestation of outside control over the market." "Tentative Typology," p. 44.

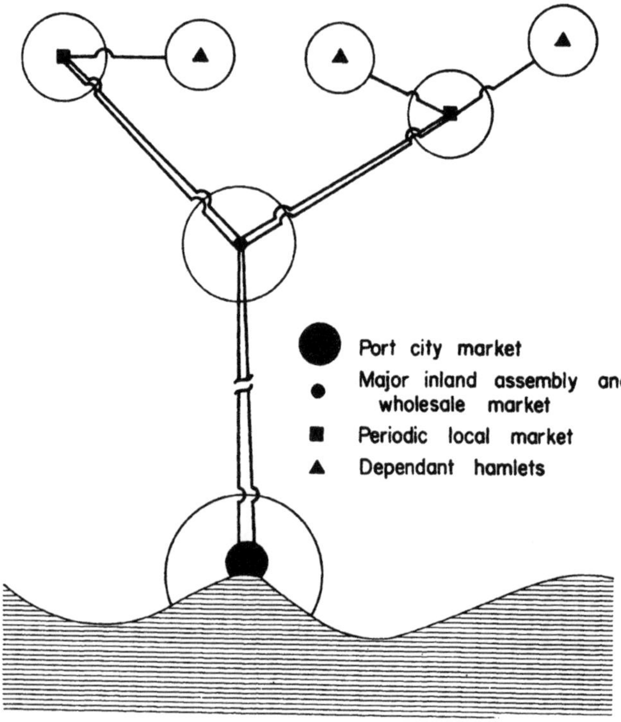

Figure 3–5 Elements of a Dendritic Market System

form, reflects a struggle for power, between coastal cities and their hinterlands and between the towns in such hinterlands and their rural dependent areas. The ultimate incidence of these efforts to engross the trading connections of agrarian communities with towns, cities, and overseas markets is on the peasantry, whose freedom to sell and whose capacity to buy is encapsulated by a system of markets in which producers of a wide variety of agricultural products must be content with a role that is passive, docile, and unrewarding.

The Haitian market typology deserves a somewhat fuller explanation because it is a species of a large genus. With variations, this kind of market system has emerged in scores of countries that have at some time experienced imperialistic suzerainty. The thrust in such a system is outward, whether there is now any actual "colonial" control or whether a domestic capital city has replaced an external "metropole" as a trading control center. What happens in Haiti is that licenses to trade, means of transport, and processing facilities are in the hands of nonlocal merchants (*révâdèz*). The sellers of produce are unorganized peasants who, although largely self-sufficient, nevertheless must obtain some cash income so that they can buy cooking oil, cloth, machetes, kerosine, spices, and other indispensable farm and household items. Accordingly, they bring their millet, corn, peas, yams, bananas, and beans to local rural markets and herd their hogs, goats, and cattle to larger country markets or to town markets. Since their products are perishable (or costly to feed), they are at a disadvantage in bargaining with professional buyers, who meet them before they actually reach the markets and persuade them, by all manner of chicanery, to sell. There is no supervised grading of produce, no open auctions; nor is there any effective cooperative association of sellers to offset even partially the buyers' advantages.

The compulsion to sell and the number of persons under such constraint leads to an inordinate number of sellers, wittingly or unwittingly competing with one another, while the minuteness of trading operations leads to a proliferation of the number of these inefficient periodic markets.[25] Lack of roads, carts, and pack animals limits the distance that peasants can travel,[26] although cows, horses, mules, donkeys, goats, and pigs are brought to major country markets from fairly large areas that vary in size with topography. For the most part, however, the radii of Haitian markets are short, except for the main-route extensions that the professional middlemen have established between the country towns and the "strategic" inland towns and between the strategic towns and the port cities.[27] These, of course, are not normal radii but the trunks and branches of the dendritic market system.

Although cultural, historical, topographic, and political factors will modify the particular designs of these dendritic market systems, there are usually three components: port cities, which are both export-import

25. In a large rural market where no more than 4,000 persons would congregate, Mintz counted 566 sellers; in a smaller local market where there would never be more than 250 persons, he counted 111 sellers. A count of sellers on a market day in February 1959 at Fond-des-Nègres showed "5 sellers of husked millet, each with about ten pounds of stock, 3 sellers of black beans, each with about five pounds of stock; 14 sellers of dried unroasted coffee, each with about ten pounds of stock (an unusually large quantity)." Ibid., pp. 25, 27.

26. A few handicraft products are brought long distances to important regional markets. Mintz found, for example, that broom makers came as far as 63 miles, "riding back on the burros that carried their products." Ibid., p. 37.

27. One of the major inland strategic cities Fond-des-Nègres is 106 miles from Port-au-Prince, the capital and largest port city. Another important inland market San Raphaël is 137 miles from the capital by the worst route and 274 miles by the "best" route, one that Americans would call "impassable." Ibid., p. 38.

points and consumption centers; "strategic" cities, connected with port cities by some linear form of transport and well located for bulking exports, consolidating purchases of primary products, and breaking wholesale lots of consumer goods for distribution through smaller markets; and dispersed local marketplaces, usually dependent on "strategic" cities for transport, processing, storage, bulk-breaking, and credit facilities. There is, of course, at all points in the market system a certain amount of what Mintz calls "horizontal trade"[28] exchange of agricultural products not destined for export or movement to port cities, of things fashioned by local artisans,[29] and of products available in some but not all parts of a local market area. This trade does nothing to integrate town and country, nor does it promise to make any contribution to the development of more complex, differentiated, and efficient rural economic centers.

In reality, then, in dendritic market structures two types of trade are concurrently carried on. Hundreds of small-scale traders are trying to obtain a marginal cash income to supplement their agricultural subsistence incomes so that their families can have things "produced both of materials and by methods which lie completely beyond [their] grasp."[30] Because sellers are many and urgently in need of cash, competition is fierce. If they sell (horizontally) to their village neighbors, price offers will be low because buyers' incomes are so small; if they sell to exporters or city produce-buyers they usually are the victims of some degree of monopsony. For the nonlocal traders have working capital, credit arrangements with banks, and usually also have inventories of the stocks they trade in; hence they are under no immediate compulsion to buy, whereas the small local sellers are under very real compulsion to sell. Consequently the city-centered merchant groups would have an advantage over their small-trading counterparts even if they had no special privileges acquired by political influence—privileges they usually do have in the majority of less-developed countries.

Although there are exceptions, the small rural traders cannot expand the scale of their operations.[31] They have neither the capital nor the

28. Ibid., p. 49.

29. In poor countries such as Haiti this includes many useful products made from discarded tin cans, tires, flour sacks, and other things thrown away as trash. This trade in economic collage is large.

30. Mintz, "Tentative Typology," p. 49.

31. In Nigeria and Ghana market women starting as petty traders have succeeded in expanding the scale of their operations. See Sidney Mintz, *Peasant Market Places*

entrepreneurial daring needed to restructure an inefficient market system.[32] Yet, because the swarm of small traders perform certain marketing functions (assembling, transport, and grading) at a very low price, there is no incentive for the export merchants or the city produce-suppliers to replace the small-scale traders. The city-based merchants are quite content to obtain intermediary services at the lowest possible price. This situation reveals the basic shortcoming of the colonial type of dendritic market: the small traders have no capacity to change it; the city-based merchants have no incentive to do so.

The differences between these colonial-rooted dendritic markets and other market systems are major; they are also inherent and persistent. From a colonial origin has come a dominance of "vertical trade" and limited development of "horizontal trade" not so much in volume as in composition. Two questions at once arise: "Why the undue accent on vertical trade, and why the anemic development of horizontal trade?" The answer to the first question is to be found in the economics of colonialism wherein the typical concern of decision makers was to expand the output of few specialized lines of primary production for export. To do this by means of an enterprise system, it was necessary not only to make appropriate investments in mines, plantations, and tea gardens but to arrange for a flow of payment goods to move in the opposite direction from the flow of exports to port cities.

Since the process of opening up a new trade area is both costly and risky, "it is only by offering some sort of monopolistic concessions that foreign business concerns can be induced to accept the risks and the heavy initial costs, which include not only those of setting up transport and communications and other auxiliary services but may also include the ordinary administrative costs of extending law and order."[33] And whereas transport, warehousing, and processing facilities very frequently were engrossed or controlled, this usually was only one aspect of a more

---

and Economic Development in Latin America, Vanderbilt University, Graduate Center for Latin American Studies, Occasional Paper No. 4, Nashville, 1964, p. 7.

32. In Jamaica market women, who sometimes borrow money in order to buy stocks at bargain prices, pay as much as 5 percent for a three-day loan. See Mintz, *Peasant Market Places,* p. 7.

33. H. Myint, "An Interpretation of Economic Backwardness," in A. N. Agarwala and S. P. Singh, *The Economics of Underdevelopment,* London, 1958, p. 121. The provision of some infrastructure might be undertaken by the colonizing power, depending on whether there were important military and political objectives that might by this means be advanced.

complete monopoloid configuration. A single enterprise, for example, might be the monopsonistic buyer of exportable crops, the monopsonistic employer of unskilled labor, and the monopolistic seller of the consumers goods upon which "native" workers could spend their wages. In this situation peasant producers, ignorant of market conditions, unorganized and hence incapable of resisting the pressures or importunities of middlemen, could not understand why export prices varied and were easily convinced that they were being exploited.[34] Yet as Myint has pointed out so well, "the real damage done by the middleman lies not in their 'exploitation,' considerable as it may be in many cases, but in the fact that they have put themselves between the backward peoples and the outside world and have robbed [them] of the educating and stimulating effect of a direct contact. As a consequence, even after many decades of rapid 'economic development' . . . the peoples of many backward countries still remain almost as ignorant and unused to the ways of modern life as they were before."[35]

The rather static character of "horizontal trade" has both cultural and economic causes.[36] In volume it may be quite large. Mintz estimates that in Haiti and in Jamaica the "horizontal" trade among members of the same class "surely exceeds one half [the national volume] in each instance." [37] The habit of clinging to the production of food and simple staples and hesitating to overspecialize in export products represents both peasant propensity to follow traditional production and exchange practices and, at the same time, a shrewd type of wisdom developed in the face of fluctuating export prices. For although the reward a peasant family may derive from producing millet, peas, and beans may be small,

34. This feeling of victimization is particularly acute when foreign middlemen become the operators of this type of market system: Indians and Chinese in Southeast Asia, Indians in East Africa, Syrians in West Africa. See Myint, "Interpretation of Economic Backwardness," p. 123, and Peter T. Bauer, *Economic Analysis and Policy in Underdeveloped Countries*, Durham, N.C., 1957, pp. 71–72.

35. "Interpretation of Economic Backwardness," p. 125.

36. The precise nature of this horizontal trade and the incredibly narrow profit margins have been described in graphic detail by Sidney Mintz in a chapter entitled "The Employment of Capital by Market Women in Haiti" in *Capital, Saving and Credit in Peasant Societies*, ed. Raymond Firth and B. S. Yamey, Chicago, 1964, pp. 256–286.

37. "Internal Market Systems as Mechanisms of Social Articulation," in *Intermediate Societies, Social Mobility and Communication*, ed. V. F. Ray, Proceedings of the American Ethnological Society, Seattle, 1959, p. 21.

it is dependable, and, above all, it seems to be fairer.[38] One should not, however, invest the resulting type of local, horizontal trade with virtues it does not possess. It is woefully inefficient, and by its prodigal use of intermediaries it not only reflects but helps to perpetuate the chronic underemployment characteristic of ill-organized agrarian landscapes. The produce brought to market comes in such small lots that the "movement of human beings by weight may exceed the movement of produce";[39] for each little load of corn, of millet or beans, of homemade sandals or brooms is brought by a selling intermediary. All over Latin America, the Middle East, Africa, and Asia these highly competitive markets are to be found. Wherever they exist—and that is practically everywhere in underdeveloped countries—they give living proof that (Adam Smith notwithstanding) unguided free enterprise does not necessarily lead to optimal development either of individual talents or of regional productive potentials. "The free play of economic forces in backward countries" says Myint, "has resulted not in a division of labor according to individual abilities but in a division of labor according to stratified groups."[40]

It is the structure of dendritic markets that tends to create these layered "non-competing groups,"[41] of local dealers selling foodstuffs, handicraft products, and cheap notions to the rural and urban poor; of professional traders engaged in domestic varieties of "vertical trade": buying provisions in country markets for urban middle classes or, oppositely, selling to the local markets industrial commodities or other city-supplied goods; and of exporters concentrating on the few commodities destined for foreign markets. Between these layers of entrepreneurship there is little if any transference, so that, whereas peasants (more likely their wives) have very real freedom of entry into the ranks of local traders, their prospects of becoming intermediaries in

38. "For a peasant producer of world market staples, the effort he puts into production and the reward he receives for it can sometimes seem to be connected in quixotic fashion: this is true particularly when the price of his product is subject to sharp and unexpected oscillation. . . . The connection between effort and reward he receives for the production of subsistence crops, and those he may sell locally, must seem more reasonable." Ibid., p. 26.

39. Ibid., p. 24.

40. Interpretation of Economic Backwardness," p. 129.

41. A concept which F. W. Taussig thought was basic to all social structures and hence indispensable for economic analysis. See his *Principles of Economics*, New York, 1923, II, 141–148.

village-town vertical trade are very poor, and their chances of becoming exporters nonexistent!

Types of Rural Landscape Design: Intermeshed Market Systems

Not all market systems in peasant or "traditional agrarian" societies are dendritic. In many less-developed countries—mainland China is a good example—markets have developed that have created a neatly interlocked spatial system in which essentially different functions are performed by several types of markets in a well-integrated central-place hierarchy. The smallest unit in the Chinese progression of exchange centers has been designated a "standard" rural market,[42] a local marketplace where a peasant household can dispose of produce it does not consume and buy the consumer goods it needs and can afford. Since nucleated villages are typical in most portions of the Chinese landscape, standard markets are normally located in places that Skinner has called "standard market towns." These centers are typically the smallest units of spatial economic organization, although below them are villages where a little horizontal peasant exchange occurs.[43] Above the "standard market towns" in Skinner's terminology for Chinese central places, comes, in order of size, importance, and function, the "intermediate markets" and the "central markets." Like Mintz's "strategic" cities, central markets are usually located at a point of advantage of transport, where wholesale functions can be performed—mainly a type of bulk exchange with other central markets.[44] Intermediate markets, standing between the standard market towns and the central markets, are largely concerned with vertical trade in both directions. In this inverted pyramid of marketing units the important thing is that "as one moves in this hierarchical typology from each type of central place to the next higher,

42. By G. William Skinner in his three excellent essays "Marketing and Social Structure in Rural China," *Journal of Asian Studies,* 24, (1964–1965) 3–45; 195–229; 363–401. The description of the Chinese marketing system that follows is based on these three articles.

43. In my own terminology I have reserved the term "market town" for a larger urban center which would provide a continuous daily market and a number of processing, warehousing, retailing, and banking facilities. See my *Market Towns and Spatial Development in India,* Chapters 1–3.

44. Whether still larger urban and administrative centers should be considered to be functionally distinct market centers is a matter on which there is disagreement. For the arguments pro and con see Skinner, "Marketing and Social Structure," pp. 7–9.

the number of households increases[45] while the proportion of the labor force engaged in agriculture falls."[46]

In China, as in a great many agrarian societies, local markets are held periodically and for several reasons. A coordinated schedule or cycle of market days for a number of standard market towns allows itinerant peddlers of needed household goods to cater to a total areal demand large enough to justify the variety of commodities they offer for sale.[47] Also, when markets are periodic, farmers and local artisans needed to devote only one day in twelve, one day in six, or whatever the market rhythm requires, to their marketing functions, thus leaving all other days for farming, shoemaking, and other productive activities. Moreover, periodic markets reduce the distances that peasant buyers or sellers must travel. Were markets held each day, market centers would perforce be more sparsely scattered over a landscape, or, conversely, "when markets are periodic rather than daily, market places may be distributed far more densely on the landscape so that the most disadvantaged villager can manage the trip to market in a reasonable period of time."[48] These are the main historical economic reasons for market-day cycles in Chinese rural areas. Whether the "density" of such periodic markets tends to restrain development and modernization is a question that must be very carefully analyzed in any planning program.

Skinner's findings, based on his own research and on that of Chinese scholars,[49] indicate that Chinese market areas are essentially hexagonal, even though the pattern is considerably distorted by the topography of any particular landscape.[50] (See Figure 3–3.) What is approximated is a two ring model (see Figure 3–6), which, in ideal spatial geometry, would arrange eighteen villages around a market center. That the actual Chinese ratio between villages and market towns is very near this

45. In examples that Skinner has cited, standard market towns had from 50 to 279 households, intermediate market towns from 366 to 900, and a central market town about 2650 households. "Marketing and Social Structure," p. 9, n. 19.

46. Ibid., pp. 9–10.

47. The cultural and historical factors that have influenced the market cycles are explained in detail by Skinner, "Marketing and Social Structure," pp. 11–16.

48. Ibid., p. 11.

49. Inter alia, Yang Mou-ch'un (Martin Yang), *A Chinese Village*, New York, 1945; Yang Ch'ing-k'un, *A North China Local Market Economy*, New York, 1944.

50. Only if a landscape were an isotropic plain, and only if villages were evenly distributed according to an isometric grid, would market areas conform to perfect hexagons. For detailed analysis of the geometry of spatial regions, see August Lösch, *The Economics of Location*, New Haven, 1954, Chapter 10.

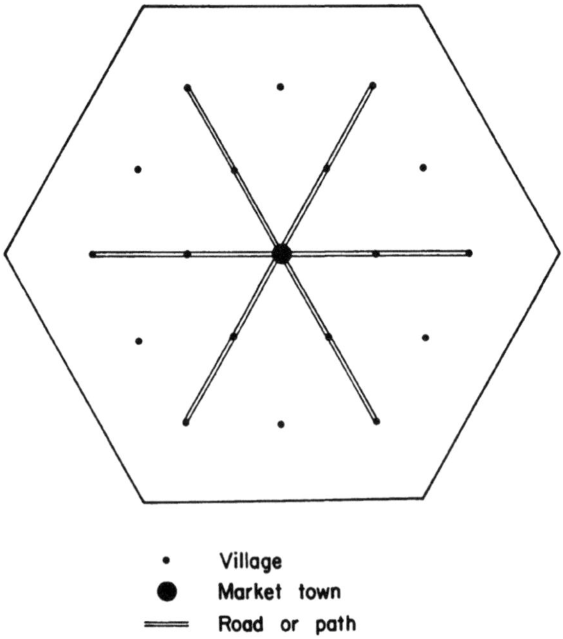

Figure 3–6 Model of a Market Area with Two Bands of Villages Linked with a Market Center

SOURCE: Adapted from a diagram in G. W. Skinner, "Marketing and Social Structure in Rural China," Part 2, *Journal of Asian Studies,* 24, No. 2 (February 1965), 197.

figure is attested by several field surveys which showed a range between 17.9 and 20.4 villages for each rural market.[51] Since roads and paths in China are not hampered by patterns as inflexible as the rectangular land survey in the United States, they tend to radiate from a market town more or less as shown in Figure 3–6. Since most produce is brought in baskets suspended from carrying poles, the market isovectures are determined by the travel time of the most disadvantaged peasant porters. A hexagonal configuration of a market area will reduce the spread between the most and the least disadvantaged villagers on the outer rim of a market area.[52]

51. See note 8 to this chapter.

52. "The appropriate model has two requirements: Markets should be so distributed that (1) the most disadvantaged villager in any given marketing area is no

The radiating paths and roads that link villages and "standard market towns" are "the arteries and veins of an economic system whose heart is the market in the town at its center. Along these paths, in the early morning hours of every market day, typically pass at least one of every five adults living in a whole array of dependent villages"[53] bringing grain, rice, chickens, eggs, pigs, and vegetables. When their produce has been sold, they can visit the stalls of the itinerant peddlers or the shops of the town artisans, buying what they need. There may be debts to pay to money lenders or credit societies or rent due at the town offices of landlords. Farm tools may in the meantime have been left for repair or sharpening while visits are made to the barber or the teahouse. Presently the outward flow of peasants will begin, while the town merchants will be busy sorting, grading, bagging, or otherwise preparing their purchases for shipment to intermediate or central markets.

The Chinese "standard market town" that serves to integrate eighteen or twenty villages is "but a subsystem of a larger structure," for it in turn is organically linked with several larger exchange centers, not merely with one, as is the case in most dendritic market systems.[54] The interesting thing to notice is that, whereas there are no villages on the perimeter of a standard market area, in the design of intermediate market centers "all dependent standard market towns are at the boundaries, equidistant from two or three higher-level market towns."[55] (See Figure 3–7, which has been drawn so that each standard market town is linked with three intermediate market towns.) This is because inter-

more and no less disadvantaged than the most disadvantaged villager in any other area, and (2) the distance from the market of the most disadvantaged villager in each marketing area is minimal. The first requirement means that all marketing areas in the model must be of uniform shape and size. Since all parts of the landscape must be in some marketing area, the only possibilities are the regular polygons which are 'space-filling', namely, equilateral triangles, squares and regular hexagons. The second requirement specifies that the more sides a polygon has the more efficient it is in this regard. To put it another way, as you move from the least advantageous position around the rim of a marketing area, the differential is maximal for triangular areas, intermediate for square areas, and minimal for hexagonal areas." Skinner, "Marketing and Social Structure," p. 17, n. 40.

53. *Ibid.*, p. 19. "Some member of almost every household," said Martin Yang of a Shantung village, "is in the town on market day." *A Chinese Village*, p. 191.

54. Skinner concludes that it is only standard market towns at upper ends of mountain valleys that are really dependent on a single (downstream) intermediate market. "Marketing and Social Structure," p. 21.

55. Ibid.

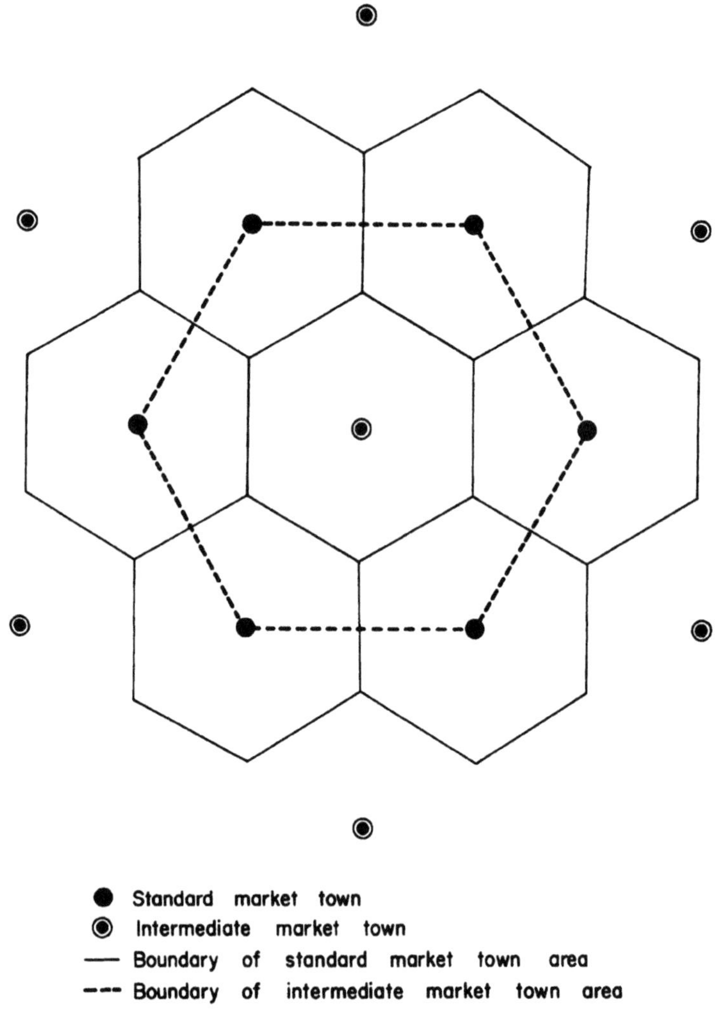

Figure 3–7 Model of a Spatial System with Market Areas of Two Sizes

SOURCE: Adapted from a diagram in G. W. Skinner, "Marketing and Social Structure in Rural China," Part 1, *Journal of Asian Studies,* 24, No. 1 (November 1964), 19.

NOTE: The intermediate market in the center hexagon serves a dual purpose: as an intermediate or secondary market for six encircling standard market hexagons and as a primary market for the standard market area of which it is the center. This circumstance gives the peasants living in the normal market reach of such a dual purpose intermediate market town a somewhat better outlet for their produce, because an intermediate market town will usually be considerably larger than the typical standard market town.

mediate markets are mainly merchants' markets,[56] and shrewd traders will want to be equipoised so that they can seek out the best prices in several intermediate markets. For this purpose the rim of an intermediate market area offers the most advantageous location. But in addition to merchants, the larger intermediate markets will attract the "local élite," whose style of life is more genteel than that of peasants, and whose incomes permit them to buy goods that are not in demand in peasant-catering standard market towns. This quasi-aristocratic demand of the elite makes it profitable for itinerant purveyors of goods or services to make a circuit through several intermediate markets, probably visiting some standard market towns *en passant*.

Although there can be varying designs of the next larger marketing unit in the Chinese central-place hierarchy, the simplest pattern (see Figure 3–8) is merely an enlargement of the intermediate market model, one in which several intermediate markets (rather than standard market towns) are on the perimeter of the spatial reach of the central market. It is these third-order central exchange centers that actually integrate activities of several intermediate markets (six in the model shown in Figure 3–8 together with their subordinate standard market towns) into a unified system.[57] Because they are larger than intermediate markets, the central markets normally concentrate on wholesale or bulk-breaking activities and accordingly have more physical facilities, such as warehouses, sheds or cellars, and a larger number of full-time resident traders.[58]

There is both downward and upward trade in the "complex of nested marketing systems." The downward flow of merchandise consists of

56. Except in those cases where an intermediate market has the dual purpose described in the note to Figure 3–7, peasants visit intermediate markets only occasionally, to make some unusual purchase or to make credit arrangements of an atypical variety. From his own experience, Skinner discovered how seldom peasants went farther afield than their local market town: "During three months when I lived with a typical peasant family in Szechwan, whose farmstead was three *li* [slightly over a mile] from one market town, Kao-tien-tzu, and five *li* [about 1¾ miles] from another, Niu-shih-k'ou, the household head and his wife between them marketed forty-six times at the former, their standard market, and only three times at the latter, their intermediate market." Ibid., p. 27.

57. Since the intermediate markets in the model are on the perimeter of the central market area, they are equally near to one or more other central market areas, thus affording a degree of flexibility and trade diffusion that is lacking in dendritic market patterns.

58. Itinerant merchants who visit intermediate and standard markets frequently use central market towns as their operation base. For highly specialized types of trade, itinerant dealers will make circuits that include several central markets.

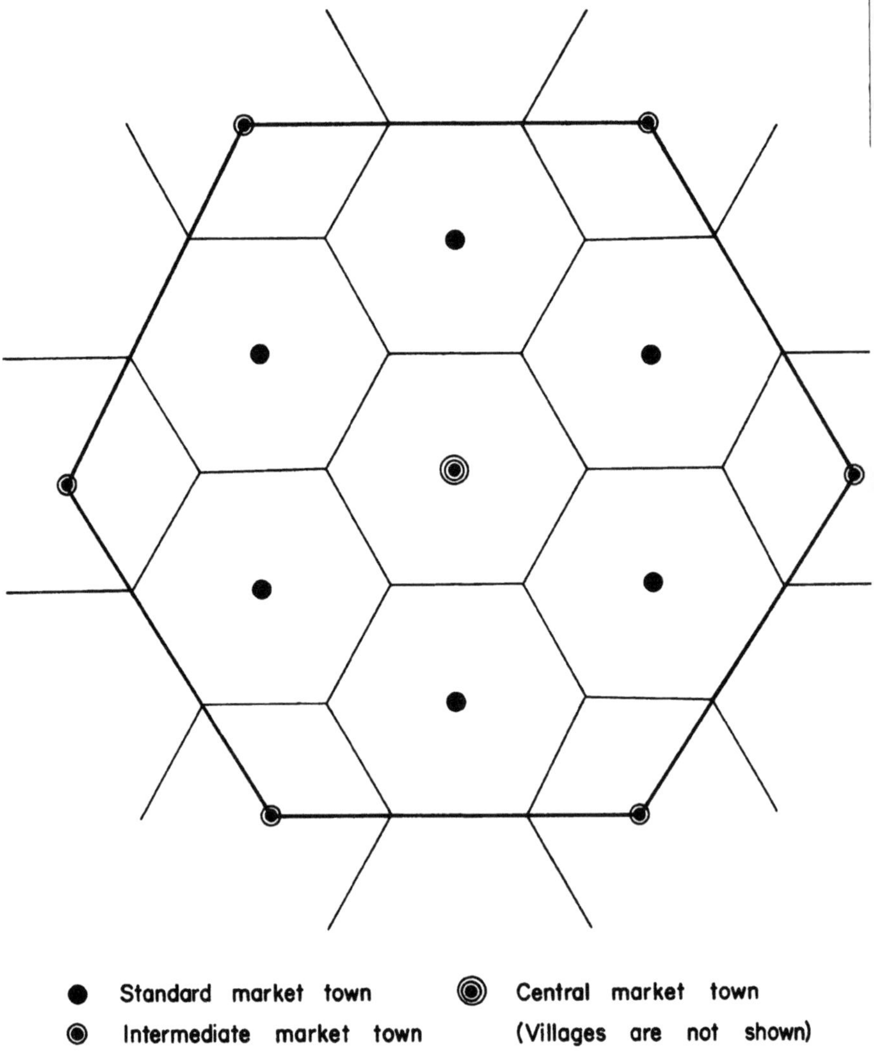

Figure 3–8 Model of a Chinese Central Market

SOURCE: Adapted from a diagram in G. W. Skinner, "Marketing and Social Structure in Rural China," Part 2, *Journal of Asian Studies,* 24, No. 1 (November 1964), 29.

several types. First there are exotic goods which central markets receive from still larger regional cities or from abroad via port cities. These goods are sold either in the central cities themselves or are passed down to intermediate markets by wholesalers or specializing itinerant merchants. Staple commodities are sold *en gros* to buyers from intermediate markets who then break bulk and sell to "firms" (either retail shops or itinerant traders) in standard markets. A sizable part of the downward trade consists of raw materials or semimanufactured components for craftsmen in intermediate towns or for petty artisans in smaller centers. It is therefore both a varied and a staggered type of downward trade: some goods go no farther than central markets, some cater to elite demand in intermediate markets, while a great many commodities that peasants need flow all the way down the three-level market structure.

The upward movement begins at the standard market town where peasants sell their farm produce or their handicraft products to traders who grade, bulk, and transport their purchases to higher-level market centers. Usually these assembling and bulking operations channel goods from standard market towns to intermediate markets, and here the buyers from central markets further grade and classify commodities destined for the more quality-conscious buyers in central markets or regional cities. Since the traders engaged in the upward traffic are dealing in sizable quantities, and since bulk-breaking wholesalers are also dealing in considerable volume, both upward and downward traders require credit accommodations; for this reason, "a hierarchy of credit arrangements parallels the hierarchical distribution and collection system."[59]

The product of thousands of years of cautious experimentation and slow pragmatic development, the Chinese marketing system has taken the form of "interlocked networks."[60] Since each standard market town is linked with two or three intermediate market systems, and since each intermediate market center is in turn functionally related to two or three central-market systems, the whole complex serves to integrate not only particular territorial regions but an entire national area. Whereas the thrust of dendritic markets is consistently outward, in the Chinese market system the outward thrusts are compensated by inward thrusts. The reciprocal upward-downward trade is more accurately describable

59. Skinner, "Marketing and Social Structure," p. 80.

60. For evidence of this growth of marketing knowledge, see Shiba Yoshinari and Yamane Yukio, *Markets in China during the Sung, Ming, and Ch'ing Periods*, East-West Center, Institute of Advanced Projects, Occasional Papers of Research Publications and Translations, Honolulu, 1967, esp. pp. 109–134.

as an outward-inward type of commodity and service flow. It is this well-articulated operation of a spatially intermeshed market system that has given such an extraordinary stability to Chinese agrarian society. Whether this is the best arrangement for Chinese growth and development is not equally clear.[61]

Since the Chinese standard market area is not only a marketing unit but at the same time the typical agrarian socioeconomic community and the basic building block out of which the spatial design of Chinese economic landscapes is formed, it is necessary to know something about its size in terms of area and population and about the travel distances from centers to perimeters.[62] It would be interesting to know also how these market areas compare, for example, with the space that was served by local British markets in the sixteenth century and how their populations compare with those of nineteenth-century American rural market centers. Their size perforce varies with topography, climate, and agronomic differences, since in the final analysis it is the richness or the poorness of agricultural resources that determine population densities.

Skinner's data indicate that Chinese standard market areas may be as large as 185 square kilometers in mountainous or arid regions and as small as 10 square kilometers in regions where the soil is exceptionally rich, where the agricultural methods are labor-intensive, and where the population is exceptionally dense. Disregarding extremes of size, both large and small, the range for 75 percent of the standard market areas is from about 90 square kilometers down to 25, and within this range four-fifths of the market areas have a median size of about 52 square kilometers.[63] The variation in population is much less. Disregarding once again the extremes of very sparsely or very densely settled areas, the range in population for 75 percent of the standard market areas is from about 5700 persons to 8,800 persons.[64] If these populations are divided

61. The present rulers of China do not think so. Their attempts to restructure agrarian landscapes are reviewed and evaluated in Chapter 10.

62. Skinner quite correctly points out that by concentrating on the village, anthropological work on Chinese society has "distorted the reality of rural social structure." The little world in which Chinese peasants live is not the village (which is by no means self-contained) but the "standard" agricultural community. "Marketing and Social Structure," p. 32.

63. This compares with an average market area in sixteenth-century England of 70 square miles. Since a square mile equals 2.59 square kilometers, the median size of Chinese standard market areas is slightly more than 20 square miles.

64. This compares with Iowa "towns" having an urban population of about 1,500 persons and a hinterland population of 2,500 to 3,000, making a "community" total of from 4,000 to 4,200 persons.

by the five to six members of a family, the model standard market community consists of about 1,500 households dispersed among eighteen to twenty villages distributed over an area of about 50 square kilometers, having a marketplace somewhere near the center of this land area. The average travel distance to a market center for the most disadvantaged villager would be about 4.5 kilometers (about 2.6 miles), which would mean that all households except those in very large, sparsely populated communities would be within easy walking distance of their respective standard market towns.

It should be emphasized that the Chinese standard market communities are very real cultural entities. By the time a peasant is fifty years old, he will have visited his standard market about three thousand times.[65] For the central place of a standard market area is not only a marketplace in which to sell and buy but a place where midwives, tailors, and porters are hired, where marriage brokers undertake to find suitable daughters-in-law, where lodges have their headquarters, and where fairs and religious festivals are held. Here in the teahouses, associations of animal breeders or fraternities of carpenters meet. Unlike the intermediate market centers, where the local elite, the traders, and the bureaucracy patronize the teahouses, the standard market towns are peasant communities, a "social structure within a marketing community"[66] sometimes with its own dialect, even its own variants of weights and measures. Its stability and unyielding quality stems from the fact that it is a basic unit of a social as well as an economic system. This is its essential virtue, although in terms of growth and development it may be a major fault.

Types of Rural Landscape Design: Contrived Market Systems

Whereas market systems such as the intermeshed Chinese variety have slowly evolved over a long period of time by a process of adaptation,[67] circumstantial mutation, and segmentation, other marketing systems have been consciously and quite deliberately contrived in order to accomplish certain explicit and definable goals. An instructive example of this type is to be found in the Indian "regulated market" system, which in certain Indian states has become a protective shield for farmers

65. Estimated by Skinner.
66. Skinner, "Marketing and Social Structure," p. 58.
67. Skinner has developed a general theory to explain this process of adaptation over some six and a half centuries. Ibid., pp. 195–211.

against the rapacity of village merchants, landlords, and usurers—triple roles so frequently played by the same persons. Regulated markets have not merely made marketing operations more equitable; the creation of daily, well-organized, efficient, and democratically supervised markets has given farmers incentives to produce more, to improve the quality of their crops, and to invest more of their savings in commercial fertilizers, improved seeds, better livestock, and more modern farm tools.

The object of the initial legislation, the Cotton and Grain Markets Act of Hyderabad Assigned District (1897), was to induce Indian farmers to raise cotton and to insure that farmers who did so would receive fair prices for their crops.[68] Accordingly, the British Resident was given authority to declare any place in the Assigned District[69] a market for the sale and purchase of certain ("notified") agricultural products and to form committees to supervise and regulate such designated markets.[70] By this means it was hoped that small farmers would not only shift away from traditional crops but would be able to escape from the clutches of the village traders and would therefore have an incentive to produce more of the cash crops that the British authorities favored. It should be remembered that Indian small farmers suffered from many handicaps. They usually had no financial reserves; indeed, they were usually in debt to village moneylenders. For that reason they were generally compelled to sell their surplus produce immediately after harvest, and because their neighbors were under the same compulsion, the village traders, singly or collusively, could offer low prices. If farmers had borrowed money locally, as most of them had, they were virtually compelled to sell to local traders in order to reduce their indebtedness, under pain of being denied further credit if they failed to do so. Without access to an open market, farmers caught in these meshes had no dependable market information on which to base their asking price.

The British authorities realized that unless some means were devised to overcome or mitigate these handicaps, small farmers could not be expected to take the risk of raising a new unfamiliar crop. They needed not only the expectation of better earnings but an assurance that the

68. Although the act was called the "Cotton and Grain Markets Act," it was only applied to cotton, which became the main cash crop of the region.

69. "Assigned" to the British for administration by the Nisam of Hyderabad.

70. India, Ministry of Food and Agriculture, *Agricultural Marketing in India: Regulated Markets,* Vol. I, *Legislation,* New Delhi, 1956, pp. 1–5.

marketing of cotton would not, like other produce, be monopolized by village traders. Farming at its best is a chancy occupation, not merely because of the vagaries of weather but because, unlike a manufacturer, a farmer has very little control over his production and distribution costs. His outpayments for seed, irrigation water, fertilizers, hired labor (if any) and rent are "outside the field of his influence";[71] so are the costs of grading, storage, and transport to wholesale and retail markets. It is final demand that decides whether all production and marketing costs will be covered. Because the distributive sector is normally much better organized than farmers are, and because moneylenders and landlords see to it that they have prior claims, in the absence of protective institutional arrangements, the farmer is a residual claimant. These inherent disadvantages would exist even if there were no deliberate "exploitation" of farmers by monopsonistic buyers of their produce. But in village societies, particularly if debt servitude is endemic, monopsony is characteristic. Village markets are too small to insure effective competition among buyers since usually the scale of operations justifies the existence of only one or two traders. In this situation there is little the small producer can do to escape from a monopsonistic impasse. For want of transport facilities he cannot travel afield in search of other buyers;[72] hence, unless some open market is created to which he has physical and transactional access, he will remain ensnarled by the local monopsonists or fall into the clutches of equally unscrupulous commission agents (*adatyas*) or other itinerant produce buyers.

Moreover, even without malice, virtually all buyers of farm produce tend to discriminate against the farmer simply because the price-making process is dependent upon ultimate demand. The retailer pays only what he can recoup from consumers, the wholesaler only what he can recover from retailers. If there are losses, they tend to be shifted back-

71. For a clear analysis of the marketing handicaps of farmers in underdeveloped countries, see Rameshwara Rao, "Under-developed Economy and Agricultural Marketing," *Indian Journal of Economics*, 40, No. 156 (July 1959), 95ff.

72. A recent survey of transport facilities in the state of Maharashtra, one of the more developed Indian states, revealed that out of 34,361 villages nearly 27,000 were not on main roads; half of the villages had no approach roads to link them with main roads; while 30 percent had no access roads whatever. For further details see Wilfred Owen, *Distance and Development: Transport and Communications in India*, Washington, 1968, pp. 52–66. In Uttar Pradesh, one of the poorest Indian states, 38 percent of the villages have no road connections with market centers. Regional Transport Study Group in cooperation with the Indian National Planning Commission, "Road Development," unpublished manuscript, n.d., p. 21.

ward to the producer. As a consequence, agricultural statistics generally reveal a high degree of stability in farm production (despite variations in weather) but wide variations in farm income. Worst of all, when the prices farmers receive for their produce fall, the terms of trade become less favorable, and producers who must then give more wheat, barley, rice, or cotton for the same quantities of manufactured goods become discouraged. The result is that producers in underdeveloped countries are reluctant to increase output however much their nation may need more food, fibers, or oilseeds. The issue therefore is whether, by proper organization and control, a marketing system can be developed which will not only reduce (or even prevent) the exploitation of farmers but can introduce enough stability in the price structure so that farmers will be encouraged to farm their land better, produce more, and be willing to experiment with new crops if they can be shown to be differentially more profitable. It was to deal with this range of vexatious problems that the regulated market system was conceived.

The original Hyderabad legislation, under which the first regulated cotton markets were established, proved satisfactory in some respects, but it soon became evident that the scheme needed improvement. It had induced farmers to raise cotton, and it had brought about an orderly procedure for the open sale and purchase of cotton by daily auctions in the regulated markets.[73] The market committees, however, had included no "cultivator-sellers," and it was therefore understandable why the committees took no penalizing action against commission men or merchants who infringed the market rules.[74] The real importance of the Hyderabad experiment was that it established a pattern of action and set some essential standards for market practices such as the determination of fees, the maintenance of accurate weights and measures, the licensing of traders, and arrangements for prompt settlement and pay-

73. A Royal Commission (1928) found that 68 percent of the cotton grown in the "Assigned District" was sold in regulated markets, whereas in a neighboring district in the state of Bombay only 8½ percent of the cotton was brought to large markets. Royal Commission on Agriculture, *Report,* India, Bombay, 1929, p. 389.

74. Another defect of the Hyderabad legislation was that it allowed the municipality in which a regulated market was held to pocket all the surpluses left after all expenses had been paid (out of revenues derived from market fees). The Royal Commission which reviewed the operation of the system sharply criticized this policy, taking the position that regulated markets should not be sources of municipal revenue, and recommended that all surpluses should be used for developing services or providing facilities that would benefit the users of the markets, particularly the producers. See Johnson, *Market Towns and Spatial Development in India,* pp. 44–45.

ment. When other jurisdictions enacted legislation governing regulated markets, the good features of the Hyderabad experience were incorporated, and the shortcomings corrected. Thus, when Bombay passed its Cotton Markets Act in 1927, it was stipulated that a majority of the Market Committee members should be cotton growers and that all surpluses earned by the markets should be spent for improving the market facilities.[75] Following the Royal Commission Report of 1928 which pointed out the putative advantages of regulated markets and recommended that not only cotton but many types of agricultural products should be sold under the open, regulated, auction system, enabling legislation was passed in Hyderabad proper (1930), the Central Provinces (1932), Madras (1933), Punjab (1939), and Mysore (1939). Meantime, new and improved legislation was agreed upon in Bombay (1939) and in the Central Provinces (1935). After India became independent, market acts were passed in Madhya Bharat (1952), Kerala (1957), and Orissa (1957). After the repartition of the country, Andhra Pradesh adopted the Madras legislation, Gujarat and Maharashtra inherited Bombay laws, while Delhi and Tripura passed legislation based on the Bombay model.[76]

Whether regulated markets have yielded benefits—real social benefits—depends on the degree to which the traditional handicaps of small farmers have been mitigated. It depends on the extent to which village cultivators have been released from the monopsonistic power of village traders. Above all, it hinges on the effect that regulated markets have had in creating larger, more efficient rural communities, thereby bringing about a much-needed spatial restructuring of Indian landscapes. Before even tentative conclusions can be hazarded concerning the meliorative impact of regulated markets, the structure, organization, and operation of India's thousand and more regulated markets must be briefly described.

Since in India agriculture is, with but few exceptions, the responsibility of the individual state rather than of the central government, the legislation under which regulated markets are created and operated varies from state to state, even though there is a great deal of simi-

75. India, Ministry of Food and Agriculture, *Agricultural Marketing in India*, Vol. I. *Legislation*, p. 5.

76. The best account of the history of Indian regulated markets is to be found in Rameshwara Rao, "Regulated Markets in India with Special Reference to Andhra Pradesh," Ph.D. dissertation, University of Allahabad, n.d.

larity.[77] But it is not so much the differences in legislation that are really important; what really distinguishes one state from another is the extent to which regulated markets have come into existence. My findings in 1964–1965 were that 79.8 percent of India's regulated markets were then located in five states, Maharashtra, Gujarat, Mysore, Punjab, and Madhya Pradesh.[78] If one were to add the 14.5 percent in two other states, Andhra Pradesh and Madras, then no less than 94.3 percent of the markets would have been found in seven out of the seventeen states. Part of this skewness was no doubt caused by the role that cotton had played in the early development of regulated markets, but this is not the only reason why almost 80 percent of the markets were in the five western states with but 30 percent of the population. In these states agriculture is technically more advanced, more commercialized, and better organized, and there is good reason to believe that the whole level of husbandry has been improved because of the incentives that regulated markets have supplied.[79] It was perhaps a fortunate historical accident that an effort to increase cotton growing led to the establishment of regulated markets in the Greater Bombay region. Once begun, however, their general utility became apparent; more than that, once begun the village traders could not prevent the enlargement of items salable in the regulated markets. In northeastern India, in contrast, the opposition of the local traders not only delayed the passage of enabling legislation for over thirty years but has continued to frustrate the efforts of those who hoped to restructure archaic marketing procedures even after belated legislation had been reluctantly passed by reactionary legislators.[80]

The basic idea underlying the regulated market system is that the sale and purchase of certain designated items ("notified commodities")

77. In an effort to achieve greater similarity, a "model bill" was prepared in 1938 by the Central Agricultural Marketing Department (now the Directorate of Marketing and Inspection), and this model has no doubt had an influence on the legislation adopted since 1939 and particularly after independence.

78. Johnson, *Market Towns and Spatial Development in India,* pp. 47–48.

79. Some striking contrasts between the relative fairness of marketing practices in Maharashtra and Mysore and the prevailing exploitation of farmers by private produce buyers in Uttar Pradesh is explained in Chapter 7.

80. For the 12,000 villages of the Kanpur region not a single regulated market had been established in 1967, although permissive legislation had been passed by the state of Uttar Pradesh three years before (November 1964). See Ronald G. Ridker, "Prospects and Problems of Agriculture in the Kanpur Region," in *Regional Perspective of Industrial and Urban Growth,* ed. P. B. Desai, I. M. Grossack, and K. M. Sharma, Bombay, 1969, pp. 55–73.

should be supervised by "market committees" charged with responsibility for insuring orderly and fair marketing procedures. The composition of these market committees, whose members are elected by ballot, has varied from time to time and from state to state, but the consistent trend since the 1930's has been to balance traders with producers[81] and to add, usually, single representatives from cooperative societies, local governments, and state governments. The committees' tasks (for which the members are paid) are to enforce the provisions of the legislation under which a given market was created, to insure that marketing procedures are orderly and fair, and to construct, maintain, and improve the yards, warehouses, auction halls, platforms, and other facilities needed by buyers and sellers. To carry out these functions a committee is empowered to levy fees and charges that will make a market self-supporting.[82] The jurisdiction of a committee extends throughout a "notified area," and it is this control over areal marketing which makes it possible for a regulated market to influence spatial economic development.

Before a regulated market opens, farmers arrive and display their produce on the selling platforms or in designated parts of the market yard.[83] When the opening bell sounds, the auctions begin, and the commission agents (*adatyas*), acting on behalf of the sellers, receive the bids of the merchants or commissioned buyers. In a large market a number of auctions are being "cried" concurrently, and at each one clerks are busy recording the names of the sellers, the buyers, and the selling prices. Authorized weighers or measurers certify the quantities that have

81. Except in Punjab where producers, by legislative intent, constitute a majority of the committee members.

82. The committee chairman is the chief executive. He exercises general supervision over the market yard, maintains order, and adjudicates minor disputes. He must see to it that sellers and buyers who use the market pay the appropriate fees and that all traders are licensed. He is the custodian of the market committee funds, and he must pay the officers and employees of the market. He is responsible for the accuracy of all weights and measures, for the maintenance of proper records, and for the expeditious payment of all obligations of buyers and sellers. He must carry out the wishes of the committee for the construction, repair, or improvement of market facilities. He is, in short, the general manager of the market, the legal agent of a corporate entity.

83. When grain and pulses are sold by the "open heap" method the produce is spilled out on the selling platforms so that the quality of the entire lot offered for sale can be examined. *Gur* (home-boiled brown sugar) is sold in blocks which are split open to enable buyers to judge the consistency. Cotton is sold by an "open cart" system where samples can be drawn at random.

been sold; couriers transmit the price and weight information to the market secretary's office, where receipts are then issued payable upon presentation at the commission agents' offices. The whole procedure is businesslike, impersonal, and—if the market committee is vigilant—equitable and impartial.[84]

The location of India's regulated markets will determine their capacity to integrate town and country and to become nuclei for agro-urban communities which can provide greater occupational choices for young men and women, thereby better utilizing talents, aptitudes, and skills. It must be recognized at the very outset that the actual location of a market may not necessarily be a truly rational one. There may be a host of political, military, or other historical explanations for the development of an urban settlement at a particular place and for the establishment of a market there.[85] One must therefore "try to envisage a model which would be primarily economic, and then attempt to test actual locational patterns by this nonpolitical touchstone."[86] Because agriculture normally uses agronomic space for its operations, it is essentially "areal," with production units diffused in terms of some given pattern of land tenure. Yet whatever this pattern may be (for it is inevitably a product of many political, social, military, and economic factors), a proper marketing system should be one that will draw out the largest possible marketable surplus from the producers so that they in turn will have the largest possible claim on purchasable goods and services.

There are at least four possible forms that a marketing system can take.[87] There may be no marketplace whatever to which sellers would physically bring their produce and alienate it to buyers, and marketing would consist only of random sales by individual farmers and random

84. Like every other institution, regulated markets may be compromised by forms of subtle dishonesty hard to detect. In his study of regulated markets in Andhra, for example, Rao found two types of commission agents. One maintained close ties with his ancestral village and was trusted by village sellers because they knew he was diligently and conscientiously protecting their interests. Yet in the same market Rao found other commission agents who seemed to work hand in glove with buyers, collusively selling produce entrusted to them at lower prices than the sellers should have received. Rao, "Regulated Markets in India," pp. 351–352.

85. The possibility that actual location is not a rational location is, according to Lösch, the very circumstances that poses the "location problem," since, in his view, "the question of the best location is far more dignified than determination of the actual one." *Economics of Location,* p. 4.

86. Johnson, *Market Towns and Spatial Development in India,* p. 51.

87. The terminology used in this discussion follows that employed by Lösch in *Economics of Location,* pp. 10–11 for somewhat different purposes.

purchases by itinerant buyers.[88] A second possibility would be for every village to provide a marketplace serving a small area; such a market would probably be unregulated by any public authority and would very likely be dominated by one or two traders. If each village had such a marketplace, there would exist, in a village-studded landscape, a loose "areal market network." A third possibility would be a "cluster" of unregulated traders located near the center of a farming region attracting sellers from as wide an area as transport facilities would permit, and where presumably there would be some reasonably effective competition among the buyers in the market cluster.[89] The fourth type would be a "punctiform" market where all potential buyers would be found at a single place near the center of a production area, and where there would be enough potential buyers to ensure an adequate degree of competition, thus obviating the danger of monopsony.

It should be quite clear that the Indian regulated market belongs to the fourth category, the "punctiform" type. If such a market attracts enough buyers to insure a fairly effective degree of competition, it ought to be more instrumental in attracting marketable surpluses than type one (no market agglomeration) or type two (local networks). Whether a punctiform market is superior to a (type three) cluster is not so evident; that would depend on the number of (buying) units in the cluster, the proximity of the units, and the prospects of fair practices. Two basic issues arise when cluster markets and punctiform markets are compared. The first is whether a cluster of private competitive markets will better reflect locational advantages than a governmentally located punctiform consolidated market.[90] The second issue is the comparative effect which a cluster or a punctiform market center will have on maximizing the

88. Since time immemorial live animals have been "marketed" by this simple and direct method.

89. The traders constituting the market cluster, or the separate markets that might constitute a larger cluster, would need to be near enough to one another so that sellers could compare price offers before consummating their sales. If this condition were not met, the market cluster could be as monopsonistic (or duopsonistic) as a village market.

90. One can visualize a cluster of markets so arranged near the center of a circular producing region that one or more buying units would be located within each quadrant. Each "market" would then be at the least distance from the sellers in each of the quadrants. Yet since the cluster of buyers would be near the center of the whole circular producing area, all the buying units would be potentially within reach of all the areal sellers, thus preventing any one buyer from exercising monopsony power. See Johnson, *Market Towns and Spatial Development in India*, pp. 52–53.

marketed surpluses of the producers within the isovectures of either market area.[91]

Before there can be a discussion of the extent to which the Indian experience throws light on these issues, something needs to be said about the size of the population centers wherein Indian regulated markets have been established and about the coincidence or lack of coincidence between the "notified" market area and the actual transactional areas. The size of a population center wherein a regulated market is located will perforce affect a market's general attractive power and may, more particularly, influence its centripetal pull on particular "notified commodities." A large city, for example, might be a better place in which to sell industrial crops such as cotton, jute, oilseeds, and tobacco than a medium-sized town, which might be an entirely satisfactory selling place for grain, pulses, poultry, and eggs. The effective "reach" of a market will therefore depend on a number of variables: the crops grown in its immediate (or extended) hinterland, the relative transport costs of the marketable commodities, or the range of goods available on which sales proceeds can be spent. Because of these variables, legislative or administrative efforts to delimit the spatial boundaries of regulated markets have not been successful; the jurisdictional and the transactional boundaries seldom coincide.[92] The Indian experience is consistent and convincing: the majority of successful regulated markets have grown up and flourished in medium-sized cities in the 20,000 to 50,000 population range;[93] very few—only about 5 percent—are to be found in cities over 100,000 people, and even fewer—about 4 percent—in towns with less than 5,000 people. Regulated markets have therefore demonstrated their capacity to integrate rural hinterlands

91. These concentric perimeters, which are not necessarily circular, are determined by equal unit transport costs. They represent therefore, *as far as transport costs alone are concerned,* the centripetal pulls of a market center on its hinterland. For details see Lösch, *Economics of Location,* p. 19.

92. Narela market (Delhi Territory) has a jurisdictional radius of five miles, but produce from at least forty villages is brought to this market, despite the octroi charges that are levied on sellers coming from outside the 5-mile radius. The market clerk estimated (September 14, 1964) that the transactional radius was at least 15 miles.

93. In Andhra Pradesh 70.5 percent of the markets are in cities of this population range, in Maharashtra 64 percent, in Gujarat 74.3 percent, in Mysore 70 percent. Punjab and Madhya Pradesh, less urbanized states, have the bulk of their regulated markets in towns and cities with a population range from 10,000 to 50,000 people: 71.6 percent for Punjab, 87.5 percent for Madhya Pradesh. Only Madras has as many as 20 percent of regulated markets in cities with from 50,000 to 100,000 residents.

with what I have called "market towns" and helped to develop something that can properly be called "agro-urban communities."

Since the transforming effects of regulated markets depend on their number and their respective "reach," both these aspects should be briefly appraised. Obviously, the adequacy of their numbers depends on the territory each can serve. Rao's investigation of forty regulated markets in the Telengana area of Andhra Pradesh indicated that the jurisdictional radius was 5 miles for twenty-two markets (55 percent), 7 miles for two markets (5 percent), and 10 miles for sixteen markets (40 percent),[94] an average of 6.6 miles. My survey of 100 regulated markets throughout India suggests that one should at least double these jurisdictional radii to discover the "reach" of Indian regulated markets.[95] My findings were that wheat traveled as far as 23½ miles to (regulated) markets, *gur* 21 miles, *jower* 23, and cotton 27½. These data, supplied by knowledgeable secretaries of market committees, would seem to indicate that the "reach" of regulated markets is much greater than that of most unregulated market clusters, since the reach of a surveyed large Uttar Pradesh cluster indicated average isovectures of about 13 miles.[96]

If a complete network of markets exists, an economic landscape will be made up of contiguous market area hexagons.[97] Whereas this condition can be fulfilled in a more or less satisfactory way by an unplanned proliferation of private uncontrolled periodic markets,[98] when markets are formally established at divers places by some administrative decision, the probability is that instead of contiguous hexagons, a landscape will consist of circular market areas often separated one from another by unserved interstices. This situation is illustrated by Figures 3–9 and 3–10, which contrast one Maharashtra district (Nanded) where almost seven-eighths of the total area is within reach of regulated markets with

94. "Regulated Markets in India," p. 342.

95. The survey was based on visits and information supplied on a questionnaire, December 1964.

96. A traffic check over several weeks made by the Uttar Pradesh Traffic Survey in the Kanpur region (1966) revealed that 90 percent of the trips transporting the following goods were for less than the kilometers shown: milk and milk products, 15; poultry, 18; raw cotton, 20; fruits and vegetables, 21; leather, 22; food grains, 22; *gur*, 23; groundnuts, 23; oilseeds, 24. The average isovecture would therefore be about 21 kilometers (about 13 miles).

97. For detailed geometric explanation see Lösch, *Economics of Location*, Chapter 10.

98. Such as the mainland China market system.

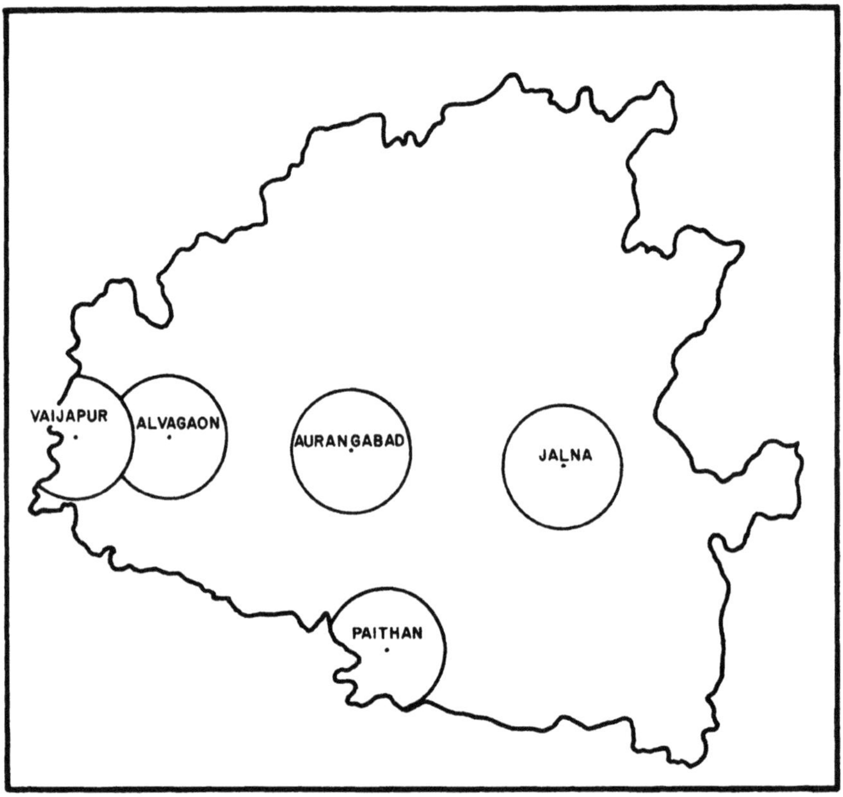

Figure 3–9 Regulated Market Coverage in District Aurangabad, India
SOURCE: E. A. J. Johnson, *Market Towns and Spatial Development in India,* New Delhi: National Council of Applied Economic Research, 1965, p. 59.

another district (Aurangabad) where less than a quarter of the area is provided with regulated markets within normal travel distance.

It would, of course, be erroneous to assume that the interstices (which seem so empty in Figure 3–9) are wholly bereft of marketing facilities. Small periodic markets (*painths, hats, shandies*) allow farmers to sell produce and livestock to traders who resell in larger markets (*mandies*). These ill-organized local trading operations have had virtually no transforming effects on rural areas,[99] and like the local components of dendritic market systems, they are frequently blemished by corruption, collusion, and monopsony. One need only visit a few such primitive markets to see the difference between the acrimonious bargaining that

99. For information on the regional distribution of *hats* and *shandies* in India, see K. R. Kulkarni, *Agricultural Marketing in India,* Bombay, 1958, II, 13 ff.; B. B. Mukherjee, *Agricultural Marketing in India,* Patna, 1937, pp. 33–51.

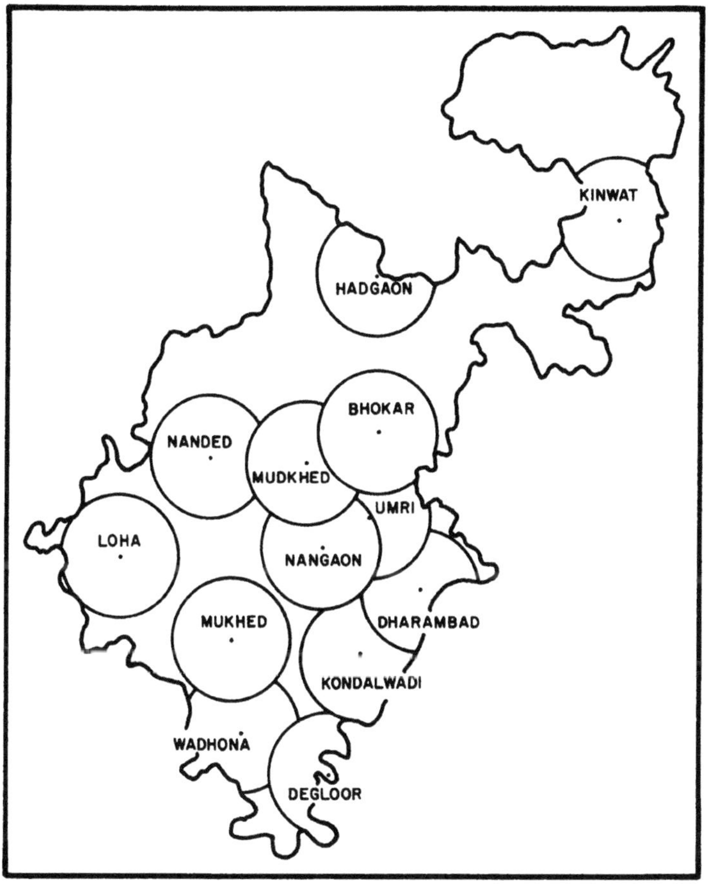

Figure 3–10 Regulated Market Coverage in District Nanded, India
SOURCE: E. A. J. Johnson, *Market Towns and Spatial Development in India,* New Delhi: National Council of Applied Economic Research, 1965, p. 55.

one encounters there and the orderly, impersonal, well-disciplined procedures in regulated markets. Yet until the regulated-market system expands to cover entire landscapes, millions of Indian farmers must be content with quite unsatisfactory market outlets for their laboriously produced marketable surpluses.[100] Even in a progressive state such as

100. Studies of living standards among small farmers indicate that much of their marketed produce is not real surplus over and above their family needs. By reason of debt servitude they are often compelled to market more than they should alienate. For details see Dharm Narain, *Distribution of the Marketed Surplus by Size-Level of Holdings in India, 1950–51,* Institute of Economic Growth, Occasional Paper No. 2, 1961, Chapter 7. See also Chapter 5 of the present work.

Maharashtra, which had in 1964 over 28 percent of the regulated markets in India (although its share of population was only 9 percent), the areas unserved by regulated markets varied, district by district, from a low of 19 percent (Kolaba) to a high of 75.6 percent (Aurangabad) and averaged 58 percent. It seems evident then that, unless motor transport can in India (as it did in the United Sttes) greatly lengthen the radii of existing (regulated) markets, even an Indian state most advanced in market development would need to double or more than double the number of its regulated markets (and deploy them properly) to achieve a network of market hexagons with 20-mile diameters. The trouble is not merely that there are too few regulated markets; the real difficulty is that there are not enough existing towns in which to locate such markets. To this vexatious problem, which is encountered throughout the underdeveloped countries of the world, some of the analysis in Chapter 5 is directed.

Market Systems as Incentives for Output and Productivity

Whether a market system is dendritic, intermeshed, or regulated is not merely a taxonomical issue, since on the nature of the marketing system may largely depend a nation's capacity for development. The basic determinants of economic progress and human well-being are increased output, improved productivity, and a will to intensify human effort and creativity. In rural societies that are only partially monetized and that lack adequate or fair marketing facilities a great deal of potential productive power is wasted, not because there is endemic lassitude or indolence, but because there are no compelling incentives that will galvanize people into productive action. The greatest possible production is not achieved; hence the potential marketable surplus is not brought to market. As a result, both the individual producer and the nation suffer an opportunity loss.

Since, for purposes of contrast, three types of agricultural marketing systems have been analyzed in this chapter, a summary word about each and its relation to productivity is in order. The dendritic type does not stimulate or impel producers to put forth their best efforts. The local markets, the only ones in which producers can in any way participate, are but the capillary extremities of market structures calculated to pay the least for agricultural produce and charge the most for payment goods. The system is so structured that the terms of trade will be consistently adverse for the rural population. Not only does this scheme of things take away the incentive to produce as much as possible but, by limiting rural savings, it drastically limits rural capital formation, which is indispensable for improved productivity.

The virtue of the intermeshed market system, such as that perfected so patiently by the Chinese, is its spatial comprehensiveness, its flexibility, and the reciprocal interaction which it facilitates between town and country. But it suffers from overbureaucratization in that far more traders and intermediaries are involved than the marketing tasks really require. Successive profits in a long chain of exchange produces two unfortunate results: the ultimate consumer pays more than necessary, and the producer receives less than he deserves.[101] It is, in short, correctly structured but wastefully staffed. A prodigal use of intermediaries tends to keep the market areas too small to allow economies of marketing scale to be realized. Nor does it have built-in measures for the protection of sellers against fraud, chicanery, or outbargaining. As a consequence, it fails to provide strong incentives for maximum production and the largest possible marketed surplus.

The contrived and democratically supervised type of market, well-illustrated by the Indian example, has overcome the imperialistic limitations of dendritic markets and the overstaffing so characteristic of private market networks. There is evidence to demonstrate that Indian regulated markets have stimulated greater (hinterland) output, increased the marketed surplus,[102] and drastically reduced the volume of farm produce sold to itinerant traders and village petty merchants. Rao's interviews led him to conclude that, before regulated markets existed, less than 40 percent of sellers in some thirty-five market centers were producers, whereas after regulated markets had been established,

101. From the days of Henry C. Carey, an original and neglected American economist of the early nineteenth century, this basic anomoly has been emphasized by perceptive economists. Too often the issue has been stated in terms of a theory of deliberate exploitation, a simplistic explanation used by politicians to curry favor with rural constituents. But the trouble is more frequently institutional than personal, and imperfections in the marketing system are far more often the cause of the spread between what the consumer pays and what the producer receives than the malevolence of merchants. For Carey's basic thesis see his *Principles of Social Science*, Philadelphia, 1858–1859, Chapter 10.

102. As the number of regulated markets in the Telengana district of Andhra Pradesh increased from twenty-five in 1951 to forty in 1959, the marketed surplus rose without break year by year so that the 1959 figure was 2½ times that of 1951. For details see Johnson, *Market Towns and Spatial Development in India*, p. 65, n. 1.

over 70 percent of the sellers were producers.[103] Yet for all their virtues the contrived markets also have their shortcomings. They do not grow up in the same organic way that private, unregulated markets do. They must be "established" on a given initial scale, at a chosen place. And just here errors are not only possible but likely. Moreover, because they need to be located in sizable urban centers, suitable sites are by no means adequate in most underdeveloped areas.[104] If the unserved spatial interstices between market areas are to be brought within reach of regulated markets, a comprehensive town-centering plan must be foreseen.[105] A beginning can be made by locating suitable "growth points" and by agglomerating various types of both public and private-sector capital formation into investment clusters[106] at places that can become the nuclei of new agro-urban communities. It is in this larger context of spatial and regional planning, which is discussed in Chapters 7 and 8, that the full potential of a contrived and regulated market system as a stimulant to production, a goad to greater productivity, and a smooth operating means for distribution can be realized. It must be recognized, however, that even the best-designed marketing system will never become automatic. The proper functioning of a regulated market system will depend on the integrity, the dedication, and the wisdom of the men who are charged with supervision.

103. Rao, "Regulated Markets in India," p. 362.

104. There were in 1964 about 1,000 regulated markets in India, and the creation of about another 1,000 was being planned. Since there are only some 1,927 towns and cities that appear to be appropriate sites, an impasse will soon be reached. If my estimates are anywhere near right, India needs, for tolerable commercialization of her rural areas, some 14,000 to 16,000 regulated markets. Where are they to be located? Very clearly, a town-building program must be part and parcel of a sound development plan. This has been the consistent experience of developed countries. See Chapter 2, see also Chapter 5 on central-place deficiencies.

105. The urgency of this problem was quite properly stressed by John P. Lewis in his splendid book *Quiet Crisis in India,* Washington, 1962, Chapter 7.

106. For India I have explored this subject in Chapter 5 of my *Market Towns and Spatial Development in India.*

CHAPTER 4 CENTRAL-PLACE THEORY AND REGIONAL ORGANIZATION OF SPACE

The Beginnings of Locational Theory: von Thünen's Concept of Functional Concentricity

General theories designed to explain the structure and function of economic landscapes stem from the seminal work of Johann Heinrich von Thünen whose first version of his *Isolated State* appeared in 1926.[1] A student of agricultual science (what little there was of it around 1800), of mathematics, philosophy, and economics, von Thünen became an estate farmer in a remote, essentially agrarian region of Mecklenburg, an area with fair soil but wholly unsatisfactory roads and no navigable rivers. It was, in short, an underdeveloped region, and von Thünen's restless mind constantly puzzled about how to utilize natural resources and manpower to best advantage.[2] The outcome was his general locational theory.

In order to clarify the quintessential relations that should exist between town and country, von Thünen imagined a "large town" located at the center of a plain of uniform fertility bounded by an uncultivated wilderness which separated the hypothetical agro-urban com-

1. *Der isolierte Staat in Beziehung auf Landwirtschaft und Nationalökonomie,* Rostock, 1826. At long last this book, which so many writers have cited and so few have read, has been translated into English by Carla M. Wartenburg and published as *Von Thünen's Isolated State,* with an introduction by Peter Hall, Oxford, 1966. (Subsequent references are to this translation.)

2. He carried on painstaking research into costs and returns on his estate over a ten-year period. What he was seeking, as Peter Hall has said, was "an abstract model of an economy, based upon actual facts." Introduction to *Isolated State,* p. xvii.

munity from the outside world.[3] Since there were, by assumption, no other towns on the plain, the single central town would have to supply its rural hinterland with all needed manufactured goods and serve as a market for all the marketable surpluses of the rural population. The problem to which von Thünen addresses himself is the "pattern of cultivation" that should be followed, assuming that "farming is conducted absolutely rationally." On this assumption, said von Thünen, it should be "obvious" that commodities that are heavy or bulky in relation to their value should be produced near the town since it would be more expensive for the more remote districts to deliver them. Perishable goods should also originate near the town to obviate losses by spoilage or dehydration. Land more distant from the town ought to be devoted to products that are lighter in relation to their value and can therefore incur greater unit transport costs. On the basis of this reasoning, von Thünen conceived of concentric rings, or functional belts, around the town, each devoted to particular types of agricultural produce (see Figure 4–1). It is, however, very difficult to present von Thünen's locational scheme graphically without oversimplifying or distorting his rigorously analytical conclusions. The proportion between "farm-based" costs (e.g., farm labor) and "town-based" costs (e.g., implements) varies not only from crop to crop but with degrees of intensity of cultivation for the same crop. Basically it is unit costs in relation to town prices that determine the optimally profitable locational production belts, although in von Thünen's model the calculations that are involved in deciding to produce a certain crop in a particular belt must take cognizance of the opportunity cost of not producing another crop.

Yet if there is any one dominant locational force, it is transport. This is why forestry should, in von Thünen's view, be carried on quite near the town, whereas light industrial crops, such as flax, ought properly be raised in the outer ring. The general thesis is that production costs decrease with distance (although this depends on the intensity of cultivation), whereas transport costs rise. Because of this general relation, products with the higher yields ought to be produced nearer the market. At issue are not the usual transport costs per unit of product but the transport costs per unit of area, since it is the optimal use of economic space which should be the desideratum of policy.

3. *Isolated State* p. 7.

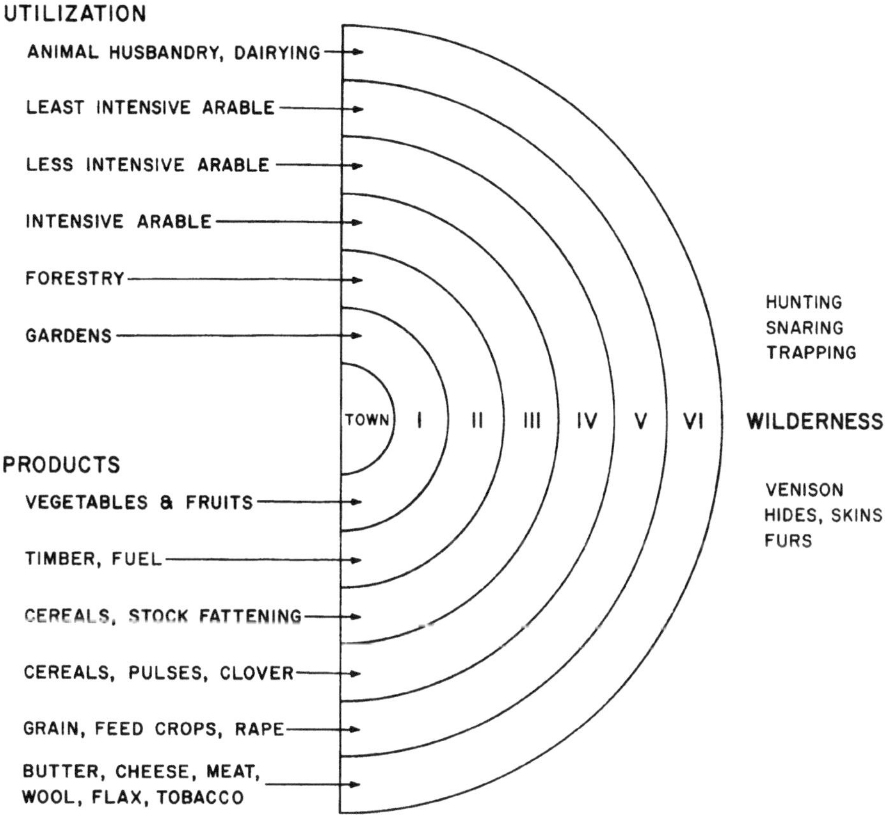

Figure 4–1 Von Thünen's Land Utilization Belts

It is inappropriate here to explore much further the subtleties and nuances of this remarkably imaginative book, which not only wrestles with the tendentious problems of land rent[4] and wages[5] but, by means of an analysis of diminishing and increasing returns and by an emphasis on margins of productivity of units of labor applied to land, fore-

4. Both the recognition and the criticism which von Thünen's work received in the nineteenth century centered around this aspect of his theory. For his views on rent see *Isolated State,* Chapters 5a, 5b, 12, 14a, 25, and 38.

5. For which he proposed a formula he considered so important that he asked that it be engraved on his tombstone.

shadows a concept of marginal productivity.[6] Yet for all its originality, the *Isolated State* oversimplified the relation between the rural and the urban by assuming that a single town could integrate so complex an agrarian economy on so large an isofertile plain. As early as 1892, a critic pointed out that agriculture tends to generate petty industrial centers where weight-losing processing occurs[7] (e.g., sugar mills, distilleries, and oil-pressing plants), and, as later writers pointed out, these lesser urban centers will in turn relate themselves to larger urban places by some hierarchical interconnections.

It would not, however, be fair to criticize von Thünen for his underlying assumptions of constant ton-mile transport costs, since this was a wholly appropriate assumption for the primitive type of land transport employed in eighteenth-century Mecklenburg. Admittedly this condition has been ameliorated by improved roads, railways, canal systems, and the substitution of natural energy for draft animals. Yet, for all that, transport systems in most underdeveloped countries are very similar to that of Mecklenburg in the 1820's, thus making much of von Thünen's analysis of basic determinants of market isovectures still pertinent.[8] The real shortcoming of von Thünen's enquiry was his failure to explore the manifold demand functions for the agricultural output of his isofertile plain, since these market forces would very greatly influence the profitability of alternative varieties of agricultural production.

To the consistent criticism made of von Thünen's work, namely, that it is *zeitgebunden,* might well be added a second shortcoming: it is also *gebietgebunden.* National agricultural policy is implicitly presumed to be essentially a spatially enlarged form of estate management, and since in semifeudal North Germany all towns except capital cities were by implication dull, artless, and inelegant, von Thünen denigrated the possible economic utility of small towns while extolling the putative virtues of a centrally located single large town. Not only was the large

6. Alfred Marshall by his own admission borrowed the concept of a margin from von Thünen and said, "I loved von Thünen above all my other masters." See *Memorials of Alfred Marshall,* ed. A. C. Pigou, London, 1925, pp. 359–360.

7. Eugen Duhring, *Kursus der Nationalökonomie,* Berlin, 1892, pp. 251–253.

8. "Wheeled traffic in rural India [1967] is principally the bicycle and the bullock cart. An estimated 12 million bullock carts are in operation, the majority used exclusively for agricultural operations." Wilfred Owen, *Distance and Development,* Washington, 1968, p. 53.

town (regional capital?) the residence of the head of government and "the seat of the highest offices of justice and administration" but a military headquarters, an educational and cultural center, and a place where rentiers, landlords, and "rich citizens" lived. Consequently it was a place to which merchants, craftsmen, artists, domestic servants, and laborers were always attracted. It was, in short, the only urban community that was well diversified occupationally, and for that reason a landscape with a single large town was much to be preferred to one with many small towns.[9]

This emotional preference for a large town with theaters, museums, and "many more social attractions and amenities" leads, alas, to some ill-supported conclusions on industrial location. Arguing that only a large town can provide a market wide enough to permit economies of scale and that only a large town can attract "outstanding talents" (businessmen, artisans, laborers, scholars, civil servants), von Thünen asserts that these advantages of industrial location in a capital city will more than neutralize the added transport cost of bringing raw materials to the large town and distributing the manufactured end-products in the rural hinterland.[10] But whereas this part of the *Isolated State* is dogmatic, no one will challenge the contention that the likelihood of competition among merchants will be greater in the capital city than in small provincial towns; since "in the presence of so many competitors," as von Thünen said, "the attempt to cheat the customer would be scarcely worth the trouble."[11] Nor can one object to von Thünen's explanation of the danger of monopsonistic or collusive acts of produce buyers in small towns when the transport cost of seeking a possible alternative buyer may easily be a greater penalty than accepting an unfair low price at the nearest sales point. This does not necessarily prove, however, that it will always be to a farmer's advantage to sell his produce in the central town. By some strange quirk, von Thünen's relativism, which makes his analysis of alternate patterns of land utilization so penetrating and so modern, seemed to desert him when he dealt with the urban part of the town and country syndrome. He realized very clearly that agrarian regions must be reciprocally inter-

9. Von Thünen's sketchy analysis of the role of urban areas is found in *Isolated State*, pp. 285–291.

10. Ibid., p. 287–288.

11. Ibid., p. 288.

related with "manufacturers, craftsmen, miners and so forth—in such a ratio that every member of the community is fully occupied."[12] But even though he grudgingly granted that some factories and workshops "processing raw materials of little value in relation to their bulk and weight, which need no complicated machinery, no extensive division of labor" could properly be located in provincial towns, his general assumption was that small communities were seldom efficient and that to obtain "the right ratio" between occupations "the community will have to be large."

In one of the fragments of the unfinished Part 2 of the *Isolated State,* published posthumously,[13] von Thünen recognizes that despite their disadvantages there will be some country towns in the "Isolated State" and that their number and spatial distribution will be a function of the density or sparseness of population. He apparently thought that towns with less than 2,000 inhabitants would have no "advantages of association in trades and industries." As to the agrarian hinterland of such a town, he estimated it would have a population of 1,500 people per square mile if it were "in the section of the ring of the improved system nearest to the [great] town," whereas "at the edge of the cultivated plain" the hinterland would contain only about 500 people per square mile. Assuming next that a [minimum-sized] country town would need at least 10,000 rural people for its market, von Thünen's arithmetic indicates that since the country-town communities should have uniform populations of not less than 12,000 persons (2,000 in a town, 10,000 in the hinterland) depending on population density, they would therefore encompass from 6.6 square miles (in the inner rings) to 20 square miles (in the outer rings). But he takes pains to point out that in these micro-communities there would be some inescapable social and economic inequalities. The more sparsely populated and more remote communities would be faced with higher costs for artisans and physicians, and the cost of education would be higher in direct proportion to the decrease in population density.[14]

Having factored out a best possible distribution of country towns, von Thünen relaxes his austere assumptions and admits that "provincial

12. Ibid., p. 290.

13. Ibid., pp. 291–292.

14. "And since we have seen that the education of the common man becomes progressively more difficult and costly the sparser the population, we arrive at the painful conclusion that even within the restricted confines of the Isolated State the level of education and intelligence will differ in the different districts." Ibid., p. 294.

towns" will not all be of uniform size. "It seems likely," he wrote, that "diverging tendencies will yield a compromise" because "the advantages of association [external economies?] grow with the increasing size of towns." As they grow, however, "the increasing distance between towns, a corollary of their growth in size, is a drawback for the country." Hence, once again, von Thünen poses the need for balancing the advantages of increasing scale, diversification, and external economies against the disadvantages of transport costs. Only the provincial towns that were near the capital, were large enough, and were located on good roads, in von Thünen's opinion, would be "suitable as industrial centers." It is in these last random jottings written just before his death in 1850 that a skeletal theory of industrial location is found. It took a half century before another German, Alfred Weber, attempted to unravel this complex problem.[15]

Christaller's Symbiotic System of Central Places

Although von Thünen's theories were original and seminal he did not really succeed in explaining the spatial structure of a functioning economic system. His main concern was to discover, if possible, the optimal way to distribute various types of agricultural production within a single market area having a large town as its center. Yet, von Thünen's book was "the fundamental and guiding work"[16] that inspired the far more comprehensive enquiry of Walter Christaller and of a great succession of geographer-economists who further refined and more precisely analyzed the theory of central-place functions. The basic question Christaller posed was, Are there any general principles which determine the number, size, and distribution of human settlements? Are the locations of towns, large and small, merely a chance outcome of history whereby they have been distributed in some "apparently senseless manner"? Might they be merely an inevitable response to peculiar topographic or geographic configurations or to population density? Is

15. See Alfred Weber, *Theory of the Location of Industries,* trans. C. J. Friedrich, Chicago, 1929.

16. These are Walter Christaller's words in the introduction to his *Central Places in Southern Germany* trans. Carlisle W. Baskin, Englewood Cliffs, N.J., 1966, p. 5. (Subsequent references are to this edition.) Christaller's book first appeared as *Die zentralen Orte in Süddeutschland: Eine ökonomisch-geographische Untersuchung über die Gesetzmässigkeit der Verbreitung und Entwicklung der Siedlungen mit städtischen Functionen,* Jena, 1933.

there one explanation for village agglomeration, another for the emergence of towns, cities, and metropolitan centers? Or is there to be found behind all these seemingly causal forces something more fundamental and organic? Christaller was convinced that the whole process was holistic and that the task of analysis was to discover the "symbiotic pattern of dependence and interdependence"[17] of various units of spatial economic organization.

Christaller begins his analysis by asserting that "the crystallization of mass around a nucleus" is "an elementary form of order," and that this "centralistic principle" of natural science is equally applicable to some "forms of human community life." Thus the chief function of a town is to be the center of a region. But towns may be of many sizes and of variable extent, as may the regions that surround them, and useful terminology must describe such differences. The generic term chosen by Christaller to denote all urban agglomerations is "central place," since the word "place" is essentially neutral, neither implying a "settlement" in any concrete sense nor having any particular political or economic meaning.[18] Central places will be of different sizes and will perform varied and even quite dissimilar functions. How then can they be systematically classified for scientific study? Christaller's answer is to regard central places in terms of their hierarchical functions. There are "central places of a higher order" below which are found "central places of a lower order," and beneath these are "central places of the lowest order." Farther downward in the basic gradation are "smaller places that usually have no central importance," which Christaller calls "auxiliary central places."[19] Yet for all the neatness of this taxonomy, Christaller recognizes that these graduated functions are not necessarily

17. Brian J. L. Berry and Allen Pred, *Central Place Studies: A Bibliography of Theory and Applications,* rev. ed., Philadelphia, 1965, p. 7. This annotated bibliography is an invaluable guide to the very large literature dealing not only with locational theory but with the "size, spacing and functions of cities; trading areas and urban spheres of influence; fairs and markets; consumer shopping and travel behavior" as well as with town-country relations, medical service areas, shopping centers, measurement of trade areas, and urban land use. Published originally in 1961, it has been supplemented by a listing of writings published through 1964, compiled by H. C. Barnum, R. Kasperson, and S. Kuichi.

18. Christaller, *Central Places,* pp. 15–16. In addition to farmsteads in the hinterland of a central place there very often are a number of "dispersed places." These may be nucleated farmsteads (small agricultural villages or hamlets), or they may be "point-bound" places such as settlements at mines, bridges, and harbors. Similarly there may be dispersed monasteries or shrines (sometimes "point-bound" by a legendary miracle) and small settlements at scenic or recreational sites.

19. Ibid., p. 17.

correlated in any determinable way with the size of central places. "Size" and "importance" are not synonymous;[20] indeed, relatively small central places may perform functions of "a higher order" while, conversely, relatively larger central places may perform functions of "a lower order." "Importance" is therefore a behavioral concept, and the test is not the physical dimensions or the population of a central place but the "combined economic efforts of the inhabitants" and the "degrees of intensity" with which they apply themselves to certain essential tasks.[21] This does not mean, however, that there is no correlation whatever between the "importance" of a central place and the size of the region for which the town serves as a center. "Importance" has a double connotation because it appertains partly to the population of a central place itself and partly to the inhabitants of the hinterland. The latter variety of "relative importance" Christaller considers to be the "centrality" of a place, and, consistent with his hierarchical gradations, central places may have higher, lesser, increasing, or decreasing centrality.

By the "centrality" of a place Christaller means that certain functions are performed because some of the inhabitants have "central professions"; and certain goods are produced or offered for sale ("central goods"), as are certain peculiar services ("central services"). These central goods and services that are produced or sold in a few central points of a region are consumed at many scattered points, and they are requited with money derived from the sale of payment goods, which Christaller designates as "dispersed goods and services" or "indifferent goods and services."[22] And because there is a gradation of central places, there is a corresponding gradation in the nature of central goods and services. Since the least-cost location of an industry may not necessarily be found in large central places,[23] the importance of a central place

20. Thus in India there are swollen "villages" that may be four or five times as large as some "towns"; but despite their size, these settlements may not perform any essential central-place functions.

21. Christaller, *Central Places,* p. 18.

22. "Dispersed" meaning "produced or offered at dispersed places," and "indifferent" meaning "goods which are not necessarily produced or offered centrally or dispersedly." Ibid., p. 19.

23. Because his main concern is with the general factors that determine the centrality of a town or city, Christaller does not deal with all the complex factors that should determine the best location for a particular industry or a particular plant. This is really a separate branch of locational theory, which was first explored by Alfred Weber in his *Theory of the Location of Industries.* For the further development of this body of theory, see Melvin L. Greenhut, *Plant Location in Theory and Practice: The Economics of Space,* Chapel Hill, N.C., 1956.

consists not so much in the "production" of (central-place) goods as in the "offering" of such goods and services.[24] In short it is the trading function of a place that reflects its real economic centrality, and this trading function ties each central place to its respective "complementary region," an area whose size "is different for different types of goods" and may undergo "periodic and seasonal variation."[25] In general, however, the size of a complementary region is "relatively constant," since its radius is a function of what Christaller calls "economic distance," a dimension determined by factors such as costs of freight, transit losses, travel time, and the discomfort of travel.[26] "Economic distance" determines the maximum travel a dispersed population is willing to undertake in order to purchase the goods or services offered at a particular central place.[27]

The attraction of a central place to the dispersed inhabitants of its "complementary region" does not, however, depend wholly on distance. The real attraction is the variety, quality, and price of the central goods and services available. But the range and variety of these central goods and services perforce depends on the receipts that the central-place traders, producers, and professional men may expect from the sale of their goods and services. Thus, unless the fees a doctor can hope to receive from his patients are large enough to insure a minimally satis-

24. These goods and services need not all be "offered" in a punctiform market place. Newspapers are provided by central places but delivered to the subscribers throughout a region. Farmers may use a central-place creamery by sending their cream to it by railway or truck. The majority of central-place goods and services, however, are offered centrally so that a town or a city is like a magnet with its "field" of attraction.

25. Christaller, *Central Places*, p. 21.

26. Better traffic facilities are tantamount to a reduction in economic distance; hence with better transportation in the complementary region a central place can be larger. For not only is time conserved but more bulky goods can move because transport is cheap, and more perishable goods can move because transport is swift. Ibid., pp. 48–49.

27. Because of travel costs the amount of central goods purchased is not proportionate to the size of a region. Christaller estimated that a "double-sized region" with twice as many inhabitants as a small region purchases not twice the amount of central goods but about one and one-half times the amount. Consequently, since the income of the central-place businessmen does not double, the size of the central place does not increase in proportion to the size of the region. For the illustrative arithmetic see *Central Places*, p. 44. Travel time is a function of population density; hence the consumption of central goods is relatively less in thinly populated areas; in such areas the central places are fewer and smaller. For illustrative figures and for a formula covering this declination of demand for central-place goods, see *Central Places*, p. 45.

factory income, there will be no doctor.[28] The density of population is therefore an important consideration in determining the variety of central-place functions. If the demand for certain standardized goods is great, the productive process, whether carried on in the central place or elsewhere, can become relatively more mechanized and capital intensive, thereby reducing unit costs. Numbers of people, of course, are not by themselves a measure of effective demand; this will depend on the size of incomes, the spatial distribution of incomes, and the relative number of high, medium, and low income receivers. Moreover, the income distribution will determine the relative demand for high-order central goods since these outlays will largely depend on the surpluses that remain after the necessary low-order goods have been purchased, whether in a central place or elsewhere. All these considerations led Christaller to conclude that it is the consumption of central-place goods that is "decisive in the development of central places."[29] Thus there is a mutual interdependence between any central place and its complementary region.

To demonstrate the possible hierarchical interrelations between central places in an economic landscape Christaller constructed geometric models that have now become quite familiar. They picture two types of economic spatial systems, each of which is equally defensible since the "rationality" of a spatial structure depends on the economic purpose for which it is designed.[30] If the main object is the largest provision of central-place goods by the minimum number of central places, Christaller shows how the "market principle" can best accomplish this. But if the main object is to satisfy the maximum demand for transportation

28. Using this illustration Christaller has shown that economic distance will limit the use that persons in outlying areas of a region will make of medical services and that calculations of possible income for central-place professional people must be made on a consultation scale that descends with distance from the doctor's office. The same type of recession will occur in the demand for all "low order" central goods.

29. *Central Places,* p. 35. This is symptomatic of Christaller's prevailing emphasis. For whereas von Thünen was so interested in rural economic order that he neglected to analyze his central town, Christaller was so much concerned with his central places that he often overlooked the stimulating effect that towns can have on their "complementary regions."

30. A third method would be to establish central places primarily for political reasons. This may lead to wholly different designs of landscapes. For the nature and effects of such political configurations on central places, see Christaller, *Central Places,* pp. 77–80; and for my brief summary of the economic consequences of this "sociopolitical separation principle," see pp. 130, 137 of this volume.

of goods at minimum cost, then as many central places as possible should lie on each traffic route. Since this will not result in an adequate dispersion of central places, relatively more towns will be needed to supply an area with central-place goods than would have been necessary under the "market principle." The contrast between the two spatial systems can be seen by comparing Figures 4–2 and 4–3.

In Figure 4–2 only three orders of central places are shown, even though in an economic landscape there may be many more.[31] The

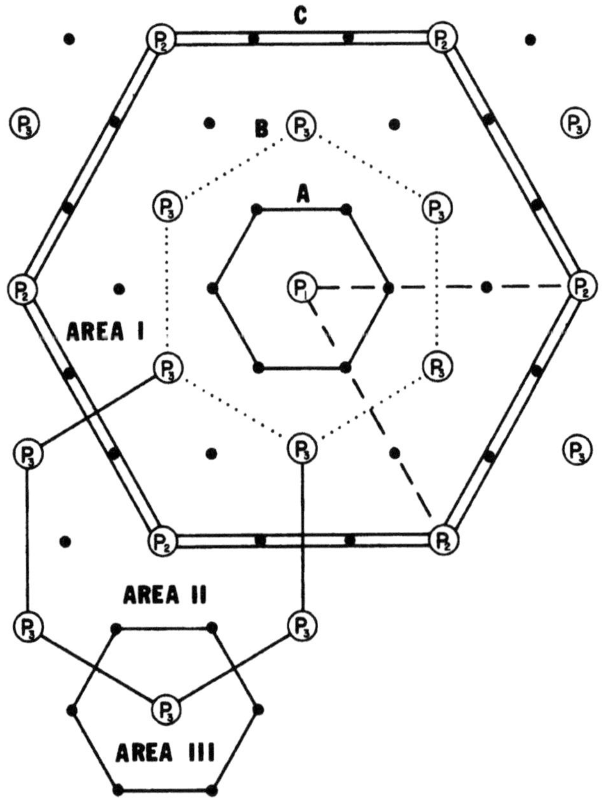

Figure 4–2 Christaller's Dispersion of Central Places under the "Marketing Principle"

SOURCE: Adapted from a diagram in Walter Christaller, *Central Places of Southern Germany*, trans. Carlisle W. Baskin, © 1966, p. 61. Reprinted by permission of Prentice-Hall, Inc., Englewood Cliffs, New Jersey.

31. The number of orders will depend on what Christaller calls the "range" of each type of central goods. There can be as many perimeters of high-order central

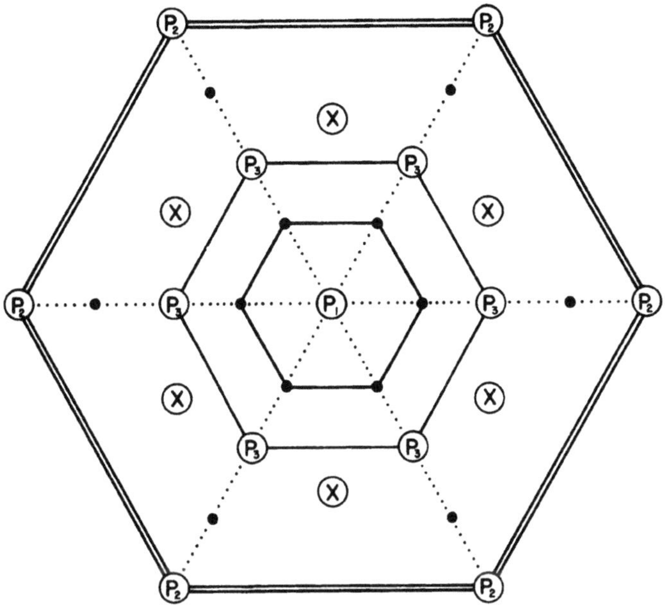

Figure 4–3 Christaller's Dispersion of Central Places under the "Traffic Principle"

SOURCE: Adapted from a diagram in Walter Christaller, *Central Places of Southern Germany,* trans. Carlisle W. Baskin, Englewood Cliffs, New Jersey, © 1966, p. 73. Reprinted by permission of Prentice-Hall, Inc., Englewood Cliffs, New Jersey.

largest central place, P_1, can supply "highest order central goods" for the entire area bounded by the P_2 perimeter (Area I), and all P_2 centers will be corners of six equilateral triangles centered on P_1. The P_2 centers (second largest) will have complementary regions bounded by P_3 perimeters (Area II) and will supply central goods of a "lower order." Following this regression, the P_3 places will be centers of regions (Area III) bounded by P_4 places (shown on the diagram as dots) and supply the "lowest order" of central goods. Each of the P_4 centers will have their respective minuscule market areas in which "dispersed goods" will be distributed. Here then is envisaged a comprehensive functional organization of an economic landscape wherein each type of central place can provide distinct types of central goods to markets which indicate preferences for each central-place size by travel willingness and

places as there are "ranges" of central goods. For details see Christaller's diagrams in *Central Places,* pp. 61, 66.

price willingness. The largest places, P_1 in Figure 4–2, would be encircled by a succession of urban wreaths: a P_4 wreath surrounded by a P_3 band that, in turn, is enclosed by a P_2 ring. These wreaths are marked A, B, and C in Figure 4–2.

"The fundamental difference between the traffic principle and the market principle," said Christaller, "is that the former is linear and the latter spatial"; as a consequence there is "a basic incongruity between these principles."[32] For whereas the market principle would posit that central places should be dispersed in a hierarchical arrangement over a landscape so as to maximize the distribution of various types of goods (both "central" and "dispersed") with the least number of central places, the traffic principle would seek to maximize the movement of goods at minimum cost. To this end it would obviously be desirable that as many central places as possible should lie on major traffic routes and that these routes should be as nearly straight as possible. What happens when this rearrangement has taken place may be seen in Figure 4–3. From P_1, the largest central place, traffic routes would fan out to the P_2 cities at the perimeter angles of the P_1 (hexagonal) complementary region. Topography permitting, there would be six radial main transport routes, and these six routes would pass through all the P_4 centers (shown by dots in Figure 4–3) of the innermost wreath of central places around P_1. The trouble arises with the P_3 places (the third largest centers). That band of towns will have to be rotated (from their positions in Figure 4–2) so that all the P_3 places will lie on direct routes between P_1 and P_2 places. But when this has been done, all the six triangles, whose acute angles are labeled P^2, P^2, P^1, no longer have medium-sized places (P_3) at their centers, and if the entire hexagonal landscape is to be adequately provided with central places (for the distribution of center-place goods), six more P_3 centers will be needed at the places marked X on Figure 4–3. This will mean that twice as many P_3 places will be required as in the dispersion shown in Figure 4–2.[33]

Both of the foregoing forms of spatial organization are equally "rational" from economic points of view, the difference arising from the

32. Ibid., p. 77.

33. If the position of the P_3 bank of center places, as shown in Figure 4–2 were to remain unchanged, and the radial roads were to pass through the P_3 places, and the band of P_2 places were rotated so that all P_2 places would be on the radial roads, then the central place deficit would consist of six P_2 places, and twelve P_4 places, an even more serious disadvantage.

primacy of goals. The same degree of rationality cannot be expected, however, if central places are the result of a "sociopolitical separation principle." For when central cities are chief administrative centers, and subordinate centers are dispersed for governmental, juridical, or other essentially noneconomic purposes, there may be no necessary economic logic in the resulting pattern. Thus sizable cities may grow up for defensive purposes on national boundaries, where they may have only fractional hinterlands.[34] Or cities that once had a "complementary region" may lose virtually all of their economic market areas when drastic revisions of political boundaries occur.[35] Border cities are inherently fragile economically since national borders artificially cut up geographically complementary regions. The only general conclusion one can draw is that when space is organized by what Christaller calls the "sociopolitical separation principle," many more central places will be required to obtain the same spatial efficiency that would have been attained had the "market principle" been the architectonic guide.

The Economic Landscapes of August Lösch

Christaller visualized an overlay of urban-centered market areas descending in size from a very large territory to a spatial area so small in scope and population that it was only minimally profitable for anyone to operate a business there or to maintain a professional office. In contrast August Lösch visualized a system of production and marketing centers from exactly the opposite point of view.[36] Instead of beginning, as Christaller did, with a metropolitan center, Lösch started his analysis from nucleated agricultural villages distributed in triangular fashion over an agrarian plain. Assuming a continuous and even distribution

34. Until 1918 Belgrade, in the northeast corner of Servia, had only slightly more than a third of the circle of land around it as its politically controlled hinterland.

35. Trieste had most of the Austro-Hungarian Empire as its hinterland before 1914. After the dismemberment of the Dual Empire only small fragments of the 50-million person market belonged to Trieste, and after World War II even less, because Yugoslavia has now sharply limited Trieste's trading privileges by expanding the port facilities of nearby Rieka to rival those of Trieste.

36. *Die räumliche Ordnumg der Wirtschaft, Zweite neu durchgearbeitete Auflage* 2d ed. rev., Jena, 1944; translated by Wolfgang F. Stolper, as *The Economics of Location,* New Haven, 1954. (Subsequent references are to this translation.) It should be pointed out that Lösch's work is much more than a theory of central places. It is a very ambitious attempt to interlard the concept of space into the entire corpus of economic theory. Only the portions of this towering enquiry that deal with the theoretical structure of a marketing system will be explained in this brief summary.

of an agricultural population and uniform nucleation, three basic types of market areas can be posited. The three types are shown in Figure 4–4, a, b, c. The smallest of these hexagons (Figure 4–4a) may have had an even smaller origin. A single farmstead A_1 might have produced some industrial good, selling it to farmsteads A_2 or A_3, thus creating a triangular market area. If A_1 expanded its nonfarm output, it could become a central place (B_1) in a hexagon consisting of six triangles. More market space could be obtained by invading the trade areas of neighboring centers either by rotating the hexagon (Figure 4–4b) or by partially rotating and further enlarging the market configuration (Figure 4–4c).

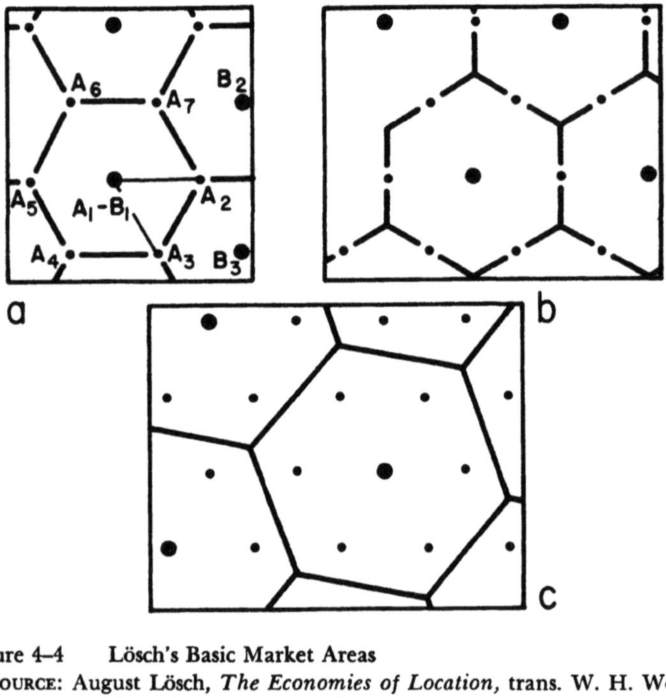

Figure 4–4 Lösch's Basic Market Areas
SOURCE: August Lösch, *The Economies of Location,* trans. W. H. Woglum, New Haven: Yale University Press, 1954, p. 117.

How this process might be further articulated is shown in Figure 4–5, where various-sized hexagons have a common center.

It should be evident then that for Lösch there is no necessary hierarchical progression of central places. What will occur is an "equilibrium of locations," provided certain assumptions can be made.[37]

37. *Economics of Location,* p. 94.

Presumably each entrepreneur will seek a location which is as advantageous as possible, and the locations in terms of their market reach will be numerous enough so that the entire space will be occupied. It is further assumed that entry into productive activities is free, so that abnormal profits will disappear and prices will approximate costs. This prospect of free entry will tend to make areas of supply, production, and sales as small as possible, and these market areas will have boundaries where it is a matter of indifference to which of two neighboring trade areas a producer or consumer belongs.[38] Since the trade area needed to permit a producer to obtain a minimal profit will vary from one commodity to another,[39] a complex network of market areas will result (Figure 4–5). But since there are indisputable advantages derivable from "numbers and association," as well as of "site and source

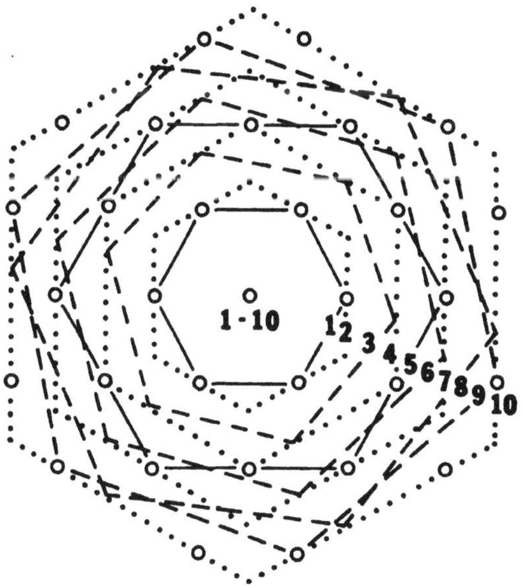

Figure 4–5 A Network of Common-Centered Market Areas
SOURCE: August Lösch, *The Economics of Location*, trans. W. H. Woglum, New Haven: Yale University Press, 1954, p. 118.

38. Ibid., pp. 95–97.
39. Data compiled by Lösch show that in the United States in 1929 74 percent of wholesale groceries were sold in a market area with a radius of less than 75 miles, whereas an equivalent percentage of hardware required a radius up to 500 miles. Ibid., p. 405.

of supply," an empirical process is set in motion tantamount to the rotation of the varying-sized hexagons in such ways that a landscape will tend to take the form shown in Figure 4–6b. What has happened is that locations have tended to cluster into those sectors of a trade area circle particularly well served with transport and other facilities, so that in the ideal case half of the sectors will tend to have many settlements, and half will have very few.[40] It is to describe this sectoral arrangement of locations that Lösch employs the phrase "economic landscape" as a technical term. Evidence that such a pattern of settlements is approximated in the real world is supplied by Lösch's findings concerning the dispersion of settlements within a 60-mile radius of Indianapolis and Toledo respectively (Figure 4–6, c and d.)[41]

It should not be assumed, however, that such landscapes are necessarily geometrically regular or that they have single metropolitan centers as their cores. They may actually have several eccentrically located main places, and Lösch concludes that this type of larger spatial entity might best be described as an "economic region," because "whereas every regional system has a large town for its center, every large town is not the center of such a system."[42] The essential, comprehensive Löschean spatial structure is therefore one that begins with the small and simple and grows, by a series of stages, into patterns that are progressively larger and more complex.[43] The entire spatial structure must therefore include "simple market areas, regional networks and regional systems." These, however, are only very general and convenient taxonomical distinctions. Skinner has shown that local and small regional markets are not as simple as one might assume,[44] and both Christaller and Lösch have demonstrated the multiple dimensions of regional net-

40. "Of the thirteen . . . first class state and federal highways that run out from Indianapolis, ten pass for the most part through the thickly settled sections, and eight of these . . . along or near their borders." Ibid., p. 439.

41. In the sectors around Indianapolis Lösch found (see Figure 4–6c) that whereas the crosshatched area was 45 percent of the territory, these sectors had a little more (48 percent) than their share of small places (fewer than 500 persons), a clear majority (53 percent) of places between 500 and 1,000 persons, and a dominant share (81 percent) of places with more than 1,000 inhabitants. Ibid., p. 439.

42. Ibid., p. 216.

43. Lösch illustrates this by showing how a very large number of cotton-growing farms are dependent on some 15,000 cotton gins, which provide cottonseed for about 500 oil mills. Yet these are only two parts of a much larger network that includes collecting depots, cotton sorting and storage centers, export points, and cotton mills. Ibid., p. 217, n. 6.

44. See pp. 93–98.

a

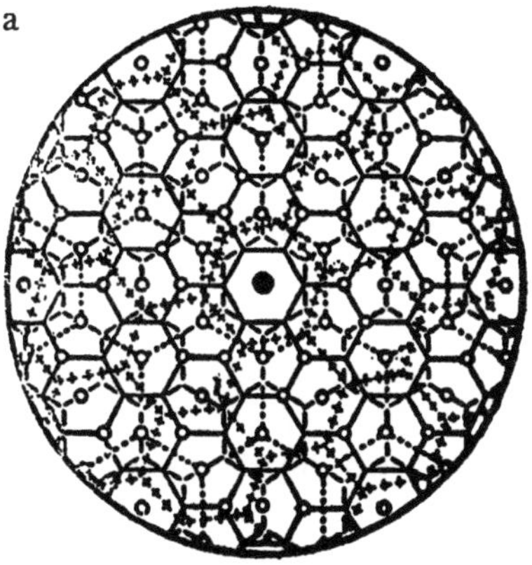

Theoretical pattern of an economic landscape

b

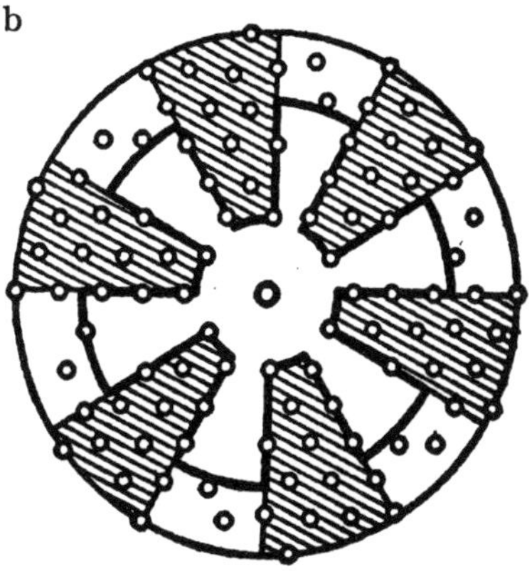

Theoretical pattern of an economic landscape, but without nets

c

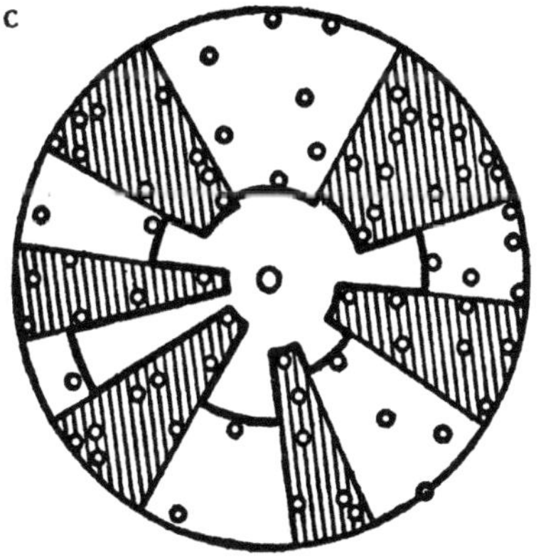

Indianapolis and environs within a radius of 60 miles. (From Andree's *Handatlas*, 8th ed., p. 198.)

d

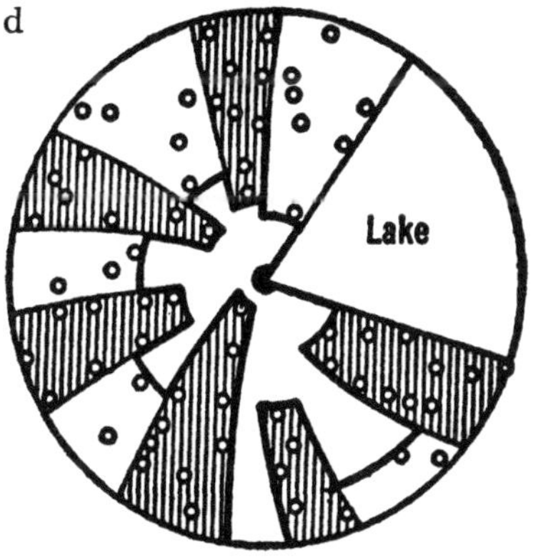

Toledo and environs within a radius of 60 miles. (*Ibid.*)

Figure 4–6 Lösch's "Economic Landscapes"

SOURCE: August Lösch, *The Economics of Location*, trans. W. H. Woglum, New Haven: Yale University Press, 1954, p. 125.

works. Yet the regional networks are reducible to demand and supply functions for single products or product mixes. When one reaches the "economic landscape," such simplification can no longer be employed. For as Lösch has so clearly explained, an "economic landscape is a system of different markets; an organism, not merely an organ."[45]

45. *Economics of Location*, p. 219.

The Utility of Classical Central-Place Theory as a Guide to Developmental Policy

However much Lösch may contend that the main purpose of locational theory is to improve the utilization of space,[46] the great bulk of central-place theory is essentially descriptive, not necessarily as a mirror of reality (although Lösch was able to document his theory remarkably well) but as an effort to depict what an ideal relation between central places and their hinterlands might be. And however valiantly Christaller has tried to introduce dynamic ingredients, his theory is essentially static.[47] There are, moreover, among the three leading classical theorists very real differences stemming from the dissimilar purposes of their analyses which necessarily influence their conclusions. Von Thünen takes the large town in the center of his agricultural plain as given and addresses himself to the task of explaining the most rational use of the town's hinterland for agricultural purposes. In a sense this is macro-estate management, since presumably by following his prescriptions the best use would be made not only of natural but of human resources in the area functionally related to the central town. But once this optimal utilization has been reached, then what? Von Thünen does not explain how there can be further development beyond this ideal equilibrium or how new generations of farm folk will be employed. He hazards no guesses about whether growth will be a balanced urban and rural phenomenon with no changes in factor proportions. He offers no opinions as to whether the urban and rural changes will be harmonious with parallel increases in capital intensivity. We look in vain for any explicit theory of development in the von Thünen model.

Christaller's approach is quite different. Whereas von Thünen devoted almost all of his attention to the countryside, Christaller's main concern is urban—with "central places." Admittedly, these places have grown up historically in response to the need for "centrality" by the inhabitants of each center's complementary region. But beyond this statement of town and country interdependence and a few references to the Roman origins of some German towns, the central places are largely assumed to exist; hence the main task is to delineate the urban mor-

46. "The real duty of the economist is not to explain our sorry reality, but to improve it. The question of the best location is far more dignified than determination of the actual one." Ibid., p. 4.

47. See *Central Places,* Chapter I, Part C, "Dynamic Processes."

phology in a structurally differentiated landscape. The analytical route Christaller takes is downward. Thus a central place of a "high order" will offer a variety of "high order central goods" to a large hinterland, each good having a measurable "range." The "market principle" next reveals smaller spheres of spatial influence exercised by "central places of a lower order," and within their configurations, in turn, can be found the "central places of the lowest order" with their correspondingly smaller "complementary regions." But what if these neatly superimposed hexagonal areas are not to be found? Can they be created by building urban networks from the top downward? In the one example that he offers of a genetic nature, Christaller actually follows a reverse procedure and shows how a small railway station might grow into an important central place.[48] The really important inference pervading Christaller's analysis is that there are economic ways of creating a rational network of central places, and there are wasteful ways. His analysis shows that if maximum commercialization of a landscape is the goal of policy, then random, sociopolitical decisions concerning central places should be scrupulously avoided. But this, alas, is not the procedure that most underdeveloped countries are following; they dream of splendid capital cities—Brazilia, Chandigarh, or Islamabad—rather than of a hierarchical network of spatially dispersed market towns. Or if they do apply tests of economic rationality, it is more likely to be Christaller's "traffic principle" rather than his "market principle" that will govern. The neglect of central-place analysis in the planning techniques of underdeveloped countries is doubly unfortunate: opportunities are lost, and resources are devoted to less than optimal uses, perhaps far less.[49] The urgent need for an increase in the number of central places will be made clear in Chapter 5. With very few exceptions—Israel and Lebanon, for example—the huge areas of the "third world" are woefully underurbanized, and, sooner or later, this structural deficit must be faced. The basic question is whether economic policy can be so designed as to increase the number and improve the

48. Ibid., p. 105. "Next to it [the railway station] a restaurant may be opened and perhaps a post office and most likely a storehouse of an agricultural cooperative will be added. Thus, we already have three or four kinds of central goods which are offered at the station place rather than at the central place. . . . Perhaps a veterinarian . . . may be added, together with a construction materials store, a coal yard and a transfer company. Perhaps living quarters and stores for railroad employees may be added. The station place may develop, in this manner, into a central place."

49. Israel is an outstanding exception. See pp. 301–304.

functional interrelations of central places. On this score, Christaller is optimistic. "When one recognizes," he writes, that the development of central places "is not haphazard, but is ruled by forces of economic laws and propositions, then the possibility exists for actively promoting and influencing this development by planning."[50]

Lösch is less disposed to trust the planners. He inverts Christaller's progression, moving in his analysis from small to larger market configurations.[51] His main object is to explain the complexities of market "nets," and since the smaller hexagons are the basic building blocks of economic landscapes, he proceeds from smaller to larger configurations. This procedure has one very clear advantage; it can begin with partial commercialization of a landscape and gradually envisage full spatial commercialization. The genetics of the process, however, are not often revealed, only the theoretical possibilities. The concern is with what the market network could be when the process is completed, and in this sense Lösch has created an architectonic masterpiece. The only trouble is that he has said almost nothing about the policy paths that less-developed countries must follow if they too are to have such a beautifully balanced market structure. Indeed the peroration of his great treatise is a defense of the "powerful forces of spontaneity,"[52] which, "if rightly guided," can be an "ally to national economic policy" and thereby save the policy makers from "the superhuman task of planning everything down to the very last detail." All this is good enough general advice—no policy maker wants to plan everything "down to the very last detail"—but it is necessary to know much more about how the forces of spontaneity are to be "guided" in order to make them "an ally to national economic policy."

Central-Place Analysis from Rural Points of View: The Social Topography of Galpin, Sanderson, and Kolb

Eighteen years before Christaller published his *Central Places in Southern Germany,* and twenty-nine years before the first edition of Lösch's treatise appeared, a thirty-four page "Bulletin" was issued by the Agricultural Experiment Station of the University of Wisconsin

50. *Central Places,* p. 124.

51. This is the method followed by Skinner in his explanation of the Chinese market network. He moves from the "standard market" to the intermediate and then to the central market (see pp. 95–99 of the present volume).

52. *Economics of Location,* p. 508.

analyzing the functions of central places in Walworth County, Wisconsin. This modest and unpretentious publication summarized the research findings of C. J. Galpin, whose interests in the interrelations of town and country had persuaded him that an effort should be made to measure the more important linkages between rural dwellers and their nearby central places in order to discover whether such an institution as a "rural community" actually existed. The little essay, which Galpin entitled *The Social Anatomy of an Agricultural Community*,[53] proved to be a trail-blazing document that led sociologists, political scientists, geographers, and economists to explore more thoroughly the social, economic, and political interrelations between villages and their hinterlands, between towns and their markets; and to appraise the spatial range of the services that were, or might be, performed for the rural population by central places. Owing partly to the impact of forces exogenous to Walworth County (such as World War I and the rapid introduction of the automobile) the community structure that Galpin quite accurately measured and described (between August 1911 and July 1913) was soon to be rather markedly altered. These changes were evaluated in two "restudies" of Walworth County made respectively in 1929–1930 and in 1947–1948.[54] Galpin's survey is therefore less noteworthy for its specific findings than for the methodology which it pioneered.

The task Galpin set for himself was to ascertain where farm families in a typical midwestern dairy region did their marketing and their banking; where they sold their milk; where they attended church services; where their children went to high school; what town or village newspaper they read, and which libraries they used. In a county 24 miles square with only twelve major villages and cities, it was possible to gather the essential data by personal interviews with merchants, bankers, clergymen, high school principals, librarians, newspaper publishers, and some 600 farmers.[55] From the data, maps were constructed showing the spatial extent of trade zones, banking areas, milk zones, church

53. Agriculture Experiment Station, Research Bulletin 34, Madison, 1915. With some small modifications and some minor additions the text of this Bulletin is reprinted in Galpin's *Rural Life*, New York, 1923, pp. 71–100.

54. J. H. Kolb and R. A. Polson, *Trends in Town-Country Relations*, University of Wisconsin, Agricultural Experiment Station, Research Bulletin 117, Madison, 1933; J. H. Kolb and Leroy J. Day, *Interdependence in Town and Country Relations in Rural Society*, University of Wisconsin, Agricultural Experiment Station, Research Bulletin 172, Madison, 1950.

55. Hamlets and small villages were not surveyed.

membership territory, newspaper distribution, high school attendance, and library usage.

Although Galpin was the first to schematize the theoretical form of what became a Löschean K = 7 central-place configuration (see Figure 4–7),[56] his empirical exploration showed that topographic factors—undulations, lakes, marshes—and agronomic variations distorted the theoretically circular (trade, banking, church, and school) zones into very irregular patterns. He anticipated Christaller's thesis that central-place services have differing perimeters[57] by the simple expedient of showing, via his "social topography," that the banking areas did not exactly coincide with the trade zones and that the milk zones and the high school zones were much smaller than the newspaper, trade, and banking areas. The trade zones (see Figure 4–8) of the twelve central places covered well over 90 percent of the total area of the county and the outer edges of the trade areas tended to overlap a little, indicating that about 7 or 8 percent of farm families traded at two or more centers.[58] The banking zones (see Figure 4–9), which, like the trade zones, surrounded each of the twelve villages and cities, were very nearly coterminous with the trade zones, and the overlaps, although somewhat different in location and design, were about as extensive. The newspaper zones, however, were considerably larger than the banking zones, for whereas all the twelve central places had banks, only seven of the Walworth County central places published newspapers. The twelve milk zones were much smaller than the trade zones because small creameries and skimming stations were scattered through the open country; hence only the farmers living fairly near to central places brought their milk to village or town creameries and condensaries.[59] Churches in the twelve villages and towns attracted their attendants from short-radius areas; this was because most hamlets had churches and because some congregations had their local churches in the countryside. For much the same reason,—namely, foreshortened travel—the milk zones and the church zones were rather similar.

56. A configuration wherein one major central place, with its own hinterland, dominates a band of six equal-sized contiguous areas, each with its (smaller) central place. For fuller explanation, see Lösch, *Economics of Location,* pp. 131–132.

57. *Central Places,* pp. 60–63.

58. About 6 or 7 percent of the farmers living near the Walworth County borders traded at central places in other counties.

59. The average radius of a milk zone was about 3 miles, whereas the radii of the trade and banking zones were often twice that distance.

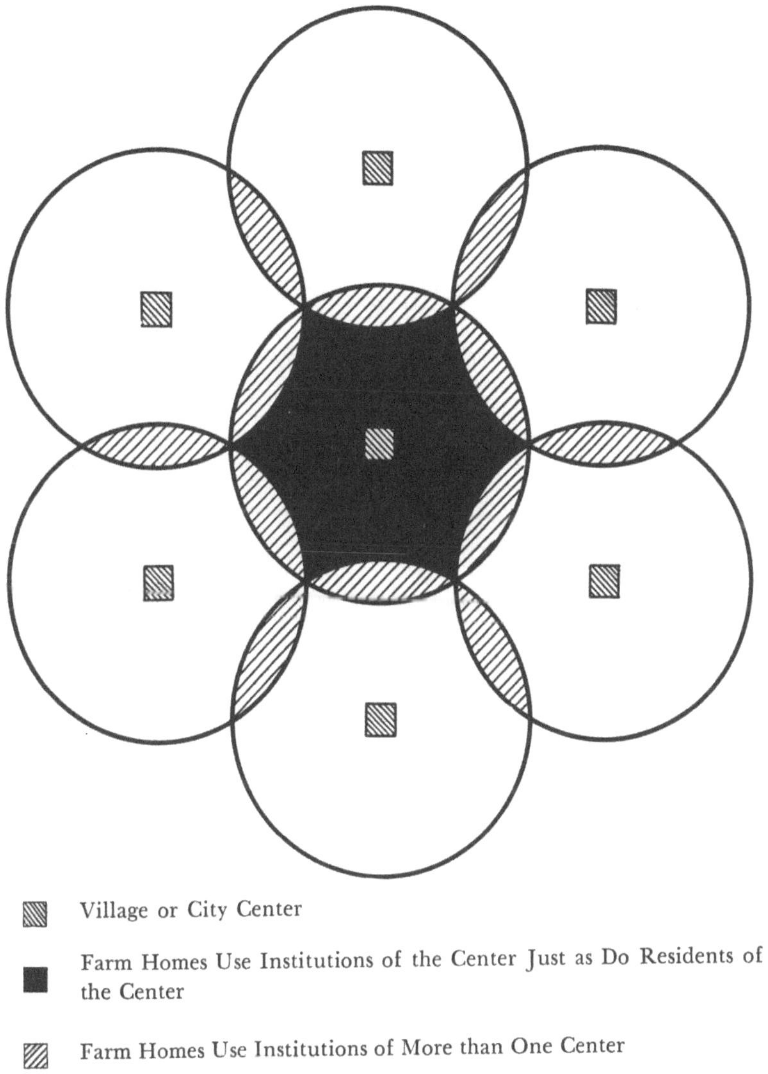

Figure 4–7 The Theoretical Form of an Agricultural Community

SOURCE: C. J. Galpin, *The Social Anatomy of an Agricultural Community,* University of Wisconsin, Agricultural Experiment Station, Research Bulletin 34, Madison, 1915, p. 17.

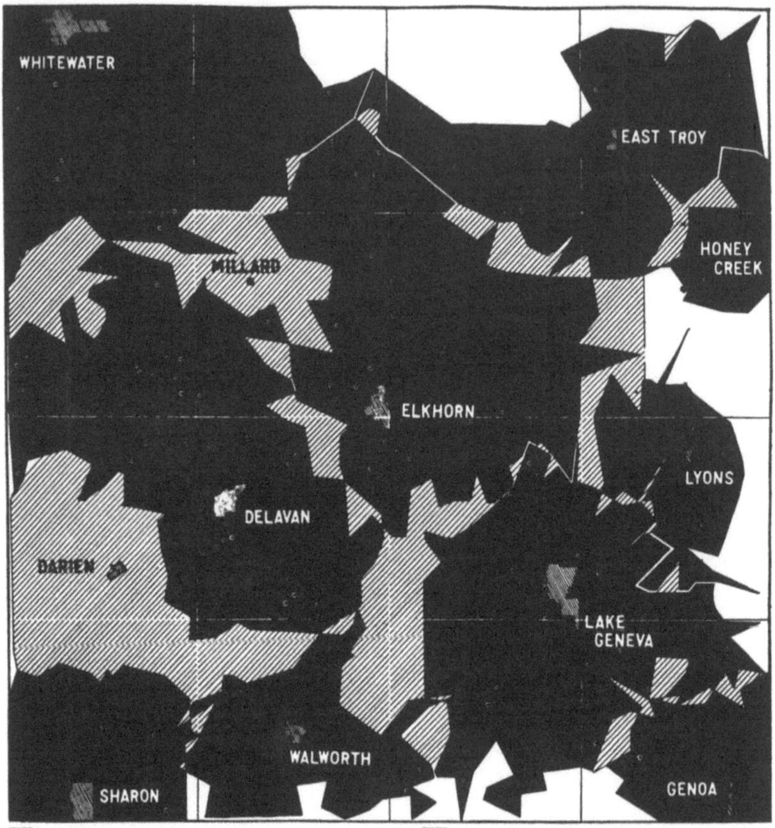

Village or City Center — Trade at One Center
Trade at Two or More Centers — Trade Outside the County

Twelve villages and small cities situated in the county serve as trade centers for the farm homes precisely as for the village and city homes and all the homes trading at the same center form a trade community. Township lines six miles apart indicate the distance.

Figure 4–8 Trade Communities in Walworth County, Wisconsin

SOURCE: C. J. Galpin, *The Social Anatomy of an Agricultural Community,* University of Wisconsin, Agricultural Experiment Station, Research Bulletin 34, Madison, 1915, p. 17.

Perhaps the most saddening finding of Galpin's survey was that only nine of the twelve central places had high schools and that less than 15 percent of the farm families sent children to high schools, even though no farm in Walworth County was more than 5 miles distant

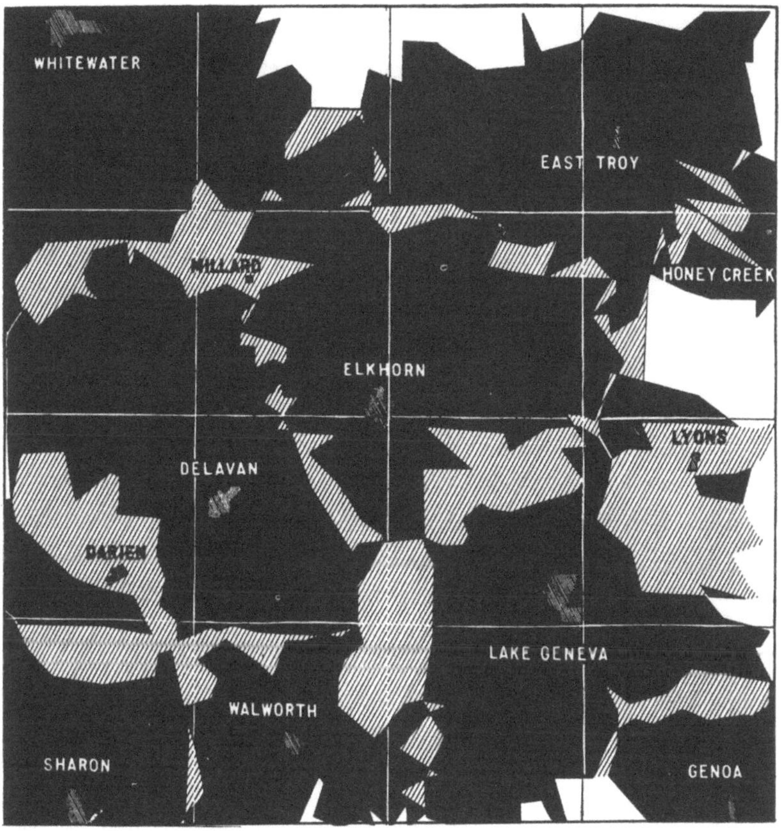

Village or City Center — Bank at One Center

Bank at Two or More Centers — Bank Outside the County

Farm homes use the banks at the village and city centers just as do the village or city residents. The homes banking at the same center form a banking community. Township lines six miles apart indicate the distance.

Figure 4–9 Banking Communities in Walworth County, Wisconsin
SOURCE: C. J. Galpin, *The Social Anatomy of an Agricultural Community,* University of Wisconsin, Agricultural Experiment Station, Research Bulletin 34, Madison, 1915, p. 8.

from one of the nine high schools.[60] In Figure 4–10 there are no overlaps; instead there are wide interstices between the high school zones, large areas that made no use whatever of the educational facilities avail-

60. At this time (circa 1914) about twice this percentage of Danish farm boys and girls were attending the "Peoples High Schools."

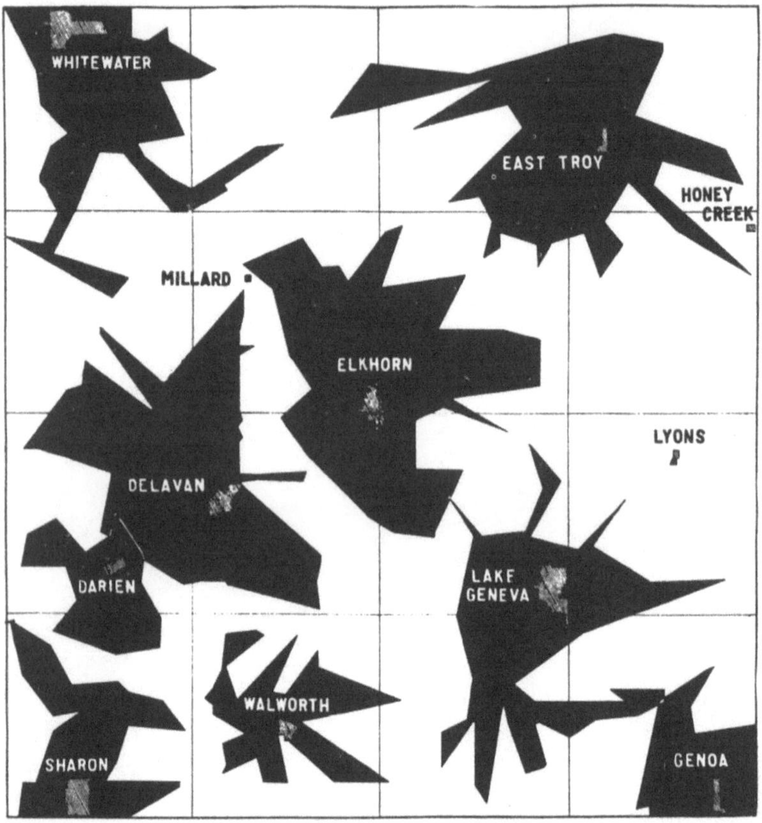

Village or City Center

Send Children to the High School of One Center

Do Not Send Children to Any High School in the County

Notice the fact that the trade-center high school is used by farmer and villager alike; that there are wide farm-land areas making no use of the high school. Compare with township areas.

Figure 4–10 High School Communities in Walworth County, Wisconsin
SOURCE: C. J. Galpin, *The Social Anatomy of an Agricultural Community*, University of Wisconsin, Agricultural Experiment Station, Research Bulletin 34, Madison, 1915, p. 13.

able in villages and towns. If there was enough mobility for farmers to visit stores and banks, why were the range limits so short for schools and libraries?[61] The presumed indifference of farmers to education

61. Galpin put the issue somewhat ruefully when he said, "It is plain that a fair percentage of the farm families *within two miles* of each high school recognizes its value." *Social Anatomy*, p. 15. (Italics mine.)

would not be an adequate explanation of this anomalous situation. Perhaps fully as responsible, in the era before consolidated schools, was the legal separation of villages (and towns) from townships. The farmer, as Galpin said, was virtually "a man without a legal community," who paid taxes to his township but was asked to pay tuition for his children in village or town high schools.[62] The consequence was that in 1910–1913 most Wisconsin farmers' children were not availing themselves of educational facilities within easy travel distance. It was very evident that the "powerful forces of spontaneity" that Lösch was later to extol had provided Walworth County farmers with satisfactory trade and banking zones but had signally failed to widen the high school zones. It was only after new consolidated school districts had been deliberately planned and financed by the common action of farmers and townsmen that farmers began to have a sense of participation in new types of educational programs that progressively integrated town and country. Schools could now offer instruction in subjects that had direct relevance to the needs of all their students; and their laboratories, libraries, and teaching staff could be far more adequate and specialized.

It was not only in the field of education that an integration of town and country seemed necessary to Charles Galpin. His maps had convinced him that "artificial" village, township, and county boundaries were obscuring realities and obstructing the emergence of true communities actually "situated on the slopes of social watersheds" of villages and small cities.[63] A policy was required that would materialize a more effective interrelation in which farmers would not be "aliens" in nearby villages; to end the "legalized insulation" of villages from farms and of cities from their economic hinterlands. "Pure ruralism," which segregated farmers from townsmen, all too often led to both biological and social inbreeding[64] and failed to give full scope and range for the talents of farm-born children. Both the desirability of greater regional efficiency and the hunger for a more genuine democracy called for a closer economic and social partnership[65] between farm and village and be-

62. The townships provided elementary education in "district school houses." In fairness it should be pointed out that the village or town communities planned, built, organized, and financed their high schools for their legal inhabitants; hence there seemed to be no equity in opening them up free of tuition to pupils from farm areas beyond their corporation limits.

63. Galpin, *Social Anatomy*, p. 22.

64. Ibid., p. 21.

65. Ibid., p. 33.

tween farm-village communities and small cities. This new regional structure, which Galpin called "rurbanism," would not, however, come into being by means of Adam Smith's "invisible hand."[66] It would have to be consciously visualized, planned, and contrived.[67] A truly functional economic landscape called for an appropriate structure, one in which central places would serve as co-ordinators, thereby developing integrated spatial social organizations that could properly be called "communities."

The methods and techniques that Galpin used in his pioneering experiment in "social topography" were employed and further developed in a series of studies of rural society undertaken by the Wisconsin Agricultural Experiment Station and Extensive Service.[68] Among these publications were the two "restudies" of Walworth County mentioned earlier.[69] The first restudy revealed that considerable progress had been made in improving town and country relations. The most noticeable

66. I first heard the term "rurbanism" used by Professor Radhakamal Mukerjee of Lucknow University, and I assumed that he had coined the word. It seems not unlikely, however, that he derived it from Galpin, as the following excerpt would suggest: "'Rurbanization' or multiplication of small agro-towns will stimulate commercial farming, modernize agricultural methods and practices, and adjust caste and occupations—primary, manufacturing, and tertiary—to the new social milieu. Extension and welfare services from city and 'rurban' centers will stir new ambitions and introduce new patterns of living and culture; there will be a fresh synthesis of the values of modern science and technology with those of a predominantly rural civilization." Indian Institute of Technology, International Seminar on Urban and Industrial Growth of Kanpur Region, Presidential Address, Kanpur, February 4, 1967, in *Regional Perspective of Industrial and Urban Growth,* ed. P. B. Desai, J. M. Grossack, and K. N. Sharma, Bombay, 1969, pp. 386–392.

67. Galpin suggested certain "steps" for planning "a comprehensive community." Areas should first be carefully mapped. Once that had been done, discussions could begin concerning a suitable "form of community government." Only after these essential steps had been taken could specific problems be considered, such as how to establish better markets for the benefit of farm producers and city consumers, how to provide rest rooms for farmers and their families for use when they come to town, how to finance and construct agricultural processing industries, how to create consolidated school districts and establish multipurpose free high schools. *Social Anatomy*, pp. 28–32.

68. Included were studies of rural clubs, churches, high schools, fairs, service relations of town and country, and many other facets of urban-rural interdependence. For a checklist of these publications from 1915 to 1957 see "A Chronology of Publications of Group Relations in Rural Society," in John H. Kolb, *Emerging Rural Communities: Group Relations in Rural Society: A Review of Wisconsin Research in Action,* Madison, 1959, pp. 187–189. Kolb was one of Galpin's students.

69. Kolb and Polson, *Trends in Town-Country Relations,* and Kolb and Day, *Interdependence in Town and Country Relations.* See note 54 in this chapter for full reference.

change was that by 1929–1930 country-dwelling pupils constituted 50 percent of high school enrollment as contrasted with 15 percent in 1911–1913. Many new rural community associations had emerged in the interval, organizations concerned not only with marketing and farm credit but also with a range of social and cultural activities. Villages and towns had become somewhat more specialized, a trend which the general usage of automobiles had helped to promote. Service areas had increased in size. Thus for all twelve central places, the average library areas had increased (1929 over 1914) 143.3 percent, the milk marketing zones 63.7 percent, the high school regions 48.7 percent, the grocery zones 22.4 percent, and the banking zones 3.1 percent.[70]

The second restudy examined this trend toward urban specialization by more precisely testing the hypothesis that central places were becoming increasingly differentiated and interdependent.[71] Greater mobility had widened the reach of larger market centers so much that only 6 percent of trade contacts were now in places with fewer than 500 people, while 54 percent were in places where the population ranged from 2,000 to 10,000. About two-thirds of all social and business contacts were with nine central places, and the trend toward larger areas and greater overlapping was consistently mentioned in the testimony obtained from 1,625 families. High school areas had greatly enlarged, particularly in the five larger centers. Three distinct types of agro-urban communities could be clearly differentiated by 1947–1948; the larger spatial units comprehending from 75 to 95 square miles (equal to the area of from 2 to 2½ standard townships), intermediate units covering from 62 to 82 square miles (about two townships), and the smaller units spread over about 36 square miles (the equivalent in size, but not in shape, of a standard midwestern township).

The research techniques developed by Galpin and his students soon spread farther afield. At Cornell University, Dwight Sanderson, who heralded Galpin as the "pioneer in discovering the structure of the rural community,"[72] began mapping "communities" in western New York and, with the aid of his many graduate students, soon opened up new vistas in town and country relations. Following ideas first advanced by

70. Edmund de S. Brunner and John H. Kolb, *Rural Social Trends,* New York, 1933, p. 99.

71. A summary of the findings of this second restudy is available in Kolb, *Emerging Rural Communities,* pp. 111 ff.

72. In Sanderson's dedication to Galpin of his *The Rural Community: The Natural History of a Sociological Group,* Boston, 1932.

R. M. MacIver, Sanderson pointed out that "communities" were distinct from "neighborhoods."[73] He also concluded that they might sometimes have more than a single center.[74] The Cornell studies carefully analyzed the reach of community centers, measured the average radii in relation to the size of central places,[75] and appraised the genetics of community growth, development, and contraction. Meanwhile, studies in Texas, Michigan, Missouri, California, Massachusetts, Utah, Oklahoma, Iowa, Minnesota, and Washington, showed many regional and ecological differences influencing the size and structure of agro-urban communities.[76] In view of all the surveys that were made in the twenties and thirties one can understand why it was easier for Lösch to find concrete verification for his general spatial theory in the United States than in Europe.[77]

73. "For the unity which the large community attains is not the unity which the smaller community [neighborhood] had previously attained. . . . It cannot take the place of the new community, but can only supplement it. . . . The service of the large community is to fulfill and not destroy the former." R. M. MacIver, *Community: A Sociological Study,* London, 1917, pp. 259–260.

74. For details see Sanderson, *Rural Community,* pp. 485–488.

75. B. L. Melvin's studies made in 1925 indicated that average distances were three miles between villages of 250 people or fewer, 3–5 miles between centers with populations of 251–750 persons, and 5–7 miles between centers of 751–1,250 people. Thus in New York State a fairly consistent hierarchical structure existed at the time that Melvin made his surveys. See *Village Service Agencies,* Cornell University Agricultural Experiment Station Bulletin No. 493, and *Rural Population: New York, 1855–1925,* Cornell University Agricultural Experiment Station, Bulletin No. 116, Ithaca, 1925.

76. Lewis H. Henry and George S. Wherwein, eds., *A Social Economic Survey of Southern Travis County,* University of Texas, Bulletin No. 65, Austin, 1916; C. R. Hopper, *A Study of Town-Country Relationships,* Michigan State College, Bulletin No. 181, Lansing, 1928; B. L. Hummel, *Community Organization in Missouri,* University of Missouri, College of Agriculture, Circular No. 183, Columbia, 1926; Bessie A. McClenahan, *The Changing Urban Neighborhood,* University of Southern California, Social Science Series, No. 1, Los Angeles, 1929; E. L. Morgan, *Mobilizing the Rural Community,* Massachusetts Agricultural College, Extension Bulletin No. 23, Amherst, 1918; Lowry Nelson, *A Social Survey of Escalante Utah,* Brigham Young University Studies, No. 1, Provo, 1925; James F. Page, *Relation of Town and Country Interests in Garfield County,* Oklahoma Agricultural and Mechanical College, Agricultural Experiment Station, Bulletin No. 194, Stillwater, 1930; Paul S. Pierce, *Social Surveys of Three Rural Townships in Iowa,* University of Iowa Monographs, Vol. 5, No. 2, Iowa City, 1917; H. Bruce Price and C. R. Hopper, *Services of Rural Trade Centers in Distribution of Farm Supplies,* University of Minnesota, Agricultural Experiment Station, Bulletin No. 249, Minneapolis, 1928; E. A. Taylor and F. R. Yoder, *Rural Social Organization in Whatcom County,* State College of Washington, Agricultural Experiment Station, Bulletin No. 215, Pullman, 1927.

77. *Economics of Location,* p. 389.

Recent Trends in Central-Place Studies

Not all the social topographers who modeled their studies on Galpin's Walworth County survey were equally fruitful. Many of the surveys were amateurish descriptions that contributed little to an analysis of the role and function of central places. Moreover, efforts to include a widening range of sociological aspects of rural communities led to such a growing diffuseness that it was indeed fortunate that the appearance of Christaller's work in the mid-thirties emphatically called attention to the need for a more rigorous understanding of underlying principles, a type of critical reorientation further stimulated by Lösch. Modern central-place analysis consequently stems partly from the empiricism of Galpin and his followers and partly from the abstract currents of thought that can be traced from von Thünen through Christaller and Lösch. These two currents are very evident in the dual character of the growing central-place literature. On the one hand are encountered a large number of essentially descriptive studies, no longer confined to the American locale but made by scholars in a large number of countries, indicating an increasingly global interest in rural-urban problems. In sharp contrast to these empirical studies are the abstract, increasingly mathematical models that are being constructed in an effort to comprehend the subtle interrelations of a larger number of social and economic factors.

The range and scope of the first type, the essentially descriptive studies, can readily be seen from the carefully selected and well-annotated bibliography prepared by Brian J. L. Berry and Allen Pred.[78] The listings indicate a surge of worldwide interest in central-place studies particularly since 1950. Among the more general descriptive sources listed under the heading "Studies of Systems of Central Places" and among some of the less-specialized essays under other headings, such as "Studies of Urban Spheres of Influence and the Trade Area of Cities" and "Town-Country Relations, Rural Neighbourhoods and Communities," are to be found books and articles dealing with central-place developments in more than thirty countries. Studies of Japanese cities, trade areas, and communities are far and away the most numerous,[79] although the United States, the United Kingdom, and Germany each

78. *Central Place Studies*. For full reference see note 17 in this chapter.

79. There are over thirty major entries, and the total is more than twice that number.

have more than a dozen major sources listed.[80] A perusal of the listings reveals quite promptly, however, that the great bulk of the studies deal with "developed" or "mature" countries. Multiple listings are therefore noticeable for Japan, Sweden, the United States, the United Kingdom, Switzerland, Germany, the Netherlands, France, Canada, Denmark, and Belgium; and also for such well-advanced countries as Australia, South Africa, New Zealand, Finland, Poland, the USSR, and Spain.[81] What is glaringly evident is that only a handful of countries from the underdeveloped parts of the world are represented: India and Brazil (each with three entries), Mexico and Morocco (each with two), and Haiti, Pakistan, Ghana, Uganda, and Inner Mongolia (each with one). Admittedly there are many more central places in developed countries than there are in underdeveloped parts of the world,[82] but for that very reason the study of central-place functions becomes all the more important for the less-developed countries. It must therefore be regretted that virtually no attention has been given to central-place analysis in Latin America[83] and the Middle East, and very, very little in Africa and Asia. This indifference to spatial problems, despite the vast outpouring of books and articles concerned with economic development in the "third world," is to some of us who have lived and worked in underdeveloped areas deeply disturbing. For genuine development cannot possibly be disassociated from geography; investment, if it is to be fruitful, must be made at "growth points," and industrialization will have little meliorative effect unless low-cost marketing can widen demand. Each critical measure of development is influenced by spatial factors; hence it is the underdeveloped countries that stand in most urgent need of central-place studies and careful spatial analysis.

It is much too early to know whether the model builders with their abstract conceptualization of areal design can be helpful to the planners in underdeveloped countries. It is surely conceivable that general theory

80. The listings on the United States include studies of central places in Washington State, North Dakota, South Dakota, Wisconsin, Illinois, Tennessee, Nebraska, Iowa, Idaho, Indiana, Utah, Minnesota, Michigan, Alabama, Texas, Ohio, Maryland, New York, Oklahoma, North Carolina, Louisiana, and California. The twenty-three sources concerning the United Kingdom include studies of central places not merely in several English regions; some deal also with Scottish, Welsh, and Northern Irish town-country problems.

81. In this group Poland is accorded the largest number of listings.

82. For a rough index see Chapter 5, pp. 174–175.

83. John Friedman's *Regional Development Policy: A Case Study of Venezuela*, Cambridge, Mass., 1966, is an outstanding exception.

can suggest particularly fruitful areas for empirical research,[84] and if it can also set up warning signals that may prevent the hasty and foolish commitment of scarce resources to far less than optimal yields, it could be very serviceable indeed. If, on the other hand, it lures some of the limited number of first-class minds into sterile intellectual exercises when they are urgently needed to make practical decisions, the utility may be more doubtful.[85] There is moreover, the ever-present danger that models that are useful in raising fundamental policy issues in highly industrialized countries may be singularly inapplicable in countries that are mainly agrarian and where the countryside is only fractionally commercialized.[86] But these caveats should not lead one to scorn, belittle, or ignore the imaginative approaches which have been and are being made to an understanding of all spatial aspects of development. General systems theory may prove to be more important for the future progress of underdeveloped areas than the vast amount of energy that has been so prodigally devoted to village studies.[87] But as Walter Isard, one of the foremost exponents of spatial theory, has wisely said, "it is fully recognized that a general theory of location and space economy is of little direct use in treating concrete problems of reality" unless it has been "supplemented by techniques of regional analysis which are operational."[88] This task clearly calls for earnest efforts to integrate empirical and theoretical aspects of central-place research.

84. A suggestion I was happy to find in H. C. Bos, *Spatial Dispersion of Economic Activity*, Rotterdam, 1965, p. 92, a book which is otherwise almost forbiddingly theoretical.

85. My experiences in Korea, Greece, Yugoslavia, and India lead me to believe this outcome is not at all unlikely. There is an innate romanticism in underdeveloped areas that tempts intellectuals to believe that there are shortcuts to development and that their duty is to find these esoteric ways of bypassing the traditional methods of development. For a fuller analysis, see my "Problems of 'Forced Draft' Industrialization—Some Observations Based on the Yugoslav Experience," in *Contributions and Communications*, First International Conference of Economic History, Paris, 1960, pp. 479–488.

86. Thus the arguments that are advanced against industrial dispersion in Japan may have no relevance whatever in India and Pakistan, where it seems most unlikely that "pushing ahead with the concentration policy will rectify inter-regional differences," as Takashi Fujii argues in his *Economic Space in the Japanese Archipelago*, Nagoya, n.d.

87. For a succinct exposition of the objective and techniques of general systems theory, see Brian J. L. Berry, *Geography of Market Centers and Retail Distribution*, Englewood Cliffs, N.J., 1967, pp. 76–79. For a much fuller analysis see Walter Isard, *Location and Space-Economy: A General Theory Relating to Industrial Location, Market Areas, Land Use, Trade, and Urban Structure*, Cambridge, Mass., 1956.

88. Walter Isard et al., *Methods of Regional Analysis: An Introduction to Regional Science*, New York, 1960, p. vii.

CHAPTER 5 GREAT CITIES AND THE MACROECONOMIC CONSEQUENCES OF DUAL ECONOMIES

Political and Economic Polarizing Forces

In less-developed, village-structured economies cities are usually relatively few and inordinately large; consequently a satisfactory interconnection between town and country by means of a hierarchy of central places, functionally dispersed over a landscape in descending scale of utility and size, is either lacking or so imperfectly developed as to leave large unserved interstices.[1] There are two major reasons for the disproportionate size of the relatively few cities. In the first place a primate city is customarily a capital city, an administrative center where the ruling classes reside, together with their entourage, their retainers and servants, and where artisans, politicians, and professional people who cater to the needs, desires, and whims of the patricians will perforce also congregate. Since the lesser aristocracy, with homes elsewhere, will need to curry favor with the dominant aristocracy, they may find it expedient to establish part-time homes in a central administrative center.[2] In large countries several such administrative centers may grow

1. In the region of India for which Kanpur is the central city only 24 towns (with 2,500 people or more) exist to link almost 12,000 villages with the central regional city, an average of 1 town for every 480 villages. The consequence is that thousands of the villages have virtually no reciprocal relations with the urban portions of the region.

2. If part-time residence is required, as was the case in Tokugawa Japan, the capital city can become far larger than it would have been if only economic factors were operative. Thus Edo (Tokyo) in mid-Tokugawa (1731) was a huge city of more than a half million people, and most of this exaggerated urbanization had a wholly factitious political rather than any real functional economic origin. The politically inspired concatenation had, however, very far-reaching economic consequences.

up, and the linkage of provincial capitals with a central capital will usually be more political than commercial.[3]

A second reason for the disproportionate size of large urban centers vis-à-vis smaller cities or towns in less-developed countries is to be found in the polarizing influence of linear forms of transport facilities that connect a primate city, or any other large city, with portions of village-structured rural landscapes.[4] This second agglomerating force, which is more economic than political, tends to exaggerate investment at the poles of a transport axis, concentrate enterprises of many varieties at such terminal sites, and lure talented and adventurous people to the larger cities by leading them to believe that differentially higher incomes are to be found there—a hope that may or may not materialize. All too frequently the migrants find themselves unemployed, underemployed, or precariously employed with incomes so low or so uncertain that they must live in the jungle of slums, which are, unfortunately, so characteristic of great cities in underdeveloped countries. Nonetheless, these two agglomerating forces, one mainly political, the other chiefly economic, largely explain the dichotomous character of settlement in Africa, Asia, the Middle East, and Latin America. One need only visit these great cities to see that they are at once splendid and pathetic, magnificent and wretched, elegant and ugly! But their influence is spatial, since very often they are related to village-studded agrarian landscapes by a dendritic, export-oriented market system, which results in exchange procedures that may keep the terms of trade

3. Australia provides one of the most vivid examples of political urban polarization. Thus in New South Wales, Sidney (population 2,183,000) is ten times as large as the next largest city, Newcastle (209,000); in Victoria, Melbourne is twenty times as large as Geelong, the next largest. The same pattern is repeated in Queensland, where Brisbane is twelve times as large as Townsville; in South Australia, where Adelaide is thirty-nine times the size of Mt. Gambia; in Western Australia, where Perth is nine times as large as Kalgoorie; and even in Tasmania, where Hobart is more than twice the size of the next largest city, Launceston. It should be noted that all the metropolises are provincial capitals. Here then, as G. M. Neutze says in a quaint understatement, "A state-by-state examination shows that . . . there is a high concentration of population in the state capitals and a dearth of medium-sized centres." *Economic Policy and the Size of Cities*, Canberra, 1965, p. 7.

4. Although railways represent the most influential polarizing force, roads and rivers can produce a similar effect. Thus in Mogul times the Great Trunk Road through the Gangetic plain produced bulbous developments at Kabul, Delhi, Agra, and Benares; and the debouchment of rivers was responsible for such great cities as Shanghai and Alexandria. There are, however (see pp. 155–156), some essential differences between the spatial effects of railways and roads.

persistently adverse for the agricultural producers.[5] Yet, as will be seen, it is not only the export sector of the large city that may cause a spatial economic disequilibrium.

There is probably no general explanation that can adequately account for the high degree of political polarization so often found in less-developed areas. But even though cultural and historical factors undoubtedly provide elements of uniqueness to these centripetal forces, for the most part it may be said that underdeveloped countries are not merely economically backward; the chances are that local and provincial government is not well articulated, and this, in turn, explains why authority tends to be centralized rather than delegated and diffused. Moreover, very often a "government" depends on a military rather than a popular sanction, and most governments so enthralled will tend to follow the military precedent of pyramidal centralization.[6] For the purposes of this enquiry, the influence of political centrality on the emergence of great cities is simply taken as part of the given data. Jakarta, Rangoon, Belgrade, Accra, Lagos, Baghdad, and Cairo are large cities not merely because they happen to be trade and manufacturing centers but also because they are the foci of political forces; for the nonce we must accept this political centrality as a factor that influences the way an underdeveloped economy functions. But policy shculd concern itself with the question of whether the persistent process of superurbanization should be encouraged or restrained. The problem is one of proportion. How large should the great cities be in relation to other central places in order to insure a tolerable macroeconomic functioning of the total economy of which they are such strategic parts?

The economic aspect of this puzzle is perhaps partly amenable to appraisal inasmuch as certain polarizing factors can be isolated and

5. "In a typical process of 'development' the backward people have to contend with three types of monopolistic forces: in their role as unskilled labour they have to face the big foreign mining and plantation concerns who are monopolistic buyers of their labour; in their role as peasant producers they have to face a small group of exporting and processing firms who are monopolistic buyers of their crop; and in the role of consumers of imported commodities they have to face the same group of firms who are the monopolistic sellers or distributors of these commodities," H. Myint, "An Interpretation of Economic Backwardness," in A. N. Agarwala and S. P. Singh, *The Economics of Underdevelopment,* London, 1958, p. 122.

6. The abandonment of parliamentary forms of government by so many states recently "liberated" from colonial control attests either to the need for military elements in their governmental systems or to the incapacity of people to resist the militarization of their governments. For illustrations one need only notice the political trends over the past decade in Burma, Korea, Pakistan, Irak, Egypt, Congo, Nigeria, and many other countries.

analyzed. Moreover, by means of appropriate counterfactual assumptions, some of the economic consequences of a drift of rural population to great cities can be at least fractionally measured.[7] First a few words about the influence of linear forms of transport on the costs of goods movements and the resultant polarizing effects.[8] More than anything else it has been railways that have enlarged, or even created, large cities. This is because each railway line constitutes a traffic axis along which traffic (and therefore trade) can flow more cheaply in a linear path than it can be diffused over an economic landscape. Some "spread effect," to use Myrdal's terminology,[9] can be achieved by branch lines, but since such lines will have lighter traffic than the main lines, the unit costs of transport on the branch lines will be higher, and these relatively higher transport costs will operate to the disadvantage of the producers and consumers outside the belts of influence of main lines.[10] Moreover, railway builders instinctively conceive of branch lines not as independent transport routes but as the means of feeding more traffic into main lines, thus creating a unified transport system which accents polarized development at the great city terminals.[11]

7. A very earnest effort to do this has been made by Jal F. Bulsara in his *Problems of Rapid Industrialization in India. Being a Memorandum based on the findings of the socio-economic surveys of nine Indian cities, viz., Baroda, Gorakhpur, Hubli, Hyderabad-Secunderbad, Jamshedpur, Kanpur, Lucknow, Poona and Surat, carried out by various authors under the auspices of the Research Programmes Committee of the Planning Commission of India,* Bombay, 1964, to which reference will be made throughout this chapter.

8. This problem was analyzed with care quite some time ago by J. Edwin Holmstrom in his *Railways and Roads in Pioneer Development Overseas: A Study of Their Comparative Economics,* London, 1934, a seminal work that has been strangely ignored by most writers on economic development. The term "polarize," as Holmstrom points out in this work, is derived from the language of physics wherein "a material is said to be polarized when its properties along one dimension differ from those along another dimension" (p. 265).

9. Gunnar Myrdal, *Economic Theory and Underdeveloped Regions,* London, 1957, pp. 31–32.

10. The higher costs will be reflected in the lower profitability of branch lines as compared with main lines if the same tariffs are charged as on main lines.

11. Holmstrom, citing A. M. Wellington's *The Economic Theory of the Location of Railways,* New York, 1914, points out that the economic considerations underlying the location of branch lines "differ fundamentally from those of main lines." The chief goal in locating a branch line should be "to strike the main line as soon as possible and enjoy the benefit of the reduced costs which result thereon from higher traffic density." Moreover, main lines cannot profitably be built into areas of low population density because of "Wellington's well-known law that traffic varies as the square of the tributary population per mile of line." *Railways and Roads,* p. 265–266.

Although modern highways can and do provide an increasing volume of linear traffic and consequently have certain polarizing effects, a road system "is not a line having only one dimension, but a network having in effect two dimensions along either of which (or along any component of which) the ease of transportation is not greatly different."[12] Whether the potential spread effects of a road system will be realized depends, of course, on whether the road-building authorities do or do not develop a road network rather than a road axis. All too much money has been spent by less-developed countries in connecting large cities by means of paved roads, and entirely too little has been allocated to building a network of roads that can help commercialize and invigorate rural landscapes,[13] and at the same time stimulate the development of many smaller, multisized urban communities rather than a few turgescent cities, thus increasing the spread effects of given amounts of investment. For it should be noted that roads have a technical-financial advantage over railways. Because a railway cannot operate without a graded and ballasted roadway, or without bridges, rails, ties, switches, "back-shops," stations, marshaling yards, nor, of course, without locomotives and cars, the whole apparatus—the "way" and the "works," to use British engineering terms—must be concurrently provided, involving an initial cost per mile that may be inordinately high in relation to the initial volume of traffic. In the case of a road, the investment in the "way" may be gradually increased as the traffic grows,[14] thus obviating the tying up of capital in underutilized transport capacity[15] and releasing the saved capital for other high-priority uses. In the majority of underdeveloped

12. Ibid., p. 266. It is, of course, possible to visualize roads that are unidimensional. As Holmstrom observes, a single trunk road "passing through an otherwise impenetrable jungle" might have polarizing effects comparable to those of a railway. Ibid., p. 267.

13. In India less than 25 percent of funds appropriated for public roads were spent on farm-to-market or other rural network roads. See E. A. J. Johnson, *Market Towns and Spatial Development in India,* New Delhi, 1965, p. 149.

14. Traffic may begin moving over smoothed earth roads, crossing creeks by paved fords. As traffic increases, increments of investment may be made pari passu in the form of ballasting, bridging, paving, reduction of gradients, widening, and other means.

15. The Yugoslav government built in the late 1940's a paved road from Belgrade to Zagreb, a distance of 250 miles. So few vehicles used this road for the next decade that on a strict cost, maintenance, and depreciation calculation, the use of the road (in 1953) by each car involved a social cost of $276 per one-way trip. See my "Problems of 'Forced Draft' Industrialization," in *Contributions and Communications,* First International Conference of Economic History, Paris, 1960, p. 484n.

countries, the potential spread effects of road transport have been very feebly realized, while the polarizing effects of old railways are being exacerbated by the additive polarizing effects of intercity highways. As a consequence, the movement of goods, capital, people, and entrepreneurship to great cities continues, unwittingly leading to frightening and seemingly unmanageable social problems and furthering an unwanted structural dichotomy, which economists have labelled a "dual economy."

Some Social and Economic Consequences of Polarized Urbanization

There is a widespread belief in underdeveloped countries that poor countries are poor because they are inadequately urbanized—an all too common example of "misplaced concreteness." It is of course quite true that in "advanced countries" a much larger fraction of the population is urban than is the case in underdeveloped countries. Thus, India with less than 18 percent of the population "urbanized" in 1950 was admittedly not as "developed" as the United States with 64 percent urbanized by the same type of measurement.[16] But it does not follow that urbanization will by some automatic process necessarily lead to "development"; it is entirely conceivable that certain types of urbanization may actually arrest rather than stimulate development. More than one Asian or African country is discovering that a planless drift of workers in the prime years of their potential productiveness to sprawling, slum-cursed cities, where huge manpower reserves already exist, may mean not only a tragic misuse of human resources but an equally prodigal wastage of scarce capital by reason of unwarranted pressures on all varieties of municipal facilities. Maintenance, repair, and depreciation costs accelerate; the costs of public surveillance, sanitation, and welfare escalate at rates wholly out of proportion to the growth in the public-revenue yielding capacity of the urban economy. The presumed beneficence of urbanization is not very evident in Manila, Jakarta, or Calcutta!

What Lord Bacon said about money can be said about urbanization.[17] It all depends how the urban structure is distributed in a functionally spatial pattern. And there are, as John P. Lewis has pointed out, "cen-

16. Namely, the fraction of population living in places with more than 2,500 people.

17. "Money is like muck, not good unless spread."

tering alternatives open to a developing economy" which "constitute a continuum that stretches from the smallest villages to the largest metropolis."[18] The trouble is that so little attention has been paid by planning or executive governmental authorities to the possibilities of controlling, directing, and manipulating the movement of population in terms of some visualized pattern of central-place urbanization. In most developing countries the process, wittingly or unwittingly, has actually been the very opposite. On the presumption that industrialization is good for all countries and particularly beneficial to economies with endemic underemployment, far-reaching programs of planned investment in selected "key" industries have been launched. A very large number of the resulting new enterprises tend to be established in or near existing large cities to obtain locational advantages, particularly from transport and external economies.[19] But in computing these locational advantages virtually no consideration has been given to the total macroeconomic costs that may be involved. Thus an enterprise need not consider as a cost the probability that it may soon contribute to an overloading of a city's housing, its sewage system, or its capacity to generate electric power; and because cost-benefit analysis has not been employed, the new firms are not asked to bear any special responsibility for the rapidly rising costs of fire protection, police, sanitation, public health, and water supply. They may actually be exempted from tax liability for a number of years.[20]

The serious social and economic incidence of India's unplanned population drift to large cities has been described and partially measured in Bulsara's study of nine large municipal areas, chosen as samples of regional urbanization, together with Bombay as an illustration of the even more acute problems of great cities.[21] All these ten cities expanded very rapidly during the first half of the nineteenth century, some doubling, others tripling, and one (Jamshedpur) increased its population almost fortyfold. After liberation the townward drift was complicated by a massive refugee problem, and the crush of urban-

18. *Quiet Crisis in India,* New York, 1962, p. 171.

19. Enterprises located in or near Manila, for example, account for over 50 percent of the total industrial payroll in the Philippine Islands. See Aprodicio A. Laquian, *The City in Nation Building: Politics and Administration in Metropolitan Manila,* Manila, 1966, p. 2.

20. How tax exemption has been more wisely used as an effective stimulus to overall development in Puerto Rico is explained in Chapter 9.

21. *Problems of Rapid Industrialization.*

ization quickened so much that in the single decade 1951–1961 Bombay's population increased 46 percent, while that of the nine provincial cities grew by 38 percent. Since India's overall population growth during this period was about 15 percent, it is clear that these ten cities were growing 2½ to 3 times as fast.

With what consequences? Most easily measured are the changes in social structure. The city population becomes steadily more masculine, thereby altering the nation's work force composition, directly in cities, inversely in rural areas.[22] Moreover, a disproportionate fraction of the city-dwelling males are in the 16–45 age bracket—not a cause for complaint if these most productive years are well utilized, but, unfortunately, this was not what the Indian investigators found. Whereas the overall unemployment figures were not dangerously high,[23] the percentage of unemployment that fell on the "Freshers," as recent arrivals are called, has been shockingly high, ranging from a low of 33.4 percent (Surat) to a high of 52.8 percent (Gorakhpur).[24] Unemployment is not a brief or transient experience; 73.7 percent of men out of work in Lucknow had been unemployed for more than a year, as had 70 percent in Surat, 46.2 percent in Gorakhpur, and 38.5 percent in Kanpur.[25] Since the largest fraction of the migrants to the cities consisted of males in the 16–40 age bracket, and since the heaviest and longest unemployment was consistently found in this "Fresher" age bracket, the wastage of the productive power of these men in the very prime of their life must be considered a serious national loss attributable to a planless cityward drift.

Although it is not possible to measure all the counterproductive results of this unbalanced urbanization, a few more aspects are revealed by the Indian evidence. If literacy is some measure of a person's potential usefulness in a nation's development program, then accelerated urbanization is failing to utilize the fruits of education. The in-migrants who suffer so disproportionately from unemployment have a higher

22. In Calcutta the number of males per 1,000 females increased in four years (1954–1958) from 1,595 to 1,876; in Bombay 78.8 percent of the immigrants (1961) were males; in Kanpur males outnumbered females by 25 percent, in Lucknow by 20 percent (India, Office of the Registrar General, *Census of India, 1960*). Bulsara, *Problems of Rapid Industrialization*, pp. 8–9.

23. The range was from 4.3 percent of the "employable" in Hyderabad-Secunderabad to 7.8 percent in Baroda. Ibid., p. 25.

24. Percentage of "Freshers" among the total unemployed.

25. Bulsara, *Problems of Rapid Industrialization*, p. 57.

literacy rate than the (more fully employed) town dwellers.[26] Moreover, the incidence of unemployment is higher among the educated and highest among migrants who hold secondary school certificates.[27] Since the majority of migrants have come from rural areas,[28] the townward drift acts as a "brain-drain," luring from farming areas and small towns the talents and the energy of the young people that are so urgently needed in rural areas and so ineffectually utilized in the large cities.[29]

One distressing consequence of the rush to cities in India and in other Asian cities is the inadequacy of housing. The Bulsara report revealed that single-room tenements sheltered 77 percent of the population of Bombay and 67.3 percent in Kanpur. Smaller cities were not so crowded: Surat had 33 percent in single room tenements, Hubli only 27.4 percent. The actual crowding would, of course, depend on the size of the rooms and the number of occupants, and here the data are truly depressing. Seven to ten persons to a room was not an atypical finding, and about 30 square feet of room space per person (an area 4 x 7½ feet) seems to be the usual allotment.[30] Even more indicative of the hardships that result from overurbanization is the inadequacy of facilities for cleanliness and for the maintenance of public health. In Kanpur, for example, only 9.3 percent of the tenements had water taps of their own, only 23.6 percent had latrines, and only 5.3 percent were provided with electric lights.[31] The lack of facilities was, of course, complete for the 70,000 pavement dwellers. The Town and Village Planning Depart-

26. Ibid., pp. 20, 35.

27. Ibid., p. 55.

28. The percentage of migrants into Bombay from rural areas was 78.3 percent. For the other nine cities see Bulsara, *Problems of Rapid Industrialization,* p. 28, Table XLV.

29. It may be well to recall that developing European countries were often careful to conserve their human resources. Thus in sixteenth-century England, convicted literate criminals were exempt from the death penalty because of their presumed national usefulness; Ben Jonson was saved from the gallows when he took a proffered book, and "read like a clerk."

30. In Gorakhpur, where 48 percent of the households live in single rooms, only 16 percent had as much as 50 sq. ft. per person. In Jamshedpur 55.6 percent of the families has only 30.33 sq. ft. per person. For other unpleasant details, see Bulsara, *Problems of Rapid Industrialization,* p. 65. In the eight largest Indian cities the density per room ranged from a low of 3.84 to a high of 4.79. India, Office of the Registrar General, *Census of India, 1961.*

31. Agnihotri, V. B., *Survey of Labour Housing and Overcrowding in Kanpur,* Lucknow, 1954. Households without independent water taps ranged from a low of 54 percent (Surat) to a high of 87.6 percent in the other eight cities covered by the Bulsara study.

ment of the Uttar Pradesh Government believes this figure will more than double by 1991.

This vignette of the social and economic hardships caused by unplanned polarized urbanization suggests some fairly clear policy implications. For the evidence rather consistently shows that the larger the city, the worse the conditions. In Hubli (population 171,326) only 13 percent of houses were without bathing facilities, whereas in Baroda (population 298,398) the fraction was 65.8 percent, and in Lucknow (population 594,440) the figure was 86.4 percent. Or, taking another test, in Hyderabad-Secunderabad (population 1,251,159) only 43 percent of families were without independent kitchen facilities, whereas in Bombay (population 4,152,056) the corresponding figure was 71.4 percent.[32] Only in the provision of electric energy for lighting did the great cities show a better record than the smaller ones, but this is a rather special situation that has peculiar political overtones.[33]

In practically all less-developed countries the trend is the same. Relatively fewer migrants now go short distances to nearby towns and relatively more move longer distances to metropolitan centers. Some undoubtedly earn more in cities than they did before and have more variety in their pattern of consumption, but whether they have achieved a better, fuller, more useful life is by no means certain. There is indisputable evidence of physical, mental, and moral deterioration.[34] The causes are not hard to find; there has been no preparation in the cities for this flood tide of migrants, no planning to control the resulting urban sprawl, no adequate fiscal provision to meet the escalating costs of municipal services, no appropriate increase in personnel to cope with increasing crime and juvenile delinquency. Because these social costs have been ignored by most macroeconomic planners, the migration of people from rural villages and small towns has been "uncontrolled, unregulated, unchecked and unguided,"[35] a cruel process of disorderly social change that has led to the waste of vast amounts of productive

32. India, Office of the Registrar General, *Census of India, 1960*.

33. The uneconomic distribution of electric energy in underdeveloped countries is considered in Chapter 8.

34. In Calcutta, where the population is about 65 percent male and 35 percent female, over 10 percent of the female income earners list prostitution as their occupation. In Kanpur there are virtually no recreational areas for the slum-dwelling and pavement-dwelling children; land set aside for recreational use is less than ½ of 1 percent of the municipal area.

35. Bulsara, *Problems of Rapid Industrialization*, p. 128.

energy and creativity, which could have been utilized for constructive developmental tasks. Worst of all, the unchanneled drift of people to the relatively few cities has frustrated and counteracted any prospects of a diffused type of orderly urbanization whereby a vitalization of rural landscapes could be set in motion by the location of new industrial establishments, processing plants, and service industries at carefully selected growth points. It has allowed the nations that most urgently need an organically integrated regional development to weaken the links between town and country and allow an unplanned dual economy to emerge.

Spatial Aspects of Economic Dualism

Economic development is never a uniform meliorative process. Even in advanced and mature countries there are persistent backwaters such as Appalachia in the United States,[36] or the *Mezzogiorno* in Italy;[37] and in developing countries preferential policy efforts to homogenize the regional rates of economic development have usually failed despite the disproportionate assistance given to the laggard or disadvantaged regions.[38] A whole series of factors are responsible for these differing rates of development. Some regions may be poor in resources, or their people may suffer from endemic diseases which weaken them and reduce their productive capacity. Associated with such resource deficiencies are other root causes: low rates of capital formation, inadequate education or training of the work force, inefficient scales of production. All these factors, by compounding their effects, eventuate in low productivity. Regional growth differentials must therefore be expected; the policy problem is not how to eliminate these differences, since that is probably impossible, but how to reduce them, if that can possibly be done, and how to prevent them from becoming wider.

36. "An oblong patch of mountains and misery, stretching from a corner of Mississippi on the south to a corner of New York at its northern end. For at least a century it had been distinguished mostly for having the densest concentration of poverty in America, and since World War II it had been getting worse." John Fisher, "Can Ralph R. Widner Save New York, Chicago, and Detroit?" *Harper's Magazine,* October 1968, p. 17.

37. "Estimates of the regional distribution of national income indicate that, taken per head of the whole population, income in the *Mezzogiorno* in the 1950's was not much above 45 percent of that in the North." Vera Lutz, *Italy: A Study in Economic Development,* London, 1962, p. 91.

38. In Yugoslavia, despite the preferences accorded to Montenegro and Macedonia, growth rates have been much higher in Croatia and Slovenia.

With the very best of intentions, all too many developing countries have embarked on investment policies that are widening rather than narrowing regional differences. This is largely because they have over-theorized their planning and neglected to consider the spatial consequences of their investment programs. No one will quarrel with the thesis that the main object of planning in underdeveloped countries should be "to increase the total amount of investment aimed at raising the productive powers of the country."[39] But it is not enough to allocate the intended investment between economic sectors or to distribute the funds between new plants, infrastructure, housing, public health, and education.[40] It is fully as necessaary to select the geographical places where the investments are to be made, and these critically important decisions have too frequently been left to logrolling politicians.

As an illustration of what can happen when the spatial aspects of investment are not carefully considered, the Indian experience with industrial estates is rather pathetically instructive. Because industrial estates had proved to be useful means for establishing new manufacturing enterprises in Canada, Ireland, Puerto Rico, and elsewhere, the Government of India, beginning in 1955, decided to "programme" industrial estates in their development "Plans."[41] Provision was made for 10 estates in the First Plan (1951–1956), for 87 in the Second Plan (1956–1961), and for 300 in the Third Plan (1961–1966).[42] From the

39. Myrdal, *Economic Theory*, pp. 80–81.

40. "The concentration on national income accounts as a tool of development policy has blotted out the crucial significance of the regional element in national planning . . . and the newly evolving nations of Africa, Latin America, and Asia are beginning to appreciate the fact that national investment strategies require a sub-aggregation along regional lines." John Friedmann, *Regional Development Policy: A Case Study of Venezuela*, Cambridge, Mass., 1966, pp. 3, 5.

41. Although privately financed "industrial parks" are widely employed in developed countries to obtain advantages of agglomeration, in developing countries "industrial estates" represent a deliberate blending of public and private investment. Governments usually provide production facilities (sheds, warehouses, offices, yards, ingress roads, railway sidings, and loading piers) together with the needed public utilities (e.g., water, gas, electric power), thus relieving the private entrepreneurs (who can rent the proffered production facilities) from the necessity of locking up their limited capital in fixed plant and leaving them free to devote all their resources to machinery, inventories, and working capital. For further details see my *Market Towns and Spatial Development in India*, pp. 80–93. The role that industrial estates can play in developing, or creating, agro-urban communities is further considered in Chapter 7.

42. Only one of the 10 programmed estates had been completed when the First Plan ended in 1956; hence the other 9 were carried over into the Second Plan, making the estates in the Second Plan total 96.

moment the new venture was announced sharp disagreement arose about the location of the structures. The initial decisions, made by the respective planning authorities of the state governments, were to locate most of the industrial estates near large cities (e.g., Delhi, Madurai, Madras, Allahabad, Hyderabad), thus contributing to the rampant urban sprawl which was already giving rise to such vexing social and economic problems. A few estates were located near medium-sized cities, but no clear and consistent policy of spatial development had been formulated which could serve as a reference against which locational decisions could be tested. This lack of a clear "spatial dimension" led to a blundering procedure, which very seriously reduced the contribution to India's development program that this type of investment might have yielded.[43] When the political representatives of smaller communities protested loud and strong against the way in which large cities had grabbed a lion's share of the Second Plan funds allotted for industrial estates, an even more impulsive decision was made to locate a majority of Third Plan estates in rural communities, many of which were ill-equipped in terms of transport, public utilities, man power, and entrepreneurship to utilize the "sunk costs" so carelessly and cavalierly allocated. The consequence was that a hasty attempt to offset the trend toward economic dualism largely misfired and resulted in a further waste of resources that capital-poor India could ill afford.[44]

The trend toward economic polarization in great cities cannot be so easily averted by a random scattering of investment throughout an economic landscape, with locational decisions impulsively made by politicians wholly unprepared or unwilling to engage in the kind of studies needed for wise and perspicacious spatial investment choices. This is a really complex task that calls for technical judgment involving geographic, economic, sociological, and other scientific aspects of prospective "growth points." The resolution of such problems calls for

43. "Any development plan has a spatial dimension in the sense that each newly established installation or activity requires a locational decision." Lewis, *Quiet Crisis in India,* p. 167.

44. The average utilization for 3,540 sheds (as of 30 June 1964) was only 67.1 percent, a clearly unsatisfactory performance except for four states which had creditable records (Delhi, 91.7; Madras, 88.2; Andhra Pradesh, 83.9; and Gujarat, 79.3). The utilization rate in "rural locations" (places with less than 5,000 persons) was only 62.6 percent, but even worse was the occupancy in medium-sized communities (places with from 5,000 to 50,000 persons), where only 52.4 percent of the sheds were being used by functioning enterprises. For further details see my *Market Towns and Spatial Development in India,* pp. 83–87.

planners properly trained, experienced, and motivated. Yet for all the specialized aspects of the work, the basic challenge to planners in underdeveloped countries is essentially philosophical. The task is to visualize a process of transformation that will widen the occupational opportunities for millions of village-born young people, increase total employment, and give greater scope for the adventurous and the ambitious without overpopulating the already exploding few large cities. In countries as densely populated as India, for example, the relief which migration to large cities can bring to rural areas is really quite insignificant,[45] while the planless urban concentration of very imperfectly utilized man power creates problems that are rapidly becoming unmanageable.[46] It should be apparent that the uncritically assessed assumption that urban industrialization will gradually "modernize" the economies of the "third world" is a baneful variety of romanticism which needs to be exposed not only for its naïvité but for its inherently mischievous consequences.

The deliberate or unwitting polarization of industry, trade, professions, and service industries in large cities is rapidly dividing underdeveloped countries into two societies which are "separate and unequal." To the large cities are lured the abler, brighter, more courageous, venturesome, and creative, leaving the less fit, the duller, more timid, and tradition-bound in the villages, which are so urgently in need of modernization. This unfortunate dualism, so aptly described[47] by

45. Even if the annual migration to cities were 10 million persons, and even if every migrant came from a rural village, such a massive movement could reduce the village population only by about 2.3 percent; and if the annual population increase continues at the current rate of 2½ percent, the net relief could be almost zero.

46. Calcutta is an example of a metropolitan area whose municipal facilities are so overstrained that the maintenance of minimal health, sanitation, and security has become virtually impossible. For a very charitable appraisal see S. N. Sen, *The City of Calcutta,* Calcutta, 1960. It is not only large Indian cities that face these problems stemming from overimmigration. Manila "with its 2.7 million people needs an estimated 300 million gallons daily of clean water, approximately 1,150,000 cubic meters per day. The best that the city's waterworks system can offer is 170 [million gallons] (650,000 cubic meters). Even this needs a near miraculous straining of the system's capacity for it was originally built to serve only 700,000 people." For more and equally frightening evidence of the overstraining of housing, police, transportation and sanitation facilities, see Aprodicio A. Laquian, *The City in Nation Building: Politics and Administration in Metropolitan Manila,* Manila, 1966, pp. 53–72.

47. "Most disturbing of all, metropolitan-centering maximizes India's drift toward the condition of a polarized 'dual society.' . . . one cannot escape the dichotomy between the new and the old, the scientific and the traditional, the experimental and the fatalistic, the achievement-oriented and the status-dominated. Instead of

John P. Lewis, constitutes the major unwanted by-product of a misguided attempt to emulate what has been mistakenly believed to be the process whereby developed countries modernized their economies. But, as was explained in Chapter 2, the countries that succeeded in expanding and restructuring the industrial components of their economies were the very ones that had first commercialized their major agrarian areas (unfortunately not all) by a network of interrelated market towns, of which a great many became progressively more complex, industrial, commercial, financial, and agricultural-processing centers. This hierarchy of multipurpose central places, which in older industrial economies admittedly emerged by a rather wasteful process, has been strangely overlooked in the macroeconomic blueprints of most of the third-world planners.[48]

What are the alternatives to the threatening economic dualism, with stagnant villages as one dimension, teeming great cities as the other? To visualize alternatives takes no burst of creativity, but to do so critically and constructively calls for a searching re-examination of the preconceptions that lie behind a planned modernization program. Moreover, it takes considerable courage to recognize and admit that a backward country may never become "modern," efficient, truly productive, and capable of providing any significant change in the standard of living for its people unless drastic changes are made in the reorganization of economic space. This means that the beneficiaries of the old order must, in some way, be stripped of their advantages or their inherited privileges. It should also be recognized that the migration of the abler young people to the cities provides the entrepreneurs in great cities with cheap, docile labor, and it should not be forgotten that if the local monopoly of village traders, money lenders, and landlords is unchallenged by the competition of regulated markets, banks, and small-scale manufacturers in some larger agro-urban center, the time-sanctioned exploitation of the village poor will continue indefinitely.

---

narrowing and bridging this gap, metropolitan centering widens it by tending to polarize the demographic spectrum. Its effect is to gather the progressive elements in the society into metropolitan concentrations that, in terms of income and ideas, pull farther and farther away from the traditional rural mass." *Quiet Crisis in India,* p. 178.

48. This is not true of Puerto Rico, where spatial aspects of development were perceived when undue polarization began to strain municipal facilities in San Juan and in Ponce; nor is it true of Yugoslavia, where the failure of a Russian type of program for a townless countryside was jeopardizing the vitality of the entire agrarian sector of the economy until it was recognized, in 1952, that a wholly new spatial pattern was necessary. For further details see pp. 282–285, 318–319.

Alternatives to Polarized Dualism

The indifference in most underdeveloped countries to the social costs of creeping economic dualism exists, in my opinion, for four principal reasons. The first is the temptation to visualize all aspects of development in terms of macroeconomic models, the assumptions apparently being that, if this methodology is serviceable in developed countries, it must, ipso facto, be equally useful for the less developed and that any structural differences (such as the absence of enough market towns) are unimportant.[49] A second reason seems to be a belief in industrialization not as a mundane productive process but as a redemptive mystique—a form of veneration which invests large-scale automation with mysterious transforming powers regardless of where particular plants may be located. The all-important consideration is to have a steel mill, an aircraft factory, or a machine tool industry; the exact locations can presumably be determined by a few technical desiderata, and if these happen to be satisfied by a site in or near a large city, there should be no objection. A third reason has already been mentioned: the emulative desire to attain the demographic patterns of the more developed countries, wherein urban populations have progressively grown as a percentage of total population while rural population fractions have declined. Here the assumption is rather pathetically simplistic, namely, that urban polarization will automatically help modernize an economy. The fourth reason is the most troublesome, particularly because it has become so fashionable in the swiftly crystallizing folklore of development. This is the contention that the inherited village structure of underdeveloped countries is quintessentially good, culturally, morally, and spiritually, and should therefore be preserved.[50]

49. "Anyone who has lingered in those New Delhi offices where the Third Five Year Plan outlines were being fitted together . . . could only judge that most of the key planners were relatively unexcited about the average geographical scale of developmental activities. They acted as though they thought either that they had other more important things to worry about, or that there was comparatively little . . . they could do . . . to control this aspect of the development pattern." John P. Lewis, *Quiet Crisis in India,* p. 168.

50. There is a huge literature concerning this cult of the village community, some based on scientific study by well-trained and seasoned sociologists and anthropologists, some based on village dimensions by protagonists of community development, and a great deal that is sentimental and essentially romantic. Joel Martin Halpern, *A Serbian Village,* New York, 1958, is a good example of the first type; *Approaches to Community Development: A Symposium Introductory to Problems and Methods of Village Welfare in Underdeveloped Areas,* ed. Phillips Ruopp, The Hague, 1953, of the second; and William H. and Charlotte V. Wiser, *Behind Mud*

Presumably village organization conserves the wisdom of centuries and provides an essential stability and cultural continuity without which a society would disintegrate into a condition of confusion and chaos. Out of this admiration for village values arises a schizophrenic attitude toward social change: admittedly the nation must be "modernized," but the inherited village structure must be preserved; most certainly the nation's standard of living must be raised, but the small scale of village economic activity is not considered to be a serious constraint on the requisite improvement in per man productivity. This compartmentalized variety of thinking is reinforced by some quite evident political considerations. A political party that hopes to acquire and retain control over the machinery of government in a village-structured society must have the support of village leaders. What better tactic for the politician than to assure these leaders that no social change is contemplated which will in any way weaken or erode their local authority? As a consequence, a self-deceiving political program is promulgated. Local government, so long controlled by village landlords, traders, and usurers, will be "democratized," thereby inaugurating a new era in village life which will release creative energy and make moribund villages dynamic instruments of constructive social change.

The only thing wrong with this blissful thesis is that by reason of their inherited privileges, consisting of landownership, trade monopoly, and a powerful creditor position in village communities, it will be the landlords, traders, and usurers who will be elected to the village offices, who will control the village cooperatives, and dominate the village councils. *Plus ça change, plus c'est la même chose.* For however well intentioned the regional development planners and the architects of a brave new world of small-scale village industries may be, they will have to obtain the approval of the old village regime if their programs are to be more than paper plans. The theoretically restructured democratic village is therefore largely a fiction. It is not and never will be a realistic counterpoise to the powerful centripetal force of municipal polarity. For a single village, as Lewis has so wisely said, cannot "hope to supply the managerial skills, the financial, professional, and business services or the social overheads and amenities needed to serve any significant array of industrial activities." Nor can the indi-

---

Walls, Berkeley, 1963, of the third type. More than anyone else Gandhi spread this quasi-religious cult of the village. See M. K. Gandhi, *Village Swaraj,* Ahmedabad, 1962, which summarizes his views.

vidual village "meet the minimum-scale requirements of many modern agricultural processing operations."[51] In spite of all the sentiment, idealism, and empathy that have characterized the many sincere efforts to make transformed villages the means for rural reconstruction of underdeveloped countries, these programs will never succeed. The modernization of developing countries calls for spatial economic units larger in size than villages and their minuscule hinterlands; it demands technical, organizational, and business leadership which the village landlords, petty traders, and usurers cannot possibly supply.

It seems clear, then, that what is needed to moderate, blunt, reduce, and, ultimately, check the planless drift of a nation's best man power to great sprawling, slum-infested cities is the development of graduated hierarchies comprising towns, small cities, and medium-sized cities that can become production, trade, and service centers offering employment and other opportunities for young people who now are migrating to large cities. But whereas it is easy enough to recognize the need for a recentering of economic activity, finding a solution for this problem is very difficult for the simple reason that the existing number of central places is entirely inadequate, and any program contemplating a wholesale town-building operation looks like a town planner's dream because the fiscal burden involved would seem to be completely unmanageable in virtually every poor country.[52] Yet the problem cannot be swept under the rug, and planners sooner or later must face this enigma with intelligence and imagination. How this complex, costly, but necessary infrastructure could be gradually created by a flexible, phased program of joint public and private endeavor is discussed in subsequent chapters. For the moment it need only be pointed out that the first tasks must be to identify the number of central places that will be needed, to set up proper tests for the

51. *Quiet Crisis in India,* p. 174.

52. In India (1960 Census) there were only 2,690 urban centers with populations larger than 2,500 people. Of these, 248 were cities with populations ranging from 50,000 to over 4 million. Of the remaining 2,442 centers, 515 were cities with populations from 20,000 to 50,000 leaving only 1,927 smaller market towns. Since it is these smaller towns that are normally most closely linked with village communities, the complete inadequacy of their number becomes apparent when one considers that there are 564,718 villages in India. One town for every 293 villages does not constitute a satisfactory spatial pattern! Only a small number of villages (about 20 to 35) actually have any real functional relations with a market town, which means that the vast majority of Indian villages have only a shadowlike connection with the urban economy, the industrial economy, or the world economy.

selection of promising growth points, and to lay plans for a coordinated and phased program that will coagulate many types of capital formation, made by both public and private agencies, into seminal "investment clusters," which can become the nuclei for new agro-urban communities.

Such a program must look forward to new spatial designs, properly adapted to topography and resources, to climate, cropping patterns, cultural differences, and other factors that will have to be carefully evaluated in the requisite regional planning. It should envisage a new type of dispersed industrialization, not the random scattering of new plants that politicians advocate in order to share in developmental patronage but a well-planned grouping of industries in or near towns or small cities that will "supply the necessary frame for the whole network of development sequences, linkages, and feedbacks upon which the successful transformation of the . . . countryside so largely depends."[53] Temporarily, such a policy of dispersed industrialization would need to make only modest demands for housing and other amenities since many workers could continue to live in their homes in nearby villages.[54] Electric energy, transport facilities, and other required utilities would have to be provided, however, and this would call for a much more selective infrastructural program than is needed when the serving of emergent growth points is not a major policy consideration. Yet this might not make a transport program or an electrification program much more expensive; from a developmental standpoint a great deal of resources are now very poorly utilized in supplying electric energy to household consumers, and a reconsideration of priorities for public utilities could sharply reduce these less important uses and release energy for productive purposes.[55]

53. Lewis, *Quiet Crisis in India,* pp. 179–180.

54. This is not a mere supposition. My findings in 1964 were that in some progressive South Indian industrial estates as large a fraction of the work force as 30 percent commuted from their village homes. See my *Market Towns and Spatial Development in India,* Appendix 2. In Puerto Rico there is even greater mobility.

55. It is saddening to realize that countries in serious need of electric energy for production (e.g., lifting water, driving mills, pressing oil) are often using electric current for consumption purposes in comparatively prodigal volume. In India, for example, the household consumption of electric energy amounts to 70 percent of output contrasted with 25 percent in the United States. For details see National Council of Applied Economic Research, *Demand for Energy in India, 1960–1975,* New Delhi, 1960, p. 8.

Central-Place Inadequacy in Underdeveloped Countries

There is a really astonishing difference between developed and underdeveloped countries in their relative number of central places and in the dispersion of these towns, small cities, medium-sized urban centers, and still larger cities. In the developed countries the varied hierarchy of central places has not only made possible an almost complete commercialization of agriculture[56] but has facilitated a wide spatial diffusion of light manufacturing, processing, and service industries. These establishments provide employment of a differentiated variety, thereby utilizing the manual dexterity and skill of some workers as well as the care, precision, and judgment of others engaged in clerical, administrative, and executive duties. As a consequence, a much fuller use can be made of a nation's total work force, and, with a wider choice of occupations, the chances are that work will be more suited to strength, aptitude, and latent ability, thus making tasks easier and more pleasurable.

The relative lack of such a central-place infrastructure in underdeveloped countries leads to serious handicaps. Because the countryside is inadequately provided with accessible market centers where farm produce can readily be sold and where shops filled with consumer and producer goods can exert their tempting "demonstration effects," the incentives to produce more for the market and the inducement to invest in better tools, fertilizers, or better livestock in order to generate a larger marketable surplus are weak.[57] Moreover, it sometimes happens that, when prices rise, farmers in poor underdeveloped areas instead of selling more may actually sell less farm produce.[58]

56. In the United States farming has become so commercialized and so thoroughly specialized that producers of fluid milk find it more economical to buy their cream and butter rather than separate some of their milk and churn their own butter.

57. In Kanpur a small factory that produces excellent, low-priced farm tools is unable to sell more than 5 percent of its output in India. It is nothing short of a tragic paradox that this backward portion of India, which needs improved farm tools and implements so badly and which can produce them, should find it necessary to seek a market for plows, cultivators, harrows, and water-lifting machines in Africa.

58. Shao-er Ong, a very astute and knowledgeable expert on Asian small farm practices, explained to me that small Asian farmers have a quite different set of goals than commercial farmers in developed countries. Because their farms are very small, the first object must be to obtain the largest productivity per unit of land in

These "backward bending supply curves" suggest that debt-harassed small farmers have probably been forced to sell more than they can really spare, and consequently, if prices rise, they can, by alienating less produce, receive the same cash income as before and in the meantime have more food for themselves and their hungry families.[59] This tendency to reduce rather than to increase the marketed surplus cannot be considered irrational conduct as far as the poverty-racked small farmer is concerned, but to the extent that an inadequate marketing system generates indifference toward producing as much as possible for the market, the nonfarm portion of the national economy will have less produce available and must pay relatively more for the inadequate supply of farm produce that such an imperfect marketing mechanism can provide.

A second handicap that stems from an inadequate number and a faulty distribution of central places is rural unemployment, underemployment, and a wanton dissipation of ability and talent. In a developed country, well supplied with a hierarchy of towns and small cities, a farm boy with mechanical aptitude need not waste his talents on a farm, be underemployed, or face the risks of migrating to a distant large city in search of work. Within a range of ten or twenty miles he can most likely find employment in a garage, a printing plant, a machine shop, or a small furniture factory. By apprenticeship,

---

order to feed their families. And since the basic concern must always be with the security of the farm family, persistent efforts will be made to buy more land whenever possible and to raise a large enough family so that, by even more intensive use, the land will yield more produce. The sale of farm produce is therefore only an instrumental and secondary consideration, not a primary one. Cash income that is not needed for indispensable consumer goods is saved, with the hope that the family can, sooner or later, buy more land. But not quite all savings can be so used. Hemmed in by close neighbors, living in an agrarian economy where group action is regularly required for use of water, threshing machines, and other facilities, it is imperative that certain social obligations be met in order to insure congenial community relations. Consequently, the small Asian farmer does not really lack incentives to produce, since family responsibility provides this compulsion. The real difference between an Asian and a European farmer is that the latter has strong incentives to produce *for the market,* whereas the Asian farmer's marketing propensity is very much weaker.

59. The statistical evidence for this type of behavior in India has been assembled by Dharm Narain. See his *Distribution of the Marketed Surplus of Agricultural Produce by Size-Level of Holdings in India, 1950–51,* Institute of Economic Growth, Occasional Paper No. 2, New Delhi, 1961, p. 35. For a succinct analysis of "forced marketable surplus" see J. N. Chaturvedi, *The Theory of Marketing in Underdeveloped Countries,* Allahabad, 1959.

formal or informal, he will be trained in a short time for a nonfarm career, something that is being denied to thousands upon thousands of equally trainable young men in scores of underdeveloped countries. One reason for Japan's accelerating modernization was that so many of her young men before leaving rural areas were half-trained for the more demanding tasks in urban industry by reason of their employment in the smaller castle-town light manufacturing establishments, where they had already acquired "a certain quickness of hand and eye, a respect for tools and materials, [and] an adaptability to the cadences and confusion of moving parts."[60] Young people have no way of knowing what talents they may actually possess unless they have some opportunities for experimenting. If their lives are confined to a rural economy where the only thing visible on the horizon is a landscape of villages, their latent proficiencies, unperceived aptness, and unsuspected creativity may never be released.[61] Yet here is a vast repository of productive power which underdeveloped countries so signally need to use.

The foregoing handicaps—lack of strong incentives for increased output and waste of human resources—are only the most glaring consequences of an inadequate number of central places. There are many other unfortunate consequences. Since only marginal produce is sold by operators of near-subsistence farms, there need be no systematic adaptation of products to consumer wants. There is little or no quality control; hence the value of salable produce is low.[62] Without access to truly competitive markets, farmers can be victimized by monopsonistic village traders while their urgent need for cash income usually compels them to sell their produce immediately after harvest when prices are lowest. All these factors limit the income and thereby the saving and investment that farmers in underdeveloped countries can make, thus perpetuating a low-productivity type of technology. Until more and better market centers are developed there is no escape from

60. Thomas C. Smith, *Agrarian Origins of Modern Japan,* Stanford, 1959, p. 212.

61. Psychologists and anthropologists have convincingly demonstrated that inventive and innovative capacity is not unusual but is widely diffused. For a brief summary of their findings, see Abbot Payson Usher, *A History of Mechanical Inventions,* Boston, 1959, Chapters 1, 2, 3, and 4. On the need for releasing latent creativity, see Chapter 11 of this volume.

62. Contrast the ungraded apples, poultry, eggs, vegetables, and fruit sold in Indian markets with their counterparts in countries where quality control is used to keep a share of the market. For the producer who hopes to increase his part of market demand this control is steadily growing more exacting.

this web of chronic adversity. To evade the clutches of rapacious village monopsonists, travel over long distances may be necessary with increased transport costs neutralizing potential gains.[63] To reach any market at all is a time-consuming, labor-wasted practice in townless underdeveloped countries such as Nepal, where farmers spend not days but weeks carrying small quantities of farm produce to most unsatisfactory markets in India or Tibet to buy a little salt and a few other indispensable consumer goods.[64]

What rough tests can be employed to measure the deficiency of central places in the underdeveloped countries? Is there any proximate correlation between underurbanization and low per capita incomes? These awkward questions cannot much longer be burked. However crude the figures may be, however loose the comparisons or tentative and jejune the inferences, some global contrasts must be attempted in order to indicate, however provisionally, the need for a fresh new look at the whole problem of economic development, the need to recognize that development will require a spatial reconstruction of economic landscapes.

The only universal yardstick that seems useful in measuring the degrees of central-place abundance or deficiency is the ratio between villages on the one hand, towns and cities on the other. From the application of this test, it becomes quickly apparent that developed countries have a very low ratio. Thus, Table 5–1 shows that no European country has a higher village-town ratio than 1 town to every 72 villages (Austria), and in some countries the ratio is as low as 1 to 5 (Switzerland). The median figure is 16.

The contrast in the village-town ratio between Europe and the Middle East may readily be seen by comparing Tables 5–1 and 5–2. Except for Israel with its very low ratio (which compares with that of Switzerland) and Lebanon (approximately on a par with Ireland) all the other countries save Kuwait (which is sui generis) have ratios

63. For sample transport costs in an underdeveloped country see Wilfred Owen's estimates in *Distance and Development*, pp. 29–33, and p. 164, Tables A-14, A-15. These figures indicate that transport by bullock cart may be about 2½ times as expensive as by truck, but since India in 1964 (see p. 161, Table A–10) had only 1 truck for every 2,000 people (as contrasted with 139 trucks for 2,000 people in the United States), it would be the inferior form of transport that would mainly influence the unit cost of transport and limit the profitable travel range.

64. For a graphic account of this woefully inadequate level of commercialization, see Toni Hagen, *Nepal*, Bern, 1960, pp. 108–109.

Table 5–1 Number of European Villages for Each Central Place with over 2,500 Inhabitants

Country	Census	Villages	Central places	Ratio
Switzerland	1963	1,209	233	5
Luxembourg	1964	67	9	7
France	1964	5,075	489	10
Denmark	1963	1,117	98	11
Sweden	1963	2,053	165	12
United Kingdom	1964	4,337	277	16
Netherlands	1964	2,378	147	16
Irish Republic	1964	3,077	122	25
Portugal	1964	2,810	74	37
Belgium	1963	1,931	49	39
Norway	1963	4,819	83	58
Finland	1964	3,445	59	58
Austria	1961	4,881	67	72

SOURCE: *Collier's Encyclopedia,* New York: Crowell-Collier & Macmillan, 1966; United Nations, Statistical Office, *Statistical Yearbook, 1967,* New York, 1968.

Table 5–2 Number of Middle Eastern Villages for Each Central Place with over 2,500 Inhabitants

Country	Census	Villages	Central places	Ratio
Israel	1963	209	49	4
Lebanon	1963	243	10	24
Kuwait	1961	68	1	68
Muscat and Oman	1962	1,682	16	105
Saudi Arabia	1963	11,193	71	157
Turkey	1964	44,175	219	201
Iraq	1963	9,186	45	204
Syria	1963	7,540	25	301
Yemen	1962	9,532	15	635

SOURCE: *Collier's Encyclopedia,* New York: Crowell-Collier & Macmillan, 1966; United Nations, Statistical Office, *Statistical Yearbook, 1967,* New York, 1968.

over 100. The median is 157. Roughly then, using only the median as a measure, Europe has ten times as many central places as the Middle East.

If isovectures were used as a more exact test of central-place market influence, the comparison would be much more unfavorable, because once the village-town ratio rises much above a 50 to 1 ratio, the "reach" of a market becomes so weak that the towns exert only a very feeble influence on more outlying villages.[65]

The difficulty is not the lack of scattered periodic produce and peddlers' markets, for as Sidney Mintz has shown, they may exist in large numbers.[66] The real deficiency is in towns large enough to maintain daily, competitive produce markets, supplied with shops where farmers can buy the consumer goods they need and with stores where inputs such as fertilizers, pesticides, and other farm supplies can be purchased. A rough correlation between the number of towns and per capita gross national product is shown in Table 5–3. From it one can readily see that countries with relatively more towns have higher

Table 5–3 Village-Town Ratios Compared with Per Capita Gross National Product (GNP)

Country	Ratio	GNP
Israel	6	$ 1,504
Sweden	23	22,735
Lebanon	23	427
Italy	24	1,182
Uruguay	36	611
Greece	41	764
Chile	77	588
Argentina	86	826
Malaysia	87	308
Iraq	98	254
Syria	99	187
Egypt	108	179
Turkey	117	322
Yemen	146	62
India	185	92
Algeria	218	228
Sudan	262	101
Iran	269	239
Indonesia	355	95

SOURCE: United Nations, *Demographic Yearbook, 1966,* New York, 1967; *World Almanac,* New York: Doubleday, 1968.

65. Except, of course, for a few high-value, small-bulk commodities that can profitably be carried long distances.

66. "A Tentative Typology of Eight Haitian Market Places," *Revista de ciencias sociales,* 4 (March 1960), 16.

per capita GNP figures and that GNP falls as the number of market towns decreases. Thus in the Middle East, Yemen with one town (under 2,500) for every 146 villages has a GNP of $62, whereas Lebanon with a town for every 23 villages has a GNP of $427. In Asia there are equally revealing contrasts: Indonesia with but one town for every 355 villages has a GNP of $95, while in Malaysia with a town for every 87 villages, the figure is $308. To be sure these are very crude indexes, but the consistency with which they indicate the depressing influence that lack of towns and small cities can have on personal incomes cannot be ignored. The raising of average incomes in underdeveloped countries will require town-building programs; and until this task of spatial restructuring is understood, resources will continue to be wasted in fruitless efforts to find some quick and easy route to modernization.

CHAPTER 6 THE CRITICAL ROLE OF MARKET TOWNS IN MODERNIZING THE LANDSCAPES OF UNDERDEVELOPED COUNTRIES

Basic Aspects of Agrarian Economies

In Asia, Africa, the Middle East, and Latin America a majority of families derive their real income from farming operations. The form that agriculture takes may be a near subsistence hoe culture, a semicommercial variety of farming, or a more specialized kind of primary production; but these differences do not qualify the basic reality that in underdeveloped countries agriculture is the occupation of a very large part of the active population. Because this situation will continue for a long, long time to come, even though, with an increase in secondary and tertiary types of employment, the agricultural fraction of the work force will be gradually diluted, development will very profoundly depend on the ways and on the speed with which agricultural operations are "modernized" and on the extent to which a "progressive rural structure" is painstakingly, systematically, and successfully brought into being.[1] This aspect of development will have none of the dramatic appeal that glamorous projects such as the Aswan Dam or the Volta River projects can provide. But prosaic agrarian changes may be far more important because they will directly influence the lives and visibly improve the welfare of millions of people.

Except for the very minor exceptions, agriculture is a space-using productive operation, and this is the case whether the crops are grains, pulses, fruit, vegetables, meat, or industrial crops such as soy

1. For this very useful concept I am indebted to Arthur T. Mosher, who has given me permission to quote from his book *Creating a Progressive Rural Structure to Serve a Modern Agriculture,* New York, Agricultural Development Council, 1969.

beans, fibers, or rubber.[2] Consequently, efficient farming depends on a judicious use of agronomic space, and this involves, inter alia, the adaptation of crops to soils; a prudent cycle of crop rotation, preferably one involving the periodic planting of a soil-building crop to compensate for the agronomic damage caused by soil-exhausting crops; a scale of operations large enough so that some surpluses over and above the food, fuel, and fiber needs of the cultivating family will be available for sale to nonfarmers; a system of land tenure that will permit such a minimally necessary scale of operations—all this together with a technology and a body of knowledge, however acquired, that can be used by a properly skilled work force to make it possible for cultivators to draw effectively upon available natural productive powers (soil fertility, moisture, sunshine, temperature) thereby combining natural and artificial factors into a productive process that can be sustained for a long time. Even in simple peasant societies, farming is a many-sided, complex interaction of many forces.[3] But whether farming is primitive, more advanced, or modern, the motivation which animates the whole process will depend upon the incentives existing in different forms of agricultural organization. None of the rationally purposeful and socially beneficial agricultural effectiveness just envisaged will materialize unless cultivators and their families believe it worthwhile to work hard and are willing to use their land, their savings, their manpower, and above all, their time to best advantage.

In peasant societies two varieties of incentives can be logically differentiated: the familial and the pecuniary, although they are interblended in varying but normally not greatly changing proportions. The familial incentives stem from a sense of duty and responsibility to a cultivator's family.[4] To the end that all members can be fed, clothed, and housed, land will ordinarily be cultivated intensively in order

2. The development of hydroponics has shown that certain types of agriculture, particularly the production of vegetables in chemically enriched trays or basins, can be as space saving as an industrial operation. The production of eggs or broilers in multistory installations or the fattening of hogs or cattle in small-area structures or yards is not really comparable, since these operations are merely stages in much larger production processes, which still involve the extensive use of space for producing poultry or animal feed or for raising young stock for the cattle feeders.

3. The varied character of subsistence and near-subsistence agriculture in worldwide contexts has been analyzed with great care and extraordinary insight in Colin Clark's and Margaret Haswell's richly documented, *The Economics of Subsistence Agriculture*, London, 1964.

4. Which in many societies is a social group much larger than a conjugal family.

to obtain the largest possible amount of produce per unit of land.[5] But for all the outpouring of labor and energy, this type of cultivation may not result in an efficient utilization of agronomic resources. Throughout the underdeveloped regions of the earth frantic efforts to increase family landholdings have resulted in so much land fragmentation that landscapes have become crazy-quilt patterns that can only be cultivated by a prodigal expenditure of family labor power.[6] Moreover, if the main object of farm operations is to feed a conjugal family, and if landholdings are small, only occasional surpluses that can be spared from family needs will be brought to market. In such a context there will be little or no systematic adaptation of salable produce to consumer preferences.[7] A small volume of marketed produce is one consequence, indifferent quality resulting in low prices another; and in near-subsistence agrarian economies it is hard to say whether it is the absence of markets which holds down the marketed surplus or whether it is the low volume and poor quality of the goods which impedes the development of a network of marketplaces for agricultural produce. What is abundantly clear is that where there are spatially dispersed, well-organized, competitive markets, a wholly different variety of incentives are operative. When incentives become mainly pecuniary, they tend to have persistent stimulating effects on the methods, organization, and technology of agricultural production.

The most serious limitation of a familial type of near-subsistence agriculture is the unavailability of certain critical inputs needed to increase productivity. Commercial fertilizers, improved seeds, pesti-

5. In areas where the land-man ratios are ample this compulsion is, of course, weaker. For examples of varying labor inputs and contrasting land-man ratios, see Clark and Haswell, *Economics of Subsistence Agriculture*, pp. 121–138.

6. For an evaluation of the constraints still imposed by land fragmentation in contemporary Europe, see Folke Dovring, *Land and Labor in Europe in the Twentieth Century*, The Hague, 1965, pp. 39–56. Not only does fragmentation increase the distance factor and reduce the chances of a satisfactory scale of operations, but, as Dovring points out, "Maps of fragmented villages reveal many other features of bad land layout which are less easy to interpret than number and size of plots and more difficult to express in quantitative terms. Irregular layout, sinuous roads, excessive intermingling of holdings, and enclaved parcels, raise numerous obstacles to rational systems of drainage and irrigation, mechanical operations and to rational work planning in general." Ibid., p. 45.

7. One need only compare the fruit available in Japan with that sold in India. The Japanese apples, pears, and persimmons are skillfully grown to meet exacting market specifications, whereas Indian oranges, apples, and other fruits are mostly ungraded and of very poor quality. Only in a few areas such as Himachal Pradesh has fruit growing become a specialized branch of agriculture.

cides, tools, implements, and irrigation water must be purchased. But these inputs cannot be acquired in local "horizontal trade" markets where peasant farmers buy from one another crops they do not themselves produce or such things as handicrafts or draft animals. The critical inputs must be obtained from "vertical trade," and they will only be available (normally through the medium of money) in exchange for agricultural produce of satisfactory quality. On both sides of the exchange process, then, a degree of specialization is requisite. The makers or the sellers of agricultural inputs will constitute a nonagricultural group of people who, with their families, will be consumers of regularly marketed agricultural produce. Hence it is quite clear that a modern type of agriculture not only presupposes the existence of markets where produce can be sold, as well as of markets where inputs can be purchased, but it is necessary that both types of markets should be spatially dispersed in such a way that they will be within satisfactory distance and travel time of farmers, for the simple reason that farmers' relative mobility is always limited by the very nature of their space-bound occupation.

Modern agriculture, as A. T. Mosher has so vividly made clear is a synthetic operation somewhat comparable to the "assembly line" of a factory.[8] Certain inputs of an intellectual character are made available by the culture and by the economy: knowledge, skills, incentives, and technology. Other inputs are provided by nature: solar energy, soil nutrients, moisture, air and soil temperatures, and crop-inducing weather.[9] But these "free" inputs cannot be fully utilized unless certain man-made inputs are incorporated into the assembly-line process. These critical inputs, fertilizers, pesticides, tools, implements, improved seeds, irrigation water, which can so markedly improve productivity, simply will not be available unless a "progressive rural structure" is brought into existence (see Figure 6–1). This process of change involves the interdependence of at least five basic elements which are needed to create a "functional economic area."[10] There must be (1) a market center that will provide an outlet for farm produce and make available the critical inputs that farmers need. Yet market centers can have

8. Mosher, *Creating a Progressive Rural Structure*, p. 3.

9. Cold weather as well as salubrious spring and summer weather is a necessary "input" for many types of agriculture. Freezing kills insect pests, and thawing mellows and fines the soil.

10. Karl A. Fox, "Toward a Policy Model of World Economic Development with Special Attention to the Agricultural Sector," quoted in Mosher, *Creating a Progressive Rural Structure*, p. 4.

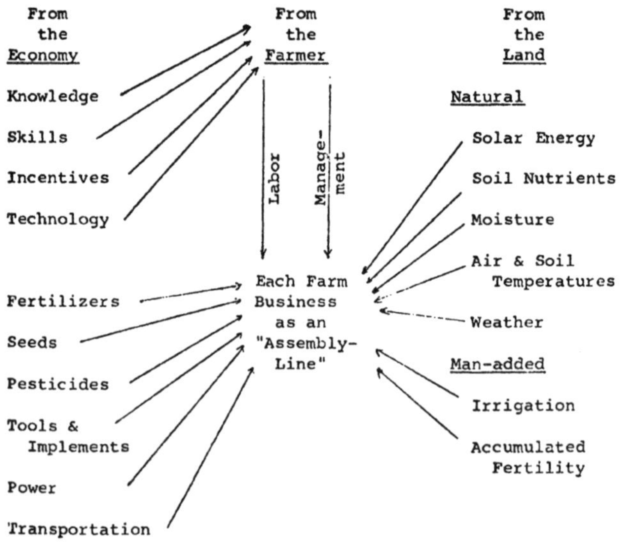

Figure 6–1 Inputs into Modern Farming

SOURCE: A. T. Mosher, *Creating a Progressive Rural Structure to Serve a Modern Agriculture,* New York: Agricultural Development Council, 1969, p. 2.

little or no influence unless there are (2) roads connecting farms to these market centers. But markets and roads are not enough. Farm products must be adapted to consumer wants, and this will necessitate (3) local verification trials of improved farm practices. Real progress will involve the utilization of the best available scientific knowledge, which will call for (4) the services of agricultural experts, and experience has shown that guidance can best be made available by means of an agricultural extension service. Lastly, improved agricultural technology will require certain types of investment, and this, in turn, will make necessary (5) some suitable form of farm production credit. All the five basic elements are so highly complementary that "there is little point in improving market outlets for farm products unless there are locally proved methods of increasing production (local verification trials) and unless the farm supplies and equipment needed to increase production are locally available. Improving roads has little consequence unless there are services nearby which . . . can lead to increased production. All extension service is of minimum effectiveness except in localities where all the other four elements are present."[11]

*The Inseparability of Agrarian and Industrial Development in Progressive Economies**

Whoever coined the classic French warning to public administrators, "*pauvre paysan, pauvre roi; pauvre roi, pauvre royaume*," had a profound and correct understanding of economic development. For unless farmers and other rural-dwelling people are prosperous, there can be no effective demand for the products made by industrialists and sold by traders. In the vast reaches of the underdeveloped portion of the world, the lack of vigor, vitality, and progress of national and regional economies is inescapably bound up with the unsatisfactory economic conditions of the inhabitants of hundreds of thousands of agricultural village communities.[12]

Since in the last analysis development depends on investment and production decisions, it follows that growth, economic improvement, and transformation will be affected not merely by the investment and production decisions of city-dwelling industrialists and traders but also by the far more numerous although relatively modest individual decisions of cultivators, rural artisans, and local traders. It is incorrect to assume that urban entrepreneurial decisions are wholly discrete and separable from rural decisions and choices. If an urban pattern of investment results in a neglect of a city's hinterland, not only will the organic growth and development of a region be arrested but the whole areal economy will be fragile and unbalanced, depending more on external demand than upon the more regular and dependable interchange made possible by growing home markets.[13] For this reason the

* First versions of this and the following two sections were prepared for the International Seminar on the Urban and Industrial Growth of Kanpur held at Kanpur, India, January 2 to February 4, 1967, in which I participated, and have been published in *Regional Perspective of Industrial and Urban Growth*, ed. P. B. Desai, I. M. Grossack, and K. N. Sharma, Bombay, 1969, pp. 171–187.

11. Mosher, *Creating a Progressive Rural Structure*, p. 5.

12. India alone has more than a half million villages, Pakistan over 100,000, Indonesia almost 185,000, Turkey about 45,000, the Sudan 25,000, Iran 40,000.

13. The innate wisdom of American economists like Matthew Carey and politicians like Henry Clay led to a policy emphasis on developing home markets which perhaps more than anything else helped move nineteenth-century America out of the underdeveloped category.

first priority of regional development plans should be to impart a continuously stimulating influence on the production and investment decisions of cultivators and other rural entrepreneurs who live within the economic reach of towns or cities. For unless urban investment and production decisions have a meaningful and genuinely reciprocal effect on an agrarian hinterland, all the familiar evils and disadvantages of a dual economy will emerge. The fact that cities have the power to attract the ablest young persons from outlying villages may prove to be an illusory advantage. Wresting farm boys from their village homes by the lure of better incomes only to plunge them into city slums already overburdened with excessive numbers is not a benefit to these hopeful young workers; nor is it a benefit to the nation or to the receiving city, which must bear the incidence of the mounting cost of municipal services. This leeching of the countryside cannot improve the productivity of cultivators or village artisans; the "brain-drain" and "labor scouting" will certainly not increase the effective rural demand for urban merchandise and manufactures.

A central concern of judicious and truly purposeful regional planning must therefore be to determine the extent to which *tranches* of investment and the associated production decisions are amenable to manipulation, with the conscious and explicit objective of shaping and influencing, directly or indirectly, the investment and production decisions of an ever increasing number of cultivators and other rural residents living within the actual or potential hinterlands of towns and cities. Ideally, the investment and production decisions of urban entrepreneurs should trigger a chain reaction of differentially smaller investment and production decisions in town hinterlands, which would manifest themselves not merely in random, unplanned, ribbon-pattern developments, extending outward from urban centers along already crowded transport routes, but in more purposefully deployed investment clusters properly located at promising growth points in the widening angles of economic landscapes between main lines of travel and transport.[14]

The beacon-light object of developmental policy in a nation, a region, or a "functional economic area"[15] should be to increase the total areal volume of economic activity. More specifically, in both urban

14. "Economic landscapes" used here in the technical Löschean sense.

15. To obviate the risk of confusion, Mosher avoids the term "community" (which Galpin and MacIver used to designate a local spatial economic, social and cultural entity) and uses instead "functional economic area" a term suggested by Karl Fox.

and rural parts of an economic landscape it should envisage an increase in the output of goods and services, an expansion of total employment, an improvement in productivity, a wider usage of progressively improving technology, a steady growth in consumption attesting progress in general welfare, and a systematic enlargement of educational, medical, and other social amenities and facilities. Part of this intermeshed program will very likely have to be undertaken by the public sector, leaving another, usually much larger part, to be implemented by the private sector. A very major problem in every developing country, therefore, is whether the agrarian private sector will voluntarily assume responsibility for a substantial fraction of the entire development burden.[16] This will very certainly depend on whether adequate incentives can be held forth that will induce farmers to raise more produce, market a larger quantity, improve the quality of what they sell, earn more, and hence be able to invest more. It is the argument of this essay that a proper spatial manipulation of investment decisions within a "functional economic area" can have a profound influence in generating stronger incentives for farmers and can thereby exert a meliorative effect on every affected village community. In the process regional agriculture would be progressively commercialized, and as a result, a larger marketed national supply of agricultural produce would be available for the benefit of all sectors of the entire economy.

Incentives for Farmers: Their Essential Nature and How They Can Be Changed and Strengthened

It is seldom accurate to make a sharp distinction between subsistence farming and commercial agriculture since virtually all cultivators sell some fraction of their crop, however small. The great majority of farmers in underdeveloped areas are therefore engaged in "semicommercial" agriculture. Ordinarily a major fraction of farm output is consumed by farm families, and only marginal amounts are marketed.[17]

"Community" in the Orient, particularly in India usually means a caste or a social group. Thus the Harijans (former "untouchables") are a "community," as are the Anglo-Indians, although they are not a caste.

16. The Chinese "Great Leap Forward" was an impatient attempt to compel the agrarian private sector to assume very promptly a large measure of responsibility for an overall development program. The undue haste set up an adverse reaction.

17. Estimates made by R. C. Desai (*Standard of Living in India and Pakistan, 1931–32 to 1940–41,* Bombay, 1953, p. 121) showed that, whereas village retention of wheat for the whole subcontinent was 49.3 percent, for Orissa it was almost 100

It is therefore not merely distance disadvantages that limit the salable fractions. Small landholders do not produce very much over and above their family consumption needs. Table 6–1 shows the rising marketable percentages (last column) that went to market in Iraq from four types of farms.

Table 6–1 Marketed Fractions of Output from Four Types of Iraqi Farms (kilogram equivalent per person per year)

Type	Net farm product	Amount marketed	Remaining product	Percent marketed
1	500	13	487	0.026
2	737	203	534	27.5
3	1089	446	643	40.9
4	1820	1042	778	52.0

SOURCE: Data from Colin Clark and Margaret Haswell, *The Economics of Subsistence Agriculture*, London: Macmillan, 1964, p. 54.

What we do not know from these data is whether the net farm product was as great as it might have been, whether smallness of landholdings was the chief reason for the low output in Type 1 farms, or whether a preference for leisure might have been partly responsible. What is abundantly clear, however, is that as output rose (whatever the cause), there was an increase not only in the marketed surplus but in the share of net product that remained and was available for family consumption. This example suggests that there may well be a triple gain from a fuller commercialization of an agrarian area: the cultivator would have a cash income which he could spend for the consumer or producer goods he wanted; at the same time he would have a larger quantity of farm produce available for consumption by his family and himself; thirdly, a larger quantity of produce would be delivered to urban and industrial centers for the alimentation of the country's nonagricultural population. For these three reasons a major object of economic development policy should be to increase progressively the commercial fraction of farm output.[18] The problem is how to do this.

---

percent; and that whereas the average retention of rice was 58.6 percent, for Assam the amount withheld from market was 94 percent and for Uttar Pradesh 64 percent.

18. This may require land reform, changes in land tenure, and land consolidation, if it can be shown that the low marketed fractions are the consequence of dwarf or fragmented landholdings.

Very clearly an expansion of the commercial portion of farmers' output, their "marketed surplus," will not occur unless adequate incentives are provided by one means or another, and, contrary to what occurs in thoroughly commercialized and developed countries, prices may not be effective inducements. There are several reasons why higher prices may not lead an increase in supplies brought to market, and they may perhaps be itemized in this order: a preference for leisure, a high priority for increased consumption, and an inadequacy of requital goods. The first is a cultural phenomenon: production of farm produce over and above what is needed for subsistence mortgages time, strength, and wits, which may provide greater happiness if devoted to play, sleep, or some other type of nonproductive activity. In many underdeveloped areas want scales are often short in range; and until the "demonstration effect" of goods can change comsumption habits, leisure may be psychologically more rewarding than work.

The second reason for the failure of higher prices to elicit a larger market surplus is more institutional than cultural. Narain has shown rather convincingly that there can be such aberrations or "backward bending supply curves" in situations where debt servitude has compelled small (Indian) farmers to bring more produce to market than a family could really spare.[19] If prices rise, relatively less produce needs to be sold to obtain the cash income so urgently needed, and this reduction in forced selling will allow relatively more produce to be devoted to consumption. Higher prices in such a situation may not increase the marketed surplus; they may reduce it. For a time at least, then, higher prices could conceivably be a disincentive. But here one must be careful not to reach hasty conclusions. For, whereas the higher prices might release the small farmer from the necessity of selling as much as before, the very fact that more can be retained might suggest the wisdom of producing more.

Throughout the annals of economic history it has been the proffer of requital goods that has induced farmers to grow farm surpluses which might be exchanged for nonagricultural commodities, whether consumer or producer goods. Conversely, it has been the insufficiency of requital goods that has deterred the production of agricultural surpluses. If there are no buyers proffering payment goods, directly or

19. Dharm Narain, *Distribution of the Marketed Surplus of Agricultural Produce by Size-Level of Holdings in India, 1950–51,* Institute of Economic Growth, Occasional Paper No. 2, New Delhi, 1961, Chapter 7.

indirectly, (via money) it is of course, quite pointless to produce more grain, meat, or vegetables than a family can consume. Thus pioneer American farmers, hundreds of miles from urban concentrations, produced only the number of bushels of potatoes they needed. It would have been quite foolish to use land and labor to produce more potatoes. Contrast this with farmers with land suitable for potato growing near large cities. Output far in excess of family needs can be wisely produced because potatoes can be exchanged for a wide variety of desirable payment goods. Universally it has been the spatial availability of such payment goods that has provided the incentives for an increased output of farm produce.

Agricultural economists agree that farming involves (1) a biological production process, which depends for its efficiency partly on (2) the behavior of farmers, partly (3) on the layout and the agronomic potential of physical farms, and is (4) an operation that is measurable in terms of costs and returns.[20] But if these four "elements of farming" are to be effectively coordinated so that real "development" can be set in motion, there must be properly organized and satisfactorily administered markets for farm produce within reach of the cultivators, a constantly changing and progressively improving technology, local availability of farm supplies and all other necessary inputs, and serviceable (preferably all-weather) means of transport for outgoing farm produce and incoming farm supplies.[21] Above all, as has already been explained, there must be incentives that will induce farmers to use better tools, improved seeds, superior breeds of cattle, sheep, hogs, and poultry, and to employ the best-known farm practices, so that they will be able to produce as much as possible at lowest possible unit prices and to market a larger quantity of produce. The critical factor is therefore evident: since the great majority of people in underdeveloped areas are farmers, development involves changing the behavior of farmers with respect to production.[22]

In agrarian societies where technology is primitive, farmers will seldom inaugurate changes in farming methods. Consequently, if any

20. U.S., Panel on the World Food Supply, *The World Food Problem: A Report*, Washington, 1967, II, 506.

21. The large volume of goods that must be moved in commercial farming operations is not generally appreciated; Mosher points out that "an average of 4.5 tons of produce moved to market in the U.S. per acre of crop land, and about 1.3 tons of farm supplies and equipment per crop acre moved from industrial centers to U.S. farms in 1964–65." *Creating a Progressive Rural Structure*, p. 6.

22. U.S., Panel on the World Food Supply, *World Food Problem*, I, 77–79.

technical progress is to occur, farmers must be induced, by one means or another, to alter their customary or traditional practices. Not that their time-honored behavior is stupid or irrational. Limited experimentation with new crops and inputs may be all well and good, but certain canons of conduct have demonstrated their capacity to insure a degree of stability of agricultural output, and these "well-tested rules for living and working" ought not be abandoned unless it is very certain that, in addition to something better being possible, the new techniques will be equally dependable. To vary from established patterns is risky business; consequently, farmers in low-technology cultures must be convinced beyond any doubt whatever that deviation from tradition (such as the use of new inputs) will not bring loss or ridicule. It is not only the cultivator who must be convinced. Members of an "extended" family, particularly the older and more respected ones, must approve any deviation from customary practices. For the first duty of a cultivator is not to contribute to a nation's commercial food supply or even to make a personal profit; his first duty is to his family. It is for the family to say what should be produced, not an extension worker or an outsider from a community development headquarters.

If these deeply ingrained conventions prevail in low-technology, low-yield communities, how then can change occur? It has been wisely said that "if a new practice can have an old sanction," change is not difficult to accomplish.[23] Thus a new kind of water-lifting machine equipped with rubber valves that can be operated manually[24] needs no new sanction since by making possible the irrigation of more land it will better insure that family needs are met and at the same time release, without peril to family food needs, a new increment of marketable surplus. The problem is largely one of demonstrating how the device can indisputably increase the productivity of a farm family. Obviously the machine cannot exert any "demonstration effect" if it is only to be found miles away from farms in a city display room never visited by farmers.[25] Like other new tools, implements, and machines, they should be displayed

23. Ibid., II, 512–513.

24. Such as the excellent but simple machines I saw in the factory showroom of Cossul & Co. in Kanpur, India.

25. About 90 percent of the current production of these Cossul & Co. machines, which have a technological capacity to improve to a marked degree the wretchedly inefficient agriculture in the Kanpur region, was exported in 1967. Whereas such implements could be sold in Africa, the Middle East, and Northeast Asia, lack of markets, marketing techniques, farm credit, demonstration facilities, and roads made it almost impossible to sell any within the immediate (75-mile radius) hinterland of the city where they were manufactured.

and demonstrated at dispersed places located within walking distance of potential buyers, at local market places or in other customary meeting places in the countryside.

There is, however, no single point of leverage which can be used to change the cautious behavior of fretful farmers worried about weather, taxes, debts, and the prices of the little they have to sell. What needs to be done is to convey patiently to local leaders an understanding that there really does exist a "package of practices" that farmers can utilize to their advantage.[26] The package is a large one, which involves at least the following: locally verified new departures in technology and farm practices, tested both in terms of agronomic response and economic suitability; provision for a continuing flow of farm supplies (e.g., pesticides) needed to put the improved technology (e.g., sprayers) into use; marketing facilities that are efficient, economical, and fair by reason of proper supervision; a growing network of transport facilities that can put farmers within reach of markets and make it possible for a visible supply of requital commodities to stimulate production of farm produce; agricultural credit impartially administered; and systematic means for diffusing knowledge of improved farm practices.

The foregoing can be melded together into a regional plan, because all the elements can be manipulated within a chosen compass of space without very much reference to other disinterested regions. There are, however, other indispensable elements in a wholly adequate "package of practices" that are not regionally determinable. Such prerequisites for a "progressive rural structure" as more equitable landownership and land tenure arrangements have political and legal implications which call for statewide or nationwide legislative changes. So do such considerations as legally enforceable security of tenure for cultivators, equitable division of harvests between landlords and tenants, clear title to land for farm owners, tax policies that will not dampen or discourage investment, crop insurance that can protect farmers against uncertainties, arrangements for irrigation water,[27] and other pertinent elements whose determination cannot be made by local or regional decision makers. Yet the fact that only some parts of a whole "package"

26. Although I have taken this phrase from U.S., Panel on the World Food Supply, *World Food Problem,* (I, 89) the content of the term has been restated to support the argument of this section.

27. Depending on the sources of water this factor might be within the control of local or regional planners.

can be dealt with in local or regional spatial planning does not make these parts less important. Indeed, it is just the reverse. The elements that are exogenous to a "functional economic area" will presumably be approximately uniform throughout a nation or, at least, throughout a state), whereas variations in the endogenous elements will depend on the imagination, foresight, courage, and will of the local or regional planners. These, then, are the really manipulative elements in the "package of practices" which can be used to change the behavioral patterns of farmers. They can be, and they should be, incorporated in programs which can be implemented by some combination of public and private activities.[28] A great deal of flexibility will be essential in such programs because they will perforce have to be adapted to the degree of commercialization existing in the several localities that constitute a larger "functional economic area." Thus the localities near a city or served by paved roads will normally be more responsive to price inducements than localities less well provided with transport facilities, because the former are already fairly well market-oriented.[29] But it is a cardinal error to assume, as all too many policy makers have done, that all localities in a region will be equally responsive to price inducements.[30]

Spatial Aspects of the Farmer Incentive Problem Illustrated in an Indian Sample Area

The "package of practices" just described cannot be provided at the village level because the average population and the average number of farms are insufficient to warrant a continuous market for agricultural produce, a profitable outlet for farm supplies, a center for farm practice verification, a cadre of extension workers, or genuinely impersonal facilities for making farm credit available.[31] If, for example, India's

28. See Chapter 7.

29. There may be exceptions, as P. K. Mukherjee and S. C. Gupta have shown, *A Pilot Survey of Fourteen Villages in U.P. and Punjab*, New Delhi, 1969, pp. 66–68.

30. The World Food Problem analysts concluded that price increases for farm produce operate as incentives only (1) where farmers are free from both general and specific cultural restraints, (2) have production alternatives made possible by facilities for processing or for selling the alternative products unprocessed, and (3) are already operating largely in a market economy. U.S., Panel on the World Food Supply, *World Food Problem*, II, 523–532.

31. Using India as an example, the average population of all villages was 637 persons in 1960. In Uttar Pradesh, the average village population was 551, but in the

564,718 villages were each to be provided with all the requisite facilities involved in such a "package of practices," the cost would be astronomical. So for all the sentiment that has been lavished on the village,[32] it is clear, from locational theory as well as from empirical evidence, that some "community" or "functional economic area" larger than the average "third world" village must be the unit of organization if agrarian economies are to become technologically efficient and interrelated in a genuinely complementary way with the urban and industrial sectors, or if they ever hope to become functionally linked with the world economy. The urgent need for creating the necessary components of a "progressive rural structure" in agro-urban "functional economic areas" can be made much more convincing by examining the Kanpur region of northern India as a sample rural area.

Kanpur with almost a million inhabitants is the major city of the most populous Indian State.[33] It serves as a metropolitan center for a region that covers approximately 17,000 square miles inhabited by about 10 million people. Structurally, the region consists of 11,239 villages very imperfectly linked to its metropolis by a skeletal hierarchy of 24 urban centers that are legally recognized as "towns," plus 28 (census-unrecognized) smaller urban centers. If one follows the official census definition of a town, the urban hierarchy of the region would consist of 1 central city (Kanpur), 24 towns, and 11,239 villages; which means that there would be but 1 town for every 468 villages. The 24 towns vary in size from around 5,000 people to 95,000, with the median population in 1960 about 16,000.[34] In terms of size, then, these towns

---

Kanpur region, which is used as a regional sample in this section, the average village population was 717 persons. India, Office of the Registrar General, *Census of India, 1961, Final Population Totals,* pp. lxi–lxii.

32. As already pointed out, much of the romantic idealization of village organization stems from the writings of M. K. Gandhi. "I am convinced" he said, "that if India is to attain true freedom, and through India the world also, then sooner or later the fact must be recognized that people will have to live in villages, not in towns, in huts, not in palaces. Crores of people will never be able to live in peace with each other in towns and palaces." One can readily agree with Gandhi when he said that India is essentially a "rural civilization," but it does not follow that the inherited small-village pattern is the best recipe for agrarian progress and well-being. For Gandhi's views see *Village Svaraj,* Ahmedabad, 1962, especially Chapter 4.

33. Since no census has been taken since 1960, the total population of Uttar Pradesh can only be estimated by adding to the 1960 figure of 73,746,000 persons about 2½ percent each year thereafter for annual growth.

34. The smallest (Rajapura) had 5,089 persons, and the largest (Farrukhabad-cum-Fatehgarh) 94,591 persons in 1960.

seemingly are suitable centers for markets, farm-supply dealers, banks, and other market-town facilities. But the glaring weakness in this regional urban hierarchy is the utter inadequacy of the number of towns, since none of them could possibly service 468 villages, even if one were to assume a complete network of good roads, which, as will presently be explained, would be completely unwarranted. Nor is the spatial prospect really very much improved if one considers the twenty-eight "declassified towns"[35] as functional components in a regional "urban" hierarchy. Their inclusion would, of course, reduce the average number of villages per town from 468 to 216, but it is very doubtful whether many of the 28 "declassified towns" could perform central-place functions. In the first place most of them are small; the largest three, averaging about 11,000 inhabitants, are not at all typical, since the median size is around 5,000. Fully half of them are little more than swollen villages, and one need only visit them to see that they have virtually no facilities that could qualify them as functional urban centers. The most generous concession would be to presume that about five or six of the 28 "declassified towns" might be considered as probably capable of performing a few central-place functions. Adding these to the census-recognized towns would give a total of 30 central places to serve 10,000,000 people (one-third of a million per town) living in 11,239 villages (374 villages per town) dispersed over 17,000 square miles (566 square miles per town).[36] This illustrative arithmetic shows better than words the flagrant inadequacy of the urban structure to provide markets, supplies, or incentives for the millions of farmers in the Kanpur region.

It is difficult to say how many of the 11,239 villages are in any meaningful contact with these 30 market towns because of the varying distances that commodities travel in search of markets. But data gathered by the Uttar Pradesh Traffic Survey in 1966 indicate that

35. This term merely means that, whereas in the 1950 census these centers had been classified as towns (according to size), in the judgment of the 1960 census enumerators they did not seem to merit consideration as "towns" and were accordingly "declassified."

36. The small market centers in Western Iowa described in Chapter 2 had market areas of about 70 square miles, which was about the size of English market areas in the late sixteenth century. The larger Iowa market towns served as much as 200 square miles, but they could do this through the intervention of the smaller markets, even as cities could serve an area of up to 1,000 square miles by means of intermediate and small market centers. In the absence of such a hierarchy, the Kanpur rural areas are vastly beyond the market reach of the towns.

virtually no produce in the Kanpur region is brought further than 25 kilometers (about 15 miles) and that milk, poultry, fruits, vegetables and grain, in that order, have much shorter isovectures. Marketing is seriously limited by the insufficiency, poor quality, and seasonable impassibility of roads, and this infrastructural deficiency means that villages can be isolated even though they are not very far from towns. This is, to be sure, an endemic problem throughout India but is particularly acute in Central and North India.

When one learns that Uttar Pradesh, a region of rich land with great productive potential, is so lacking in surfaced roads that it has only $\frac{1}{32}$ the mileage per 100 square miles of area that Japan has and only $\frac{1}{224}$ of Australia's similarly calculated mileage, the incapacity of thirty random-sized cities to provide central-place goods and services in the Kanpur region for more than eleven thousand villages becomes painfully evident. Over one-third of these villages (36.6 percent) have no roads whatever; another third have the benefit of unsurfaced roads that are usually impassible in monsoon season; and only 28.7 percent have access to surfaced roads.[37] The distances that separate villages from a market are not negligible; 42.2 percent of the villages are more than 5 miles from any market, and almost 18 percent are more than 10 miles distant. (See Table 6–2.) Yet these figures do not really reveal the basic problem. The greatest handicap is the distance that must be traveled

Table 6–2 Distance from Any Market of Kanpur Region Villages

Distance	Percent of villages
1 mile or less	19.2
1–3 miles	21.7
3–5 miles	16.9
Total	57.8
5–10 miles	24.3
10 miles or over	17.9
Total	42.2

SOURCE: "Road Development," Report prepared by an Uttar Pradesh Regional Transport Study Group, Mimeographed, n.d., p. 20.

37. These figures were derived from an unpublished report entitled "Road Development" prepared by a regional transport study group that worked in cooperation with the Government of India Planning Commission.

by villagers who are without roads or who are served by poor unsurfaced roads if they are to be in contact with any market. Let us look first at the villages served by poor roads. About 71 percent of the villages on unsurfaced roads are within a 5-mile market diameter; if the average travel distance is about 4 miles, then these villages (71 percent of 34.7 percent, or roughly a fourth, of the Kanpur region villages) have reasonably adequate market contact in dry weather, since bullock carts can make a round trip in something less than a work day. For the 29 percent of villages on unsurfaced roads more than 5 miles from market the access is less certain, while for the 8.4 percent of villages more than 10 miles removed, a road trip of 20 miles or longer may deter many cultivators from undertaking so unpleasing a journey very often.

The crux of the spatial problem, however, centers around the villages that are not served by any roads whatever. This involves 36.6 percent of the Kanpur region villages, some 4,100 communities with a population exceeding three million people. This immense group of people, as large as the total population of Norway, are very imperfectly related to the market economy. The degree of their handicap (how far they must transport small quantities of produce or their purchases by pack animals—if they have any—or carry burdens on their backs or on their heads) should be apparent from Table 6–3. Nearly one-half of the villages (47.2 percent) are more than 5 miles from any market, and almost a fifth of the villagers (18.3 percent) must travel twenty miles or more (round trip) without benefit of roads. Even if one tries to put the

Table 6–3 Distance from Any Market of 4,100 Kanpur Region Villages without Roads

Distance	Percent of villages
1 mile or less	10.5
1–3 miles	18.1
3–5 miles	24.2
Total	52.8
5–10 miles	28.9
10 miles or over	18.3
Total	47.2

SOURCE: "Road Development," Report prepared by an Uttar Pradesh Regional Transport Study Group, Mimeographed, n.d., p. 25.

most charitable construction on these figures by noticing that some of the villages are not very far from markets, the bald fact remains that less than a third (28.6 percent) are within a 3-mile radius. Some of the villagers, to be sure, are nearer to metaled roads than markets, which means that only part of their journey to market will be without benefit of roads. But this correction does not materially modify the gloominess of the picture because almost a third of these roadless villages are more than 5 miles from any surfaced roads, and only a little over a fifth (21.2 percent) are within a mile of such a road.[38]

No econometric model is needed to indicate what changes are called for in a context such as this, one that repeats itself with variations in almost every underdeveloped country. The remedies for the unhappy situation are mainly roads, market centers, local investment clusters, technical advice, and agricultural credit. But the complementarity between these remedies is so great that it is difficult to arrange them in a meaningful order of priority. Perhaps the lack of roads is the greatest handicap to a productive economy, because physical isolation means not only an inability to sell produce and to buy necessary consumer goods but involves an intellectual separation of the roadless villages from currents of thought and action in urban areas and from information and ideas in those rural areas that are in better contact with towns and cities. How widespread can be this ignorance of what is occurring outside of the isolated villages was revealed in a 1966 study of a village only 23 miles from a large Indian city, Allahabad.[39] The survey had limited and modest objectives: merely to ascertain what the occupational groups in an Uttar Pradesh village knew about India's development plans and planning procedures. The findings, say the authors, can be easily summarized: "a shocking degree of ignorance, indifference, and psychological blackout."[40]

Less than a third of the interviewed villagers knew that India had Five-Year Plans, and those who did had "very superficial knowledge about their objectives, or their main features, or their achievements." Housewives, laborers, and artisans revealed the greatest ignorance; in contrast, teachers were quite well informed, and about 40 percent of the cultivators had some knowledge of India's plans and policies. The most

38. "Road Development," pp. 20–25.

39. A. N. Agarwala et al., *Plan Consciousness in a Rural Area: A Survey of Dhatarpur Village,* University of Allahabad, Agro-Economic Research Center, Allahabad, 1966.

40. Ibid., p. 6.

saddening conclusion the investigators reached was that about three-fourths of the people reflected "complete indifference and did not care as to whether the plans failed or succeeded."[41] About a fifth of the 188 interviewed persons had a feeling that most of the benefits from economic planning had been received by manufacturers, industrial workers, salaried people, and traders, although over a fourth of the cultivators (28 percent) thought the plans might in some way have helped them. About one-half of the farmers knew about the existence of plans, about 40 percent had a "fair knowledge" of plan objectives, and 30 percent gave "tolerably satisfactory" answers as to whether the plans had succeeded. This sample survey made not in a roadless, remote, or "shut-in" village but in a community with road connections to a large city has both a depressing and a hopeful side. The want of knowledge, the indifference to a great national undertaking—all this was understandably disappointing. The hopeful aspect was the far higher than average responses of the farmers, indicating that their habits and viewpoints could be changed if a systematic effort were made to bring them into some participatory relation with a development program. Surely the simplest way to do this would be to draw more and more village people into the intellectual orbit of market towns.

It is all well and good to assert that the behavior of farmers in underdeveloped countries, or in backward areas of any country, can be changed if roads are built and market centers are visualized in some ideal spatial pattern. This type of drawing-board reform unfortunately fails to ask a major question: who will plan, finance, and build the market center facilities to which the projected roads will presumably give access?[42] Very clearly, the problems that face the regional planners are how they can concentrate some public-sector investments at selected growth points and how they can persuade processers, manufacturers, merchants, and service providers to make investments at these chosen places, induce them to institute labor training programs, and by these means begin the process of establishing agro-urban centers to which farmers within travel range will be attracted as sellers and buyers. In the example of the Kanpur region just described, spatial geometry would indicate that full commercialization of the 11,239 villages would

41. Ibid.

42. How effective state and local governments can be in this type of planning has been critically appraised by R. Roy in his "Administration of Industrial Development in U.P.," in *Regional Perspective of Industrial and Urban Growth*, Desai, Grossack, and Sharma, eds., pp. 262–279.

require (unless means of transport are radically changed) the ultimate establishment of about 300 more market centers. Phasing this over a ten-year period, such a town-building program would call for the creation of about thirty new market centers each year. Provided there were agreement that this was a worthwhile regional goal, such an objective is not at all fanciful.[43] It could be done if a truly coordinated effort were made. But viewing the spatial problem in this light shifts the center of attention from the farm to the emergent market center, from the cultivator to the small-town investor, and indicates that paralleling new incentives for farmers there must also be opportunities proffered to investors and entrepreneurs to encourage them to embark on a regionally functional, sustained market-center building program. How this might be done is considered in the next chapter. For the moment it should be emphasized that policies are not enough. Effective regional planning calls for the creation of appropriate institutions that can shape and steadily stimulate a developmental process and make possible the attainment of carefully estimated targets and goals. The process must combine a planning and an implementing procedure in which goals would be phased not rigidly and invariably but in an experiential-projective way, so that the movement of change would be sustained while the restructured area progressively widened. For in development one of the most important elements is momentum.

Structural Choices in Rural Reconstruction

If the village, which has so long been the traditional unit of organization in agrarian societies, cannot make possible a progressive type of agriculture that will permit improvement in living standards and promote cultural and intellectual development,[44] if it cannot by reason of

43. Each unit of local government, the district, would have to assume responsibility for its quota of new market centers. This would involve about four new market centers per district per year.

44. "The village of a few hundred people cannot survive as a healthy organism. . . . It cannot maintain any of the social services; it must send its senior, and sometimes all, its children away for their schooling; it must share the services of a district nurse; it cannot bear the overhead costs of water supplies, sewage and lighting; it has few shopping facilities." *Country Planning: A Study of Rural Problems,* ed. C. S. Orwin, Oxford, 1944. This passage from a survey of rural Britain is even more apposite for underdeveloped countries, which must by some means develop new social organizations capable of providing urgently needed economic and social amenities.

its minuscule market allow an adequate commercialization of farming and provide farmers with cash incomes with which to finance the necessary inputs that will make a tolerably satisfactory productivity possible, then what are the choices? To my mind there are only three. Rural society can be restructured on some new peasant-plantation basis; it can be centered around collective or cooperative organizations; or it can be less formally integrated into agro-urban "functional areas" by a gradual but well-planned sequence of changes.[45] All three have their merits, all their limitations. But they are not all equally feasible in relation to cultural residues, ethnographic traits, social preferences, or stubborn ecological factors. A few illustrations may help to make this clear.

From a technological viewpoint a plantation type of agrarian restructuring has indisputable merit.[46] Large areas shown to be agronomically suitable for the production of certain crops (for which there is strong demand) could be consolidated into farming units large enough to justify the employment of at least some modern, power-drawn farm tools. Former peasants could become either share-participants or wage-compensated workers. Technical training could be supplied as needed so that the work force would be capable of following new farming methods and able to operate, service, and repair implements. Long-distance transport equipment, railways or trucks, could carry produce to large urban markets, thus eliminating the need for so many local market centers. A swift transition could conceivably be made from traditional to modern agriculture; but such a venture would require outside direction and outside capital supplied either by government or some quasi-public corporation. It is highly unlikely that it could be a community-inspired or self-generated enterprise.

It was the hope of such a new agrarian design that prompted the several British attempts to restructure portions of African agriculture.[47] These ventures, begun with great enthusiasm, were sometimes rather

45. Some interblending, particularly of the last two is possible. See pp. 205–206.

46. "Plantation" in this context refers to the attempted scale of productive operations and does not comprehend the type of labor exploitation which has been long associated with the historical plantation. In my sense a Yugoslav state farm or a large California orchard in which the workers are completely organized in a powerful trade-union may be called a plantation. Failing protective measures, modern plantations might easily revert to traditional type, a tragic fourth alternative.

47. See Alan Wood, *The Groundnut Affair,* London, 1950; Sir Oliver Franks, *Central Planning and Control in War and Peace,* Cambridge, Mass., 1947; West African Oilseeds Mission, *Report,* Colonial Report No. 224, London, 1948.

unwittingly based on "a fallacious notion that the bigger the scheme the better the results likely to be obtained."[48] One venture of this type, the Niger Agricultural Project, planned a new type of farming operation on 32,000 acres (about 50 square miles) involving a capital investment of £450,000 jointly contributed by the Colonial Development Corporation and the Nigerian Government. The project was to be administered by a corporation known as the Niger Agricultural Project, Limited. The main crops were to be groundnuts (peanuts) for commercial sale, and sorghum for local consumption.[49] Altogether some 9,652 acres of land were actually cleared and put into cultivation. It was estimated that by aid of modern implements each "settler," who had previously farmed about 4 acres, should be able to cultivate 24 acres. Model villages were built for the settlers with houses that "bore little resemblance" to the type to which they had been accustomed and which became causes of complaint and disaffection.[50]

The history of this venture can be quite quickly summarized from the Annual Reports of the Colonial Development Corporation. From the beginning, in 1950, serious difficulties were encountered in finding the right types and varieties of crops suitable for mechanical cultivation.[51] By 1951 it had become clear that it would take more time than had been expected to increase yields, reduce production costs, and obtain the anticipated worker productivity, and the corporation was warned that it could expect losses for at least another year. By 1952 real storm clouds had gathered. A large proportion of the settlers were proving to be "unsatisfactory"; it was now estimated that revenues per acre would have to be quadrupled if a "break-even" point was to be

48. K. D. S. Baldwin, *The Niger Agricultural Project: An Experiment in African Development,* Cambridge, Mass., 1957, p. 1.

49. Small acreages of several other industrial crops were planted: sunflowers, soya beans, tobacco, cotton and rama; and a few food crops in addition to sorghum (cowpeas, maize, and millet) were raised. Ibid, p. 86.

50. Ibid, p. 4.

51. The experienced farmer does not impulsively change crops or crop strains, although he cannot be accused of being either hidebound by tradition or simple-minded. As a Malaysian advocate of progressive farming has so well pointed out, a peasant farmer "has an enormous number of techniques to master and decisions to make. He has to think of soil and weather conditions. He has to select . . . varieties . . . which he knows from experience will succeed." He must "think twice about changing to a new variety," and if he does make an experiment he will "try it in a corner of a field—or on a plot of poorer lands where the risk is not so great." Tun Abdul Razak bin Hussein, "A Drive for Greater Progress," *Development Forum,* No. 3 (April 1968), 2.

reached, and doubts had begun to emerge about the wisdom of using expensive mechanical equipment for producing subsistence crops. Losses continued in 1953, and whereas the Nigerian Government regarded the scheme as useful for "rural welfare" purposes, the Corporation watched with growing impatience the mounting costs and the failing revenues. On July 1, 1953, it notified the Nigerian Government that it would have to withdraw from the venture. Accordingly, the Project was liquidated with a net loss to the Colonial Development Corporation of £123,494, over 55 percent of the initial capital contribution.[52]

A great number of reasons can be offered to explain the failure of the venture. In the first place, even though an earnest effort was made to distinguish this new type of extensive agriculture from the bitterly hated colonial plantation, the mere fact that it was said to be "cooperative" or "communal" tillage did not suppress a suspicion that it was still a colonial type of agricultural regimentation.[53] The major difficulty probably stemmed from the very nature of the project itself, which required a continuity of operations unprecedented and unfamiliar to the African peasants who wanted to be free to absent themselves for ceremonial events or simply to be idle if they wished.[54] In the new scheme of things the settlers in new (unfamiliar) villages were told where to live, where to farm, what to grow, and when to plant, weed, and harvest. They were asked to change their whole way of life, and whereas they may have appreciated "the kindness of the Europeans in providing them with houses and making available very expensive equipment," this did not prevent them from feeling that "they were working in the interests of Europeans and not of themselves."[55] Disagreements consequently arose about an equitable division of crops, and

52. For a comprehensive analysis of cost and revenue data and for a critical evaluation of the project, see Baldwin, *Niger Agricultural Project,* Chapters 2–8, 12.

53. "It is open to question . . . whether West Africans really object to plantations as such or whether they only object to plantations being in the ownership of Europeans or of a government identified in their minds with Europeans." *Ibid.,* p. 26.

54. The attitude of Africans toward work, wages, and leisure has been very carefully examined by Elliot J. Berg in an excellent article entitled "Backward-Sloping Labor Supply Functions in Dual Economics: The African Case," *Quarterly Journal of Economics,* 65 (August 1961), pp. 468–492.

55. Baldwin, *Niger Agricultural Project,* p. 54. This "colonial" aspect of the Africans' disaffection undoubtedly increased the difficulties of the Project managers, but the basic complaint was probably against the discipline that the peasant-plantation type of farming involved.

suspicions that the settlers were being cheated led to pilferage, chronic absenteeism, and an increasing withdrawal of peasants from the Project. As more and more peasant participants abandoned their new 24-acre farms, replacements had to be found, many of whom were marginal;[56] and "the rest of the story of the relations between the settlers and the management is largely one of mutual frustration, misunderstanding, and irritation."[57]

The trouble was that large-scale mechanized farming demands the completion of tasks "at the right places at the right time," and the only disciplinary action the company could take against uncooperative or truant farmers was to evict them, a penalty that proved to be wholly ineffective. As a result, this experiment, which had envisaged not only a substantial increase in output but much higher cash incomes and a new spatial design of agriculture in "model villages" ended with virtually none of its aims achieved. There had been, to be sure, a steady increase in the amount of food crops (particularly sorghum), but the production of groundnuts was most disappointing, and the costs of production consistently exceeded the value of the crop. "Mechanical farming," as Baldwin has said so laconically, "was certainly not combined happily with the agricultural skill of the settlers."[58] The effort to forge a new society in new villages, equipped with meeting halls, schools, mosques, slaughter houses, and market stalls, ran afoul of a local (Nupe) traditional practice of integrating villages with dependent hamlets into a collectivity wherein marriages, feasts, and other ceremonies were systematically supervised. The new large compounds, with rectangular rather than circular houses and with entrances facing outward rather than inward in the African custom, were not "homes" to the African settlers who scornfully referred to them as "cantonments." Surely the moral of this story is that changes cannot be drastic, and that progress in agricultural productivity will depend on adaptation rather than displacement of time-trusted institutions.

For some underdeveloped countries a restructuring of agrarian landscapes can probably be achieved by means of cooperative institutions, and the rapid progress that Israel has made in modernizing agriculture seems to confirm this belief. It may be objected that, since Israel is

56. Ibid., p. 50. By the end of the second year, a third of the original settlers had been replaced and the remainder were considered "unsatisfactory." Ibid., p. 57.

57. Ibid., p. 47.

58. Ibid., p. 174.

largely a nation of immigrants, it has not really restructured an existing agricultural pattern but has brought new institutions into the country for an immigrant population.[59] In a sense this is true; but it ought not be overlooked that "much of Israel's growth has been accomplished by relatively primitive people, immigrants . . . reared in a patriarchal tradition,"[60] and that an existing Palestinian agricultural pattern was superseded by a new arrangement. At any rate a novel design has emerged, one in which the object of agricultural planning has been to obtain benefits comparable to those that are technologically possible in efficiently operated plantations and yet allow most of the farmers to have continuous and secure land tenure, thereby strengthening their incentives for good husbandry and intensifying their patriotism by assuring to them actual, if not legal, possession of a part of the Jewish homeland. As a consequence of these innovations, Israel's agriculture is largely now organized along cooperative lines, and three kinds of agricultural communities have evolved: the kibbutz (collective), the moshav shitufi (collective village), and the moshav (cooperative village).

Whether large or small,[61] the kibbutz is "a true collective and functions as a single democratic unit."[62] Following Marxist theory, it asks each member to contribute "according to his ability," rewarding him, not with money or profits, but by communal services "according to his need." The moshav shitufi[63] is similar to the kibbutz in that "lands are collectively cultivated, the dairy is collectively owned, and the work is organized by one elective works manager."[64] But profits are distributed in equal amounts to member families, who live in separate households.[65] In both the kibbutz and the less rigid moshav shitufi there are disciplinary, educational, and didactic purposes interblended with economic functions. In the third type, the moshav, the emphasis is primarily economic; and since most of the recent settlements are of this

59. Between November 1948 and January 1963 the population of Israel increased almost threefold, from about 810,000 persons to 2,332,000; but of this growth about two-thirds was from immigration. See Eliezer Brutzkus, *Physical Planning in Israel: Problems and Achievements,* Jerusalem, 1964, p. 13.

60. Mordechai E. Kreinin, *Israel and Africa: A Study in Technical Cooperation,* New York, 1964, p. 7.

61. A small kibbutz may have only 60 members, a large one over 1,000 members.

62. Kreinin, *Israel and Africa,* p. 24.

63. As of 1964 only twenty existed.

64. Kreinin, *Israel and Africa,* p. 24.

65. Since families in a moshav shitufi have cash incomes, which members of a Kibbutz do not have, village stores are part of the collective villages.

type, the moshav has had a far more important spatial influence than the kibbutz or the moshav shitufi. Whereas the moshav shitufi is a "collective village," the moshav is a "cooperative village." Up to 150 farm family units make up a community, one in which each family lives in its own house and works its own fields.[66] But although each farmer is an entrepreneur who manages his farm independently, all purchases of inputs (seeds, implements, and other farm supplies) are made through a cooperative society, and all farm produce is marketed by the society. As in the Danish system, the village cooperative societies (which are multipurpose) are federated with nation-wide cooperative societies so arranged that there are separate societies for particular functions. The location of all cooperative villages as well as the major productive purpose they are to perform (e.g., mixed farming, industrial crops) are matters decided upon by the national Central Planning Authority. This supervision is legally possible because moshav land is nationally owned, although it is rented to participating farmers on long leases.[67] The leases forbid fragmentation of holdings and stipulate the proper type of crop rotation, the arrangements for irrigation water, and other technical requirements. Plots of land are laid out in such a way that they are parts of larger contiguous areas, to make possible large-scale, cooperative, mechanized operations.[68]

The establishment of the several types of collective and cooperative institutions and their dispersion over Israeli landscapes has helped to materialize a national spatial plan, which is flexible as regards specific locations of new settlements but nevertheless has had very clear and consistent objectives. Since these spatial achievements will be reviewed in more detail in Chapter 9, it need only be pointed out here that the Israeli planners, who had to formulate a settlement policy once an independent state had come into existence, realized that the trends which had developed in the Mandate period were dangerously polarizing the population in metropolitan areas. Tel Aviv with its five suburbs had almost 44 percent of the nation's Jewish population, while the country's three largest cities (Tel Aviv, Haifa, and Jerusalem) together accounted for over 70 percent. So that national defense could be insured and some necessary degree of national self-sufficiency achieved, a popu-

66. The hiring of farm laborers is prohibited except under unusual circumstances.

67. Which are extendable to a lessee's heirs.

68. Kreinin, *Israel and Africa,* p. 25. For further details see E. Yalan, *Planning of Agricultural Settlements in Israel,* Jerusalem, 1960.

lation-dispersal program was decided upon. In considering all the implications of such a program, the planners came to the conclusion that mere diffusion of arriving immigrants would not suffice; a proper hierarchy of urban centers would be needed to link the collective and cooperative-farming units with the large cities. The upshot was a veritable town-building program, with a state-making importance probably unparalleled since the early years of Tokugawa Japan. The spatial structure envisaged by the Israeli planners included four major components: A, B, C, and D centers. Smallest were to be the A centers, which might be moshavim, kibbutzim, or old Palestinian villages. The B types were regarded as local service centers that would link together from four to six moshavim. Next in the hierarchy came the C centers, areal market towns with planned populations of from six to twelve thousand people, serving a rural hinterland with diameters of from 12 to 20 kilometers. Here would be located not only workshops and service institutions but some of the smaller industrial plants, particularly processing industries. The D centers were envisaged to be as much as five times the size of the C centers, from about fifteen to sixty thousand people. In them would be located a variety of manufacturing enterprises "not necessarily dependent on regional resources" together with such marketing financial and service facilities as would be necessary for cities conceived as regional capitals.[69] How this spatial design was modified in the Israeli efforts to implement it is explained in Chapter 9. Here it is only necessary to remark that the extraordinary success of Israel's land reclamation and settlement program, carried out despite exasperating political difficulties[70] and seemingly unsolvable irrigation problems, which were both technical and political, is attested by the growth in agricultural product per person employed,[71] a remarkable achievement when one considers that so many of the immigrant farmers came from technically backward areas of Asia and Africa.[72]

69. The best account of this imaginative planning has been written by one of the planners. See Eliezer Brutzkus, *Physical Planning in Israel,* pp. 13ff.

70. Many settlements in remote and unpromising areas were considered imperative for security reasons.

71. The annual rates of growth range from a low of 5.4 percent (1950–1955) to a high of 11.1 percent (1955–1960) and average 8.3 percent for the 1950–1965 period. For details see Nadav Halevi and Ruth Klinov-Malul, *The Economic Development of Israel,* New York, 1968, p. 135.

72. From 1955 on, about 28 percent of the Asian and African immigrants were employed in agriculture. Ibid., p. 79, Table 21.

The Israeli success story in restructuring agriculture by means of collective and cooperative institutions is really quite unique and probably can be largely explained by the discipline, devotion, and dedication of homeless people zealously determined to have a Jewish homeland at long last. Despite the achievements in the USSR, most other experiments with collective and cooperative agriculture have been beset with difficulties or have been abandoned. In both China and Yugoslavia, although both were declaredly socialist societies, efforts to restructure agriculture by collective organizations have been signally unsuccessful. I was a witness to the dismemberment of collectivized agriculture in Yugoslavia, and there can be no doubt whatever that the Yugoslav government was compelled to liberalize its agricultural program in order to obtain a tolerable measure of cooperation from the peasant farmers.[73] Consequently, the extensive, ambitious, and sometimes coercive attempt to follow the Soviet pattern was abruptly ended by the simple expedient of allowing the members of collectives to revert to small-scale private-enterprise farming.[74] With the wholesale dismemberment of the collectives (or their consolidation with or conversion into state farms) the spatial theory on which the collectivization of agriculture had been based had to be superseded by a new schema.[75] The socialist thesis had been that collectives would restructure agrarian space in two main ways: by combining the population, fields, and appurtenances of several villages, collectives would create communities larger than the hamlets and villages that had grown up historically; and, secondly, many of the functions of towns and small cities in "bourgeois" societies would presumably be performed by a spatial hierarchy of collectives. All these theoretical projections ran afoul of the increasing opposition of the Yugoslav peasants to which the government finally had to come to terms. A new spatial theory was now needed, one that would make it possible for the government to provide satisfactory incentives for farmers and thereby convert a stagnant agri-

73. Estimates I made in 1952, when the average agricultural output of the OEEC countries was 18 percent above prewar production, indicated that Yugoslav output was pre-war minus 9 percent and falling.

74. Lest a resurgence of "bourgeois" organization should follow the dissolution of the collectives, legislation stipulating a maximum size of farms (about 25 acres) was hastily enacted. See Albert Waterston, *Planning in Yugoslavia,* Baltimore, 1962, p. 23.

75. The withdrawal of the peasants from the cooperatives was so nationwide and so swift that only 6 percent of the cultivated land remained in cooperatives and 3 percent in state farms. Ibid.

culture into a scheme of things that would make possible satisfactory increases in output and productivity. The outcome was a somewhat reluctant acceptance of a market-town concept of spatial organization, which will be explained in detail in Chapter 9. There were, however, some new factors, mainly an interblending of the roles of public and private sectors in the "communes," so that the result was a defensible synthesis of Christaller-Löschean principles and Marxist revisionism. But the hope of following the Soviet policy of organizing the rural economy on a townless, peasant-plantation scheme was abandoned in favor of a less drastic, more familiar, and, above all, more flexible arrangement.

Some tentative conclusions seem warranted about the available options for restructuring agrarian landscapes in underdeveloped areas. Because a peasant-plantation type of agriculture is a rather unlikely prospect, and because a collective (or systematically cooperative) organization, except in very unusual situations, is congenitally unacceptable to most peasant communities, the modernization of agriculture in a majority of underdeveloped countries will have to be a gradual process of cumulative change. Policies will have to be carefully formulated that look toward a progressive commercialization of the farming areas already provided with some market facilities, toward the creation of new, more, or better markets in areas now very poorly served. Roads must be planned to link farms with market towns; suitable institutions (private or cooperative) must be formed to make available needed farm inputs. All these essentials are dependent on an appropriate spatial restructuring of economic landscapes, a task that must be clearly visualized and then gradually implemented. Regional theory, in short, must become something operational.[76] Some of the ways in which this might be done are explained in the next chapter. First, however, it is necessary to show why this spatial restructuring will not occur by what Lösch called the "powerful forces of spontaneity."

76. As Walter Isard has so wisely pointed out. See his *Methods of Regional Analysis,* Cambridge, Mass., 1960, p. vii.

CHAPTER 7 SPATIAL RECONSTRUCTION: SOME POLICY ASPECTS

The Need for Planning and Prescriptive Intervention

If progress is to be made in developing poor and technically backward countries, the reasons why they have remained backward must be explored. Answers must be found to a number of awkward questions, since, apparently, in some economies development does not spread naturally like outgoing ripples from places where it has begun to contiguous areas. It would seem that when competition in the more-developed areas of a country has led to falling returns on investments, the decreasing yields would tempt investors and entrepreneurs to redirect their funds to spatial frontiers. On that assumption, it could be argued that, if nature were left to take its course, inexperienced governments in less-developed countries would not need to embark on their uncharted experiments with "induced" development. Rather good theoretical answers to such issues have been given in a few succinct pages of carefully reasoned analysis by John Friedmann, who crisply asserts that "a major difficulty with the equilibrium model," which posits that capital will spontaneously flow from lower to higher productivity areas and thereby animate development in spatial backwaters, is simply "that historical evidence does not support it."[1]

Like many other regional analysts,[2] Friedmann employs a "center-periphery" model which abstractly describes an inevitable polarity

1. *Regional Development Policy: A Case Study of Venezuela,* Cambridge, Mass., 1966, pp. 14–18.

2. Among whom may be listed François Perroux, Rául Prebisch, Gunnar Myrdal, Albert Hirschman, T. W. Schultz, Gerald M. Meier, Robert E. Baldwin, and Harvey Perloff.

recognizable in every nation's economic development and calls attention to a tendency for dual economies to emerge as investments are concentrated in location-favored "core-region" centers, which, as they grow, not only drain off the best manpower from outlying "peripheries" but restrict investment in those hinterlands by luring both capital and entrepreneurship to the more dynamic "centers." As a consequence, the centers benefit from an agglomeration of enterprises (both similar and dissimilar) and in the process acquire external economies that give them further advantages.[3] Since the periphery has ordinarily only primary products to exchange for center-produced (or center-assembled) manufactured goods and center-supplied services, the regional terms of trade will tend to favor the centers, and the peripheries will presently find themselves in a quasi-colonial relation vis-à-vis the more prosperous centers. For the resulting inequality of wealth and income and for the differential rates of economic progress in center and periphery, two explanations have been advanced, each with its accompanying policy prescription.

One school argues that the advantage which the centers have acquired is only temporary. As more investment funds are attracted and employed, the marginal efficiency of capital will decline, and, presently, when yields fall (or threaten to fall), investors and entrepreneurs will begin to seek higher-yield outlets for their capital and managerial skills in the peripheries. Reflecting a conviction that there is an unfailing tendency of every economy to find an equilibrium, this school, as Friedmann has put it so neatly, "soothes policy makers by reassuring them that the unhindered operation of market forces will inevitably tend to establish a spatial equilibrium (and thus the highest degree of social well-being."[4] In time, presumably, the investment contours will widen until there will be spatial equalization of rates of return on capital and on managerial compensation. No intervention is needed because the true productive potentials of the peripheries will presently be discovered by the enterprise system. What is needed is patience and faith!

The opposing school, with which I ally myself, rejects these blissful forecasts categorically, insisting that "disequilibrium is built into tran-

3. Walter Isard distinguishes "localization economies," which result from the clustering of plants of like character at one site, from "urbanization economies," which emerge when unlike plants congregate around one site. Both types, which collectively Isard has called" spatial-juxtaposition economies," are unlike "scale economies" because they are independent of the firms' output capacities. See *Methods of Regional Analysis,* Cambridge, Mass., 1960, p. 404.

4. Friedmann, *Regional Development Policy,* p. 14.

sitional societies from the start"[5] and that historical evidence reveals that after almost two centuries of industrialization the presumed spatial equalization has occurred neither in Western Europe nor in the United States. Instead, the depressing spectacle of endemic and seemingly permanent poverty in the Borinage region of Belgium, Appalachia, South Wales, and elsewhere has aroused public opinion to such a degree of indignation that demands for governmental remedial measures can no longer be ignored! Market forces have not generated a demand for the services of the unemployed (or underemployed) labor even though wage rates have been lower in these pockets of poverty. Capital has not flowed to the low-wage areas, nor have underpaid workers migrated to higher-wage locations and thereby equalized wage rates in centers and peripheries. Since there has been no regional convergence of factor compensation in "mature," completely commercialized, and industrialized countries, it seems rather illogical to expect neat equilibria to emerge in underdeveloped countries. The predictions of equilibrium theory refuse to correspond to economic reality for several puissant reasons.

The diminishing returns for investments in metropolitan areas, forecast by the equilibrium theorists, rather consistently seem to be offset by growing external economies or are neutralized by technological or managerial innovations; consequently, since profits can continue to be made by investing in "centers," any strong incentives to seek investment opportunities in peripheries are lacking.[6] Moreover, because investors and entrepreneurs are familiar with business opportunities in large metropolitan centers, and since data relevant to new ventures can be readily assembled there, it is always much easier to establish new enterprises (or expand old ones) in center locations than to launch new projects in smaller, less-familiar locations in the peripheries. And when center-located industries find export outlets for some of their products, their decision makers may tend to regard domestic peripheries as merely one of several market areas and may consider the establishment of foreign subsidiaries more important than building new plants in an already controlled domestic market. In the meantime, as more industries seeking "urbanization economics" congregate in centers, it may well be that only those industries whose input requirements indicate a location near weight-losing materials will tend to be found in periph-

5. Ibid.
6. Friedmann, *Regional Development Policy*, p. 15.

eries. In addition, because a center "is almost always the high citadel of finance, education, research, planning, and control services,"[7] it will have many advantages over simpler hinterland towns and small cities. Its population will be more skilled, varied, versatile, and innovative. In contrast to all these cumulative advantages of the center one usually finds in the peripheries overpopulation and underemployment leading to outmigration, which leeches rural communities of their ablest young persons; lack of capital, since much of the available savings tends to find investment outlets in centers; and relatively inexperienced and cautious entrepreneurship. For all these reasons the prospects of income convergence between centers and peripheries are remote,[8] and Myrdal's "spread effects" an unlikely eventuality, as he himself apparently recognized.[9] The trend toward income convergence (for in halting ways there is such a trend) is therefore very slow, one that is often arrested by technological and managerial innovations before it has produced much effort, and since the centers of "core regions" of developing countries are much more likely to develop or borrow technological innovations, particularly when they will consistently be favored by foreign investors and promoters, Lösch's presumed "powerful forces of spontaneity" are unlikely to initiate a transformation of village-structured peripheries in underdeveloped countries.[10]

This universal trend toward economic polarity, which has been documented in so many contexts that its pervasiveness cannot be denied,

7. Ibid., p. 16.

8. For a well-reasoned explanation why "growth impulses" have not "trickled down" to Indian peripheries, see Brian J. L. Berry, "Policy Implications of an Urban Location Model for the Kanpur Region," in *Regional Perspective of Industrial and Urban Growth: The Case of Kanpur*, ed. P. B. Desai, I. M. Grossack, and K. N. Sharma, Bombay, 1969.

9. "Even in such countries as the United States or Sweden, where in the last century business enterprise has been able to exploit a particularly favorable situation as regards natural resources, and where other unusually advantageous conditions for economic growth have also been present, not least in the general cultural situation, developments have not been such as to draw the whole country into a more or less equal and simultaneous expansion process." Gunnar Myrdal, *Economic Theory and Underdeveloped Regions*, London, 1957, pp. 31–32.

10. For a fuller explanation, see Friedmann, *Regional Development Policy*, pp. 14–19; Rufus B. Hughes, "International Income Differences: Self-Perpetuation," *Southern Economic Journal*, 37 (1961), 41–45; Bernard Okun and R. W. Richardson, "Regional Income Inequality and Internal Migration," *Economic Development and Cultural Change*, 9 (1961), 128–143; Richard A. Easterlin, "Long-Term Regional Income Changes: Some Suggested Factors," Regional Science Association, *Papers and Proceedings*, 4 (1958), 313–325.

indicates that planning will be imperative if the great interior spaces of the "third world" are to be modernized.[11] The question no longer is whether to plan but rather how to plan, what to plan, and with what primary spatial goals and targets. It is the thesis of this essay that unless underdeveloped countries are prepared to adopt the Soviet type of spatial policies, which envisage few cities and are content with virtually townless agrarian landscapes, the first objective of regional planning must be a visualization of systematic projections for the progressive development and numerical increase of properly dispersed agro-urban central places.

The lack of towns and small cities must by some means be corrected; the void between the ubiquitous villages and parasitic great cities must be bridged.[12] Obviously, a whole hierarchy of central places cannot be preplanned or quickly built. What can be done, however, is to coagulate programmed investments, both private and public, into new, well-located capital clusters that can become nuclei around which the "powerful forces of spontaneity" can gradually begin to exert their influence. Just as a handful of honeybees, if provided with a fertile queen, can in a short time become a vigorous colony of twenty-five thousand or more worker bees,[13] in much the same way one can visualize a genetic process whereby contrived investment clusters can become the nuclei for almost any desired number of new agro-urban center places in underdeveloped countries. It is here that the process of town building must begin; on this score the Löschean sequence from small to larger central places should be the prescription, because the larger, intermediate central places will have no true function unless the smaller market towns have begun to take form.

Creating an Investment Climate in Rural Areas

If a town-building program is to be launched, and if, once started, its momentum is to be maintained, a number of planning steps must be

11. On the limitations of general equilibrium theory and the necessity of planning, see François Perroux, *Les Techniques quantitatives de la planification,* Paris, 1965, p. 6ff.

12. See Bert F. Hoselitz, ed., *Sociological Aspects of Economic Growth,* Glencoe, Ill., 1960, pp. 185–216.

13. If, by proper planning and parthenogenetic arrangements, fifty queens have been raised and fertilized, it would be possible for a normal-sized colony to be divided into as many nuclei, and by this means the number of colonies might be increased fiftyfold. See Lorenzo L. Langstroth, *Langstroth on the Hive and Honey Bee,* revised by C. P. Dadant, Hamilton, Ill., 1913, Chapter 7.

systematically taken in each region whose transformation is contemplated. Because there are in every landscape some well-located villages, strategic road crossings, important river-road junctures, or places where the population exhibits better than average energy and drive, such locations can become particularly promising growth points. In these, certain already programmed investments can be coagulated into what I have called "investment clusters."[14] Here regulated markets can experimentally be established to see whether they will create a "field of attraction." If they do, then a road-building or road-improving program and a selective electrification expansion can be undertaken to stimulate some measure of local subpolarization. The process might well be quickened if appropriate coordinating and capital-assembling institutions are established, competent to guide and assist the whole town-building program. A distinction will need to be made between "town founders" and "town fillers," although both groups will be equally essential.[15] But these several steps in the planning enchainment, which will be discussed seriatim, are all dependent on the success with which an investment climate can, more or less artificially, be produced so that private investors will voluntarily conjoin *tranches* of their capital with public-sector capital inputs, thereby setting in motion a cumulative and multiplying type of capital formation. It is quite feasible to create such an investment climate, one that can attract capital from outside a local community and by that example induce wary local propertied people to venture capital in a development program.[16]

The amazing progress of Puerto Rico indicates not only that such a program is possible but also that, once begun, it can acquire considerable momentum. This poor, backward island created an investment climate that has already attracted over fifteen hundred American enterprises and lures millions of dollars of overseas capital each year for starting new enterprises and expanding existing ones.[17] The strategy

14. *Market Towns and Spatial Development in India,* New Delhi, 1965, Chapter 5.

15. This distinction was explained as a historical factor by Werner Sombart. For details see August Lösch, *Economics of Location,* New Haven, 1954, p. 76.

16. On this subject see Friedmann, *Regional Development Policy,* p. 22. The conclusions of the Kanpur International Seminar were that "the industrial climate in Kanpur seems to be dominated by pessimism." Local owners of capital appear reluctant to take risks, while conversely, a greater reliance on "State assistance, concessions and guarantees" has developed. See Kamta Presad, "Industrial Prospects of the Kanpur Region," in *Regional Perspective of Industrial and Urban Growth,* ed. Desai, Grossack, and Sharma, pp. 78–79.

17. In 1968–1969 arrangements were made for 551 new factory projects that will provide about 42,000 jobs. Of these 551 projects, 212 were new factories; 162, expan-

of the planners was to convince external investors that there were advantages in directing some of their funds to a low-wage Caribbean area. This, to be sure, required special inducements, certain protective assurances, and, above all, guaranteed boundaries of entrepreneurial freedom. But the program was not based on mere permissiveness. The kind of industries that were suitable and desired were suggested by the planners, and since Puerto Rico had long suffered from endemic underemployment it was the labor-intensive industries, producing goods for which demand was elastic, that were initially favored. As development took root, relatively more capital-intensive industries seemed to be justified,[18] and now, a quarter century after the development program began, the emphasis can more and more be laid on capital-intensive projects.[19]

At the beginning of the capital-attracting venture the object was to induce entrepreneurs to start industrial plants anywhere on the island, and although the employment thereby created was gratifying, the planners soon realized the dangers that might result from a rapid overconcentration of industry and population in the island's two large cities, San Juan and Ponce. The program was therefore reconsidered in spatial terms, and this reconsideration of goals progressively converted the investment operation into a town-building program. For the planners now sensed the weaknesses of a center-periphery type of development and boldly decided that their efforts would be directed toward a spatial diffusion rather than a polarized concentration of manufacturing. Since the unit of local government is the "municipality," of which there are seventy-six in Puerto Rico, the planners set as a minimum goal the establishment of at least one factory cluster in

---

sions of existing plants that are branching into new product lines; 160, enlargements of operating plants, and 17 new joint ventures between Puerto Rican and United States investors. For fuller details see *New York Times*, July 13, 1969.

18. So many underdeveloped countries have failed to understand this progression. Dazzled by the seeming transforming power of capital-intensive industries, they opt for these long before adequate preparation has been made by labor-intensive industries.

19. Such as the petroleum-processing industries and petro-chemical plants now being established in Ponce and elsewhere, representing a $200 million investment. These are not the only large-scale capital installations: Union Carbide will have a $225 million complex completed by 1970, and International Fibers, a subsidiary of Phillips Petroleum, is expanding its facilities by a $41 million investment. See *New York Times*, July 13, 1969. PPG Industries has earmarked $150 million for new chemical plants in Puerto Rico. See *PPG Shareholders News*, April 1969.

each municipality to provide employment in the overpopulated rural areas and to help commercialize farming in the mountainous interior municipalities. This dispersion of industry into country communities called for differential subsidies, larger tax abatement, together with certain special inducements and rewards for meritorious achievement. As a result of this imaginative type of "induced" development, there is not a single municipality that does not now have an industrial estate.[20] The thrust of development policy has been to create agro-urban communities in all parts of the island and to persuade more and more businessmen to locate either new enterprises or branch factories in the poorer interior municipalities.[21]

Led by an inspired and dedicated man, an imaginative planning agency, by dreaming up lures and incentives, has created an appropriate investment "climate" that has not only channeled to Puerto Rico an ever-growing stream of capital imports[22] from the United States and Europe but, as the success of these foreign-financed enterprises has become evident, has persuaded Puerto Rican monied people to abandon their traditional landlord and money-lending activities and enter into joint ventures with foreign entrepreneurs or launch their own industrial ventures. Thus, cold, calculating businessmen have been persuaded to establish canneries, glass factories, foundries, needlework shops, knitting mills, pharmaceutical plants, shoe factories, and a wide range of other industries in this poor tropical island. Moreover, it has been possible to prevent a concentration in core-region centers, such as San Juan and Ponce, and to induce investors to engage in developing dozens of interior market towns. The general inducements comprised tax exemptions, rent abatement on industrial space, and low-interest loans. Of the three, the main inducement was complete (100 percent) tax exemption, and this relief was from income tax, municipality fees, customs duties, personal income tax on dividends, and from real and personal property taxes. The standard period of

20. The Puerto Rican Industrial Development Corporation has built the industrial estates so that small industries can rent their needed facilities. For more details see Chapter 9, especially Figure 9–5.

21. Of the new projects for fiscal year 1968–1969, thirty-three will be located in small towns "where hard-core unemployment is most acute." *New York Times*, July 13, 1969.

22. Puerto Rico, Administracion de Fomento Economico, Oficina de Estudios Economicós, Divisiόn de Economia General, "Fabricas establecidas bajo el programa de industrializacion, enero de 1966," Mimeographed, San Juan, 1966.

tax exemption was ten years. The second general inducement took the form of rent abatement: one year's use of an industrial-estate "shed" rent-free. This third inducement, a low-cost loan, was provided by the Puerto Rico Development Bank, which stood ready to loan incoming enterprises up to 50 percent of the value of their (uninstalled) machinery and equipment.

Since there was originally no locational variation in this pattern of subvention, practically all the early new enterprises were established in or very near the two largest cities, San Juan and Ponce, where some skilled labor was to be found and where reasonably satisfactory external economies were available. But, whereas the program was generating employment opportunities, increasing the island's exports, and helping to enlarge the effective demand of city-dwelling wage earners, it was soon realized that, at the same time, unfortunately, it was doing little to correct the inequalities of a "dual economy." Indeed, the surge of urban industrialization was creating very difficult housing, sanitation, and educational problems. Because the growth of industry in the two largest cities did not promise to bring about an island-wide development, a decision was therefore reached to graduate the inducement program so that small manufacturing plants would ultimately be dispersed throughout the entire Puerto Rican landscape.

Accordingly, the Industrial Incentives Act of 1954 established a variable schedule of tax and other inducements. Tax exemptions now ranged from ten years in the more developed areas to seventeen years in the most disadvantaged areas. The island was zoned into different tax-exemption belts[23] after careful "regional profiles" had been made, and the differential tax exemptions were related as closely as possible to profitable entrepreneurial risk.[24] But variable tax exemptions were not the only advantages proffered to industrialists who agreed to establish plants in country towns. The rents on government-owned industrial estates were also graduated, with enterprises in the large cities paying almost twice as much rent (95¢ per square foot) as was charged in the least-advantageous locations (50¢). The effect, of course, was to compel the city enterprises to subsidize rural enterprises by means of the differential rental. But this was not yet all. To overcome the handicap which rural industries would encounter by reason of the lack of skilled labor,

23. See Chapter 9, especially Figure 9-4.

24. The basic theory and the Puerto Rican experience with locational incentives are well summarized in Puerto Rico, Administracion de Fomento Economico, *"Proposed Revisions in Policy,"* Memo No. 4, Mimeographed, San Juan, 1962.

the Puerto Rican Industrial Development Corporation made cash grants to country-located enterprises for use in training workmen and to compensate for the temporary lower productivity of apprentices.[25]

The Puerto Rican experience shows that agro-urban industrial centers can be developed if there is the requisite will, vision, imagination, and perseverance. There must be a recognition that core-region centers may frustrate diversified development of peripheries unless positive action is taken to create an equally attractive or more attractive investment opportunity in the rural or outlying communities. In this connection the Puerto Rican experience is exceptionally instructive. The "seed money" that has been spent to bring manufacturing enterprises to every part of rural Puerto Rico is yielding an ever-growing harvest of employment, rising productivity, larger incomes, improved standards of living, and, perhaps best of all, better housing, more schools, and more varied patterns of consumption.

Choosing Promising Growth Points

Assuming that all the regions of an underdeveloped country stand in need of modernization, the question arises as to where to begin. Should planners accord both advisory and fiscal priority to the most-backward regions, or should efforts be first directed to areas where returns will be larger,[26] earlier, and more probable? The latter course, as I have pointed out elsewhere would seem best "if the swiftest possible increase in national output is the chief objective."[27] But "short-run wisdom may be long-run folly." If growth points are sought only in the relatively less-backward regions, then regional differences in productivity, in marketed fractions of farm output, or in incomes, standards

25. For the rural shoe industry, on which major emphasis was laid in 1966–1967, the Development Corporation established special training schools for workers.

26. A committee appointed to study the dispersal of Indian industries (1960) listed the following regional "criteria of backwardness:" low per capita income and consumption; a high ratio of population to cultivable land; low per capita values of agricultural output; absence or underexploitation of mineral or forest resources; dearth of transport facilities as indicated by low mileage of roads or railways in relation to acreage or population; high incidence of employment or underemployment; low consumption of artificial energy. India, Small-Scale Industries Board, Committee on Dispersal of Industries, *Report*, New Delhi, 1960, pp. 5–6.

27. *Market Towns and Spatial Development in India*, p. 107. This was the policy that Italy chose in the immediate postwar years when, despite protests, recovery efforts were concentrated in northern Italy where both agricultural and industrial output seemed much more promising than in southern Italy or Sicily.

of living, and education may widen further, "presaging not only more misery and inefficiency in the 'most-backward' regions but stopping these (usually) heavily-populated areas from becoming reciprocal trading partners with the more-favored regions."[28] The choice is not simply one between regions. A decision has to be made whether a "saturation" technique will be followed in a chosen area with enough growth points selected so that something similar to a classical landscape of market hexagons might result; or, conversely, whether growth points should be chosen at random on the assumption that wherever they are they are worthy of development and that their improvement will benefit not only a particular locality but, in some way, the national economy as well. The virtue of the latter procedure is that it might make it possible for the more backward areas to share modestly in a town-building program (provided they have any eligible growth points) ab initio rather than be forced to wait until the less backward regions have first been favored.[29]

Because every development project has political implications, it is always difficult for decision makers to follow any neat economic prescriptions. But favoritism for the politically vocal, most backward areas may lead to the placement of industrial estates or other sunk-cost investments in wrong places, just as the artificial establishment of market stalls or produce warehouses may involve a waste of resources if they are not adequately utilized because hinterland farm techniques are too primitive, the fragmentation of land too limiting to permit the production of marketable surpluses, or the cultural constraints so stultifying that prices have no luring effect on production. And yet the poorer, less-promising areas cannot be ignored or neglected. The same troublesome issue that always arises concerning the allocation of resources between the more-backward and the less-backward areas will necessarily complicate the planners' tasks when they try to select growth points. Perhaps the best compromise would be to "saturate" portions of one or more of the better regions while randomly chosen growth points are used as "pilot projects" in the more-backward areas. The decision is essentially political, and all the economist can do is to estimate the relative cost-benefit consequences of alternative action programs. But he will be remiss if he does not point out that the

28. Ibid., p. 107.

29. The economic justification for favoring the less-backward areas is the presumption that their quicker development might increase the national resources subsequently available for improving the more-backward areas.

selection of growth points is not something that can be dealt with on a crude patronage basis. However heartless a well-grounded decision to favor less-backward areas may appear to be to those who are distressed by the sight of poverty, there are rigorous criteria that must be applied if the waste of resources is to be avoided. For if growth points are to have a cumulative, transforming effect, they will have to be places where successive *tranches* of investment can prudently be made. It is of the greatest importance, then, that their initial selection should be made by rational, objective, clear-headed, and far-sighted planners in terms of probable long-run advantages.

In selecting rural sites that have better than average prospects of becoming future agro-urban communities, two locational considerations arise. What should be the characteristics of the region in which such a growth point will be sought, and, secondly, what special features should a particular site within a region possess? Since geographic, agronomic, and ethnographic factors will influence the choice of both region and site, it is not easy to isolate general determinants. But there are some. Because the function of the emergent "rural growth center"[30] is to bring country-dwelling people into a market economy in a more complete and truly functional way, the growth potential of any chosen site will perforce depend on the productive capacity of the region in which it is located, for the very obvious reason that in an agrarian economy the future prospects of a market center will depend on its capacity to assemble or process crops that are important not only to the local area but to the entire economy. The first criterion for evaluating a region will therefore be its present crop-producing performance, the second, its potential future productive capacities.

Bennett Harrison has suggested that these two crop "indicators" can be used in conjunction with an index of regional rural population density to determine the relative promise of regions as areas in which to seek suitable sites for rural growth centers.[31] Regions so near to large

30. I have borrowed this useful term from a very imaginative and thoughtful unpublished paper by Bennett Harrison, entitled "Rural Growth Centers: A Strategy for the Rural Development of Low-Income Countries." This paper was prepared for the United States Agency for International Development, Office of Program and Policy Coordination in 1967.

31. "Through a study of a country's comparative food crop advantages, a set of critical crops is specified. Each region of the country is then assigned a quantitative . . . index reflecting its present and potential contribution to national production of these critical crops. The indicator of present 'regional economic importance' (A) is recent average annual percentage contribution by the region to national production of the critical crops. The indicators of potential 'importance' are (B) regional land

cities that some of their villages might become suburban "dormitories" for city workers ought not be equated with genuinely rural regions since it is unlikely that satellite regions can develop semiautonomous centers that will counteract the polarity of large cities. On the other hand, remote regions that have no "transport access" to the urban portions of a national economy will not be very promising places to select as prospective rural growth centers.[32] What Harrison has tried to do is to devise a set of tools which would make it possible to make an algorismic catalogue of the comparative capacities of regions to generate and support rural growth centers, and of the comparative promise of particular places within regions to qualify as sites for future agro-urban communities. The methodology is very imaginative and can without doubt be very useful. It does, however, have some limitations. It does not, for example, come to grips with the most backward–least backward syndrome, and it cannot, by reason of its indifference to where growth points are focused, estimate the possible cumulative effect of a "saturation" approach to town building in a chosen area. For if a saturation method seems worth trying, and a strong case can be made for it, then in all likelihood some sites will have to be included that will have lower algorithms than sites in other regions that may have to be excluded. The merit of the Harrison technique, however, is that planners would at least have some estimate of the disadavantages involved in selecting enough sites that would lead (it might be hoped) to contiguous, spatial, hexagonal hinterlands.

The saturation approach is based on the expectation that the whole will be greater than the sum of its parts. More particularly, it rests on the assumption that the deliberate creation of a polka-dot pattern of rural growth centers in a chosen area will be more likely to result in a regional urban hierarchy than would be the case if rural growth centers were scattered at random over a large economic landscape. This likelihood stems from a corollary assumption that a network of rural growth centers will give greater scope and opportunity for what Lösch has called the "powerful forces of spontaneity."

---

capacity for future expansion of critical crop production, and (C) regional rural population density." "Rural Growth Centers," Chapter 5, pp. 1–2.

32. In his model (which is formally developed in the appendix to his "Rural Growth Centers") Harrison has therefore given a "quantitative dimension" to the "degree of access," and by this means "it becomes possible to rank all existing market towns in the basic set of regions according to their relative transport access." Ibid., Chapter 5, p. 4.

Moreover, since one of the first objectives of a rural growth center program is to increase the degree of areal commercialization, regional congeries of such centers might permit their spatial dispersion according to Christaller's "traffic principle" and thereby reduce the unit cost of transport (by increasing the volume shipped) to the advantage of both rural producers and urban consumers. The basic purpose, however, should not be to develop assembling and loading points for primary commodities; this pattern of rural structure, with its very serious limitations, has been described in a foregoing section on "dendritic markets." The thrust of the emergent "rural growth centers" should be much more centripetal than centrifugal, looking toward the progressive development of places where trade, service, and some appropriate manufacturing facilities will be within access of agricultural hinterlands, thereby providing not only markets for farm products but employment for farm-born young people who prefer nonfarm occupations. This manpower criterion ought not be neglected in the selection of sites for rural growth centers. An International Labour Office (I.L.O.) document has put this issue very succinctly: "An even development of the whole country requires a balanced rural-urban distribution of the requisite skills. As long as urbanization and migration continue as in the past, this will not be achieved."[33] It follows that employment aspects of town-centering development policy may well justify some experimentation with a "saturation" choice of rural growth center sites on the presumption that there will be more variety in the mercantile, service, and manufacturing activities in a dozen closely nested market-town areas than there could be in any single rural growth center.[34]

Of the three general determinants that Harrison has proposed for the selection of regions, the B indicator (regional land capacity for future expansion of critical crops)[35] is clearly the most important.

33. I.L.O., Advisory Working Group on Rural Employment Problems in Tropical Africa (English Speaking Countries). "Discussion Guide." Mimeographed, Lagos, 1965, p. 15.

34. Whereas a single growth center might not have a printing plant, a foundry, or a pharmaceutical laboratory, a group of market towns might possibly develop all these varied enterprises, in which young persons might find employment and in-service training.

35. The "critical crops" may not be the ones that have traditionally been grown. Hybrid corn, "miracle rice," soy beans, or other "new" crops may be better suited to climatic or agronomic potentials than "old" crops such as millet, sorghum, and barley. Proper land-use planning should attempt to appraise the full potential.

Ideally, this forecast would involve estimating for each crop the potential capacity of the region and measuring the optimal regional productivity by "crop trade-offs,"[36] which would reveal the possible gains and the probable opportunity costs. Fuller utilization of agricultural resources will, of course, involve greater inputs (of irrigation water, fertilizers, tools); and to obtain organic spatial development appropriate credit arrangements will be needed to enable farmers to make necessary investments to parallel the investments made in infrastructure and in growth center facilities.[37]

Regional profiles of resources ought to be made together with projections of what these resources might reasonably be expected to produce under a feasible degree of technical guidance. Once these potentials are estimated, the search for best sites can begin. Just here the A indicator (recent average annual agricultural contribution) can be usefully employed to make comparisons between alternative sites, and market contribution maps could be prepared showing the differential capacity of areas within a region to deliver market surpluses to sales points.[38] It should not be forgotten, however, that there are social criteria that are sometimes as important as physical factors. Even deep rich soil, suitable terrain, or salubrious climate and adequate rainfall will not suffice unless there is "evidence of a rising civic spirit,"[39] of ambition and drive on the part of a majority of the people, a willingness to work, save, and invest. Like all other aspects of progress, the development of rural growth centers will very much depend on the quality of leadership a community can muster and on the ability of leaders to inspire confidence and kindle the enthusiasm of their fellow-citizens.[40]

36. Harrison, "Rural Growth Centers," Chapter 5, p. 8.

37. "Public works are only economic if they are integrated into the overall development plan. Constructing a road without improving agriculture or developing industry which can make use of the road is a waste of resources." I.L.O., "Discussion Guide," p. 23.

38. This type of analysis was used to sample and measure marketing volume in the (Indian) Punjab. See Walter C. Neale, Harpal Singh, and Jai Pal Singh, "Kurali Market, A Report on the Economic Geography of Marketing in Northern Punjab," *Economic Development and Cultural Change,* 13 (January 1965), pp. 153–159.

39. Ford Foundation, International Perspective Planning Team on Small Industries, *Development of Small-Scale Industries in India: Prospects, Problems and Policies: Report to the Ministry of Commerce and Industry, Government of India,* New Delhi, 1963, p. 122.

40. For a vivid account of how civic leaders in nineteenth-century America planned country communities and thereby hastened development, see Milton Heath, *Con-*

Coagulating Investments into Punctiform Clusters

Although the site for a rural growth center could be out in open country at an important road junction or at a riparian location where piers, docks, and loading and unloading facilities could be built, it will ordinarily be found in an existing village or small town where some marketing, merchandising, and service facilities already exist.[41] The planning task is to devise ways and means for improving the facilities that already exist, adding new capital installations, providing minimally necessary public services, and establishing such educational, health, and other institutions as will be necessary to make the center a place that will attract buyers and sellers from a widening hinterland, and thereby hasten the process of areal technical and economic improvement and modernization.

An investment cluster is a punctiform grouping of business enterprises that can, by the communicative power of its proffered goods and services, stimulate greater agricultural production, improve the quality of farm produce, and induce farmers to augment their marketable surpluses. Unlike a cluster of similar industries (shoe factories in Brockton, Massachusetts, or cotton textile mills in Ahmedabad, India) an investment cluster in a rural growth center will consist of varied and different enterprises, their number and variety articulated largely to the needs of the hinterlands which are to be served. But though dissimilar, the enterprises will nevertheless derive benefits from association and proximity to one another. These advantages of agglomeration are real and fairly predictable.[42] As the number of mercantile, manufacturing, and service industries that coexist in the same locality increase, there is a very strong probability that total

structive Liberalism: The Role of the State in Economic Development in Georgia to 1860, Cambridge, Mass., 1954, pp. 151–156.

41. If a site has a real marketing advantage, this will no doubt have been discovered long since. Thus Singh has shown that small central places in the Gangetic region of northern India have served as sites for periodic markets since circa A.D. 1290 See Shiw Mangal Singh, "Turrufs Babhnauti and Raotar in the Ganga-Ghaghara Doab West (India): A Study in Land Settlement, Social Geography and Rural Central Places," *National Geographical Journal of India,* 11, Parts 3 and 4 (1965), pp. 185–197.

42. Some analysts make a distinction between "agglomeration" and "nodality," using the former in a regional or subregional sense, the latter as "an orientation toward a central place or node." See Harvey Perloff et al., *Regions, Resources, and Economic Growth,* Baltimore, 1960, pp. 81–84.

demand for all the several products and services will expand because more buyers will be attracted by the prospect of wider choice. Moreover, since a cluster of enterprises attracts more young workers than a single store or workshop can do, and since varied types of businesses will involve different training and skills, a work force will presently come into being that will be versatile and adaptable to a changing set of tasks and responsibilities.[43] The result will normally be greater productivity, which can lead to high wages and lower prices concurrently. A punctiform clustering of workshops or small manufacturing plants will also lead to the emergence of repair and maintenance facilities as well as financial institutions that can provide short-term and intermediate credit accommodation. All these economies, generally called "external economies" since they are not the result of any single firm's managerial decisions, can emerge in varied degrees as investment clusters are formed.[44] As more enterprises congregate in a central place, the total demand for water, electricity, and other "utilities" will grow, permitting better scale economies in the production of such services and reducing the unit costs to the benefit of all users.[45] This would be essentially an advantage of "numbers"; in contrast, the advantages of "association" are largely on the demand side. The production of a variety of products at a spatial "node" will attract buyers because of the sheer convenience of being able to purchase a range of commodities in a single central place; furthermore, there is another quite different benefit which a cluster of different enterprises can confer on a community. Because the types of business—mercantile manufacturing, processing, service—are dissimilar, the probability is that their seasonal and cyclical variations will not coincide; hence a community with a cluster of dissimilar enterprises will have the likeli-

43. In the United States during the last fifty years, perhaps the most important technical training institution has been local (village or town) garages, where thousands and thousands of farm boys received mechanical training on an in-service basis.

44. Walter Isard, who prefers to call these advantages "urbanization economies," has attempted to show the effect of an enlargement of urban size on such economies. See his *Location and Space Economy*, Cambridge, Mass., pp. 182–188.

45. August Lösch has quite properly pointed out that this cost-reducing process will continue only up to an optimal point, after which agglomeration may raise the costs of many services and utilities. See *Economics of Location*, p. 75. But the rural growth centers need have little fear of this constraint since for a long time in this regard they will enjoy the advantages of "increasing returns."

hood of greater stability in output and employment.[46] Thus an industrial estate with small industries operating continuously can be a stabilizing counterpoise to a highly seasonal cannery, rice-hulling mill, or slaughterhouse.

Once astute and careful planners have chosen a site for a rural growth center, the problem is how to materialize these potential "advantages of numbers and association." Obviously, an underdeveloped country cannot patiently wait for the "powerful forces of spontaneity"[47] to set this process in motion, since the unpleasant truth is that these forces have not been "powerful" enough in the past, and unless an investment stimulus is provided by some "change agent," they will not be any more "powerful" in the future. The "operational" task of the planners, whoever they may be—and it should be emphatically pointed out that they need not necessarily be bureaucrats of some central governmental ministry—the really critical responsibility for the planners is to find the needed "change agents." I say "find" because the change agents may be local entrepreneurs who can be "induced" to undertake some new venture, they may be outside investors who are "attracted" by certain concessions, or they may be certain institutions that can "extend" their activities to new growth centers. The methods and techniques will vary from country to country, from region to region. Puerto Rican planners have mainly relied on "attracting" foreign entrepreneurs, Israel has "induced" change by means of collective cooperative institutions, while Yugoslavia has allocated investment funds to new "communes." Whatever strategy is employed, the basic task is to get a few key enterprises started at the chosen growth center sites.

This raises at once the question of whether the initial impetus must come wholly from the public sector or whether some interblending of public and private activities may be feasible. This will largely

46. An extreme example of the dangers to a community that can result from reliance on a single type of enterprise is provided by the history of Cripple Creek, Colorado. When gold mining was booming, over 45,000 people lived in Cripple Creek. As gold-bearing resources were exhausted, the population steadily decreased, so that by 1934 only 4,000 people remained in the community. In that year the United States Government raised the price it would pay for newly-mined gold from $18.67 an ounce to $35.00 an ounce. Mining of hitherto marginal ores now became suddenly profitable, and the population quickly rose to 7,000. Such wide swings in employment do not permit organic central-place development.

47. Lösch, *Economics of Location*, p. 508.

depend on the "investment climate." Whatever the strategem, some adventurous innovators must be found who will assume the initial risks. Only when they have taken the first steps can one expect more conservative people to make parallel investments or establish enterprises of an ancillary or secondary character.[48] It should be noted that what most businessmen do is essentially imitative rather than creative. This is not said to belittle such emulative propensities, quite the contrary. One of the really important functions of a development planning operation is to set this wholesome process of apish investment into vigorous motion.[49] For it is the "town fillers," to use Sombart's term, who will organize and operate the wide variety of local industries, the little shops, the modest service activities, and all the other small enterprises that diversify a community, widen employment opportunities, and complement in countless ways the activities of key industries, so that the entire industrial and business service matrix becomes one of mutually reinforcing enterprises.

One of the simplest and least expensive ways to develop new rural growth centers has been strangely neglected. Each developing country has certain already programmed capital projects. In India, in 1964–1965, for example, plans had been laid for building grain-storage facilities, plants for mixing and distributing commercial fertilizer, modern rice-processing mills, central-government warehouses, state-financed warehouses, solvent-extraction oilseed-processing plants, subdepots for the distribution of seeds, pesticides, and farm implements, village water filtration and distribution systems—all these rural improvement ventures were included in the Third Plan (for the period 1961–1966) as were village-to-town roads, schools, health centers, sanitation projects, and a rural electrification program.[50] The tragic discovery I made was that no effort had been made to coordinate these improvements so that there might by punctiform coagulations that might lead to the creation of new rural growth centers or that might invigorate

48. The important role played by innovating businessmen has been carefully analyzed by Joseph A. Schumpeter. See his *Theory of Economic Development*, Cambridge, Mass., 1934, pp. 156, 217, and 228.

49. "Without . . . a spatial frame of reference . . . the selection of growth points and the identification of less-developed areas could hardly be expected to result in integrated development." L. S. Bhat, "A Regional Approach to the Urban and Industrial Development of the Kanpur Region," in *Regional Perspective of Industrial and Urban Growth*, ed. Desai, Grossack, and Sharma, p. 286.

50. For further details about all these programmed projects see my *Market Towns and Spatial Development in India*, Chapter 2.

well-located, already existing small central places. Instead, each of the planning agencies deployed their installations without reference to the spatial plans of other agencies. The most important function of central planning, the task of coordination, had been woefully neglected because of the indifference of the planners to geographic and spatial factors.[51]

The reason for this neglect, which is by no means merely an Indian failing, is usually twofold. The first is the narrow training of many planners, who become so model-minded that locational theory and geographic factors in economic development are blithely ignored.[52] The second reason is somewhat less innocent. What happens is that every development program becomes a pork barrel, from which politicians dole out projects without reference to the cumulative benefits that might result from a spatial coagulation. Admittedly, there would be favoritism involved in allowing a single site to have not one but a half-dozen programmed capital installations plus lead-in roads, electrification, a modern water system, and a health center. But the favored site might then have a really good chance of becoming an agro-urban center, which could attract private capital and, by a further diversification of shops, industries, and service industries, develop into a truly functional central place.[53] There should therefore be no attempt to conceal the public-sector favoritism; rather, as I have said, "it should be flaunted in order to induce private investors to add to the marketing, processing and light manufacturing facilities."[54]

51. See John P. Lewis' cutting comments on the smug satisfaction of the Third Plan planners, *Quiet Crisis in India*, Washington, 1962, p. 168.

52. The fissiparous outcome of expertise freedom has been vividly explained by Laurence Hewes in his *Study on Integrated Rural Development in Developing Countries* (ACC/WGRCD/XVI). United Nations, Working Paper No. 2, Geneva, 1969, p. 43 ff who points out that the result has been "a proliferation of partial and imperfect . . . theories and strategic concepts, each designed to support a particular undertaking."

53. "As the hinterland farmers come with increasing regularity to the new market town, the possibilities of a wide range of sales and service activities will reveal themselves. Poultry-producers will need feed-mixers, incubators and insecticides; fruit-growers will come into the market for sprays and sprayers, pruning shears and grafting tools. The ever-increasing number of bicycles will require tyres and replacement parts; while, as farmers find better markets for their produce, their spending power will expand not only for necessities such as matches or soap but for a wide range of semi-luxuries such as flash-lights, transistors or household gadgets, provided their desires are whetted." E. A. J. Johnson, *Market Towns and Spatial Development in India*, p. 22.

54. Ibid., pp. 21–22.

CHAPTER 7

Markets and Submarkets as Town-Building Agencies

The greater majority of underdeveloped countries are agricultural economies that can only be transformed and modernized if farming can become increasingly commercialized. Every farm locality that hopes to develop will therefore need access to markets where farm produce can be sold for cash without the danger of monopsonistic exploitation and where there are enough sellers of farm supplies to prevent monopoly. Such markets and farm supply outlets should be punctiform,[55] so that buyers will not have to go to one place for farm supplies, to another for credit, and to still a third place to sell their crops. What is essential, therefore, is a unified market town where appropriate facilities are congregated. Historically, investment clusters have grown up around markets; the Greek agora was a forum, a market, and an artisans' center, even as a cathedral in the medieval world was not merely a place for worship. The enclosure wherein the cathedral stood (the "close") was a meeting place for buyers and sellers, and around it the shops of artisans and the warehouses of merchants crowded so closely that it was difficult in most medieval towns to view the glories of ecclesiastical architecture. Thus, in a sense markets created the towns, although, conversely, it was the towns that made the markets famous.[56]

If markets have been so instrumental in developing towns in the past, there is no reason they cannot now become magnets that will attract investments in the underdeveloped countries and set in motion a town-building process that development so urgently requires. They must, however, be something better than the petty, periodic, exploitative markets that are, alas, all too characteristic of most underdeveloped areas.[57] They will need to be market places and market systems supervised by a governmental authority that is genuinely solicitious of

55. Arthur T. Mosher, by use of another term, "single market center," has very properly emphasized this point in his *Creating a Progressive Rural Structure*, New York, 1969, p. 5.

56. Toledo, Sheffield, and Solingen for steel products; Norwich, Florence, and Leeds for woolen cloth; Lyons for silk; Sevres for porcelain; Faenza, and Burslem (Stoke-on-Trent) for earthenware; Cremona for violins; Prague and Venice for blown glass—almost an endless list could be compiled.

57. In a study of the marketing of *gur* at a *mandi* (an unregulated market) in Uttar Pradesh, India, it was discovered that sellers were required to pay the following types of charges, all subtracted from the alleged market value of the *gur:* octroi charges to enter the market, weighing costs, a commission to the selling agent (*kachcha arhatia*), a charity contribution, a deduction for the (dealer-estimated)

farmers' interests (which will be difficult to insure) or they must be controlled by some organization in which producers are themselves well represented. They history of regulated markets in India demonstrates that a wholesale cooperation between traders, producers, and local government can be effected with great benefit to the direct participants, to the communities in which such regulated markets are located, and to the entire nation. In a sample survey that I made in 1964 of 100 regulated markets, 83 percent of the respondents asserted that market arrivals had markedly increased (estimates ranged from 25 percent to 85 percent) since the establishment of their respective regulated markets, and 55 percent of the respondents listed the kinds of new processing industries (e.g., cotton gins, oilseed-pressing plants, decorticating mills) that had grown up near the market yards subsequent to the establishment of the regulated markets.[58] The data derived from this survey showed that there is an indisputable correlation between the existence of regulated markets and degrees of agrarian commercialization. This inference is confirmed by other studies, indicating that it was precisely those Indian states in which there were the better networks of regulated markets that have shown, since liberation, the highest growth rates in agricultural output.[59]

The skeptic may argue that the foregoing argument merely proves that where there are towns there can be markets and that no causal connections can be inferred. Markets and agrarian commercialization, he will say, are always complementary phenomena. If towns create a demand for farm produce (whether from local consumers or from merchants, commission agents, or brokers who reflect demand external to the towns), markets can and will be established. But only if farmers are producing marketable surpluses. The process is both organic and reciprocal: demand might increase, and supply might be a response;

---

moisture in the *gur*, and interest on the money value of the credit presumably extended by the commission agent to a city buyer of the *gur*. See Tej Vir Singh, "Market Study of Gur in Bulandshahr Mandi," Master's thesis, Government Agricultural College, Kanpur, 1965. This type of market cannot be expected to give farmers very strong incentives for increasing marketable surpluses. For the most part, distress sales of petty surpluses are brought to such markets, and no shops or farm-supply distributors grow up around them.

58. Since there were then only about 1,100 regulated markets in the whole of India, this was a large sample, and I therefore consider the data gathered dependably representative, especially because the information was prepared by the secretaries of the markets and was in most cases approved by the market committees.

59. India, Ministry of Food and Agriculture, Economics and Statistics Adviser, *Growth Rates in Agriculture*, New Delhi, 1964, pp. 44–46, 54, 60.

or surpluses might be produced, and the available supply might attract buyers. There is, of course, much truth in this argument. In India the regulated markets, which were established in existing towns and small cities, first regularized and systematized existing trading operations; then, by developing certain supervisory and protective features, they were soon instrumental in increasing the volume of trade. By doing so they enlarged producers' spending capacity, which, in turn, had a stimulating effect not only on retail trade but on agrarian capital formation, on productivity, and on the volume of production. All this seems very clear. The sequence was towns, establishment of regulated markets, greater agricultural production, larger trade volume, greater areal prosperity.

There are, I think, two reasons why the regulated market system did not expand over the whole subcontinent of India and modernize one area after another. In some states, and in parts of others, the movement was opposed by vested interests that stood to lose monopoloid advantages by the establishment of a regulated-market system. In other states, as regulated markets grew in number, there were fewer and fewer appropriate central places in which to locate new regulated markets. Two quite different problems consequently arise: the first is political, the second largely, but not wholly, economic. For the political problem, stemming from the opposition of an entrenched group of skinflint local merchants and usurers, only political remedies are possible, and how long it will take for an effective political opposition to crystallize is a question on which I am not competent to offer any opinion. I can only assume that information about how regulated markets operate in these parts of India where they now exist will not remain a local secret and hope that, as the public in other regions is made aware of the very substantial benefits such markets can confer, this will lead to a demand for legislative and administrative change in the unregenerate areas. The second problem, which stems from the inadequacy of existing central places, calls for an entirely different solution. Once the programmed expansion of regulated markets visualized by the Directorate of Marketing and Inspection is completed, the meliorative process will grind to a halt unless new rural growth centers are found and developed.[60]

60. Projections made in 1964 foresaw an increase in the number of regulated markets from 1,078 to 1,787, and this expansion would largely exhaust the available sites in the thirteen states that planned to increase their regulated-market coverage.

That regulated markets themselves can provide the Promethean creative fire would seem to be indicated by the Indian experience in Maharashtra. Yet it was pointed out in Chapter 3 that one limitation of contrived markets is that they may leave sizable portions of a landscape without satisfactory market facilities. Thus, in Aurangabad District (see Figure 3–10) 75 percent of the agrarian area was unserviced. To correct this kind of a situation a new trend began (though unfortunately not in Aurangabad District); existing regulated markets started to establish "subyards" in smaller communities. This movement has spread from Maharashtra into several other Indian states, and Table 7–1 shows that almost a third of the markets that existed in six states (when the data was gathered in December 1963) were subyards. The new departure has many advantages: it is simple, inexpensive, not difficult to initiate, and it is an experiment that can be easily terminated if it proves unsuccessful.

Table 7–1 Regulated Market Subyards: Number and Distribution

State	Main yards	Subyards	Ratio of subyards to main yards
Mysore	80	65	80.1%
Gujarat	96	76	79.2
Orissa	16	10	62.5
Maharashtra	182	70	38.3
Madhya Pradesh	98	12	12.2
Andhra Pradesh	91	8	8.8
Total	563	241	29.1 (average)

SOURCE: E. A. J. Johnson, *Market Towns and Spatial Development in India,* New Delhi: National Council of Applied Economic Research, 1965, p. 77.

The way the process operates is illustrated in Figure 7–1. Before the new movement began, the Poona District had eight, spatially distinct regulated markets in operation, each with its controlling committee, on which both farmers and traders were represented. And whereas these eight regulated markets served portions of the landscape

But two very populous states, Uttar Pradesh and West Bengal, both of which have several score of suitable sites, had no plans even to begin the reconstruction and supervision of their archaic and cruelly exploitative unregulated-market structures. The same negativism persisted in Assam and, in a somewhat lesser way, in Orissa, where only a feeble expansion was contemplated. For details see my *Market Towns and Spatial Development in India,* p. 144, Table 21.

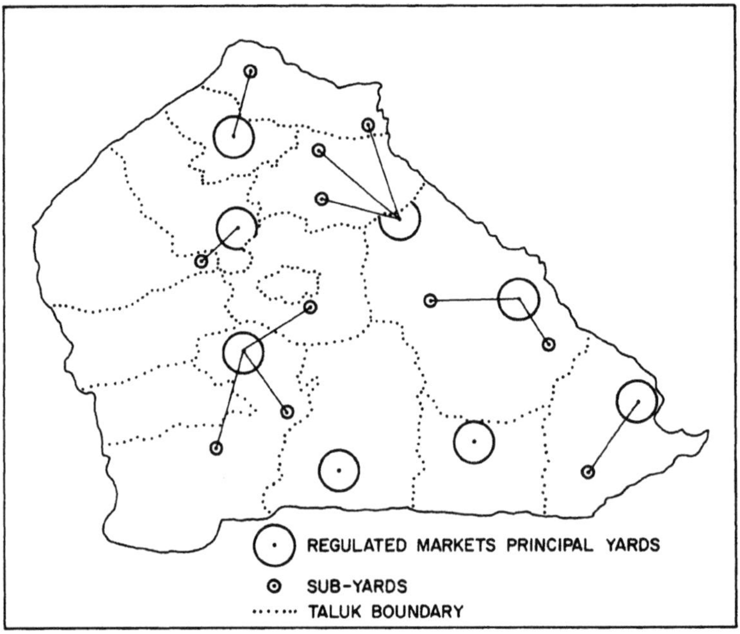

Figure 7–1 Sketch Map Showing Regulated Markets and Subyards in Poona District, India

SOURCE: E. A. J. Johnson, *Market Towns and Spatial Development in India*, New Delhi: National Council of Applied Economic Research, 1965, p. 81.

very well, great stretches of the countryside remained unserviced by regulated-market facilities. Then, one by one, the existing Poona District markets began to establish subyards, so that by 1964 six of the eight regulated markets had such subyards: three had one subyard each, one had two subyards, and two had three subyards each. The effect was to increase the number of supervised marketplaces in the district from eight to nineteen, and by this process of experimental segmentation the total area served by regulated markets probably doubled. As I have already said, the technique is simple, inexpensive, and rather easy to begin. A market committee in one of the larger towns, after having made arrangements with the appropriate officials in a smaller place, sometimes in a different taluk (local government unit), simply begins a branch variety of market operations on an experiential basis. A small market yard is rented, a few tentative structures are built (selling platforms, commission agents' offices), necessary control devices are provided (approved scales, measures, testing devices) and an experienced market secretary is put in charge. Commission agents licensed in the parent market are then authorized to carry on business in the subyard. If the venture fails to attract a large enough clientele to make the market self-supporting, it can easily be terminated. If it succeeds, the facilities can be enlarged and expanded. When that moment is reached, some or all authority over the subyard can be transferred to a new local market committee. The new controlling group may elect to remain in a satellitic relation to the parent market, or it may decide to sever the umbilical cord and become a wholly autonomous regulated market.[61]

Once a suitable site for a rural growth center has been found, it would seem both wise and proper for regional planners to consult with the supervising committee of a reasonably nearby regulated market to see whether or not the establishment of a subyard might be feasible. Government assistance might be available to launch such a venture. Indian market committees, as corporate entities, can and do borrow funds from their chartering (state) governments, and since they may borrow funds for "initial expenditures" on buildings and facilities, they could, if they wished, enter into a joint effort with a (state) government to establish new regulated-market subyards in well-chosen rural sites and thereby contribute a much-needed impetus to a town-making process.[62] Were a subyard to attract enough salable produce,

61. I found examples of both types. The regulated market of Hubli established two subyards, one at Kalaghatagi (18 miles distant, serving 136 villages) the other at Shiggaon (40 miles distant, serving 124 villages). Both of these subyards have continued to be satellites of Hubli. By contrast, Unjha, which had established a subyard at Sidhpur, relinquished control over the 53 villages serviced by the Sidhpur subyard, thereby making two independent regulated markets of what had been one entity. It is this type of cellular division that might facilitate a continuing increase in the number of rural growth centers. For further information on subyards and their relation to their parent markets see Dyal Singh Dhillon, "Detailed Note on the Working of the Agricultural Produce Market Committee, Hubli, District Dharwar, Mysore," and Surjit Singh Randhawa, "A Detailed Note on the Working of the Agricultural Produce Committee, Unjha, District Mahesana, Gujarat State." Both reports are in the files of the Indian Directorate of Marketing and Inspection, Nagpur. For a brief summary of Indian experience with regulated market subyards, see my *Market Towns and Spatial Development in India,* pp. 76–80.

62. The language of the Mysore Act No. XVI, 1939, (which is representative of the provisions in the regulated-market acts of other states) provides that "every market committee may, with the previous sanction of the Government, raise the money required for carrying out the purposes of this Act on the security of any property vested in or belonging to the market committee. . . . The committee may, for the

certain small processing industries would undoubtedly come into being,[63] and the emergent nucleus might eventually appear to be a proper place for the establishment of an industrial estate. Once the trade volume were large enough, cooperative societies would consider the advisability of starting a sales office, and as the business of the subyard grew, certain service industries would spring up: restaurants, hostels, and small workshops.

Two interrelated consequences may therefore be expected from a well-planned program of regulated-market subyard expansion. A larger farming area will be more completely commercialized, since all producers within travel range of parent markets or subyards will have both the opportunity and the incentive to enlarge their marketed surpluses. The second effect will be to provide incentives for entrepreneurs who contribute *tranches* of capital toward the gradual development of a new investment cluster. The parent market, or more particularly its market committee, can therefore be considered to be a "change-agent," since its decision to establish a subyard might very well induce *tranches* of both government and private investment at a chosen site.[64] Yet in establishing a subyard all that the market committee has done is to make a locational experiment. Undoubtedly certain shortcomings of the site will soon reveal themselves. If no electric energy is available, that lack will have to be promptly corrected. Certain local public utilities—water supply, sanitary facilities—must be provided if the site is to develop into a real market center. Storage facilities will become necessary if commission men and producers are to hold their stocks for the best possible prices. But to do these things will require credit, which

purpose of meeting the initial expenditures on lands, buildings and equipment required for establishing the market, obtain a loan from the Government." India, Ministry of Food and Agriculture, *Agricultural Marketing in India: Regulated Markets*, Vol. I, *Legislation*, New Delhi, 1956, Appendix VI, pp. 119–120.

63. If cotton is brought to a market it must be ginned and baled; similarly, rice must be husked and polished, oilseeds crushed, and the oil prepared for sale in suitable containers.

64. Except in a few "orthodox" socialist countries, it will be this emulative semi-autonomous or wholly autonomous investment that will determine the transformation of central-place nuclei into agro-urban market towns. The actual investment that grows up around a flourishing wholesale produce market is often underestimated by casual observers. My enquiries in India showed that the investment clusters are quite impressive. Hubli market in 1963 had no less than fifty-four processing plants within its legal jurisdiction (10-mile radius): twelve cotton gins, fifteen pressing plants, fifteen rice mills, six decorticating mills, three solvent-extraction oil plants, two pulse-preparing factories, and one textile mill. Dhillon, "Detailed Note on Hubli," p. 11.

means that the center will need a credit cooperative or a bank, probably both.

Planning Subregional Polarization by Proper Transport Design

The only practicable counterpoise to the growing metropolitan polarization, which has become such a characteristic trend in all underdeveloped areas, will be the generation of countervailing centripetal forces that can converge on regional and subregional central places. But because the forces making for great-city polarity are so pervasive and so strong, unless the peripheries can soon protect themselves they will become increasingly enfettered in an unplanned domestic variety of neocolonialism, which will unwittingly further intensify the already acute problems of slum-cursed cities[65] and, with corresponding lack of intent, perpetuate rural stagnation, underemployment, low productivity, and chronic undercommercialization of the main occupation of the great bulk of people.

In beginning the requisite subpolarization effectively, and in giving it momentum once it has begun, reliance will have to be placed for the most part on roads (although the local centralizing influences of electric power and other utilities ought not to be overlooked), since it is entirely feasible to develop road systems which can increase the attractive power of regional and subregional central places. Indeed, no planning task is more urgent than the designing of a transport matrix that can begin to generate resistance to the dangerous trends toward metropolitan polarity. Wilfred Owen has pointed out that "the individual city is helpless to reverse the present trends in urban settlement," even though population densities have become intolerable.[66] Relief must therefore come from "more desirable spatial concepts,"[67] from counterbalancing subpolarization, and the solution will largely depend

65. Professor Aprodicio Laquian, an authority on metropolitan Manila, estimates that out of a total population of 3.7 million (1968), about 1.2 million were slum-dwellers. The spectacle of every third person living in a jungle of flammable shacks is doubtful evidence of "development," even though Laquian believes that slums can be, at least for some "escalator" types of displaced or migrant rural-born persons, fairly effective "zones of transition" from traditional to modern modes of life. "The 'Rurban' Slum as 'Zone of Transition,'" paper read February 3, 1969, at Institute of Advanced Projects, East-West Center, Honolulu, Mimeographed.

66. *Distance and Development,* Washington, 1968, p. 94. Calcutta, with 294 persons per residential acre, has reached the highest population density among world cities, a doubtful distinction.

67. Ibid., p. 95.

on the wisdom, insight, and daring of the designers of rural road systems.

The barest essentials of the proximate goals[68] of regional and subregional transport planning can be readily perceived from an examination of Figure 7–2, which pictures three separable forms of transport that could, given proper design, converge on a rural growth center. The population center visualized is small, and the several isochrone[69] perimeters are rough estimates of distances (round-trip) that could be traversed each day by different forms of transport if suitable roads were available. The three rings are distinct, reflecting rather obvious requisites; if a rural growth center is to "grow," it will need at least these three logically separable types of converging transport axes. Most numerous and relatively shortest will be the commuting routes. Fewer in number but considerably longer will be the roads or other transport facilities used to bring agricultural produce to a central-place market.[70] Much longer, better surfaced, and less numerous will be the highways that connect a growth center with larger urban centers; these "truck routes" will be used mostly by merchants (or cooperative societies) engaged in wholesale in-shipments or out-shipments. A few words should be said about each of these road systems.

If the rural growth center is going to become a production, processing, and service center, and if it hopes, by the establishment of even a modest range of diversified enterprises, to increase the total areal employment, then very careful attention should be given to developing a truly functional constellation of commuting routes. If feasible, they should radiate in all directions from the center, making it possible for village-dwelling workers to travel swiftly, easily, and directly to their places of employment. For most underdeveloped countries, the means of travel for these commuters in the foreseeable future will be on foot, by bicycle, or by pedicycle. What is needed, therefore, is not expensive, wide, paved roads but a star-shaped arrangement of firm paths, paved bicycle lanes, or well-ballasted and properly bridged narrow roads. Developed countries such as Denmark, Belgium, and the Netherlands

68. For planning operations that recognize the organic nature of human societies there can never be final goals.

69. Points equidistant from a center in terms of travel time, shown in Figure 7–2 as circles, on the (unreal) assumption of level terrain and no obstruction to shortest travel.

70. Whereas normally these transport facilities will be roads, they could be railways, rivers, or even coastal waters.

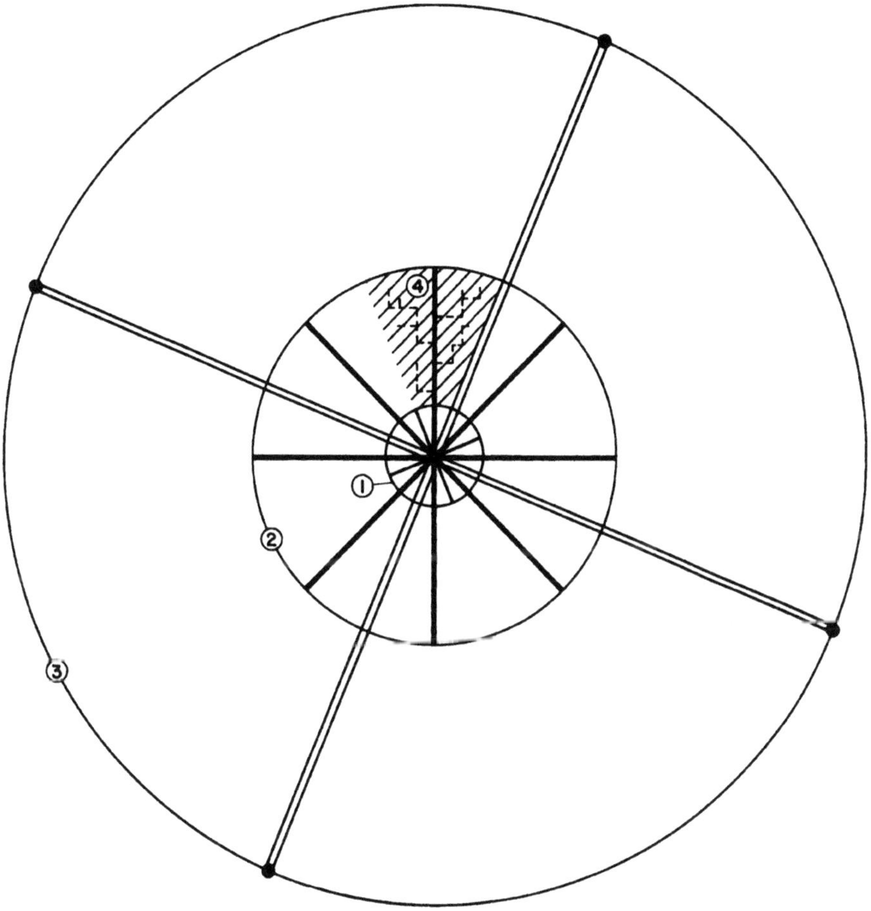

① MAXIMUM ISOCHRONE FOR COMMUTERS

② MAXIMUM ISOVECTURE FOR AGRICULTURAL PRODUCE MOVEMENTS

③ PROXIMATE LIMITS FOR IN-BOUND & OUT-BOUND TRUCK TRAFFIC

④ FEEDER ROADS (SAMPLE WELL-SERVICED AREA)

Figure 7–2 Road Convergence Schema for a Rural Growth Center

have for a long time made abundant use of such commuting routes, to the advantage of towns and cities on the one hand, farms and outlying rural hamlets on the other. There has been a signal neglect of this simple and obvious form of transport development in all too many underdeveloped countries, reflecting once again the romanticism of planners who dream of a system of latest-variety paved roads teeming with automobiles. A well-planned radial system of bicycle paths is a far wiser alternative, because it is fiscally manageable, and because there is a reasonable chance that people in outlying villages and hamlets will be able to afford bicycles if the rural growth centers provide employment.

The spokes of the wheel representing the farm-to-market roads could be fewer than those in the commuting-path wheel for two reasons. In the first place the market roads might well be designed to follow the Christaller "traffic principle" and, accordingly, pass through the largest possible number of villages. The second reason is more important. Each incoming hinterland-to-market road ought to have a complement of dendritic feeder roads branching out into the widening angles between the major road-system spokes. The general design of a single such centripetally planned road with feeder branches can be seen in Figure 7–3.[71] Whereas the commuting paths, lanes and roads seldom need have radii much longer than 5 miles,[72] the farm-to-market roads ought to have isovectures of about 20 miles. This estimate is made on the (very realistic) assumption that for a long time to come draft animals will continue to supply motive power for the marketing of agricultural produce. These roads will not need to have as smooth surfaces as the (shorter) commuting roads (where maintenance of moderate speeds for bicycles or pedicycles will require the minimization of friction), but they will need to be well-graded, diked in places where water will be high in rainy seasons, solidly ballasted, and adequately bridged.

The limited number of "truck roads" that ought to link an emergent rural growth center with a regional urban hierarchy will, in a sense, be to a rural growth center what import and export channels are to a port city. These are the transport links of an agricultural community with neighboring regions, with inland industrial cities, with port towns, and

71. For a fuller analysis of feeder roads see Mosher, *Creating a Progressive Rural Structure*, pp. 16–29.

72. In an area as densely populated as the Kanpur region of India a 5-mile radius might link as many as thirty or forty villages to a rural growth center and allow enterprises in such a center to recruit workers from a rural population of from two to three thousand people.

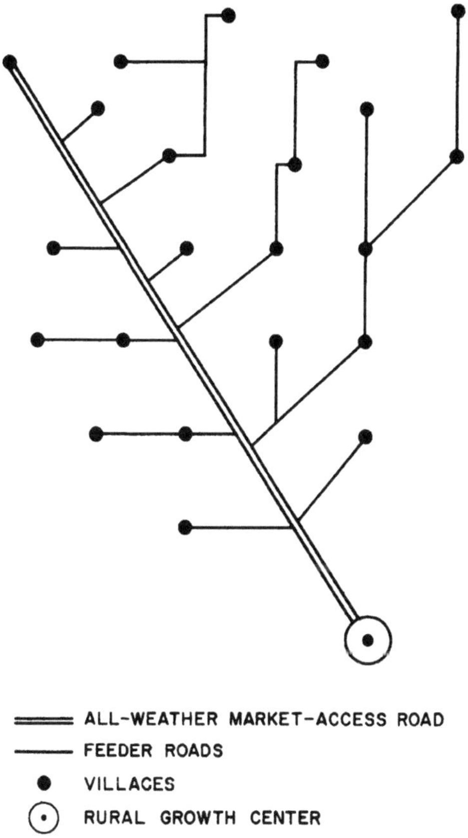

Figure 7–3 A Spatially Adequate System of Feeder Roads

through them with the world economy.[73] These roads will need to be progressively improved as traffic increases, permitting the movement of heavier loads at greater speeds and thereby minimizing the transport cost of out-going and incoming merchandise. The thrust of these transport facilities must be inward as well as outward. The inbound transportation ought to consist of an increasing movement of necessary

73. Wilfred Owen has shown that unit transport costs by truck are markedly lower than bullock-cart costs. Hence, to the extent to which some (longer-distance) traffic can move by truck, there will be a net economic advantage. The limitation, of course, is the investment involved in truck transport, which will for a long time restrict the use of this more capital-intensive (and more specialized) form of transport. But on the longer hauls the truck will more readily prove its cost advantage. See "Transport and Communication in Kanpur's Future," in *Regional Perspective of Industrial and Urban Growth,* ed. Desai, Grossack, and Sharma, pp. 92–104.

agricultural inputs, raw materials, and semifinished components for the emergent small industries, as well as larger inventories for workshops and local retail outlets. Outbound transportation would move the agricultural produce (gross or processed, as the case may be) that is surplus to the center's consumption needs. This outbound volume of traffic should grow, as more feeder roads are built reaching out into hitherto uncommercialized interstices. Moreover, as some measure of industrialization develops in growth centers, these truck roads will carry out manufactured goods, moving to consumers through wholesale channels.

Such an integrated network of bicycle paths, bullock-cart roads, and motortruck highways will call for extremely careful preplanning and judicious phasing, so that the most necessary mileage of each type is annually programmed and actually built. It will call for coordination of national, regional, and local planning, with an agreed and clear division of responsibility for construction and maintenance. Here again the vexing problem will arise as to whether the less backward or the more backward areas should be favored in phasing the road-building and road-improving program. Admittedly, the ultimate goal is the "development" of all the space comprehended in a planning effort, and Mosher is quite right when he says that "agricultural development is only instrumental; its object is welfare, the welfare of farm and non-farm people alike."[74] But fiscal limitations demand that projects such as roads will have to be locationally selective, and the proper choice of the initial sunk-cost capital inputs will to a large extent determine whether the road-building program not only can continue but will steadily enlarge.

A very useful key to the problem of less backward and more backward areas has been provided by Mosher's analysis of "place priorities for a progressive rural structure."[75] To insure that the yields on development capital inputs will be as large and as immediate as possible, Mosher has suggested that a regional land-classification cadastre could very likely reveal where investments (such as roads) might be most fruitful. Any region can fairly easily be classified into areas of immediate high agricultural potential (IP areas),[76] areas of future high potential (FP

74. *Creating a Progressive Rural Structure,* pp. 45–53.

75. Ibid., Chapter 5.

76. Relevant factors would be soils, rainfall, irrigation facilities, technological aids, and the progressiveness of farm practices.

areas),[77] and areas of low agricultural potential (LP areas).[78] Once a region has been mapped in terms of these prospects, cost-benefit analysis could be employed to determine the location of roads that would most promptly increase farmers' incentives to produce more, to improve the quality of their produce, and to enlarge their marketed surpluses. Such studies might indicate that roads into FP areas could yield as large or even larger benefits than road expansion in the IP areas.[79] In the LP areas certain preparations ought to be made for their ultimate commercialization: improvement of elementary schools, establishment of some secondary schools, and the staffing of health centers.

A road system is something more than prepared surfaces on which porters, pack animals, or wheeled vehicles (whether animal-drawn or self-propelled), can move. A road system can become a unifying instrumentality that consolidates the productive power of an area and releases a latent social dynamism. The universal handicaps of all underdeveloped areas are low agricultural yields, low productivity per worker, and waste of manpower stemming from underemployment. A properly planned road system must try to ameliorate all three of these endemic shortcomings. This is why a regional transport plan must be more than a farm-to-market network. It must be this plus a set of commuting configurations and a number of "through" roads that can connect "functional economic areas" with other such spatial organizations and link peripheries with core-region centers, in ways that will make them complementary rather than dependent, coordinate rather than satellitic—a wholesome relation that countries such as Denmark and the Netherlands have demonstrated to be quite possible.

77. Here soils and climate may be satisfactory, but lack of irrigation or of transport facilities may prevent proper utilization of natural resources.

78. Topographic features and shallow soils may make field-crop agriculture expensive and inefficient. Proper land usage may call for different farm practices, altered cropping patterns, and more animal husbandry.

79. Mosher has proposed a somewhat more exact and rigid sequence. His "first stage" of road building would connect the market centers in an IP area with a larger central place. In the second stage, a start would be made on access roads to the market centers in the IP area. In a third stage, more access roads in the IP area would be built and more market centers would be connected with the largest central place. Only in a fourth stage would skeletal road building begin in the FP area. I find this sequence rather arbitrary, and I feel confident that careful cost-benefit studies might very likely show the wisdom of building some roads in the FP areas in one of Mosher's earlier stages. For illustrative maps of Mosher's sequence see his *Creating a Progressive Rural Structure*, pp. 71–74.

CHAPTER 8 FUNCTIONAL ECONOMIC AREAS AS SPATIAL ENTITIES

Contrasts between Developed and Less-Developed Countries

It could be that all the historical illustrations that have been interlarded in the foregoing chapters have little relevance to modern realities. It could be argued that rapid changes in transportation and communication, the development of industrial estates or industrial parks permitting areal dispersion of manufacturing, and the swift progress of automation and computerization—that these present trends have so drastically altered the structure of every economy that the historical patterns of classical spatial theory are now archaic and obsolete. Certainly, spatial units much larger than those envisaged by Christaller, Galpin and Lösch are emerging. This does not necessarily imply, however, that efforts to persuade developing countries to launch town-building programs are merely backward-looking manifestations of atavistic nostalgia, nor does it contradict Kierkegaard's wise observation that, although "life can only be understood backward, it must be lived forward." The evidence is quite clear: the underdeveloped countries cannot create tolerably satisfactory market economies without a spatially dispersed hierarchy of rural growth centers, market towns, small cities, and other central places that collectively can counterbalance the pull of their voracious metropolitan centers. This structural paraphernalia is needed for its immediate functional utility, not as a device that will permit underdeveloped countries to enter into some mandatory "stage" of development so that they will be able, sometime later on, to advance to a "higher" stage in a teleological progression.[1] But

1. For an exposé of the naïveté of this simplistic thesis, which permeates the literature of development from Marx to Rostow, see my "Nature and Price of Economic Progress," *SAIS Review*, Summer 1962, pp. 3–18.

because town-centering is a condition of development, it ought not be hastily assumed that there is one old-fashioned economic polity appropriate for underdeveloped countries and a quite different one for developed countries, nor does an insistence on agrarian commercialization imply that, although imperialism has been repudiated politically, it is still very much alive as an intellectual device and as an article of faith.

There is no doubt but that the traditional urban hierarchical pattern is being reshaped in developed countries. Commuting zones that once had 5-mile radii may sometimes today reach out as far as 50 miles. Industrial parks are built in open country, miles from cities or towns. In the United States, residential farms have increased so rapidly during the past two decades that for perhaps as many as a million rural-dwelling families farming has become a side occupation pursued on summer evenings and on Saturdays, Sundays, and holidays. As the working population continues to spread out over widening, partly industrial landscapes, new societal units are coming into existence that have been described as "low density cities."[2] As farms become more mechanized, fewer and fewer people are needed to cultivate fields, harvest crops, or feed livestock, thus releasing more and more manpower for industrial, service, and professional activities.[3] The boundaries between town and country are therefore becoming less and less distinct, leading some analysts to allege that in economies such as that of the United States "the rural community has ceased to exist as a separate and definable entity."[4] There is, of course, no mystery involved whatever. When Galpin gathered data for his *Social Anatomy of an Agricultural Community* in 1911, only 618,727 automobiles and 20,773 trucks were registered for use on American highways.[5] In 1966 the total registration, in round numbers, was 78,332,000 automobiles and 15,845,000 trucks,[6] an increase (1911–1966) of over 125-fold for passenger cars and more than 765-fold for commercial vehicles. But this remarkable numerical increase does not in any way measure the actual change. The average

2. Karl A. Fox, "A Program to Promote Maximum Employment, Human Dignity, and Civic Responsibility in the United States," Cyclostyled, Ames, Iowa, 1968, p. 11.

3. An Illinois farmer who has an automatic silo and a mechanized feed trough told me (1969) that all he needs to do to feed four hundred steers each day is to press four buttons.

4. Fox, "A Program to Promote Maximum Employment," p. 4.

5. U.S., Bureau of the Census, *Historical Statistics of the United States*, Washington, 1960, p. 462.

6. U.S., Bureau of the Census, *Statistical Abstract of the United States, 1967*, Washington, 1967, p. 562.

speed of wheeled traffic has increased 10-fold in the sixty-five years, and the average carrying capacity of each truck may have increased as much as 20-fold. If centers of areal social and economic activity now have as much as 50-mile radii, rather than the 5-mile radii they usually had in 1911, then trade areas have increased from about 50 square miles (with from 2,000 to 4,000 people) to about 5,000 square miles (with 100,000 to 200,000 or more people). And since manufacturing, processing, service, and merchandising enterprises have been dispersed throughout many of these enlarged areas, "a new synthesis of rural and urban society"[7] seems to have come into being.

From the home-to-work commuting data contained in the 1960 census, Berry has delineated 358 of these new spatial entities, which, following Fox's terminology, he calls "functional economic areas."[8] Berry's maps indicate that about half of these economic configurations have populations in excess of 50,000 people, about a fourth range between 50,000 and 250,000, leaving another fourth with populations of from 250,000 to 1 million or even more. A very remarkable and far-reaching de facto restructuring of the American landscape has occurred that has rearranged 3,000 counties and 18,000 incorporated places into some 350 or more nonmetropolitan, multicounty, functional economic areas.[9] The integration of town and country, for which C. J. Galpin argued so passionately,[10] has materialized on a rather more elaborate scale than the Wisconsin rural sociologist could possibly have foreseen. Shopping centers have developed a powerful variety of "centrality," while the mobility provided by automobiles, traveling swiftly on arterial highways and on well-paved branch roads, has allowed industry to relocate in places to which manpower can be attracted from all directions. Hamlets and villages that have survived this drastic restructuring of the countryside are now mostly residential places that have lost their earlier agricultural processing, manufacturing, or consumer-oriented enterprises. The whole thrust of structural evolution seems to be just

7. Karl A. Fox, "Agricultural Policy in an Urban Society," Paper presented at the Annual Meeting of the American Agricultural Economics Association, Bozeman, Montana, August 19, 1968, p. 8. Mimeographed.

8. Brian J. L. Berry et al., *Metropolitan Area Definition: A Re-evaluation of Concept and Statistical Practice,* U.S., Department of Commerce, Bureau of the Census, Working Paper 28, Washington, 1968.

9. Fox, "Agricultural Policy in an Urban Society," p. 13.

10. *Social Anatomy of an Agricultural Community,* Madison, 1915, pp. 22, 23, 25, 26, 30, 34.

the reverse of the prescriptions that have been offered for underdeveloped countries in the preceding chapters. How can this awkward contradiction be resolved?[11]

One must first realize that a dramatic transformation of rural landscapes such as has occurred in the United States requires vast amounts of capital. The farm machinery and equipment which enables a farm family to operate a typical Midwestern American 400-acre farm and to prepare several hundred hogs and cattle for market may have a value, per farm, of over $100,000. For the entire country the value of farm implements and equipment has risen from less than 1½ billion dollars in Galpin's day to over 27½ billion in 1966, a twenty-two-fold increase.[12] The value of the 80 million automobiles which make it possible for American workers to commute to their work up to distances as great as 50 miles represents an investment that might range from 40 to 80 billion dollars. To these totals must next be added the value of the trucks, buses, and specialized motor vehicles that allow the new functional economic areas to "function." A conservative estimate for the value of this automotive equipment would range from 15 to 30 billion dollars, and the road system, on which the "new synthesis of rural and urban society" depends, represents a fantastic investment.[13] But the creation of modern types of functional economic areas has called for huge expenditures far beyond these few samples. Involved for a single year (1966) were a large share of the more than 60 billion dollars invested in new industrial plant and equipment and the 30 billion devoted to retail store inventories, representing just two of the capital inputs needed for the functioning of the new urban-rural spatial entities.

These few illustrations should make it crystal clear that the underdeveloped countries of the "third world" are not going to have "functional economic areas" with 100-mile diameters for a long, long time.

11. Particularly when some analysts go so far as to assert that "there is some empirical evidence which suggests that cities or functional economic areas with less than 250,000 population are too small to accomplish self-sustaining economic growth," a thesis advanced with some reservation by Karl Fox in his "Program to Promote Maximum Employment," p. 18.

12. *Statistical Abstract of the United States, 1967,* p. 621.

13. In a single year (1965) the states disbursed over 11 billion dollars of their own funds and received over 4 billion dollars of Federal Funds. To this must be added, for that single year, all county, township, and municipal expenditures on roads and streets. Ibid., pp. 556, 558.

When one considers the progress that has been made in the past twenty years in some "liberated" and "independent" countries, one hesitates to say that structural changes paralleling those in the United States can never occur in the less-developed countries; to deny that the prospects are remote, however, would be a foolish variety of self-deception. Until productivity on farms, in workshops, and in factories very greatly increases, the savings simply will not be available for building the paved roads, buying the automobiles to travel on them, or for developing the vast infrastructure that a mechanized agriculture and a motorized market system requires.[14] Given time, progress toward mechanization, motorization, and overall economic modernization can and will be made. But the immediate task, and the really urgent one, is to take stock of the resources that are now available and to take steps that will insure proper and fullest possible utilization of these resources so that output can increase on farms and in industrial establishments; and to make proper institutional arrangements so that agrarian regions will become progressively more commercialized, thus making possible a little more saving and a little more investment. All of this indicates that functional economic areas in less-developed countries will for a long time have to be relatively small spatial entities, probably nearer 100 square miles than 5,000 square miles. More, not less, central-places must therefore come into existence if an appropriate and suitable "synthesis" of rural and urban activities is to be achieved. There is really no fundamental difference between the basic ends of spatial units in developed and in less-developed countries. What is different is the scale of operations in farming, in a great deal of manufacturing, in merchandising, in service industries, and these factors, in turn, will influence the size of spatial units. Until domestic capital formation is far more abundant in underdeveloped countries, functional economic areas will continue to be relatively small, and each area will need a central place as a focal point where the basic activities of the economic sectors—agriculture, industry, trade, education, welfare—can be interrelated and coordinated in ways that will advance economic development, growth, and transformation.

The size of these functional economic areas, in territory and in popu-

14. The modest amounts that are available for investment in less-developed countries can be seen from the findings of the very careful studies made in India concerning the propensity and the ability to save. See National Council of Applied Economic Research [N. C. A. E. R.], *Savings in India During the Plan Periods*, Occasional Paper 16, New Delhi, 1966; and N. C. A. E. R., *All India Rural Household Survey*, Vol. II, *Income, Investment and Savings*, New Delhi, 1965.

lation, will, of course, vary from country to country and from region to region within countries. Transport isochrones and isovectures will be the more important determinants of spatial extent. If a central place (whether it be a rural growth center, a market town, or even a small city) is going to be a genuine integrating force, a "social unit," as Frank Pick once said, must come into existence, one that is "not too large to destroy personal contact" and yet large enough "to afford variety and diversity."[15] Ideally, such a social unit should "involve all classes" and thereby elicit the vital forces and latent creativity that reside in an area's human resources. Whether a growing and much fuller participation by all groups of people can be achieved will depend on cultural, political, and educational factors. The willingness of almost all emerging countries to explore the usefulness of community integration as a device for stimulating growth and development may indicate a guarded admission that rigid caste distinctions are luxuries that countries which hope to develop can no longer afford.

The crux of the matter is just this. If an area that is spatially definable by transport perimeters is to become truly "functional," it will need to develop what McCarty has called an "occupational pyramid."[16] The base of this pyramid will consist of the several types of primary production that natural resources make possible: farming, mining, fishing, and lumbering;[17] these "basic" operations will profoundly influence the superstructure that can be built upon them as social and economic foundations. Processing industries will form an important section of the pyramid, but only if outreaching market and transport facilities exist, so that semimanufactured agricultural, mineral, marine, or forest products can be "exported" from the area. Such market linkages will determine the location of another range of industries catering to the needs of the primary producers. If there are but few "export" outlets for primary goods, there will be little income to spend on either consumer or producer goods, whereas, if the processing industries flourish, an expanding range of local industries can develop. Moreover, as the

15. Frank Pick, *Britain Must Rebuild*, London, 1941, quoted in Robert E. Dickinson, *City, Region and Regionalism: A Geographical Contribution to Human Ecology*, London, 1947, p. 4.

16. H. H. McCarty, "A Functional Analysis of Population Distribution," *Geographical Review*, 32 (1942), pp. 282–293.

17. Whereas in Thailand, Korea, India, and Burma the basic occupation will be farming, in parts of Zambia, Peru, and the Philippines the occupational pyramid may rest more on mining, fishing and lumbering.

basic industries become more commercialized, a widening variety of local services will be purchased, leading to the expansion of many other segments of the pyramid; as man power is lured to an emergent urban center from the rural hinterland—and once this work force acquires skill, and enough external economies have begun to emerge—certain "footloose" industries[18] may be attracted, providing still further employment opportunities and more area "exports." The growing pyramid will, in addition, include more specialized merchants, traders, brokers, and other persons engaged in transactional activities, thus further diversifying the occupations in what is emerging as a functional economic area.

Advantages and Disadvantages of Industrial Dispersion

In both mature and emergent countries effective development will involve appropriate spatial combinations of agriculture and industry, of primary, secondary, and tertiary occupations within "functional economic areas" of economically justifiable size. There is, however, one important difference. Since the majority of underdeveloped countries are not willing to wait for the uncertain remedial influence of the "forces of spontaneity" to overcome their rather obvious structural deficiencies (nor would they, in my opinion, be well-advised to do so), they must adopt the right kind of corrective areal industrial policies.[19] But a major question arises. Policy makers must decide how much dispersion to promote. Whether every developing country can follow the example of Puerto Rico, which has lured some "foot-loose" industry into every rural area, is problematical, since they do not have the unrestricted access to markets in a developed country that Commonwealth status has given Puerto Rico. Moreover, it might become possible for one Hong Kong after another to undersell the Puerto Rican manufacturers, the very success of whose industrial program lies in the reduction of the local level of underemployment and the raising of wage rates. It might therefore be wiser for most developing countries to adopt slower but safer courses, relying largely on an expansion of domestic rather than of foreign demand.

18. Such as printing, pharmaceutical, needlework, knitwear, and clothing industries. The availability of semiautomatic machine tools has widened the range of metal products that can be produced almost anywhere that transport and electrical power are adequate.

19. For the argument supporting this thesis see Chapter 7, and John Friedmann, *Regional Development Policy*, Cambridge, Mass., 1966, pp. 14–19.

Whatever tactics are chosen, the main goal of an industrial dispersion policy in every underdeveloped country should be a permanent increase in areal employment, for the very simple reason that man power is a ubiquitous, underutilized resource. To try to determine whether the marginal productivity of certain fractions of a rural population is zero is a sterile exercise.[20] It is patently evident that underemployment is endemic in the villages of Asia, Africa, the Middle East, and Latin America and that the drift of young people to the cities does little or nothing to reduce this wanton waste of productive power. The solution of this problem, if ever there is to be one, must be sought not in core-region metropolitan centers but in the peripheries. Employment, in short, is basically a spatial problem. But it must be emphatically pointed out that no solution for this deep-seated economic malaise is likely to be found in village communities; the checkered history of mis-spent money and wasted personnel on cottage industries has proved this again and again.[21] Staley and Morse have rather succinctly given a general answer to the troublesome question of where the needed employment should be provided: "The village is too small and the supercity too large. What is needed is an active program to foster small industry . . . in intermediate cities and towns and to link this program to the surrounding rural areas by promotion of trade and other interconnections. This indirect approach is . . . likely to prove the best way to bring the benefits of modern industrialization to the villages."[22] Whether the type of industrial dispersion recommended by Staley and Morse is economically defensible, or whether the putative benefits would be more than offset by local disadvantages, is largely a factual question that calls for empirical answers. There are, however, some general factors that shoud be carefully considered before any extensive experimentation is attempted which involves large sunk costs. Certain

20. For a refreshing commentary on this overdebated subject see Theodore W. Schultz, *Transforming Traditional Agriculture*, New Haven, 1964, pp. 52–70. His conclusion is that "it is a false doctrine" whose roots "make it suspect," whose "theoretical presumptions" are "shaky," and which "fails to win any support" when tested by an actual situation wherein a labor force was drastically reduced.

21. That village industries, so long favored in India for employment purposes, are woefully inefficient and inconsequential as a transforming force is guardedly and reluctantly admitted in each recent *Annual Report* of the Directorate of Publicity, Khadi and Village Industries Commission. This type of industrial organization makes little appeal to workers or entrepreneurs, and the end-products can only be marketed by appealing to consumers' patriotism.

22. Eugene Staley and Richard Morse, *Modern Small Industry for Developing Countries*, New York, 1965, p. 311.

presumptions are warranted. Wage rates ought to be lower in country towns than in metropolitan areas, but if out-migration has screened out the brightest and the quickest workers, the low latent productivity of those who remain might make the low money wages really high wages in terms of the costs of units of output. The normal probability, however, is that few rural communities will have been very seriously leeched of superior grades of labor and that most country towns will be able to provide fairly representative labor samples. Whether this is actually the case will largely depend on the size of a country. In a spacious and populous country, such as India, out-migration could not possibly lure all able workers out of country towns and villages. On the other hand, in a very small country, where distances between farms, inland villages, and major cities are not great, there can be, as there actually was in Puerto Rico, a great deal of pre-empting of top-quality labor by city enterprises.

The fact that a country town may not have many skilled laborers need not be a lasting locational handicap. Modern small-scale industry that uses mechanical equipment driven by electric motors can normally train machine operators in a surprisingly short time; oddly enough, the training of a complement of truly skilled handworkers may take more time. The real discovery that has been made again and again is that talent is very widely diffused, and one of the very strongest arguments for the dispersion of industry into rural growth centers and country towns is that hidden resources of innovation and creativity might thereby be released.[23] In the benefit-cost balance sheet, there is yet another important "benefit" of industrial dispersion. If workers can be persuaded to commute from their village homes to a workshop or small factory in a nearby town, little or none of a developing country's limited capital need, in the short run, be devoted to housing, a social advantage that is often overlooked by the advocates of city concentrations of industrial enterprises.[24]

Industrial dispersion will undoubtedly involve some disadvantages such as the absence of large-city external economies, an initial shortage of skilled labor and experienced key personnel (e.g., foremen, foundry-

23. For a fuller development of this point see Chapter 11, the section "Releasing Creativity."

24. See, for example, Vera Lutz, *Italy: A Study in Economic Development*, London, 1962, Chapters 2, 3; Takashi Fujii, *Economic Space in the Japanese Archipelago*, Nagoya, n.d., pp. 1–3.

men, pattern makers, electricians), and very limited financial and technical services. All these deficiencies will make industrial dispersion difficult in underdeveloped countries. Granting that electric power, internal combustion engines, motor vehicles, telephones, and machine tools make possible a degree of decentralization of industry that was impossible fifty years ago, and that modern business machines and control devices can expedite routine administrative procedures and simplify many managerial tasks, it does not follow that industrial plants, even small ones, can be established just anywhere. Staley and Morse have wisely differentiated "traditional manufacturing of the artisan and household type," catering to narrow markets and using relatively few outside-the-locality inputs, from "modern" small-scale industry.[25] Locational requirements for the artisan and household industries are not very demanding, except for a few crafts (e.g., pottery) that must be located near raw materials. Modern small industries, in contrast, need considerably larger local markets to insure reasonably full utilization of tools and machines and adequate transport and marketing facilities, particularly if a major part of the output is going to be "exported" from the production site, or if a sizable volume of in-shipments of materials and components will be involved.

If an industry hopes to find its main market among country dwellers, and if a rural site seems feasible, then the chosen location must be in a farming area that is either already pretty well commercialized or in one that bids fair to become progressively interlinked with its nearby market towns. Unfortunately, relevant degrees of social dynamism are extremely difficult to measure. Yet, a small modern industry has a distinct advantage in discovering this agrarian adaptability; it is mobile enough to make locational experiments without encountering heavy losses if the market response is sluggish.[26] A well-planned small-industry

25. *Modern Small Industry,* p. 305. They have also very properly eschewed the ambiguous term "cottage industry" which sometimes is used to designate manufacture performed in or near a family house by family members (household industry) but may, in other contexts, refer to production by specialized artisans working at home (artisan homework) or in a putting-out system (industrial homework) coordinated by owners of the materials on which artisans work. All these distinctions, and others that could be made, have been "fuzzed over by the term cottage industry." Ibid., p. 8.

26. A small tomato purée plant, for example, like those being established when I was in Greece in the 1950's, could be moved from one location to another if farmers near the first site were unwilling to produce tomatoes rather than tobacco or other customary crops.

program will, of course, attempt to evaluate the probable local demand for its products before any structures are built and before any machinery is installed. A great deal of skill was built up in this type of market analysis in Puerto Rico, where it was discovered that fairly accurate projections of local demand were possible. But even then considerable imagination and entrepreneurial judgment was called for in this important task, which has very aptly been called "locational pioneering."[27]

There are, to be sure, some industries for which small towns or even villages have distinct locational advantages. If the processing of agricultural or other primary materials involves considerable weight or bulk reduction, an optimum location will ordinarily be near the production areas. Cotton gins not only remove seeds but greatly reduce the bulk of the cotton by compressing it into tight bales. Sugar cane and sugar beets lose both weight and bulk in first-phase processing. If an adequate supply of water is assured, and if electric power is available for refrigeration rooms, slaughter houses can be located in small towns near to animal herds, with consequent locational advantages, provided refrigerator cars or trucks are available for marketing the "exportable" output. Perishablė vegetables and fruits must often be processed near the producing fields or orchards, fish close to landing piers, and sawmills may find their best location near the forests. Many other examples can be cited. But an industrial dispersion program that attempts to blot up an appreciable fraction of chronic rural underemployment and to enlarge incomes and spending power must go beyond these basic agro-industries. A variety of small industries not immediately bound to the areal primary products can and should be established.

What these industrial undertakings ought to be cannot be specified, since this will depend not only on a transport matrix[28] but on a number of environmental factors, not least of which are such considerations as the security of persons and property, the withering away of caste distinctions that restrict or limit the demand for industrial products, and the willingness of people to modify their traditional patterns of life.[29] New

27. Staley and Morse, *Modern Small Industry*, p. 308.

28. See Chapter 7. For listings of small industries appropriate for the Kanpur region of India, see Krishna Roy, "Prospects of Urban Growth in the Kanpur Region," in *Regional Perspective of Industrial and Urban Growth: The Case of Kanpur*, ed. P. B. Desai, I. M. Grossack, and K. N. Sharma, Bombay, 1969, pp. 139–140, 156.

29. When the *Times of India* describes a district in Uttar Pradesh in as gloomy terms as the following two excerpts from an October 27, 1966 dispatch indicate, the

products (transisters) and new services (a cinema) have, to be sure, subtle communicative and change-making powers, but their transforming effects will vary from place to place depending upon the rigidities of cultural constraint. Problems of this kind, of course, are not peculiar to an industrial-dispersion program; they are the troubles that confront architects of modernization whenever they are faced with cultural congealment. If modernization is going to be set in motion, there must be receptivity to innovations, a growing awareness of the importance of time, a propensity to plan, a recognition of the social utility of achievement, and an admission that social roles need not be the exclusive privilege of an elite. Basic to the whole process, therefore, is a new concept of participation. Unless some of these new attitudes can be expected to gain currency, an industrial dispersion program may have but feeble influence and a problematic future. For, if it is really to succeed, it must be accepted as a necessary part of a new social coherence, superseding an older, traditional pattern of rural life which had its own essential coherence.

In addition to all these complex cultural complications, which wise regional planners must consider carefully, once a decision to proceed with an industrial dispersion program has been made, a number of far more concrete issues arise. One must decide, for example, what type of small, modern industry should be emphasized in a little town that is the central market for a farm area of 50 square miles, and, if an industrial estate is built with public funds, which kind of industries should be accorded priority in the assignment of factory space. There are really two basic choices. Preference might be given to enterprises that would manufacture products salable in the immediate hinterland (e.g., soap, matches, shoes, kitchen utensils, and hand tools), on the presumption that they might constitute incentive goods which would help to widen

---

prospects for industrial experiments there would seem highly unpromising. The area, according to the *Times,* "is notorious for its criminal record. One hundred and fifty murders are committed in the district every year. . . . The number of breaches (in irrigation canals) made by village toughs run into hundreds." Of a total district population of 144,000 some "42,000 Kols and Bhils [are] virtual slaves of Brahmins and Thakurs who have been owning large holdings of lands for centuries. . . . Thakurs and Brahmins inherit Kols and Bhils as slaves along with ancestral property and the slave-master relationship grows stronger with every generation."

For a thoughtful analysis of the importance of good government and orderly processes on development, see Laurence Hewes, *Study on Integrated Rural Development,* Geneva, 1969, pp. 61–63. "Only when citizens can engage in transactions without fear or fraud," Hewes argues, "is there a basis for widespread commercialization."

and deepen the commercialization of the farming community. The other choice would be to give priority to enterprises that promise to employ the largest possible number of local workers. Whether the enterprises produced goods wanted by the surrounding farm population or whether their products would all be "exported" to cities would not enter into the decision.

Although these two options seem rather innocent and unimportant, they raise, in my opinion, a really profound policy question, a conclusion I reached from my analysis of "rural" industrial estates in India.[30] Because the main emphasis of the Indian industrialization drive during the Second and Third Plans was macroeconomic and very much concerned with India's international accounts, small industries were usually authorized only if they could produce commodities which would replace or substitute for goods imported from abroad. As a consequence, not only those enterprises that were seeking space in city-located industrial estates but new business undertakings about to begin operations in "rural" industrial estates were encouraged, sometimes even required, to produce such things as cosmetics, opera glasses, tape recorders, typewriters, automobile accessories, and air-conditioning equipment, all eminently useful items but hardly well chosen to serve as incentive goods for farmers. Nor were these industries (as contrasted with those the Puerto Rican government sought to attract) chosen because of their employment-yielding capacities. Few were really labor-intensive, and, as a consequence, the rural industrial estates did little to supplement the earnings of farm or village families. Because the main objectives of the Indian small-industry program apparently were not to provide rural employment or to provide incentives for more commercial farming, almost without exception the industrial operations accorded space in government-owned industrial estates were fairly capital-intensive manufacturing enterprises. A study based on data from 206 enterprises revealed that almost half employed less than ten workers.[31]

In defense of the Indian policy it should be said that what the planners had in mind was a clear separation between "modern" small industries on the one hand and "make-work" industrial operations on the other. The new industries were to strive for high productivity per worker, on the assumption that, in time, these new, low unit-cost

30. *Market Towns and Spatial Development in India,* New Delhi, 1965, pp. 80–93; 146–149; and Appendix 2.

31. P. N. Dhar and H. F. Lydall, *The Role of Small Enterprises in Indian Economic Development,* Bombay, 1961, p. 55.

industries, in conjunction with new large-scale industries, would have a transforming effect upon the whole economy and in the process generate on a national scale the much-needed volume of employment. In the meantime cottage industries, using very labor-intensive hand operations, together with equally labor-intensive public-works programs, would provide transitional employment. The emphasis on per-worker productivity in the new "modern" small industries was certainly proper, since it is this stress on productivity that has made the small factory such an important part of the techno-economic apparatus of all flourishing nations.[32] The mistake the Indian planners made—and from my analysis of the investment-estate performance I do not hesitate to call it a mistake—was to ignore the possible spatial transforming effects that "rural" small industry might have had. The authorized enterprises could have been more labor-intensive and yet "modern," and they should most certainly have been interrelated with the (unfortunately quite separate) programs designed to increase agricultural output and commercialization.[33] A golden opportunity to use industrial estates as town-making "change agents" was largely lost.

The contrasts between the Indian and the Puerto Rican small-industry programs are very instructive. The location of rural industrial estates in Puerto Rico was decided upon only after careful "regional profiles" had been prepared, indicating as accurately as possible the types of enterprises that would be suitable to each locality. In India, sites for rural industrial estates were not systematically chosen; rather, they were too often the chance consequence of "ill-informed popular clamour for location of industrial estates in various places without any regard to the conditions and considerations necessary for their success."[34] And whereas the Puerto Rican plan was to concentrate on the types of manufacturing which would use power-driven machines but

32. For the impressive role of small factories (establishments with fewer than 100 workers) in the United States, see the data prepared by the Stanford Research Institute neatly summarized in Staley and Morse, *Modern Small Industry,* pp. 106–135.

33. "A preoccupation with certain mechanical, chemical and electrical industries by the officials who have had the responsibilities for assigning shed space, has tended to establish a pattern of [industrial] estate use which has signally failed to develop the needed link between town and country. What has happened, therefore, is a high-cost, spatial dispersion of city-oriented small industries, and very little concern with agro-industries, or with plain, inexpensive consumer goods that country people can afford to buy." Johnson, *Market Towns and Spatial Development in India,* pp. 91–92.

34. These are the words of P. C. Alexander, sometime Development Commissioner of Small-Scale Industries, in his *Industrial Estates in India,* Bombay, 1963, p. 55.

would at the same time be as labor-intensive as possible, the fallacious hope in India was that cottage industries would cope with rural underemployment, and this unwarranted assumption led Indian planners to ignore or neglect the employment possibilities of "modern" rural industry. But neither the Puerto Rican nor the Indian programs adequately related local manufacturing operations to areal needs. This was less necessary in Puerto Rico, a compact island only 100 miles long and 35 miles wide, where most things farmers need are within their travel range. For the vast rural stretches of India, miserably served by sparse urban centers, this was a most unfortunate oversight. Both experiments, however, confirmed certain caveats that need clear statement. The clinical history of rural industries has shown that it is difficult to launch industries in communities where there is little entrepreneurial experience, and virtually impossible to do so where necessary transport, marketing, and financial facilities are lacking. Rural industry is therefore not an independent prescription; it is only a part of a more comprehensive development program.[35]

Large Enterprises as Urban Nuclei

Despite the Japanese precedent and the more recent achievements in Israel, it seems unlikely that any underdeveloped country can afford to undertake the building of an interchained hierarchy of central places even if this were considered to be a high development priority.[36] Occasionally new capitals are established, such as Canberra, Islamabad, Chandigarh, and Brazilia, and in some countries new towns have been established on settlement frontiers. But those very few exceptions inversely testify to an almost universal belief that central places are expected to grow up by some organic historical process. Yet in sharp contrast to the instinctive reluctance to plan an urbanization program, is an almost world-wide acceptance of the idea that certain basic industrial plants or complexes, often called "key industries," should not only

35. On this see Arthur T. Mosher, *Creating a Progressive Rural Structure,* New York, 1969, pp. 45–53; see also I.L.O., Advisory Working Group on Rural Employment Problems in Tropical Africa (English Speaking Countries), "Discussion Guide," Mimeographed, Lagos, 1965, p. 13: "Industrial development is impossible without the necessary supply of food and raw material from the agricultural sector and without an ever-increasing purchasing power on the home market, which is largely constituted by rural populations."

36. For the Swedish experience see Chapter 10.

be programmatically developed but ought to be spatially deployed, in one way or another, over a national landscape. But almost never does one encounter central planners who give any thought to the questions of whether "key industries" might be structured in such a way as to create an interlocked spatial industrial hierarchy or whether they might serve as nuclei for much-needed new central places.[37]

Yet here is a realm of planning that deserves extremely careful consideration. Without much mental strain one can visualize a number of new, large-scale industrial establishments that could constitute nodal points for systematically integrated "functional economic areas." Since there has been considerable misgiving about the wisdom of an atomistic dispersion of small industries in minor central places, some of the feared handicaps might be forestalled if large and small industrial establishments were reciprocally interrelated in a larger spatial configuration, and urban nuclei of several orders of importance might thereby be created. This is an unexplored subject, but one that may hold great promise particularly when there are in most underdeveloped countries two chance developments that could make experiments with spatial arrangements of large and small industrial enterprises quite feasible. The first of these is the popularity of macroeconomic planning and the merit planners consistently find in "key industries" and "leading sectors."[38] The other is the strong trend toward political authoritarianism which has swept over large parts of the "third world" with surprising celerity. How permanent this brand of political centralization will be is anyone's guess. Yet however much it may be lamented as a constraint on democratic and libertarian political processes, it has, for all its shortcomings, one signal advantage: it allows nation-wide decisions to be made without much delay or compromise. Hence, in many underdeveloped countries, I suspect that governments would have the power, if they elected to exercise it, to establish unified and interlinked spatial industrial structures.

This potential leverage has not been used, and the only reasons I can suggest to explain this inaction are lack of imagination on the one hand

37. In Uttar Pradesh, as a fearless critic has said, "it is notable that none of these [large-scale, public-sector, new] projects is capable of forming a nucleus around which diverse ancillary units can be built." R. Roy, "Administration of Industrial Development in U. P.," in *Regional Perspective of Industrial and Urban Growth*, ed. Desai, Grossack, and Sharma, p. 269.

38. See for example W. W. Rostow, *Stages of Economic Growth*, Cambridge, 1960, p. 52–57.

and the political necessity of spatial patronage on the other. As to the first of these explanations, it does not appear to be appreciated that whereas the autonomous development of towns or small cities may take generations or even centuries, an industrial complex which might quickly become an urban nucleus can be built in a matter of a few years, sometimes in one or two years.[39] All over the "third world" key industries are being built, the underlying justification being that a modernizing nation must have its own steel mills, chemical plants, aircraft factories, paper mills, and machine-tool, electrical, and metal-forming industries. The planners are undoubtedly right; "modern" nations will need an essential group of industries consistent with their natural resource endowment and their capacity to import the inputs they cannot themselves produce. No one can quarrel with this general thesis. But if these new industries are doled out to regions so that a ruling ingroup can obtain greater nation-wide political support, locational considerations may become secondary, and the resulting industrial structure may be far less efficient than it might otherwise have been. Some industries will, of course, be "point-bound" by reason of their dependence on localized raw materials; this will be the case particularly if the manufacturing process involves weight or bulk reduction.[40] But many industries have a wide choice of location, and political distortions all too frequently interfere with optimal choice of location.[41]

Politics, it has been said, is the art of the possible, and one must recognize the very great importance of repressing the fissiparious forces

39. In Yugoslavia, for example, despite the drastic dislocation of plans by the break with the Cominform in 1948 and the resulting loss of very large prepayments on industrial equipment which was never delivered by the Soviet Bloc, it was still possible, albeit by very onerous forced saving, to complete more than a hundred "key industries" in less than a decade.

40. Among the new large-scale enterprises established in India since liberation, advantages of location near sources of raw material determined the sites for Travancore Minerals (near mineral sands yielding almandite, rutile, zircon, monazite, sillimanite, garnets), Hindustan Salt, Hindustan Steel, National Mineral Development Corporation (iron ore, diamonds), and Neyveli Lignite Corporation. For details see India, Cabinet Secretariat, Central Statistical Organization, *A Brochure on Principal Public Sector Undertakings in India,* New Delhi, 1961.

41. The Yugoslav "key-investment program" offers illustrations of both wise and unwise locational decisions. No one can criticize the choice of southeastern Macedonia for a leather industry (the herds are there) or of Voyvadina for a starch factory (near the corn fields). But to understand why a precision tool factory should be located in the barren hills of Montenegro rather than in Slovenia (where skilled labor is available), or why the five republics should each have its own steel complex (regardless of the quality of the ore or the nearness of coal), one has to invoke a political rather than a techno-economic explanation.

that are ever present in newly formed countries.[42] Concessions, therefore, will have to be made, and it is foolish to assume that patronage can be eliminated from a national capital-formation program. I am only arguing that, if it is necessary for political reasons to put a machine tool factory in the foothills of the Himalayas or a rayon fiber mill in a small Bosnian town, then this necessity might be made an advantage if such large plants were to become the regional centers of investment clusters which could stimulate the growth of functional economic areas.

There are very important lessons that underdeveloped countries can learn from the industrial experience of mature countries, not least of which is that high costs may be involved if large enterprises attempt to produce all the components their end products require. This striving for complete enterprise autonomy, so prevalent in emergent industrial countries, has long since been abandoned by West European and American large-scale enterprises. In Germany purchases of components from 17,760 firms by the Daimler-Benz motorcar company represent about 65 percent of production costs; in France Renault, the leading automobile manufacturer, buys more than 20,000 components from over 5,000 suppliers and subcontractors; in the United States the Raytheon Company, one of the large electronic manufacturing firms, purchases 65 percent of its components from small enterprises; the du Pont company depends on over 30,000 other firms for its supplies, and of these "other firms" 93 percent are small, by American definition.[43] There is no charity or condescending solicitude for small business involved in these arrangements. The "other firms," many of which are small enterprises, can produce industrial components at lower costs; hence it is to the pecuniary advantage of the large enterprises to buy rather than manufacture a large proportion of the parts their end products incorporate.

Purchase of components is not the only variety of complementarity that exists in mature countries between large and small enterprises. The great majority of small manufacturing firms buy semifinished

42. Nigeria is a tragic example of a failure to work out a political basis for economic development.

43. For much further documentation see the excellent chapter "The Complementarity of Small Industry and Large" (Chapter 9) in Staley and Morse, *Modern Small Industry*. For an interesting account of the relocation of the American meatpacking industry see *Time*, December 6, 1968. Armour and Company is closing 250 antiquated city plants and will spend $143 million on new decentralized slaughter and packing houses.

goods from large enterprises. Thus builders of television or radio cabinets purchase plywood from large companies, and all small firms that fabricate metal obtain their basic materials from large companies. In this type of "direct complementarity" the small factories and artisan workshops are engaged in what has been called "further manufacturing," and since in this interrelation the small firms are really the customers of the large, it is to the interest of large enterprises to provide technical advice for the small firms, engage in research on their behalf (which could be prohibitive for the small firm), share the findings with their customers, and even make loans to the small firms so that they can expand the scale of their operations. Unfortunately, these linkages between large and small enterprises, so typical in advanced countries, are rarely being forged in emergent industrial countries. There is, consequently, much less "subcontracting," a familiar interrelation between large and small firms that is just the opposite of "further manufacturing," since in subcontracting operations it is the large firm that buys from the small. The reluctance of large firms in newly industrialized countries to integrate their activities with those of smaller enterprises apparently has its origins not only in vanity or distrust but in a mistaken view of the economics of scale—a negativism which contrasts strikingly with the willing acceptance of crisscrossing purchase and sales arrangements in developed countries.[44]

Small firms can very often produce at lower unit costs than large firms. Their overhead costs are consistently less per unit of output, and their direct labor costs may be considerably lower, particularly if plants are located in small cities or towns. Nor do they always suffer from a handicap of scale. By concentrating on a particular product (or on a group of products) they can, if they sell to a number of buyers, sometimes have a much larger volume of production than any single large manufacturing firm could have if it were to make particular components for its end products.[45] Moreover, a very rigid

44. "Large plants probably could not operate efficiently . . . if their production were not integrated with the production of hundreds or even thousands of other plants, both large and small. . . . The ten-man shop could not produce an automobile (or airplane) except at astronomical cost, but the assembly-line plant would also be less efficient (and much larger) if it produced all the components of an automobile (or an airplane)." Robert W. Oliver, *The Role of Small-Scale Manufacturing in Economic Development: The Experience of Industrially Advanced Countries as a Guide for Newly Developing Areas,* Washington, D.C., 1957, p. 71.

45. American rubber tire companies buy their valves from specializing manufacturers of metal products, since a valve maker who sells to a number of tire companies achieves greater economy of scale than a single tire company could do.

quality control will ordinarily be instituted in a relatively small, specialized enterprise whose repeat orders depend on the complete satisfaction of its large-scale customers. Since the experience of Western Europe, Japan, and the United States has shown that the production of components for large enterprises, whether by subcontracting arrangements or by wholly independent operations, can "add substantially to the flexibility and efficiency of the industrial system",[46] it seems very likely that the tendency in newly industrializing countries for each large enterprise to aim at completely centralized manufacturing operations may lead to unnecessarily high manufacturing costs and a waste of resources caused by less than optimal use.[47]

Those who cannot learn from history, it has been said, must repeat the mistakes of yesteryear. With their scanty resources, their overwhelming problems of poverty, low productivity, and endemic underemployment, the underdeveloped countries cannot afford this foolish luxury. In the industrial realm, they should encourage the maximum degree of complementarity between large and small industrial firms. Only to a very limited extent are such links being forged in underdeveloped countries;[48] this is mainly because there is little or no appreciation of how a systematic areal interconnection between large and small industries can be the means for creating dynamic functional economic areas. Since in so many developing countries the industrial structure is largely being created de novo, it is the more to be regretted that attempts are not being made to intermesh large and small enterprises, whether public or private. It would be entirely possible to do this in conjunction with agricultural development activities,[49] infra-

46. Staley and Morse, *Modern Small Industry*, p. 261.

47. Describing the operations of metalworking firms in Madras, James J. Berna noted that "the smallest unit must have its own foundry . . . even though it remains unused nine-tenths of the time." *Industrial Entrepreneurship in Madras State*, Bombay, 1960, p. 11.

48. For an account of a few examples in Brazil and India see Staley and Morse, *Modern Small Industry*, pp. 265, 267–268.

49. The indispensability of agricultural improvement in a national industrialization effort has been forcefully stated by W. Arthur Lewis: "Measures to increase the productivity of manufacturing industry," he said prophetically fifteen years ago, "must be paralleled by measures to increase the demand for manufactured products. This demand comes only to a small extent from industrial producers themselves, who are only a small proportion of the population. . . . It comes to a greater extent from all other classes, of whom the farmers are far and away the largest category. If capital is being put into developing manufacturing industry while the country's agriculture remains stagnant, the result is bound to be distress in the manufacturing sector." *The Theory of Economic Growth*, London, 1955, pp. 140–141.

structural investments, and educational programs in spatial patterns that could have transforming effects on entire economic landscapes.

Some possible interrelations between large and small industrial enterprises are skeletally pictured in Figure 8–1. Large enterprises are designated by capital letters (A, B, C, D, E), small enterprises by arabic figures. Places where end products are sold, within the inscribed "functional economic area," whether they be stores, manufacturers' sales offices, or any other outlets, are designated SP (selling places). Three kinds of interfirm transactions are depicted, involving the sale of materials or semiprocessed goods by larger firms to small firms for "further manufacturing"; the sale of components by small firms to large enterprises; the flow of end products to selling places within the functional area. In addition, the figure indicates that both

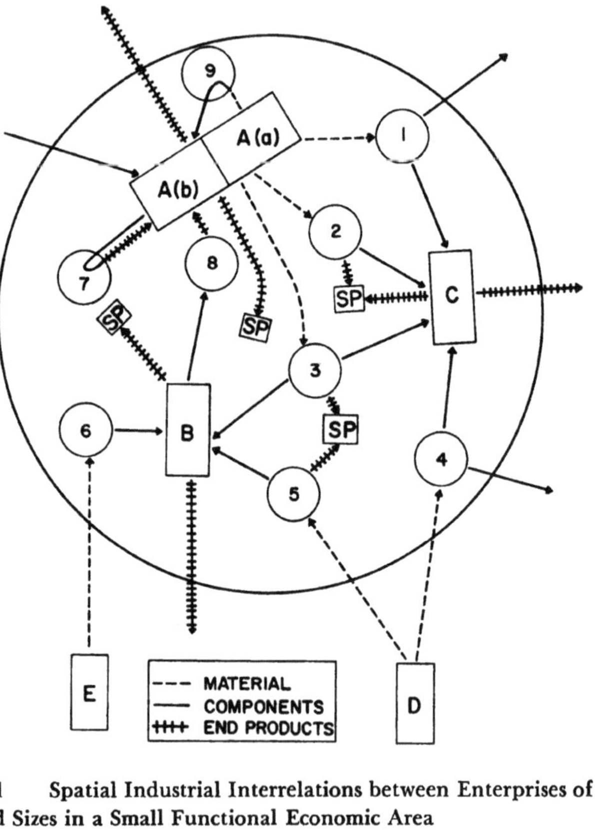

Figure 8–1 Spatial Industrial Interrelations between Enterprises of Varying Types and Sizes in a Small Functional Economic Area

materials and components are received from places outside the (circled) area and that both end products and components are "exported" to buyers outside the area. The interstices are, by assumption, devoted to agriculture, and the selling places (SP) are located in market towns.

Even in this simplified model the wide range of choices of interfirm relations that are possible in a well-planned spatial network of industrial units is evident. Firm A, for example, has two major activities. In part (a) it produces semifinished materials (which are purchased by firms 1, 2, and 3 in order to manufacture components for firms C and B, and for "export"). In part (b), its finished goods division, firm A employs two types of subcontracting arrangements. Firm 9 buys semifinished materials from A(a), "further manufactures" them, and sells them as components to A(b). The arrangement with firm 7 is technically more advanced: partly completed end products made in A(b) are sent to firm 7 where the manufacturing is completed; hence they are returned to A(b) as finished end products. Firm A's end products (whether finished in A(b) or by firm 7) are sold partly in the (circled) area and partly outside. It will be noted that firms 7 and 9 confine their business dealings to firm A and are therefore what has sometimes been called "captive subcontractors,"[50] as contrasted with the somewhat more independent firm 8, which buys components from firm B and sells end products to firm A. But firm 8 nevertheless relies exclusively on firm A as a buyer of the products it makes. Firm 3 is less dependent on a single buyer; it sells components to firms B and C and also produces some final end products which it markets at SP. Firm B's interfirm arrangements show how industrial linkages can be both intra-areal and interareal. It should be noticed that firm B buys components from firms 5 and 6, both of whom "import" materials, and from firm 3, which buys materials intra-areally from firm A(a). Firm B sells components to firm 8 for "further manufacture" (before they are, in turn, sold to firm A) and markets its finished end products at selling places both in the area and outside the area. In these several ways Figure 8–1 provides an illustration of the kind of spatial industrial planning that might contribute to a far-reaching transformation of an economic landscape. As the whole interlinked system grows—and this growth will partly depend on the way it is articulated to serve the needs of

50. By Staley and Morse, who point out that this variety of subcontracting is much more commonly used in Japan than in Europe or America, *Modern Small Industry*, p. 252.

the agricultural interstices—the volume of employment will expand not merely at a few nodal points but throughout the whole "functional area." Furthermore, by reason of the interareal linkages, the increased industrial activity will contribute to the macroeconomic objectives of national plans.

The Politics and Economics of Energy Distribution

Perhaps the greatest technical advantage that newly industrializing countries have in launching spatially dispersed industrial enterprises and in developing a more modern and efficient agriculture is the ease with which energy can now be supplied almost wherever it is needed. In the earlier phases of European, American, and even Japanese industrialization, reliance on waterwheels or turbines limited the number of sites where power-driven machinery might be installed. Steam power widened the locational choices,[51] but the relatively high costs of a dependable power plant and the necessity for transmitting power to machines by elaborate systems of wheels, belts, shafts, and gears made for relatively large, unified industrial establishments in which machines, materials, and workers were crowded together. One need only examine drawings or photographs of early factories or visit some of the nineteenth-century examples that still survive in Asia to see how unpleasant, noisome, and depressing they were, or still are. Not all the responsibility for these insalubrious conditions should be charged up to the greed, avarice, and insensitivity of factory owners or superintendents. A great deal of the overconcentration and interior congestion in steam-power factories was the inevitable consequence of the inflexibility of the energy-providing system.

Electric power has not only made possible wholly different locational patterns for a nation's industry; it also permits experimentation with new departures in plant layout and design. Power lines, graduated to suitable voltages, can dependably transmit power over long distances, and motive power for a great variety of purposes can therefore be instantaneously available at the turn of a switch. If the building of a

51. On the early history of the spatial dispersion of energy supply as a consequence of improved steam engines, see Erich Roll, *An Early Experiment in Industrial Organization: Being a History of the Firm of Boulton and Watt, 1775–1805*, London, 1930, Chapters 3–5.

regional transmission grid is economically feasible, neither large nor small industrial enterprises need devote any capital for constructing power plants; all they need do is to purchase the necessary transformers and install the motors that are appropriate in size for operating the manufacturing equipment. Since each machine can now have its own motive power, operators can start and stop their machines at will and are no longer the human robots they were when whole banks of machines were driven by connecting shafts transmitting power from dangerous, swift-moving wheels and flying belts. Best of all, machines can now be properly located in relation to light, air, and materials, so that modern factories can be comfortable and even pleasant places in which to work.

In view of these very real possibilities for designing factories that will reduce the physical hardships of work, minimize fatigue, and virtually eliminate occupational hazards, the critical role of electricity production and distribution becomes a matter of paramount importance. The tremendous potential of electric energy as an aid to agricultural progress should not be underestimated. Tube wells with pumps driven by electric motors can greatly widen irrigated areas; tedious and laborious farm tasks such as grinding, decorticating, and sawing can be easily and better performed by electrically powered equipment; and a whole group of processing industries can quickly develop in central places if electric power is available. Two essential operations are therefore involved: the generation of adequate electric power and its most effective spatial distribution. For technical reasons the production of electricity calls for plants, whether hydro or thermal, that are located at proper sites and built with capacities which will promise to result in lowest possible unit costs. The building of conventional power plants is now a very precise branch of engineering, and the technological uniformities are so well recognized that it makes little difference whether an underdeveloped country engages an American, French, Belgian, German, Japanese, British, or Yugoslav firm to design and construct a hydro or a thermal power plant. Whatever energy sources a country may have can be utilized, even volcanic steam. Almost any type of coal or lignite[52] will serve as fuel in steam-power plants, while new developments in water turbines now allow hydro plants

52. The great soggy beds of lignite in Greece and Yugoslavia have become the sites for large, technically efficient, thermal power plants.

to capture the energy of even sluggish rivers. In view of these physical factors, there is fortunately little room for politics in the determination of the technically proper locations for conventional power plants.[53]

If a developing country is small, it might be possible to locate all electric power plants at optimally low-cost locations, since transmission lines could be relatively short, and "line losses" of electricity would therefore be negligible. Moreover, it ought not be prohibitively expensive to unify the transmission lines into a grid, into which all generating plants could feed in energy and from which all users could obtain current. The problem is very different in a large country, particularly if it contains great stretches of poor lands that are sparsely settled. Decisions mainly political will then have to be made concerning which region to favor and, oppositely, which areas to neglect. Once again the least backward most backward syndrome crops up to harry and perplex the decision makers. All too frequently the importunities of particular groups, enterprises, or ambitious politicians may determine why a particular area is favored. In the process large cities usually take precedence over small central places and always over country regions, except for some narrow rural belts on city outskirts. Yet this type of .chance favoritism may be quite irrational from a macroeconomic point of view. For if a national increase of per capita income is allegedly the major object of economic policy, then the distribution of energy ought to be based on rigorous spatial productivity criteria.[54] All too often the provision of electric energy to a city or to a favored area is not functionally related to productivity, and although there may be some consumer comfort derived from electric lights or even some instruction as well as pleasure from radios, the opportunity costs of using electric current mostly for consumptive purposes needs to be carefully considered if one is seriously concerned with optimal use of resources.

53. In the siting of nuclear plants, where there is no compulsion to locate near fuel supply, I suspect political considerations will rather vigorously intrude themselves. It does not follow that this is wholly undesirable; "political" factors might prevent the location of nuclear power plants where they might be considered dangerous to public health and safety.

54. "It may be taken for granted that no country . . . can enjoy a high per capita income without becoming an extensive consumer of energy." Edward S. Mason, "Energy Requirements for an Expanding World Economy," in *The Changing Environment of International Relations*, Washington, 1956, p. 9.

The great paradox is that poor, underdeveloped and often wretched countries "consistently use a far greater fraction of their energy output as a consumer item than mature countries do."[55] Studies made in India by the National Council of Applied Economic Research revealed that about 70 percent of total energy production was consumed in the domestic and service sectors of the economy, leaving less than a third for the productive sectors.[56] In the United States the situation is just the reverse; about 75 percent of energy is used for production, and, despite the vast number of automobiles and household appliances, only about 25 percent in the domestic and service industries. There are, as I have pointed out elsewhere, two main reasons for this paradox.[57] In underdeveloped countries the energy-intensive industries (mechanical transport, mining, and manufacturing) are few and small, while the labor-intensive occupations (agriculture and services) employ the largest fraction of the work force and make the major contributions to national product. The second reason for the disproportionate share of energy output devoted to consumption has a totally different cause. However charismatic politicians may be, they must nevertheless offer some proof that under their governance their countries are modernizing and improving. Hence, they are under considerable compulsion to provide visible amenities to as many voters as possible. Electric lights, radios (that depend on electric current), city and intercity buses, motorcycles, and kerosene stoves—all these good things—can be cited as indisputable evidence of progress. But these "good things" have only one common quality: they are all essentially consumer goods, and the understandable solicitude of politicians for the welfare of voters contributes to the energy paradox. One finds, therefore, that poor countries, which ought to devote every precious unit of energy to increasing production, waste energy with seemingly prodigal indifference while their political leaders, virtually without exception, keep promising their constituents still more energy for consumptive purposes.[58]

55. Johnson, *Market Towns and Spatial Development in India,* p. 105.

56. N. C. A. E. R., *Demand for Energy in India, 1960–1975,* New Delhi, 1960, p. 8. See also N. C. A. E. R., *Demand for Energy in Southern India,* New Delhi, 1962, pp. 10–11.

57. *Market Towns and Spatial Development in India,* p. 105.

58. The waste of energy, as the National Council of Applied Economic Research studies of India have shown, is by no means confined to the electrification of mud-wall villages. The use of dung cakes as domestic fuel and the dependence on draft

The resulting high "propensity to consume" electric energy confronts policy makers with awkward questions. They must decide whether an electrification program that merely makes it possible for more people to have the convenience of electric lights helps or hinders development, and whether, in building a distribution grid, they should or should not follow practices used in developed countries. They must decide, for example, whether rural electrification will really help to develop a backward country or whether it will merely waste resources that could yield returns many times as high (in real output) if devoted to some unequivocally productive purpose. Public policy should adopt a rigorous technical approach to the energy distribution problem, based on the thesis that the real purpose of a distribution system should be to convert energy into "work." If this criterion is applied, there must be a clear understanding of the concept of "useful energy" (energy generated less all losses involved in producing, transporting, and converting energy materials into work)[59] and some agreement about the nature of "useful consumption." An ill-planned spatial distribution of electric energy may not only reduce available "useful energy" by increasing losses and leakages but at the same time may expand "useless consumption."[60]

---

animals for most transport may constitute the greatest national waste of energy. The so-called "free fuels" are by no means "free"; when dung is burned, the opportunity cost of the vaporized nitrogen may exceed the cost of alternative fuel by a large margin. Similarly, the draft energy of bullocks is not "free," since young bullocks must be fed for over three years before they can perform any productive work. Hence bullock power may be "the most expensive of all India's sources of power." N. C. A. E. R., *Demand for Energy in Southern India,* p. 1.

59. "As a percent of energy produced or consumed, these losses are the product of a large number of influences including the 'mix' of energy materials, the extent of processing, increases in efficiency, changing difficulties of extracting energy materials, the average length of haul of energy materials or transmission of converted energy." Mason, "Energy Requirements," pp. 6–7.

60. No technical definition of "useful" or "useless" consumption is possible, although technical data help to reveal the opportunity costs that are involved in one type of energy consumption when compared with another. Indian studies have shown that in the production of heat (for cooking purposes) electricity is seven times as efficient as dung cake and (given distribution lines) about 30 percent less expensive. Furthermore, these differentials in heat generation and cost would not fully measure the advantages of electricity. The released dung could be utilized for fertilizer, and its application would markedly increase agricultural yields. Despite these technical findings, the traditional preference for cooking with dung cakes may be so deep-rooted as to make a rational definition of "useful consumption" inapplicable. For further details see N.C.A.E.R., *Domestic Fuels in Rural India,* New Delhi, 1959, p. 23.

Proper criteria must be used in planning, phasing, and building an electricity production and distribution system. Electric current is such an extraordinarily flexible form of energy usable in so many ways that every economic sector can benefit from its availability. Because it can be used not only for light, heat, and power but also for such tasks as chemical separation or synthesis, efforts to specify or define geographically the areas where electricity will make the greatest contribution to growth and development are beset with bristling difficulties. Clearly, some kind of benefit-cost analysis is called for. If it can be assumed that the approximately proper share of total annual investment has been earmarked, by macroplanners, for electricity production and distribution facilities, then the major intrasector investment decisions will be to ascertain the most fruitful activities to be favored and the ranking of geographic areas in some tolerably satisfactory order of priority. In dealing with the latter of these two dimensions, benefit-cost analysis will be particularly helpful. For, whereas the rationality of supplying electric energy to an industry or a group of enterprises can be measured at least partially by the expected revenues of the electricity generating system, the provision of electric current for a spatial area cannot similarly be estimated. It is entirely possible that it would be in the national interest to provide electricity at a net loss if the resulting annual increment of areal development far exceeded such annual light and power losses.

The benefit-cost technique is essentially an engineering-economic technique that was first developed by United States governmental agencies for forecasting the putative regional benefits that might accrue from river basin or other water resource improvements.[61] Total costs were laid alongside the estimated value of all foreseeable benefits, and normally no projects were undertaken unless the benefits exceeded the costs. In calculating benefits, all possible economic improvements that might logically be ascribed to the particular increment of investment were footed up into a credit item.[62] Because developing countries are

61. See Otto Eckstein, *Water Resources Development: The Economics of Project Evaluation*, Cambridge, Mass., 1958; John V. Krutilla and Otto Eckstein, *Multiple-Purpose River Development: Studies in Applied Economic Analysis*, Baltimore, 1958; and U.S. Federal Interagency River Basin Committee, Subcommittee on Benefits and Costs, *Proposed Practices for Economic Analysis of River Basin Projects*, Washington, 1950.

62. Thus, as Eckstein has pointed out, the benefit of an irrigation project will not be measured by the revenue that the irrigation district derives from the sale of water

constantly faced with a chronic scarcity of investment funds, benefit-cost analysis can be a most useful technique for making reasonably accurate evaluations of the potential yields (in national benefit) of every increment of investment outlay. The ever emergent question in such a context will be: Which project is most worthy? By means of benefit-cost calculations it may well be possible to rank all projects in terms of their potential contributions to development.

There are, however, many difficulties. A policy maker must decide which of two projects to choose if both promised equally satisfactory benefit-cost ratios but if for one the foreign-exchange cost were greater. It must be determined whether the second of these projects, which promised very clear domestic benefits, should be downgraded because of its probable impact on the nation's international accounts and replaced (in the implementation order) by a project with lower prospective "benefit" but no foreign-exchange cost. There is also the question of how low-cost, high-benefit projects that involve considerable uncertainty should be ranked,[63] whether they should give way to lower-benefit, higher-cost projects that are almost riskless. Even presumed experts seem to have trouble in devising criteria that will take account not only of cost and benefit but of risk.[64] There are also, as I have explained elsewhere, many other difficulties:[65] slow-maturing projects can be compared with quick-ripening ones; whether electric-power facilities should be built far ahead of demand on the presumption that there will be real benefits from increasing returns on a given investment as the percentage of capacity utilization increases; whether it is possible to weight benefits as between economic sectors on a presumption, for example, that an increase in manufacturing is x times as important as an increase in primary production or agriculture. The most perplexing question of all, to be sure, is how to define what "economic benefits"

---

but by the "extra-total value attributed to the water supply, as measured by the changed income of farmers." "Benefit-Cost Analysis and Regional Development," in *Regional Economic Planning: Techniques of Analysis,* Papers and Proceedings of the First Conference on Problems of Economic Development Organized by the European Productivity Agency, Bellagio, 1960, ed. Walter Isard and John H. Cumberland, Paris, 1961, p. 361.

63. Such as the building of a road to an unproved coal mine, a decision that proved unwise in Korea, when actual mining operations showed the unreliability of the geological estimates on which the project had been based.

64. As Eckstein does; see his "Benefit-Cost Analysis," p. 366.

65. *Market Towns and Spatial Development in India,* p. 111.

actually are. Is public health more important than mineral output? Is education to be preferred over better nutrition? Decisions about such questions must be made by a nation's political leaders, and all that economists can do is to remind them that if they do one thing, however useful it may be, they will not be able to do something else that is also very important. Hence, although the presumed purpose of benefit-cost analysis is to show why "this is better than that," it cannot answer the more difficult question of whether a nation should do this or that. Despite this handicap, it is a technique which can help a nation to channel limited resources into certain activities that are comparatively more productive than other alternatives. Its greatest virtue may be that it is a device that would put policy makers on notice that, if they do certain things (however much they may be importuned and however enthusiastically the public might applaud), there is a social opportunity cost involved that will fall somewhere on the economy if the benefit from one project is less than the benefit that an alternative project can yield.

When one attempts to apply benefit-cost analysis to infrastructural projects, spatial considerations are clearly unavoidable. Whether a new nation should have a synthetic fiber factory or a pharmaceutical plant may create few if any spatial problems since either enterprise would produce a high value, small bulk product; hence transport would be a negligible locational factor. A light and power system is very different, since wherever it is built it will be related to a certain area and will therefore involve spatial sunk costs. The capacity of one region rather than another (or of one functional economic area rather than another) to yield higher benefits in relation to costs becomes therefore an essential factor in deciding where an increment of investment ought to be made. Will an expansion of a power distribution grid in a particular area, for example, "further complicate or help correct the overconsumption of energy by the household and service sectors of the economy?"[66] Will such an investment favor growth points or "will it squander resources on unpromising areas and places?" Some basic problems involved in the spatial allocation of electric energy are shown in simplified pictorial form in Figure 8–2. For convenience it is assumed that a generating plant already exists with a capacity to produce energy for any portion of a given economic landscape without serious line losses. The issue to be settled is where to build further distribution

66. Ibid., p. 112.

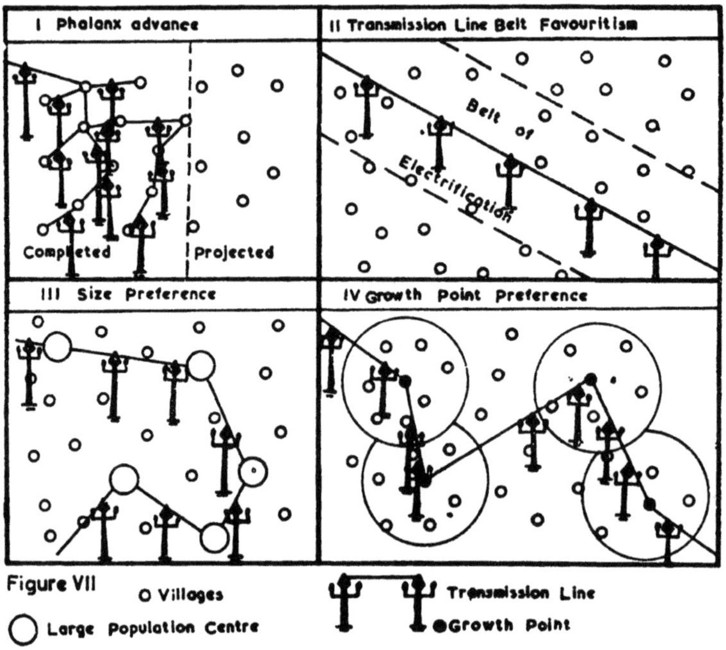

Figure 8–2 Possible Ways of Electrifying an Economic Landscape
SOURCE: E. A. J. Johnson, *Market Towns and Spatial Development in India,* New Delhi: National Council of Applied Economic Research, 1965, p. 119.

facilities. Four spatial possibilities are illustrated. In the upper left picture the existing distribution network is expanded by the least possible outlay on poles and wire. Such a "phalanx advance" of transmission facilities would involve electrifying each and every population center that was located near an existing network. The consequence might be a relatively high per capita electrification opportunity cost, since every village and hamlet in the enlarging circle of electrification would be eligible for electrification. Whether any corresponding benefits would accrue would be problematical; that would depend on whether there was or was not an increase of "useful consumption of electric energy." If this simple centrifugal type of grid expansion were compared with any of the other alternatives pictured in Figure 8–2, the chances are that in the "phalanx advance" the costs would be high and the benefits low. Yet this type of transmission-line expansion is occurring in every underdeveloped country. Without worriment about benefit in relation to cost, suburbs and satellites of great cities are steadily being electrified, usually guaranteeing that a very high proportion of electric energy will continue to be used for consumption.

A second possibility is illustrated in the upper right-hand picture in Figure 8–2. Here the assumption is made that, since a "high line" has been built connecting a power plant and a large city, it might be feasible to electrify some of the intervening space without great cost. To be sure, some branch lines will need to be built, and transformers would have to be installed. What might benefit-cost studies indicate concerning the economic propriety of providing service in such a "belt of electrification?" Once again the question arises as to who the users of energy will be. There is little reason to believe that hamlets and villages that chance to be near a high-voltage transmission line will be more deserving of electrification than hamlets and villages that are nowhere near the "belt of electrification." But for politicians to deny electricity to villages through which (or near which) transmission lines are built is not easy!

In an effort to develop some more equitable means of allocating transmission lines spatially, the idea has been advanced that communities with population over a specified size should be granted priority. Thus in India, under the Third Plan (1961–1966), the declared objective was to electrify all population centers having more than five thousand people (and some twenty thousand places with less than five thousand inhabitants).[67] But, although the lower left-hand picture in Figure 8–2 seems to make sense, it really doesn't. The size of a population center is a very doubtful indicator of factors which might magnify the benefits of an investment *tranche*. Most underdeveloped countries have relatively few towns, but they often have many villages with populations in excess of five thousand people.[68] There are few reasons for

67. For the statement of general objectives see India, Planning Commission, *The Third Five-Year Plan*, New Delhi, 1961, pp. 403–405. The Plan established no criteria whatever for selecting the 20,000 villages with less than 5,000 inhabitants from the more than 500,000 Indian villages. One must assume therefore that what really occurred was that the Plan recognized that a certain number of villages would be electrified by the process I have called "phalanx advance," and that some villages in "belts of electrification" would be similarly favored. If these assumptions are valid, then it seems somewhat absurd to say that the electrification of 20,000 villages had been "planned."

68. The census of 1961 showed that whereas India had a grand total of 2,690 towns and cities, she had 4,169 villages with populations that exceeded 5,000 people.

believing that the large, swollen villages are necessarily more efficient or dynamic than the smaller. Very frequently it is just the reverse; large villages are crowded with poor, marginal producers. Even if this is not the case, there is little reason for believing that every village or settlement with more than five thousand people is for that one reason particularly productive. Once again, the costs will be certain, the benefits unmeasured and uncertain.

The real trouble with pictures I, II, and III in Figure 8–2 is that in these methods of public utility allocation there has been no concern with a "functional economic area" and hence no consideration of the potential transforming effect that the provision of electricity might set in motion. This method of electrification, which is shown in picture IV of Figure 8–2, would have to be highly selective. Efforts would need to be made to locate really promising growth points, and on the basis of benefit-cost analysis the comparative claims of one emergent functional economic area for electrification could be compared with the claims of another. Indeed, the benefit-cost studies ought not be confined to estimating the possible benefits attributable to electrification alone. For in the same way that investment clusters can do more than single enterprises in setting areal development in motion, a number of functionally interrelated infrastructures can have perhaps an even greater multiplying effect. How the estimated benefits and costs of outlays on roads, electric transmission lines, and a warehouse may be calculated and compared for a small (Indian) functional economic area of twenty-five villages is illustrated in Table 8–1.

Change-Inducing and Development-Directing Institutions

The decentralization of planning and the implementation of regional and local plans have proved to be among the most difficult problems faced by countries that are attempting to coordinate their investment and resource allocation procedures with the object of hastening development. Highly centralized techniques, such as those initially used in the Soviet Union, and imitated with many variations in a number of other countries, have not only proved to be arbitrary and often rigid and inflexible as plans, but have usually relied for implementation on administrative decrees rather than on the voluntary response of pro-

---

Among these were 773 with over 10,000 inhabitants. India, Office of the Registrar General, *Census of India, Final Population Totals,* 1961 Census, pp. lxi–lxii.

Table 8–1 Condensed Cost-Benefit Calculation (in rupees)
Direct and Indirect Benefits

Infrastructure projected	Input returns and beneficiaries	Estimated net benefits
Transport village to market center rock-ballasted roads (75 miles) connecting 25 villages with new regulated market subyard	Higher prices obtained by producers at subyard	71,428.50
	Producer's revenue from increased output of customary crops induced by new subyard	142,857.00
	Producers income from new crops now saleable	95,238.00
	Additional net profits of market center merchants (less losses of village artisans)	76,190.50
	Reduction of transport cost of village cooperative societies	17,857.00
Power construction of high-tension transmission line to provide electric power in new market center where subyard will be established	Increased extraction of oil from oilseeds as a result of power-driven equipment	13,333.00
	Net revenues of operators of new agricultural processing industries	76,190.50
	Increased income of small-scale market center industries	52,381.00
	Wages of increased work force that power-driven industries will provide with employment	66,667.00
Warehouse Facilities building of a 1,500-ton general purpose ware-house near new subyard	Prevention of losses by heat, moisture, rodents, and pests	21,428.50
	Increased returns to producers by distribution of sales over crop year	52,381.00
	Increased returns to merchants from holding of stocks	100,000.00
Total Estimated Annual Benefits, All Beneficiaries		785,952.00
	Annual Costs	
Amortization and interest, at 6 percent, on total (5,595,238) investment		335,714.00
Operation and maintenance costs of new infrastructure		123,809.00
Total Annual Average Cost		459,523.00
Net Agro-Urban Community Annual Gain (benefits minus costs)		326,429.00
Benefit-Cost Ratio	785,952.00 ÷ 459,523.50 = 1.71	

ducers, traders, and consumers motivated by economic incentives. Yet, since this variety of centralized macroeconomic planning was the tool which made it possible for the Soviet Union, in a short span of forty years, to become the second industrial nation of the world, no one can contest the importance of such techniques.[69] The question, therefore, is not whether centralized planning and centralized resource allocation will work, but whether a more decentralized system might not work much better.

Whether plans are implemented by paramilitary techniques, as they often were during the Stalinist era in the USSR and during the "Great Leap Forward" in Mainland China, or whether, in contrast, they can be enforced by much gentler compulsions, as they have been in Sweden or Norway, they will inevitably have to be concerned in one way or another with at least three spatial dimensions: the nation, the economic regions into which the whole country is divided, and smaller spatial areas within regions.[70] It is the argument of this essay that the quintessential vitality of a developmental effort will in the final analysis depend on the extent to which total planning operations actually influence the behavior of people in subregional spatial units. For if the dreams of release from poverty are going to be realized, planning activities and the implementation of plans must in some way enlist the participation of the bulk of people who live in hamlets, villages, towns and small cities if only for the simple political reason that they are now, and for a long, long time will continue to be, a majority. Only by their cooperation and sustained interest can an action program be set in motion that will not merely progressively modernize portions of an underdeveloped country but can gradually transform whole national economic landscapes. Over the past fifty years, and particularly during the last twenty years, central planning procedures have been explored with great zest, insight, and imagination,[71] in three main political contexts: the so-called "capitalist"

69. It should not be overlooked, however, that very important industrial beginnings had been made in Imperial Russia before the Communists took power. In steel, coal, and textiles, Russia was already in about fifth place.

70. An Indian geographer has suggested that these three facets of planning might be designated as "macro planning" (of a nation or a group of constituent states), "meso planning" (of a state or its subregions), and "micro planning" (of districts or blocks of villages). See L. S. Bhat, "A Regional Approach to the Urban and Industrial Development of the Kanpur Region," in *Regional Perspective of Industrial and Urban Growth,* ed. Desai, Grossack, and Sharma, p. 231.

71. The literature is so huge that hundreds of pages would be needed for listing the major books and articles alone.

variants in Western Europe or North America; the "socialist" types, whether of Eastern Europe, Scandinavia, or elsewhere; and the eclectic forms employed in countries recently "liberated" from colonial rule.[72] In contrast to the attention devoted to central planning, regional planning, despite its manifest importance, has been until quite recently relatively neglected, and although its tentative character is still evident,[73] very real progress is now being made in the analytical elucidation of this very important subject. Unfortunately, the most serious shortcoming of development plans has been their ambivalent attitude toward subregional areal planning. All too often the presumption has been that if the macroeconomic plans are properly textured, development benefits will automatically "trickle down" to the smaller spatial units of an economy; hence, aside from some restrained enthusiasm for the loosely structured programs of community development, development planners and analysts have largely ignored subregional areas as basic elements in their planning procedures. Yet it is in the thousands upon thousands of socioeconomic groupings, comprising one, two, or three scores of villages, that the majority of people in a majority of underdeveloped countries actually live. These are the areas that must be made more productive if poverty is to be overcome, if underemployment is to be reduced, if the welfare, education, and the quality of life for most people are to be improved. These backwaters will need to be galvanized into action by dedicated leaders using institutions appropriate for their historic tasks. An almost zealous desire for improvement will be called for in order to convert listless local economies into truly functional economic areas.

The question is how this critically important part of a nation's planning program can be coordinated with regional and national planning. The ivory tower theory so popular two decades ago, which posited that planning must always start with global targets and goals,[74] has too often become an exercise far removed from any prospect of realization.

72. This separation, which is not very exact but is nevertheless useful, has been interestingly employed by Oskar Lange in his *Essays on Economic Planning*, New York, 1960.

73. From such books as *Regional Economic Planning*, ed. Isard and Cumberland, which contains essays by scholars from ten countries. For a penetrating appraisal of the status of regional analysis, see J. G. M. Hilhorst, *Regional Development Theory: An Attempt to Synthesize*, The Hague, 1967.

74. See, for example, W. Arthur Lewis, *The Principles of Economic Planning*, London, 1949, Chapter 9, "How to Plan."

National aggregates are basic, to be sure, but they must be formulated by using the potentials of regional and subregional resource and population units as building blocks. It is not the present productive capacity of regional or subregional areas which are most relevant, however. The problem is how to aggregate the potentials of the totality of prospective spatial units, and relate these to nationally possible innovations such as key investments or infrastructure. This is why the concept of emergent functional areas is so important. A proper analysis must be both an inventory and a projection, and the right type of planning must be at once locality-centered and region-oriented.

When Charles Galpin began his pioneer enquiries in Wisconsin, his concern was with measuring the "centrality" of the main towns of a single county. In doing so he discovered, much as Christaller and Lösch later did, that central-place functions have differing perimeters and that, whereas for some functions (e.g., trade) the areas served might be large enough to make possible a tolerable degree of efficiency, for others (e.g., high schools) the areas were wholly unsatisfactory. What Galpin's "social topography" revealed was the need for a functional adaptation of space in order to improve the economic, cultural, and educational possibilities of rural communities. This is precisely the problem that confronts the underdeveloped countries. The task is to create appropriate modern types of centrality and to restructure economic landscapes into more integrated, more diversified, and hence more productive functional economic areas.

Policy makers must therefore discover the appropriate institutions that can be usefully employed in helping to convert a promising rural growth center into a multifunctional central place which will begin to aggregate and unify an agro-urban community. The really important institutions will be those that can exert a stimulating or transforming influence on trade and trading areas, on nonagricultural employment, on the improvement of agricultural resources, on the training of an areal work force, on widening and enriching the general education of the population, and on saving, lending, borrowing, and investment activities. More specifically stated, the indispensable institutions would be properly supervised markets, suitable investment-stimulating instrumentalities (such as industrial estates), vocational and general schools, together with banks, credit unions, and other impersonally conducted financial institutions. To this basic list can be added, when resources permit, a number of other institutions whose purpose would be to improve welfare and the quality of life: clinics and health centers, cultural and social assembly facilities, libraries, and sewage and water-purification systems.[75] Energy supply, on the other hand, will be an indispensable factor, and its provision to every qualified growth center should be a matter of the highest priority.[76]

One need only list the minimally necessary change-making and development-directing institutions to realize the inseparability of national, regional, and small-area planning. Technological factors will dictate that electricity supply should be met on a regional basis, and whereas a farming community of perhaps fifty villages dispersed over 50 square miles can without much trouble establish a central market yard and perhaps build a cooperative warehouse, it ordinarily cannot finance an industrial estate or raise the capital needed for a modern oil-seed crushing and processing plant. If a truly functional economic area is to be created, this will call for a joint effort involving planning operations that acquire their real strength because they are laminations of spatial purposes, because the local community assumes responsibility for certain change-inducing institutions, the region for others, and the central government for still others. The key to the problem is the achievement of some comprehensive agreement concerning a hierarchy of responsibility for modernization.

Because they involve human reactions and responses, development techniques are only partially transferable. Methods readily acceptable in Taiwan may not be feasible in Ghana or Egypt. Industrial disciplines suitable to India may be bitterly resisted in Nigeria. Planning must take cognizance of a wide variety of cultural attitudes. For these reasons it is foolish to try to specify the precise means that should be employed to

75. Despite their good intentions, advocates of community development programs have, I fear, largely confused means and ends. Most of the good things they urge so passionately can be afforded only after the "communities" have been made much more efficient by means of markets, irrigation districts, industrial estates, and other productivity-increasing institutions.

76. One cannot expect small towns, to say nothing of rural areas, to be transformed if a lion's share of a nation's energy supply is engrossed by a few large cities. Thus, at the end of World War II two cities in China, Shanghai and Tientsin, utilized 74.3 percent of the nation's manufacturing motive power; and if one were to add the consumption in Tsingtao (7.4 percent) and Peking (6.3 percent), then four cities engrossed 88 percent. The likelihood of any very vigorous industrial development in the rest of China under such circumstances was certainly not great. For more details see Yuan-Li Wu et al., *The Spatial Economy of Communist China,* New York, 1966, p. 9.

increase the degree of commercialization of a near-subsistence economy, or the exact institutions needed to diversify the occupational pattern of what has been a monoculture. But given institutions which can, by reason of their demonstrated utility, acquire widening sanctions, it is entirely possible, as the experiences of Taiwan, the Indian Punjab, Puerto Rico, and Yugoslavia have demonstrated, to change the behavior of large numbers of people and make them more productive, more critical of traditional practices, more prosperous, and by these means more contributory to a macroeconomic program of development.

CHAPTER 9 SPATIAL EXPERIMENTS: AREAS OF PROGRESS

The Yugoslav Communes as Functional Economic Entities

The three major experiments with the organization of economic space briefly described in this chapter are essentially discrete as to purpose. The main objective of the Puerto Rican program, gradually structured in ways that would develop the local "municipalities," was employment. This contrasts with the chief goals of Israeli spatial design, which were settlement, defense, resource development, and conservation. Whereas some comparable ends are involved in the far-reaching Yugoslav experiments with "communes," these long-debated, ambitious undertakings have a number of political, cultural, sociological, and ideological objectives in addition to their economic purposes. Intended to be much more than functional economic areas, the communes were conceived by the theoreticians as essential instruments whereby a new type of socio-economic organization could be established.[1]

Even at the risk of reckless oversimplification, I must try to summarize the events which led the Yugoslav Government, in 1952–1953, to abandon their unsuccessful efforts to operate a Soviet type of centralized economy and to launch their program of decentralization. For it was this drastic change in economic policy that led to experiments not only with the now familiar workers' councils but with "communes" as politico-economic spatial units.[2] A change was necessary because the Stalinist program hadn't worked. One cause of its failure was that

1. Edward Kardelj, who in 1952 was among the leaders of the movement for decentralization, conceives of the commune as a planning unit, a form of local self-government, and as a carrier and improver of the material-technical content of the economy. See his *Samopravljanje u Komuni,* Materijali sa godišnje škupstine stalne konferenceje gradova Jugoslavije, Niš, 1952.

2. "Drastic" is not too strong an adjective to use. Federal employees who had numbered more than 43,000 in 1948 had by 1955 been reduced to less than 8,000.

administration was grotesquely overcentralized: all planning and virtually all implementation decisions were made in Belgrade.[3] Under the Federal Five-Year Plan, with which the parallel plans of the Republics and districts were presumably coordinated, judgments were made concerning what was to be produced, consumed, saved, and invested. Output quotas were assigned not merely to Republics and districts but to particular factories or to specific farm areas, and all conditions of work, credit, costs, prices, and distribution were factored out by the planners.[4] When such a completely centralized bureaucracy was expected to handle all the details of a quite complex economy, it was not surprising that "serious mistakes were made in planning amounts and kinds of goods needed for the home market."[5] Moreover, because "marketing was separated from production, the system of distribution was chaotic, bedevilled by poor communications, inexperience and an inefficient zoning system. There were gluts in some places, scarcity in others. . . . There was a staggering increase in officials and paper work."[6]

These shortcomings of the Soviet-inspired economic scheme of things did not go unnoticed by the extraordinarily talented Yugoslav leaders. They realized that "the whole system tended to defeat its own aims."[7] Even more disturbing than the increasingly evident deficiencies of the industrial and the mercantile sectors was the growing opposition of the

3. The actual enforcement of policies was entrusted to People's Committees, of which there was a pyramidal structure beginning with the local *savet* (committee) in the *opština* (village or group of hamlets) and laddering up through committees in the *srez,* (district) the *okrug,* (circuit) the *oblast,* (region) and the republic. Since the committees in this hierarchy were all too large to perform the requisite executive functions, the implementation of policy fell largely into the hands of full-time chairmen, secretaries, inspectors, and other officials. It was this new élite who exercised power, often with favoritism, sometimes with ruthless discrimination.

4. For a clear, nontechnical account of this critical period in Yugoslav history, see Phyllis Auty, *Yugoslavia,* New York, 1965, Chapters 4 and 5. See also Albert Waterston, *Planning in Yugoslavia,* Baltimore, 1962, Chapter 2.

5. Auty, *Yugoslavia,* p. 135. "Some items, needles, combs, razor blades, for example, had been omitted, but hats and slippers of inferior quality that none would buy flooded the market." Ibid.

6. Ibid., pp. 135–136. "Centralization of planning and execution and the subdivision of the federal annual plans into 'basic' and 'operational' plans, republican annual and quarterly plans, district and communal plans, and enterprise monthly, 10-day and daily plans, required a great deal of paper work and a large bureaucracy. It has been estimated [by Rudolf Bicanić] that the completed annual plan weighed about 3,300 pounds! There were over 215 federal and republican ministers issuing orders for enterprises to carry out." Waterston, *Planning in Yugoslavia,* p. 14.

7. Auty, *Yugoslavia,* p. 137.

great majority of Yugoslav peasants to the centralized economy. Farmers had real grievances, since they found themselves the victims of a Soviet type of "scissors" policy, whereunder the selling prices of their farm produce were artificially held down while the prices they had to pay for any and all industrial products were arbitrarily kept at levels the peasants considered extortionate. Nor was this all; to purchase nonfarm products both money and "bons" (coupons doled out in proportion to agricultural deliveries) were needed. Against these discriminations, Yugoslav farmers took typical peasant countermeasures. Without formal collusion they progressively reduced the amount of land cultivated, lowered the intensity of their farm practices, and slyly connived at the growing disregard of the traditional care of fields and farm animals. Despite the fulminations of the government press, the consequence was that the volume of agricultural production not only failed to reach prewar levels but by 1952 was far below and steadily declining.[8] In the meantime, the members of farm communities who had joined one or another of the several varieties of agricultural collectives grew more and more disenchanted when the predicted paradise proved to be an unpleasant, increasingly authoritarian regime, characterized by more venom and conflict than happiness and harmony. Task assignments were considered unreasonable,[9] and efforts to avoid work were evident in the rapid deterioration of farm equipment—a crass indifference toward maintenance that seemed wholly out of character for traditionally frugal peasants. In both the collectives and in the private agricultural sector a relentless peasant "slow down" occurred, and by 1952 it was patently clear that some wholly new economic policy was necessary if farm output was ever to increase.

Behind the failure of the Yugoslav attempt to emulate the Russian agrarian policy there were undoubtedly many subtle political and cultural complications that the outside observer could not understand.[10]

8. Estimates made by the U.S. Aid Mission in 1953 indicated that Yugoslav agricultural output was about 93 percent of prewar output and falling, whereas farm output in Western European countries (O.E.E.C. estimates) averaged about 18 percent above prewar and was rising.

9. On many occasions when I attempted to discuss assignments with work gangs, I found it prudent to take a worker's heavy hoe and keep up the pace of hoeing (sugar beets, for example) so that the field workers who were willing to talk could not be accused by their supervisors of idleness.

10. Not merely the constantly heard complaint that people from Montenegro had far more than their aliquot share of government positions and other preferments; or the still smoldering oppositions of Croats toward Serbs and of Serbs toward

But there is no doubt whatever in my mind that the major reason was the inability of the government to provide the necessary incentives for an instinctively conservative, bourgeois-minded, land-loving peasantry. With them, the right to plant the crops they thought best, the freedom to sell their crops or animals when they thought prices were satisfactory, and their right to be part of a market economy in ways of their own choosing were all-important considerations. The farmers who had not joined collectives bitterly resented the inspectors who visited their farmsteads without warning, who told them what to produce, and who earmarked hogs, sheep, cattle, or geese for mandatory delivery to the market at prices fixed by Belgrade planners. After more than five years' experimentation with agricultural collectives, involving large sums of money spent on consolidated farm structures and the allotment of precious foreign exchange for the purchase of thousands of tractors (which became inoperative with distressing rapidity for want of proper maintenance and lack of spare parts), it was belatedly realized that some very different new program was needed,[11] one that would provide incentives to induce Yugoslavia's capable peasants to farm better, grow more crops, raise more livestock, and deliver more produce to the market voluntarily.[12] Out of this reappraisal came the commune.

Decentralization called for wholesale political and economic change. The 1946 constitution was superseded by a "New Fundamental Law" allegedly designed to set in motion the "withering away of the state." And if "state" meant the central administration, this proved to be much more than a promise. Planning now became the responsibility of repub-

---

Croats and Slovenes; or the accusation in the villages that local Communists were seldom capable farmers or artisans but ne'er-do-wells. Undoubtedly some of the prewar opposition to Serbian political dominance survived, and to many people a centralized system was considered to be a new attempt to "Serbianize" the whole country.

11. To fend off Russian propaganda alleging that the Yugoslavs had never been true Communists, the Yugoslavs put on a drive to increase agricultural collectivization in 1949, 1950, and even in 1951, although the indications were already pretty clear that the existing system was honeycombed with inefficiency.

12. Just after the decision had been made to allow members of collectives to withdraw, I made a long field trip and talked with scores of farmers who had joined collectives and were now extremely eager to opt out. "All I want to do is to get out so I will be free to farm as one ought to farm" was a typical reply to my query about whether my informant planned to leave the *zadruga* he had so hopefully joined. "I contributed four horses, a plow, a harrow, and a wagon," said one hard-bitten farmer. "They can keep it—what's left of it—all I want is my freedom."

lics, of districts, and particularly of communes, which became the basic new units of local government.[13] Behind this new departure lay both political and economic ambitions of the Communist Party, which in 1952 had been renamed the League of Communists. Their most important aim, as Phyllis Auty has said, was to "protect the revolution."[14] To do this, concessions had to be made to a belligerent peasantry; in addition, something had to be done to compensate for the utter disregard of spatial factors that had characterized the centralized macroeconomic era and had sapped whatever vitality and will to develop that the local communities might have possessed when the German invaders had been finally overwhelmed. To revive that unity, spirit, and zest, which had been so intense in 1945, there had to be, said the theoreticians, an institution that could integrate industry and agriculture locally, that could meld the public and the private sectors, that would bring memories of the historical *zadrugas*,[15] and that recognized the relation of clans and neighborhoods.[16] It was envisaged that the new communes would consolidate villages and hamlets into larger politico-economic units, or, oppositely, divide cities into smaller population aggregates. Moreover, pending further experience in the "building of socialism," the communes contemplated the coexistence of public-sector modern industry with private-sector agriculture. These new spatial entities would not only be forms of local government but, in the terminology I have employed in Chapter 8, would be "functional economic units" properly related to larger economic and political entities and to a hierarchy of central places.

It is, of course, both jejune and hazardous to ascribe economic progress to a single innovation or to a limited number of institutional

13. First under 1952 legislation, which specified the rights and duties of People's Committees in *srez* (district) and *opština* (commune) and then, far more specifically, under the 1955 Law on the Organization of Communes and Districts. There had been communes under the 1944 constitution, but they were small, unimportant governmental units inferior to village committees.

14. *Yugoslavia*, p. 119.

15. The historical South-Slav extended family. For an illuminating account see Philip E. Mosely, "The Peasant Family: The Zadruga, or Communal Joint Family in the Balkans," in *The Cultural Approach to History*, ed. Caroline Ware, New York, 1940.

16. The cultural importance of communities that were both kinship and geographic units has been well explained by Joel Martin Halpern in *A Serbian Village*, New York, 1958, pp. 157ff.

changes. Yet, very promptly after 1953 something was responsible for a striking increase in both industrial and agricultural output, a trend that began its upward course almost immediately after planning was decentralized, after workers' councils came into being, and after communes began to integrate town and country activities spatially all over the country.[17] The evident vitality of both the public-sector industrial enterprises and of private-sector agriculture must have had some common cause, and it seems not unreasonable to attribute the surge of productive activity to incentives that were in some way provided by the increased role of local administrative institutions in the fifty-five Yugoslav cities with populations over twenty thousand, and in the more than 500 other communes that became basic politico-economic units mainly responsible for "coordinating and supervising all economic activity and social services" in their jurisdictional areas.[18] The nature of these building blocks of the post-1952 decentralized economy, therefore, deserves rather careful analysis.

First, a word about the concept of the *komuna*. Although the basic idea can be traced to the Paris Communes of 1871, the proposal for reorganizing the whole country on a communal plan reflected the interest of influential Yugoslav leaders in successful forms of local government in Sweden, Switzerland, and England. And whereas the prewar unit of local government (*opština*) had been purely administrative, the new spatial unit, the commune, was conceived to be "a defined socioeconomic community and not merely a political machine and an autonomous political organization."[19] To create these new spatial units two processes were set in motion, one aggregative, the other divisive. By the first procedure small *opštine* were consolidated into larger

17. "In the 1948–52 period the rate of growth remained at the pre-war level of 1.9 percent; in the 1953–56 period it rapidly increased to 8.4 percent, and in the period of the third Five-Year Plan, 1957–60, it reached 13 percent." Janez Stanovnik, "Planning through the Market—The Yugoslav Experience," *Foreign Affairs,* 40 (January 1962), 263. For comparative data for the period 1953–1960, indicating that the Yugoslav growth rate "heads the list of fastest growing countries," see Branko Horvat, *Note on the Rate of Growth of the Yugoslav Economy,* Belgrade, 1963, p. 2.

18. George Macesich, *Yugoslavia: The Theory and Practice of Development Planning,* Charlottesville, 1964, p. 2. The best account of the factors that shaped this new administrative system is in Jack C. Fisher's *Yugoslavia—A Multinational State: Regional Differences and Administrative Response,* San Francisco, 1966. See especially Chapter 5, "The Communal System," and Chapter 3, "Socioeconomic Variation and Urban Structure."

19. Jovan Djordjević and Najdan Pašić, "The Communal Self-Government System in Yugoslavia," *International Social Science Journal,* 13, No. 3 (1961), p. 390.

spatial units,[20] while by the second procedure the major Yugoslav cities (Belgrade, Zagreb, Skoplje, Sarajevo, and Ljubljana) were divided into communal fractions. This attempt to make the commune an inflexibly uniform organizational form reflects the strong penchant for symmetry in Yugoslav planning. The decision to convert cities into communes was probably a mistake; a better appreciation of central-place theory would have indicated the economic usefulness of unified cities. The rather doctrinaire attempt to insist on multicommunal cities has occasioned the complaint that urban communes have militated against maximum metropolitan, urban, and macroeconomic efficiency. Cities are functional entities; they cannot be expected to operate as a cluster of smaller spatial units.[21]

In rural areas, in contrast, the role of the communes was of salutary importance. In the first place, as the very negation of centralized planning and administration, the commune, by emphasizing local self-government, gave nationwide evidence of "citizens' fundamental political right to govern themselves."[22] But the commune was to be much more than a device for local self-government: it has been described as "the fundamental cell of future socialist society," because in such a socioeconomic community new social relations would be estab-

20. This consolidation occurred in several stages. The 7,085 *opštine,* into which the kingdom of the Serbs, Croats, and Slovenes had been divided under the Vidovdan Constitution (1921), had already been considerably reduced by 1955, by which time they numbered 4,519. Consolidations in that year reduced the number sharply to 1,479 (in 107 districts). By 1960 there were about 800 communes (in 75 districts); in 1961 the number was 611, and by 1963 further consolidation reduced the number of communes to 581 (in 40 districts). See Fisher, *Yugoslavia,* pp. 150, 154–155; and Macesich, *Yugoslavia,* p. 11.

21. Because the overall plan called for municipal fragmentation, the *srez* (district) in Zagreb had to assume responsibility for providing water, gas, and electricity for the whole, multicommunal city. As Fisher has pointed out (*Yugoslavia,* p. 115), the division of cities into communes "has often resulted in duplication of various administrative functions at greatly increased costs coupled with the growing tendency towards localism: attempts to maximize one commune's advantage over another. This has led . . . to a lack of cooperation among urban communes within the same metropolis."

22. Djordjević and Pašić, "The Communal Self-Government System in Yugoslavia," p. 390. The 1955 legislation made all *opštine* (the term is now synonymous with *komune*) equal in status, whether rural or urban. More important was the stipulation that the *srez* (district) was no longer a superior administrative unit but merely an "association of independent communes." Some analysts contend (see Fisher, *Yugoslavia,* p. 149, note 9) that it was the elimination of the districts that gave the communes the real incentives needed to begin solving their economic, cultural, and public health problems.

lished "on the basis of social ownership of the means of [industrial] production" and on "different forms of [agricultural] socialization or cooperation" whereby some socially useful "limitation of individual ownership of land among peasants" could be agreed upon.[23] The planners implied that the commune, as a true symbiosis, would establish harmonious reactions between all the organisms of local society, and this would find material expression not merely in productive investments but in schools and hospitals, and in artistic and cultural institutions. A sample commune statute indicates that a commune is "completely autonomous" as regards the establishment of its economic plans and budget and the setting up of enterprises and communal institutions.[24] It can adopt its own regulatory provisions, decide on "the organization and operation of its organs and institutions, appoint its employees, and appeal [to a higher authority] for the protection of the rights of self-government" should any other organs of the State "violate one of its legal rights."[25]

Fully as important are the economic rights and responsibilities of the emergent communes. The overall pre-1952 macroeconomic planning had failed "to come to grips with the problems resulting from the geographically uneven economic development that had taken place in the country over the centuries,"[26] despite the earnest efforts of the planners to disperse the "key investment" program in a way that would favor the less-developed parts of the country.[27] Decentralization was

23. Ibid. In 1959, for example, an Agricultural Land Use Law gave communes the power "to acquire land compulsorily from private owners who do not use modern agro-technical methods to ensure the full and rational use of their land." As a consequence, the amount of arable land lying fallow has been reduced by about a half since 1957. For details see F. E. Ian Hamilton, *Yugoslavia: Patterns of Economic Activity,* New York, 1968, p. 168, Table 15.

24. See Macesich, *Yugoslavia,* Appendix I, "Extracts from the Statutes of the Commune of Kranj," pp. 211–216.

25. Djordjević and Pašić, "The Communal Self-Government System in Yugoslavia," p. 398.

26. Macesich, *Yugoslavia,* p. 13.

27. After the break with the Cominform the consequent heavy loss of export proceeds in the Soviet-bloc countries, the urgent need for defensive outlay occasioned by the threat of Soviet invasion, and the very unsatisfactory diplomatic relations with Western European countries (largely caused by the nationalization of all foreign investments) compelled the Yugoslavs to strip down their original Five-Year Plan investment program to 90 "key industrial projects." Of these, 59 were in such basic industries as electric power (25 projects), coke (2), iron and steel (4), nonferrous metals (5), nonmetallic minerals (6), cement (4), engineering (5), electrical industries (5), chemicals (3), oil refining (1); 15 were processing industries such as timber-

based on an assumption that local initiative might be a more dependable motivating force for economic development than "republic or federal impulsion."[28] But poor regions with low capacities to save cannot be expected to develop unless capital becomes available. Certain revenues were accordingly reserved for the communes,[29] and some of these resources have been and are being used to finance projects, particularly of an infrastructural character. But it was recognized that unless communes in less-developed areas could, in some way, attract capital from outside their boundaries, their chances of keeping pace with more advanced areas, to say nothing of catching up, would be meager indeed. A system of tax-free and interest-free loans was therefore authorized in 1954, whereby disadvantaged communes could obtain capital from the General Investment Fund under suitable arrangements with either the federal or a republic investment bank.[30] But aside from these preferences for less-developed communes, normal capital allocation was entrusted to market forces, the presumption being that, given freedom to plan, each commune ought to be able to bid for its proper share of the national aggregate of investment capital. To do this, a commune's leaders would have to prove the *rentabilnost* (rentability) of any new or expanded enterprise, demonstrating to the satisfaction of the investment banks that the project was competitively capable of generating income commensurate with the anticipated fixed and variable investment.[31] The economic vigor of a commune will therefore

---

processing (3), paper and cellulose (3), textiles (8), and leather (1). Of the 90 projects, 72 were allotted to the less-developed areas (Macedonia 19, Bosnia-Herzegovina 21, Montenegro 3, Serbia 26, Kosovo-Methoija, 3). For details see Hamilton, *Yugoslavia*, pp. 237–239.

28. Macesich, *Yugoslavia*, p. 13.

29. Derived from taxes on workers' personal incomes and on the incomes of enterprises, as well as from taxes on land, inheritance, and transactions (turnover). Kiro Gligorov has estimated that communes, and economic organizations within them, are together the beneficiaries of about 45 percent of public revenue. "The Communal Economy," *International Social Science Journal*, 13, No. 3 (1961), p. 409.

30. Hamilton, *Yugoslavia*, p. 112.

31. As Hamilton has pointed out (*Yugoslavia*, p. 114, note 14), the word *rentabilnost* is not synonymous with profitability in the "capitalist" sense. It is "a balancing of the least investment and production costs" of a particular project with the "least costs of the macroeconomic and macrogeographic situation of the project within the total system of the social and economic structure of the state." For a comparison of the Soviet and the Yugoslav systems of capital allocation, see Svetozar Pejovich, *The Market-Planned Economy of Yugoslavia*, Minneapolis, 1966, Chapter 2, particularly pp. 50–57.

hinge on whether its projects are promising enough not only to persuade the commune authorities to invest locally generated funds but to attract funds from republic and federal authorities. There is, however, no longer any patronage basis for the allocation of such "outside" funds; the commune as a responsible legal entity must underwrite all new ventures, thus sharing the risks with the enterprises that are launched or expanded.[32]

Polycentric planning, self-government of enterprises, and increasing reliance on the "market principle" are therefore now focused on the communes. It is the communes that are responsible for "organizing and starting new economic enterprises within their areas,"[33] thus vesting in their communal councils the power to determine the kinds of diversification or specialization that a community will have. If the communes are to shape community development plans prudently and contribute to an integration of town and country, they will have to correct the spatial deficiencies of the prewar structure. They must take steps to increase the degree of commercialization of agriculture and thereby stimulate the production of an enlarged marketable surplus of farm produce. Concurrently they will need to promote an employment-generating type of industrial dispersion. If they are to meliorate the backwardness of the less-developed areas,[34] they must help to develop a truly functional hierarchy of central places. The evidence seems to indicate that the communes are making important contributions to all the foregoing, although in the compass of this brief account only a very limited amount of documentation can be supplied.

That the new order of things has had a stimulating effect on agricultural production is very evident from the data in Table 9–1. For all

32. On the role of the firm in the Yugoslav scheme of things and its relation to the commune, see Pejovich, *Market-Planned Economy,* Chapter 4.

33. Macesich, *Yugoslavia,* p. 62.

34. As in other countries where there are marked regional variations of wealth and income, a development program may widen the differences rather than reduce them. In Yugoslavia the "advanced" republics (Slovenia, Croatia, and Vojvodina) have gained relatively over the less-developed regions. See Hamilton, *Yugoslavia,* p. 139, Table 11. But the "absolute progress in increased employment, production, and income in the backward areas . . . has been very substantial—indeed monumental when compared with the total neglect of these areas before 1945." Ibid., p. 151. For a detailed analysis of per capital income by regional clusters of communes, see Hamilton, *Yugoslavia,* pp. 327–332, 340–350; and p. 328, Fig. 27. On the statistical and methodological difficulties involved in measuring variations in regional growth, see Fisher, *Yugoslavia,* pp. 74 ff.

the major crops except sugar beets the 1947–1956 output was less, often far less, than the prewar (1930–1939) output. What a contrast the figures for 1966 reveal! Ten years after decentralization the output of wheat and maize had more than doubled; barley output had increased more than 80 percent, oats almost 60 percent. For every major crop the output in 1966 shows a dramatic increase over the depressed and stagnant levels of 1947–1956. There can be little doubt but that better agro-technical methods were largely responsible for this remarkable increase in output. The yield of wheat (quintals per hectare) increased from 9.9 quintals to 20; maize from 13.1 to 26.3; barley from 9.7 to 16.3; oats from 8.7 to 14.0; sugar beets from 163 to 316; potatoes from 81 to 93. The figures for agricultural investment offer even better proof that the communal system had given farmers incentives to buy more tools and fertilizers, thereby further commercializing their operations. Between 1954 and 1963 investment in the agricultural sector increased almost eight times,[35] whereas investments in industry and mining increased less than 2½ times. It cannot be assumed that the bulk of this investment occurred on the surviving collectives and the state farms. Despite all the publicity given the socialist sector, these are the minor components of Yugoslav agriculture; the peasants who own 71 percent of all farmland, 86 percent of cultivated land, and 91 percent of the livestock[36] have been mainly responsible for both the increase in output and the growth of agricultural investment.

Table 9–1 Output of Selected Yugoslav Crops, 1930–1939, 1947–1956, and 1957–1966 (thousands of tons)

	Wheat	Maize	Barley	Oats	Sugar beets	Potatoes
1930–1939	2,430	4,300	410	310	616	1,658
1947–1956	2,040	3,370	332	285	1,240	1,690
1957–1966	4,450	8,000	620	400	3,240	2,820
Increase in 1957–1966 over 1947–1956	2,470	4,630	288	115	2,000	1,130

SOURCE: F. E. Ian Hamilton, *Yugoslavia: Patterns of Economic Activity*, New York: Praeger, 1968, p. 159.

35. From 20,496 million dinars in 1954 to 157,329 million in 1963. See Pejovich, *The Market-Planned Economy*, p. 68, Table 6.
36. Hamilton, *Yugoslavia*, p. 170.

These buoyant changes in agriculture can be attributed mainly to two post-1952 developments: the first comprised the reforms that made it possible for farmers to buy or lease land and that reintroduced a market-determined price system to provide price incentives; the second was the progressive dispersion of industry by means of communal decisions.[37] Both city and town industries have steadily absorbed the rural underemployed: they have drawn off some four million people from farms. As rural communes have established local industrial enterprises, the off-farm incomes of thousands of farm families have steadily increased, and these nonagricultural incomes have helped to make it possible for thousands of Yugoslav farm families to buy more land and invest in better farm tools and equipment. The importance of this new town and country interrelation is illustrated not only by the expansion of commuting zones around large cities but by similar belts around about sixty-five other urban centers.[38] Thus in Kraljevo, a relatively small Serbian market town, about 500 of the 1,200 people employed in the Magnohrom Works live in their village homes.[39] This arrangement, as I have already explained, has a double advantage: it increases the cash income of farm families and at the same time relieves the economy from the necessity of using its scarce capital for building urban industrial housing. It ought not be assumed, however, that the communal system has brought about a complete commercialization of Yugoslavia's landscapes.[40] This will take time, more industrial dispersion, more agricultural investment, more land consolidation (whether by purchase or lease), and, above all, the development of better-organized marketing facilities at more central places.

The real structural change that the Yugoslav communal system will progressively make cannot yet be predicted. Not all the 581 communes

37. Using 1961 census data for the then existing 611 communes, Jack C. Fisher, by means of factor analysis, has measured the level of urbanization and development by communes for the whole country. His findings are contained in his *Yugoslavia*, Appendix 3, pp. 204–221.

38. These commuting zones have been very carefully analyzed and mapped by Fisher in his *Yugoslavia*, pp. 187–195. This analysis, based on figures that are now badly out of date (April 1957), indicated an industrial commuting work force that comprised 18.8 percent of the workers in Serbia, 18.1 percent in Croatia, 17.9 percent in Slovenia, 25.4 percent in Bosnia-Herzegovina, and 22.4 percent in Montenegro. Only in Macedonia, where the commuting fraction was only 3.8 percent, was there any great deviation from the national average of about 16.3 percent.

39. Macesich, *Yugoslavia*, p. 29.

40. Petar J. Marković estimated (1963) that 36 percent of all farmland yielded no net marketable surplus. See his *Strukturne promene na selu kao rezultat economskog razvitku, 1900–1960*, Belgrade, 1963, p. 127.

will develop central-place cores with full complements of necessary processing, manufacturing, service, and mercantile enterprises. But that the communes are promoting and will further expand intermediate urbanization seems beyond any doubt; a strong subregional centripetal force is at work throughout the entire country that will progressively correct many of the marketing disadvantages with which Yugoslav farmers and merchants have long been confronted. Although socialist Yugoslavia inherited a fairly satisfactory hierarchy of central places from the nation's turbulent history, a look at Figure 9–1 quickly reveals that only the two metropolitan areas (Belgrade and Zagreb) have suitable wreaths of well-developed regional service centers surrounding them. Fisher has pointed out that whereas the north Yugoslav cities and towns exhibit a fairly satisfactory progression of sizes, the southern part of the country reveals a "primate-type" urban pattern "where a stratum of small towns and cities is dominated by one or a few very large cities without intermediate size groups."[41] Here are landscapes that need well-planned investment clusters, together with the appropriate educational, medical, and cultural facilities that can help to release the latent

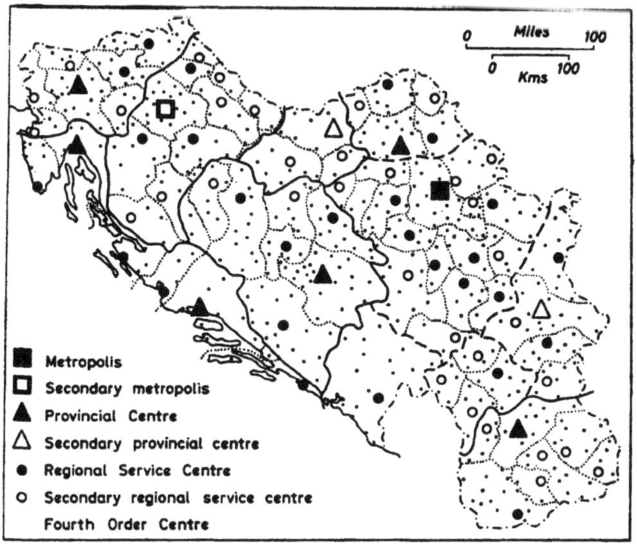

Figure 9–1 A Hierarchy of Yugoslav Central Places
SOURCE: F. E. Ian Hamilton, *Yugoslavia: Patterns of Economic Activity.* New York: Praeger, p. 333.

41. *Yugoslavia,* p. 4.

creativity of every young man or woman in a communal area. Here is where a judicious juxtaposition of large industries (planned by the republics) and small industries (developed by the communes) can bring about a fairly swift conversion of a "fourth order" center into a "secondary regional service center" or into an urban settlement with even more varied central-place functions.

Dividing the total land area of Yugoslavia (98,766 square miles) by 581 *opštine* gives the average size of a commune as 170 square miles, an area equivalent to a 13 x 13 mile square. There are, of course, variations in size caused by topography and wasteland, but, as Figure 9–2 shows, except in the barren mountainous region of the Dinaric Karst, the areal differences are not very great.[42] These are, therefore, manageable spatial and social aggregates that ought to be able to function as communities.[43] In population, however, the variations are considerable. Thirty-seven of the communes are fractions of the five largest cities, while about fifty other communes are dominated by cities with populations of 20,000 persons or more. Although the average population (19,958,000 ÷ 581) can be said to be 34,350 persons,[44] this average is not really very meaningful. The important consideration is that, if the representative range is from 10,000 to 75,000 persons, such population aggregates can be effective planning units for a wide variety of industrial enterprises, and a proper scaling of enterprises to communal market requirements could do much to obviate the criticism that the artificial fragmentation of market areas will lead to inefficiency.[45] It is incorrect to assume

42. In the mountainous areas of Bosnia, Herzegovina, and Montenegro communes have areas far above the average. Thus, the commune of *Nikšić* extends over 797 square miles.

43. The assembly is the commune's representative body. It consists of a communal chamber or council (elected by all adult citizens) and a chamber of working associations (elected by all workers whether employed in industry, commerce, or in educational, public health, or welfare activities). The executive, the president of the assembly, holds office for a maximum of four years.

44. Population estimates for 1967. United Nations, *Demographic Yearbook*, New York, 1968, p. 112.

45. As Fisher fears. See his *Yugoslavia*, pp. 165, 173. See also Hamilton, *Yugoslavia*, p. 162. For an opposite view, see Kosta Mihailović, "The Regional Aspect of Economic Development," in Radmila Stojanović, ed., *Yugoslav Economists on Problems of a Socialist Economy*, New York, 1969, pp. 41–42: "Though scattered location of the factors of production and their lack of linkages are shortcomings . . . they also offer advantages since they allow bolder moves in the building of an economically rational structure . . . which will . . . take into account the specific conditions of individual areas."

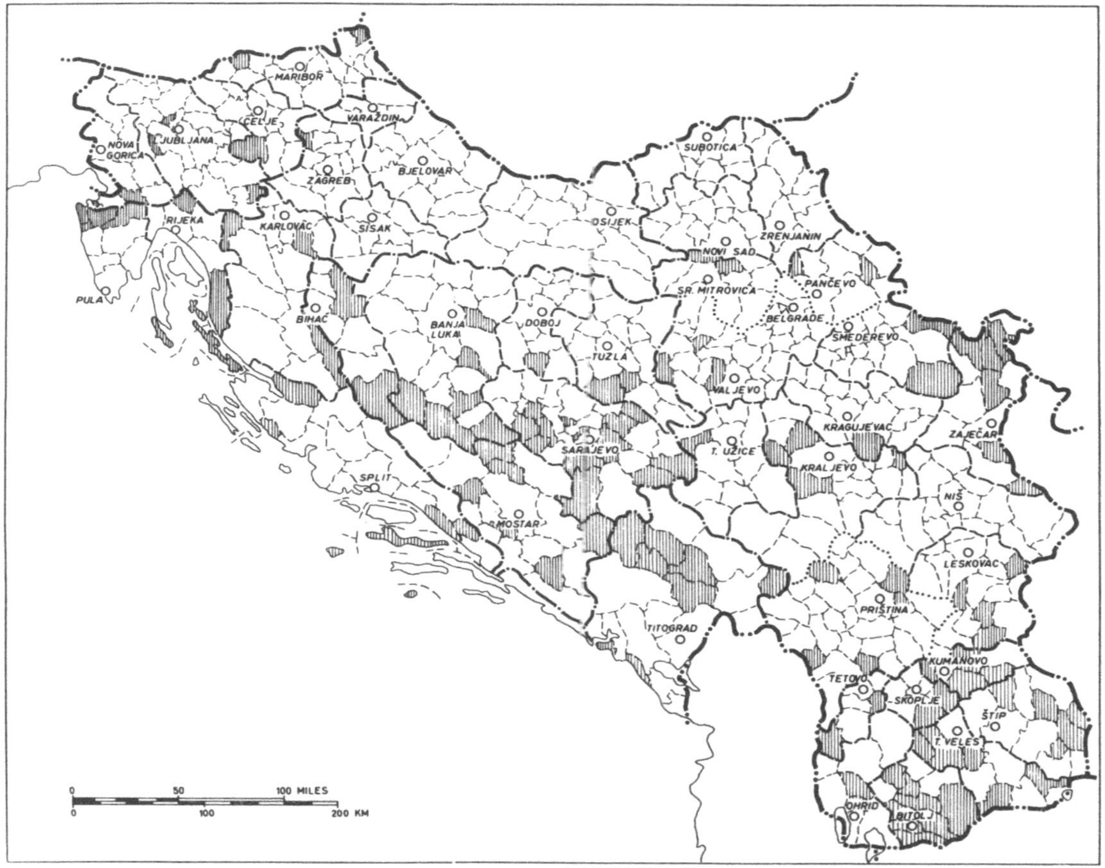

Figure 9–2 Distribution of Yugoslav Communes and Districts, January 1, 1963

SOURCE: Jack C. Fisher, *Yugoslavia—A Multinational State; Regional Difference and Administrative Response*. San Francisco: Chandler Publishing Co., © 1966. Figure 35. Reprinted by permission.

NOTE: The less-industrialized communes are shaded.

that the size of a given commune market imposes a top limit on the demand for the products of an enterprise located within that commune. The "market-planned economy" allows every enterprise to compete, if it can, within the entire national market. Processing industries within easy travel range of producers and small manufacturing plants catering to local demand can quite successfully accommodate themselves to areas of about 150 square miles and about 15,000 people.[46] The real virtue of the communal system is that it tends to create investment clusters in every possible eligible location, thereby increasing employment opportunities, widening occupational choices, and helping to draw out more of the talents of Yugoslavia's energetic and gifted people. In the long stream of history the commune as an instrument of modernization might therefore be much more important than it will be immediately as an economic catalyst.

The Israeli Social Policy Underlying Spatial Design

There are interesting similarities between the problems of societal organization that faced the Yugoslavs and the Israelis in the postwar era. The Yugoslav socialists have been confronted with the difficult task of melding together various ethnic groups, people with differing religious persuasions (and those who disavowed religious beliefs), groups and even families sharply divided by ideological disagreements, country people who distrusted city people, and city people who looked down on rustic peasants. Faced with all these fissiparous tendencies and with the historical "nationality" conflicts, the Yugoslavs, after their unhappy experience with Stalinist programs, have since 1953 sought integration "through controlled differences" and "ordered local diversity," encouraging mass participation of all citizens in local government organizations and in local enterprises.[47] Although communal amenities of a cultural and educational nature have been strongly emphasized, it has been increasingly appreciated that economic

46. The new constitution of 1963 encourages intercommunal cooperation, the thesis being that the grouping of communes might lead to the development of larger, more diversified economic regions. On the prospects of such development, see Hamilton, *Yugoslavia*, pp. 350–357.

47. The problem, as Fisher has properly implied, is to discover how much diversity can be tolerated in order to obtain the desired degree of participation. *Yugoslavia*, p. 8.

integration must "precede further development of local autonomy and well before social integration can be expected to take place."[48]

Despite an assumed unity stemming from a single religion, the Israeli leaders have been confronted with a range of problems that are in many ways rather parallel. Even though the immigrants almost without exception have been Jews, they have come from widely differing cultures and out of contrasting economic and political milieus. Moreover, the presumed unifying influence of a single religion has not prevented deep doctrinal differences. Nor has there been ideological agreement; Marxists from Russia, Poland, and Germany found themselves at odds not only with migrants from "capitalist" countries but with oriental Jews from North Africa or Yemen. From the beginning of immigration the town and city problem has been a troublesome one; indeed, the problem of how to combine the latent contributions of illiterate farmers from primitive Middle Eastern backwaters with those of soft-handed scholars from Western European and American cities has called for cautious, prudent, and imaginative answers. All those problems have had to be dealt with in spatial terms because, from the moment it became an independent state, Israel has of necessity been concerned with settlement, reconstruction of primitive areas, resource development, and the territorial deployment of population for political and defensive purposes.

The Israeli planners had to decide which economic and social goals should have priority, and their spatial experiments have been organically related to these goals. But cultural, political, and economic purposes had to take account of technological capabilities. Out of these considerations has come a logical development program which has emphasized "gathered agricultural settlements" whether they take the form of moshav (cooperative village), moshav shitufi (collective village), or kibbutz (egalitarian collective). But beyond these agricultural settlements, the planners envisaged "agrotowns," "settlement service centers," and "regional service centers." And in all this planning, decisions had to be made about the interrelations between the public sector and the private sector, so that appropriate developmental tasks could be wisely assigned to each. Because it was quite early appreciated that a heavy reliance on what Lösch called the "powerful forces of spontaneity" would have created an unequal, fragile, dual economy

48. Ibid., p. 185.

of well-to-do burgers and poor, illiterate peasants, it was decided that a dispersion of population and a spatial allocation of resources would have to be carefully planned.[49] In this complex venture attention had to be centered on communities of varying sizes, each with appropriate functions.

The proceedings of the International Seminar on Rural Planning, held in Israel in 1961,[50] which is a mine of information on agricultural settlement and physical planning, appropriately begins with this quotation: "In country planning the interests of the countryman must be the first concern, and any attempt to reconstruct the country-side will fail if it does not take into account all the circumstances of his life. . . . The problem . . . is how to put within reach of the country dweller all the amenities, and the opportunities of life, which are regarded nowadays as the normal inheritance of every townsman."[51] Thus for Israel a proper resolution of the town-country syndrome becomes the very essence of the planning task. Rational planning must not only concern itself with ways and means for achieving efficient agricultural production; it should, at the same time, envisage communities that can assure a measure of social equality if a nation is to have unity and social stability, if it is to illicit a maximum of effort, ingenuity, and loyalty from all of its citizens. With such ends in view, microplanning should concern itself with designs that will reduce fatigue and help to safeguard the health of workers,[52] while macroplanning must integrate all requisite economic, welfare, cultural, and educational components into a meaningful and purposeful system that will galvanize people into social action which can accomplish the agreed national goals.

The overall purpose of Israeli spatial planning has been to prevent overurbanization in the metropolitan areas and in the heavily populated Coastal zone[53] by developing throughout the country a hierarchy

49. "The aim of planning in Israel was thus contrary to the spontaneous trends in most countries where the populations tend to concentrate in privileged regions, and within the confines of metropolitan areas." Eliezer Brutzkus, *Physical Planning in Israel,* Jerusalem, 1964, p. 3.

50. Edited by E. Yalan under the title *Private and Cooperative Settlement: Physical Planning,* Haifa, 1961.

51. The quotation is from *Country Planning: A Study of Rural Problems,* Oxford, 1944.

52. Illustrated by a poultry house for a moshav settlement farmstead, in Yalan, *Private and Cooperative Settlement.*

53. Brutzkus, *Physical Planning,* p. 3.

of properly dispersed urban centers of varied sizes capable of performing certain appropriate central-place functions. Whereas for a large country such an undertaking might have been unduly complex and very costly, for Israel, a country of 7,993 square miles, of which only 1,930 square miles are suitable for cultivation, a systematic attempt could be made to stud the countryside with suitable urban centers, particularly when some of the needed capital was obtainable from benevolent Jewish communities abroad. It is understandable why the program could be launched; the remarkable thing is the imagination and sagacity with which the task was approached. The Coastal zone, stretching from the Gaza region in the south to the Lebanon border in the north, constituted "the backbone of the whole state";[54] it had to serve as a main agricultural producing region while the hill areas of Judea and Galilee were improved, and, of course, while the arid Negev was slowly reclaimed.[55] Hence the nation's entire village, service-center, and town-building program had to be properly phased.

Although the legal basis for planning had been established under the British Mandatory Government in Palestine,[56] and although the expropriation of land for public purposes was then authorized,[57] very little spatial restructuring occurred before the creation of the State of Israel in 1948. A number of local town-planning areas did come into being, some of whose officials helped to plan the Jewish colonies that were established in the Coastal zone.[58] But, for the most part, the British Mandatory Government restricted itself to regulatory functions: setting planning standards and supervising the activities of local or district planning commissions. The government did, however, permit Zionists to experiment with wholly new designs for agricultural settlements, projects which attempted to cope with the agro-technical

54. Ibid., p. 4.

55. The Coastal zone also had to serve as a source of water for the new irrigation districts and as a conduit for water flowing south from the Jordan and Yarkon rivers to the Negev.

56. By the promulgation of a Town Planning Ordinance in 1921.

57. By the Land and Expropriation Ordinance of 1943.

58. The Jewish population of Palestine, which had grown quite rapidly before World War I (from 24,000 in 1882 to 85,000 in 1914), had declined to 65,000 by 1919. It tripled by the early 1930's and grew rapidly after 1939, reaching a total of 650,000 on the eve of the establishment of the State of Israel, so that 33.2 percent of the Palestine population was then Jewish. See Nadav Halevi and Ruth Klinov-Malul, *The Economic Development of Israel,* New York, 1968, p. 15, Table 1.

needs of new communities and at the same time were planned in terms of soil conservation, health, security, and social effectiveness.[59] The shortcoming of this early planning was that each rural settlement was a separate entity. There were no designed linkages between settlements; nor was there any formal tying-in of new colonies with existing urban centers. This lack of understanding of the need for regional interrelations between settlements has been called by an Israeli expert on planning "the outstanding deficiency of Jewish rural colonization work" during the mandate era.[60]

The arrival of over a hundred thousand immigrants in 1948 started the upward surge of the Jewish population, which by 1967 surpassed 2½ million.[61] At the same time, the nonJewish population was sharply reduced by the mass exodus of Palestinian Arabs, so that, whereas two-thirds of the population had been nonJewish in May 1948, by 1951 the proportion had fallen to 11 percent, a level which has continued up to the present. It was this drastic change in the demographic composition of Israel that both required and permitted the far-reaching spatial restructuring that occurred once the austerity period from 1948 to 1951 was over, and after a cluster of important policy decisions had resolved some of the most pressing problems of inflation, foreign-exchange shortages, and distorted price structures. The immediate problem facing the planners[62] was, of course, the absorption of the first waves of immigrants that poured into the country: 101,800 in 1948, 239,600 in 1950, 170,200 in 1951, and 175,100 in 1952.[63] Because the newcomers were almost completely dependent on the government for housing and employment, the planners were given a unique opportunity to experiment with geographic distribution of the growing work force.[64] By good fortune many of the planners were familiar

59. Brutzkus, *Physical Planning*, p. 10. The pioneer in this new type of community planning was Richard Kaufman, whose plan for Nahalal in 1921 served as a model for many later moshavim.

60. Brutzkus, *Physical Planning*, p. 11.

61. Halevi and Klinov-Malul, *The Economic Development of Israel*, p. 52, Table 7, and p. 54, Table 8. The U.N. estimate for 1967 was 2,669,000.

62. A National Planning Department created in 1948 soon came under the joint control of the office of the Prime Minister and the Ministry of the Interior. Hence the Planning Department was never in full control over development projects, although its initiatory work cannot be discounted.

63. Thereafter immigration drops off, averaging about 39,000 a year, 1952–1965, with peaks of over 70,000 (1957) and lows of 11,000 (1953).

64. Only about 15 percent of the immigrants during these first few years found places of abode without public help. Yet even this small fraction brought great

with the hierarchical patterns of urban centers that had proved their usefulness in Europe, and some of them were aware of the locational studies of Christaller and Lösch. There persisted, however, an idea that a new country should try new ideas. As a result, some consideration was given to more-polarized urban structures such as had developed in Canada and Australia. But these urban patterns seemed inappropriate for a country as small as Israel, in which population could certainly become quite dense, even if well-distributed. Moreover the mandate era had revealed the serious imbalance that polarizing forces were already producing,[65] and for all their virtues, the kibbutzim and moshavim, in which the Zionists had placed such reliance, were not systematically or effectively organizing the agrarian landscapes.[66]

What emerged in the mandate period was a "primate-city" type of economic landscape: a pattern involving the kibbutz (or moshav) and the city, with virtually no intermediate urban linkages. Worst of all, this dualism was regarded by many as the inevitable consequence of technological developments such as trucks and paved roads. It took courage for the planners to challenge this intellectual flabbiness, but they realized that if Israel was to become an intensively developed economy, every farmstead would have to be linked with a community, and every community would have to become an organic part of a unified spatial system. Marketing facilities and service industries would need to be diffused throughout the agrarian economy, and the whole central-place structure hierarchically interrelated. There were, in addition, other considerations: for security reasons, population would have to be pressed outward toward Israel's frontiers, and the resulting relatively remote settlements would have to be interrelated with the more secure areas by effective economic links.

These fundamental considerations produced a development program that envisaged not merely a dispersal of population but an effective integration of this scattered population by means of a size-graduated system of urban and semiurban centers. Articulating this thesis, the planners visualized the need for areal subdivisions, and, after rigorous

pressure on urban facilities, since the majority of the self-financing immigrants took up residence in the three major cities. See Brutzkus, *Physical Planning*, p. 13.

65. The three metropolitan areas, Tel-Aviv, Haifa, and Jerusalem, accounted for over 70 percent of the Jewish population of the country.

66. Many of the Zionists held rather doctrinaire views about how a good society should be organized, and "viewed with reservation and even animosity the very idea of creating an urban center within a rural area." Brutzkus, *Physical Planning*, p. 15.

consideration of suitable boundaries, they recommended, in 1953, a division of the country into six districts and fourteen subdistricts. Within this administrative structure four levels of settlement were initially envisaged: the A, B, C, and D centers, graduated in size and in hierarchical function. The smallest units, the A centers, could be surviving Palestine villages, moshavim, even hamlets or minuscule settlements. Next would come the "rural service centers,"[67] the B centers, which would cater to the areal needs of four, five, or six moshavim (or hamlets) by providing the appropriate commercial or artisan type of facilities that a relatively small number of farmsteads (or cooperatives) might need. The C centers would service a number of B centers, extending their functions to perhaps six to twelve thousand persons living within a radius of from 3 to 7 miles. Such a center might include not only produce markets and retail shops but processing plants, service industries, or even a few simple manufacturing operations. The C centers, in turn, would be linked with the D centers, middle-sized towns of from fifteen to sixty thousand people. These regional capitals (actual or emergent) would provide more varied and more specialized services and be the sites for dispersed manufacturing. This, then, was the general plan; the actual progression, except for the A centers, went from large to small, and this concession to Perroux's development theory might have introduced some unintended elements of polarity. Yet, even in its incomplete form, the central-place matrix, which is still in the process of construction, has revealed its economic, social, and political utility.

Since a presumption prevailed that most new industries would be light manufacturing enterprises of types that are neutral as to location,[68] there was general agreement that new towns could be built mainly for their service functions to an agrarian hinterland, and that once established they could gradually attract industries and thereby diversify occupations. This premise gave the planners flexibility in interrelating local service centers, agrotowns,[69] and regional service centers to the

67. Defined as "a place comprising all needed facilities such as trades, industry, commerce, economy, technical instruction, administration, health, security, education, cultural and social, serving the needs of the surrounding area and the local inhabitants." Yalan, *Private and Cooperative Settlement*, p. vi.

68. "Being independent . . . of raw material sources or sea ports they can, at least theoretically, be moved to any place where labor, metalled roads, water supply and electric current are available." Brutzkus, *Physical Planning*, p. 21.

69. Defined in Yalan, *Private and Cooperative Settlement*, p. v, as "the largest pattern of agricultural settlement consisting of farmsteads and homesteads of

marketing, welfare, and educational needs of various-sized rural communities. Pending the attraction of industries, which might take two, three, or even more years, a majority of the settlers in new towns were employed either in construction or in seasonal agricultural work. The planning of the new towns called for coordination between the Planning Department and the Housing Department (Ministry of Labour) and involved such tasks as regional resource analysis, population estimates and forecasts, the determination of demographic targets, employment requirements and forecasts (both short- and long-range); it was also concerned with zoning for residential and industrial purposes, open spaces, public institutions, density standards, roads, streets, water supply, electricity, and land-use surveys.[70] Not all immigrants, to be sure, were dispersed to the new settlements; many self-financed newcomers took up residence in the large cities (even though a minimum number of new housing units were built there) or in existing towns in the coastal zone. But from 50 to 60 percent of immigrants were regularly directed to the peripheral districts. The effect became steadily noticeable; whereas 70.4 percent of Israel's Jewish population resided in the three main cities in 1948, by 1963 only 51.5 percent lived in these metropolitan centers.[71]

Although the spatial planners had new structural patterns in mind, one difficulty was how to relate the existing urban centers to the new ones. Below the three metropolitan areas, the planned hierarchical network of urban centers was envisaged as consisting of three major components: the urban centers of the agricultural colonies that had been established under the British mandate, the historical towns, and the new towns and regional centers. No wholly "new" towns were to be built in the central coastal area, where the network of private agricultural colonies was already fairly well provided with market centers. Here, only enlargement was needed. The southern part of the country needed C centers to service a complement of B centers, and it was becoming increasingly appreciated that there were locational advantages in centering more processing, service, and repair enterprises in somewhat larger centers,

artisans grouped around their service center," these communities were expected to have populations of not less than 2,000 people.

70. Between 1949 and 1963 the overall scheme for population dispersion was revised six times on ten- to twenty-year projections. For details of how these "working hypotheses" were developed and used, see Brutzkus, *Physical Planning*, pp. 23–24.

71. Nevertheless, the large cities, by reason of the total increase in population, grew throughout this period.

rather than attempting to develop them in smaller centers, or in moshavim or kibbutzim. This shift in emphasis was in many ways something that happened by chance; the C and D centers became "absorption centers for relatively large numbers of immigrants,"[72] and, to provide them with employment, enterprises that might very appropriately have been established at B centers emerged in the C or D centers. The resulting enlargement of the C and D centers, even when wholly justified economically, had some undesired social consequences: rural communities, particularly those composed of immigrants from "oriental" countries, tended to segregate themselves from the emergent urban communities, thus retarding the social integration in the newly created settlements that had been visualized by the planners.

The choice of sites for new towns or for the modernization of old ones often led to sharp disagreements, and two schools of thought emerged. One group of planners emphasized physical factors: climate, topography, or agronomic qualities. Centers that were to become industrial, they said, should seek locations where temperature, wind direction, or humidity were favorable, so that industrial efficiency would be the highest possible. Hill or hillside locations recommended themselves on this score, and also because fertile valley soils would then not be withheld from agriculture by urban uses.[73] The other school emphasized "centrality," insisting that since an urban center would be dependent on its rural hinterland as a source of food and as a market for central-place goods and services, the urban center must "dominate" its surrounding areas. Regardless of soil, climate, or prevailing winds, rigorous locational considerations should govern. So bitter were the disagreements that sometimes the Prime Minister had to adjudicate disputes.[74] The trend, however, in recent years has been

72. Brutzkus, *Physical Planning*, p. 28.

73. Brutzkus explains that when the school that emphasized physical features prevailed, some waste of resources was often involved. Thus the town of Affule, originally founded in 1925 in the rich land of the Valley of Jezreel, was moved 4 kilometers in 1950 to the slopes of Mount Moria. In much the same way this attitude toward urban location was responsible for the building of Upper Tiberias on a plateau 200 meters above sea level because the climate of Old Tiberius, 200 meters below sea level, was hot and enervating. For details see Brutzkus, *Physical Planning*, pp. 29–30.

74. As he did in the case of Beth-Shean. This four-thousand-year-old town is located on fertile soil that could be used for intensive agriculture, and it also has an unpleasant climate. A proposal to raze the old city and rebuild on an infertile hillside site was vetoed by Ben-Gurion because the new location would have isolated the city from the area it was to service. Ibid., p. 30.

away from the emphasis on centrality because, as Israel becomes more and more industrialized, a concern for the comfort and happiness of workers and their families must receive more and more consideration. These concessions, however, have not changed the basic thesis, germane in Israeli planning, which insists that urban expansion ought not be allowed to trench upon Israel's precious agricultural soil. It was the encroachment of housing projects on orange groves, for example, that led to the appointment of a special committee for the "Preservation of Agricultural Soil," which must now be consulted whenever a town-planning scheme is proposed. In the meantime, land reserves under public ownership have been created, and strict control over land speculation in existing towns has been instituted.

Industrial location has not created any very troublesome problems in Israel. Certain heavy industries are either point-bound by raw materials (cement, potash, phosphates) or so closely dependent on foreign trade that they require seaport locations (oil refineries, motorcar assemblies, or foundries).[75] Most light industries, however, are amenable to dispersion, since distances from raw material supplies, whether domestic or imported, are not great, and because all the towns, old and new, are interlinked with roads and provided with water and power. The problem is rather one of persuading entrepreneurs, investors, and the *Histadruth* (Labor Federation) that new enterprises should be established in smaller urban centers that urgently need employment and occupational diversification. Subsidies have been necessary in some instances, but only in very stubborn situations has resort to direct government investment been necessary. Much in the same way that Puerto Rico has graduated inducements and preferences to induce businessmen to locate in disadvantaged "municipalities,"[76] the Israeli government has given the largest preferences for projects in the Negev and in Galilee. Land allocation, income-tax reduction, and government loans on favorable terms have been the inducements proffered to businessmen to lure them into the Negev, where external economies are few, skilled labor scarce, and where repair facilities, spare-part stores, or vocational education are all unsatisfactory. Obviously, such disadvantages must be compensated by something more material than an appeal to patriotism.

75. For data on the major manufacturing categories and their relative importance, 1951–1963, see Halevi and Klinov-Malul, *Economic Development of Israel*, p. 108, Table 38.

76. See Figure 9–5.

Whereas spatial planning in Israel has been ever mindful of economic considerations, at the same time it has been very much concerned with preserving natural and historical landmarks and with providing a large number of recreational areas.[77] A very special problem in spatial planning has arisen from the need for properly utilizing and distributing Israel's water resources. Not only have canals and conduits been constructed to channel water from the rivers in the north to the citrus orchards in the Coastal zone, and beyond that area to the Negev, but every possible effort is being made to impound rain water so that runoff losses can be held to a minimum. In a country as arid as Israel successful rural expansion can only occur if water for irrigation can be made available, and the more than two hundred rural settlements that have been established since 1948 (moshavim, kibbutzim, and shitufi moshavim) have made this part of planning an extremely critical factor.

A great deal of experimentation with various designs for rural communities has occurred. No single plan would serve, because topographic and agronomic differences existed, and because security was an important consideration not merely on threatened frontiers but almost everywhere. Yet, despite differences, certain basic principles have been followed. Since the presumption has been that Israel's rural economy ought to be one with a minimum of hired labor and a maximum of family participation in agricultural tasks, fields should be as close as possible to farmhouses. But whereas this might be best accomplished by a "scattered settlement," (see top diagram in Figure·9–3) where both the "work activities distances" (WAD) and the "family and personal activities distances" (FPD) would be short, a wide dispersion of farmsteads would weaken the chances for social integration because "community activities distances" (CAD) would be long. Since in Israel a main object of spatial design has been "a high degree of community interdependence for social, economic, security, and other reasons, it seems that scattered settlements will not be suitable."[78] Accordingly, gathered cooperative settlements" (see middle diagram, Figure 9–1) and

77. Included were places of "geological, morphological and botanical interest; antiquities sites and holy places; forest reserves; beaches; walking trails; and places of picturesque value and outstanding natural beauty." Brutzkus, *Physical Planning*, p. 40. The initial 1948–1950 plans involved more land that Israel could spare, and many of the reserved areas were subsequently reduced. Under the 1964 allocation about 9.7 percent of the land area has been reserved for the categories just listed.

78. Yalan, *Private and Cooperative Settlement*, p. 3.

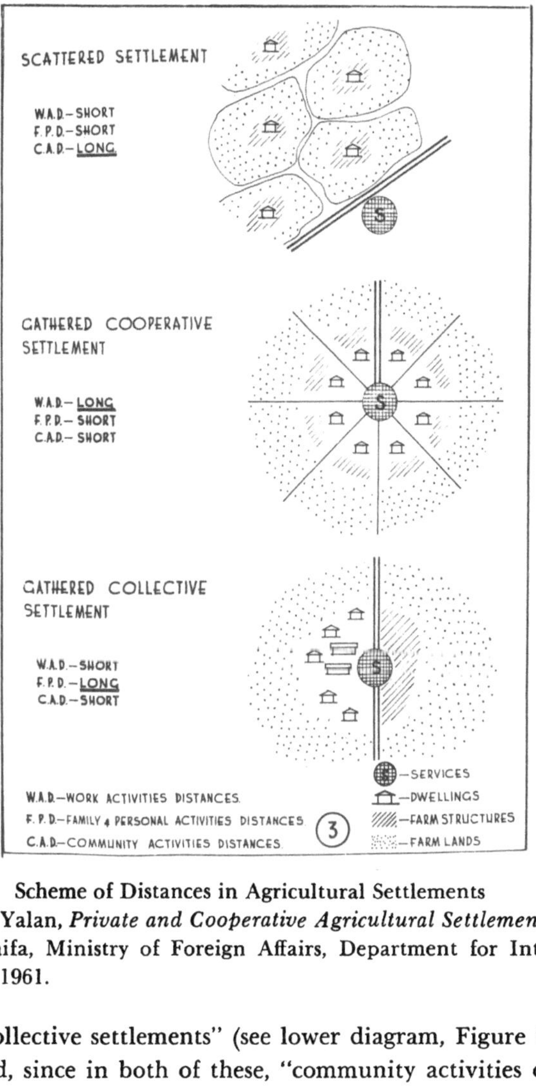

Figure 9–3 Scheme of Distances in Agricultural Settlements
SOURCE: E. Yalan, *Private and Cooperative Agricultural Settlement: Physical Planning,* Haifa, Ministry of Foreign Affairs, Department for International Cooperation, 1961.

"gathered collective settlements" (see lower diagram, Figure 9–1) have been favored, since in both of these, "community activities distances" (CAD) are short. But of the two forms of gathered settlement, as Table 9–2 shows, moshavim have expanded faster than kibbutzim.[79] Planning the new agricultural settlements has not been an easy task. Security

79. For historical and descriptive details and for diagrams and photographs of moshavim, see Yalan, *Private and Cooperative Settlement,* pp. 14–48. For a critical evaluation of the advantages and disadvantages of gathered settlements, see Brutzkus, *Physical Planning,* p. 44–45.

factors often determined the optimum size of villages (about eighty to one hundred farmers), and this sometimes led to the establishment of schools, workshops, health centers, tractor stations, and other service institutions in moshavim or kibbutzim rather than in B centers, as had been initially planned. These unintended microcentripetal forces have only been overcome in certain areas,[80] where rural service centers now cater to the economic, social, and cultural requirements of four, five, or more moshavim, and where truly functional towns have attracted enough enterprises, so that some of them have already grown beyond the C-center size and are gradually becoming the D type of regional cities.

Table 9–2 Agricultural Settlements in Israel

Type of settlement	Before 1948	After 1948	Total
Private	42	0	42
Moshavim	107	262	369
Shitufi Moshavim	7	12	19
Kibbutzim	142	93	235
Total			665

SOURCE: E. Yalan, *Private and Cooperative Agricultural Settlement: Physical Planning, Haifa,* Ministry of Foreign Affairs, Department for International Cooperation, 1961, p. 3.

Two major problems have bedeviled the planners: how to modernize the historical towns, and how to prevent "creeping urbanization." The old towns and cities are crowded and unsanitary; moreover, many buildings are dangerously deteriorated. Yet if they are "historical towns," they cannot be leveled without precipitating strong opposition inside and outside the country. An ancient city such as Acre, the old capital of the Crusaders, was spared for posterity by surrounding it with a green belt beyond which a new city was built. A similar plan has been developed to protect Safad, a famous Jewish spiritual town in Upper Galilee. But whereas a few of the older cities can be made into historical shrines, other old towns present vexing difficulties.

Far more serious is the second problem: how to cope with urban sprawl and creeping urbanization. The population density in the coastal zone already compares with the more densely populated areas

80. Notably in the Lakhish region in the southern Judean plain. For details see Brutzkus, *Physical Planning,* p. 46.

of the Netherlands.[81] Middle-sized towns have developed there as more industrialization has occurred in the large private colonies in the citrus-growing area, and these "urbanized colonies" are steadily changing into something analogous to low-density cities, mortgaging more and more land for nonagricultural purposes. The Israeli planners and architects had originally tended to follow the British "garden-city" designs for new towns, emphasizing open spaces, single-storeyed houses, or semidetached bungalows. Considering the scarcity of arable land, this policy has recently been drastically changed, and small houses are being replaced by apartment houses with three or four storeys or even ten or more. New towns are now being designed by experienced town planners who reserve areas for shopping centers and playgrounds and allocate at least 12 percent of the building budget for public facilities: schools, synagogues, clinics, and community centers. As urban areas increase, certain social tensions develop. Newly arrived immigrants are settled in outlying villages or in new towns. Contrasts between rural and urban areas are becoming more evident, and there is considerable "back flow" from the rural areas to the urbanized Coastal zone. As this occurs, agriculture tends to become more capital-intensive, and the fraction of the work force engaged in farming declines. All of this has led planners to favor more industrial dispersion into D centers and C centers and to cherish the hopes that even "industrial villages" might emerge.

The two distinguishing aspects of Israeli spatial planning have been an insistence on the creation of a hierarchy of central places[82] and a firm belief that a primate-city type of urbanization can be prevented. Both objectives have been largely, although not completely, attained. In the planned hierarchy of central places only the C centers have failed to materialize in the way initially visualized.[83] The D

81. About 800 persons per square kilometer. The forecasts indicate an average density in the central Coastal zone of 1,080 by 1980. See Brutzkus, *Physical Planning*, p. 52.

82. The success of the Israeli central-place program was probably responsible for the effort of Hungary to restructure its urban pattern. In 1961 a national planning policy was adopted that envisaged 8 provincial capitals, 74 medium-sized regional urban centers, and 900 larger rural service centers, with which the collectives would be organically linked. In addition to the systematic hierarchy, there would be 27 mining and heavy industry towns. Ivan Gyarfas, *The Economic Basis of Urban Development Policy and Planning*, Warsaw, 1962, cited by Brutzkus, *Physical Planning*, pp. 71–72.

83. Recently, however, in the Arab-populated parts of the country some of the larger villages are earmarked as future central places of the C type.

centers, however, have developed vigorously, not only as processing and service centers but as industrial sites. Indeed, it is the vitality of these centers, with populations of from 10,000 to 50,000, that has been mainly responsible for arresting the polarizing forces that have produced a primate-city type of urbanization in most other developing countries.

The Israeli effort at rational spatial planning has been remarkably imaginative, admirably tough-minded, and, despite some unavoidable compromises, exceptionally consistent in its emphasis on objectives. It has prevented an exaggerated concentration of the urban population in a few huge cities.[84] It has succeeded in dispersing a stream of immigrants into well-designed agricultural settlements which are systematically linked with a spatially distributed and size-graduated hierarchy of central places. New towns have been planned, located, and built, and by this means unplanned creeping urbanization in the coastal zone, although not wholly prevented, has been greatly arrested. The central-place matrix is adequately interconnected with roads (and with some new railways) and provided with water and power. Industries have been decentralized, thereby creating employment in the D and C centers. Recreational areas, national parks, and land reserves have been set apart and protected from encroachment. Like the Yugoslavs, the Israelis have emphasized decentralization, although the instrumentalities they have used have been not only different but for the most part more flexible and adaptive to place, time, and circumstance. Even though one of the planners rather modestly avers that "Israel has still much to learn in the field of physical planning from other countries,"[85] I suspect that other developing countries have even more to learn from this uniquely seminal Israeli experiment.

The Puerto Rican Program of Areal Transformation

In a single generation the Puerto Rico per capita gross domestic product increased from less than $100 to over $1000,[86] over 1,500 new

84. From 1948 to 1952 the growth of Greater Tel-Aviv was held down to about 50 percent of the average annual population increment. Thereafter the growth of Tel-Aviv, though less than the national growth rate, was only slightly less. See Brutzkus, *Physical Planning*, p. 50.

85. Ibid., p. 85.

86. The $100 figure is an average for the period 1932–1936 from the estimates made by Frances Horning in *El ingreso insular y la economía puertorriqueña,* San

permanent foreign-financed manufacturing enterprises were established, the percentage of children in schools more than doubled, while new opportunities for employment throughout the island not only reduced the emigration of thousands of the most productive members of the population but set the stage for repatriation of men and women who had gone abroad when their prospects for employment at home seemed hopeless.[87] The near miracle performed under the guidance of gifted leaders was a bold experiment that progressively emphasized a dispersion of investment among all the spatial jurisdictions into which the island state is divided.[88] In contrast with Yugoslavia and Israel, where the small spatial units which were to become the nodal components of their decentralized economies were literally created, in Puerto Rico very little revision was made in local political structure. The seventy-six spatial areas, the "municipalities," were accepted as adequate in size and number. As products of history they were familiar units of local government and tolerably satisfactory as to area and population. What really caused concern were the wide differences in income, infrastructure, resource endowment, and levels of literacy and education. Fortunately, distances are not great in an island 100 x 35 miles and consequently not much attention needed to be paid to town building, particularly since colonial development in Puerto Rico had provided the island with two metropolitan port cities. Moreover, since there were ten other urban centers of medium size and a goodly number of small cities and towns, there seemed to be no urgent reason for enlarging the hierarchy of central places.[89] The development task, as Muñoz Marin and his advisors saw it, was primarily one of diversifying and increasing

Juan, 1951. The United Nations estimate for 1961 was $761 (U.N., *Yearbook of National Accounts*, 1962, New York, 1963), and the $1,000 is based on a 1967 estimate of $1,047 (see *World Almanac*, 1969, p. 380). A recent estimate (*New York Times*, July 13, 1969) indicates that personal income has risen from $118 a year in 1940 to $1,200 in 1968–1969.

87. In 1958 some 85,000 migrants left the country, and 59,000 returned. By 1963 the returnees exceeded the departees, but this reversal is not yet a dependable trend.

88. Too often the credit for this remarkable event has been given to a single person, Governor Luis Muñoz Marin. There can be no doubt of his brilliance, dedication, and rare insight, but he had the assistance not only of a gifted lieutenant, Theodoro Moscoso, but of an organization that included many talented planners and administrators.

89. An analysis of the 1960 population data reveals a rather nicely graduated hierarchy of urban centers. There were thirty-two centers in the 2,000–5,000 range, twelve with populations from 5,000 to 10,000, eight from 10,000 to 40,000, and two large port metropoli: San Juan with 432,379 inhabitants, Ponce with 114,286.

production, thereby widening employment, and articulating new production to overseas markets in order to earn sorely needed foreign exchange.

The result was "Operation Bootstrap," basically an investment-luring and employment-increasing program but one which presently became an experiment in dispersed capital formation. Proper business management was recognized to be an indispensable and critical input and, like capital, one that initially and temporarily would have to be brought in from overseas. But it was realized that it takes more than persuasion to induce hard-nosed businessmen in mature industrial countries to risk their capital, personnel, and time in economic peripheries, where labor is unskilled, industrial discipline unfamiliar, and where business practices, customs, and traditions are wholly different from those in Milwaukee, Patterson, or Birmingham. A great deal of stage setting and very careful training of the actors was needed before the show could begin. Because the preparations were careful, and because there was flexibility in the program so that it could be readily reshaped as experience was gained, *Fomento* became much more than a Spanish word for an impersonal developmental effort; it stood for something that presently intrigued overseas businessmen, gradually induced some wealthy Puerto Ricans to risk their capital in nontraditional investments, and brought hope to plain and ordinary workers not only in cities but in all the *barrios* of the island. *Fomento* became a synonym for the government's effort to improve the economic life of every community "whether done by *Fomento* proper, by the Water Resources Authority, the Land Authority, the Aqueduct and Sewer Authority, the Department of Public Works, the Department of Education, or other agencies."[90] But to everyone in Puerto Rico, *Fomento* meant, first and foremost, the new industrial estates that housed the workshops and small factories where jobs were available, where both men and women could find steady work and earn wages paid in cash, regularly, without argument, and without fail.[91]

The tremendous importance of employment stemmed from population density and particularly from its incredible increase after 1900. When the United States took over responsibility for Puerto Rico in

90. William H. Stead, *Fomento: The Economic Development of Puerto Rico*, National Planning Association, Planning Pamphlet No. 103, Washington, 1958, p. 3.

91. For an analysis of the employment aspects of *Fomento* through 1957, see A. J. Jaffe, *People, Jobs, and Economic Development*, Glencoe, Ill., 1959.

1899, there were already 278 people for every square mile of land, but as public health measures reduced the death rate, the density burgeoned up to 451 persons per square mile in 1930, 672 persons in 1958, 687 in 1960, and 785 in 1967.[92] With very limited subterranean resources,[93] and with most of the timber long since cut down, the great bulk of people were dependent on the soil for their livelihood. But with not more than a million acres of land serviceable for any type of agriculture, the land-man ratio (2.2 persons per acre in 1949) was not one-sixth as favorable as the corresponding ratio in the United States, a country highly industrialized and consequently far less dependent on agriculture. Moreover, only a small part of Puerto Rico's arable land consisted of high-productivity soils,[94] and these better lands had mostly been co-opted for raising sugar cane, a cash crop whose output increased fifteen times between 1899 and 1930. Although expansion of the sugar industry did provide employment for thousands of Puerto Ricans, it was a most unsatisfactory kind, not merely because cutting and loading cane was brutally hard work at low wages[95] but also because of its seasonality.[96] For most rural families life was precarious, even when supplemental incomes could be earned by women and children at home from needlecraft, work which was, unfortunately, also highly seasonal.[97] All these factors produced a distressing level of unemployment (and

92. The average emigration of over 40,000 persons a year for the period 1945–1957 was, of course, one of the reasons for the slowing down of the density growth. In the 1950's, for example, the annual out-migration was almost equal to the annual population increase. For the annual figures see Jaffe, *People, Jobs and Economic Development*, p. 65.

93. For a succinct evaluation of known minerals and earths at the time when "Operation Bootstrap" began, see Harvey S. Perloff, *Puerto Rico's Economic Future: A Study in Planned Development*, Chicago, 1950, p. 46, Table 2.

94. For productivity rating of grades of soil on a percentage basis, see Perloff, *Puerto Rico's Economic Future*, p. 48, Tables 3 and 4.

95. "A man would be loading at least 24, 25, 26 and up to 28 tons of cane a day, by hand. . . . The tonnage was paid at 9, 10, up to 12 cents; that was the wage rate." For a depressing picture of work and working conditions in the cane fields, based on oral and written testimony, see Sidney Mintz, *Worker in the Cane*, New Haven, 1960. The quoted passage is from p. 132.

96. Employment on tobacco farms and on coffee plantations, however, was even more seasonal. Data compiled by the Bureau of Statistics of the Puerto Rican Department of Labor in 1947 indicated that whereas suger provided average employment for 8.7 months, for tobacco the average employment was only 5 months out of the year, and for coffee 6.8 months. For details see Perloff, *Puerto Rico's Economic Future*, p. 146.

97. For a graphic account of life and labor in a Puerto Rican village, see Mintz, *Worker in the Cane*.

underemployment), which ranged on the eve of "Operation Bootstrap," according to the data compiled by the Puerto Rico Department of Labor, from 27 percent to 36 percent and averaged 31 percent. In view of Puerto Rico's resource inventory, the outlook in the 1940's was bleak; the island had no known mineral resources of commercial importance, no fuels except bagasse,[98] very limited forest resources, wholly inadequate arable land, poor fishing potential, and an almost fully utilized hydroelectric capacity. It did have a good climate and, as the only resource really capable of "development," 2,300,000 people, all of whom needed food, shelter, clothing, education, and, above all, employment. Two events occurred in 1941 which led to a studied approach to the basic problem: the appointment of Rexford Tugwell as governor, and the election of enough Popular Democrats under the leadership of Luis Muñoz Marin to give that party control over the Puerto Rican legislature.[99] It was this dual change in leadership which really made the difference: "Governor Tugwell persuaded some of the able men on the University of Puerto Rico faculty and others from business and the professions to take important government positions and devote their talents to the great program of political, social and economic development."[100] At the same time, Muñoz Marin began the difficult task of planning a frontal attack on poverty, ignorance, and hopelessness.

Any attempt to evaluate the macroeconomic consequences of the *Fomento* effort would be far beyond the scope of this brief essay. I am concerned here with the Puerto Rican experience only to the extent that it throws light on the problem of how space can be better organized to the advantage of inhabitants of particular areas and at the same time to the benefit of all the citizens of the larger economy to which all lesser spatial units can be and ought to be functionally related. For Puerto Rico, therefore, the question that Muñoz Marin posed was really this: how could a development program be designed that would benefit not only city dwellers but village and farm people, one that would not merely improve conditions but would have some chance of transforming the economy of every one of the seventy-six Puerto Rican municipalities? The ultimate answer to this question was found in industrial dispersion, but it took some years to forge the right keys and to fit them

98. Residue of sugar cane after juice has been extracted.
99. Stead, *Fomento,* p. 7.
100. Ibid., p. 9.

to the economic and cultural locks that had long kept the Puerto Rican people in abject poverty.[101]

From 1898 to 1940 probably the chief economic contribution that the United States made to Puerto Rico was to include the island within the American tariff wall. In consequence, capital began to flow to the island as American businessmen invested in sugar plantations, raw sugar mills, access roads, warehouses, irrigation works, and power plants.[102] This kind of investment, primarily concerned with the exploitation of natural resources (land) to produce an export crop (sugar) and to build infrastructure (roads, irrigation canals and conduits, warehouses, port facilities) that would further such export-oriented enterprises, generated profits which were mostly repatriated (by the American entrepreneurs) rather than re-invested in a broad spectrum of domestic industries that would diversify occupations, utilize the productive and mental potential of the Puerto Rican people, and provide them with goods and services they so desperately needed to improve their wretched standard of living. In view of this pattern of investment[103] and the consequent engrossing of more and more of the best land by the big mainland sugar companies, the first program of Muñoz Marin's Popular Democrats was an attempt to protect the small farmers and the farm workers. An effort was therefore made to limit the size of the holdings of the large land-

101. The first U.S. military governor, Brigadier General George W. Davis concluded (*Report on Civil Affairs of Puerto Rico,* Washington, 1902) after his first survey of the island: "So great is their poverty that they are always in debt to the proprietors or merchants. They live in huts made of sticks and poles covered with thatches of palm leaves. A family of a dozen may be huddled together in one room, often with only a dirt floor. They have little food worthy of the name and only scanty clothing, while children of less than seven or eight years of age are often entirely naked. It is hard to believe that the pale, sallow, emaciated beings are the descendants of the conquistadors."

102. For details see Arthur D. Gayer, Paul T. Homan, and Earl K. James, *The Sugar Economy of Puerto Rico,* New York, 1938. For a very brief account of the "dominant role of sugar" in the Puerto Rican economy in the 1940's see Perloff, *Puerto Rico's Economic Future,* Chapter 5.

103. For a critique of this kind of investment see Oscar Lange, *Essays on Economic Planning,* New York, 1960, p. 6. H. Myint has pointed out that the failure of this type of investment (in mines, plantations, or other varieties of primary production) to animate an entire economy was really not because of its concentration on primary products for export but because with it was associated a "cheap labor policy," which resulted not only in low wages and low productivity (for want of adequate tools per worker) but low spending power of the recipients of low wages. See *The Economics of the Developing Countries,* New York, 1965, p. 64.

owners by enforcing existing legislation that stipulated a 500-acre maximum, a law long on the statute books and long ignored. Acreages in excess of 500 were sequestrated and placed under the jurisdiction of the Puerto Rico Land Authority, which in turn devised a system of "proportional profit farms" to be cultivated by tenants who were to share in the profits of sugar cane production in proportion to the tonnages they produced. Associated with this scheme were provisions for the allotment of small parcels of land to field workers.[104] But it soon became clear that even though the number of participants in "proportional profit farms" increased,[105] efforts at land tenure reform would not have a very great meliorative impact on the rural economy. Something more than distributive justice was needed; if ever the rural poor were to be rescued from their poverty-stricken condition, some new, additive sources of family income would have to be provided.

Three new agencies were therefore authorized in 1942: the Puerto Rico Industrial Development Company (PRIDCO), the Puerto Rico Planning Board, and the Government Development Bank. To assist these agencies other complementary agencies were associated: The Land Authority and the Water Resources Authority (both of which already existed), the Transportation Authority (1942), the Communications Authority (1942), and the Aqueduct and Sewer Authority (1945). The interlocking of these governmental organizations was based on a conviction that Puerto Rico could only cope with its population problem by developing new industries and that industrial expansion would have to be intermeshed with the land reform program. PRIDCO's task was to establish new industries, and an initial attempt was therefore made to set up plants owned and operated by the government.[106] But this statist industrial venture was so patently inadequate and beset with so many bureaucratic difficulties that within the next three years the leadership came to realize that a comprehensive program of industrialization would depend on the ability of *Fomento* to persuade foreign business-

104. For more details about this part of the Puerto Rican "New Deal," see Perloff, *Puerto Rico's Economic Future*, pp. 38–39, 73, 219, 303. One object of the small-plot allocations was to arrest the migration of rural poor to the city slums.

105. From 3,604 in 1944 to 15,953 in 1947. Whereas this would appear impressive, the annual profit per tenant was very small, rising from $12.44 in 1944 to $23.07 in 1947. Ibid., p. 77, Table 17.

106. Beginning in 1942, four PRIDCO-owned plants were established, one each in the glass, shoe, paperboard, and clay industries. An existing cement plant was also taken over by PRIDCO. See Stead, *Fomento*, p. 14.

men to establish branch factories (or wholly new enterprises) in Puerto Rico. To give overseas entrepreneurs an incentive to launch such operations, a law exempting new manufacturing enterprises from taxes was therefore enacted by the Puerto Rican legislature in 1947.[107] The five PRIDCO-owned factories were sold in 1949 and 1950, and instead of an agency of state socialism, PRIDCO now became a construction company engaged in building factories and other facilities to be sold or leased to private entrepreneurs. The consequence was that *Fomento* now represents a flexible mix of public and private enterprise. Thus, although there are many differences, there is some similarity between the Puerto Rican and the Yugoslav experiments.

There would be no point in building industrial estates, neatly divided into sheds of variable sizes and properly serviced by access roads, water, and electric power, unless there were some measure of certainty that enterprises to occupy the sheds could be attracted. An intensive promotion program was required, and a corps of salesmen had to be recruited who could visit mainland factories and persuade the managers thereof to make modest experiments in the use of Puerto Rican facilities and Puerto Rican labor. The main inducements offered were low wages and no taxes.[108] Although the process of attracting industries was slow in starting, by mid-1950, when the Economic Development Administration (EDA) integrated a number of disparate components of *Fomento* into a single organization, a total of sixty-one private industrial plants had begun operations.[109] But it was the annual increase of new factories that showed that the *Fomento* operation was gathering momentum.[110] From 1950 onward the transmigration of

107. Exemption was authorized until 1959. Since this would discriminate in favor of the early established firms and discourage the later established, the law was amended in 1948 to provide for complete tax exemption for ten years from the time an enterprise began operations.

108. Because of the apprehensions entertained by American businessmen that Puerto Rico would "go socialist," it became evident that very few "private" plants would be established until PRIDCO had divested itself of its "socialist" factories. "We had to find buyers for the Development Company's plants," said Theodoro Moscoso, "convince the legislature that more capital appropriations were necessary, and organize ourselves for a different kind of development effort." From an address given October 1957, quoted by Stead, *Fomento,* pp. 15–16.

109. This included the five government plants that had been sold to private interests.

110. The number of factories promoted by *Fomento* operating at the end of each year was as follows: 1946, 10; 1947, 13; 1948, 24; 1949, 52; 1950, 83; 1951, 114; 1952, 167; 1953, 229; 1954, 280; 1955, 303; 1956, 371; 1957, 446; 1958, 512; 1959, 576; 1960,

American industries to Puerto Rico becomes really impressive, something unique and unparalleled. One need only scan the full-page advertisement that appeared in the *New York Times,* June 24, 1965, to appreciate what had happened in fifteen years. No less than 752 American-financed plants were included in the official Commonwealth of Puerto Rico list (dated May 31, 1965) representing an investment of over $800 million.[111] Nor were these sweat-shop operations by small and obscure American companies; no less than 60 of America's 500 largest corporations had branch factories in Puerto Rico. In addition to the mainland ventures, 404 locally financed industrial operations were in existence in 1965, and 51 non-American plants, making a total of 1,207 plants altogether.

By the early 1950's the macroeconomic contributions that the industrial program was making to the Puerto Rico economy were already evident. National income was increasing more than 5 percent yearly;[112] industrial employment had expanded fivefold in as many years; and benefit-cost analysis led the planners to believe that for every dollar the government had spent on the *Fomento* program, benefits at least thirty times as large could be attributed.[113] Nevertheless, it was quite apparent that the meliorative effects of industrialization were confined to a few urban areas, particularly to San Juan and its satellite communities. Nor was it all clear gain! As more and more people thronged into the San Juan slums in search of employment, housing and sanitary problems, already acute, became rapidly much worse. This foretaste of an emergent economic dualism[114] persuaded the planners that a change in policy was needed, and beginning in 1954 *Fomento* became a far-reaching experiment in industrial dispersion.

635; 1961, 723; 1962, 809; 1963, 879; 1964, 943; 1965, 1,054; 1966, 1,207. (Data from Puerto Rico. Administracion de Fomento Economico, Oficina de Estudios Economicos, Division de Economia General. "Fabricas establecidas bajo el programa de industrializacion, enero de 1966," Mimeographed, San Juan, 1966.)

111. Distributed among types of manufacture as follows: chemicals, 28; electrical, 85; metal fabricating, 34; food processing, 36; furniture, 6; leather, 60; machinery, 15; paper, 17; petroleum, 6; primary metals, 10; printing, 6; precision manufacturing, 31; rubber, 25; ceramics, 13; textiles, 304; tobacco, 19; miscellaneous, 47. For the complete list see *New York Times,* June 24, 1965, p. 48.

112. Fuat M. Andic, *Distribution of Family Incomes in Puerto Rico,* Rio Piedras, 1964, p. 12.

113. Puerto Rico, Office of Economic Research, Economic Development Administration. The estimates are given in Stead, *Fomento,* p. 46, Table 3.

114. See Chapter 5.

Whereas the initial object of the "Bootstrap" program had been to create an investment climate that could attract mainland capital and entrepreneurship anywhere in Puerto Rico,[115] the new policy was designed to promote the establishment of new industries in particular parts of Puerto Rico. Accordingly, instead of a uniform tax exemption for ten years, the Industrial Incentives Act of 1954 established a variable schedule of tax exemptions and authorized other subventions for those businessmen who were prepared to begin industrial operations (in PRIDCO-built industrial estates) not in San Juan but in outlying rural municipalities. Careful "profiles" were prepared to measure the comparative disadvantages of the parts of the island, and on the basis of these studies the seventy-six municipalities were classified into the three "zones" shown in Figure 9–4. The urban municipalities—San Juan and its satellites—continued to offer the original ten-year tax exemption to "new enterprises," while most of the riparian municipalities on the north and south coasts of the island, plus a few adjacent inland municipalities, now offered twelve-year tax exemption. In sharp contrast to both of the foregoing, the inland, hilly municipalities (diagonally striped in Figure 9–4) were authorized to offer seventeen-year tax exemption and to extend, in addition to freedom from taxes,[116] other inducements to mainland or local entrepreneurs who were willing to join forces with the Puerto Rican authorities in developing the more backward and disadvantaged areas of the island.[117] PRIDCO, which had long been attentive to the technical requirements of "new enterprises," now became even more solicitous, inasmuch as it was given the responsibility of assuring, in out of the way places, the needed amount of electric energy, peak-hour water requirements,[118] the requisite sewer facilities, fire protection, and other facilities.

115. This aspect of the Puerto Rican policy was described in Chapter 6.

116. The tax moratorium covered exemption not only from real and personal property taxes but from the corporate income tax, the personal income tax, from customs duties on imported machinery or equipment, and from municipal license fees.

117. These additional inducements comprised lower rentals for factory space, loans at favorable interest rates, cash grants to cover industrial training of workmen, and arrangements for assigning workers to mainland factories to be trained as foremen and for other supervisory positions.

118. Not only in volume but in purity, salinity, pressure, temperature, and chemical content. "Locational questionnaires" were therefore prepared, which prospective tenants of yet unbuilt industrial estates were asked to fill out. A sample questionnaire is reproduced in Appendix A.

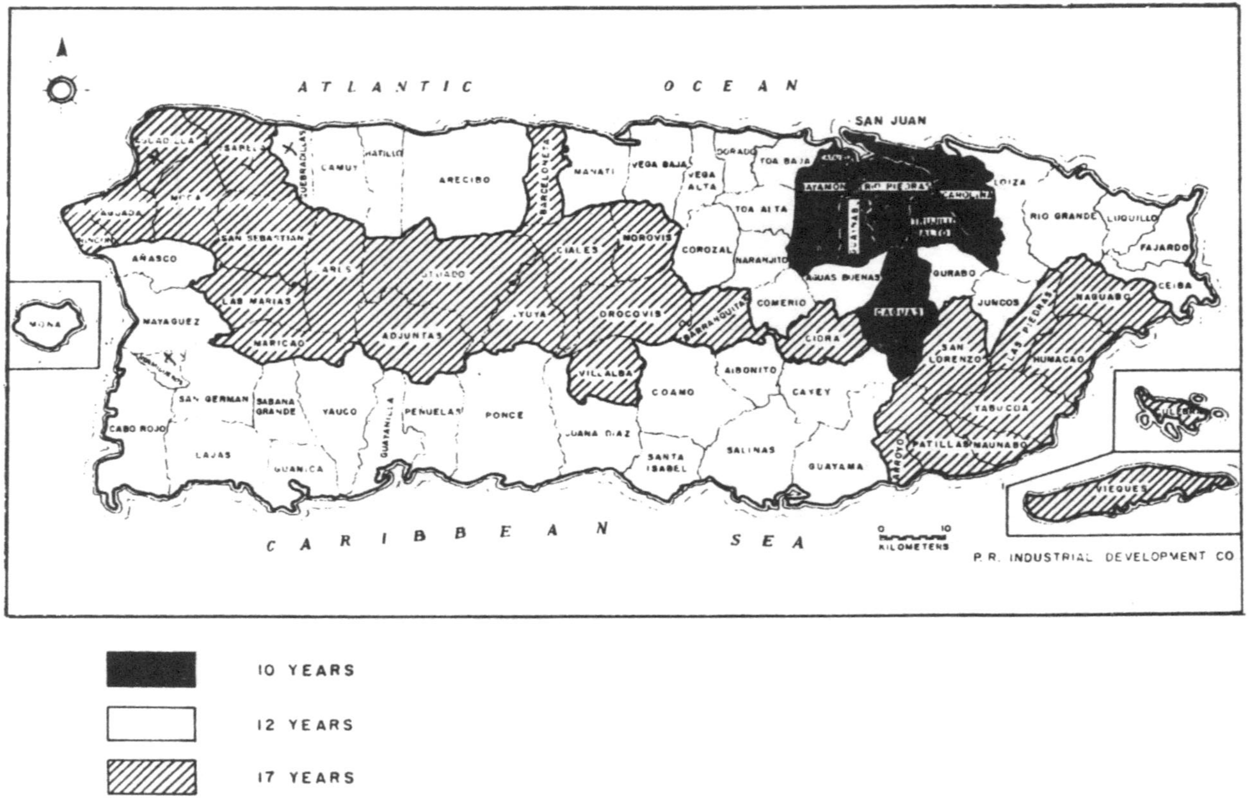

Figure 9–4 Puerto Rican Tax Exemption Zones
SOURCE: Puerto Rico Industrial Development Company, San Juan, 1963.

The fruits of this new policy can be seen by looking at Figure 9–5, which shows that by 1969 one or more industrial plants had been established in all of the seventy-six Puerto Rican municipalities. The empty spots on the map have been eliminated, and the "locational incentive program" has convincingly demonstrated not only its economic importance but an increasing educational utility. And whereas the first target of the industrial dispersion program had been the establishment of at least one plant in each municipality, it was soon realized that some more appropriate and equitable measure of optimal industrial dispersion was needed. In a memorandum dated June 14, 1962, the thesis was advanced that the number of industrial plants in the seventy-six municipalities should "bear a relationship to the number of inhabitants in each municipality" and that the "minimum goal" ought to be "one *Fomento* job per 100 inhabitants."[119] This proposal epitomizes better than anything else the spatial objectives of Puerto Rican planning. Provision of employment is implicitly assumed to be a governmental responsibility, and in assuring an equitable sharing of employment opportunities it is considered proper that the government should continue to make the necessary investments and solicit the requisite capital and management, so that employment facilities can be made available within convenient travel distance of every community. This isochronic concept of industrial location, scaled to the size of local populations, represents the quintessential democracy and humaneness of Puerto Rican economic liberalism.

This new concept of a planned pattern of industrial dispersion may well be the most important contribution that Puerto Rico is making to the theory and practice of economic development. The 1962 memorandum surveyed the whole island in terms of *Fomento* population-job ratios and discovered very wide variations. In 33 municipalities, for example, the ratio was nearer to 250 residents per job than 100 to 1, although in 15 more fortunate municipalities the ratio was approaching a ratio of 1 *Fomento* job for every 50 persons, and in 7 well-industrialized municipalities the ratios ranged as low as 1 job for 13 persons and averaged 1 to 32.[120] On the basis of these findings the memorandum

119. Puerto Rico, Administracion de Fomento Economico, "Proposed Revisions in Policy," Memo No. 4, "Special Incentive Program," Mimeographed, San Juan, 1962, p. 1.

120. Ibid, pp. 2–3, wherein the ratio between the (1960) population and the (1962) *Fomento* employment is tabulated (Tables 2 and 3) for all the municipalities, with the job deficits calculated on the basis of 1 job for 100 residents for rural municipalities and on a 1 to 50 ratio for the more urbanized.

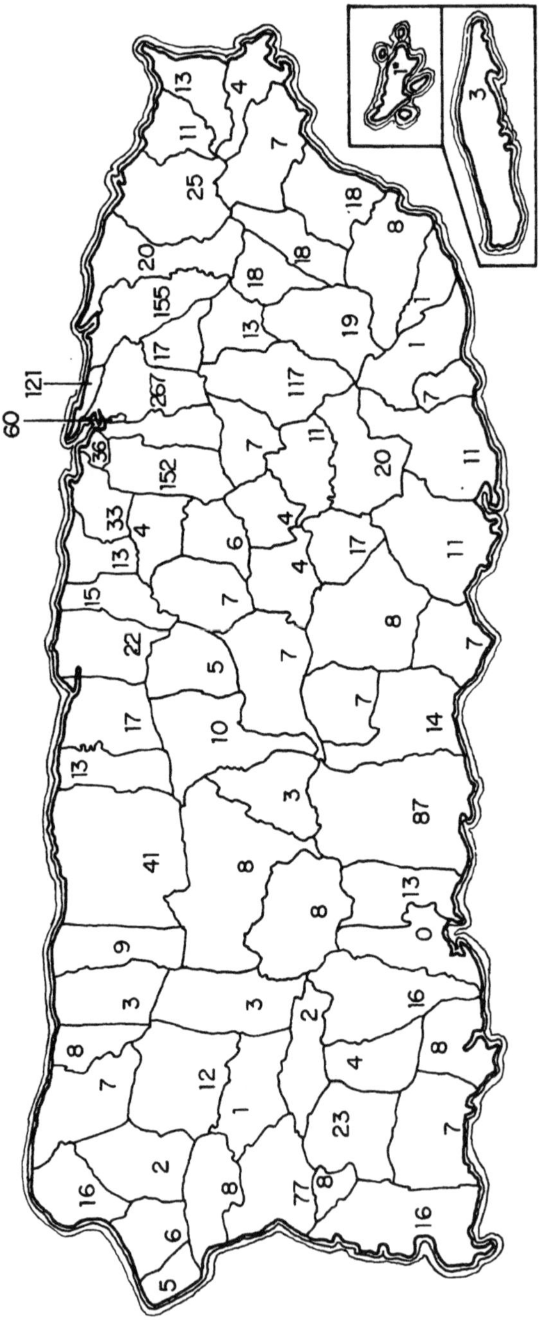

Figure 9–5 Number of Factories in the Puerto Rican Municipalities
SOURCE: Puerto Rico Industrial Development Company, San Juan, 1969.

proposed a review and a revision of the entire incentive program and recommended that "locational grants" should be spatially graduated in terms of job deficits.[121] Those municipalities with the largest deficits would be eligible for the largest locational grants; municipalities that had already exceeded the minimum target of 1 job for every 100 residents would receive smaller "incentive" payments; while for municipalities where the ratio was below 50 to 1 there would be no incentive grants. The incentive payments would be further graduated within each zone (see Figure 9–6), with the maximum grants proffered to enterprises that would be prepared to provide 100 or more jobs (within one year of the beginning of operation in one zone, within three years in another, where industrial recruitment would be slower),[122] and with lesser grants for proportionately smaller contributions to optimal spatial employment. What basically was involved in this new trend in policy was an appreciation of the need for a "saturation" approach to the establishment of investment clusters similar to the thesis I have advanced in Chapter 7.

Granting that there has been visible proof of the macroeconomic benefits of the Puerto Rican industrial dispersion program, the question remains as to the impact it has had on the quality of life, particularly in the rural areas once so poor, and, more particularly, whether there has been greater improvement in those municipalities (and within them, in those *barrios*) wherein industrial plants have been established. Obviously, not all progress can be attributed to the presence of a factory in a rural area, inasmuch as a number of facilities (roads, electric grids) and a variety of welfare services have been provided for the entire island. Studies such as that of the Bournes', however, indicate rather clearly that communities that now have factories and other communities within commuting distance of *Fomento* industrial estates have progressed far more than communities that are still essentially agrarian.[123] The Bournes were able in 1962 to replicate surveys of ten communities that had initially been appraised in 1932. Their findings

121. Since 1954 special inducements had been proffered to entrepreneurs who would begin industrial operations in less-developed municipalities. In addition to tax exemption the "inducements" included lower rental rates on factory space, cash grants, and reimbursement for costs of training workmen.

122. Many other variations were recommended. See Puerto Rico, Administracion de Fomento Economico, "Proposed Revisions in Policy, Memo No. 4, pp. 3–5.

123. Dorothy D. Bourne and James R. Bourne, *Thirty Years of Challenge in Puerto Rico: A Case Study of Ten Selected Rural Areas,* New York, 1966.

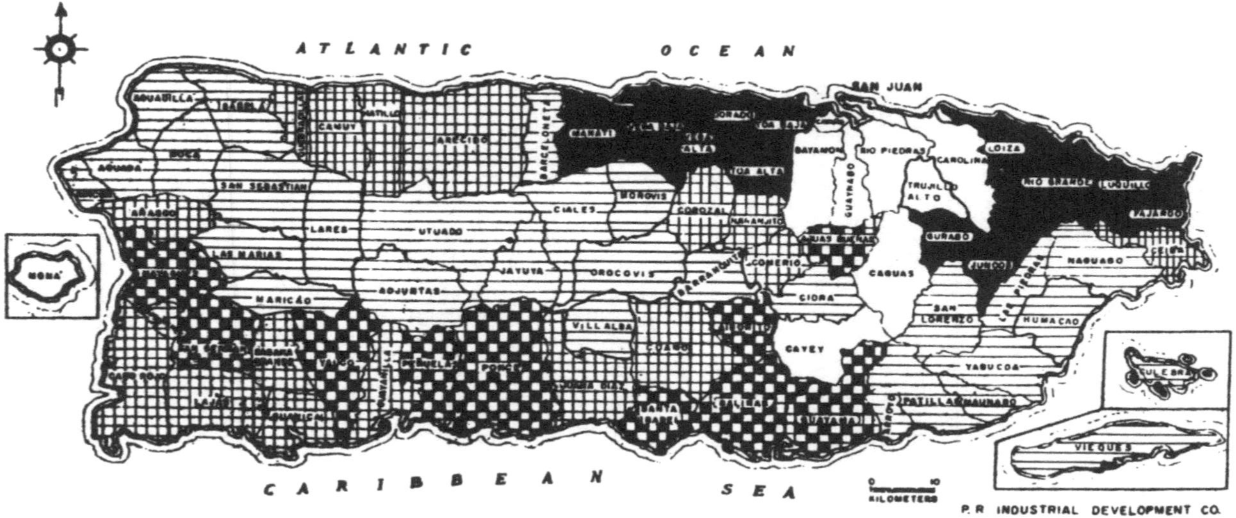

Available Incentives

Category		Basic per 30 employees	Additional per employee	Total per 100 employees	For each 100 additional
	I	$30,000	$300	$50,000	$30,000
	II	20,000	200	35,000	20,000
	III	15,000	150	25,000	15,000
	IV	5,000	75	10,000	7,500

Figure 9–6 Incentives for Factory Location

SOURCE: Puerto Rico Industrial Development Company, San Juan, n.d.

NOTE: These zones would not coincide with the tax-exemption zones shown in Figure 9–4, since there would be four zones (plus ineligible areas), and the determinants would

are, to say the least, most revealing. In a *barrio* in the mountainous municipality of Cidra, average monthly income had increased almost 2½ times (1932–1962) and there can be little doubt but that the three factories operating in this small community of 3,040 persons were mainly responsible.[124] By contrast, in a *barrio* of the municipality of Loisa, which had no factory, and where the nearest industrial plant was 10 miles distant, the average monthly income in 1962 was 2.4 percent less than in 1932. Poverty still lingered here, and few changes in housing, education, or sanitation have occurred. Compare this with a *barrio* in Bayamon municipality within 3 miles of industrial estates that house sixty-two factories: here, monthly income had doubled, school enrollment had quadrupled, and every house had running water and electricity.

Circumstantial developments, such as the expansion of a metropolitan area or the building of military installations, can speed up the development of a few villages, but for most communities, progress is a function of a diversification of occupations resulting from imaginative investment. Where this has occurred, in Puerto Rican rural landscapes, a process of transformation has been set in motion. The huts of 1932 have been replaced by houses with floors and tight roofs, equipped with electricity and running water. Diseases such as malaria, tuberculosis, gastroenteritis, and pellagra have been overcome or greatly reduced. Paved streets, obstetrical care, school buses, and houses provided with hygienic latrines are evidences of genuine progress. So is the decline of home needlework at sweatshop wages, the diminution or termination of overseas migration for seasonal employment, the increase in school population, and, not least important, the higher levels of aspiration that parents have for their children. To say that "there has been great improvement," a phrase that repeats itself in the testimony the Bournes gathered, would be a grave understatement. In many instances there has been a veritable transformation that can to a very large extent be attributed to the imaginative, flexible, yet persistent Puerto Rican policy of industrial dispersion and spatial restructuring of the island's economy.

124. For monthly income figures, 1932 vs. 1962, see Bourne, *Thirty Years of Change*, p. 288, Table 20. For a description of the ten communities in 1932 and the 1962 contrasts, see Chapter 5 of the same work.

CHAPTER 10 SPATIAL EXPERIMENTS: TENTATIVE AND PARTIAL

Efforts at Spatial Reform in Mainland China

The declared goals of the locational and spatial policies of the People's Republic of China were to correct the "irrational" structures that the pre-Communist economy had created, to establish new industrial centers near raw materials and consumers, to achieve a proper balance between intraregional self-sufficiency and interregional specialization, to develop a hierarchy of medium-sized and small cities in the interior, and to locate certain critical installations where their contribution to national security would be maximized.[1] The first four of these goals certainly had merit; pre-1949 Chinese industries were concentrated in coastal areas, in Manchuria, and in a few riverine cities. In 1948, for example, only eighteen cities outside of Manchuria "had sufficient manufacturing capacity to be considered even modest industrial centers."[2] Moreover, among these industrial centers the concentration was so great that the five largest accounted for 85.6 percent of the factories, 90.7 percent of motive power used, and 85.5 percent of the manpower employed in mechanized manufacturing operations. For a country as large as China, this degree of industrial polarization and the lack of interior cities meant that vast areas were backward, poor, minutely fragmented, agrarian landscapes,[3] handicapped by their remoteness from diversified

1. Yuan-li Wu, H. C. Ling, and Grace Hsiao Wu, *The Spatial Economy of Communist China: a Study on Industrial Location and Transportation*, New York, 1966, p. 200.

2. Ibid., p. 8.

3. For measurements of the degrees of underdevelopment of the Chinese provinces, see T. H. Shen, *Agricultural Resources of China*, Ithaca, 1951, Appendix Tables 2 and 5; and Wu, *Spatial Economy of Communist China*, p. 12–15.

industrial centers,[4] and by adverse terms of trade. All these disabilities the First Five-Year Plan proposed to correct: "We shall locate the productive forces of industry in different parts of the country," said the planners," in such a way that they will be close to producing areas of raw materials and fuel and also to consumer markets."[5] More specifically, Li Fu-ch'un, chairman of the State Planning Commission, explained that 472 out of 694 industrial projects planned for the first five years would be located in interior provinces, as contrasted with 222 new installations in the developed areas.[6] In view of this confident outlook, it will be interesting to see how well these promises were kept and how accurate were the planners' predictions that by constructing inland industrial centers they would "develop medium and small cities in the interior" of China and "restrict . . . the expansion of the large cities."[7]

Although a number of new inland industrial plants were built with forced-draft vigor, getting them into any tolerably satisfactory degree of utilization once they were built proved difficult, and by 1956 Li Fu-ch'un reported to the First National People's Congress that it would be necessary to place more reliance than had been initially planned on the coastal industrial areas.[8] Soon thereafter Chou En-lai explained to the National Congress of the Chinese Communist Party that "Those who expect a rapid and general establishment of many industrial bases in the far reaches of western China are unrealistic in their outlook."[9] Perhaps it was the inability to integrate the new dispersed plants into the existing overall national economy that led to the announced division of the country (July 1957) into seven economic regions and the consequent publicity devoted to the desirability of regional autonomy. At any rate, the thesis now was that, in order to reduce long-distance transport and cross-country hauls, the several regions should adopt policies that would make them increasingly self-sufficient. Each region,

4. Nearly half of China's railway mileage was in Manchuria, and since the coastal provinces had a dominant share in the remaining trackage, large areas were very poorly served. Eight of the twenty-six provinces had no railways in operation in 1949–1950, while of the mileage in operation, 77 percent was located in the more developed regions of Manchuria and northeast China. Wu, *Spatial Economy of Communist China*, p. 199.

5. China. *The First Five-Year Plan of the People's Republic of China*, Peking, 1956, p. 31.

6. *People's Handbook, 1955*, Tientsin, 1955, pp. 59–60.

7. Ibid.

8. *People's Handbook, 1957*, Shanghai, 1957, p. 192.

9. Ibid., quoted by Wu, *Spatial Economy of Communist China*, p. 19.

for example, should have its own iron and steel complex,[10] its own machine-tool factory, and other such secondary enterprises as would be appropriately tributary to the steel mills. In carrying out these policies it was recognized that not only would proper cognizance have to be taken of locational considerations such as the proximity to raw materials, fuels, and markets but, for the short run, attention would need to be paid to the "proper balance between intraregional self-sufficiency and interregional specialization and exchange."[11] The long-term goal, however, seems to have contemplated a gradual reduction of interregional trade as each region succeeded in diversifying its enterprises and improving its infrastructure.[12] It ought not be overlooked, however, that one object of developing certain basic industries deep in the interior of China was strategic, the object being to reduce the vulnerability of important industrial installations from enemy attacks.[13]

Immediate and insistent needs for industrial output seem to have rather promptly compromised the plans for economic regionalism and dimmed the hopes for a swift industrialization of a number of interior areas. Using urban population growth as one index, Wu has shown by a study of 117 cities that, although from 1948 to 1953 the medium-sized cities (300,000 to 1 million) grew more rapidly than the large cities (over 1 million), after 1953 a strong trend toward "metropolization" set in, so that by 1958 the number of small cities (less than 300,000) had actually decreased by 16 percent, whereas the number of large cities had increased by 67 percent.[14] Apparently the promises made by the leadership that the expansion of large cities would be arrested had not been achieved. Nor had the development of economic centers in the underdeveloped regions materialized as forecast. Wu's findings are that twenty-three cities in the developed regions experienced intensive growth as against twelve in the less-developed regions.[15] The population data therefore provides no evidence that the program of regional counter-polarization was being fulfilled.

10. Compare with Yugoslavia, where each "republic" has its own iron and steel complex.

11. Wu, *Spatial Economy of Communist China,* p. 20.

12. For the iron and steel program, see Yuan-li Wu, *The Steel Industry in Communist China,* New York, 1965.

13. This is not the only element of the Chinese program that seems to have been modeled on a USSR precedent.

14. Wu, *Spatial Economy of Communist China,* p. 29, Table 2–1.

15. Ibid., p. 201.

Even though the migration of people to the large cities (which must have been induced by the prospects of relatively more employment) had not been arrested, this might have been merely a short-run tendency. Perhaps a better test of the success of the Chinese decentralization policy would be the extent to which industrial plants were actually built in the interior areas. But once again the evidence is not very impressive. The "Great Leap Forward," which involved extensive experimentation with rural "communes" and the building of a very large number of small industrial projects, seems to have required so much capital that some scaling down of the originally planned industrial program for the interior provinces was inevitable, and it was this circumstance that made greater reliance on the "going concern" in the older industrialized regions more and more urgent, particularly when tensions between China and the USSR clouded the political horizon. Industrial concentration, which had been so pronounced in pre-Communist China, was therefore very little changed. Wu's "industrial profile" of some 328 industrial locations indicates that half of China's industrial capacity is still (1966) in three provinces (Kiangsu, Hopeh, Liaoning), as it was before 1949; that two-thirds of the capacity is in five provinces (Kiangsu, Hopeh, Liaoning, Hupeh, Szechwan) and that seven coastal provinces have twice as many industrial centers as all the inland provinces.[16] Largely because of the forced-draft efforts to industrialize underdeveloped areas as an integral part of the "Great Leap Forward," a majority of industrial plants built in the interior were very small, and consequently these plants, many of which are no longer in operation, did little to offset the dominant role of the coastal industrial centers.[17] Hence, despite the exaggerated publicity given to the "Great Leap Forward" and to industrial decentralization, there has actually been, according to Wu's findings, a "greater relative emphasis on the establishment of industrial centers in the developed regions."[18]

It ought not be concluded, however, that the Chinese efforts to develop backward areas have all misfired. There has been enough

16. Ibid., pp. 201–202.

17. During the "backyard furnace" drive of 1958 an enormous number of small blast furnaces were built, the estimates running up to 2 million, which is probably a very much exaggerated figure. There is rather good evidence, however, that at least 370,000 furnaces were built, and of these about 50 percent were set up in the east and northeast region. For details see Wu, *The Steel Industry in Communist China*, p. 223.

18. Ibid., p. 60.

capital formation in at least three provinces (Honan, Hunan, Anhwei) to move them "from the ranks of the industrially underdeveloped and agriculturally developed" classification into a category "in which both industry and agriculture are relatively more developed," while in two other provinces (Shansi and Inner Mongolia) so much investment has been made that they can now be considered "industrially developed."[19] Yet, despite these instances of success in transforming a few specially favored enclaves, relatively few of the spatial goals of the First Five-Year Plan seem to have been realized. The failure of the (1958) "Great Leap Forward" produced a "great depression" (1960–1962) which was largely responsible for a hasty shift from long-term planning to "near-term improvisation." One mistake the Chinese leaders made was to overestimate their ability to kindle popular support for the "Great Leap Forward" and thereby galvanize millions of people to such heights of patriotism that they would not only work harder than ever before but scrimp and save so that the rate of investment could very greatly increase. What became patently clear was that the incentives for such an unparalleled intensity of effort were lacking. More than that, the Communists' overambitious efforts to restructure the rural marketing system were even more counterproductive, not only because they were drastic, but because the planners signally failed to appreciate the operational merits of the existing spatial design.

The neatly intermeshed Chinese rural market system was the product of generations, even centuries, of adaptation to the needs of peasant communities.[20] Prior to the Communist envelopment in 1949 a considerable amount of cautious restructuring was occurring. Markets grew larger, and new "standard markets" were established, although some were absorbed by larger intermediate markets. Market-day schedules were better adapted to the increasing volume of activity,[21] and, in the opinion of a careful scholar, "in most parts of China the apparent state of the periodic marketing system was one of robust health."[22] In the process of gradual "modernization," largely made possible by better means of transport, many smaller markets had dis-

19. For details see Wu, *Spatial Economy of Communist China,* p. 90, 204, and p. 91, Fig. 4–2.

20. For a summary picture of this market structure see Chapter 3.

21. For very precise and explicit details, see G. William Skinner, "Marketing and Social Structure in Rural China, Part 2," *Journal of Asian Studies,* 24, No. 2 (February 1965), 211–228.

22. Ibid., p. 211.

appeared,[23] but even so about 58,000 "standard marketing systems" still remained.[24] It was this far-flung, delicately balanced rural marketing system that the Communist planners began to "socialize" by means of two major institutions: the state trading companies, and the marketing cooperatives. The first of these, the state trading companies, wholly owned by the state, were specialized by commodities (e.g., grain, vegetable oils, fish), and their branches were soon established in the larger market towns. When they were accorded monopoly privileges after 1953, they were soon able to control the wholesale trade in farm produce.[25] At the same time, marketing cooperatives were being established "under the guidance of Communist cadremen in market towns throughout China,"[26] and, although they were presumably "autonomous associations unattached to the state apparatus," they collected local produce and distributed industrial products in close connection with the state trading companies. Threatened by this competition, some small storekeepers and pedlars became employees of the cooperatives, although a majority of the 2½ to 3 million traders resisted in one way or another the attempted "socialist transformation" of the rural market system, carrying on their buying and selling operations as best they could alongside those of the cooperatives.

The efforts of the planners to correct the allegedly "irrational" market system that the bourgeois society had created were to have profound effects on the structure, reach, and effectiveness of China's rural markets. After a brief relaxation of close surveillance during 1956–1957, a real change in policy was announced in August 1958. Skinner has put the issue succinctly: in an agrarian economy "still largely unmodernized, with a rural market network over seven-eighths of whose nodes were traditional periodic markets, the regime attempted not merely to reform, not gradually to obviate, not eventually to bypass, but to *dispense altogether* with the traditional institutions of peasant marketing."[27] Marketing and supply cooperatives, merged to form single organizations within each of the emergent communes, now became the

23. Skinner's estimate is 5,300. Ibid., p. 228.

24. Ibid.

25. Skinner, "Marketing and Social Structure in Rural China," Part 3, *Journal of Asian Studies,* 24, No. 3 (May 1965), 363. See p. 364 of the same work for an illustration of how state trading company branches were distributed in the central-place hierarchy.

26. Ibid., p. 363.

27. Ibid., p. 371. (Skinner's italics.)

local agencies of the state trading companies. The thousands of periodic markets that had operated over the centuries in China were abruptly closed, and the consequence was a "near paralysis in commodity distribution."[28]

This impulsive and ill-considered effort to supplant the traditional marketing structure neutralized many beneficial improvements that the new regime had been making. Real progress, for example, had occurred in building transport facilities. Railway extensions helped to triple the volume of railway traffic (1952–1958), while the volume of coastal and inland waterway trade quadrupled. A doubling of the mileage of improved roads facilitated the movement of agricultural produce by trucks, particularly between central market towns and industrial centers. All these changes helped to commercialize agriculture. Unfortunately, little attention was paid to local road improvement, so that the potential "spread effects" of the very large investments in transport facilities were not spatially realized. Yet the assumption in 1958 was that the whole delicate local market system, which had been functioning smoothly despite the primitive character of its transport facilities, could be summarily scrapped.

The results were not long in revealing themselves. Fertilizers and farm supplies were not distributed, seasonal fruits rotted in the orchards, untended livestock in the impersonal new market system died before they reached their slaughterhouse destinations. This part of the "Great Leap Forward" was sullied before it was really begun! Capitulation was inevitable, and in September 1959 the State Council authorized the reopening of rural markets with the schedules to be set "in accordance with old usage." But although some forty to forty-five thousand markets were reopened, very strict controls were devised to prevent the re-emergence of "the spontaneous force of capitalism." Committees representing various departments of the communes controlled "prices, participants, and market practices,"[29] all of which introduced elements of rigidity into an exchange and supply system that had been eminently flexible. Moreover, attempts to harmonize the administrative and the market-town hierarchy often tended to force trade into unfamiliar and less efficient channels. Thus, one attempt to link an intermediate market with a central market within the same administrative area increased the travel distance by 30 percent and lengthened the travel

28. Ibid., p. 372.
29. Ibid., p. 373.

time fivefold.[30] Neverthless these foolish efforts to force a marketing system to fit an administrative spatial structure continued until 1962, and "imposed an enormous additional burden on China's meager transport and storage facilities."[31]

Yet, whatever their ideology, the Chinese are an extraordinarily practical people. By 1962 both the central planners and the local cadremen were ready to correct their mistakes. Confessing error, the government formally conceded that "historical, logical supply relations must be rediscovered," and admitted that when administrative and economic areas did not coincide, to insure effective marketing and distribution of goods, the economic areas must take precedence.[32] Accordingly, local leaders were instructed to engage in field research, so that they could properly define market areas, ascertaining the traditional routes, commodity flows, and trading patterns. Armed with their findings, the local leaders were expected to make recommendations concerning the boundaries of "rational economic-area divisions."[33] In the meantime, the share of trade conducted by private businessmen steadily increased, more roads were improved, and even the neglect of local transport facilities was being corrected as village roads and bicycle paths were mended. But despite the injunction that "more rational" market patterns should be created, it would appear that the "basic-level supply points" (in Communist terminology these constitute the substructure on which a rural market system rests) consist of some thirty-two to thirty-four thousand standard markets. Consequently, although there are many new actors on the local stage—agents of state trading companies or cooperative societies, communal and other governmental officials—and although there are fewer itinerant traders, the spatial patterns are much the same as they were before 1949. Wholesale trade, however, is almost entirely monopolized by the state, so that in intermediate and central markets heavy invasions have been made on the former prerogatives of the private traders. One can scarcely avoid the conclusion that the Communist planners rather badly bungled a golden opportunity to re-

30. For more illustrative details, see Skinner, "Marketing and Social Structure in Rural China," Part 3, p. 74. One estimate computed the ton-kilometers involved, in making one trade and administrative area coincide, to be 485,100 as contrasted with the former 277,200 ton-kilometers.

31. Ibid.

32. The official sources authorizing these concessions are listed by Skinner, in "Marketing and Social Structure in Rural China" Part 3, p. 376.

33. Ibid., p. 377.

structure the rural economy into more effective functional economic areas. By attempting too much they achieved little. Rural marketing today, Skinner concludes after his searching explorations, "bears the unmistakable stamp of traditional custom and premodern practice." Admittedly, by "electing to work through rather than against the inherited system," the Chinese have probably "enhanced their chances of ultimate success," but the rationalization of space in rural China has not yet really begun. This is partly because the drastic policies of 1958–1959 actually delayed rather than hastened modernization. Perhaps the most serious shortcoming was the failure to better integrate town and country by means of industrial dispersion. The hastily planned and programmatically propagated commune was a miserable alternative to an organically integrated community in which agriculture and industry are reciprocally related in a genuinely functional sense. The feckless history of the Chinese communes contrasts strikingly with the far more realistic organization of communes in Yugoslavia. Since the cartographic exercise of dividing China's agricultural landscapes into communes presupposes some proper-sized spatial unit, it is appropriate to inquire how large the Communist planners thought the communes should be. If Skinner's estimate of about 58,000 "standard market areas" is correct, and if some 21,600 rural communes were established, then each commune would, on the average, encompass an area about three times the size of a standard market area. It would be roughly equivalent to the area served by an "intermediate market town." This would mean an area that might include 4,000 to 6,500 households, or about 24,000 to 39,000 people living in some fifty to sixty villages.[34] Such a spatial unit could have had a large enough market to support a sizable number of local industries, while the transport matrix could have permitted an adequate (commuting) work force and short enough farm-to-market distances; and since an organized central place staffed with traders and provided with market facilities already existed, a commune might therefore have become a functional economic area. This suggests that the failure of the commune as an integrating force can be attributed far more to operational than to structural factors. Functional economic areas cannot be created by administrative fiat. They must grow, gradually interrelating a variety of economic activities over an expanding

34. Skinner has shown, however, that there were quite wide regional variations in both the area and the population size of communes and that many bore no relation to a possible trading system. Ibid., p. 388.

spatial area. Skinner has shown how reckless was the attempt to cobble together townships into communes, with little or no endeavor "to align the new unit with the natural socioeconomic systems shaped by rural trade."[35] Perhaps the Chinese Communists would have been better able to deal with the problems of spatial restructuring if they had read Charles Galpin rather than Karl Marx.

Contrasts in Spatial Planning among the Indian States.

Although the central planners of India have largely ignored the spatial dimensions of their task, sometimes acting as if geographical factors were too unimportant to merit their attention,[36] some of the more progressive Indian states have made rather notable beginnings in restructuring their economic landscapes. Precisely why most of these changes have occurred in western India is not wholly clear, but there is a marked contrast between the spatial developments occurring in a belt of territory that stretches north from Mysore through Maharashtra, Gujarat, and Madhya Pradesh to the Punjab and the relative changelessness in a parallel eastern belt extending north from Madras through Orissa and Uttar Pradesh to Bihar. Farther east, Assam and West Bengal are perhaps even more resistent to spatial restructuring. Although it may have been cotton growing that was historically responsible for the initial establishment of regulated markets,[37] a number of other factors, ethnic, cultural, and political, have been responsible for the fairly rapid spread, particularly in the western states, of these well-organized, impersonally conducted, and competitive outlets for agricultural produce. The incentives that these markets have given farmers for commercializing and modernizing farming operations have led them to increase their marketed surpluses.

That this change in the organization of marketing, which has steadily weakened the monopsonistic power of village traders and money lenders and increased the demand of farm families for industrial products, has occurred mainly in the western states is evident from the data (for 1964) in Table 10–1. Five states (Maharashtra, Gujarat, Mysore, Punjab, and Madhya Pradesh) together accounted for 79.8 percent of

35. Ibid., p. 394.
36. John P. Lewis, *Quiet Crisis in India,* Washington, 1962, p. 133, 168.
37. See Chapter 3; for more details see my *Market Towns and Spatial Development in India,* New Delhi, 1965, pp. 44–47.

Table 10–1 Distribution of Regulated Markets in the Indian States

State	No. of Markets	Percent of national population	Percent of all markets
Maharashtra	311	9.0	28.4
Gujarat	169	4.7	15.5
Mysore	147	5.4	13.3
Punjab	137	4.6	12.4
Madhya Pradesh	111	7.4	10.2
Total	875	31.1	79.8
Andhra Pradesh	94	8.2	8.6
Madras	65	7.7	5.9
Orissa	26	4.0	2.4
Bihar	10	10.6	.9
Rajasthan	8	4.6	.7
Kerala	4	3.8	.4
Total	207	38.9	18.9

SOURCE: E. A. J. Johnson, *Market Towns and Spatial Development in India,* New Delhi: National Council of Applied Economic Research, 1965, p. 47.

NOTE: It will be noted that Andra Pradesh seems to be more similar to the states of western India than to those in the eastern part. Her share of regulated markets is fairly impressive in numbers and quite credible in relation to her population. But, despite this median showing, the spatial organization in this province has not been outstanding. For a searching analysis, see Brian J. L. Berry and V. L. S. Prakasa Rao, *Urban-Rural Duality in the Regional Structure of Andhra Pradesh: A Challenge to Regional Planning and Development,* Mimeographed.

India's regulated markets, although they had only 31.1 percent of the nation's population. By comparison, six other states that also had regulated markets in 1964 had only a fourth as many (18.9 percent), although their share of population (38.9 percent) was larger. The contrast with the remaining Indian states, which had 29 percent of the nation's population, was much greater. This group of states, which included population-dense Uttar Pradesh and West Bengal, had no regulated markets whatever in 1964, and, as a result, the spatial organization of the countryside was much more primitive and far less efficient than that in the western states.

Instructive evidence can be presented to show the effect that regulated markets in the western states have had in integrating town and country, in diversifying occupations, and in quickening investment. The data in Table 10–2 indicate that the majority of regulated markets have been located in small and medium-sized cities: an average of 34 percent in

Table 10–2 Distribution of Regulated Markets According to Size of Central-Place Sites

	Percent of markets in urban centers with populations between 5,000 and 100,000 (in thousands)					
State	Over 100	50–100	20–50	10–20	5–10	Under 5
Maharashtra	6.5	9.4	25.9	38.1	19.4	0.7
Gujarat	4.3	8.5	40.0	34.3	11.4	1.4
Mysore	7.1	8.6	25.7	44.3	12.9	1.4
Punjab	3.4	11.2	26.0	21.5	24.1	13.8
Madhya Pradesh	4.2	1.4	16.6	31.9	39.0	6.9
Average			26.8	34.0	21.3	

SOURCE: E. A. J. Johnson, *Market Towns and Spatial Development in India*, New Delhi, National Council of Applied Economic Research, p. 54.

the small cities (of the 10,000–20,000 range) plus an average of almost 27 percent in the medium-sized cities (with populations of 20,000–50,000). Only in the two more rural states, Madhya Pradesh and Punjab, were there significant fractions (39 percent for Madhya Pradesh, 24 percent for Punjab) in quite small central places (5,000–10,000 people). But even in the other three states an average of about 15 percent of the regulated markets were in small market towns. The important thing to notice, therefore, is that the great bulk of the regulated markets, (about 81 percent) are in urban centers with populations ranging from 5,000 to 50,000. Because they are located in centers of several differing sizes, that ladder up from rather small rural centers to fair-sized cities, they are helping to develop, not merely random market towns, but a hierarchy of central places.

Had the central planners appreciated the critical importance of what John P. Lewis has called "the town-centered alternative" to "village-centered" and "metropolitan-centered" development policy,[38] the Indian government, by a proper use of industrial estates, might have greatly strengthened the vitality of every urban center that contained a regulated-market yard. Unfortunately, instead of dispersing industrial estates to the urban centers that were already making important strides in reorganizing rural economic areas, the planners' first policy was to cluster industrial estates on the outskirts of large cities, thereby un-

38. *Quiet Crisis in India*, pp. 179–202.

wittingly aggravating an already excessive urban polarization and exacerbating acute problems of housing and sanitation. When, by 1959, the planners "had developed guilt feelings about the way the program was compounding metropolitan centered industrial location,"[39] an even more fatuous decision was reached, namely, to establish "rural industrial estates" but only in places with less than 2,500 persons. If this hasty solution, which resulted in a planless scattering of industrial estates, had any locational basis whatever, it must have rested on a belief in the desirability of village-centered industry. Yet it should have been clear to anyone who had had any experience or familiarity with industrial operations that not enough enterprises could be attracted to use all the "sheds" (which usually ranged from 50 to 100) of a village-located industrial estate. The consequence, as I have pointed out elsewhere,[40] was a scandalously wasteful underutilization of factory space, for the reason that a small center with less than 2,500 people simply could not supply the versatile manpower needed for a range of industrial enterprises and was utterly incapable of providing the requisite marketing, transport, repair, and credit facilities which a group of small shops would require.

The result was that the small and medium-sized cities in which regulated markets had already been established by civic leaders who recognized the desirability of diversifying employment in their communities were compelled either to rely on the "forces of spontaneity" to develop local industry or to organize groups of investors who could build private industrial estates. But however chequered the history of government-built industrial estates, and however unwisely many have been located, at least the government experiments did call to the attention of alert civic leaders in the market towns of western India the advantages of clustered small industrial enterprises. During my visits to Indian regulated markets the discussions with market committees would invariably involve the role of industrial estates in spatial development; the subject always came up. In some towns there already

39. Ibid., p. 186.

40. See my *Market Towns and the Spatial Development of India,* p. 86, Table 9. Since the utilization data available to me made no distinction between urban and rural industrial estates, the percent of utilization shown in that table, which ranged from a low of 44.1 percent (Rajasthan) to a high of 88.2 percent (Madras) and averaged 67 percent does not by any means reflect the far greater than average underutilization of the rural estates.

existed industrial estates, which I was asked to visit;[41] in other urban centers estates were under construction or being planned.[42] Little by little, albeit in an undramatic way, these pragmatic and variable interblendings of private and governmental activity are increasing employment and diversifying occupations. In the Punjab some restructuring has taken the form of industrial "ribbon development" along major paved highways, and it remains to be seen whether this will have as appreciable an impact on adjacent rural areas as a more spatially-centered industrial estate might have. In a number of ways Punjab has exhibited rather exceptional dynamism, reflecting quite possibly the disciplined mentality of the Sikhs and their burning desire to prove that their value system can demonstrate signal advantages in coping with modern problems.[43]

It is not only in the Punjab where structural rural changes are occurring. Rajasthan, handicapped by poor natural resources, has launched a systematic program for providing itself with properly trained personnel to staff the new regulated markets that are being established.[44] Gujarat planned to increase the number of regulated markets (1964) from 169 to 200 (18.4 percent), but this is minuscule when compared with the expansion contemplated by other states: Andhra from 94 to 247 (163 percent), Madhya Pradesh from 111 to 255 (130 percent) and Rajasthan from 8 to 74, a ninefold increase. It should be pointed out that it is not only the western states that plan to enlarge

41. In Sangli (Maharashtra) 157 persons and eleven cooperative societies combined their contributions to create the initial capital for an industrial estate. More funds were obtained by the sale of additional shares to the (state) government and to the Life Insurance Company of India. Ninety-four sheds were built within easy walking distance of the regulated-market yard, and in these facilities fifty-six types of enterprises were operating when I visited the estate in 1964. Most of these were agro-industries catering to the needs of nearby farmers and farm families. Altogether 483 persons were employed in the industrial activities carried on in the estate sheds. For further details see my *Market Towns and Spatial Development in India*, pp. 161–162.

42. In Jalgaon (northern Maharashtra), where the activities of the regulated market had outgrown the space available in the original site, a new market yard was being built. Directly opposite the entrance to the new market yard, a 100-shed industrial estate was under construction.

43. For a vivid picture of Sikhism, see Khushwant Singh, *The Sikhs Today: Their Religion, History, Culture, Customs and Way of Life*, Bombay, 1959; or his *A History of the Sikhs*, Princeton, 1963.

44. In 1964, when I visited the training school for regulated market secretaries (conducted at Sangli by the Government of India Directorate of Marketing and Inspection), more than 75 percent of the trainees were Rajasthani.

their regulated-market networks. Bihar projected an increase from 10 to 150, Tripura from 1 to 15, and Kerala from 4 to 64.

What is saddening in India is to contrast those rural landscapes that are being gradually vitalized by better markets, modern processing industries, and dispersed light industries, with the stubborn resistance to change in the densely populated, poorer, and more primitive areas of northeast India.[45] Here one encounters, on the part of both city and village leaders, not so much an inability to institute changes as an unwillingness to do so. Thus the carefully considered proposals, by both Indian and foreign experts, for a planned dispersion of small industrial plants among the twenty-four towns (imperfectly serving almost 12,000 villages) of the Kanpur region were rejected categorically by the spokesmen for the Kanpur business community, whose only counterproposal was that all new industrial plants should be located on the outskirts of their regional metropolis. They seemed singularly unimpressed by suggestions that there was anything functionally inadequate with a near-subsistence farming hinterland for their bloated, slum-cursed city, whose industries were almost dying from lack of wider markets, new capital, advanced technology, and alert, modern management. They were not the slightest bit interested in the areal changes that were occurring in Punjab, Gujarat, and other progressive parts of the Indian economy. Yet for them to see, within easy travel distance, were communities that were being transformed by means of regulated markets, industrial estates, and agricultural-extension programs. For them to visit, were convenient clusters of industries located in market towns within the convenient isochrones of country people from thirty or forty villages; there were shops and small factories making inexpensive commodities within the range of farmers' modest incomes, things country people could see when they came to market. It is the "demonstration effect" of these physical goods—the work shoes, wire screens, farm tools, galvanized pails, or the spectacle frames, kitchen utensils or raincoats—that really provides incentive for better farming and induces an enlargement of almost every farmer's market surplus. Moreover, in a regulated-market yard, only a few paces from the commission-agent offices where farmers receive payment for their

45. For evidence of this apathy or resistance, in the Kanpur region, see *Regional Perspective of Industrial and Urban Growth*, ed. P. B. Desai, I. M. Grossack, and K. N. Sharma, pp. xiv, 10, 21, 78, 96–97, 109, 112, 134, 135, 136, 144, 155, 159, 178–182, 219, 227, 263, 265, 269.

produce, are the retail outlets of the cooperatives. Here farmers can buy fertilizers, pesticides, and other inputs with some of the money they receive for their tumeric, sorghum, rice, or *gur*. Here too are the rodent- and vermin-proof warehouses, where commission men or farmers can store produce in anticipation of better prices, and nearby in the market town are the retail stores, repair shops, restaurants, and banks which are slowly helping to convert the agro-urban communities of western India into functional economic areas.

There is hope in these portions of India because there is vision. Admittedly, the undramatic experiments have none of the programmatic niceties of the Yugoslav attempt to polka-dot a whole national landscape with symmetrical communes. Nor do they have the architectonic qualities of the Israeli efforts to create a graduated enchainment of central places. Indeed, the Indian tentatives even lack the instrumental consistency of the overall Puerto Rican plan. If the Indian experiments have any historical counterparts, perhaps they might be the pragmatic American procedures, essentially local in scope and experimental in method. Like the civic leaders in nineteenth-century America, who adopted any scheme that would work, who had no doctrinaire views about public or private contributions,[46] and who quietly consolidated local sentiment for structural change, some contemporary Indian leaders are earnestly trying to persuade people to join forces and make the kind of local investments that will knit communities together into something that may evolve into genuine functional areas. This empiric process I consider far more promising than the much-publicized but pattern-bound attempts that are being made to integrate spatial economic activities by means of artificially imposed "block" activities, or by the nebulous and amorphous "community development" programs. Whether this commendable, locally inspired, gradualist process can ultimately overcome the total inadequacy of India's central-place matrix is another question. That depends

46. That nineteenth-century America was a classic example of laissez-faire and private enterprise is a long-cherished myth, which no one who can read American history need any longer believe. For documentation concerning the actual role of the state during the nineteenth century, see Oscar and Mary Handlin, *Commonwealth: A Study of the Role of Government in the American Economy: Massachusetts, 1774–1861*, Cambridge, Mass., 1947; Milton Heath, *Constructive Liberalism: The Role of the State in Economic Development of Georgia to 1860*, Cambridge, Mass., 1954; and Louis Hartz, *Economic Policy and Democratic Thought: Pennsylvania, 1776–1860*, Cambridge, Mass., 1948.

on whether functional areas will be created that can transmit part of their dynamism to outlying growth points and, by a process of segmentation, actually propagate some of the urgently needed additional central places.

Two African Efforts at Spatial Innovation: Djoliba and the Volta River Resettlement

Djoliba, Mali. To test the feasibility of a proposal for the ultimate establishment of some 150 rural centers that would service Mali's more than 10,000 villages, the government of Mali, with the assistance of the American Agency for International Development undertook, as a pilot operation, the planned development of a community about 28 miles from Bamako, the nation's capital city. Djoliba was chosen from six eligible sites because its location between the Niger River and the Bamako-to-Guinea road made it "a natural market and distribution center."[47] There seems to have been some disagreement, however, concerning the major purposes of the venture. Thomas Callaway, who has been called "the project's most important propagandist,"[48] avers that the main object was to create a "countermagnet" that would reduce the flow of migrants to Bamako, a rapidly expanding city that was fast becoming unable to house, feed, and care for its rapidly growing population.[49] Bennett Harrison contends, on the other hand, that the Malians' intention was merely to "create a suitable environment for increased, diversified economic development" in one portion of Mali's poor rural landscapes.[50] The issue arose from a rejoinder by William I. Jones to Callaway's account of the project in the *International Development Review.*[51] Jones attempted to demonstrate that urban "congestion costs" in Bamako would be much lower than the cost of "industrial job creation" in country towns. He argued that pilot ventures such as the Djoliba type ought not be undertaken unless

47. U.S. Department of Housing and Urban Development, Division of International Affairs, *Aided Self-Help in Housing Improvement,* Ideas and Methods Exchange No. 18, Washington, 1967, p. 48.

48. Harrison, Bennett. "Rural Growth Centers: A Strategy for the Rural Development of Low-Income Countries," Mimeographed, Washington, D.C., 1967, Chapter 4, p. 10.

49. Thomas Callaway, "A Countermagnet to the Capital: The Case of Djoliba," *International Development Review,* September 1966, pp. 18–21.

50. "Rural Growth Centers," Chapter 4, p. 10.

51. "A Countermagnet to the Capital," pp. 18–21.

it could be clearly demonstrated "that they provide sites for industries and jobs at lower net social (or public) cost than cities can." The expense of providing a country town with power, water, paved streets and housing, Jones said, "must be balanced against the costs of urban congestion."[52]

This was really a rather unfortunate controversy that stemmed from a failure of the disputants to agree on a time horizon. For the short run it may well be that Jones is right, since the cost of creating a job in a country town might, at a given moment of time, be greater than the corresponding urban "congestion cost." But if the problem is viewed over a ten- or twenty-year period, the need for "countermagnets" may become much more apparent. The population of Bamako (about 120,000 people in 1960) already accounts for one-third of Mali's urban population (which is about one-ninth of the country's total population).[53] Were the capital city's poulation to double because there were no countermagnets, congestion costs might rise very sharply, and any short-time advantages the city might now have could be rather rapidly eroded. But congestion cost versus rural-center development cost is really not the essential issue. The bulk of Malians, as Harrison properly emphasizes, are not going to migrate to the capital city.[54] The great majority will remain in the country, and the primary purpose of developing occupationally diversified agro-urban communities ought to be to increase the incomes, widen the occupational choices, and improve the educational and public health facilities of those who do not migrate. Callaway is quite right in asserting that this type of desirable areal development just cannot occur if "the countryside is drained of its youth and skills, making it increasingly difficult to maintain the land, which is the basic wealth of agrarian societies."[55]

At any rate, Djoliba was chosen as the site for a pilot experiment, not only because it had a good agricultural hinterland and was served by road and river transport but because it was far enough away from the capital city so that it would not become a "dormitory" satellite. With about 1,600 people, Djoliba was already a market center for a dozen or more outlying villages and a potential market for many more villages

52. "Congestion Costs and Countermagnets," *International Development Review*, June 1967, pp. 42–43.

53. United Nations, *Demographic Yearbook, 1967*, New York, 1967, p. 140.

54. "Rural Growth Centers," Chapter 4, p. 11.

55. "A Countermagnet to the Capital," p. 18.

on both sides of the Niger River. The problem was how to convert a swollen rural village into an agro-urban community, and the conclusion reached by the Malian authorities and by the United States Agency for International Development (AID) was that this called for several layers of investment. If country people were to be attracted to Djoliba, certain institutions and amenities would be necessary. Accordingly, a mall was laid out near the mosque, and along it were built a permanent market yard, a medical center,[56] and a youth center. The existing school was enlarged, and alongside it a training institute for small industries was constructed. A second layer of investment was devoted to new streets (that would accommodate motor vehicles), to improving sports areas, and to creating a parkland reserve. Beyond the reserved park area, where the industrial facilities were to be located, a third layer of investment was used to build mills for processing millet and corn, oil-crushing presses for producing peanut oil, and a plant for producing animal feed. It was hoped that this basic industrial nucleus would soon be enlarged by the establishment of (private) light industries, but no attempt was made to lure enterprises to Djoliba by tax exemptions or by building an industrial estate, although water, power, and access roads were provided for eight industrial sites. Construction of the processing industries was based on the assumption that farm produce could be attracted from an encircling area with about a 10-kilometer radius.[57] A fourth layer of investment was devoted to housing, and here it seems quite clear that a conscious effort was made to persuade potential migrants that they would be better off in a model rural agro-community than they would be in the overcrowded capital city. The housing program was rather skillfully intermeshed with voluntary work and with technical instruction: some 400 people were allowed to learn rudimentary construction skills on a well-planned rotation basis that still allowed normal farming operations to continue.[58] By 1966, technical training had been expanded in the new institute to include formal training in carpentry, blacksmithery, mechanics, and electricity.

56. This included a two-ward maternity section.

57. The isochronic basis was neatly stated, "Dix kilomètres est une distance raisonnable pour un homme à pied transportant des produits à la communaute et retourner chez-lui le même jour." Thomas Callaway, *Village Development Program: A Report on Djoliba,* U.S. AID/Mali, Bamako, 1963, quoted by Harrison, "Rural Growth Centers," Chapter 4, p. 12.

58. Callaway, "A Countermagnet to the Capital," p. 20.

Paralleling the industrial training program, a master agricultural plan was unfolded for the Djoliba area. New crops such as the Congo bean, excellent for both human nutrition and for poultry feed, were introduced, and encouragement was given to farmers who would grow tomatoes for processing into purée, thereby giving them an "export crop." Poultry husbandry blossomed into a new industry, while better animal feed enlarged the cattle herds and, as a consequence, expanded the leather industry. With improved productivity in the countryside it is expected that marketed surpluses will steadily increase, permitting Djoliba to grow into a regional city of about ten thousand people. Present plans call for making housing available for about three thousand people, each house consisting of three bedrooms and a kitchen, and provided with a granary, adequate storage space, a place for cottage industries, and enough land for kitchen gardens. Residents can either rent these model houses or they can build their own homes in special areas reserved for the purpose. Some twenty-five deep wells have been bored, septic tanks have been built, and about 5 kilometers of drainage ditches are now in operation. Altogether, from 1962 to 1966, about a half million dollars have been spent on this project.[59] What benefits seem to have emerged and what may be expected? Before one shares the skepticism of Jones or the optimism of Callaway, one must examine the limited evidence of emergent benefits. It is probably much too soon to form any dependable judgment, but Harrison has nevertheless tried to do so. He shows first of all that millet production in the Djoliba area has increased (1962–1965) 2½ times and that groundnut output has expanded over 5 times.[60] By assuming that only a little more than half of the increased agricultural output can be attributed to the project, a conservative estimate of the benefit reflected in enlarged farmers' income is reached. To this can be added the benefit from the technical training institute; this would be reflected, at the very least, in the saving of wages previously paid to foreign advisors. Only these two measures of the benefit would more than equal the annual imputed interest on the total investment in the project. Such a calculation, however, does not attempt to appraise the conceivable cumulative impact the project may have on farmers' incentive or on the outlook of people who had not

59. Data from a series of AID reports quoted by Harrison, "Rural Growth Centers," Chapter 4, p. 16.

60. "Rural Growth Centers," Chapter 4, p. 17.

before sensed that changes could be made in the countryside—changes that would affect the welfare of almost every member of a better-organized community. Not least important is a growing awareness that ordinary farm boys can become mechanics or electricians. Jones's short-run calculations, I fear, are very myopic. In Puerto Rico the benefits of dispersed industrialization have sometimes been shown to be more than twenty-five times the costs. Admittedly, Mali suffers locational disadvantages by comparison; even so, the chances are that the Djoliba project will some day pay handsome dividends in net social benefits.

The Volta River Resettlement Program. Far more ambitious than the single pilot venture in Mali was the enforced resettlement of some 80,000 people in Ghana, whose ancestral lands, comprising an area of about 3,275 square miles, are now being engulfed by a widening lake forming above the enormous multipurpose Volta dam.[61] The problem was how all these people, who had been living in some 739 villages, should be resettled: whether they should again be reclustered in village communities of about a hundred people, or whether wholly new kinds of population units should be formed. Since the aluminum plant for which the dam will generate power will require a permanent work force of only about 1,600 people, there was no prospect that the displaced farmers could be absorbed in local industrial activities. It was clear from the time the project was first considered, therefore, that thousands of farmers would have to be resettled somewhere. The problem was finally resolved by a decision to create for the displaced people a "network of rural towns or 'townships' . . . connected . . . with one another and with the rest of the country."[62] Starting in 1962 work began on the construction of new towns and access roads, and about three times as many workers (about 15,000) were employed in these resettlement preparations as were used in building the Akosombo dam.[63] Altogether

61. The main dam, 440 feet high and almost a half mile long, is the world's seventh largest. For a compact but well-documented account of the Volta River project, its history, costs, industrial purposes, and its economic importance, see Tony Killick, "The Volta River Project," in Walter Birmingham, I. Neustadt, and E. N. Amaboe, eds., *A Study of Contemporary Ghana,* Vol. I, *The Economy of Ghana,* London, 1966.

62. Harrison, "Rural Growth Centers," Chapter 4, p. 2.

63. About one-third of the local-currency costs of the Volta dam (Akosombo Hydro-Electric Project) was budgeted for resettlement costs. For estimated cost figures of the project, see Birmingham, Neustadt, and Amaboe, *Contemporary Ghana,* p. 395.

fifty-two new "townships" were selected as resettlement sites. All costs of housing, roads, wells, and other basic facilities were born by the government, and the displaced farmers were given the option of receiving property in the new townships or, if they chose to relocate themselves, compensation for their (flooded) lands at thrice the current market value.[64]

It is interesting to notice the interplay of locational ideas that were involved in the thinking about possible settlement sites, most of which were to be existing villages. Much in the spirit of Christaller, the first test was "centrality"; hence the task was to choose for each township a site with an encircling compass of land that would lend itself to a more modernized type of agriculture than was being typically used in Ghana. A second criterion may well have come out of the Israeli experience: the thesis was that town sites should not engross rich agricultural land and that, consequently, wherever possible, the urban settlements ought to be located on poor land. Admittedly, there were some purely technical determinants of town sites that were stubbornly inflexible: there would have to be a dependable water supply, and the public health authorities were insistent that demonstrably unhealthy places must be avoided.[65] A third factor given careful consideration was transport, since it was assumed that the new spatial pattern would make agriculture much more commercialized than the old near-subsistence type. Here again, one detects a Christaller flavor in the thinking of the planners: the new towns should be related to one another in such a way that a majority of settlements would be on or near major roads.[66] Two other closely related spatial ideas were involved in the preplanning of the new townships: they should be of adequate size to make possible satisfactory scale economies, and they should be interrelated in some logical hierarchical gradation.

As contrasted with the sentimental admiration for village-structured agrarian economies that had muddied thought and stymied progress in so many parts of the world, the concensus in Ghana seems to have been

64. E. A. K. Kalitsi, "Organization and Economics of Resettlement," in *Volta Resettlement Symposium Papers,* Kumasi, 1965, p. 20, quoted in Harrison, "Rural Growth Centers," Chapter 4, p. 3.

65. J. St. George Warmann, "Public Health Problems of Volta Resettlement," in *Volta Resettlement Symposium Papers,* p. 151, quoted by Harrison, *"Rural Growth Centers,"* Chapter 4, p. 3.

66. For Christaller's theoretical solution of the "traffic principle" problem see Chapter 4.

very much in favor of "town-centered" new communities. To reproduce 739 villages made no appeal. A new type of agriculture, it was hoped, would employ machinery for some tasks, and a full utilization of tractors or gangplows would call for spatial patterns larger than single villages. Proper marketing would require all-weather roads, and such access roads would patently be cheaper to build if fewer settlements had to be served. But beyond these technical considerations was the expectation that the new "townships" would interblend agriculture and industry and that machine operators, mechanics, workers in small industries, and an increasing number of people engaged in service occupations would form an important nonagricultural group of townsmen.

After careful resource and land-use studies, and after repeated solicitation of the views of the affected farmers, the Volta River Authority proposed that the fifty-two townships should have central places of four sizes: "central towns" with populations ranging from 8,000 to 10,000; "service centers," 5,000 to 8,000; satellite villages, 5,000 or less; and below these, village clusters. It is evident how similar this pattern was to the D, C, B, and A nuclei proposed by the Israeli planners, and since the "bond between tiny Israel and the vast reaches of Black Africa" has been called "one of the strongest unofficial alliances in the world,"[67] it seems not unlikely that the planners in Ghana were modeling their resettlement program on Israeli precedents.[68] To be sure, the hierarchical model was not slavishly adhered to; rather, as an observer has neatly said, "the model gave a theoretical framework against which proposals [for sites] were weighted."[69] Some towns were enlargements of existing towns, others were built de novo; but when the resettlement operation had been completed, instead of the previous 739 villages there were 52 "new" townships ranging in size from 14 to 816 houses. Since the average new township population has been estimated to be 1,320 persons,[70] almost 69,000 out of the 80,000 displaced persons must have elected to accept supervised resettlement.

The "standard house" with two rooms and with "cooking and sitting" porches had to be modified; consequently the one-room nuclear home

67. "A Surplus of Brains," *Newsweek*, August 20, 1962, p. 44.

68. For a survey of Israel's advisory role in Africa, see Mordechai E. Kreinin, *Israel and Africa: A Study in Technical Cooperation*, New York, 1964, particularly Chapter 4 on "Land Settlement."

69. E. A. K. Kalitsi, "Organization and Economics of Settlement," quoted in Harrison, "Rural Growth Centers," Chapter 4, p. 6.

70. Ibid.

became the typical structure. By 1964 over 11,000 houses had been erected in forty-four settlements, and 275 miles of new roads gave the new towns access to the national highway system. By 1965 all fifty-two settlements had been completed, each with septic latrines and water supply; with primary and middle schools, community centers, civic buildings, and churches; with market yards equipped with selling platforms, granaries and warehouses. To permit fuller use of the agronomic resources of the fifty-two townships, three experimental farms were established where field tests in plant breeding could be made for maize, sorghum, cowpeas, tobacco, and yams, and where experiments for the purpose of improving livestock strains could be carried on. A mechanical cultivation service was also provided by the establishment of eight "machine tractor stations" of the Soviet type, equipped with several hundred tractors and with the appropriate cultivating tools.

It remains to be seen how successful this rather drastic restructuring of the living and working patterns of 70,000 people will be, whether the settlers will adapt themselves to larger social aggregates, or whether the townships will soon subdivide into traditional village communities. It will be interesting to see whether the settlers consider that the advantages of scale can produce benefits that will seem worth preserving. However meritorious it may appear to adopt some device or tactic that promises to transform a rural society quickly and to overcome the poverty, squalor, and illiteracy of the peasants (particularly a plan that appears to make it possible for subsistence farmers to modernize their agricultural technique, thereby benefiting not merely the farm families but the entire national economy), however desirable all these changes may appear, success will ultimately depend on the attitudes of the farmers, their families, and their leaders. The easy, borrowed assumption that peasant proprietors will promptly respond to profit stimuli has been quite properly challenged.[71] My erstwhile colleague Shoa-er Ong of the East-West Center, Honolulu, who is a very close student of small-scale farming, has pointed out that money income is seldom the first goal of the 650 million people who live on 100 million small Asian farms.[72] But may it not be that it is a faulty structure of the agrarian

71. Notably by A. V. Chayanov in his *The Theory of Peasant Economy*, ed. Daniel Thorner, Basile Kerblay, and R. E. F. Smith, Homewood, Ill., 1966. For an opposite view see Theodore W. Schultz, *Transforming Traditional Agriculture*, New Haven, 1964, Chapter 3.

72. "Be he a Muslim, Hindu, Buddhist, Taosit, or Christian or be he a Chinese, Afghan, Indian, Laotian, or Filipino, an Asian farmer operating a small production

economy, both in a land-tenure and in a market sense, that has encrusted peasant thinking? Perhaps the great virtue of an experiment as massive as the Volta River Authority resettlement venture is that it may give a great many farmers, long shackled by the limitations of a near-subsistence peasant economy, an opportunity to visualize alternatives. And whereas the Djoliba experiment in Mali will offer this opportunity to only a single community of 1,600 people, the Ghana resettlement will enlarge the same fortyfold. It is an experiment worth watching.

The International Labour Office Pilot Project in Nigeria: An Exploration of Some Spatial Aspects of Rural Employment Promotion

In Nigeria, as in many other developing countries, some of the unforeseen and unwelcome side effects of a development program have emerged. Increased productivity and resulting higher incomes in the relatively small "modern" sector of the economy have widened the gap between the new and the old, and particularly between the more dynamic parts of the urban economy and the unchanged villages. As the government, with the very best of intentions, has made grade-school education available for more and more rural children, there have arisen an aversion to farming and a hunger for white-collar jobs, which are leading a large number of young persons to seek their fortunes in Nigeria's few and already overcrowded cities. By reducing death rates, public health measures have permitted population throughout the country to increase by over 2 percent annually, probably nearer to 2½ percent. The resulting enlargement of the rural population, far in excess of rural employment opportunities, has led to a rampant surge of hopeful school leavers migrating to the large cities.[73] New agencies for social control to replace the traditional institutions of rural society have not grown up swiftly enough in the burgeoning cities, which are

---

area has four common goals, namely: increased land productivity, expanded family security, maximum farm income and congenial community involvement." "Management Dilemma of Small Farms in Asia," Mimeographed, Honolulu, East-West Center, 1969, p. 27.

73. This polarization of population has occurred in almost all the new African states. Thus, in the short space of seven years, 1955–1962, the population of Monrovia (Liberia) doubled, that of Lusaka (Zambia) tripled, while Nairobi (Kenya) increased by 58 percent, Freetown (Sierra Leone), 65 percent, and Lagos (Nigeria), 36 percent. United Nations, *Demographic Yearbook, 1963,* New York, 1963, Table 6.

now confronted with steadily intensifying problems of slums, crime, delinquency, unemployment, acute poverty, and political radicalism.[74]

These rather unexpected concomitants of what had been considered a well-planned development program led the Nigerian government to seek the help and collaboration of the International Labour Office (I.L.O.) in studying the overall rural employment and manpower situation with the hope that international labor experts might be able to suggest suitable methods for coping with the growing problems of rural unemployment, underemployment,[75] low productivity, and the widening gap between rural and urban per capita income. Plans were accordingly made for a "pilot project" in which all these problems could be studied in depth for several years with the object of exploring and demonstrating "the most effective methods, techniques and schemes . . . for the best possible use of underemployed rural labor with a minimum contribution of scarce capital."[76] But even the first attempt to visualize the task revealed the baffling complexity of the many relevant elements of the problem. Before any prescriptions could be made, the nature of this endemic and increasingly malignant rural economic pathology had to be carefully diagnosed. Essentially this is what the I.L.O. experts, in collaboration with their Nigerian counterparts, have been trying to do.[77]

An I.L.O. Advisory Working Group delineated (without reference to the specific area subsequently chosen for the pilot project) the major factors that were complicating rural employment difficulties not merely in Nigeria but all over Africa.[78] Despite cityward migration, the net growth in rural population was increasing the number of persons

74. Very vividly and succinctly explained in International Labour Office [I.L.O.], Advisory Working Group on Rural Employment Problems in Tropical Africa (English Speaking Countries), "Discussion Guide," Mimeographed, Lagos, 1965, (hereafter cited as I.L.O., "Discussion Guide") pp. 5 ff.

75. P. Mueller and K. H. Zevering, "Employment Promotion through Rural Development: A Pilot Project in Western Nigeria," *International Labour Review*, 100 (August 1969) 113–114.

76. I.L.O., "Pilot Project for Rural Employment Promotion, Western Region of Nigeria: Tentative Plan of Work," Mimeographed, Geneva, 1965.

77. The initial survey plan (March 1963) called for a team leader (who ought to be an economist), one or two agricultural experts, a person with experience in rural cooperative and mutual aid, an expert on small-scale industries, and an expert on rural education and training. For further details, see I.L.O., "Rural Development Programme, Pilot Project for Rural Employment Promotion, Preliminary Project Statement: Nigeria, Mimeographed, Geneva, 1963, pp. 9–12.

78. I.L.O., "Discussion Guide."

dependent on farming. But since techniques and land-tenure patterns have remained virtually unchanged, the consequence has been a reduction in per man productivity, largely because the selectivity of migration leeches away the ablest young people in the most productive age group.[79] Two factors are mainly responsible for this trek to the cities: the inability of young men to see any future in traditional village-centered agriculture, and a snobbish disdain of farming (and indeed of any kind of manual labor) on the part of young school leavers, who, as "educated persons," think they should have only white-collar jobs. Yet, since so many of the migrants actually fail to find continuous employment in cities, what actually happens is that by their migration they are converting rural underemployment into urban unemployment.[80] For, as contrasted with outright urban unemployment, rural underutilization of manpower most frequently takes the form of pervasive underemployment.[81]

This can represent a huge opportunity loss; indeed, it may be one of the greatest obstacles to progress, since it is patently clear that an increase in national output, so urgently needed to raise living standards,

79. Similar to Bulsara's findings in India (*Problems of Rapid Industrialization in India,* Bombay, 1964), the I.L.O. Advisory Working Group concluded that, whereas young school leavers formed the majority of migrants from rural areas, they were, unfortunately, "the core of the urban unemployed," and the report pointed out that a survey by the Food and Agriculture Organization (F.A.O.) *Report on the Possibilities of African Rural Development in Relation to Economic and Social Growth,* Rome, 1962, p. 17, had estimated that the number of unemployed school leavers in Western Nigeria would exceed 800,000 by the end of 1966. I.L.O., "Discussion Guide," p. 6.

80. Ibid., p. 10.

81. The I.L.O. Advisory Working Group report makes a useful distinction between "visible" and "invisible underemployment." "Visible underemployment results from an insufficiency in the volume of employment opportunity," compelling people to cease working for a time altogether (as in seasonal agricultural operations) or to accept an involuntary reduction of working time, a situation that may be caused by any number of factors, among which should be noted a reduction of processing tasks that once were labor-intensive rural activities. "Invisible" underemployment by its very definition is harder to detect and consequently to measure. Either the full skill or the potential energy of a worker is not really used, even though his time may seem to be utilized. In either case, the actual contribution of a worker to national output is only some fraction of his real productive capacity. In Africa such "disguised unemployment" is widespread largely because of a faulty system of land tenure. (For details, see I.L.O., "Discussion Guide," pp. 8–9.) But the migration of school leavers to cities is adding another variety of invisible underemployment; since young persons are, more often than not, unable to find work commensurate with their skills and capacities, they are forced into the less productive city employment.

cannot be achieved unless a nation's resources are fairly well utilized. Yet for a long time to come, in the developing countries of Africa, it will not be possible to employ large numbers of people in industry; consequently, the bulk of the population will "have to find a living on the land." The important question therefore is not how large a fraction of the surplus agricultural population can find industrial work but rather "how fast can the rural sector be developed to absorb as much as possible of the growing labor force."[82] Unfortunately, this most commendable goal is now being unwittingly compromised to an unknown but appreciable extent by Nigeria's educational policy. As the I.L.O. Working Group has pointed out, "if people regard primary education as giving a claim for an urban life, they overestimate their knowledge and misinterpret the prospects of the economy and the needs of the country."[83] A genuine "development" of a country "requires a balanced distribution of the requisite skills," but as long as the present type of pre-emptive urbanization continues, this cannot be accomplished.

From these observations, the I.L.O. Working Group reached certain general conclusions that had much to do with shaping the western Nigerian pilot project. In their opinion very careful thought should be given to labor-intensive techniques, particularly in country towns.[84] They recognized, however, that labor-intensive production methods usually require a relatively larger supervisory force, which may be hard to find and to train. They reminded their readers that I.L.O. studies have shown that whether labor-intensive or capital-intensive production methods will be more economical depends upon a large number of variables, all of which must be carefully evaluated.[85] But since the nub of the Nigerian employment problem is centered in rural areas, fuller utilization of man power might very likely involve "major structural changes," and these structural changes would probably involve the creation of secondary employment in processing, transport, and trade within some more efficient patterns of rural community organization.[86] Lastly, the I.L.O. Working Group took pains to point out that,

82. I.L.O., *"Discussion Guide,"* p. 14.

83. Ibid., pp. 14–15.

84. They noted that capital-intensive techniques are often introduced by management (or technical staffs) trained in industrial countries with labor shortages, and that sometimes ambitious entrepreneurs in countries with redundant labor choose capital-intensive methods merely "for prestige purposes." Ibid., p. 18.

85. Ibid., p. 19.

86. Ibid., p. 20.

whereas the promotion of rural industries can be one of the best ways for "creating permanent non-agricultural employment opportunities for the rural population," cottage industries suffer from a double disadvantage. They normally cater to limited markets and consequently cannot achieve satisfactory economies of scale. When they do attempt to enlarge their operations, they are unable to compete in price or quality with more modern types of production, because their productivity is so low.[87]

At the request of the Nigerian government, the International Labor Office assigned a seven-man team of experts to plan and implement a pilot project. An area for study and experimentation was chosen which would "reflect the major rural employment problems in Western Nigeria," be large enough to test the "impact of various action programmes," include a number of towns that would "function as poles" where the utility of certain institutions could be tested, and have reasonably good communications.[88] By a variety of surveys—of households, agriculture, education, handicrafts, small industries, and public works—a comprehensive overview of the pilot project area was obtained. Comparatively well served with electricity, water, schools, health services, railways, and roads, the area included some thirty market places arranged in a tolerably satisfactory hierarchy. About 138,000 people lived in the area, making the average density about 170 persons per square mile. The density varied considerably, however, for whereas about a fifth of the total population lived in three rural towns with populations ranging from 7,500 to 13,500, about half of the people lived in small villages averaging less than 1,000 people per settlement.

Some 47,000 young people who had been born in the pilot area were living outside the area in 1966. The "hollowing" effect of this outmigration is shown in Figure 10–1. Of the migrants in the two most productive age groups (15 to 19, and 20 to 29), 38.5 percent were from the villages as contrasted with 17.5 percent from country towns. Evidently the towns were acting as partial "countermagnets," although they were net losers of young man power to the large cities. The 47,000 young persons who had left the pilot area were mostly in the prime of

87. Ibid., p. 25.

88. Mueller and Zevering, "Employment Promotion through Rural Development," p. 114. Ecologies best suited for the pilot venture were found within a "transitional zone between the Cocoa Belt and the Savannah," an area that contained most of the towns and half of the population of Western Nigeria. Ibid.

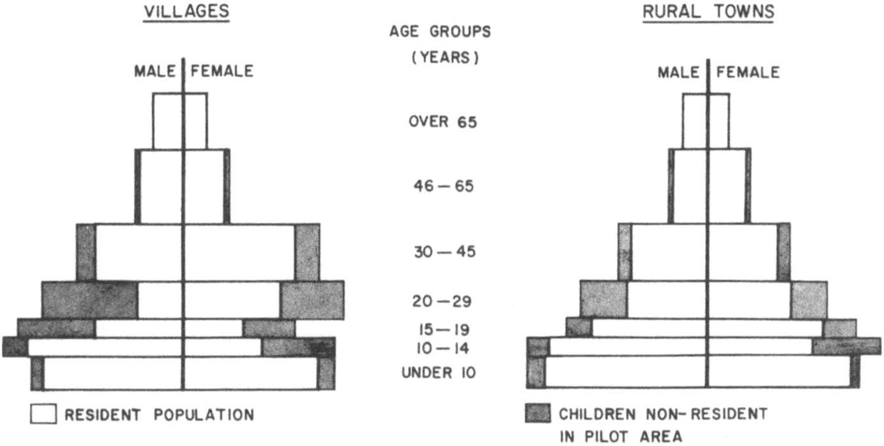

Figure 10–1 Sex and Age Distribution in the Nigerian Pilot Area, 1966
SOURCE: P. Mueller and K. H. Zevering, "Employment Promotion through Rural Development: A Pilot Project in Western Nigeria." *International Labour Review,* 100, No. 2 (August 1969), 116.

their productive years: 57.7 percent in the 15 to 29 age group, and 76.5 percent in the 15 to 45 bracket. (See Table 10–3.) Sixty-one percent of the migrants had gone to the capital city (Lagos), 16.5 percent to the two major provincial cities (Abeokuta and Ibadan). Of the remaining 22.4 percent, about 16.1 percent had migrated beyond the boundaries of the western state, and only 6.3 percent had gone to small places within their own state. Two very evident consequences of out-migration from these Nigerian villages were emphasized by the I.L.O. experts:

Table 10–3 Age and Sex of Migrants from the Pilot Area in Nigeria (percent)

Age	Male	Female	Total by major age group
Under 10	3.6	4.3	
10–14	3.0	8.8	
Total under 14	6.6	13.1	19.7
15–19	9.2	7.1	
20–29	23.8	17.6	
Total 15–29	33.0	24.7	57.7
30–45	8.7	10.1	
46–65	2.1	1.7	
Total each sex	50.4	49.5	

because the young were leaving, the villages now had aging populations; and because the better-educated and more ambitious were moving away, rural productivity was falling.

Over 75 percent of the 36,350 households in the pilot area derived their main income from farming, and in the village communities more than 80 percent of the males were engaged in agriculture. By contrast, for the towns the average percentage of those deriving their income from farming was 44 percent, although in the main commercial center (Ifo Town) less than 10 percent of the male working population was employed in agriculture. Since a considerable amount of agricultural processing and many of the trading activities were performed by women,[89] it was only in the larger villages and the rural towns where any appreciable amount of nonagricultural work for males was to be found. The I.L.O. experts estimated that in villages only 2 percent of the male work force was engaged in artisan, commercial, and service occupations, while in population centers with more than two thousand people this fraction was about 15 percent. From these findings it became quite clear that any improvement in income and employment called for structural changes in the Western Nigerian countryside. To the I.L.O. experts the major problem was how to reduce the ubiquitous underemployment.

As was expected, "open unemployment" was small in the pilot area (probably not more than 1.9 percent of the active population) but underemployment was endemic. Part of it had seasonal causes, and a great deal stemmed from the fragmentation of land holdings.[90] Large acreages were held by land-owning kinship groups, and this engrossing of resources made it difficult for small farmers to enlarge their holdings. The effect of this land limitation was reflected in underemployment. Instead of working seven or eight hours a day, farmers more often spent only four or five hours at their farm tasks. Figure 10–2 shows the I.L.O. estimate of the waste of man power that was occurring. The monthly

89. An I.L.O. study in the pilot area found that 34.7 percent of interviewed women gave "trading in self-processed agricultural products" as their main occupation, while another 29.1 percent said "trading in agricultural produce" was their primary employment. K. Poulsen, *Survey of Women in Some Locations of the I.L.O. Pilot Area,* Ibadan, 1967.

90. An I.L.O. "household survey" found that land under cultivation averaged 4.9 acres per family, and that 65 percent of heads of families had no gainful occupation other than farming. See "Employment Promotion through Rural Development," p. 119.

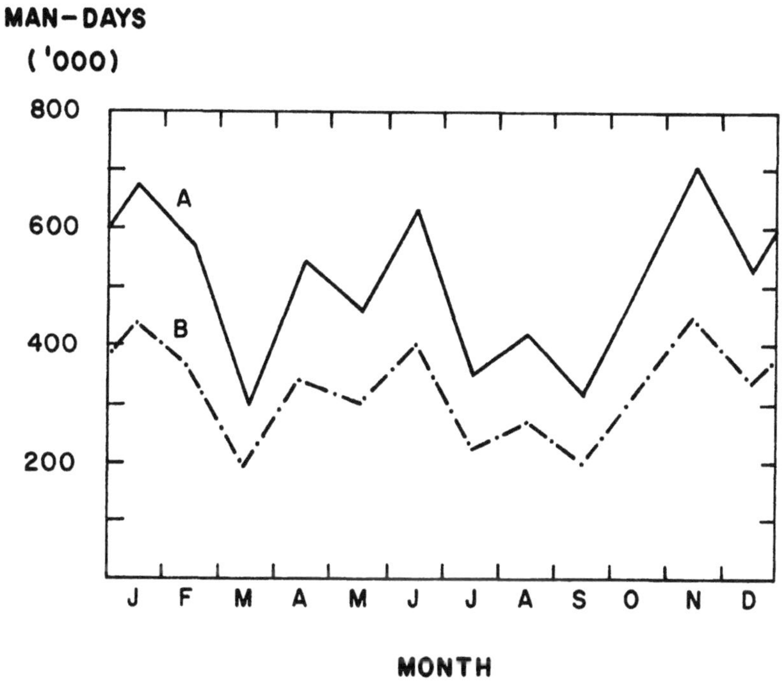

Figure 10–2 Estimated Monthly Distribution of Agricultural Labor Requirements in the Nigerian Pilot Area, based on 1965–1966 crop acreages

SOURCE: P. Mueller and K. H. Zevering, "Employment Promotion through Rural Development: A Pilot Project in Western Nigeria," *International Labour Review,* 100, No. 2 (August 1969), 121.

agricultural labor requirements for the whole pilot area, based on a seven-hour working day, are shown by the A curve, the actual (5.4 hour) inputs in man-days are shown by the B curve, and the deviation of the two curves gives some quantitative measure of the waste of labor time.[91] Since out-migration is not correcting this situation, some rural solution for the underemployment problem, involving some changed village-town reciprocity, would seem to be needed.

91. Although there was, by any reasonable working-day definition, a large surplus of labor over requirements, seasonal work peaks nevertheless created periodical labor shortages. Here three difficulties arose: by reason of petty scale and low productivity, small farmers lacked the cash income with which to hire migratory labor; meantime, the movement of young persons to cities was reducing the town supply of labor that used to work at agricultural tasks; while the "education" of some who remained made them disinterested in farm work.

A theoretical solution is, of course, easy to visualize. If the farm population were to devote the unused time to more intensified farm practices, increments of marketable surplus would be available to feed an enlarged nonagricultural population in the rural towns. The cash incomes thereby derived would give the farmers spending power with which to buy the goods and services proffered for sale by the town-dwelling nonagricultural workers. But whether this conceivable chain of events could materialize would depend on the nature of existing nonagricultural town activities and whether they were capable of expansion. According to the I.L.O. survey there were only about 3,200 craftsmen in the entire pilot area. About 40 percent of these journeymen and apprentices were employed (by 815 small entrepreneurs)[92] in the three larger towns, leaving only about 1,900 in the other twenty-seven market centers. But the distribution of the nonagricultural workers was not the only difficulty; the real trouble was that there were simply not enough industrial, mercantile, and service workers to make it worth while for farmers to apply more labor on their little farms and enlarge their marketed surpluses.

Like the farm population, the craftsmen and small entrepreneurs also suffered from acute underemployment. Farmers, who were their main customers, had money to spend after they had harvested their main crops (cocoa, kola, coffee, citrus fruit, maize, rice, and yams).[93] Moreover, since the more important religious festivals came around harvest time, this introduced another seasonal factor in the farmers' spending cycle. The effect of this on artisan employment was revealed in an I.L.O. survey of 584 small enterprises. In the "slack season," from May to August, 40 percent of the entrepreneurs worked less than three hours a day.[94] The effect of this inadequate and inconstant demand was visibly evident in the poor premises and the primitive equipment of the craftsmen, and was reflected in careless work and low productivity. Young men who wanted to become artisans could therefore get only indifferent apprenticeship training. As the I.L.O. investigators said, "it is not surprising that some 6,000 young people—over 90 percent coming from villages—have taken up an apprenticeship outside the pilot area.

92. If I.L.O. figures are correct, 815 employers were hiring only 1,305 workers, not quite 1.6 employees per enterprise.

93. There were two major farmer income peaks. Arable crops were mostly harvested in August–September; major tree crops (cocoa and kola) in November–January.

94. Mueller and Zevering, "Employment Promotion through Rural Development," p. 123.

Most of them went to the cities to become mechanics, electricians, carpenters or bricklayers."[95] As contrasted with most of the "educated" school leavers (who look with disdain on manual work),[96] the young men who are ready to become apprentices in order to learn a trade are the critical manpower components that the rural areas can least afford to lose.

In approaching the "over-riding problem . . . of low productivity and underemployment" in Nigeria's rural sectors, the I.L.O. experts have isolated the major causes: low yields of tree and field crops, lack of knowledge about better agricultural techniques, unsatisfactory marketing facilities, and inadequate transportation.[97] Yet here is a case where the spatial pattern is fairly satisfactory. In the pilot area, the average population served by the existing market towns would be near 4,500, and the potential clientele of the three largest towns, were they related to smaller towns by some degree of Löschean functionalism, would be around 46,000. Hence, in this context, it is not really the lack of central places that is the seat of the difficulty. The task that challenges the I.L.O. and Nigerian planners is how to develop the central-place functions of the existing central places while concurrently improving farming techniques, so that agricultural productivity will markedly increase and a genuine functional reciprocity between town and country can be established. This will call for more things than feeder roads or regulated markets; it will involve, among other things, new patterns of agriculture that can convince the haughty school leavers that scientific agriculture can be a profession eminently worthy of an "educated" man. The main task is therefore what the I.L.O. experts have called "employment promotion," and for this there are no simple recipes or prefabricated models with magic remedial powers. Instead, there must be a carefully coordinated program of which all the interrelated parts are visualized, phased, manned, financed, and imple-

95. Ibid.

96. "Only 1.3 per cent of children attending the sixth form of primary schools in the pilot area want to take up farming, while just under half of the sixth form pupils in the villages and two-thirds in the rural towns aspire toward some form of professional, technical, administrative or clerical post." Ibid., p. 126.

97. They believe that "open unemployment" can be safely ignored, since so much of it represents a refusal of (nonmigrant) school leavers to take jobs below the status level they think they deserve. Creating work places for this dissatisfied group of young persons would not, in the opinion of the I.L.O. experts, be a wise expenditure. Ibid.

mented with enough flexibility and resilence so that continuous consideration can be taken of the participation of the farmers, artisans, entrepreneurs, and tradesmen, who must be both actors and beneficiaries.

Some of the specific I.L.O. recommendations need listing if only to show the many factors that must be integrated. Better seeds, cultivating techniques, and cropping patterns will require enough extension workers to deal directly with all farmers.[98] But unless feeder roads are planned in such branchlike designs that entire farm areas are linked in suitable isochrones with market towns, there will be no incentives for increased labor-intensity and greater farm output. Open-minded farmers must be found who can be persuaded to make experiments with new crops, improved seeds, and different tillage methods, but the chosen innovators must be people respected by their neighbors for their good judgment. Extension workers must demonstrate that better techniques need not be a change that only large farmers can adopt. Some seasonal unemployment can be meliorated by public works programs, particularly by the construction or improvement of feeder roads, ideally by voluntary village labor—a dream that can easily dissolve. But the I.L.O. analysts have wisely reminded us that "public works are only economic if they are integrated into the overall development plan. Constructing a road without improving agriculture or developing industry which could make use of the road is a waste of resources."[99]

Concurrently, a well-planned action program for the parallel modernization and vitalization of rural towns must be set in motion. It must be recognized that feeble and inconstant demand stemming from the inadequate buying power of the farm population is not the only reason for low productivity among craftsmen and local artisans. Lack of skills, the use of outmoded and inefficient equipment, and an inability to obtain credit in order to enlarge inventories are characteristic handicaps. Intensive training programs can correct the want of skill, while

98. Over 70 percent of the farmers interviewed by the I.L.O. agricultural experts had never seen, much less talked with, an extension worker. Nor is there anything odd about this: only six extension workers had been assigned to the pilot area, although the farms numbered almost 28,000.

99. I.L.O., "Discussion Guide," p. 23. The I.L.O. Advisory Working Group on Rural Employment Problems point out also that public works projects provide only temporary employment; once a specific project is completed, unemployment will re-emerge unless the public works, in conjunction with other structural changes in the local economy, have permanently increased the demand for labor.

the systematic provision of credit can allow craftsmen to buy modern equipment and enlarge their inventories of materials. Education needs to be more closely interrelated with the immediate community objectives, but this does not mean that the whole emphasis should be laid on vocational training. Perhaps the most important task of a school system in a country such as Nigeria is to reveal vistas of creativity, to convince young people that they can become change-agents, and to "detect managerial and entrepreneurial talents"[100] that are so urgently needed in rural towns.

Very wisely, the I.L.O. experts have avoided any inference that there are easy solutions for rural underemployment and the ever-associated low productivity: "Complex measures are required; piecemeal efforts promise but little success."[101] Reasonable output targets must be determined, methods for attaining them carefully chosen, specific activities to be emphasized must be programmed and phased. The main goals toward which the adaptive and flexible program is directed must be constantly publicized, so that more and more people will come to realize that their well-being can be improved not by clinging to a subsistence-oriented agrarian economy but by adopting methods that lead to a progressive expansion of an exchange economy.[102] The defeatist view that poor peasant cultures are not responsive to profit opportunities has all too often been an excuse for inaction. It is understandable that farm families with small land holdings will consider the production of food for family members a first priority.[103] But it does not follow that, because peasants have an instinctive distrust of a market system, they cannot be persuaded by demonstration that they can have both nutritional security and additional income if they produce a marketed surplus. Studies made by the University of Ibadan have shown that

100. "Employment Promotion through Rural Development," pp. 129–130.

101. I.L.O. "Rural Development Programme," p. 2.

102. How such a change in peasant attitude was achieved in a backward Tuscan community has been very vividly explained by C. Pellizzi, "Some Sociological Implications of the Borgo a Mozzano Centre of Agricultural Studies," in L. E. Virone et al., *The Transformation of Rural Communities,* World Land Use Survey, Occasional Papers, No. 7, Tonbridge, 1966, pp. 17–28.

103. When Nigerian farmers in one of the poorer areas were asked whether they thought it was more important to produce enough food for their families or to make a lot of money, 75 percent of the farmers said that food production was more important. Martin Upton, "Recent Changes from Subsistence to Commercial Agriculture in Southern Nigeria," in Virone et al., *The Transformation of Rural Communities,* p. 35.

Nigerian farmers will and do respond to economic incentives. But "the benefit or profitability of an innovation cannot be assessed" unless the efficiency of existing methods is first thoroughly understood by the technical-assistance personnel. Only if an innovation can repeatedly show an advantage will it have a fair chance of adoption—demonstrating that people who live on the thin edge of subsistence cannot afford to take many risks. Asked to explain the difference between "farming" and "agriculture," a Nigerian houseboy answered without hesitation, "farming is what farmers do, agriculture is what the government does."[104] The ambition of the I.L.O. experts is to convince the people in the pilot area that "agriculture" is an activity that farmers can engage in to their increasing advantage.

The Swedish Program of Spatial Reform and of Locational Aid to Disadvantaged Areas

Whereas most countries are confronted with vexing problems that result from high population densities, one of the most troublesome and overriding problems in Sweden stems from a low density of population, in the vast stretches of land north of Stockholm. Historically, thinness of population in northern Sweden resulted from the limited areas suitable for farming and grazing,[105] a topographic factor that led to a dispersion of population in small villages and isolated farmsteads.[106] Tiny fishing villages and small settlements of forest workers and miners further accentuated the demographic dispersion. The consequence was "long distances between farms, between urban centers and between capitals and borderlands." As cities grew, the economy came to be organized around two "core areas," one with Stockholm as the main center, the other dominated by Göteborg.

These core areas as well as a number of smaller provincial centers developed "at the expense of surrounding rural areas and smaller local

104. Upton, *"Recent Changes,"* p. 39.

105. Small patches of land along the coasts, on the shores of inland lakes, in narrow valleys, or on the tops of small hills.

106. T. Hägerstrand, "General Geographical and Economic Background of the Scandinavian Countries," in Organization for Economic Cooperation and Development [O.E.C.D.], "Statements of the Swedish Delegation at the Meeting of 7–9 June, 1967, with Working Party No. 6 of the Industry Committee of O.E.C.D.," Mimeographed, Paris, 1967. For this paper and the others cited in this section I am indebted to Professor Thomas Thorburn of the Stockholm School of Economics.

agglomerations,"[107] and as a result of this dualism, not only are there "certain problems of pressure in the few metropolitan areas" but "problems of unemployment, depopulation and inadequate social and commercial services within the wide, sparsely populated regions."[108] Rural problems in Sweden are probably more acute than in other industrializing countries because small-scale farming and small-scale forestry operations are so seriously hampered by the great intersettlement distances which are imposing ever increasing disadvantages on isolated marginal farms and which led to the closing of some 2,600 scattered sawmills between 1958 and 1965, almost a third of all the mills that were operating in 1958. The rural problem is therefore complicated by inadequate scale, historical dispersion, and technological obsolescence. As profits have declined and local employment has decreased, young people have deserted the stagnating villages, leaving an aging population for whom even a progressive welfare state such as Sweden finds it extremely difficult to provide social facilities and medical care.

Many of the dispersed small settlements now faced with growing unemployment were minuscule industrial centers established to exploit forest or ferrous products, and a large number of them are still dependent on single enterprises. Prudent policy must consider what these small, declining, obsolete industrial centers should become; whether the atrophy now in progress be allowed to run its course; whether young men and women should be encouraged to drift off to the overcrowded core regions; and whether such a negative policy can insure the most beneficial development of the rich natural resources in the sparsely populated areas which comprise almost three-fourths of Sweden's land area. For long-term objectives it might be better to attempt a broader spatial distribution of capital by finding growth points where industries of proper scale could be established[109] and where proper community services—schools, hospitals, utilities, transportation—could then be provided. At once the complex spatial aspects of the problem reveal themselves. It has become very evident that local government boundaries must be revised to permit "better regional control" and to provide more appropriate planning units.[110] Better coordination between

107. Hägerstrand, "General Geographical and Economic Background," p. 8.

108. Ibid., p. 9.

109. R. Olsson, "Regional Policies in Sweden," in O.E.C.D., Statements of the Swedish Delegation," p. 22.

110. Ibid.

different sectors of public activity will be needed—housing, communications, welfare, resource conservation—before suitable types of investment can be induced. Moreover, some agency will have to resolve "complicated conflicts concerning the utilization of natural resources." Someone will have to determine, for example, whether forests should be converted into pulp wood or preserved for recreational purposes.

The first frontal attack on these rural problems was made in 1952 when the Swedish government sharply reduced the number of primary local jurisdictions from 2,500 to just over 1,000. The object of this structural reform was to create "communes" with populations of at least 3,000 people, and only in exceptional cases was a minimum of 2,000 persons to be approved. But as Table 10–4 shows, there were 77 communes in 1952 with less than 2,000 inhabitants and by 1962 the number of these dwarf-sized communes had risen to 118. Indeed, the figures indicate that during the decade of the fifties the number of communes with less than 3,000 inhabitants increased (by almost 17 percent),[111] as did the communes with more than 10,000 inhabitants (by over 5 percent).[112] The little shrinking that did recur took place in communes ranging in size from 3,000 to 10,000 inhabitants.

Many critics of the local government program argued that the 1952 revision was "not radical enough," and as the number of small communes increased, this feeling was reinforced. Moreover, there were

Table 10–4 Distribution of Swedish Communes by Population Size

Inhabitants	1952	1962	Change in Number
Less than 1,999	77	118	+41
2,000–2,999	249	273	+24
3,000–3,999	252	205	−47
4,000–4,999	147	120	−27
5,000–5,999	85	81	− 4
6,000–9,999	131	118	−13
10,000–14,999	40	42	+ 2
over 15,000	56	69	+13
Total	1037	1026	−11

SOURCE: R. Olsson, "Regional Policies in Sweden," in O.E.C.D., "Statements of the Swedish Delegation at the Meeting of 7–9 June, 1967, with Working Party No. 6 of the Industry Committee of O.E.C.D., Mimeographed, Paris, 1967, p. 25.

111. Ibid., p. 25.

112. Of the 1,037 communes in 1952, the truly rural communes numbered 816, and more than a third of these had populations of less than 3,000 inhabitants.

reservations about the means which had been employed to reduce the number of local government units from 2,500 to 1,037. All too often several settlements were merely combined to bring the population up to an acceptable minimum, and the result was that in these communes there were "no natural centers where administrative and commercial functions could be located."[113] It became more and more evident that the 1952 revision had been inadequate, and for several main reasons.

In terms of population most of the new communes are still too small to be able to finance the nine-year compulsory schooling or to care for the aged "in a socially acceptable and rational economic manner."[114] Because the communes near expanding cities are legally separate jurisdictions, they are unplanned or badly planned, and their random growth prevents the formulation of any coherent plan for urban areas that from a functional standpoint should become single entities. Far too little attention had been paid in the 1952 consolidation to economic geography and demography. In view of these considerations the general opinion at the end of the fifties was that "a population base of 6,000–7,000 was the minimum number of inhabitants for the proper functioning of a civic administrative unit."[115] Accordingly, in the autumn of 1959 the government appointed a commission to ascertain whether further redesigning of local government areas was needed. The commission reported that a revision of local government boundaries "was a matter of the utmost urgency"[116] but strongly recommended that changes "should not be imposed from above," since really functional areas could only come into being if very close cooperation between neighboring areas was amicably achieved.

Out of the commission's recommendations came the idea of a new spatial pattern based on the *kommunblock,* the presumption being that blocks of communes would gradually be formed by joint planning and by means of a collaborative and voluntary process of amalgamation of existing communes. As a target, the commission proposed that by 1975 a population of 8,000 should be the "lowest permissible number of inhabitants for the new communes."[117] The general plan of reorganiza-

113. R. Olsson, "Regional Policies in Sweden," p. 23.

114. Ibid., p. 24.

115. Ibid., p. 24. It will be noted from Table 10–4 that 797 communes out of 1,026 in 1962 (77.6 percent) had less than 6,000 inhabitants.

116. Ibid.

117. Ibid., p. 27. The responsibility for making initial projections of the new blocks of communes was assigned to the governor's office of each län (administrative area), but any amalgamation plan required the approval of the merging communes.

tion was approved by the Swedish *Riksdag* in 1962. Consultations with communes began promptly, and by April 1964 plans for the new commune blocks were accepted by the Swedish government. As Table 10–5 indicates, the plan called for the division of the entire Swedish landscape into 282 commune blocks, with median populations of about 17,500 persons. The target of 8,000 as the "lowest permissible number of inhabitants" was considered achievable in all except 27 blocks, most of which would be those located in thinly populated areas where transportation facilities were very inadequate.

Table 10–5 Swedish Commune Blocks: The 1964 Projections

Inhabitants	Number	Percent	
4,000– 5,999	8	2.8	
6,000– 7,999	19	6.7	
8,000– 9,999	49	17.0	
10,000– 14,999	75	26.6	56.4
15,000– 19,999	36	12.8	
20,000– 29,999	33	11.7	
30,000– 49,999	36	12.8	
50,000– 99,999	19	6.7	
100,000–800,000	7	2.5	
Total	282		

SOURCE: R. Olsson, "Regional Policies in Sweden," in O.E.C.D., "Statements of the Swedish Delegation at the Meeting of 7–9 June, 1967, with Working Party No. 6 of the Industry Committee of O.E.C.D., Mimeographed, Paris, 1967, p. 25.

NOTE: It will be noticed (last column) that 56.4 percent of the projected commune blocks would have from 8,000 to 20,000 inhabitants.

By the end of 1967 amalgations affecting 167 communes had taken place.[118] The total number of communes had therefore fallen from 1,026 (in 1962) to less than 900, and consolidations had already created 64 "blocks." The integrating process is therefore in motion, and there is every expectation that a great many more amalgamations will occur by 1970. In 1967 a commission recommended that the number of läner (counties) should be reduced from twenty-four to fifteen with the view of creating better administrative units and, presumably, more efficient functional economic areas. But any changes in provincial structure must

118. Ibid., p. 27.

await careful analysis of population trends and tenable forecasts of regional economic development.[119] In both commune amalgamation and in county restructuring, estimates will need to be made concerning the probable expansion of built-up areas as well as the growth of motorized commuting. As in other modern countries, many new industrial installations in Sweden are now being located at a considerable distance from built-up areas. Secondary investments in housing, utilities, schools, and shopping areas are thereby made necessary, and all too often new centers have been very imperfectly planned. As more industrial installations become necessary, far more careful planning will become increasingly important.[120]

It will be evident from Figure 10–3 that the restructuring of Swedish landscapes resembles the structural changes that have occurred in Yugoslavia, where, by a process of unification, the number of opštine were reduced from 7,085 to 581.[121] Two contrasting aspects of the Swedish reforms should, however, be noticed. In the first place, the emphasis in Sweden has seemingly been more with administrative rationalization than with economic vitalization; and, secondly, it has been mainly in the more compactly settled areas such as Skåne (see Figure 10–3) that scale economies and market perimeters have been rationalized. Rather little attention seems to have been paid to the creation of an interlinked urban hierarchical structure. Furthermore, it is not clear that the programmed reduction in the number of communes has greatly increased areal employment in the face of a persistent trend toward the closure of small, dispersed, marginal plants.[122] Yet the acid test of the national and local benefits of spatial reorganization will be the capacity of the new commune blocks to absorb more and more of the labor that is being steadily displaced. The "power of the man-power policy"[123] to find new and profitable employment for the now re-

119. This research is now in progress. For a description of types of calculations that have been made since 1965, see Olsson, "Regional Policies in Sweden," p. 29.

120. It has been estimated that southern Sweden will need between thirty and sixty new industrial clusters during the next two decades, comprising nuclear power plants, oil refineries, tank farms, oil depots, pulp mills, and paper mills. The location of these complexes cannot be left to chance.

121. See Chapter 9.

122. Between 1956 and 1964 an average of 80 factories were closed each year, while in 1966 over 10,000 workers lost their positions as 220 factories suspended operations. See C. Canarp, "Regional Development Policy in Sweden as an Instrument for Manpower Policy," in O.E.C.D., "Statements of the Swedish Delegation," p. 33.

123. Canarp, "Regional Development Policy in Sweden," p. 33.

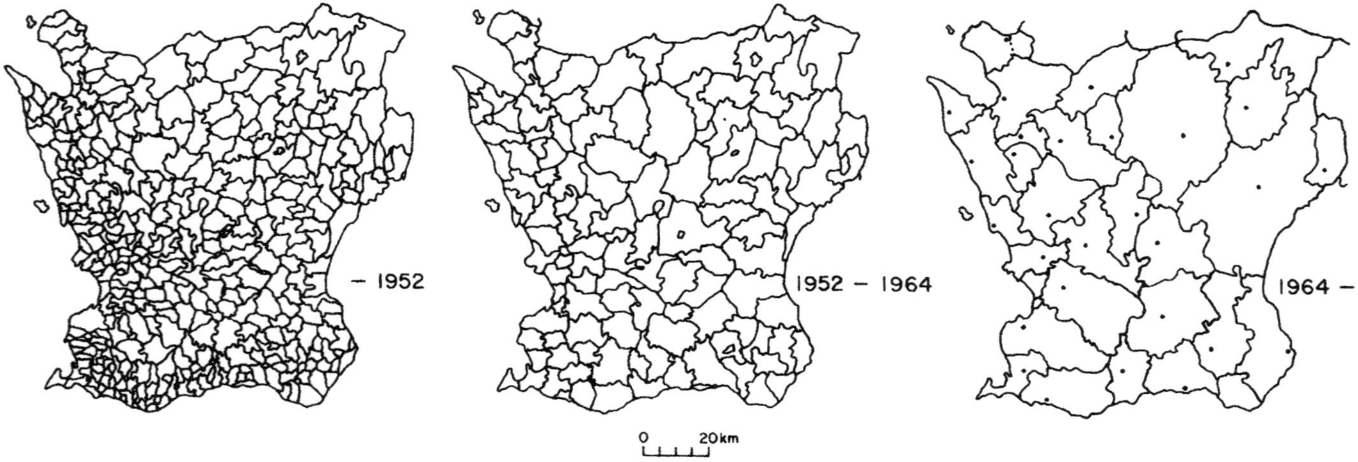

Figure 10–3 The Communes in Skåne, Southern Sweden

SOURCE: O.E.C.D., "Statements of the Swedish Delegation at the Meeting of 7–9 June, 1967, with Working Party No. 6 of the Industry Committee of O.E.C.D.," Mimeographed, Paris, 1967.

dundant labor in the declining or distressed areas is therefore being tested.

Since the old traditional small-scale industrial operations are failing in the forest and mining areas of northern Sweden, there seem to be some reservations among the experts as to whether economic incentives can be developed that will attract new private industry to distressed areas or enlarge, modernize, and vitalize already existing industries. Canarp, for example, feels that in northern Sweden the employment problems "cannot be solved only through measures aimed at creating new job opportunities" and argues that a concurrent object of manpower policy" must be to promote the mobility of labor from the northern regions to the expanding regions in central and southern Sweden."[124] Public works expenditures for roads, schools, and drainage systems offer only a "temporary solution to the employment problem." It was for this reason that the Swedish Parliament, in fiscal years 1963–1964 and 1964–1965, authorized an expenditure of 50 million Swedish crowns for the construction of industrial buildings "to be rented or transferred to private firms on easy terms."[125] But this would seem a modest experiment with a device which Puerto Rico has found to be very useful in luring enterprises to labor-redundant areas. Other tentatives were equally cautious. The government authorized the Labour Market Board to use some of its investment funds for regional development. When the foregoing expedients seemed to make an inadequate impact on the stagnating northern Swedish economy, the government, beginning in July 1965, made available investment grants and loans to enterprises prepared to open new ventures or to expand existing ones. For a five-year period 60 million crowns were made available annually in investment grants and 100 million annually in the form of loans.[126] A detailed ordinance on "state location aid" stipulates how these grants and loans are to be administered. Grants may be used to cover up to 35 percent of the costs of constructing, enlarging, or converting buildings or plants, whereas loans are given for the purchase of machinery and tools. Exemption from payment of interest

124. Ibid., p. 35. Canarp points out that from 1960 to 1965 more than 10,000 persons per year have obtained special transfer grants (when they have taken jobs in central or southern Sweden) and that over 75,000 people, representing 5.5 percent of the total population of the northern Swedish provinces had moved south in search of work.

125. Ibid., p. 36.

126. Ibid.

may be granted for a maximum of three years and relief from amortization payments for a maximum of five years.[127]

It has been estimated that since 1963 some 23,000 new jobs have been created,[128] that about 630 establishments have been assisted, and that over 2,000 million crowns have been invested in building and machinery. These figures suggest that the average investment needed to produce each new job has been in the neighborhood of 100,000 crowns (about $20,000). About a fourth of the new jobs were in newly established enterprises, while the remainder were the result of enlargement of existing plants, and about 60 percent of the new jobs emerged in the metal and engineering industries. These rather modest achievements lead one to believe that the number of growth points in northern Sweden are relatively few. Careful studies of the Labour Market Board seem to indicate that the really promising communities (classified as A centers) may not exceed twenty. These centers, with population levels of over 30,000, seem to account for about 75 percent of the new job opportunities.[129] It is therefore these relatively few growth points that might become the centers of emergent functional economic areas. Hence efforts are being made to encourage the migration of rural man-power to these centers rather than to the southern Swedish core regions.[130]

It is in these A centers that a really purposeful interaction between the process of administrative amalgamation and the program of "location aid" has a possibility of achievement. The creation of commune blocks has not only increased the size of market areas but strengthened the "centrality" of the emergent areal business centers. Swedish economists are devising statistical procedures[131] that will more accurately reflect the resource base of the A centers and are computing data which will make possible tolerably accurate economic and demographic forecasts. Most important, of course, is the need to evaluate the investment prospects, since employment promotion will obviously depend on

127. Ibid., p. 37. These investment incentives are offered to foreign individuals or corporations as well as to Swedish subjects.

128. About 17,500 in the aided areas and about 5,500 in other parts of the country. Ibid.

129. Ibid., p. 39.

130. This involves the training or retraining of workers for unfamiliar jobs and a considerable improvement of the infrastructure in the A centers.

131. R. Olsson, "Investigations and Research for Regional Development in Sweden," in O.E.C.D., "Statements of the Swedish Delegation," p. 42.

the expanding volume of prudent investment. Yet the spatial problem is not merely an enterprise problem, resolvable in terms of costs and profits. It is fully as much a sociological problem, and Swedish scholars are giving a great deal of thought to this dimension. They are asking what pattern of urbanization should Sweden seek, what relations should exist between "the level of training and urbanization,"[132] what size of region will offer suitable "openings in life" for individuals. On all these facets of spatial restructuring more research is needed. What is envisaged is "a physical organization model for an urban community" that will comprehend lines of communication, places of work, dwellings, teaching, curative institutions, and recreational facilities as well as shops and service centers. What is needed, in short, is a critical appraisal of the economic, sociological, and psychological effectiveness of alternative forms of spatial organization.[133] By conducting this type of research, the Swedish scholars are again demonstrating their capacity for intellectual pioneering.

132. Ibid., p. 44.
133. Ibid., p. 45.

CHAPTER 11 SOME GUIDELINES FOR SPATIAL POLICY

Rejecting Myths and Obsolete Doctrines

In an activity as complex and many-sided as economic development it is understandable why preconceptions, aspirations, fears, hopes, dreams, and longings can color attitudes and influence public policy. Because of the deep emotions which the vision of human betterment can excite, a host of myths have grown up. But not all have aspirant or romantic origins; some are the unfortunate offsprings of simplistic theories that promise easy routes to growth and development; some have hidden political purposes; while others are poorly disguised efforts to protect the interests of the privileged. From all these origins the folklore of development is growing so rapidly that whole books will soon be needed to describe it. Almost all developing countries are becoming pluralistic, and as a consequence a growing number of interest groups become increasingly articulate. Some of the mythology of development has origins in the egocentric views of entirely well-meaning but anthropologically untrained, technical "experts" from "mature" countries who fail to understand why Asians, Africans, or South Americans refuse to adopt techniques that have proved so useful in Peoria (Illinois), Montgomery (Alabama), or Stuttgart (Germany). Out of such incomprehension other myths are derived about why underdeveloped countries are underdeveloped. Among more sophisticated specialists there is another somewhat similar reason for the pervasive tendency to oversimplify the prescriptions for social and economic change. Few economists, political scientists, and even fewer students of public administration have devoted much time to the study of history. Yet history, and particularly economic history, is mostly a record of development, laden not with lessons but with data, evidence, or information concerning episodes and experiments chronicling the successes and failures of plans and policies. All too many designers of development plans have approached their complex tasks woefully underprepared, and sometimes they have therefore found it necessary to invent imaginary economic history to justify their policy recommendations.

Faced with this encircling and ever growing folklore and mythology of development, it is not easy for policy makers in developing countries to deal forthrightly with problems of spatial restructuring. Among the many troublesome myths that they must try to dispel there are, I think, seven beliefs that are extremely persistent and probably the most antagonistic to constructive policies. Together these seven myths form a subtle, albeit naïve, argument for rejecting any and all proposals for industrial dispersion or for better spatial patterns of villages, towns, and cities. Merely by listing them one can see how they are intertwined. There is (1) the village myth, a belief that small human aggregates have mysterious social, political, economic, and spiritual values that must be preserved. Closely linked is (2) the thesis which avers that where landholdings are small and population pressure strong, agriculture can never be commercialized. Since the village ought not be supplanted, and since the subsistence farm can be only marginally changed, development cannot begin in rural areas. Change must therefore (3) originate elsewhere, in cities of core regions, and "trickle down" to peripheries. Moreover, virtually all changes that induce growth will (4) be a result of industrial investment, and the greatest transforming effect will be derived from large-scale industrial ventures which can (5) always be best advanced by private enterprise. The coexistence of relatively few large cities and thousands of small villages will create no special problems, since migration is constantly redistributing manpower in a rational way, and if (6) education is made widely available every person will ultimately find his proper place and progress will be assured, provided (7) democratic processes are inculcated into the villages by programs of community development. But, as my foregoing chapters have demonstrated, the reality does not square with the folklore, and the worst trouble is that myths are so much easier to invent and to propagate than to challenge or disprove. Yet, unless policy makers are prepared to reject the persuasive, fanciful, and misleading folklore of development, the long overdue spatial restructuring of the underdeveloped world that is so urgently needed to achieve any tolerably satisfactory improvement in efficiency and output will be so limited, so slow, or so territorially unpredictable and accidental that any modernization that does occur may easily be neutralized by the deepening stagnation of the unchanged backwaters.

The village myth is probably the most firmly entrenched and the hardest to dispel. As I have already mentioned, Mahatma Gandhi, more than anyone else, popularized this romantic myth which, in true folklore fashion, allegedly explains how once happy, creative, and harmonious village communities were rendered wretched, listless, and insecure because they quite innocently fell into a trap set for them. Scheming imperialists, by proffering cheap factory-made consumer goods, skillfully persuaded hapless villagers to abandon their traditional creative craftsmanship and become producers of raw materials and other primary goods whose prices could be maliciously manipulated by foreigners. There is no way of knowing how much of this fanciful story Gandhi himself believed. Nor does it matter. The object of the fabrication was to convince the leaders of over half a million villages that they should join the independence crusade, since Gandhi knew full well that without the support of the rural people, who constituted 85 percent of the subcontinent's population, passive resistance could never succeed. Very artfully, then, the village myth has become a subtle form of political propaganda, and as such it has been used in many other countries in "liberation" programs. The cult of the village soon begins to grow, flattering every village headsman, who can now justify his inherited or usurped authority by explaining that the nation's progress depends on his local leadership. The outcome has been that a specious theory of development has very often been used to confirm the privileges of landlords who rack-rent their poverty-stricken tenants and of village moneylenders who keep their borrowers in a condition of permanent debt peonage. Yet it is not wholly such shameless chicanery that perpetuates the cult of the village. To many national planners it seems quite hopeless to even dream of supplanting the thousands of villages that historical forces have multiplied and dispersed. Like Everest, the village is there! Perhaps it can be modernized, democratized, and regenerated by schools, health centers, or local cooperative societies. Oddly enough, however, all the valiant efforts and all the resources devoted to "community development" on a village basis have their policy origins in an essentially defeatist doctrine. Since the villages exist, all one can do is to help them. But this path leads nowhere. In the world as now economically organized the village of four or five hundred people is an archaic extravagance that a developing country really cannot afford. It wastes land, limits capital formation, and above all misuses manpower. The right policy implications are very clear: villages must be progressively integrated into larger functional economic units. But this process, so urgent, so potentially meliorative, cannot even begin until policy makers are prepared to expose the village myth and are willing to retrain leaders and restrain misleaders.

The folklore surrounding subsistence farming confronts the policy makers with a rather different challenge. Here the allegation is that peasant farmers by reason of certain quaint psychological quirks will not respond to price incentives and that by their stubbornness and incompetence they not only hinder macroeconomic development but, by clinging to their traditional *petite culture,* prevent any rational restructuring of rural landscapes. This is a complicated, treacherous subject, which the unitiated should scrupulously avoid; hence, all I dare do is to venture a few comments borrowed from close students of subsistence agriculture. The studies of Sol Tax have shown that Guatemalan Indian farmers "are remarkably efficient in allocating the factors at their disposal"[1] and that within the market structures in which they live they "are always looking for a new means of turning a penny." Thus, a farmer buys goods he can afford "with a close regard for price in various markets" and "calculates with care the value of his labor in producing crops for sale or for home consumption."[2] By standard terminology this agrarian economy is "traditional," and it is presumably for this reason that the farmers are extremely poor. Yet Professor Tax found no evidence that Guatemalan small farmers were indifferent to any opportunities for improving their output or their income; instead, they were constantly "on the lookout for new and better seeds, fertilizers, ways of planting." W. David Hopper's findings in an Indian village are remarkably parallel to those of Professor Tax. In the village that Hopper studied, resources were used with great

1. *Penny Capitalism,* Smithsonian Institution, Institute of Social Anthropology, Publication No. 16, Washington, 1963, analyzed and interpreted in Theodore W. Schultz, *Transforming Traditional Agriculture,* New Haven, 1964, pp. 41–44.

2. Tax, *Penny Capitalism,* p. 13.

skill: "age-old techniques have been refined and sharpened by countless years of experience."[3] By a very precise algorithmic method, Hopper tested the rationality of factor allocations in relation to actual prices and reached the conclusion that there is "no evidence that an improvement in economic output could be obtained by altering the present allocations as long as the village relies on traditional resources and technology."[4] A third study by Raj Krishna explained the supply responses of Punjab farmers to market demand for a new crop (cotton) which they could produce after an irrigation canal had brought water into their community.[5] Krishna discovered that the time lag involved in shifting from grain to cotton in the Punjab was just about what it had been for farmers in the United States to make a similar transition. The myth about the unresponsive subsistence farmer, therefore, doesn't seem to square with the facts. The trouble is not that the subsistence farmer lacks pecuniary motivation but that he lives within a spatial land-tenure and market system which holds down the scale of his operations. He does not need education or psychological reorientation; what he lacks is a wider market system in which his uncanny skill in combining productive factors can be more profitably exercised.

The thesis that economic change cannot begin in agrarian sectors but must always "trickle down" from industrial and urban core regions is not only an article of faith among the city-dwelling bourgeoisie; unfortunately, it is also a doctrine that has become the "conventional wisdom" of scores of influential planners and model builders. From it springs a salutary neglect of agriculture in development programs that shrewd and really expert observers bemoan.[6] Two historical events should throw doubt on the confidently predicted metropole-periphery progression of economic development. There are countries such as Den-

3. "The Economic Organization of a Village in North Central India," Ph.D. dissertation, Cornell University, 1957, quoted by Schultz, *Transforming Traditional Agriculture,* p. 45.

4. Ibid., p. 47.

5. "Farm Supply Response in the Punjab: A Case Study of Cotton," Ph.D. dissertation, University of Chicago, 1961, quoted by Schultz, *Transforming Traditional Agriculture,* p. 50.

6. See Schultz's penetrating criticism of "growth economists" who have "been producing an abundant crop of macromodels that are . . . neither relevant in theorizing about the growth potentials of agriculture nor useful in examining the empirical behavior of agriculture as a source of wealth." *Transforming Traditional Agriculture,* p. 6.

mark where change originated in rural areas in the face of strong urban opposition; there are also dozens and dozens of instances where, despite an expansion of core-region centers, development has shown no signs of trickling down even to nearby peripheries.[7] What normally occurs when investment and planning emphasis is laid on urban centers and core regions is "a marked polarity between the dynamic metropolis and the unchanging village," not because the city cannot be a change agent but because there is no true linkage between village and metropolis. P. B. Desai put the issue in sharp focus when he said that development cannot be expected unless the polarity of metropolis and village is "replaced by a functionally integrated hierarchy of communities of varying size."[8] To wait for a prophesied, automatic seepage of benevolent transforming effects from great cities to rural villages may exacerbate an already unhappy situation. Wise policy makers will "seek out a functionally efficient level of synchronization between two spatial patterns of distribution of economic activity and of population."[9] "The major thrust of regional policy," say Berry and Prakasa Rao, "should be the fight to offset polarization, to eliminate the dichotomy," because it is only by bringing into existence "a complete spatial system of urban centers arranged in a hierarchy from agro-urban towns through several intermediate types to the metropolis that growth and development can be achieved."[10] But unless the euphoric, though false, myth of urban magnetic fields that automatically diffuse development is

7. Any number of cases could be cited, but this quotation from two perceptive geographers is apposite: "Conventional regional growth theory suggests that continual urban-industrial expansion in major central cities should lead to catalytic impacts on surrounding regions. Growth impulses and economic advancement should 'trickle down' to smaller places and ultimately infuse dynamism into even the most tradition-bound peripheries. But this has not occurred in India and particularly not in Andhra Pradesh." Brian J. L. Berry and V. L. S. Prakasa Rao, "Urban-Rural Duality in the Regional Structure of Andhra Pradesh," Mimeographed, Chicago, n.d., p. 16. Neither has it occurred in most Latin American states.

8. "Points for Consideration of the Research Cell," International Seminar on Urban and Industrial Growth of Kanpur Region, Mimeographed, Kanpur, December, 1966, p. 4.

9. Ibid.

10. Berry and Prakasa Rao, "Urban-Rural Duality," p. 17: "It is through such a system that growth impulses can be transmitted downward into the rural areas, with larger centers retaining activities of greater scale and capital intensity, and smaller centers acquiring functions that can be performed at lesser scale for more rural markets or in which the capital-labor ratio is low, and with all centers, as to the limits of their ability, spreading growth into their hinterlands."

dispelled, the tough, up-hill job of creating the needed intermediate urban structure cannot even be programmed, much less begun.[11]

No one will quarrel with the thesis that men who are equipped with tools are more productive than men who work with their bare hands; nor will anyone deny that workers who have better tools can produce more than workers with poor tools. Investment in tools, machines, or any other form of equipment is therefore an essential ingredient in any development program. But what form this labor-assisting capital should take and how much of the investment should be in industrial capital, how much in infrastructure, and how much in agriculture tools, farm equipment or other rural productive facilities is not so easily answered. Because "developed," or "mature," countries possess large amounts of industrial capital, all too many envious people in "underdeveloped" countries assume that the relative amount of industrial capital is indisputable proof of the wisdom of devoting a lion's share of savings to industrial capital formation. It seldom occurs to them to ask whether it might not be the level of development that has permitted the growth of industrial capital. An underdeveloped country needs better tools in every economic sector, and since the great bulk of the active population is engaged in agriculture, it is entirely possible that the best yield on limited investment funds can be obtained by giving farmers better tools. "There is no longer any room for doubt whether agriculture can be a powerful engine of growth," writes one of our wisest agricultural economists; but in order to acquire such a growth-making engine, "it is necessary to invest in agriculture."[12] Yet, because of a prevailing belief in the peculiar, almost magical transforming powers of large industrial establishments, the allocators of capital in national or state planning departments (in which farmers and small businessmen are seldom if ever represented) may actually be making quite unwise decisions by following wholly inapplicable investment patterns modeled on those countries that already have a modernized agriculture and a very elaborate network of small business enterprises. The most effective use of a large share of a developing nation's scarce investment funds might be in small indus-

11. For a very carefully reasoned regional example which precisely defines the nature of this task, see Brian J. L. Berry, "Policy Implications of an Urban Location Model for the Kanpur Region," in *Regional Perspective of Industrial and Urban Growth,* ed. P. B. Desai, I. M. Grossack, and K. N. Sharma, Bombay, 1969, pp. 203–219.

12. Schultz, *Transforming Traditional Agriculture,* p. 5.

tries[13] located in market towns and small cities, rather than in huge industrial complexes or in large-scale metropolitan industry.[14] But once again, someone must challenge the myth makers who have ascribed to large-scale industrial establishments puissant and mysterious developmental powers.[15]

The private enterprise fixation is part prejudice, part myth. The prejudice stems from a theory of human motivation, the myth from a misreading of history. It is, of course, a well-recognized fact that people husband private property more carefully than they care for communal property and that the prospect of personal gain does provide an incentive for diligence, industry, and saving. But it does not follow, Adam Smith notwithstanding, that a private-enterprise economy will necessarily generate the best type of overall development. Nor is it correct to assert that the historical record proves that growth and development have consistently occurred where the private sector was given free range and where government performed only limited functions. As the annals of economic history are critically reviewed, it becomes increasingly evident that vigorous development has in the majority of cases been the consequence of variable mixes of private enterprise and governmental subvention or assistance.[16] The advocates of private enterprise, who allege that the only dependable recipe for development is to grant complete freedom for investors and entrepreneurs to make all planning decisions, and who inveigh so emotionally against the "errors" of socialism, fail to recognize that it may

13. For a well-documented account of the historical role of small industrial enterprises in facilitating a transition to modern economics, see Eugene Staley and Richard Morse, *Modern Small Industry for Developing Countries,* New York, 1965, Chapter 6. For an analysis of "overly aggregative" and often "inapplicable" growth models "derived or based on Western European or North American" doctrines, see Laurence Hewes, *Study on Integrated Rural Development,* Geneva, 1969, pp. 41 ff.

14. It is not accidental that Småland, one of the provinces of Sweden, which was among the poorest in the latter part of the nineteenth century is now an area of vigor and prosperity. In a single small town, Anderstorp, with but 3,700 inhabitants there are 134 industries. Most of Småland's thousands of factories have fewer than fifty workers and "make everything from furniture and plastic goods to hinges and coat hangers." For details see Donald S. Connery, *The Scandinavians,* London, 1966, pp. 353–354.

15. Admittedly there are very real scale economics that enlargement of plant and firm size make possible. But as Joe Bain has shown (*Industrial Organization,* New York, 1968) it is seldom the largest plant or the largest firm that has the lowest unit costs.

16. See Chapter 10, n. 46.

be private enterprise that has kept and is keeping underdeveloped countries underdeveloped. Landlordism, which in so many countries is extortionate and heartless, is private enterprise; so are usurious money lending and skinflint village trade monopolies. Private enterprise has had adequate trial time to demonstrate whether it can by itself produce a market system that will supply incentives for "traditional" farmers and lead them to restructure their landholdings so that they can, with their acknowledged diligence and skill, increase their marketed surpluses. It has had time enough to show whether it can diversify rural occupations and thereby give scope and range for human talent; time enough for observers to see whether it can create a hierarchy of central places that can make possible, by a variety of facilities, a truly efficient organization of an economic landscape. The private enterprise myth must therefore be challenged for the very simple reason that the conventional wisdom derived therefrom has failed to develop the world's economic backwaters.

But education and democracy are generally conceded to be essential prerequisites for functional economic areas, and surely no myths can possibly falsify or distort their importance. Once again, unfortunately, the trouble is basically spatial. Education can indeed be a positive good, but its effectiveness will very much depend on how adequately the content of educational programs is correlated with current social and economic needs. Training young persons to fulfill traditional aristocratic roles or preparing them for activities that a changing culture does not urgently need, or cannot afford, may lead to the idleness of a nation's most able persons, culminating almost inevitably in frustration, defeatism, or political radicalism. The paradoxes are not confined to the idle lawyers, philologists, or students of belles lettres who return from abroad with graduate degrees only to experience the painful humiliation of being supported by their illiterate relatives. About the only kind of an education that a village-structured economy can provide is instruction in customary grammar-school subjects. It takes a larger spatial community to make available more specialized training in agriculture, elementary engineering, mechanics, and the wide range of skills that developing countries so desperately need. The consequence is that school leavers have not acquired an education that fits them for the variety of rural tasks that must be performed if real development is to occur. The need is for agronomists, entomologists, plant breeders, veterinarians, lathe operators, auto mechanics, and agricultural extension workers. Emerging market towns will, to be sure, need a few accountants, clerks, and similar white-collar workers, but it will need as many or more warehousemen, wheelwrights, toolmakers, and electricians. The education myth is that general education will equip young people to fill any of these exacting roles. The truth of the matter is that village schools cannot possibly provide the necessary education and training. But forty villages, properly linked with a market town, might quite easily be able to supply the more specialized training that properly motivated village boys and girls need to become genuinely useful key personnel in a development program. Here the underdeveloped countries can indeed learn from American experience. Until consolidated schools were created, our rural "district" schools, with but one teacher for all eight grades, were wholly incapable of training young persons for a society that was becoming increasingly technological. Yet, simply by combining resources on a larger spatial basis, a differentiated educational system, articulated to a wide variety of interests and needs, has been developed.

The spatial aspects of democracy need corresponding consideration. The importance of widening opportunities, thereby eliciting all the latent creativity that a society can release, must not be overlooked.[17] The dangerous and delusive myth is that democratic ways of life can be adopted without any structural changes in settlement patterns, even though the historical record gives little reason for such optimism. Feudal German, Polish, and Russian villages, despite all the romantic nonsense about the democratic origins of the manor, were no more democratic in the eighteenth and nineteenth centuries than stratified Indian villages are today. Democracy, as Pirenne has so ably explained,[18] was a town phenomenon, a type of occupational and intellectual freedom that could only develop when people had escaped from the restraints imposed in hamlets and villages. There can be no democracy if older citizens rule as arbitrarily as they did in the Russian *mir,* or if the low-born must perform only disagreeable tasks for the convenience of the high-born. Democracy involves replacing status by function, caste by merit. The city banker will not ask whether an applicant for credit is Brahman or Harijan (Gandhi's name for the untouchables, meaning "the children of God"); he will merely ascertain whether the prospective borrower is credit worthy. The city factory will not offer a Nigerian a position merely because he is Yoruba; it will hire him if he can prove that he can operate a turret lathe. Democracy is

17. This topic is explored in some detail later in this chapter.
18. Henri Pirenne, *Belgian Democracy: Its Early History,* Manchester, 1915.

not a myth; it is a very real and genuinely important prerequisite for development. But it demands for its functioning an area large enough to be essentially impersonal, where persons of any origin can demonstrate their utility by their capacity and performance. It thrives wherever there is a ladder of opportunity provided normally by a graduated hierarchy of villages linked with towns and towns functionally interrelated with cities.

Finding the Spatial Architects

If a nation is to develop, it must find leaders rational enough to challenge the foregoing fabric of myths, wise enough to chart new directions in policy, honest enough to withstand the temptations that confront all who hold positions of importance, fearless enough to brook the opposition of vested interests, idealistic enough to persuade others that a better society is possible. It is most unlikely that all these virtues will be found in any single leader. Moreover, it is probably unwise and sometimes even dangerous to overemphasize the leadership role. What a developing country needs much more than charismatic leaders is a cadre of earnest, properly trained, well-motivated, and, if possible, dedicated policy makers who can agree on basic objectives and define reasonable goals and targets. The dramatic aspects of revolution and liberation that produced the leaders who went into the woods with Tito or to jail with Gandhi can no longer be depended on to produce a new group of selfless idealists; and not only are the surviving leaders old and tired but many are discouraged because their dreams have not materialized. In all the emerging countries the tasks of managing development programs have proven far more difficult than had been expected. The result has been popular disenchantment, much of which stems from the exaggerated promises held out to the underdeveloped world by the development theorists and model builders, whose alluring visions of "balanced growth" and "takeoff" seemed to reduce development to a few simple macroeconomic factor allocations, prescriptions the new élite assumed could promptly be put into practice. But the plans proved to be anything but self-fulfilling; nor did the economic system respond as the model builders had predicted.

The new leaders must be wiser, less impulsive, more critical of general theories, and more attentive to the incentives that animate an economy. Above all, they must understand what John P. Lewis has stated so vividly: that any economic analysis and policy-making that deserves to be called planning "is inherently spatial in character."[19] The abstract policy prescriptions, tediously repeated in hundreds of books and articles on economic development and written mostly by pundits with little or no field experience, have proved quite inadequate. It is not enough to set up certain investment priorities or to try to allocate most resources to certain "modern" projects which are presumed to have exceptional multiplier effects and unique change-making puissance, regardless of where they might be located. Nor is it enough to give preference to chosen industries primarily because they promise to be "import savers" or "export generators".[20] The import-saving industries may require capital that would have a far greater employment-generating capacity and growth-inducing effect if invested in industries far less glamorous than plants producing air-conditioning units, opera glasses, or cosmetics cases.[21]

Perhaps the most unlikely place to look for space-conscious policy makers is in the great cities of Asia, Africa, or Latin America, where traditions are aristocratic and sometimes essentially feudal.[22] To the city-dwelling ruling classes, hinterlands have traditionally been considered dependent not reciprocal—areas for exploitation rather than for development. By contrast, it is well to remember that the leading figures in Britain's industrial revolution—Arkwright, Stephenson, Wilkinson, Brunnel, Watt, and Boulton—did not come from London; they came from the provinces, every one of them! But Britain was

19. See his preface to *Regional Perspective of Industrial and Urban Growth,* ed. Desai, Grossack, and Sharma, p. v.

20. Studies made jointly by the American, British, and French aid missions in Yugoslavia (1952–1953) showed that many of the new "export-generating" industries required so many imported supplies that the international accounts were, at least for the short run, worsened rather than improved.

21. I do not choose these illustrations carelessly. For the type of import-saving commodities favored in India see my *Market Towns and Spatial Development in India,* New Delhi, 1965, p. 92, nn. 1, 3.

22. Karl Wittfogel has pointed out (*Oriental Despotism,* New Haven, 1957, p. 85) that, historically, oriental cities "were administrative and military footholds of the government; and the artisans and the merchants had no opportunity to become serious political rivals." For a fuller analysis of the contrasts between administrative cities and economic central places, see Vatro Murvar, "Some Tentative Modifications of Weber's Typology: Occidental Versus Oriental City," in *Urbanism, Urbanization, and Change: Comparative Perspectives,* ed. Paul Meadows and Ephraim H. Mizruchi, Reading, Mass., 1969, pp. 51–63.

fortunate; she already had a hierarchy of central places that included a large number of intermediate-sized towns, essentially bourgeois in composition: cloth towns like Norwich or Leeds, metalworking centers such as Birmingham, and pottery towns like Stoke-on-Trent. Comparable urban structures are seldom found in underdeveloped countries, but if there are only a few towns of this type, city-born planners will be well-advised to suppress their prejudices in favor of a metropolitan elite and search the medium-sized towns for talent.

On the other hand the likelihood that villages can supply the needed spatial planners is very improbable, not because there is a dearth of ability there (I am convinced talent is very widely distributed), but because village leaders instinctively want to maintain their traditional privileges and will therefore tend to resist change. Landlords will not voluntarily divest themselves of their rentable land so that tenants can become owner-occupiers; nor will village traders willingly promote truly competitive markets in nearby regional towns that can undermine their local monopolies. Vigorous spatial development will require a scheme of things far more democratic than villages in underdeveloped countries are likely to provide. For, in a sense, the oriental village is the historical microcosm of the autocratic oriental city, and to assume that intruded programs of community development are going to change the mores and objectives of village leaders is a foolish, albeit popular, illusion.[23]

If the villages cannot provide the spatial policy makers, and if the city elite are congenitally indifferent to the developmental potential of rural hinterlands, then the prospects would seem rather gloomy. But it really is not quite that bad. Cities in underdeveloped countries are, after all, magnets that attract talent. They are the sites not merely of governmental departments but of schools, universities, institutes, and research agencies. They have far more than their proportionate share of trained minds. The cities must therefore provide a majority of a nation's macroplanners. But if central planners are to succeed in devising overall programs that can set development in motion, quicken its tempo once it has really begun, and diffuse it throughout a country, they will have to solicit the help of spatial planners, who are more intimately familiar with regional and local problems, and who are capable of galvanizing groups of businessmen into constructive, co-

23. For a disheartening account of built-in resistance to change in an Indian "community development" experiment, see D. P. Sinha, "Innovation, Response, and Development in Banari," *Man in India,* 48, No. 3 (July–September 1968), 225–243.

operative, or collective action. The planning function must, in short, be both shared and decentralized.

The Yugoslav experience testifies to the wisdom of such a procedure. As long as planning was centralized in Belgrade, as long as it relied chiefly on macroeconomic models, and as long as the planners regarded their work as an esoteric activity beyond the comprehension of anyone who was not a mathematician, engineer, or econometrician, the growth of the economy, despite large inputs of capital, derived from heavy forced saving, was discouragingly low. When a wiser program belatedly recognized the need for spatial improvements, and when "decentralization," by localizing and diffusing the epicenters of structural change, delegated more and more planning functions to some 55 towns and another 500 communes, the whole economy was vitalized. What occurred in Yugoslavia is therefore particularly instructive. After 1953 the central planners gradually replaced a command approach to resource allocation with a market approach and, in the process, turned more and more of the planning decisions over to communal councils and other local organizations. It was by this means that the needed spatial planners were found, bright people who could, with proper regard for the "indicative planning" of the central government, not only mobilize local resources for development purposes but bid competitively for outside capital to launch ventures that called for larger investments than a commune could itself finance. Because the Yugoslavs had developed a governmental system that involved many layers of committees, they had some experiential advantage in making a transition from command planning to planning as a collaborative process.[24]

Finding spatial planners in a country such as India has proved to be much more difficult. In the first place relatively few towns exist; hence the polarity between villages and large cities is very pronounced.[25] Yet there are, after all, some 2,000 cities and in the progressive states a new

24. Planning as a collaborative activity whereby citizens and planners are brought together in a common effort has been neatly analyzed by David R. Godchalk and William E. Mills in "A Collaborative Approach to Planning through Urban Activities," in *Urbanism, Urbanization, and Change,* ed. Meadows and Mizruchi, pp. 513–525.

25. The underurbanization can be easily demonstrated. The 1961 Indian census enumerates only 2,690 towns and cities as contrasted with 564,718 villages. There were, therefore, about 210 villages for every urban center. In the United States in the same year (1960), for 13,749 villages there were 6,041 urban centers, almost 1 town or city for every 2 villages. India, Office of the Registrar General, *Cenus of India, 1961, Final Population Totals,* New Delhi, 1961, pp. lxi–lxii; U.S., Bureau of the Census, *Statistical Abstract of the United States,* Washington, 1967, p. 16.

variety of leadership has been emerging represented particularly by the regulated-market committees who have planned their market yards and built up sales, credit, and warehousing facilities that are effectively integrating rural areas with market towns. But two circumstances have limited the planning role of these local leaders. They have been largely ignored by the central planners, and they have for the most part confined their planning to a single local activity. Whereas in the Yugoslav context it is possible for a communal council to plan industrial expansion as an integral part of a larger community program that includes markets, schools, hospitals, housing, and recreational facilities, no corresponding overall planning has yet emerged in Indian towns or small cities. Consequently, if there is to be such a thing as an industrial estate, an ad hoc group must plan, finance, and operate it. The municipal corporation ordinarily bears responsibility for schools and hospitals, while the state government will be expected to erect a warehouse, if there is to be one. Private business enterprises may commit fractions of the nation's scarce capital to whatever investment promoters believe will be most profitable, and this unsupervised capital formation may or may not be consistent with the chief goals of the national planners. Whether these uncoordinated activities will produce any satisfactory functional economic areas is highly problematical. The sad thing to observe is that quite a number of really capable potential planners are available, but their creative powers are seldom allowed very much range.

It is, of course, naïve to assume that all cultures will respond in the same way to intellectual challenges; it should be expected that the actual planning performance of any culture group will reflect certain underlying values. Thus Philip Jacob's research indicates that, whereas Yugoslav local leaders favor both economic equality and greater public participation as policy ends, American local leaders want participation without the equality.[26] Polish leaders, like Indian leaders, show little enthusiasm for broad public participation in decision making and are almost as indifferent to economic equality as the Americans. The real

26. To test and, if possible, measure the influence of values on community action, Philip E. Jacob and his associates have been conducting a comparative study of local political leadership and social mobilization in India, Poland, Yugoslavia, and the United States. Some preliminary findings based on factor analysis have been published; see Philip E. Jacob, Henry Tenne, and Thomas Watts, "Values, Leadership and Development: A Four-Nation Study," *Information sur les sciences sociales,* 7, No. 2 (April 1968), 49–92.

virtue of an increasing measure of collaboration between national and local planners (between the macro planners, who are constantly considering the kind of an action program needed for some holistic development, and the practical local planners, who know what a local community needs and how it can really be improved)—the real advantage that will spring from such a cooperation is that a development program will tend to be more nearly in harmony with deep-seated values. As more space dimensions are added, a planning program will have better chances of success because it can be better articulated to the needs, desires, and values of more people. But these spatial dimensions cannot be discovered by any general theory. They must be patiently factored out in terms of spatial growth potentials, a task that calls for the closest collaboration of well-trained economic analysts, who can blueprint an overall program of development, with pragmatic and realistic leaders, who can forecast the possible contributions that a unit of space will make to such an overall plan, and who will have to be depended on to implement an appropriate increment of the approved plan.

Mobilizing the Needed Capital

Like every other type of development, spatial improvement will require investment, some in industrial facilities, some in agricultural tools and farm equipment, and a large amount in infrastructure, both economic (roads, warehouses, electrification) and social (schools, health clinics, recreational facilities). There are several possible sources of capital, and it will become the responsibility of the planners to try to assemble it for their community from any or all of these sources. Not many developing countries will be able to emulate the Puerto Rican example and obtain a large share of the needed capital from foreign investors. But every country can try to do so, and it is interesting to note that socialist Yugoslavia has succeeded in forming joint ventures with private overseas investors.[27] What Puerto Rico discovered, however, was that certain domestic investments (in industrial estates, power facilities, roads, water supply) had to be made before foreign businessmen would venture any of their capital. The first investment *tranches* will ordinarily, therefore, have to come from domestic sources.

If local leaders can persuade the central planners of the importance

27. *New York Times,* August 19, 1968.

of their developmental plans, some grants-in-aid might be obtained from central or state governments. Although this procedure has been employed by some disadvantaged Yugoslav communes, ordinarily, except for infrastructure, it does not represent much promise, since in terms of overall national priorities most local ventures will seem marginal. The appeal to the central planners, therefore, had best be confined to requests for allocations of money for roads, warehouses, water systems, or electricity grid extensions. But strong efforts might very properly be made to attract domestic private urban capital by the proffer of special advantages such as low taxes, low wages, or industrial sites at nominal rentals. Many varieties of city-based manufacturing enterprises which operate with relatively little fixed capital might find real advantages in establishing labor-intensive branch factories in market towns, which could attract both workers and customers from twenty or thirty mile radii. Any number of assembling operations, as well as metal-forming, pharmaceutical, plastics, and other light industries can be profitably conducted in small cities, provided transportation is adequate and a trainable work force can be recruited.

The major initial impetus, however, will need to come from local entrepreneurs, and this at once raises the question of how they can proceed when they cannot afford to make all the necessary investments. In this regard some of the southern Indian experiences are very instructive. Private industrial estates have become increasingly popular, and to accumulate the capital for their construction, very flexible arrangements are being made. At Sangli (Maharashtra), for example, 157 persons and eleven cooperative societies, by purchasing membership shares, pooled their resources in order to amass the initial portion of the capital.[28] The Maharashtra government thereupon purchased enough additional shares so that the enterprise could qualify for a loan from the Life Insurance Corporation of India,[29] covering 60 percent of

28. Details concerning the enterprise's "aims and objectives," its "area of operations," its authority to raise funds, the nature of "membership," and the legal organizational and administrative structure are given in Sangli Industrial Estate Cooperative Society, *Bye Laws*, Sangli, 1963.

29. In 1962 the Life Insurance Corporation of India (which is a creation of the central government) informed the state governments that it would receive applications for loans from (private) industrial estates not to exceed 60 percent of the total cost of each estate, provided the borrowing enterprise had "raised the balance of 40 per cent either by way of capital or partly by way of capital and partly by way of state government loans", Life Insurance Corporation of India, Circular Letter, DI/143, New Delhi, 1962.

the cost of the projected fixed investments. Out of these total resources the Sangli Industrial Estate Cooperative Society constructed ninety-four sheds and proceeded to make them available to those "members" who undertook to pay for the structures in twenty-four installments, evenly distributed over twelve years.[30] What had actually occurred therefore was that capital had been assembled from three sources: a fraction from local businessmen and cooperative societies, another portion from the state government, the foregoing two fractions equal to about 40 percent of the needed capital. The remaining 60 percent was borrowed from an autonomous central government agency whose investable reserves had been acquired from insurance premiums paid in by hundreds of small policy holders, and it was therefore these small savers who were the contributors of a major part of the funds at the disposal of the Sangli corporation. In a very real sense, then, a local enterprise had been able to go to the national capital market for most of its funds.

The buildings and facilities of the Sangli industrial estate, however, represented only the fixed capital needed for the fifty-six manufacturing enterprises that were using the ninety-four sheds when I visited the estate in 1964. Working capital had to be found before enterprises could begin operations. Because most of the operations were fairly labor-intensive, the average investment in tools and machines was small, about $995 per worker. For inventories (of materials, semiprocessed, and finished goods) the investment per worker was about $460. Since the average number of workers per enterprise was 8.7, the average investment per enterprise would be in the neighborhood of $12,500.[31] Although most of the larger enterprises represented city capital that had been attracted, most of the working capital for the medium-sized and small enterprises had been accumulated by local entrepreneurs, partly from savings, partly from credit extended by banks or by (city-based) suppliers of raw materials. The important thing is that the scale of operations and the investment needed to achieve that scale were, in the majority of cases, within the financial and managerial competence of ambitious people who lived in Sangli or in the outlying villages for

30. The member-buyers were free to rent their sheds to outside entrepreneurs if they did not themselves wish to undertake manufacturing operations.

31. There were, of course, variations from the average size. Some of the larger enterprises employed more than fifty persons (metalworking and engineering); a median group employed about fifteen to twenty workers (textiles, paper products, machine parts, buckets, and utensils); while a larger number of small enterprises hired only three or four workers.

which that market town served as a central place.[32] That the demonstration effect of the estate was influencing local investment patterns was indicated by the applications the estate had received for future factory space. The twenty additional sheds under construction had been long bespoken; so had the thirty sheds for which blueprints had been prepared. Among the applicants were three sugar cane growers who had pooled their savings to make a down payment on one of the sheds. This single illustration shows how an imaginative group of local businessmen and civic leaders can interblend private and public capital,[33] attract urban capital and managerial talent, indirectly obtain investment funds from the capital markets, and induce prosperous country people to diversify their investments, thereby transmuting traditional agricultural capital into modern industrial capital.[34]

What is really needed to mobilize capital is enterprise. For as William Diamond has so vividly explained, a low level of investment in an underdeveloped country may not be entirely a consequence of poverty.[35] A complex series of political, economic, and cultural factors—instability of government, corruption, fluctuations in the value of money, limited markets, the prevalence of an illiterate and unskilled work force—may tend to channel what savings there are into "safe" investments such as land, into quickly disposable assets like inventories of consumer goods, or into high-yield, if risky, personal loans. These patterns of investment, however much they may hold down development, are nevertheless wholly "rational," since in these outlets the investor will have security, liquidity, and profitability. But real development calls for a quite different pattern of investment, and this is what the spatial planners must

32. About a fourth of the entrepreneurs were village-born, and over a third of the 483 workers commuted daily from their village homes. (Interview with the Sangli Industrial Estate Manager, November 13, 1964.)

33. Municipal contributions to ventures of this kind may not necessarily take the form of direct investments. Land for market yards or industrial estates may be given outright or leased at nominal rentals. Certain municipal facilities may be made available, such as warehouse space or buildings that can be used as showrooms or training centers for workmen.

34. The growing number and the cumulative importance of locally owned Puerto Rican manufacturing enterprises is signal proof that a spatially diffused development program can progressively change traditional agrarian investment patterns and stimulate savings. For a detailed survey see Amadeo I. D. Francis, *Locally and Nonlocally Owned Enterprises in Puerto Rican Manufacturing Industries,* Puerto. Economic Development Administration, Office of Economic Research, Small Business Management Research Report No. 144. San Juan, 1963.

35. *Development Banks,* Baltimore, 1957, pp. 10–17.

try to induce. Clearly they cannot do so alone. Government must undertake many of the most essential regional investments in infrastructure. Beyond that, government should also address itself to the problem of changing the investment climate and helping to alter the investment patterns of people who are now investing in traditional ways. This will call for institutions in which wary and conservative people with money to invest will have confidence. It is not likely that landlords, long habituated to real estate investment, will readily buy the shares of a new manufacturing corporation. But they might be persuaded to entrust some of their money to a government institution which can offer such inducements as guaranteed, or tax-free, dividends, and through such an institution traditional investors may indirectly contribute to the launching of new enterprises. The government must therefore take the initiative in a variety of programs designed to mobilize capital from all possible sources. For this task development banks have proved to be eminently useful.[36] Their main function is to provide enterprises with capital (usually long-term) on reasonable terms and sometimes to provide savers with sound and profitable outlets for their savings. Yet all too frequently, particularly when all or most of a bank's resources have been provided by a government, the large and dramatic projects so often favored by the central planners will be given priority. Unless there is an overall plan that emphasizes spatial dispersion of investment projects, as there has been in Puerto Rico, the planners of development in country towns and small cities may have difficulty in obtaining much help from development banks; hence they will have to devise their own schemes for mobilizing capital.

It seems quite obvious, then, that the creation of new growth centers and the invigoration of existing central places requires a closer coordination of public and private investment, and this calls for a better integration of local or regional planning with central planning. The really great developmental potentials of underdeveloped countries are not going to be found in a few glamorous projects but in the systematic improvement of the productivity and the spending power of the rural areas and the mass of rural people. It is the argument of this essay that in countries which for historical reasons have inherited village-struc-

36. For a clear explanation of how development banks are formed and how they operate, see Diamond, *Development Banks,* pp. 40–84. For summary descriptions of different types of development banks (in Turkey, India, and Mexico) see the same work, pp. 95–124.

tured economic landscapes, a transition to a modern economy will require the creation of a network of intermediate agro-urban centers to provide incentives capable of tempting producers to raise more and better farm crops, to induce them to sell relatively more products, so that they can spend more yet save more, invest more, and thereby raise their productivity. The critical link in this chain will be the visible supply of incentive goods that can indirectly and silently persuade farmers to produce more. Very evidently the customary and limited variety of village goods made by handicraft methods do not now make an adequate appeal. They do not whet the appetites of farm families, as cameras, transistors, or electric fans can do. A whole set of new "modern" industries are needed, producing goods that will have really powerful "demonstrating effects."[37] But these modern industries require varying amounts of fixed capital and involve certain overhead costs that must be distributed over a large enough output so that the unit costs of the end products will be low enough to fit into the small disposable incomes of country people. Hence the main technical and managerial problem is how to attain a scale of operations that will keep unit costs adequately low.

Such a scale of operations is not possible at the village level. Why then should not all such "modern" industries be located in large cities, where demand will be large enough to permit low unit costs? The answer, of course, is that such a location usually is advantageous both for the entrepreneurs and for city-dwellers. But as far as spatial development is concerned the trouble is that very, very few country people in poor underdeveloped countries ever travel to great cities. Their horizons are determined by isochrones whose lengths are the function of the speed at which people can travel by foot, by donkey, or by bullock cart. Unless modern goods are made or sold in centers within such isochrones, there is no demonstration effect. But since development requires not merely new goods but additional rural employment, so that rural spending power can grow, the widest possible dispersion of manufacturing is eminently desirable. The development and transformation of rural landscapes, therefore, calls for the creation of new industries at all central places that can consolidate a requisite amount of regional demand; at places that now are, or can become, market centers and

37. The demonstration effect of a model-T Ford car in thousands of American villages was far more important in increasing demand than all the advertising of the Ford Motor Company.

that can make available enough of a trainable industrial work force to permit a profitable scale of operation for a variety of modern industries. To make possible this metamorphosis, whereby a cluster of villages (once they obtain an organizing center) can be transformed into an occupationally diversified functional economic area, two change-making factors are indispensable: capital and enterprise. Under proper guidance, encouragement, and assistance, both can be found. If there ever is to be genuine spatial development, both must be found.

Surveying the Elements of Spatial Problems

The entrepreneurial spontaneity and vigor exemplified in the launching and expansion of the Sangli Industrial Estate convincingly show that change can be induced in agro-urban communities without waiting for any trickling down of growth-making impulses from core-region centers. This innovation demonstrates that a small group of civic leaders can become important change agents; yet however commendable and praiseworthy it has been, it should be noted that the financing, building, and opening of the Sangli Industrial Estate was a response to a comparatively simple spatial challenge. The community already was a market center attracting farm-produce sellers (who were also buyers of consumer goods and farm inputs) from a fairly prosperous agrarian hinterland. The civic objectives of the estate founders were to provide areal employment and to increase the availability of locally manufactured industrial products by the simple expedient of allowing the owner-occupiers (or tenants) of the estate sheds to make money by selling their products either outside the community or to local consumers. Although there are countless quite similar situations in scores of underdeveloped countries, most spatial problems are far more complex, and if they are to be dealt with, their nature and their complications must be systematically explored. An example from Malaysia can show very clearly that a spatial problem may require a careful preview of all relevant data before prudent policy decisions can be reached.

The Malaysian Jengka Triangle. Almost in the very center of western Malaysia is an area of 470 square miles of land considered to be capable and worthy of development. About 60 percent is under high forest,[38]

38. Dense forests composed of hundreds of timber-producing species, ranging in height from 100 to 150 feet and sometimes to 200 feet.

and of this wooded area about 75,000 acres (about 117 square miles) have been logged, leaving a balance of some 93,600 acres (146 square miles) of undisturbed forest lying within the Tekam Forest Reserve. Around the forested area stretches an irregular band of occupied or reserved land, some 112,000 acres (about 175 square miles), while another 25,000 acres have already been assigned to settlers who are part-time farmers or graziers, part-time workers on oil palm or rubber plantations. Modern all-weather highways connect the Triangle with east and west coast ports and with urban centers, and a railway passes within three miles of the western boundary. In the unforested land there is one oil palm plantation and several relatively small rubber estates, but the bulk of the land there is in the hands of small landholders. The population of the Triangle is estimated to be somewhere between 12,000 and 15,000, including the families of the 600 or more settlers who have taken up small landholdings under Land Development Authority schemes fairly recently. Here, then, are valuable resources very imperfectly utilized. To answer wisely the question of how the Malaysian economy might make better use of this whole area, the Federal Land Development Authority engaged the services of consultants who have produced a very extraordinary document, *The Jengka Triangle Report.*[39] Its contents will be very briefly summarized to indicate how thorough a spatial survey can be, and to show how wide a range of precise technical information has in this instance been laid before the Malaysian spatial policy makers.

Making abundant use of the effective communicative devices that have been called the "language of maps" and the "language of geometrical figures,"[40] and adding to these the "language" of photographs, charts, and tables, the consultants have described with great exactitude the Triangle's climate;[41] geology and geomorphology;[42] soils, classified by parent materials and illustrated by soil series distribution maps; forests, inventoried by species groups and girth classes; vegetation, and

39. *The Jengka Triangle Report: Resources and Development Planning,* prepared by Tibbetts, Abbott, McCarthy, Stratton, Engineers and Architects, New York, and Hunting Technical Services, Boreham Wood, Herts., for the Federal Land Development Authority, Kuala Lumpur, 1967. I refer to this *Report* throughout this section.

40. By Charles Sanders Peirce (1839–1914).

41. Temperature, humidity, rainfall, air movements, sunshine, and evaporation.

42. Igneous, pyroclastic, and sedimentary rocks; deposits, landforms; and landform distribution.

water resources.[43] Following this evaluation of basic areal resources comes a series of equally detailed chapters concerned with "development planning." Beginning with a chapter on "planning objectives," this section of the *Report* raises a series of extremely important questions.[44] With the objective of insuring that the resources of the Triangle make an "optimum contribution" to national progress, the analysts consider whether private enterprise can be relied on to develop them, or whether some other type of organization will result in the best land use, generate maximum possible employment, and conserve forest resources. The inference is that a mix of private and public activity will be necessary, but how the roles should be factored out is the problem. Reckless logging operations or planless extension of oil palm or rubber estates will no longer meet the developmental needs of the nation. Yet enough freedom will have to be accorded to the private sector to induce as much private investment as possible.

Having raised questions about the general objective of a master plan, the consultants next attempt to describe the technical and economic potentials of the Triangle, since, in their judgment, none of the policy issues can be decided until such data have been carefully assembled. To this end, the consultants with great care explore seriatim: land capability for producing a variety of crops;[45] the estimated volume of timber that could be obtained in coordination with a land clearing schedule; the market for sawed lumber, plywood, and veneer; logging plans for a ten-year period; and the investments needed to utilize forest products properly.[46] The use of land for oil palm and rubber trees is analyzed in terms of possible yields, markets, price trends, probable exports,[47] and estimated costs. Since oil palms and rubber have ordinarily been "estate" (plantation) operations, the consultants found it necessary to

43. Stream discharges and their monthly variations; flood measurements, groundwater, water quality, and soil infiltration.

44. *Jengka Triangle Report,* Chapters 8–26.

45. To do this a land classification system developed by the U.S. Department of Agriculture was employed, and eight land classes (and their subclasses) were graded as good, fair, marginal, or unsuitable for the production of oil palms, rubber, fruit trees, bananas, manila hemp, cassava, vegetables, legume crops, and padi. *Jengka Report,* pp. 64–71.

46. This includes recommendations not only for sawmills but for a plywood and veneer factory and a plant for making the components for prefabricated houses. Ibid., pp. 89–96.

47. Ibid., pp. 99–128.

discuss critically the comparative merits of estate farming,[48] small holdings, and communal settlements; they were inclined to favor small holdings allotted to settlers who could become owner-occupiers, provided their activities were properly coordinated. The appropriate sizes of such small holdings are discussed in terms of labor requirements;[49] gross sales needed to cover all costs, including loan repayments; and expectations for enough net profits to provide incentives for careful husbandry.[50]

The foregoing analysis of the capacity of the resources to provide satisfactory returns for settlers in small holdings is a prelude to a very searching consideration of the most desirable patterns of settlement, and the several chapters devoted to spatial design are exceptionally imaginative.[51] Since the development of the Jengka Triangle would involve the rural settlement of about 85,000 people,[52] the demographic dimensions of this Malaysian problem are very similar to those of the Volta River Resettlement Project, and it will be interesting to see how the ultimate spatial solutions will coincide or differ. Both plans contemplate an interlinked hierarchy of graduated rural and urban settlements, but whereas the Volta plan involved central places of several sizes, the Jengka Triangle consultants opted for a simpler plan of fairly uniform-sized villages (in area and population) served by relatively few towns.[53] The basic unit the consultants recommended was, therefore, a village-centered area whose center to perimeter distance could be traversed in a twenty-five-minute walk. With ten-acre holdings, plus garden allotments, such an isochronically determined area would consist of approxi-

48. Ibid., pp. 133–140.

49. "There is at present in western Malaysia a rapidly increasing rural population, much of which is underemployed. A national objective of the First Malaysia Plan is to provide the maximum number of employment opportunities." Ibid., pp. 143–144.

50. This section of the *Report* is very detailed, since it involves cost and return analysis for various crops at several assumed scales of operations.

51. Chapter 14, "Settlement Units"; Chapter 16, "Towns"; Chapter 17, "Transportation"; Chapter 18, "Roads and Ports"; Chapter 19, "Water Supply, Drainage and Irrigation"; Chapter 22, "Telecommunications and Electric Power."

52. This estimate is, of course, derived from the recommended landholding units and the estimated desirable degree of labor-intensity of the proposed farming operations.

53. The consultants were of the opinion that previous Malaysian settlement schemes had given too little attention to the proper isochronic dimensions of the "new towns" that had been designed to accommodate from 2,400 to 3,000 settlers plus their families. From these towns there was sometimes as much as three hours' travel to a settler's fields.

mately 1,200 acres of land accommodating about 100 settler families. Together with the expected village service personnel (teachers, police, midwives, government representatives) and their families, each settlement might have an aggregate population of 700–800 persons.[54] Altogether ninety-seven such basic units were proposed, of which sixty-eight would be oil palm areas, and twenty-nine rubber areas. Terrain and soil differences would result in size variations ranging from 772 to 1,957 acres for the oil palm settlements and from 785 to 2,077 for the rubber areas.

The villages would conform as closely as possible to western Malaysian cultural needs, proper consideration being given to houses, houselots, public buildings (religious, co-operative, communal), recreational facilities, wells, roads and health centers.[55] But whereas each village would have an elementary school, secondary schools would be joint ventures of six or seven basic (village) units. The same type of inter-village cooperation would be involved in the development of processing industries and "projects" (a term that in the *Jengka Report* refers to a spatial grouping of basic areas into a "geographical block for management purposes").[56] This type of coordination would be indispensable, since in oil palm and rubber operations a systematic areal policy of land clearing, tree planting, and management is required to insure a regular flow of primary products to the processing industries. The Triangle was therefore divided into six major "projects" that varied in size according to soils, terrain, and other physical factors. It was largely because of the role of "projects" in the Jengka Triangle spatial design that relatively few towns seemed necessary. Actually, four towns already exist on the borders of the Triangle, 14, 16, 18, 22 miles respectively from the center of the Triangle;[57] but since they are all peripheral, some new urban centers will be needed to provide more convenient medical, educational, industrial, commercial, and other specialized services. Based on rural-urban population ratios in fairly well-developed parts of Malaysia (where 19–29 percent of the population was urban), the consultants

54. *Jengka Report,* p. 168.

55. Essential factors are very precisely explained with illustrative maps in Chapter 14 ("Settlement Units") of the *Jengka Report,* particularly pp. 172–177.

56. *Jengka Report,* p. 178. The precise demarcation of projects is detailed on pp. 178–185.

57. Except for Temerloh-Mentekab (16,500 persons), the population of these small central places ranges from 750 inhabitants (Maran) to 1,750 (Kuala Krau) and 4,300 (Jerantut).

suggested that perhaps about 20 percent of the Triangle's population ought to be urban—somewhere in the neighborhood of 20,000 persons. Three new towns were therefore proposed, one to have about 12,000 people, two with about 4,000 each.[58] Appropriate sites were suggested, carefully chosen not only in terms of spatial geometry and their relation to the several "projects" but also in terms of topography, soil, and drainage, so as to hold to a minimum the costs of excavation and grading for building sites and roads and to insure adequate water supply and properly sloped drainage and sewage systems. In these new towns, land use could be controlled by making suitable allocations for industrial, commercial, institutional, residential, and recreational purposes—all properly served with the appropriate public utilities—and for expansion of these functional areas.

There is much more that perhaps ought to be said about this imaginative and wonderfully detailed preview of a spatial problem. The needed transportation facilities (within the village areas, between villages and towns, and from towns to ports or to Malaysia's large cities) have been completely projected.[59] Water supply, drainage, and irrigation requirements have been estimated by tested engineering standards,[60] as have the needed sanitation and health facilities.[61] Educational requirements have been less adequately examined,[62] and for some reason the role of vocational training has been overlooked. Telecommunications and electric power requirements are very thoroughly explored, as they would have to be to ensure the provision of sufficient electric energy not merely for domestic consumption but for the sawmills, oil mills, and rubber factories. If there is any technical subject that has been neglected, it is the small industries that entrepreneurs should be encouraged to establish in the emergent towns. The emphasis upon primary products (forest products and tree crops) and on the processing plants that convert them into lumber, palm oil, latex, or crumb rubber suggests a lingering preference for a type of development that belongs to an earlier time in history, when it was considered that this type of capital formation was the only one appropriate for

58. *Jengka Report,* p. 200.
59. Ibid., Chapters 17, 18.
60. Ibid., Chapter 19.
61. Ibid., Chapter 20.
62. Ibid., Chapter 21, which is very brief.

underdeveloped countries.[63] Despite this emphasis, which stems more from the potentialities of the region than from the unwitting preferences of the consultants, the *Jengka Report* is a model of orderly analysis. The projected areal development has been costed and phased. It is now up to the policy makers to decide what use they will make of this excellent and comprehensive survey. They, of course, should undertake some further research on a quite different level. It is for them to undertake, either arithmetically and formally, or intuitively and experientially, the benefit-cost analysis that is necessary to determine whether the Jengka Triangle can provide true social and economic benefits that will more than outbalance the costs.

Releasing Creativity

If there is any universal belief today, it is a tenacious conviction, shared by the leaders of all countries, that material and intellectual progress is not only eminently desirable but actually attainable for the majority of people, provided proper developmental policies are instituted. This belief in the possibility of national and, beyond that, worldwide welfare is in a way our modern ecumenical religion, leading millions of people to dream of salvation from poverty, suffering, ill health, and illiteracy! The increasing automaticity of industrial production in developed countries; the breakthrough in the substitution of synthetics for natural materials, fibres, and foods; the widening scope of education; and the improving levels of family incomes in progressive economies—all these factors, by reason of improved communication, have exerted a profound "demonstration effect" on the less-developed countries and set in motion a "revolution of rising expectations," which has led to an assumption that all countries can emulate, or even surpass, the economic well-being of the most affluent of our contemporary societies. Whether this optimism is warranted may be one of the most important questions of this moment in history. If it is justified, we can look forward to a richer, happier, and wiser world, perhaps even a more peaceful world. If the assumptions underlying this belief in progress are false, we can expect not merely disappointment but disillusionment, bitterness, despair, and rebellion.

63. See Hla Myint, *The Economics of the Developing Countries*, New York, 1965, pp. 53ff.

The progress that is so hopefully envisaged will call for changes in many action patterns, in a large number of social and economic institutions, and probably in the whole array of productive instruments, so that the entire resource base of our planet can be utilized. Nor will it be enough for the less-developed areas or countries to borrow, adopt, and introduce unchanged techniques and instrumentalities that have been economically beneficial in the more-developed countries. The history of economic development has never been a simple process of emulation of some more-advanced nucleus; it has been, instead, a complex process of diffusion and cumulative change, whereby the innovating, inventive, creative faculties of each developing country have been stimulated, utilized, and progressively enriched, thus leading to new and different institutions, machines, processes, methods, and techniques. Change has an ideational origin, and regions or countries that hope to develop will, I fear, signally fail to do so if they merely expect to indulge in intellectual parasitism.[64] To be sure, many, many discoveries, inventions and processes can be borrowed; even so, they will need to be adapted to discrete situations and to peculiar cultural propensities. Moreover, this borrowing will not by itself insure a comparably dynamic society, especially in view of the certainty that the more-developed cultures, by reason of their scientific and technical resources, will progressively increase their lead over their borrowing neighbors in the world community. A really improving global situation, therefore, calls for a universal increase in human creativity.

Why do new things happen? Why can there be novelty in thought and action? Some answer, however tentative, must be given to these questions before any plausible explanation can be found for differentials in creativity between cultures. The problem is an exceedingly complex one, since it involves psychological, social, political, economic, and ecological factors. Moreover, there may be cultural encrustations that can quite effectively inhibit the release of creative potentials. Change does occur even in societies that outwardly appear static and stagnant, but it is the rate of change that is of importance. Consequently, the problem is not merely to try to understand why the

64. In a revealing account of modern Africa, Drew Middleton (*New York Times*, May 11, 1966, p. 12) records an interview with an African leader who said, "Do you realize that there's nothing on this airfield that we Africans have invented or made? Everything from the planes to the luggage tags is made by the white man, yet we are told that this is our continent."

tendency to innovate is greater in some cultures than others but, more basically, to comprehend what it is that triggers the search for new ideas, new procedures, new techniques anywhere.

The simplistic explanation so common in folklore, and all too frequently recorded in history books, attributes discoveries, inventions, or innovations to exceptionally talented persons possessed of superior insight and imagination. But this "genius" or "great man" thesis, despite its propagation by tedious repetition, has been rejected by psychologists, anthropologists, and historians as quite inaccurate. For, whereas in the history of music, art, architecture, and science there are indeed the Mozarts, Michelangelos, Paladios, and Faradays, there are also thousands of nameless persons whose individual innovations may have been small but whose collective contributions have been tremendous. Moreover, if only rare and exceptional persons have inventive ability, why is scientific history replete with so many instances of simultaneous discoveries and innovations? And why does the successful inventor feel the need to rush to the patent office to register his new idea, unless he is really fearful that someone else might get there before him? At least thirty-five steamboats were built before Fulton allegedly "invented" his *Clermont*, and the experiments with this new type of transport were carried on not only in the United States but concurrently in England, France, and Scotland.[65] This illustration is not at all unique: the American Patent Office notes an average of about 20,000 annual duplicate inventions, attesting to the wide distribution of creative aptitude. Why, then, in the face of such evidence, does the "great man" theory of invention persist? The answer, I fear, is to be found in a false sense of patriotism, which manifests itself in a rather absurd attempt to prove that one's own nation is the greatest on earth and has produced the largest number of bright men who have invented the most important machines, made the greatest discoveries, and thereby created the best cultural, political, social, economic, and ethical milieu. *Vanitas vanitatum et omnis vanitas!*

The reality is rather different. Psychologists and anthropologists have convincingly demonstrated that inventive capacity is widely diffused, not only in human beings but in other primates, lower animals, and birds. Apes, chimpanzees, horses, pigs, and sheep can all solve problems,

65. See S. C. Gilfillan, "Invention as a Factor in Economic History," *Journal of Economic History*, Vol. 5, Supplement (December 1945), 68; and John Jewkes, David Sawers, and Richard Stillerman, *The Sources of Invention*, New York, 1959, pp. 42–43.

and carefully prepared "detour" tests have been used to measure differential inventive capacity.[66] For animals, very irritating tensions can artificially be created by an appropriate "stage setting," skillfully arranged by the experimenter. If this frustrating configuration is properly designed, it will elicit inventive responses from the tested animals which will reflect their generic resourcefulness and their individual capacity to act in new and different ways.

For people, it is history, chance, environment, and circumstances that supply the problems and set the stage for the exercise of imagination.[67] But it does not follow that creativity is itself an accidental consequence of random circumstances. Once again our folklore is more romantic than accurate. As a boy James Watt may very well have noticed that the teakettle lid tended to rise when the water boiled, but this observation had precious little to do with the mental process of the intellectually mature instrument maker who systematically utilized scientific knowledge in his attempts to improve the Newcomen engine, and who patiently continued his experiments with heat, steam, and vacuums until he visualized an entirely different type of an engine. It is true that acts of insight often have "strong emotional coloring,"[68] since the discovery of something new must perforce be a zestful experience.[69] But the transcendentalist explanation of novelty in thought and action grotesquely oversimplifies the actual process of discovery, invention, or innovation. It implies that massive creative acts occur quite suddenly, and that inventors, by means of their intuition, can conceive of automobiles, airplanes, or computers in great acts of creativity. For the most part, it is the other way round: the elements of an invention are slowly visualized in disparate chains of knowledge, and the actual invention is usually a laborious, frustrating task of synthesis.

Psychologists perceive a genetic sequence of four steps that are involved in any creative process leading to the emergence of novelty in thought and action. First, there has to be a clear perception of some

66. See, for example, Wolfgang Köhler, *The Mentality of Apes,* New York, 1926, particularly pp. 31–39.

67. In the case of Thomas Newcomen, who succeeded in building a workable atmospheric engine in 1705, which became the predecessor of the steam engine, the problem was how to pump water out of the deep tin mines in the west of England.

68. Abbott Payson Usher, *A History of Mechanical Inventions,* Boston, 1959, p. 78.

69. "The creative act is always liberation and conquest. It is an experience of power." Nicolai Berdyaef, *The Meaning of the Creative Act,* trans. Donald A. Lowrie, New York, 1962, p. 12.

vexing problem. Next, must be a "stage setting" which can reveal the essential elements of the problem and make evident the "intrinsic properties of the data."[70] Once this measure of understanding is achieved, there is a possibility that the quintessential third step can be taken, namely, an "act of insight" whereby a solution to a vexatious problem is first envisaged. Finally, after some tolerable answer has been found (after some discovery has been made, or after some workable invention has been completed), a fourth step normally follows, which Usher has called "critical revision."[71] Here, the analysis centers around the effectiveness of the way the problem has been solved, and as a result of a critical re-examination a far better solution may emerge. In contrast to the first three steps, which are historically definitive, this process of critical revision is generally continuous, with cumulative improvement increasing the social utility of an original discovery, invention, or innovation.[72]

The genetic nature of these four steps is illustrated in Figure 11–1. It should be noted that the process begins with a problem which, from a psychological point of view, constitutes an unsatisfactory configuration or gestalt. This situation is represented in the figure by an incomplete circle (1). The converging arrows represent ideas of disparate origin that have a bearing on the problem and that provide some of the potential ingredients for a possible solution. The second circle represents the "stage setting" which has supplied the missing arc of the circle (2). By reason of this conjuncture and the aid of other contributing strands of knowledge (indicated by the arrows), an "act of insight" can now occur, and this step is represented by a complete circle (3). Once such an initial visualization has occurred, the fourth step, "critical revision," can begin, leading to a (tentatively) complete and superior new configuration (4), which may persist for some time as the customary solution to a given problem or may, by progressive revision, be steadily improved.

70. Usher, *History of Mechanical Inventions*, p. 64.

71. Ibid., p. 65.

72. One need only compare the performance of a modern automobile with that of Daimler's original invention to appreciate the tremendous improvement that has been made by "critical revision." Perhaps the clearest statement of the merits of this fourth step in the creative process has been expressed by a distinguished scientist when he said, "Historically, the thesis can be maintained that more fundamental advances have been made as a by-product of instrumental improvement than in the direct and conscious search for new laws." Robert A. Millikan, *Autobiography*, New York, 1950, p. 219.

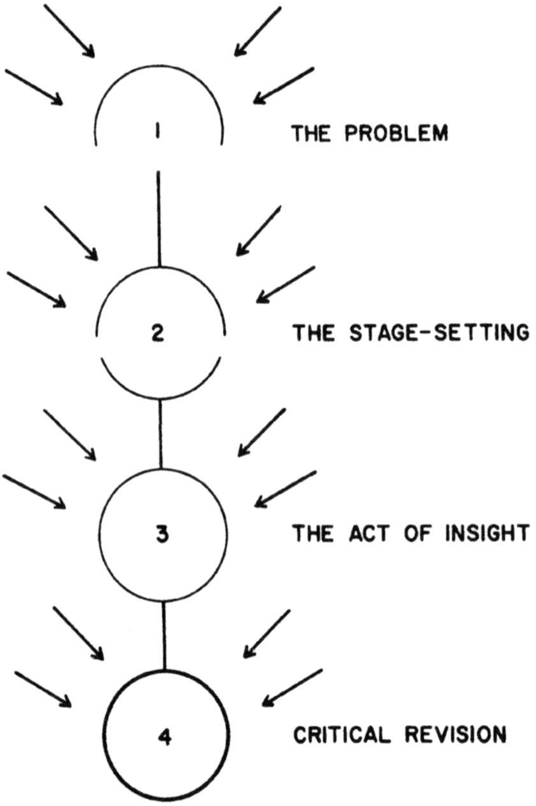

Figure 11–1 The Emergence of Novelty: Four Discernible Steps
SOURCE: Abbott Payson Usher, *A History of Mechanical Inventions,* Boston, Beacon Press, 1959, p. 66.

But as Usher has so wisely cautioned, "the action in such a process takes place against resistances of undetermined magnitude."[73] These frictions are both psychological and cultural. Some persons, for individual reasons, have but limited problem-solving capacity.[74] Other persons may prove to be creative provided the circumstances are right and the stage setting genuinely stimulating. Among imaginative persons

73. Usher, *History of Mechanical Inventions,* p. 66.

74. These "individual differences" have been the object of searching investigation by many psychologists. See, for example, the bibliography following the article on "Mental Tests" in *The Encyclopaedia of the Social Sciences,* New York, 1933, X, 328–329.

there will normally be a wide range of creativity, and this explains why particularly gifted or particularly well-trained and intellectually versatile persons can sometimes make outstanding contributions, or even quite dramatic individual discoveries.[75] This does not, however, challenge the essentially synthetic nature of the creative process, which has been so naïvely overlooked by the exponents of a heroic or transcendental theory of creativity.

Knowledge grows over time in a great number of strands. It is an inescapably multilinear process by reason of the typical preoccupation of persons with particular ideas, tasks, functions, duties, and interests. Thus, painters will be concerned with color, drawing, design, or perspective, and each of these elements will, over time, have its own history.[76] Lawyers are interested in quite different intellectual problems: in equity, contracts, trusts, property, crimes, penalties, or legal liability, and each of these components of the larger entity known as law or jurisprudence has its own history. Creativity may therefore manifest itself in two quite different ways: it may discover new links in separate intellectual strands, or it can integrate, fuse, and synthesize elements drawn from several intellectual strands. Generally, this latter type of creativity is both more difficult and more consequential—more difficult, because it requires a wider, multilinear knowledge, which is to say a more systematic body of information and understanding. But an amplitude of knowledge is not enough; there must also be a capacity to choose elements from several separate intellectual strands and to weave these selected elements into a wholly new configuration. Basically, the process is ideational and rests on a perception of some new organic relation among ideas, among material agents, or in patterns of behavior. The end product may therefore be a new theory of genetics (Mendelism), a new prime mover for transport (Trevithick's locomotive), or a new plan of government (as explained in the *Federalist* papers by Hamilton, Madison and Jay). All these "products" were syntheses of

75. Jewkes, Sawers, and Stillerman in *Sources of Invention* have described in some detail the really unique contributions of a number of successful inventors. Whereas they reject the "great man" thesis, they are less prone than Gilfillan or Usher to minimize the personal contributions of particular innovators.

76. Consequently, histories of art, such as Bernard Berenson's *Italian Painters of the Renaissance,* London, 1952, are largely concerned with describing the discovery of better techniques, both as separate elements and as contributions to an integration of better techniques into new art forms. Berenson's work is replete with illustrations of both types of creativity.

several intellectual strands, and in each case the act of insight consisted in a recognition of how hitherto discrete elements could be united into a new configuration. Such "strategic" inventions, as Usher has called them,[77] are actually the result of a cumulative synthesis, which is depicted in Figure 11–2. Merely for convenience, the contributing strands in each step of the creative process are shown as uniform in number (namely four strands). This is, of course, a wholly arbitrary scheme, since any number of strands could conceivably be melded together. The important thing to observe is that each strand has its own synthetic character, so that in each chain the four steps (as shown in Figure 11–1) have already occurred. Number 1 is therefore a convergence point, but the resulting configuration (the part circle) is as yet unsatisfactory. In number 2, additional converging strands have supplied the missing arc, thus making the "stage setting" adequate for the "act of insight," which, as number 3 indicates, requires additional inputs of ideational contributions from still other strands. The cycle completes itself in number 4, where the process of "critical revision" is expedited by means of contributions from elements drawn from still other strands of knowledge.

Recognizing, then, that creativity in a genuine social sense is a meaningful synthesis of previous discoveries, insights, and innovations, and that major acts of creativity are amalgams of lesser syntheses, one can readily agree with Whitehead's remark that the greatest invention was the "invention of invention."[78] This, however, leaves unanswered a wide range of questions. It does not explain whether certain cultures are more creative than others, whether certain institutions stimulate creativity and, oppositely, whether other institutions repress novelty in thought and action. It throws no light on why farmers in India, Egypt, and Albania scratch the soil with their wooden plows, unchanged in design or effectiveness for 2,000 years, while tilling tools are constantly undergoing improvement in Iowa, Saskatchewan, Norfolk, and New South Wales. It does not solve the riddle why some areas consistently generate creativity in toolmaking or whether certain ethnic groups lead the procession of technical progress.

The problem goes beyond these rather obvious dimensions. A few acts of insight, a few useful inventions are not enough! What is called for, if

77. Usher, *History of Mechanical Inventions,* p. 68.

78. Alfred North Whitehead, *Science and the Modern World,* New York, 1925, p. 136.

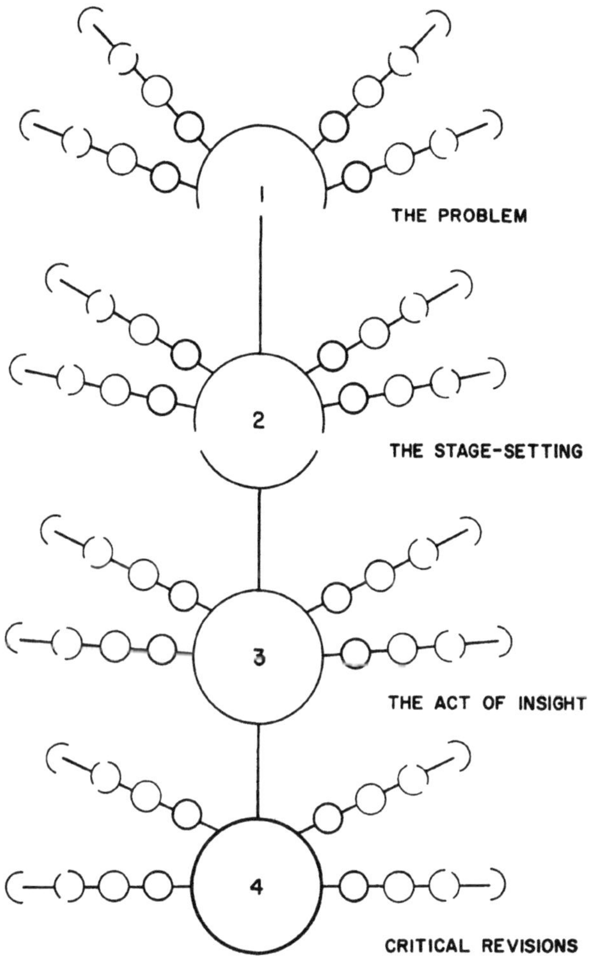

Figure 11–2 The Process of Cumulative Synthesis
SOURCE: Abbott Payson Usher, *A History of Mechanical Inventions,* Boston, Beacon Press, 1959, p. 69.

creativity is to become cumulatively beneficent, intellectually and technologically, is a cultural climate that will release whatever there is of creative potential lying hidden in the intelligence of all men, women, and children—black, brown, yellow, or white. There can be little doubt but that certain social, ideological, political, and economic contexts release more of this divine discontent than other contexts do, and in an era which believes in the possibility of induced human progress, it is highly appropriate to consider the content of milieus that retard or hasten creativity.

Insightful behavior is not an adequate explanation of innovation. Nor is mastery of certain skills enough. What is called for is a set of attitudes which will question the adequacy of existing techniques, precipitate advances in knowledge, and lead to certain value judgments concerning types of desirable social action. This last consideration is of special importance. If, for example, a culture tends to emphasize the ever latent human concern with personal salvation, it is very likely that a large share of savings will be devoted to temples, churches, shrines, monasteries, or other votive institutions. As a consequence, creative talents will tend to find expression in architecture, painting, sculpture, music, ritual, and theology. Since this variant of human expression always involves symbolism (whereas mechanical invention, which is rigorously utilitarian, does not) virtually limitless possibilities for creative acts will be provided in the sacerdotal realm. Consider, as an example, the fantastically complex proliferation of artistic forms involved in Buddhist iconography,[79] or the symbolism in art and architecture involved in the differentiation of a Christian saint for every day of the year! The limitless decorative possibilities, and the correlative number of doctrinal interpretations, could conceivably mortgage such a large fraction of creative potential that relatively little would be left for other creative outlets.

Manifestations of creativity are, to be sure, very difficult to classify. Thus, with worship as a primary purpose, churches or temples are built. But in order to construct such sacred edifices, principles of architecture and of engineering are discovered. Stonecutting and quarrying may reveal some of nature's geological secrets, while the search for more beautiful colors may open up vistas in botany or chemistry. Despite these interdependencies, levels of thought and action may nevertheless be roughly classified into certain contrasting patterns. Thus, every

79. For Lamaistic Buddhism alone, the Emperor Ch'ien-lung had cast a pantheon of 300 Buddhas and Bodhisattvas, each with their respective mudras (symbolic hand poses) and asanas (positions of lower limbs) and symbols (sacred objects). Concurrently, another collection of bronze statuettes consisting originally of 787 figures was cast, each distinct in some symbolic detail. See Walter Eugene Clark, *Two Lamaistic Pantheons,* Cambridge, Mass., 1937, I, pp. ix–xiii. For further details concerning the profusion of iconographic variations, see Antoinette K. Gordon, *The Iconography of Tibetan Lamaism,* Rutland, Vt., 1959; and Alice Getty, *The Gods of Northern Buddhism,* Rutland, Vt., 1962.

community must of necessity create certain social conventions in order to survive and to live with some degree of order. In the process, religious rituals and mystic dogmas will most likely emerge, representing an extracommunity, or otherworldly, cluster of ideas, which at the same time provide sanctions for approved modes of conduct. Puzzlement about the physical world in which men live will lead to some more or less systematic interpretation and understanding of nature, and this knowledge will sooner or later come to be expressed in abstract concepts. Social relations will call for rather different intellectual constructs, and consequently legal concepts will normally come to represent another area of invention. Even more complex will be a community's social and political ideals, and in this area great ingenuity will be called for in order to visualize or devise appropriate plans for purposeful social action.

The kind of creativity that a community (or a culture) will tend to emphasize depends largely on which of these five levels of thought predominates. Sharp antithesis can develop between religious dogmas and scientific interpretations of nature[80] or between religious dogmas and social conventions.[81] Rigid concepts of law can influence land tenure, and thereby have limiting effects on progress in farm tools or changes in crop rotations; while random inbreeding resulting from the custom of common grazing of animals can make systematic improvement of livestock impracticable, if not impossible. Creativity is therefore not so much a personal activity, as is commonly thought; it is really a social process that operates within various cultural and intellectual parameters. Thus, a political system which accords all positions of importance to an elite (whether native or foreign) and limits the occupational mobility of the majority can have an utterly destroying effect on the creative potential of the underprivileged. The slave, the serf, or the rack-rented tenant cannot be expected to invent many new tools, techniques, or farm practices; nor will a black wage earner in the depths of a South African gold mine propose very many new mining or metallurgical innovations.[82] Contrast this with the permissive climate

80. For a wealth of illustrations, see Andrew Dickson White's classic study, *A History of the Warfare of Science with Theology in Christendom*, New York, 1896.

81. A very senior Philippine diplomat said (May 1966) that no legislation designed to propagate knowledge of birth control could be introduced in the Philippine legislature until permission was received from the Vatican.

82. The bleakness of this prospect has been indelibly limned by Alan Paton in *Cry, the Beloved Country*. London, 1953.

for industrial experimentation that existed in most nineteenth-century American factories, where there were few restraints of class or craft, a great deal of freedom from traditional definitions of tasks, a high motivation for personal advancement, and an extraordinary mobility, flexibility, and movement in the working population. All these permissive factors tended to release initiation, originality, and creativity. Visitors from Europe were amazed at the ceaseless search for better production methods, not merely by management but by the entire work force. "Every workman," said John Anderson, Inspector of Machinery of the British Ordnance Department, in his 1854 report on American manufacturing techniques, "seems to be continually devising some new thing to assist him in his work."[83] Another visitor noticed "the restless activity of mind and body," the eagerness of employees to solve economic and mechanical problems. He went so far as to say that "there is not a working boy of average ability in the New England States . . . who has not an idea of some mechanical invention or improvement in manufacture by which . . . he hopes to better his position or rise to fortune and social distinction."[84] As a result of this stimulating milieu, a surge of inventions and technical improvements occurred; yet for the most part we have no record of who the inventors and innovators were, for the simple reason that there were so many of them.[85] In agricultural machinery, the story is much the same. Hundreds of blacksmiths were shaping plows, building harrows, or experimenting with grain drills or corn planters, while carpenters, school teachers, lawyers, or even preachers were toying with ideas and making working models of cotton gins, grain harvesters, or cultivators.[86]

If there is to be progress, the resources for new syntheses must be available, and, as has been shown, the basic resources for innovators

83. Great Britain, *Parliamentary Papers, Accounts and Papers,* Vol. 21 1854–1855, quoted by John E. Sawyer, "The Social Basis of the American System of Manufacturing," *Journal of Economic History,* XIV, No. 4 (1954) 377.

84. "New York Industrial Exhibition, Special Report of Mr. George Wallis," Great Britain, *Parliamentary Papers, Command Papers,* Vol. 36, 1854, p. 3, quoted by Sawyer, "Social Basis of the American System," p. 378.

85. In the case of "strategic" discoveries, particularly if they were patented, there is a better possibility for attribution of inventions or innovations to individual persons. See, for example, Joseph W. Roe, *English and American Tool Makers,* wherein leading inventors and innovators in a designated area of technology are listed.

86. See P. W. Bidwell and J. I. Falconer, *History of Agriculture in the Northern United States,* Washington, 1925; and Leo Rogin, *The Introduction of Farm Machinery,* Berkeley, 1931.

and inventors are to be found in the knowledge that accumulates in the separate intellectual chains. But the rate of accumulation of knowledge in these multilinear strands is seldom uniform; hence there may be discontinuities in the innovating process. Thus, the idea of a flying machine emerged long before properly designed airfoils or adequately powerful, lightweight motors were available. These discontinuities have helped to propagate the myth of the heroic inventor. But, as has already been explained, such a theory is really a confession that the very nature of the creative synthesis is not really understood or even knowable. Fortunately we do not have to await the chance advent of the exceptionally talented person because the creative capacity of a community (or a culture) depends on its reservoirs of knowledge and on the ability of large numbers of (intellectually discontented) people to integrate knowledge from a number of these discrete ideational strands. Normally the resources contained in these strands have been accumulated over relatively long periods of time, and in a dynamic culture these resources are constantly increasing. And whereas the magnitude of a single item of knowledge in one of these idea-chains may be small, its influence on some emergent synthesis may be critical.[87] It is not essential, however, that all the elements of a new configuration be immediately available; the important thing is that the stage setting should be effective enough to allow at least one person to appreciate what the missing ingredients are.[88] This appreciation depends primarily on the breadth of knowledge of the potential innovators. Whenever such familiarity with fields or strands of knowledge is lacking, there will be an empty harvest of missed opportunities! Conversely, once the requisite synthesis is envisaged, a search for all the necessary contributory elements can begin.[89] Usher has expressed this part of innovation in vivid language: "At low levels of empiricism, trial and error is commonly presented as aimless fumbling," whereas "at substantial levels of scientific activity, the trial and error method is described as systematic experimentation."[90]

87. Whittles jet engine was complete as a concept long before the necessary new alloys "capable of standing extreme stresses and temperature" were available. Jewkes, Sawers, and Stillerman, *Sources of Invention*, p. 125.

88. In the case of animal tests the tools which would have to be used had to be in sight when the tested animal looked hungrily at the (out of reach) food. See Wolfgang Kohler, *The Mentality of Apes*, New York, 1926, p. 39.

89. See Arthur Koestler, *Insight and Outlook*, New York, 1949, pp. 253–55, for an illustration from the age of Archimedes.

90. Usher, *History of Mechanical Inventions*, p. 65.

In the technical realm we have, after long, long preparatory stages, reached a point in our intellectual history where the innovating process is well understood. Intensified research is steadily enriching the separate strands of knowledge, and systematic integration is constantly attempted by means of systematic experimentation. Nor is the fraternity of scientific innovators an intellectual elite that is found only in so-called developed or mature countries. Modern communication has diffused both the data and the methodology of science, and the myth of creative and uncreative cultures is gradually being dispelled. It is no longer a question of whether non-Europeans can create new things; the issue is whether the rate of innovation or discovery can be as fast in developing as in developed countries. And here we must again raise the question of whether human intelligence can consciously invent an adequate number of creativity-releasing institutions. All manner of troublesome questions pop out when we make this enquiry: whether communities (states, regions, cities, towns, villages) can coordinate their activities in such purposeful ways that there will be a likelihood of an increase in creative acts; whether schools whet or dull inventive capacity; whether some types of schools are better laboratories for creative minds than others; whether bureaucracy, in the public or in the private sector limits and restrains creativity or increases it. There are still other questions: whether international contact and association quicken the rate of innovation or tend to generate a variety of intellectual parasitism; whether socialism, with its emphasis on central planning, restrains innovation and represses creativity by limiting entrepreneural freedom or, by reason of its concern with macroeconomics and macrosociology, reveals the social need for change, thereby intensifying the search for improved technology and stimulating research.

The modern concern with human resources, with social infrastructure, and with more effective and purposeful education reflects a growing awareness of the need for better instruction, guidance, and intellectual development as a precondition for a more creative world community.[91] But in the same way that a God-intoxicated Western world for a thousand years channeled so much of its creative talent to theology, to ecclesiastical art and architecture, and left the other "useful

91. That this is no merely a problem for developing countries is shown by books published in the United States and Britain, dealing with problems of education. See, for example, Francis Keppel, *The Necessary Revolution in American Education*, New York, 1966; James A. Perkins, *The University in Transition*, Princeton, 1965.

arts" relatively unchanged until a Newtonian revolution gradually corrected the balance, it may well be that we are devoting an inordinate amount of our creative talent to military and space exploration programs and far too little to less dramatic but probably more useful and socially beneficent purposes. The world community has urgent wants that are not now being satisfied. Millions of people need more food, shelter, clothing, medical care, sanitation, and education. Cities need to be cleaned of their slums, vice, poverty, and unclean air. Here are problems that might be solved by imaginative and creative innovators. Perhaps our greatest challenge today is not how to find ways of going beyond the moon but how to use the limitless creative power of human minds to solve the most urgent social and economic problems of the world community. Perhaps we should begin thinking about how we can divert the wonderful creative power of human minds from the instruments of violence and vanity to the more humane purposes of social betterment.

Directing Creative Talents to Spatial Problems

There is no want of latent creative power in the world community. The orbital flight of space capsules around the moon, the landing of earthlings on that planet, the discovery of the possibility of gravitational waves, and the prevention of German measles by innoculation are only the more dramatic recent manifestations of man's ever growing innovative and creative power. As I have said, creativity is not a rare and unusual ability limited to a few "great thinkers" or dependent on nature's chance production of an occasional genius; it is widespread throughout human society, and, as world-wide communications improve, the global creative potentials become greater and greater. It is not a monopoly of any elite group, any particular culture, or any form of societal organization. The pretense that only certain cultures can innovate, or the inference that only people with white skins and blue eyes are truly creative, is not only arrant nonsense but an insufferable variety of unforgivable vanity. Attempts to associate high creativity with inequality in wealth or income or with private property and free private enterprise are no more defensible. There are, admittedly, certain institutions that restrain creativity and others that help to release creative powers. Thus, a caste structure of societal organization that restricts the activities of some persons to prescribed repetitive tasks can quite effectively prevent the exercise of creativity by a sizable fraction of the population. Many poor countries are therefore poor because they have failed to release the full creative potentials of their great masses. Indeed, the systematic suppression of innovation may well be the greatest of all human tragedies.[92]

There are clearly two important tasks that must be faced if welfare and progress are to be advanced. The first is to facilitate the release of the greatest possible creative talent. The second consideration is to try to direct creative efforts to the most important societal problems. History has shown, again and again, that creative power can readily be channeled. Thus, in relation to prevailing value systems there have been induced bursts of invention and innovation in the fine arts, music, poetry, architecture, military engineering, sculpture, pure science, and space exploration. Traditionally it was the ruling classes that mainly determined the spheres of interest toward which creative powers were directed. They commissioned *objets d'art,* lured talent into palace and temple building, and provided the market for furniture, tapestries, jewelry, paintings—for all the lovely things now displayed with such pride in thousands of museums and private collections. But even though the aristocrats and their sycophants co-opted a major share of creative power, they could not engross it all. Wandering gypsies found an outlet for their creativity in music, Asian nomads in rug weaving, and poor highlanders of Montenegro in ballads. Underprivileged Jews, confined to ghettos, also found in music a boundless creative sphere strangely different from other areas of remarkable Jewish innovation, the world of trade, moneylending, and arbitrage. Such innovations were seldom part of any aristocratic plan; more often they were unpremeditated by-products of restriction, repression, and segregation.

It would be far too large an undertaking, in this brief discourse, to explain how and why creative talents came to be progressively directed toward the "useful" rather than the "fine" arts. To be sure, some creative talent had always been channeled toward the prosaic tasks of agriculture and manufacture, but by the sixteenth century there is clear

92. Even though slavery had certain technical advantages over free enterprise, its chief shortcoming was that it failed to utilize the creative power of the slaves. The consequence was not merely an opportunity loss to the slave owners, but an immeasurable meliorative potential that might have occurred and could have been shared by a nation's population (or even the earth's population) was foolishly sacrificed. See "Slavery as an Obstacle to Economic Growth in the United States: A Panel Discussion," *Journal of Economic History,* 27, No. 4 (December 1967), 518–560.

evidence in Western Europe that relatively more innovations were occurring in the industrial sphere.[93] Perhaps this trend was stimulated by new intellectual currents, such as the growing interest in the idea of progress that seems to have gathered momentum in sixteenth-century France.[94] Whatever the causation, the channeling of innovative and inventive talent toward industry, transportation, agriculture, banking, and other mundane and practical problems gathered momentum in the seventeenth century and reached such emphasis in the eighteenth century that, for better or worse, the resulting burst of invention and innovation has been called an "industrial revolution."[95] The cumulative and ever growing benefits of this direction of innovative propensities toward increased production and distribution of goods and services are beyond dispute. The United States alone, by reason of inventions in energy production now has available nonhuman productive power equivalent at the very least to that of five billion slaves. Gone are the days when mistreated horses suffered pain and fatigue to supply men with tractive power, and this amazing change, which has come during my lifetime, has been paralleled by equally remarkable changes in every other branch of technology. A set of values shifted Samuel F. B. Morse's creative powers from painting to telegraphy, made Burbank dream of new possibilities in plant breeding, brought Edison and Steinmetz into the early electrical laboratories, led Daimler and Ford to experiment with explosion-engine vehicles, and gave urgent new tasks to Fermi, Bohr, and Oppenheimer.

But whereas we can review with pride all the wonderful manifestations of human creativity in literature, fine arts, architecture, industrial technology, modern agriculture, engineering or science, there are, alas, neglected areas into which creativity seldom seems to penetrate. There are all too many of these bypassed backwaters. But to me the three most underdeveloped areas are politics, ecology, and what I have called "the organization of space." There are virtually no new inventions in the realm of government, and the world-wide revolt of the younger genera-

93. See, for a large number of illustrations, John U. Nef, *Industry and Government in France and England,* Ithaca, 1957.

94. See J. B. Bury, *The Idea of Progress: An Inquiry into Its Origin and Growth,* New York, 1932, Chapter 1.

95. For comprehensive account of the many interrelated innovations and their impact on the Western European economy, see David S. Landes, *The Unbound Prometheus: Technological Change and Industrial Development in Western Europe from 1750 to the Present,* Cambridge, 1969.

tions is probably a manifestation of intense dissatisfaction with archaic political systems. Only belatedly have we discovered that there have been no innovations capable of neutralizing the ecological damage caused by the recent surge of innovations in science and technology. As to the third of the neglected areas, about which I will presently have just a little more to say, it is my mature conviction that the poverty of the underdeveloped world is largely attributable to a faulty organization and utilization of space.

The consequences of the neglect of these three important areas—government, ecology, and terrestrial space—can be explained without hesitation. Failure to direct creative thought to politics has resulted in irresponsible government and an endemic distrust of politicians. Indifference toward the ecological consequences of modern mechanical and chemical processes is rapidly leading to a progressively dangerous pollution of land, sea, and air, endangering not only human life but changing the whole "balance of nature." The neglect of geo-economic structure has produced the spectacle of ungovernable, slum-cursed cities and an economic dualism, which has accentuated the poverty of many rural areas by stripping them of their best human resources and intensifying their competitive disadvantages. Surely the time is at hand when we must try to redirect our vast creative potential. The ingenuity that can devise a machine to land astronauts on the moon might be a thousand times more beneficent if it were directed to problems such as the foregoing three.

Man's material well-being depends on the effectiveness with which he uses available natural resources. Societies become prosperous by developing skill in farming, mining, forestry, fishing, and manufacturing, while the use of an exchange economy consistently widens occupational variety, thus facilitating the utilization of the varied talents of a society's population. But exchange cannot knit a whole economic landscape into a functional entity unless there are markets within reach of producers and consumers. Countries that are "developed" solved these spatial-economic problems long ago; Britain in the sixteenth century had over 760 market towns, and farmers or graziers even then were seldom farther from a market center than 10 or 15 miles. The ratio of villages to market towns is a revealing index of development: in developed countries such as Britain, the United States, Germany, France, and Japan the ratio seldom exceeds 15 villages per market town.

Contrast this with India, where the ratio is at least 200 to 1; with the portions of the Middle East, where the ratio is 150 to 1; and with Africa, where it is more than 160 to 1. The consequences are very clear. Since transport by bullock cart, pack animals, or porters can normally only relate ten, fifteen, or twenty villages to existing market centers, the great bulk of rural villages are not functionally linked with the industrial or the urban economy, and, of course, they are even more feebly related to the world economy. Without market outlets for their produce, the majority of farmers have no incentives for increasing production. Young men—always the ablest, brightest, best-educated—trek away from the outlying villages and join the hordes in the shack-town slums of Calcutta, Manila, Singapore, Cairo, Djakarta, or Johannesburg.

Imaginative thinkers who have called attention to ways of dealing with these problems have been largely ignored. The greatest of these, Walter Christaller, whose seminal work on the south German cities initiated a truly scientific approach to spatial economics and thereby laid the foundations for systematic central-place theory,[96] was repeatedly denied permission to visit like-minded American geographers because he had elected to ally himself with the German Communists.[97] Yet Christaller's perceptive mind stimulated the thinking of scores of geographers throughout the world, and their advice and guidance could have helped to create a far more efficient economic and social development had politicians not been so woefully scornful and indifferent.

Another pioneer, Charles Galpin, was a bit more successful in propagating some of his excellent spatial ideas. By carefully mapping the boundaries of trade zones, banking areas, and high-school attendance territories in a single Wisconsin county, Galpin was able to show by means of his "social topography" the imperfections of existing spatial organization. It was the evidence he produced that helped to start a movement for consolidated school districts, a type of collective action between communities that has completely transformed the school system not only in the Midwest but throughout the American continent. But the fuller integration of rural areas with a hierarchy of local market centers and regional towns was left largely to chance, and the conse-

96. *Central Places in Southern Germany,* trans. Carlisle W. Baskin, Englewood Cliffs, N.J., 1966. Originally published in Germany in 1933.

97. Peter R. Gould, "The New Geography," *Harper's Magazine,* March 1969, pp. 91–94.

quence was a blundering, wasteful, and unsatisfactory improvisation rather than the scientifically balanced spatial development that might have been attained at far less social cost.

In a brilliant study to which he devoted years of imaginative work, August Lösch formulated a general theory of spatial and locational design. Based on the work of Christaller and Galpin, it addressed itself to the problem of how truly efficient "economic landscapes" could be created. Out of this came the now familiar pattern of hexagonal market structure and a searching inquiry into the role of transport in determining the most efficient types of spatial design. The ideal goals are patently evident from Lösch's analysis. Every rural producer should be within convenient travel time of some adequately competitive selling place for his produce, some equally competitive source of consumers' and producers' goods, and some adequately diversified service center. But these market centers are only the basic building blocks of a much more complex hierarchy of central places, capable of knitting the entire spatial economic structure together in a truly functional sense. For, unless there is a graduated, interlinked, and functionally integrated market system which covers all of a nation's space, three serious handicaps inevitably result. There will be only fractional production; consequently, there can be only fractional consumption; and, even more unfortunately, there can be only fractional social and intellectual development of a nation's human resources.

The impulsive building of large industrial plants, the logrolling political decisions that determine where roads or electric power lines are to be located, the subsidization of inefficient agriculture in unsuitable areas to curry favor with voters are examples of the wrong ways to deal with spatial economic problems. What is at fault, obviously, is the incapacity of an archaic political system to deal with contemporary socioeconomic difficulties. Geographers and economists have devised tools by which the potentials of any portion of terrestrial space can be quite accurately measured. Not only can the resources, both physical and human, be evaluated but, within a given compass of space, particularly promising "growth points" can be located. Benefit-cost studies can then show, with completely acceptable margins of error, the overall effects of investments at alternative places. The necessary number of local market centers, and the requisite hierarchy of graduated central places can be factored out once the required infrastructure for provision of transport, energy supply, warehouse, and banking facilities has been calculated. These estimates can become the directing guidelines for policy, serving not as absolute and rigid parameters but as proximate goals of "indicative planning."

The goals of rational spatial policy should be the creation of truly functional economic areas, which will provide employment opportunities not merely in primary production (farming, mining, forestry, fishing) but in industry and in service activities, thus utilizing to the full the varied potential productivity of a work force. Furthermore, by creating a sense of "community" there can be a far better protection of regional ecology than is possible if "outside" enterprises without any local roots "mine" the natural resources and pollute the rivers and the air.[98] The main goal of rational spatial policy should be to improve the quality of life in a community not only by providing tasks appropriate to interests and ability but by protecting the environment, by supplying the proper educational facilities, health measures, and convenient recreational facilities. But beyond all these ends of enlightened policy should be a goal even more important: the creation of a cultural milieu that will release the largest possible amount of a community's creative power.

There is nothing visionary or fanciful about my proposals. They are attainable provided we direct our creative powers to this urgent task. As I see it, there are four dimensions to the spatial problem. First, the task must be *visualized,* by economists, geographers, engineers, and scientists. Secondly, the importance of the changes must be *explained,* which is an urgent cybernetic task. The next step is to *mobilize* the needed talent and resources, which calls for public administrators who understand the problem and a cadre of politicians who dare to risk their reputations in supporting novel proposals. Only when the preceding three steps have been taken can the program be *implemented* by technicians guided by economists, geographers, scientists, political scientists, and ecologists. What a different world we might have if only a fraction of the money spent on madcap military ventures and on vainglorious interstellar competition could be directed toward making decent places in which people could live, work, play, and study. There is still time to revise our social goals; but we must hurry, or it may indeed be too late.

98. The shocking destruction of fish in the Rhine is only one illustration of the ecological devastation that can be caused by irresponsible enterprises. See *New York Times,* June 25, 1967.

APPENDIX LOCATION QUESTIONNAIRE USED BY PUERTO RICO INDUSTRIAL DEVELOPMENT COMPANY PLANNING OFFICE

The information you are to furnish below is needed to provide our Planning Office with an intelligent basis for helping you in the selection of a suitable site for your project, or to help you evaluate a location tentatively selected. It is designed to protect you against any future inconvenience that may arise through faulty location, and to protect other firms already established in your vicinity.

Please be specific in your answers. Do not give answers such as *"normal for this type of operation,"* where you could be more specific. Please furnish information in addition to that required whenever you deem necessary. Future needs should be covered when possible.

Please *sign* this form when completed to your satisfaction. Thank you.

I. GENERAL INFORMATION:

A. Proposed local firm's name:____________________

B. Parent firm's name and address:____________________

C. Name and address of local representative or manager:__________

II. TYPE AND ACTIVITY:

A. Basic Product:____________________

B. Description of operation (use separate sheet if necessary):________

C. List of machinery with individual weight and area covered by base:

III. UTILITIES:

A. Electric power requirements:

1. Maximum demand in KVA__________ 4. Voltage________
2. Total power in horsepower__________ 5. Phases________
3. Other comments____________________

B. Water requirements:

1. Total consumption (GPD)__
2. Duration (Hours/day)____
3. Peak rate of use (GPM)____
4. Duration of peak use____
5. Pressure required____
6. Special characteristics desired (purity, chemical content, temperature, salinity, etc.)__
7. Breakdown of water uses (GPD):
   a. Industrial process______
   b. Sanitary uses______
   c. Cooling purposes______
   d. Air conditioning______
   e. Steam production______
   f. Other______
8. Type of fire protection required

____

C. Sewer Facilities:

Will your industrial plant produce any effluent other than the normal sewerage from sanitary facilities? Yes:______ No:______

If so, give details:

1. Total volume of waste (GPD)__________
2. Duration of discharge (hours/day)__________
3. Peak rate of discharge (GPM)__________
4. Duration of peak discharge__________
5. Plans for treatment of waste__________

____

6. Submit certified copy of physico-chemical analysis of waste originated in similar plant, including:
   a. Temperature
   b. pH (alkalinity or acidity)
   c. BOD (biological oxygen demand)
   d. Total solids concentration:
      1. suspended solids 2. volatile solids 3. settleable solids
   e. Chlorine demand
   f. Toxic substances (if known)
7. Description of process using water:__________

____

____

____

8. List of chemicals used:__________

IV. SITE

A. Size of lot required__________

B. Special requirements as to location (community preference, geographic orientation, climatic conditions required, proximity to waterfront, etc.)__________

____

C. Subsoil conditions, indicating soil bearing desired__________

____

V. BUILDING

A. Floor area required__________

B. Projected future expansion:

1. Size__________ 2. Expected date__________

C. Type (single or multi-story, flat roof, semi-monitor, full monitor, etc.)

D. Special requirements (floor bearing capacity, air conditioning, etc.)

E. If a special building is required, give brief description of characteristics desired:__________

VI. CHARACTERISTICS OF PROCESS:

A. Raw materials:

1. Itemize materials__________

____

____

2. Expected source__________

3. Fire, explosion or health hazards associated with materials used

____

4. Plans for storage facilities (raw materials and product)__________

____

B. Obnoxious conditions originated in proposed operation (dust, odors, fumes, smoke, noise, vibrations, etc.)__________

C. Similarly, describe possible environment factors to which operations may be peculiarly sensitive__________

D. Proposed special treatment, such as: smoke abatement, floor padding, air conditioning, etc.__________

VII. LABOR FORCE

A. Number of employees and sex distribution:

1. At full production (______months after start)__________

Male__________Female__________

B. Number of work shifts anticipated:__________

VIII. ADDITIONAL COMMENTS:

____

____

If the information above presents, in your opinion, a true picture of your contemplated Puerto Rican operation, and may be used by our Planning Office to determine the best possible location for your factory, please so signify by signing below.

Signature:__________Firm:__________

Title:__________Date:__________

NOTE: This information will be handled in the strictest confidence and will not be unduly disclosed to any personnel not related to the firm or engaged in the selection of the site.

(Revised July 1965)

WORKS CITED

Agarwala, A. N., and S. P. Singh, eds. *The Economics of Underdevelopment.* London: Oxford University Press, 1958.

Agarwala, A. N., et al. *Plan Consciousness in a Rural Area: A Survey of Dhatarpur Village.* Allahabad: University of Allahabad, Agro-Economic Research Center, 1966.

Agnihotri, V. B. *Survey of Labour Housing and Overcrowding in Kanpur.* Lucknow, 1954.

The Agrarian History of England and Wales. Vol. IV, *1500–1640,* edited by Joan Thirsk. Cambridge: Cambridge University Press, 1967.

Akagi, Roy Hindemichi. *The Town Proprietors of the New England Colonies.* Gloucester, Mass.: Peter Smith, 1963.

Alexander, P. C. *Industrial Estates in India.* Bombay: Asia Publishing House, 1963.

Allen, G. C. *A Short Economic History of Modern Japan, 1867–1937.* New York: Praeger, 1963.

Anand, Mulk Raj; Charles Fabri; and Stella Kramrisch. *Homage to Khajuraho.* Bombay: Marg Publications, 1962.

Andic, Fuat M. *Distribution of Family Incomes in Puerto Rico: A Case Study of the Impact of Economic Development on Income Distribution.* Rio Piedras: University of Puerto Rico, 1964.

Approaches to Community Development: A Symposium Introductory to Problems and Methods of Village Welfare in Underdeveloped Areas, edited by Phillip Ruoff. The Hague: von Hoeve, 1953.

Auty, Phyllis. *Yugoslavia.* New York: Walker, 1965.

Bain, Joe Staten. *Industrial Organization.* New York: Wiley, 1968.

Baldwin, K. D. S. *The Niger Agricultural Project: An Experiment in African Development.* Cambridge, Mass.: Harvard University Press, 1957.

Bauer, Peter Tomas. *Economic Analysis and Policy in Underdeveloped Countries.* Durham, N.C.: Duke University Press, 1957.

Beardsley, Richard K.; John W. Hall; and Robert E. Ward. *Village Japan.* Chicago: University of Chicago Press, 1959.

Berdyaef, Nicolai Aleksandrovich. *The Meaning of the Creative Act.* Translated by Donald A. Lowrie. New York: Collier Books, 1962.

Berenson, Bernard. *The Italian Painters of the Renaissance.* London: Phaidon Press, 1952.

Berg, Elliot J. "Backward-Sloping Labor Supply Functions in Dual Economies: The African Case." *Quarterly Journal of Economics,* 65 (August 1961), pp. 468–492.

Berna, James J. *Industrial Entrepreneurship in Madras State.* Publications of the Stanford Research Institute, International Development Center. Bombay: Asia Publishing House, 1960.

Berry, Brian J. L., and Allen Pred. *Central Place Studies: A Bibliography of Theory and Applications.* rev. ed. Philadelphia: Regional Science Research Institute, 1965.

Berry, Brian J. L. *Geography of Market Centers and Retail Distribution.* Foundations of Geography Series, edited by Norton Ginsburg. Englewood Cliffs, N.J.: Prentice-Hall, 1967.

———; Peter G. Goheen; and Harold Goldstein. *Metropolitan Area Definition: A Re-evaluation of Concept and Statistical Practice.* U.S. Department of Commerce, Bureau of the Census, Working Paper 28. Washington, D.C., 1968.

——— "Policy Implications of an Urban Location Model for the Kanpur Region." In *Regional Perspective of Industrial and Urban Growth: The Case of Kanpur,* edited by P. B. Desai, I. M. Grossack, and K. N. Sharma, pp. 203–219. Bombay: Macmillan, 1969.

——— and V. L. S. Prakasa Rao. "Urban Rural Duality in the Regional Structure of Andhra Pradesh: A Challenge to Regional Planning and Development." Mimeographed. Chicago, n.d.

Bhat, L. S. "A Regional Approach to the Urban and Industrial Development of the Kanpur Region." In *Regional Perspective of Industrial and Urban Growth: The Case of Kanpur,* edited by P. B. Desai, I. M. Grossack, and K. N. Sharma, pp. 230–238. Bombay: Macmillan, 1969.

Birmingham, Walter; I. Neustadt; and E. N. Amaboe, eds. *A Study of Contemporary Ghana.* Vol. I, *The Economy of Ghana.* London: Allen and Unwin, 1966.

Bogue, Margaret Beattie. *Patterns from the Sod: Land Use and Tenure in the Grand Prairie, 1850–1900.* Springfield, Ill.: Illinois State Historical Library, 1959.

Bos, Henricus Cornelis. *Spatial Dispersion of Economic Activity.* Rotterdam: Rotterdam University Press, 1965.

Bourne, Dorothy D., and James R. Bourne. *Thirty Years of Change in Puerto Rico: A Case Study of Ten Selected Rural Areas.* New York: Praeger, 1966.

Bowden, Peter. "Agricultural Prices, Farm Profits, and Rents." In *The Agrarian History of England and Wales.* Vol. IV, *1500–1640,* edited by Joan Thirsk, pp. 593–695. Cambridge: Cambridge University Press, 1967.

Brunner, Edmund de Schweintz, and J. H. Kolb. *Rural Social Trends.* New York: McGraw-Hill, 1933.

Brutzkus, Eliezer. *Physical Planning in Israel: Problems and Achievements.* Jerusalem, 1964.

Bulsara, Jal Feerose. *Problems of Rapid Industrialization in India, Submitted to the Research Programs Committee of the Planning Commission of India: Being a Memorandum Based on Findings of the Socio-Economic Surveys of Nine Indian Cities, viz., Baroda, Gorakhpur, Hubli, Hyderabad-Secunderabad, Jamshedpur, Kanpur, Luchnow, Poona and Surat.* Bombay: Popular Prakashan, 1964.

Bury, J. B. *The Idea of Progress: An Inquiry into Its Origin and Growth.* New York: Macmillan, 1932.

Callaway, Thomas. "A Countermagnet to the Capital: The Case of Djoliba." *International Development Review,* September 1966.

Campbell, Olive Dame. *The Danish Folk School: Its Influence in the Life of Denmark and the North.* New York: Macmillan, 1928.

Canarp, C. "Regional Development Policy in Sweden as an Instrument for Manpower Policy." In Organization for Economic Cooperation and Development [O. E. C. D.], "Statements of the Swedish Delegation at the Meeting of 7–9 June, 1967, with Working Party No. 6 of the Industry Committee of O. E. C. D.," pp. 33–41. Mimeographed. Paris, 1967.

Capital, Saving, and Credit in Peasant Societies: Studies from Asia, Oceania, the Caribbean, and Middle America, edited by Raymond W. Firth and B. S. Yamey. Chicago: Aldine Publishing, 1964.

Carey, Henry C. *Principles of Social Science.* Philadelphia: Lippincott, 1858–1859.

Catrou, François. *Histoire général de l'empire du Mogul.* Paris, 1715.

Chayanov, A. V., *The Theory of Peasant Economy.* Edited by Daniel Thorner, Basil Kerblay, and R. E. F. Smith. Homewood, Ill. R. D. Irwin, 1966.

Chaturvedi, J. N. *The Theory of Marketing in Underdeveloped Countries.* Allahabad: Kitab Mahal, 1959.

China. *The First Five-Year Plan for Development of the National Economy of the People's Republic of China, 1953–1957.* Peking: Foreign Language Press, 1956.

Christaller, Walter. *Central Places in Southern Germany.* Translated by Carlisle W. Baskin. Englewood Cliffs, N.J.: Prentice-Hall, 1966.

Clapham, J. H. *The Economic Development of France and Germany, 1815–1914.* 3rd ed. Cambridge: Cambridge University Press, 1928.

Clark, Colin, and Margaret Haswell. *The Economics of Subsistence Agriculture.* London: Macmillan, 1964.

Clark, Walter Eugene. *Two Lamaistic Pantheons.* Cambridge, Mass.: Harvard University Press, 1937.

Connery, Donald S. *The Scandinavians.* London: Eyre & Spottiswoode, 1966.

Country Planning: A Study of Rural Problems, prepared under the direction of Charles Stewart Orwin. Oxford: Agricultural Research Institute, 1944.

Davis, George Whitefield. *Report of the Military Governor of Puerto Rico on Civil Affairs of Puerto Rico.* Washington, D.C.: Government Printing Office, 1902.

Desai, P. B. "Points for Consideration of the Research Cell." Paper prepared for International Seminar on Urban and Industrial Growth of Kanpur Region, Kanpur, December 1966. Mimeographed.

Desai, R. C. *The Standard of Living in India and Pakistan, 1931–32 to 1940–41.* Bombay: Popular Book Depot, 1953.

Dhar, P. N., and H. F. Lydall. *The Role of Small Enterprises in Indian Economic Development.* Institute of Economic Growth, Study 1. Bombay: Asia Publishing House, 1961.

Dhillon, Dyal Singh. "Detailed Note on the Working of the Agricultural Produce Market Committee, Hubli, District Dharwar, Mysore." Nagpur, n.d. (In the files of the (Indian) Directorate of Marketing and Inspection.)

Diamond, William. *Development Banks.* Economic Development Institute, International Bank for Reconstruction and Development. Baltimore: Johns Hopkins Press, 1957.

Dickinson, Robert E. *City and Region: A Geographical Interpretation,* London: Routledge & Kegan Paul, 1964.

Djordjević, Jovan, and Najdan Pašić, "The Communal Self-Government System in Yugoslavia." *International Social Science Journal.* 13, No. 3 (1961), 389–407.

Dovring, Folke. *Land and Labor in Europe in the Twentieth Century: A Comparative Survey of Recent Agrarian History.* 3rd ed. rev. The Hague: Nijhoff, 1965.

Duhring, Eugen. *Kursus der Nationalökonomie.* 3rd ed. Berlin, 1892.

Easterlin, Richard A. "Long-Term Regional Income Changes: Some Suggested Factors." Regional Science Association, Papers and Proceedings, 4 (1958), pp. 313–325.

Eckstein, Otto. "Benefit-Cost Analysis and Regional Development." In *Regional Economic Planning: Techniques of Analysis.* Papers and Proceedings of the First Study Conference on Problems of Economic Development Organized by the European Productivity Agency, edited by Walter Isard and John H. Cumberland. Paris: European Productivity Agency of the Organization for European Economic Cooperation, 1961.

———*Water Resources Development: The Economics of Project Evaluation.* Cambridge, Mass.: Harvard University Press, 1958.

Economic Growth: Brazil, India, Japan, edited by Simon Kuznets, Wilbert E. Moore, and Joseph Spengler. Durham, N.C.: Duke University Press, 1955.

Encyclopaedia of the Social Sciences, edited by Edwin R. A. Seligman and Alvin Johnson. New York: Macmillan, 1930–1935.

Everitt, Alan. "The Marketing of Farm Produce." In *The Agrarian History of England and Wales.* Vol. IV, *1500–1640,* edited by Joan Thirsk. Cambridge: Cambridge University Press, 1967.

Fisher, Jack C. *Yugoslavia—A Multinational State: Regional Differences and Administrative Response.* San Francisco: Chandler, 1966.

Fisher, John. "Can Ralph R. Widner Save New York, Chicago, and Detroit?" *Harper's Magazine,* October 1968, pp. 12–36.

Ford Foundation. International Perspective Planning Team on Small Industries. *Development of Small-Scale Industries in India: Prospects, Problems and Policies.* Report to the Ministry of Commerce and Industry, Government of India. New Delhi, 1963.

Fox, Karl A. "Agricultural Policy in an Urban Society." Paper presented at the Annual Meeting of the American Agricultural Economics Association, Bozeman, Montana, August 19, 1968. Mimeographed.

———"A Program to Promote Maximum Employment, Human Dignity, and Civic Responsibility in the United States." Cyclostyled. Ames, Iowa, 1968.

———"Toward a Policy Model of World Economic Development with Special Attention to the Agricultural Sector." Paper prepared for the Universities–National Bureau Committee of Economic Research Conference, Princeton, N.J., December 1–2, 1967. Mimeographed.

Francis, Amadeo I. D. *Locally and Nonlocally Owned Enterprises in Puerto Rican Manufacturing Industries.* Puerto Rico. Economic Development Administration, Office of Economic Research, Small Business Management Research Report No. 144. San Juan, 1963.

Franks, Sir Oliver. *Central Planning and Control in War and Peace.* Cambridge, Mass.: Harvard University Press, 1947.

Friedmann, John. *Regional Development Policy: A Case Study of Venezuela.* Cambridge, Mass.: M.I.T. Press, 1966.

Fujii, Takashi. *Economic Space in the Japanese Archipelago.* Nagoya, n.d.

Galpin, Charles J. *The Social Anatomy of an Agricultural Community.* University of Wisconsin, Agricultural Experiment Station, Research Bulletin 34. Madison: University of Wisconsin Press, 1915.

Gandhi, M. K. *Village Swaraj.* Ahmedabad: Navajian, 1962.

Gates, Paul W. *The Illinois Central Railroad and Its Colonization Work.* Cambridge, Mass.: Harvard University Press, 1934.

Gayer, Arthur D.; Paul T. Homan; and Earl K. James. *The Sugar Economy of Puerto Rico.* New York: Columbia University Press, 1938.

Getty, Alice, *The Gods of Northern Buddhism.* Rutland, Vt.: Charles E. Tuttle, 1962.

Gilfillan, S. C. "Invention as a Factor in Economic History." *Journal of Economic History.* Vol. 5, Supplemental Number (December 1945), 66–85.

Gligorov, Kiro. "The Communal Economy." *International Social Science Journal,* 13, No. 3 (1961).

Godchalk, David R., and William E. Mills. "A Collaborative Approach to Planning through Urban Activities." In *Urbanism, Urbanization, and Change: Comparative Perspectives,* edited by Paul Meadows and Ephraim R. Mizruchi. Reading, Mass.: Addison-Wesley, 1969.

Gordon, Antoinette K. *The Iconography of Tibetan Lamaism.* New York: Columbia University Press, 1959. Reprint ed., Rutland, Vt.: Charles E. Tuttle. n.d.

Gould, Peter R. "The New Geography." *Harper's Magazine,* March 1969.

Gras, N. S. B. *The Evolution of the English Corn Market from the Twelfth to the Eighteenth Century.* Harvard Economic Studies, 13, Cambridge, Mass.: Harvard University Press, 1926.

Greenhut, Melvin L. *Plant Location in Theory and Practice: The Economics of Space.* Chapel Hill, N.C.: University of North Carolina Press, 1956.

Gregorian, Arthur T. *Oriental Rugs and the Stories They Tell.* Boston: Taylor Press, 1957.

Gyarfas, Ivan. *The Economic Basis of Urban Development Policy and Planning.* Warsaw, 1962.

Habib, Irfan. "Potentialities of Capitalistic Development in the Economy of

Mughul India." *Journal of Economic History,* 29, No. 1 (March 1969), 32–78.

Hagan, Toni. *Nepal: Köni greich am Himalaya.* Bern: Kimmerley & Frey, 1960.

Hägerstrand, T. "General Geographical and Economic Background of the Scandinavian Countries." In Organization for Economic Cooperation and Development [O.E.C.D.], "Statements of the Swedish Delegation at The Meeting of 7–9 June, 1967, with Working Party No. 6 of the Industry Committee of O.E.C.D." Mimeographed. Paris: O.E.C.D., 1967.

Halevi, Nadav, and Ruth Klinov-Malul. *The Economic Development of Israel.* New York: Praeger, 1968.

Hall, John Whitney. "The Castle Towns and Japan's Modern Urbanization." *Far Eastern Quarterly,* 15, No. 1 (November 1955), 37–75.

Halpern, Joel Martin. *A Serbian Village.* New York: Columbia University Press, 1958.

Hamilton, F. E. Ian. *Yugoslavia: Patterns of Economic Activity.* New York: Praeger, 1968.

Handlin, Oscar, and Mary Handlin. *Commonwealth: A Study of the Role of Government in the American Economy: Massachusetts, 1774–1861.* Cambridge, Mass.: Harvard University Press, 1947.

Harland, John, ed. *The House and Farm Accounts of the Shuttleworths of Gawthorpe Hall.* Part 1. Chetham Society 35, 1856.

Harrison, Bennett. "Rural Growth Centers: A Strategy for the Rural Development of Low-Income Countries." Prepared for the United States Agency for International Development, Office of Program and Policy Coordination. Mimeographed. Washington, D.C., 1967.

Hartz, Louis. *Economic Policy and Democratic Thought: Pennsylvania, 1776–1860.* Cambridge, Mass.: Harvard University Press, 1948.

Harvey, William J., and Christian Reppian. *Denmark and the Danes: A Survey of Danish Life, Institutions and Culture.* London: T. F. Unwin, 1915.

Heath, Milton. *Constructive Liberalism: The Role of the State in Economic Development in Georgia to 1860.* Cambridge, Mass.: Harvard University Press, 1954.

Henry, Lewis H., and George S. Wherwein, eds. *A Social Economic Survey of Southern Travis County.* University of Texas, Bulletin No. 65, Austin, Texas, 1916.

Hewes, Laurence, Jr. *Study on Integrated Rural Development in Developing Countries* (ACC/WGRCD/XVI). Working Paper No. 2. Geneva: United Nations, 1969.

Hilhorst, Jozef G. M. *Regional Development Theory: An Attempt to Synthesize.* The Hague: Mouton, 1967.

Holmstrom, J. Edwin. *Railways and Roads in Pioneer Development Overseas: A Study of their Comparative Economics.* London: P. S. King, 1934.

Honjo, Eijiro. *The Social and Economic History of Japan.* New York: Russell & Russell, 1965.

Hopper, C. R. *A Study of Town-Country Relationships.* Michigan State

University, Agricultural Experiment Station, Special Bulletin 181. Lansing, Michigan, 1928.

Hopper, W. David. "The Organization of a Village in North Central India." Ph.D. dissertation, Cornell University, 1957.

Horning, Frances. *El ingreso insular y la economía puertoriqueña.* San Juan: Centro de Investigaciones Sociales de la Universidad de Puerto Rico, 1951.

Horvat, Branko. *Note on the Rate of Growth of the Yugoslav Economy.* Belgrade: Yugoslav Institute of Economic Research, 1963.

Hoselitz, Bert F., ed. *Sociological Aspects of Economic Growth.* Glencoe, Ill.: Free Press, 1960.

Howe, Frederic C. *Denmark: The Co-operative Way.* New York: Coward-McCann, 1936.

Hughes, Rufus B. "Interregional Income Differences: Self-Perpetuation." *Southern Economic Journal,* 37 (1961), pp. 41–45.

Hummel, B. L. *Community Organization In Missouri.* University of Missouri, College of Agriculture, Circular No. 183. Columbia, Miss., 1926.

India. Cabinet Secretariat, Central Statistic Organization. *A Brochure on Principal Public Sector Undertakings in India.* New Delhi, 1961.

India. Central Committee on Cantonments. *Report.* New Delhi: Government of India Press, 1952.

India. Directorate of Publicity, Khadi and Village Industries Commission. *Annual Reports.* New Delhi.

India. Ministry of Food and Agriculture. *Agricultural Marketing in India: Regulated Markets.* Vol. I, *Legislation.* New Delhi, 1956.

India. Ministry of Food and Agriculture, Economics and Statistics Adviser. *Growth Rates in Agriculture.* New Delhi, 1964.

India. Office of the Registrar General. *Census of India, 1961, Final Population Totals.* New Delhi, 1961.

India. Planning Commission. *The Third Five-Year Plan.* New Delhi, 1961.

India. Royal Commission on Agriculture in India. *Report.* Bombay, 1929.

India. Small-Scale Industries Board, Committee on Dispersal of Industries. *Report.* New Delhi, 1962.

Intermediate Societies, Social Mobility and Communication, edited by V. R. Ray. Seattle: American Ethnological Society, 1959.

International Labour Office [I.L.O.]. "Pilot Project for Rural Employment Promotion, Western Region of Nigeria: Tentative Plan of Work." Mimeographed. Geneva, 1965.

——— "Rural Development Programme: Pilot Project for Rural Employment Promotion. Preliminary Project Statement: Nigeria." D. 8. Mimeographed. Geneva, 1963.

International Labour Office. Advisory Working Group on Rural Employment Problems in Tropical Africa (English Speaking Countries). "Discussion Guide." D. 9 (5) 1965. Mimeographed. Lagos, 1965.

Irvine, William. *The Army of the India Moghuls: Its Organization and Administration.* New Delhi: Eurasia Publishing House, 1962.

Isard, Walter. *Location and Space Economy: A General Theory Relating to*

Industrial Location, Market Areas, Land Use, Trade, and Urban Structure. Cambridge, Mass: M.I.T. Press, 1956.

———; D. F. Bramhall; G. A. P. Carrothers; J. H. Cumberland; L. N. Moses; D. O. Price; and T. W. Schooler. *Methods of Regional Analysis: An Introduction to Regional Science.* New York: Wiley, 1960.

Jacob, Philip E.; Henry Tenne; and Thomas Watts. "Values, Leadership and Development: A Four-Nation Study." *Information sur les sciences sociales,* 7, No. 2 (April 1968), 49–92.

Jaffe, Abram J. *People, Jobs, and Economic Development: A Case History of Puerto Rico.* Glencoe, Ill.: Free Press, 1959.

The Jengka Triangle Report: Resources and Development Planning, prepared by Tibbetts, Abbott, McCarthy, and Stratton, Engineers and Architects, New York, and Hunting Technical Services, Boreham Wood, Herts., for the Federal Land Development Authority. Kuala Lumpur, 1967.

Jewkes, John; David Sawers; and Richard Stillerman. *The Sources of Invention.* New York: St. Martin's Press, 1959.

Johnson, E. A. J. *American Economic Thought in the Seventeenth Century.* London: P. S. King & Son. 1932.

——— *Market Towns and Spatial Development in India.* New Delhi: National Council of Applied Economic Research, 1965.

——— *Predecessors of Adam Smith: The Growth of British Economic Thought.* New York: Prentice-Hall, 1937.

——— "Problems of 'Forced Draft' Industrialization: Some Observations Based on the Yugoslav Experience." In *Contributions and Communications.* First International Conference of Economic History. Paris: Mouton, 1960.

Kalitsi, E. A. K. "Organization and Economics of Resettlement." In *Volta Resettlement Symposium Papers.* Kumasi: Nkrumah University, 1965.

Kardelj, Edward. *Samopravljanje u Komuni.* Materijali sa godišnje škupstine stalne konferenceje gradova Jugoslavije. Nis, 1952.

Keppel, Francis. *The Necessary Revolution in American Education.* New York: Harper & Row, 1966.

Killick, Tony. "The Volta River Project." In Walter Birmingham, I. Neustadt, and E. N. Amaboe, eds. *A Study of Contemporary Ghana,* Vol. I, *The Economy of Ghana.* London: Allen & Unwin, 1966.

Köhler, Wolfgang. *The Mentality of Apes.* Translated by Ella Winter. New York: Harcourt Brace, 1926.

Koestler, Arthur. *Insight and Outlook: An Inquiry into the Common Foundations of Science, Art, and Social Ethics.* New York: Macmillan, 1949.

Kolb, John Harrison. *Emerging Rural Communities: Group Relations in Rural Society. A Review of Wisconsin Research in Action.* Madison: University of Wisconsin Press, 1959.

——— and Leroy J. Day. *Interdependence in Town and Country Relations in Rural Society: A Study of Trends in Walworth County, Wisconsin, 1911–13 to 1947–48.* University of Wisconsin, Agricultural Experiment Station, Research Bulletin 172. Madison, Wis., 1950.

——— and R. A. Polson. *Trends in Town-Country Relations.* University of

Wisconsin, Agricultural Experiment Station, Research Bulletin 117. Madison, 1933.

Kreinin, Mordechai E. *Israel and Africa: A Study in Technical Cooperation.* New York: Praeger, 1964.

Krishna, Raj. "Farm Supply Response in the Punjab: A Case Study of Cotton." Ph.D. dissertation, University of Chicago, 1961.

Krutilla, John V., and Otto Eckstein. *Multiple-Purpose River Development: Studies in Applied Economic Analysis.* Baltimore: Johns Hopkins Press, 1958.

Kulkarni, Krishnarao R. *Agricultural Marketing in India, with Special Reference to Co-operative Marketing of Agricultural Produce in India.* Bombay: Co-operator's Book Depot, 1956.

Landes, David S. *The Unbound Prometheus: Technological Change and Industrial Development in Western Europe from 1750 to the Present.* Cambridge: Cambridge University Press, 1969.

Lange, Oskar. *Essays on Economic Planning.* New York: Asia Publishing House, 1960.

Langstroth, Lorenzo L. *Langstroth on the Hive and Honey Bee.* Revised by C. P. Dadant. Hamilton, Ill.: Dadant & Sons, 1913.

Laquian, Aprodicio. *The City in Nation Building: Politics and Administration in Metropolitan Manila.* Manila, 1966.

——— "The 'Rurban' Slum as 'Zone of Transition.'" Paper read at Institute of Advanced Projects, February 3, 1969, East-West Center, Honolulu. Mimeographed.

Laska, John A. Jr. "The Development of the Pattern of Retail Trade Centers in a Selected Area of Southwestern Iowa." Master's thesis, University of Chicago, 1958.

Lewis, John P. *Quiet Crisis in India: Economic Development and American Policy.* Washington, D.C.: Brookings Institution, 1962.

Lewis, W. Arthur. *The Principles of Economic Planning.* London: D. Dobson, 1949.

——— *The Theory of Economic Growth.* London: Allen & Unwin, 1955.

Life Insurance Company of India, *Circular Letter,* DI/143. New Delhi, 1962.

Lipson, E. *History of the English Woolen and Worsted Industries.* London: Black, 1921.

Lockwood, William W. *The Economic Development of Japan: Growth and Structural Change, 1868–1938.* Princeton: Princeton University Press, 1954.

——— "The Scale of Economic Growth in Japan, 1868–1938." In *Economic Growth: Brazil, India, Japan,* edited by Simon Kuznets, Wilbert E. Moore, and Joseph J. Spengler. Durham, N.C.: Duke University Press, 1955.

Lösch, August. *The Economics of Location,* 2nd rev. ed. Translated by Wolfgang F. Stolper. New Haven: Yale University Press, 1954.

Lutz, Vera. *Italy: A Study in Economic Development.* London: Oxford University Press, 1962.

Lybyer, Albert H. *The Government of the Ottoman Empire in the Time of Suleiman the Magnificent.* Cambridge, Mass.: Harvard University Press, 1913.

McCarty, H. H. "A Functional Analysis of Population Distribution." *Geographical Review,* 32 (1942), 282–293.

Macesich, George. *Yugoslavia: The Theory and Practice of Development Planning.* Charlottesville: The University Press of Virginia, 1964.

McClenahan, Bessie A. *The Changing Urban Neighborhood.* University of Southern California, Social Science Series, No. 1. Los Angeles, 1929.

MacIver, Robert Morrison. *Community: A Sociological Study. Being an Attempt to Set Out the Nature and Fundamental Laws of Social Life.* London: Macmillan, 1917.

Manniche, Peter. *Living Democracy in Denmark: Independent Farmers, Farmers' Cooperation, the Folk High Schools, Cooperation in the Towns, Social and Cultural Activities, Social Legislation, A Danish Village.* Copenhagen: G. E. C. Gad, 1952.

Marković, Peter J. *Strukturne promene na selu kao rezultat economskog razvitka, 1900–1960.* Belgrade: Zadruzna Knj., 1963.

Marshall, Alfred. *Memorials of Alfred Marshall,* edited by A. C. Pigou. London: Macmillan, 1925.

Mason, Edward S. "Energy requirements for an Expanding World Economy." In *The Changing Environment of International Relations.* Brookings Lectures, 1956. Washington, D. C.: Brookings Institution, 1956.

Meadows, Paul, and Ephraim H. Mizruchi, eds. *Urbanism, Urbanization, and Change: Comparative Perspectives.* Reading, Mass.: Addison-Wesley, 1969.

Meeüs, Adrien de. *History of the Belgians.* Translated by G. Gordon. New York: Praeger, 1962.

Melvin, Bruce L. *Rural Population: New York, 1855–1925.* Cornell University, Agricultural Experiment Station, Bulletin 116. Ithaca, 1925.

——— *Village Service Agencies.* Cornell University, Agricultural Experiment Station, Bulletin 493. Ithaca, 1925.

Mihailović, Kosta. "The Regional Aspect of Economic Development." In Radmila Stojanović, ed. *Yugoslav Economists on Problems of a Socialist Economy.* New York: International Arts and Sciences Press, 1969.

Millikan, Robert A. *Autobiography.* New York: Prentice-Hall, 1950.

Mintz, Sidney. "The Employment of Capital by Market Women in Haiti." In *Capital, Saving, and Credit in Peasant Societies,* edited by Raymond Firth and B. S. Yamey. Chicago: Aldine Publishing, 1964.

——— *Peasant Market Places and Economic Development in Latin America.* Vanderbilt University, Graduate Center for Latin American Studies, Occasional Paper 4. Nashville, 1964.

——— "A Tentative Typology of Eight Haitian Market Places." *Revista de ciencias sociales,* 4, No. 1 (March 1960), 15–58.

——— *Worker in the Cane.* New Haven: Yale University Press, 1960.

Moral, Paul. *L'Économie haïtienne.* Port au Prince: Impr. de l'État, 1959.

Morgan, E. L. *Mobilizing the Rural Community.* Massachusetts Agricultural College, Extension Bulletin No. 23. Amherst, 1918.

Mosely, Philip E. "The Peasant Family: The Zadruga, or Communal Joint Family, in the Balkans." In *The Cultural Approach to History,* edited by Caroline Ware. New York: Columbia University Press, 1940.

Mosher, Arthur T. *Creating a Progressive Rural Structure to Serve A Modern Agriculture*. New York: Agricultural Development Council, 1969.

Mueller, P., and K. H. Zevering. "Employment Promotion through Rural Development: A Pilot Project in Western Nigeria." *International Labour Review*, 100 (August 1969), 111–130.

Mukerjee, Radhakamal. Presidential Address at the International Seminar on Urban and Industrial Growth of Kanpur Region, January 29–February 4, 1967. In *Regional Perspective of Industrial and Urban Growth: The Case of Kanpur*, edited by P. B. Desai, I. M. Grossack, and K. N. Sharma. Bombay: Macmillan, 1969.

Mukherjee, Bhupati B. *Agricultural Marketing in India*. Calcutta: Thacker Spink, 1937.

Mukherjee, P. K., and S. C. Gupta. *A Pilot Survey of Fourteen Villages in U. P. and Punjab*. New Delhi, 1959.

Murvar, Vatro. "Some Tentative Modifications of Weber's Typology: Occidental Versus Oriental City." In *Urbanism, Urbanization, and Change: Comparative Perspectives*, edited by Paul Meadows and Ephraim H. Mizruchi. Reading, Mass.: Addison-Wesley, 1969.

Myint, Hla. *The Economics of the Developing Countries*. New York: Praeger, 1965.

——— "An Interpretation of Economic Backwardness." In Agarwala, A. N., and S. P. Singh. *The Economics of Underdevelopment*. London: Oxford University Press, 1958.

Myrdal, Gunnar. *Economic Theory and Underdeveloped Regions*. London: Duckworth, 1957.

Narain, Dharm. *Distribution of the Marketed Surplus of Agricultural Produce by Size-Level of Holdings in India, 1950–51*. Institute of Economic Growth, Occasional Paper No. 2. New Delhi, 1961.

National Council of Applied Economic Research [N. C. A. E. R.]. *All India Rural Household Survey*. Vol. II, *Income, Investment and Savings*. New Delhi: N. C. A. E. R., 1965.

——— *Demand for Energy in India, 1960–1975*. New Delhi: N. C. A. E. R., 1960.

——— *Demand for Energy in Southern India*. New Delhi: N. C. A. E. R., 1962.

——— *Domestic Fuels in Rural India*. New Delhi: N. C. A. E. R., 1959.

——— *Savings in India During the Plan Periods*. Occasional Paper 16. New Delhi: N. C. A. E. R., 1965.

Neale, Walter C.; Harpal Singh; and Jai Pal Singh. "Kurali Market: A Report on the Economic Geography of Marketing in Northern Punjab," *Economic Development and Cultural Change*, 13 (January 1965), 129–168.

Nef, John U. *Industry and Government in France and England, 1540–1640*. Ithaca, N.Y.: Cornell University Press, 1957.

Nelson, Lowry. *A Social Survey of Escalante Utah*. Brigham Young University Studies, No. 1. Provo, 1925.

Neutze G. M. *Economic Policy and the Size of Cities*. Canberra: Australian National University, 1965.

Okun, Bernard, and R. W. Richardson. "Regional Income Inequality and

Internal Migration." *Economic Development and Cultural Change,* 9 (January 1961), pp. 128–143.

Oliver, Robert W. *The Role of Small-Scale Manufacturing in Economic Development: The Experience of Industrially Advanced Countries as a Guide for Newly Developing Areas.* Prepared for the U.S. International Cooperation Administration by Stanford Research Institute. Washington, D.C., 1957.

Olsson, R. "Investigations and Research for Regional Development in Sweden and the Starting of Nordic Cooperation in this Field." In O. E. C. D. "Statements of the Swedish Delegation at the Meeting of 7–9 June, 1967, with Working Party No. 6 of the Industry Committee of O. E. C. D.," pp. 41–48. Mimeographed. Paris: O. E. C. D., 1967.

——— "Regional Policies in Sweden." In O. E. C. D. "Statements of the Swedish Delegation at the Meeting of 7–9 June, 1967, with Working Party No. 6 of the Industry Committee of O. E. C. D.," pp. 21–32. Mimeographed. Paris: O. E. C. D., 1967.

Ong, Shao-er. "Management Dilemma of Small Farms in Asia." Paper read at the Institute of Advanced Projects, East-West Center, Honolulu, 1969. Mimeographed.

Orchard, John E. *Japan's Economic Position: The Progress of Industrialization.* New York: McGraw-Hill, 1930.

Overton, Richard C. *Burlington Route: A History of the Burlington Lines.* New York: Knopf, 1965.

Owen, Wilfred. *Distance and Development: Transport and Communications in India.* Washington: Brookings Institution, 1968.

——— "Transport and Communication in Kanpur's Future." In *Regional Perspective of Industrial and Urban Growth: The Case of Kanpur,* edited by P. B. Desai, I. M. Grossack, and K. N. Sharma, pp. 93–104. Bombay: Macmillan, 1969.

Page, James F. *Relation of Town and Country Interests in Garfield County, Oklahoma.* Oklahoma Agricultural and Mechanical College, Agricultural Experiment Station, Bulletin No. 194. Stillwater, Okla., 1930.

Paton, Alan. *Cry, the Beloved Country.* London: Cape, 1953.

Pejovich, Svetozar. *The Market-Planned Economy of Yugoslavia.* Minneapolis: University of Minnesota Press, 1966.

Pellizzi, C. "Some Sociological Implications of the Borgo a Mozzano Centre of Agricultural Studies." In L. E. Verone, C. Pellizi, M. Upton, and L. Marcano. *The Transformation of Rural Communities,* pp. 17–28. World Land Use Survey, Occasional Papers, No. 7. Tonbridge: Geographical Publications, 1966.

Perkins, James A. *The University in Transition.* Princeton: Princeton University Press, 1965.

Perloff, Harvey S. *Puerto Rico's Economic Future: A Study in Planned Development.* Chicago: University of Chicago Press, 1950.

——— et al. *Regions, Resources, and Economic Growth.* Baltimore: Johns Hopkins Press, 1960.

Perroux, François. *Les Techniques quantitatives de la planification*. Paris: Presses Universitaires, 1965.

Petty, Sir William. *The Political Anatomy of Ireland*. London: D. Brown and W. Rogers, 1691.

——— *A Treatise of Taxes and Contributions*. London: N. Brooke, 1662.

Pick, Frank. *Britain Must Rebuild*. London: Kegan Paul, 1941.

Pierce, Paul S. *Social Surveys of Three Rural Townships in Iowa*. University of Iowa Monographs, Vol. 5, No. 2. Iowa City, 1917.

Pirenne, Henri. *Belgian Democracy: Its Early History*. Translated by J. V. Saunders. Manchester: Manchester University Press, 1915.

Planned Society: Yesterday, Today, and Tomorrow: A Symposium by Thirty-Five Economists, Sociologists, and Statesmen, edited by Findlay Mackenzie. New York: Prentice-Hall, 1937.

Poulsen, K. *Survey of Women in Some Locations of the I.L.O. Pilot Area*. Ibadan, 1967.

Pressad, Kamta. "Industrial Prospects of the Kanpur Region." In *Regional Perspective of Industrial and Urban Growth: The Case of Kanpur*, edited by P. B. Desai, I. M. Grossack and K. N. Sharma, pp. 73–92. Bombay: Macmillan, 1969.

Price, H. Bruce, and C. R. Hopper. *Services of Rural Trade Centers in Distribution of Farm Supplies*. University of Minnesota, Agricultural Experiment Station, Bulletin No. 249. Minneapolis, 1928.

Puerto Rico. Administracion de Fomento Economico. "Proposed Revisions in Policy." Memo No. 4, "Special Incentive Program." Mimeographed. San Juan, 1962.

Puerto Rico. Administracion de Fomento Economico. Oficina de Estudios Economicos, Division de Economia General. "Fabricas establecidas bajo el programa de industrializacion, enero de 1966." Mimeographed. San Juan, 1966.

Randhawa, Surjit Singh. "A Detailed Note on the Working of the Agricultural Produce Committee, Unjha, District Mahesana, Gujarat State." Nagpur, n.d. (In the files of the (Indian) Directorate of Marketing and Inspection.)

Rao, Rameshwara. "Regulated Markets in India with Special Reference to Andhra Pradesh." Ph.D. dissertation, University of Allahabad, 1959.

——— "Under-developed Economy and Agricultural Marketing." *Indian Journal of Economics*, 40, No. 156 (July 1959).

Razak bin Hussein, Tun Abdul. "A Drive for Greater Progress." *Development Forum* (A publication of the Malaysian Center for Development Studies). 1, No. 3 (April 1968).

Regional Perspective of Industrial and Urban Growth: The Case of Kanpur, edited by P. B. Desai, I. M. Grossack, and K. N. Sharma. Bombay: Macmillan, 1969.

Ridker, Ronald G. "Prospects and Problems of Agriculture in the Kanpur Region." In *Regional Perspective of Industrial and Urban Growth: The Case of Kanpur*, edited by P. B. Desai, I. M. Grossack, and K. M. Sharma, pp. 55–73. Bombay: Macmillan, 1969.

"Road Development." A Study Made by a Regional Transport Study Group Working in Cooperation with the [Indian] National Planning Commission. Mimeographed. n.d.

Roll, Erich. *An Early Experiment in Industrial Organization: Being a History of the Firm of Boulton and Watt, 1775–1805.* London: Longmans Green & Co., 1930.

Roy, Krishna. "Prospects of Urban Growth for the Kanpur Region of India." In *Regional Perspective of Industrial and Urban Growth: The Case of Kanpur,* edited by P. B. Desai, I. M. Grossack, and K. N. Sharma, pp. 138–140. Bombay: Macmillan, 1969.

Roy, R. "Administration of Industrial Development In U. P." In *Regional Perspective of Industrial and Urban Growth: The Case of Kanpur,* edited by P. B. Desai, I. M. Grossack, and K. N. Sharma, pp. 262–279. Bombay: Macmillan, 1969.

Rostow, W. W. *Stages of Economic Growth: A Non-Communist Manifesto.* Cambridge: Cambridge University Press, 1960.

Sanderson, Dwight. *The Rural Community: The Natural History of a Sociological Group.* Boston: Ginn, 1932.

Sangli Industrial Estate Cooperative Society, *Bye Laws.* Sangli, India, 1963.

Schafer, Joseph. *The Social History of American Agriculture.* New York: Macmillan, 1936.

Schultz, Theodore W. *Transforming Traditional Agriculture.* New Haven: Yale University Press, 1964.

Schumpeter, Joseph A. *The Theory of Economic Development: An Inquiry into Profits, Capital, Credit, Interest, and the Business Cycle.* Translated by Redvers Opie. Cambridge, Mass.: Harvard University Press, 1934.

Sen, Satyendranath N. *The City of Calcutta: A Socio-Economic Survey, 1954–55* to *1957–58.* Calcutta: Bookland, 1960.

Shen, T. H. *Agricultural Resources of China.* Ithaca: Cornell University Press, 1951.

Siddiqui, N. A. "A Classification of Villages Under the Mughals." *Indian Economic and Social History Review,* 1, No. 3 (January–March 1964), 73–82.

Singh, Khushwant, *A History of the Sikhs.* Princeton: Princeton University Press, 1963.

——— *The Sikhs Today: Their Religion, History, Culture, Customs and Way of Life.* Bombay: Orient Longmans, 1959.

Singh, Shiw Mangal. "Turrufs Babhnauti and Raotar in the Ganga-Ghaghara Doab West (India): A Study in Land Settlement, Social Geography and Rural Central Places." *National Geographical Journal of India,* 11, Parts 3 and 4 (1965), pp. 185–197.

Singh, Tej Vir: "Market Study of Gur in Bulandshahar Mandi." Master's thesis, Government Agricultural College, Kanpur, India, 1965.

Sinha, D. P. "Innovation, Response, and Development in Banari." *Man in India,* 48, No. 3 (July–September 1968), 225–243.

Skinner, G. William. "Marketing and Social Structure in Rural China." *Journal of Asian Studies,* 24 (November 1964), 3–43; (February 1965), 195–228; (May 1965), 363–399.

Smith, Thomas C. *The Agrarian Origins of Modern Japan.* Stanford: Stanford University Press, 1959.

——— "Landlords and Rural Capitalists in the Modernization of Japan." *Journal of Economic History,* 16, No. 2 (June 1956), 165–181.

Sombart, Werner. *The Quintessence of Capitalism.* Translated and edited by M. Epstein. New York: Dutton, 1915.

Sombart, Werner. *Der Modern Kapitalismus.* Munich: Duncker & Humblot, 1921–1928.

Staley, Eugene, and Richard Morse. *Modern Small Industry for Developing Countries.* New York: McGraw-Hill, 1965.

Stanovnik, Janez. "Planning through the Market—The Yugoslav Experience." *Foreign Affairs,* 40 (January 1962), 252–263.

Stead, William H. *Fomento: The Economic Development of Puerto Rico.* National Planning Association, Planning Pamphlet No. 103, Washington, D.C., 1958.

Stein, Burton. "The Economic Function of a Medieval South Indian Temple." *Journal of Asian Studies,* 19, No. 2 (February 1960), 163–176.

——— "The State, the Temple, and Agricultural Development: A Study in Medieval South India." *Economic Weekly Annual,* February 4, 1961, pp. 178–187.

Stojanović, Radmila, ed. *Yugoslav Economists on Problems of a Socialist Economy.* New York: International Arts and Sciences Press, 1969.

"A Surplus of Brains." *Newsweek,* August 20, 1962.

Takenaka, Yasukazu. "Endogenous Formation and Development of Capitalism in Japan." *Journal of Economic History,* 29, No. 1 (March 1969), 141–162.

Taussig, F. W. *Principles of Economics.* 3rd rev. ed. New York: Macmillan, 1923.

Tawney, Richard Henry. *The Agrarian Problem in the Sixteenth Century.* London: Longmans Green, 1912.

Tax, Sol. *Penny Capitalism: A Guatemalan Indian Economy.* Smithsonian Institution, Institute of Social Anthropology, Publication No. 16. Washington, D.C.: Government Printing Office, 1953.

Taylor, E. A., and Yoder, F. R. *Rural Social Organization in Whatcom County.* State College of Washington, Agricultural Experiment Station, Bulletin No. 215. Pullman, Wash., 1929.

Thirsk, Joan. "Farming Techniques." In *The Agrarian History of England and Wales.* Vol. IV, *1500–1640,* edited by Joan Thirsk. Cambridge: Cambridge University Press, 1967.

Thünen, Johann H. von. *Von Thünen's Isolated State.* Translated by Carla M. Wartenburg. London: Oxford University Press, 1966.

Tomasovich, Jozo. *Peasants, Politics, and Economic Change in Yugoslavia.* Stanford: Stanford University Press, 1955.

Treat, Payson Jackson. *The National Land System, 1785–1920.* New York: E. B. Treat, 1910.

United Nations. *Demographic Yearbook, 1963.* New York, 1963.

——— *Demographic Yearbook, 1968.* New York, 1968.

——— *Yearbook of National Accounts, 1963.* New York, 1963.

United Nations. Food and Agriculture Organization. *Report on the Possibilities of African Rural Development in Relation to Economic and Social Growth.* Rome, 1962.

United States. Department of Commerce, Bureau of the Census. *Historical Statistics of the United States, Colonial Times to 1957: A Statistical Abstract Supplement.* Washington, D.C.: Government Printing Office, 1960.

United States. Department of Housing and Urban Development, Division of International Affairs. *Aided Self-Help in Housing Improvement.* Ideas and Methods Exchange No. 18. Washington: Government Printing Office, 1967.

United States. Federal Interagency River Basin Committee, Subcommittee on Benefits and Costs. *Proposed Practices for Economic Analysis of River Basin Projects.* Washington: Government Printing Office, 1950.

United States Panel on the World Food Supply, *The World Food Problem,* Washington: The White House, 1967.

Upton, Martin. "Recent Changes from Subsistence to Commercial Agriculture in Southern Nigeria." In L. E. Vezone, C. Pellizi, M. Upton and L. Marcano. *The Transformation of Rural Communities,* pp. 29–40. World Land Use Survey, Occasional Papers, No. 7. Tonbridge: Geographical Publications, 1966.

Urbanism, Urbanization, and Change: Comparative Perspectives, edited by Paul Meadows and Ephraim R. Mizuchi. Reading, Mass.: Addison-Wesley, 1969.

Usher, Abbot Payson. *A History of Mechanical Inventions.* Boston: Beacon Press, 1959.

Virone, L. E.; C. Pellizzi; M. Upton; and L. Marcano. *The Transformation of Rural Communities: Some Implications of Promoting Change from Subsistence to Marketing Agriculture in Contrasting Geographical Regions.* World Land Use Survey, Occasional Papers, No. 7. Tonbridge: Geographical Publications, 1966.

Volta Resettlement Symposium Papers. Kumasi: Nkrumah University, 1965.

Ware, Caroline Farrar, ed. *The Cultural Approach to History.* New York: Columbia University Press, 1940.

Warmann, J. St. George. "Public Health Problems of Volta Resettlement." In *Volta Resettlement Symposium Papers.* Kumasi: Nkrumah University, 1965.

Waterston, Albert. *Planning in Yugoslavia: Organization and Implementation.* Economic Development Institute, International Bank for Reconstruction and Development. Baltimore: Johns Hopkins Press, 1962.

Weber, Alfred. *Theory of the Location of Industries.* Translated by C. J. Friedrich. Chicago: University of Chicago Press, 1957.

Wellington, A. M. *The Economic Theory of the Location of Railways.* New York: Railroad Gazette, 1914.

West African Oilseed Mission. *Report.* Colonial Report No. 224. London: H.M. Stationery Office, 1948.

Westergaard, Harold Ludvig. *Economic Development in Denmark before and during the World War.* Oxford: Clarendon Press, 1922.

White, Andrew Dickson. *A History of the Warfare of Science with Theology in Christendom.* New York: D. Appleton, 1896.

Whitehead, Alfred North. *Science and the Modern World.* New York: Macmillan, 1925.

Wiser, William H., and Charlotte Vial Wiser. *Behind Mud Walls, 1930–1961.* Berkeley: University of California Press, 1963.

Wittfogel, Karl. *Oriental Despotism.* New Haven: Yale University Press, 1957.

Wood, Alan. *The Groundnut Affair.* London: The Bodley Head, 1950.

Wootton, Barbara. *Plan or No Plan.* New York: Farrar & Rinehart, 1935.

Wu, Yuan-li; H. C. Ling; and Grace Hsiao Wu. *The Spatial Economy of Communist China: A Study on Industrial Location and Transportation.* New York: Praeger, 1966.

Wu, Yuan-li. *The Steel Industry in Communist China.* New York: Praeger, 1965.

Yalan, E. *Planning of Agricultural Settlements in Israel.* Jerusalem, 1960.

Yalan, E. *Private and Cooperative Agricultural Settlements: Physical Planning.* Haifa: Ministry of Foreign Affairs, Department for International Cooperation, 1961.

Yang, Ch'ing-k'un. *A North China Local Market Economy: A Summary of a Study of Periodic Markets in Chowping Hsein, Shantung.* New York: Institute of Pacific Relations, 1944.

Yang, Mou-ch'un (Martin Yang). *A Chinese Village.* New York: Columbia University Press, 1945.

Yarranton, Andrew. *England's Improvement by Sea and Land,* or *How to Beat the Dutch without Fighting.* London: R. Everingham, 1677.

Yoshinari, Shiba, and Yamane Yukio. *Markets in China during the Sung, Ming, and Ch'ing Periods.* East-West Center, Institute of Advanced Projects, Occasional Papers of Research Publications and Translations. Honolulu, 1967.

Youings, Joyce. "The Church." In *The Agrarian History of England and Wales.* Vol. IV, *1500–1640,* edited by Joan Thirsk. Cambridge: Cambridge University Press, 1967.

INDEX

Bei Fragen zur Produktsicherheit wenden Sie sich bitte an:
If you have any questions regarding product safety,
please contact:

Walter de Gruyter GmbH
Genthiner Straße 13
10785 Berlin
productsafety@degruyterbrill.com